MUTATION AND MORPHOSIS
LANDSCAPE AS AGGREGATE

Editorial management
Amalia Bonsack with Coralie Berchtold,
Swiss Federal Institute of Technology (ETH) Zurich

In collaboration with
Lars Ruge and Laure Baretaud, Martijn Slob, VOGT

With contributions by
Maria Alexandrescu
Laure Baretaud
Coralie Berchtold
Amalia Bonsack
Maren Brakebusch
Violeta Burckhardt
Thomas Kissling
Lars Ruge
Alexandra Savtchenko-Belskaia
Roland Charles Shaw
Martijn Slob
Daia Stutz
Günther Vogt
Ralf Günter Voss

Including conversations with
Chris Dercon
Roger Diener
Olafur Eliasson
Katja Gentinetta
Dehlia Hannah

With contributions from the following artists
Julius von Bismarck
Julian Charrière
Olafur Eliasson
Andreas Greiner
Roni Horn
Marguerite Humeau
Dafi Kühne
Christian Vogt

MUTATION AND MORPHOSIS

LANDSCAPE AS AGGREGATE

EDITED BY
GÜNTHER VOGT AND
THOMAS KISSLING

LARS MÜLLER PUBLISHERS

Categories

Günther Vogt in Conversation with

Projects

Interventions

Portraits

Reflections

Mutation/Morphosis
Dafi Kühne, 2019

The typographic poster *Mutation/Morphosis* explores the reading structure of the book *Mutation and Morphosis*. Dafi Kühne challenges the medium of the printed book with its predetermined and edited sequence, and reinterprets it. No matter whether one approaches it chronologically and logically, proceeding from A to Z, or follows a nonlinear path, skipping around or following one's feelings–depending on the page you open the book at and where you turn to next, thematic and visual links, dovetails and overlaps, in contexts that are both familiar and new, are read and interpreted differently. Together, they combine to create an overall picture.

Ludlow linocut with hot-metal lines printed in letterpress, 55 × 88 cm, edition 250 copies

Landscape in Mutation

After the Party is Over

Modulus

City and Territory

Res Publica

Landscape as Aggregate

Maria Alexandrescu

Laure Baretaud

Coralie Berchtold

Amalia Bonsack

Maren Brakebusch

Violeta Burckhardt

Thomas Kissling

Lars Ruge

Alexandra Savtchenko-Belsk

Roland Charles Shaw

Martijn Slob

Daia Stutz

Günther Vogt

Mutation/Morphosis

Conversations

The Blue Fossil Entro

Reflections

Alpine Roads

Projects

Portraits

The morning small cl

Interventions

Still Water (The Rive

Monument for the 30

Julius von Bismarck

Julian Charrière

Dominions

Olafur Eliasson

Andreas Greiner

Tropisme

Roni Horn

Marguerite Humeau

Belgrad Forest, Istan

Dafi Kühne

Christian Vogt

We Are All Astronaut

8 Heads High

Landscape as Aggregate

Maren Brakebusch

Violeta Burckhardt

Thomas Kissling

Lars Ruge

Alexandra Savtchenko-Belsk

Roland Charles Shaw

Martijn Slob

Daia Stutz

Günther Vogt

Ralf Günter Voss

Chris Dercon

Roger Diener

Olafur Eliasson

Katja Gentinetta

Dehlia Hannah

Evolution Square

The Landscape Beneath the City

Erratic Giants

The Square within the Square

Views and Vistas

Your Glacial Expectations

In the Foreground of the Background

Time and Scale

The Layers of the Landscape

Rates of Change

Rehabilitating the River

Monster in the Garden

Overlooking the City

Olafur Eliasson

Andreas Greiner

Roni Horn

Marguerite Humeau

Dafi Kühne

Christian Vogt

Tropisme

Belgrad Forest, Istan

We Are All Astronaut

8 Heads High

FOXP2

Some Pigeons Are M

Detective Work

Invasive Plants

The Return of Wilderness

Creation of a Cultural Landscape

Copy Paste Paradise

Surface and Interface

City of Stone

On Creating Order in the Forest

Landscapes of Controlled Origin

The Honeyscape

Chris Dercon

Roger Diener

Olafur Eliasson

Katja Gentinetta

Dehlia Hannah

Your Glacial Expectations

In the Foreground of the Background

Time and Scale

The Layers of the Landscape

Rates of Change

Rehabilitating the River

Monster in the Garden

Overlooking the City

Landscape Model Landscape

Surveying the Territory

Miniaturized Landscape

Opushka, the Russian Forest Edge

The Value of the Existing

Measure and Interval

Green Milan and Blue Milan

Pairi Daeza

Gardens of the City

An Airfield Turned City

The Nature of the City

The Other City

Discovery of a Fluvial Landscape

Listen, Drink, Savor

The City's Collective Memory

Mutation and Morphosis

Lars Müller Publishers

Copy Paste Paradise

Surface and Interface

City of Stone

On Creating Order in the Forest

Landscapes of Controlled Origin

The Honeyscape

The Engineer's Tree

On Fashioning Boundaries

Alps

Green Belt

Bois

City Garden

Volkspark

Landscape in Mutation

After the Party is Over

Modulus

City and Territory

Res Publica

Conversations

Reflections

Projects

Portraits

Interventions

Mutation/Morphosis

The Blue Fossil Entro

Alpine Roads

The morning small cl

Still Water (The Rive

Monument for the 30

Dominions

Tropisme

Belgrad Forest, Istan

We Are All Astronaut

8 Heads High

FOXP2

Some Pigeons Are M

Landscape

as

Aggregate

Maria Alexandrescu

Laure Baretaud

Coralie Berchtold

Amalia Bonsack

Maren Brakebusch

Violeta Burckhardt

Thomas Kissling

Lars Ruge

Alexandra Savtchenko-Belskaia

Roland Charles Shaw

Martijn Slob

Daia Stutz

Günther Vogt

Ralf Günter Voss

Julius von Bismarck

Julian Charrière

Olafur Eliasson

Andreas Greiner

Roni Horn

Marguerite Humeau

Dafi Kühne

Christian Vogt

Evolution Square

The Landscape Beneath the City

Erratic Giants

The Square within the Square

Views and Vistas

Your Glacial Expectations

In the Foreground of the Background

Time and Scale

The Layers of the Landscape

Rates of Change

Rehabilitating the River

Monster in the Garden

Overlooking the City

Landscape Model Landscape

Surveying the Territory

Miniaturized Landscape

Opushka, the Russian Forest Edge

The Value of the Existing

Measure and Interval

Green Milan and Blue Milan

Pairi Daeza

Gardens of the City

An Airfield Turned City

The Nature of the City

The Other City

Discovery of a Fluvial Landscape

Listen, Drink, Savor

The City's Collective Memory

Detective Work

Invasive Plants

The Return of Wilderness

Creation of a Cultural Landscape

Copy Paste Paradise

Surface and Interface

City of Stone

On Creating Order in the Forest

Landscapes of Controlled Origin

The Honeyscape

The Engineer's Tree

On Fashioning Boundaries

Chris Dercon

Roger Diener

Olafur Eliasson

Katja Gentinetta

Dehlia Hannah

Alps

Green Belt

Bois

City Garden

Volkspark

Mutation and Morphosis

Lars Müller Publishers

Aggregare–
Collection as Inspiration

For those driven by curiosity and the urge to explore the world, collecting things is a way to explain the world to themselves. The intentional or unintentional collection of things is a cultural technique that is thousands of years old. Already as children, we are quite familiar with it: a dead insect, a stone found at the wayside, a plant we pick and dry. All this we gather and assemble in one place.

Mankind's earliest knowledge was based on such rudimentary accumulations of things. Claude Lévi-Strauss, founder of structural anthropology and a great mythologist, described this activity in his treatise *The Savage Mind:* fruits of the same color represent a class of their own among indigenous communities, seeds in the form of a tooth are regarded as medicine against toothache, and a black, reflecting stone is supposed to improve eyesight. Of course, we know that those are mere assumptions. Nevertheless, this way of thinking marks the beginning of science and relies on phenomenological or directly perceptible phenomena–shape, color, weight, etc.–as the basic principles of order.

By organizing and classifying, collections emerge from the mere accumulation of objects, such as have been spreading in cabinets of curiosity and wonder all over Europe ever since the fourteenth century. There is seldom a division between found natural objects, works of art, or artefacts–and the principle of the arrangement is not easily recognizable either. Mostly, they are the result of a collector's passion. It is this very passion that will establish relationships between these objects and create a delicate matrix that connects individual components into a conglomerate and, ultimately, gathers them into a true collection.

Every collection raises the question of its completeness. That it is, as a rule, not complete, is part of its nature. Its genesis is not solely subject to the collector's passion but depends on external factors and, depending on the object, on its nature, location, and time. However, its incompleteness is not a disadvantage. Rather, it enables the enrichment, "aggregation," reconfiguration, and creation of ever new semantic contexts. This book is a collection. It unites and connects contributions, all of which refer to the subject of landscape.

A landscape is a fragile structural fabric that is undergoing constant change under the influence of endogenous and exogenous forces causing mutations and morphosis. Above all, however, we understand "landscape" to be the work of man: a many-coded cultural construct that we perceive collectively. Eruptions and ongoing erosion leave traces in the terrain, while designed intervention is evidence of its cultivation.

Every structuring intervention changes the reality of a landscape and creates new conditions for the human habitat. The characteristics and phenomena of a place have to be identified, correlated, weighted, and rearranged with the help of our collected knowledge. These interventions have to be interwoven to continue to spin the millennia-old history of the landscape. Seen in this way, the landscape itself turns into the driving force of its own change.

Here it is essential to understand design as a process. It begins with a precise analysis of the territory given a continuous change of perspective. The shifts of thought that take place between the first encounter with a site and the communication of a design, which are reflected in sketches and models, will have to be recorded and made visible by a cartographic process. This will establish the basis and vocabulary for a broad discourse in which the participants agree on the aims and means of the creative intervention.

In our case, the argument is not limited to the employees in the offices of VOGT Landschaftsarchitekten and the ETH Zurich Chair of Landscape Architecture. It includes experts from near and more remote disciplines in order to suitably address the complex and sometimes serious issues surrounding any future landscape developments. Thinking within the microcosm and macrocosm of the overall system corresponds to the principle of transdisciplinary practice inherent in landscape architecture.

Following this credo, the contributions in this book are brought into a loose order along discussions between Günther Vogt and experts from various disciplines. The debaters ponder topics as diverse as the transformation of the global landscape as a consequence of climate change or the possibilities and problems of large-scale interventions in the city. They discuss different ways of working and the importance of the studio as a center of creative processes. They explore the European city as a grown artifact and how it could be thought of from the point of view of the landscape and reflect on public space given its increasing surveillance, while interventions by artist friends broaden the horizon and the panorama of the collective landscape.

Mutation and Morphosis: Landscape as Aggregate is a snapshot of the current analysis of the conditions of our field of work and any motivating factors. The book documents the dynamics with which the concept of landscape and, thus, landscape architecture are mutable in view of the changing climate and growing population. It depicts the extended space of thought and work characteristic of VOGT, which is reflected in the documented projects developed in the offices in Zurich, Berlin, London, and Paris and ranges from large-scale landscape spaces and complex urbanization processes to subtle and careful interventions in public space. Thus, this publication provides insights into some answers to the urgent questions faced by our discipline and puts them up for a public debate.

Günther Vogt
Thomas Kissling

Regenwald

Rosenwald

Campus, Rotkreuz, CH
Evolution Square

Öhningen during the Miocene

Cooperation:
Architecture:
Leutwyler Partner Architekten, Zurich
Scheitlin Syfrig Architekten, Lucerne
Burckhardt+Partner Architekten Generalplaner, Basel

Design/construction:
2008–2009/2010–2011

Type and size:
Square, 0.76 ha

Status:
Realized

The development of Rotkreuz has been determined in many ways by external influences. Originally a linear settlement on the connecting route between Cham and Lucerne, the present-day appearance of the town was largely conditioned by the construction of the railway. Its inclusion in the Greater Zurich Area and subsequent rapid growth have resulted in new centralities, albeit at a certain distance from the historical core of the village and without much diversity of use. There is no social and cultural center, as the realities of contemporary urban planning are unable to accommodate the desire for a village square with Rathaus, church, village inn, and linden tree.

Following the decision of an international company to transform its existing production site in Rotkreuz into its European headquarters, several administrative, laboratory, and production buildings, a staff restaurant, and a training center were built on the northern edge of the municipality within a relatively short space of time. If the area had been photographed a few years ago, the pictures would have shown several logistics and production halls, organized along purely functional lines and wedged between two freeways.

Prehistoric Landscape

The richness of the area can only be revealed by scientific maps and an in-depth survey of the site. A study of the local hydrology, geology, and potential natural vegetation reveals deposits of lake marl, high levels of groundwater, and a vegetation palette typical of what was once a low-lying moor in the vicinity of today's campus. While it cannot be seen in photographs, the reason for this phenomenon is visible in the maps: a small lake, once located here and linked to Lake Zug, that has silted up over the past millennia.

The foundation work for the new buildings was hampered by the remains of plants and seeds preserved in the soil from a landscape that has long since vanished. Despite the complications, this phenomenon also provided the basis for the landscape design. Various "inlays" are distributed throughout the square, which look like excavation sites and contain artificial fossils and models of fallen sequoia trees made of sprayed concrete. These models act like nurse logs, providing shelter and nurture for young sequoias. This has given rise to a new generation of growth that seems exotic by today's standards–a wooded area supplemented by other forest species that were native to Lake Zug at the time, such as bald cypress, wild magnolia, tupelo, and hickory. The trees are covered with creepers, reinforcing the sense of "wilderness."

Central Location

On the central plaza, whose structure is based on a square, the inlays define spaces of different sizes that respond to particular situations and can be used in various ways. For their part, the giant trees, which are now covered with mosses and ferns, point to a different temporal and climatic dimension, an impression conveyed both by their length and the girth of their trunks, whose diameter can only be guessed at.

Based on the design concept, the company itself came up with the name Evolution Square as a metaphor for the development of the site over time. And a few years after its completion, the tusk of a mammoth was found in an excavation pit on the site. (lr)

Prehistoric shoreline

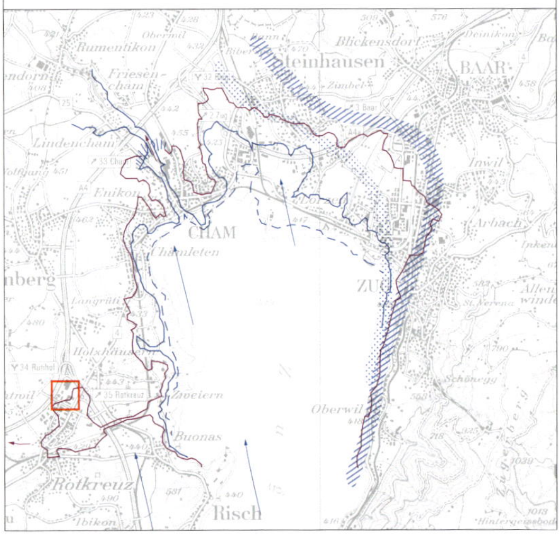

- Early ice age lake, approx. 480 m.a.s.l.
- Later ice age lake, approx. 440 m.a.s.l.
- First lakeshore, approx. 429 m.a.s.l., approx. 14,000 BC
- Suspected moraine wall as a natural dam
- Estimated lakeshore contour line, 420 m.a.s.l. (approx. 10,000 BC)
- Main flow direction of the ice
- Suspected overflow
- Lakeshore before 1592, approx. 416 m.a.s.l.

Lake Zug approx. 15,000 years ago

Land gain in Zug and Ennetsee

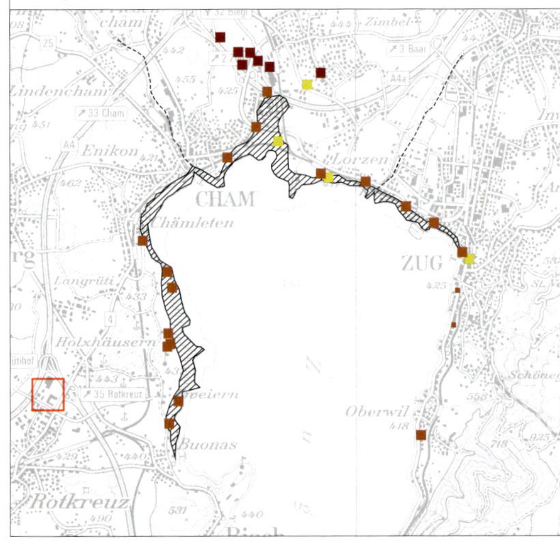

- First marsh subgrade of the sixteenth century
- Land gain by lake lowering, approx. 1.5 km²
- Mesolithic settlements
- Neolithic settlements
- Neolithic shore settlements, unsecured
- Bronze Age shore settlements

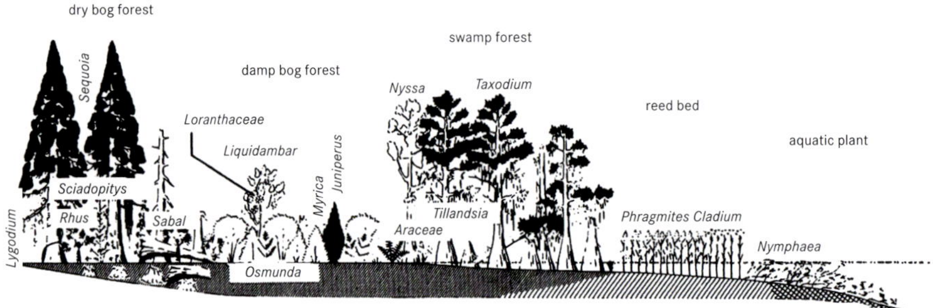

Reconstruction of the vegetation zones for a Middle Tertiary lignite moor in central Europe

Campus, Rotkreuz, CH
Evolution Square

The immense height and circumference of living sequoias still create a strong impression. What dimensions might these trees have had in earlier periods? The species seems predestined to play tricks with time and scale.

Worldwide distribution of giant sequoias

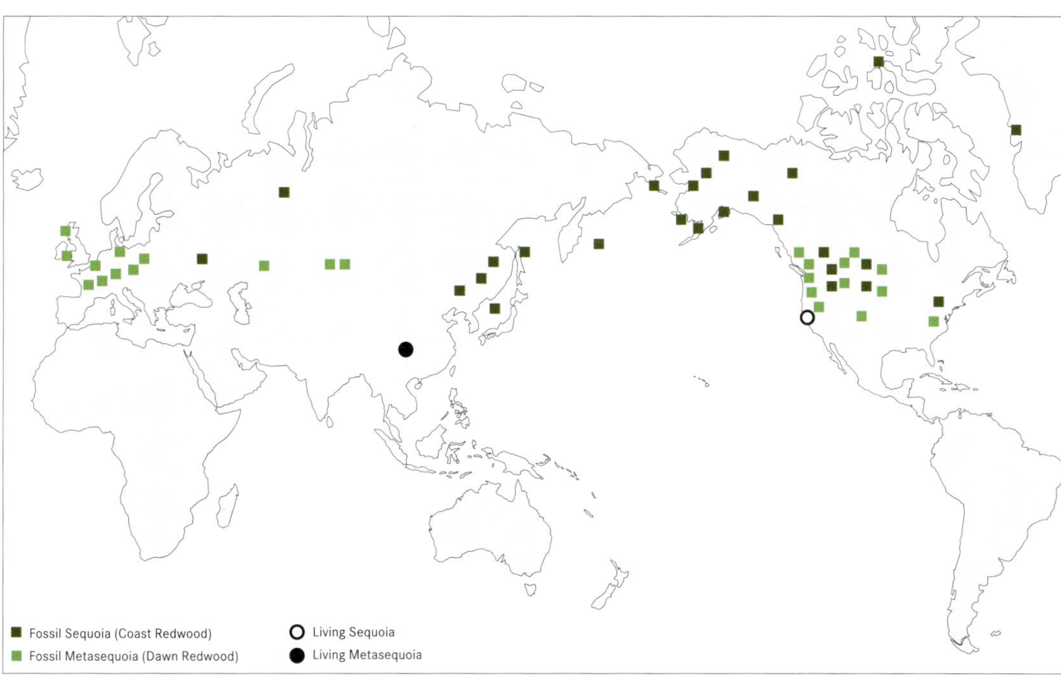

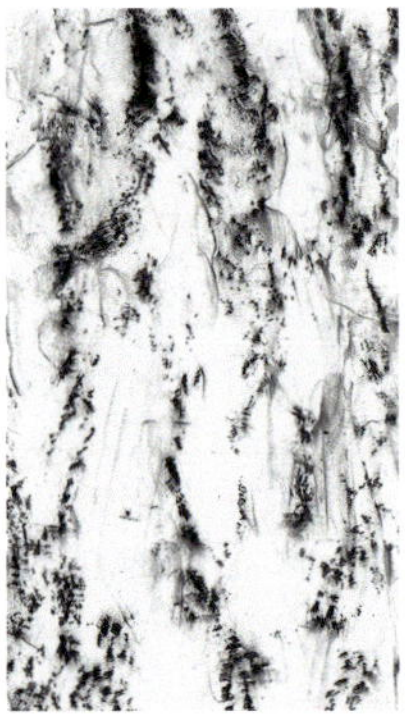

Fraxinus excelsior

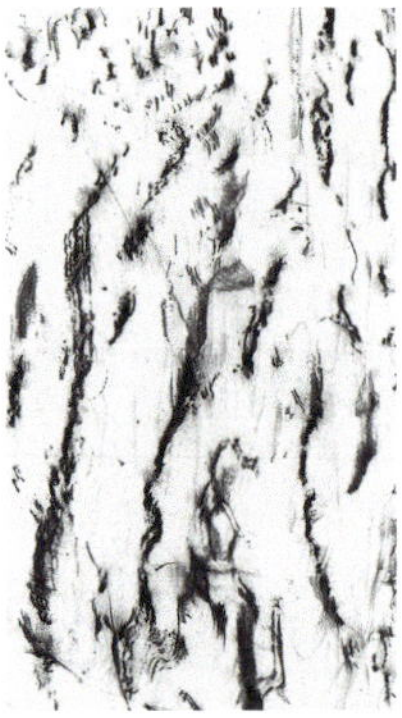

Pinus sylvestris

Taxodium distichum

Metasequoia glyptostroboides

Sequoiadendron giganteum
(Selected tree species)

Working models of the bark structure made of shotcrete

A silicone impression is used to transfer the bark structure.

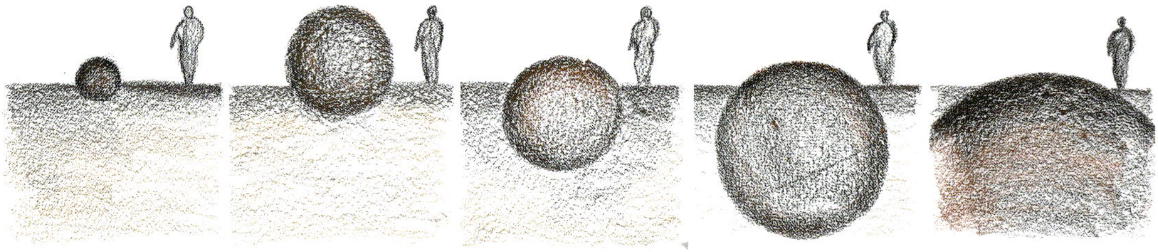

Scale studies of prehistoric tree trunks:
how much remains visible; how much is hidden?
The implied dimensions of the length of the tree and the diameter of its trunk shift the trunk and its location to a different era.

Mock-up made of shotcrete, realized by Eberle Landschaftsbau and Geotechnick AG (Herisau, CH)

Campus, Rotkreuz, CH
Evolution Square

Silicon studies of the raw edge of a fallen tree

Mock-up of the color design

The new headquarters was organized in terms of classical open-space typologies: square, courtyard, promenade, garden. The square is the central focus, serving primarily as a prestigious reception area.

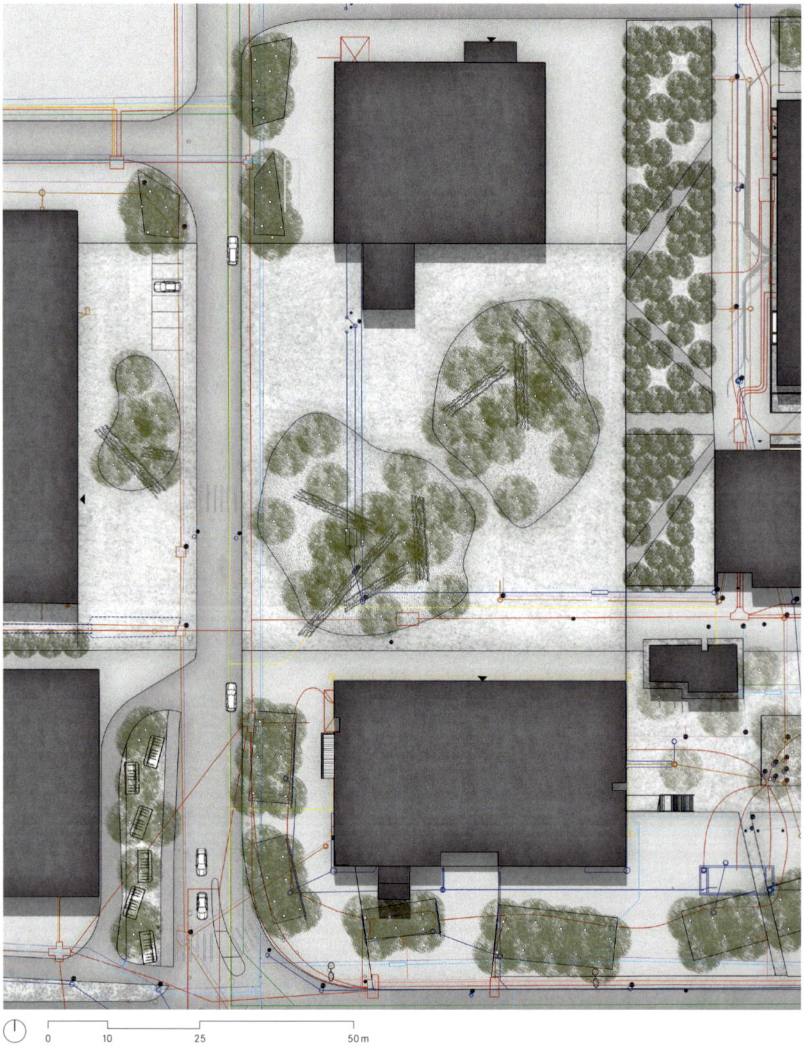

Fallen, dead trees, also known as nurse logs, help seedlings grow and regenerate the forest.

Pyramides de Terre
Detective Work

Roland Charles Shaw

Hoodoos in Euseigne

Rounding the corner to discover the alien formations at Euseigne comes as quite a shock. Peeking out from the wooded landscape with its cartoonish curves, one forgets momentarily that one is in the Swiss Alps. Is this a spray-concrete mound, grafted onto the side of the mountain to attract more tourists? In an attempt to make sense of these bizarre anomalies in the landscape, a variety of names has been ascribed to earth pyramids around the world, often imbuing them with a symbolical or religious significance in the process. America's hoodoos, thought to be etymologically linked to the word voodoo,[1] and France's *cheminées de fée* (fairy chimneys) are two such examples.

An alternative reading is that what we see is a built diagram of a number of erosion forms. The end of the last Ice Age, some 10,000 to 80,000 years ago, saw the retreat of glaciers across what we today call Switzerland. Leaving in their wake huge swathes of mixed deposits, the material at the top of these moraines, often comprising boulders, happened to be much denser than what lay beneath. Acidic rainwater, ice, and wind began the process of carving away at these deposits. This top layer's density, however, prohibited the disintegration processes, so that one thin section of the crust stayed put while the rest of the landscape sank around it. The boulders remain today, perched impossibly upon slithers of rock but often succumbing

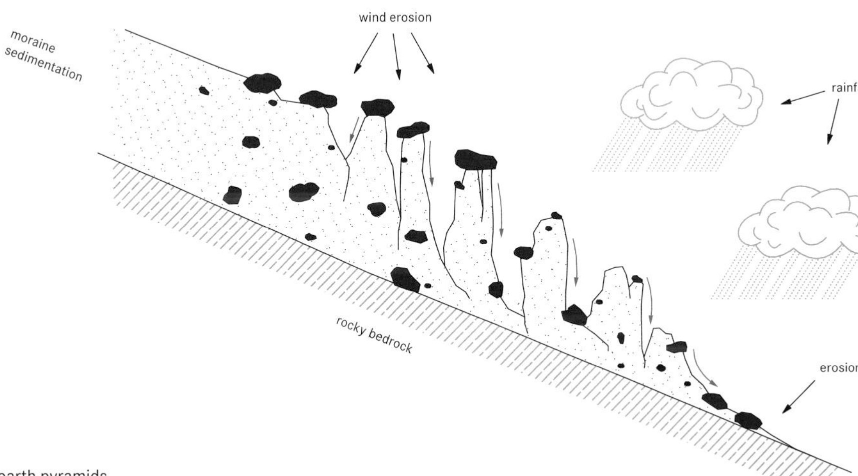

The formation of earth pyramids

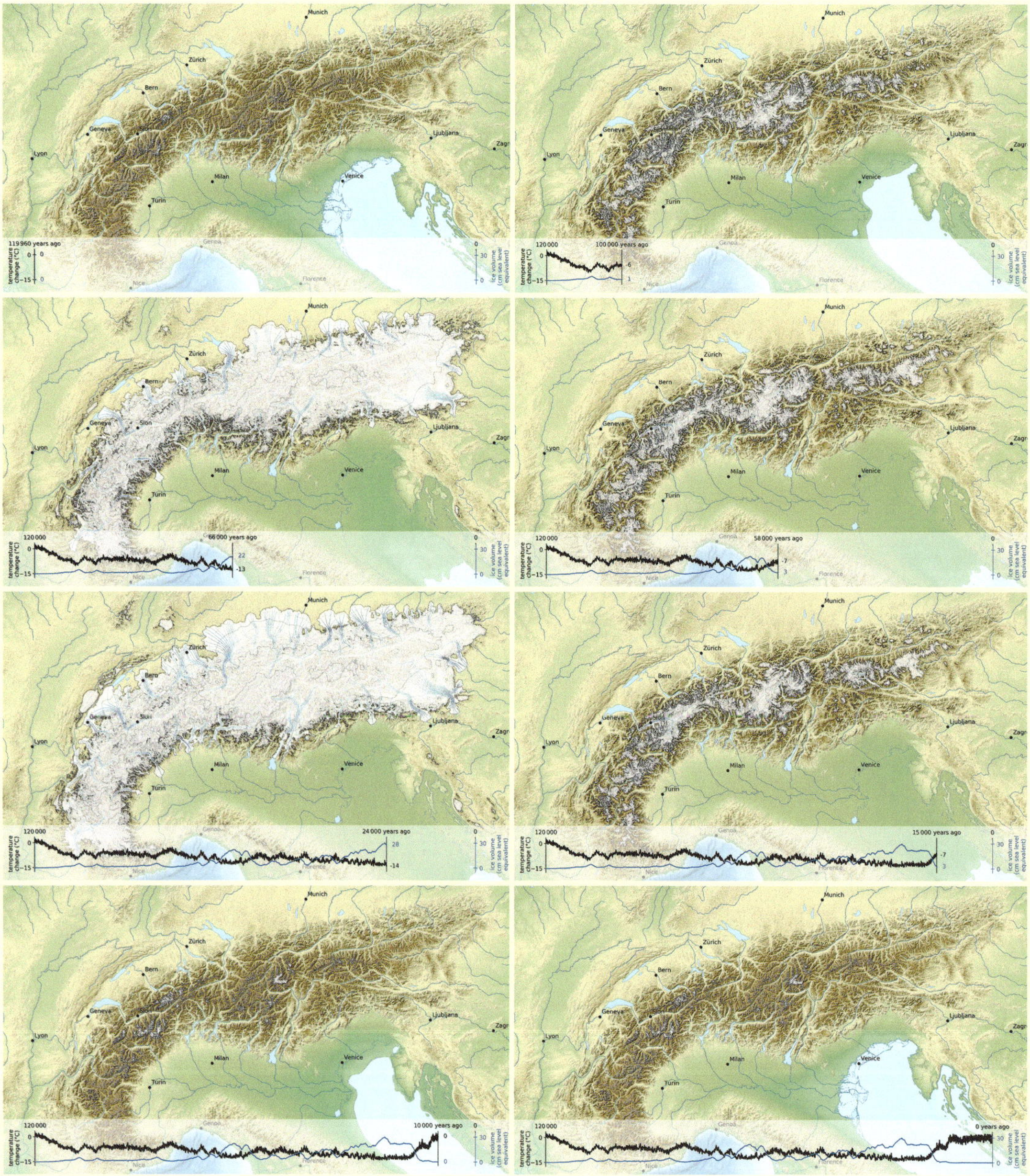

The glaciers of the Alps have successively grown and shrunk over the past 120,000 years, while only a few pockets of the original mass remain today.

themselves to the pull of gravity and eventually falling off. While geological processes originate from within the earth's core and often thrust subterranean strata skyward, as with the formation of the Alps, geomorphological processes operate on the upper crust of the Earth and in this case work downward, hand in hand with gravity.

Further up the Valais Rhone Valley, the glacier at Aletsch is the largest still in existence in the Alps, albeit steadily shrinking. Here, operating on the same principles as in Euseigne, erosion has fashioned the glacier tables–for decades the beloved subject matter of Swiss postcards–whereby stone prohibits the melting of the ice immediately below it, creating a pedestal as the surrounding glacier thaws. At the edges and through the center of this glacier run a series of dark motorway-like lines that follow the route down the valley. Here, as with the pyramids, glacial deposits have not been eroded but simply pushed to the side of the glacier as it takes its downward course.

Glacier-Table on the Mer de Glace
by James D. Forbes, 1843

Geomorphology I. Overview

Einstige und heutige Gewässer
Hydrographie ancienne et actuelle

- Einstiger und heutiger Flusslauf
  Cours d'eau ancien et actuel
- Abflussrinne von Schmelzwassern einstiger Gletscher
  Chenal d'écoulement des eaux de fonte d'anciens glaciers
- Periodisch fliessendes Gewässer im Karstgebiet
  Rivières périodiques en région karstique
- Kliff
  Falaise
- Natursee und überstauter Natursee
  Lac naturel et lac naturel avec retenue
- Stausee
  Lac de barrage

Talstufe, Talwasserscheide usw.
Rupture de profil longitudinal, ligne de partage des eaux en vallée, etc.

- Grössere Talstufe, Mündungsstufe und Riegel
  Rupture de profil longitudinal importante, rupture de profil de confluence et verrou
- Talwasserscheide
  Ligne de partage des eaux en vallée
- Talwasserscheide in tektonischer Mulde (im Jura)
  Ligne de partage des eaux dans un synclinal (Jura)
- Ehemalige Entwässerungsrichtung in Taltorso
  Direction précédente d'écoulement d'un tronçon de vallée

Vorwiegend durch die Arbeit des fliessenden Wassers oder unter Mitwirkung atmosphärischer Einflüsse entstandene Formen; zum Teil durch einstige Gletscher überarbeitet (fluviale, periglaziale und subaerische Denudation)
Formes dues principalement au travail de l'eau courante seule ou combinée avec les influences météoriques; remaniées en partie par d'anciens glaciers (dénudation fluviale, périglaciaire et subaérienne)

- Hangflächen
  Versants
- Fastebene (Peneplain) und Tafelflächen
  Pénéplaine et relief tabulaire
- Andere Verflachungen
  Autres aplanissements
- Junge Talböden und Schwemmkegel (Würm und jünger)
  Fonds de vallées, cônes alluviaux et cônes de déjection, wurmiens ou plus récents
- Fluviale Schotterflächen, älter als Würm
  Surfaces d'accumulation fluviatile à gravier, pré-Würm
- Junge, nacheiszeitlich entstandene Bachtobel oder Kerben, auch inaktive
  Torrents ou ravins torrentiels récents, postglaciaires, actifs ou non
- Schlucht, Klamm
  Gorges
- Canyon
- Klus
  Cluse

- Schichtstufe, Schichtrippe, Bruchlinienstufe
  Front de côte (relief de côte), crête monoclinale
- Gelände- und Terrassenkante
  Ligne d'intersection de terrains, rebord de terrasse
- Gratschneide, scharfer Kamm
  Arête
- Bergrücken, unscharfer Kamm
  Croupe, crête arrondie
- Flacher Bergrücken mit Verebnung
  Croupe avec aplanissement
- Bergrücken in Anlehnung an eine Antiklinale (nur im Jura)
  Croupe anticlinale (seulement dans le Jura)
- Schuttflächen, Schutthänge
  Nappes d'éboulis, versants à nappe d'éboulis
- Schwemmkegel oder Delta
  Cône de déjection ou delta
- Anrisse von Bergstürzen, Sackungen, Rutschungen
  Niche d'arrachement d'éboulements, d'affaissements, de glissements
- Bergsturz
  Eboulement
- Sackung
  Affaissement
- Rutschungsgelände
  Terrain affecté par des glissements
- Tomalandschaft
  Paysage de toma
- Erdpyramide
  Pyramides de terre
- Blockstrom („Blockgletscher")
  Coulées de pierres (glaciers de pierres)

1:500000 — 10 0 10 20 30 km

Feldaufnahmen unter der Leitung von / Levés originaux sous la direction de H. Annaheim, durch / par: H. Andresen, H. Annaheim, D. Barsch, V. Binggeli, A. Bögli, E. Bugmann, K. Erny, R. Salathé, E. Schwabe, R. Seiffert, M. Steffen, H. Zimmermann

Kartographische Bearbeitung / Projet cartographique: Eduard Imhof und / et Heinz Leuzinger, Redaktion des Atlas der Schweiz, Eidgenössische Technische Hochschule Zürich / Rédaction de l'Atlas de la Suisse, Ecole Polytechnique Fédérale Zurich

Scales of Time

Despite the pyramids' misleading artificiality, once armed with an understanding of their formation, one can easily see the effect of erosion here. More often than not, the job of the (landscape) architect starts with a form of detective work: Where are the clues as to how the landscape was formed? In an attempt to decipher the *morphos* (form) of the *geo* (earth), the architect dons the cap of the geomorphologist, so to speak.

Integral to this detective work are many leaps in scale and time. The glacier that formed Euseigne, for example, also left its mark on the other side of the Alps in what we know today as the Swiss Plateau. The retreat of this group of glaciers formed today's bumpy landscape of low hills and sporadic lakes, leaving in its wake an abundance of gravel, a vital resource to this day for the Swiss construction industry. Any attempt to understand the geomorphological history of a specific site, then, demands an understanding of the origin of Switzerland as a whole.

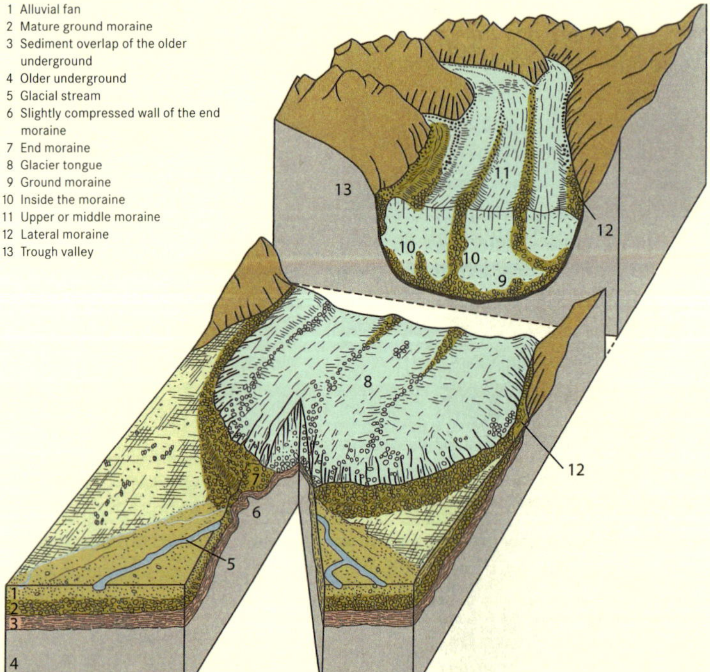

Moraines in and around a glacier, from *Geomorphologie* by Harmut Leser (Braunschweig, 2003)

Homo geologicus

Returning to the pyramids of Euseigne, there is one other form of erosion that we have so far overlooked. Wind and gravity may reform the landscape gradually and continually over millennia, but political and cultural tendencies have ruthlessly and at times irreversibly remodeled Alpine Switzerland in a matter of decades. Since 1947 a tunnel has run through the middle of the pyramids, allowing a road to continue on its way up the mountains to the ski resort

Moraines form black stripes resembling motorways that run the length of the Aletsch glacier.

Two monumental concrete structures: Walter Förderer's concrete Saint-Nicolas church in Hérémence (built from 1967 to 1971) and the vast dam at Grande Dixence (built from 1951 to 1961). At 285 m high, the Grande Dixence dam is the tallest in Europe. It is made of six million cubic meters of concrete.

at Arolla. Geomorphology is also the preserve of humankind, then. From the reservoir at Lac des Dix and Walter Maria Förderer's tectonic church at Hérémence, we continue to leave our mark here through tourism, energy production, and climate change. While the formation of our earth pyramids required many tens of thousands of years, we have ruptured the earth's crust to a comparable degree in a matter of generations.

1 "Hoodoo," Oxford English Dictionary, accessed April 23, 2019, https://en.oxforddictionaries.com/definition/hoodoo.
2 https://interaktiv.tagesanzeiger.ch/2017/gletscherschwund/?openincontroller, accessed July 17, 2019.

In spite of appearances, landscape is never a static condition, but always dynamic: the current form of the pyramids is not the end of the story. Approximately 60 percent of Switzerland's glaciers have disappeared between 1850 and 2016,[2] and we must accept that our pyramids at Euseigne will also not stand forever as erosion continues its work.

Šmartinska, Ljubljana, SI
The Landscape Beneath the City

Under the direction of architect Jože Plečnik, the city of Ljubljana has undergone major structural changes since the 1920s with the implementation of comprehensive urban renewal plans. Assertive and monumental architecture and boulevards aimed to establish links with major European metropolises such as Vienna, Berlin, and Paris. Some hundred years on, the Šmartinska project is to be another major step in the city's development–this time using different strategies. The new part of the city is shaped by organizational principles and open-space typologies such as squares, promenades, and parks. Their design does not seek to reproduce traditional patterns and images. References to the specific Slovenian landscape beneath the city are intended to characterize the open space and emphasize local differences.

Client:
City of Ljubljana

Cooperation:
Master plan:
Hosoya Schaefer Architects, Zurich

Design:
2008–2009

Type and size:
Park/Square/Promenade/Street, 230 ha (entire quarter)

Status:
Not realized

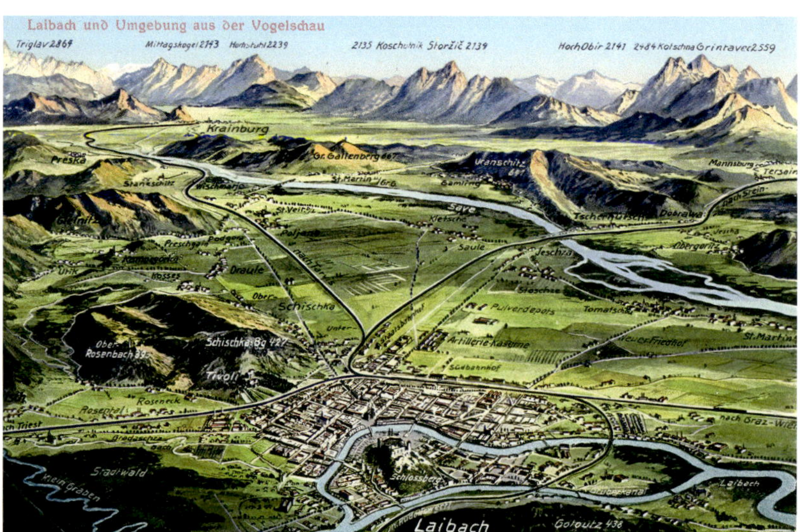

Karst landscapes can be found in various forms in many parts of the world. They invariably develop out of limestone, gypsum, or saline formations, which are dissolved by weathering or carbonation when factors such as rainwater, atmospheric carbon dioxide, and a humid climate combine to cause erosion. Because the country features a considerable amount of karst–which was scientifically examined for the first time here–this type of landscape is closely associated with modern-day Slovenia. This is also illustrated by the etymology of the term, which derives from the Slovenian *kras,* a word that has its origins in the Latin *carsus* meaning "rock" or "stony, barren soil."

While usually, a landscape can be mostly surveyed by analyzing its surface, this is not possible with a karst landscape, because a substantial part of it is below the surface, where it no longer functions as stable bedrock but is reduced to a crust between different strata. It takes a section view and scientific maps to relate the visible to the invisible. To understand the phenomenon of the Slovenian river with its seven names, you have to be aware of the invisible river stretches flowing through the karst, and partly through the famous Postojna Caves: Trbuhovica, Obrh, Stržen, Rak, Pivka, Unica, and Ljubljanica had previously been considered to be different rivers with their source and outflow in the rock, whereas in reality they are just names used to denote the visible sections of the same watercourse.

Even the vegetation of the karst can only be understood by knowing the processes that formed the landscape. An analysis of the vegetation maps and the characteristics of the tree species studied conveys a mental image of mighty forests, but what is found on-site is perplexing: the lack of soil formation and poor storage of water and nutrients result in the emergence of miniaturized forests shaped by the wind, with mature oak forests reaching a maximum height of ten meters, the same size as the native smoketrees (*Cotinus coggygria*)–the scale and species of an urban front garden transposed to the vast Slovenian landscape.

Translation into Design Principles

In order to exploit the accumulated knowledge in the design, the material had to be condensed into its essential aspects. Using simple schematic diagrams, the different geological rock formations and images of the vegetation were interpreted and translated into superordinate design principles. In the new quarter, these principles appear in different degrees of intensity in all the open spaces –parks, squares, and promenades–but are most clearly visible in the central park. The different kinds of karst provide a rich vocabulary–alpine (limestone, beech with maple), pre-alpine (dolomite, oak with hornbeam), and Dinaric (sandstone, hornbeam, poplar, and alder).

The design of the vegetation and topography from west to east shows the progression from covered to open karst. The western part, with its high proportion of trees and light depressions reminiscent of dolines (sinkholes), appears as a rather scenic playground and sunbathing lawn. In contrast to this, the eastern area shows a mineral, urban character, with the paths framed by stone walls based on the geomorphological phenomenon of limestone pavements (slabs called clints crisscrossed by deep fissures called grykes). The perception of the watercourse is reinforced by the vegetation, from hornbeam woods to groves of alder and poplar and groups of oak trees. A nutrient-poor substrate also causes a disconcerting form of dwarfism in some groups of trees. The connecting element is water: while in the western part the scenic impression is enhanced by a body of water that grows and shrinks in size depending on the quantity of rainfall, the underground watercourse in the transitional area is only partially visible or audible, before it reappears in the eastern part in the form of an artesian spring. (lr)

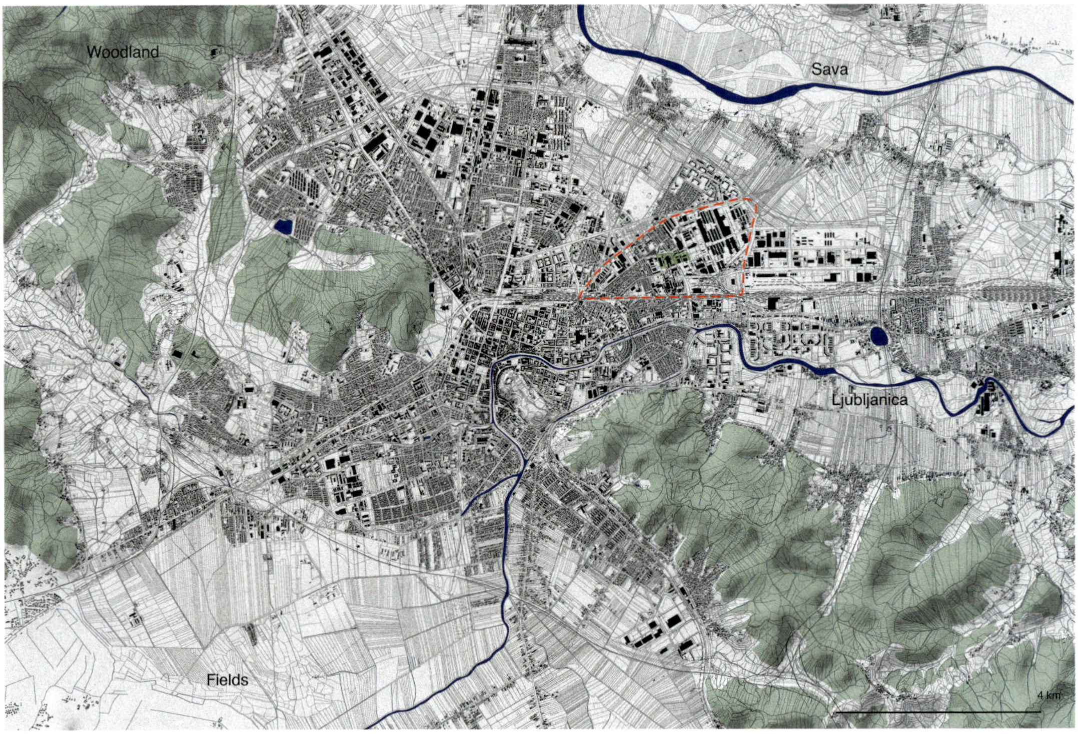

Ljubljana's urban landscape is characterized by two wooded mountain ranges that extend from the west and east to the center of the city and the two river plains of the Ljubljanica in the south and the Sava in the north.

Šmartinska, Ljubljana, SI

The Landscape Beneath the City

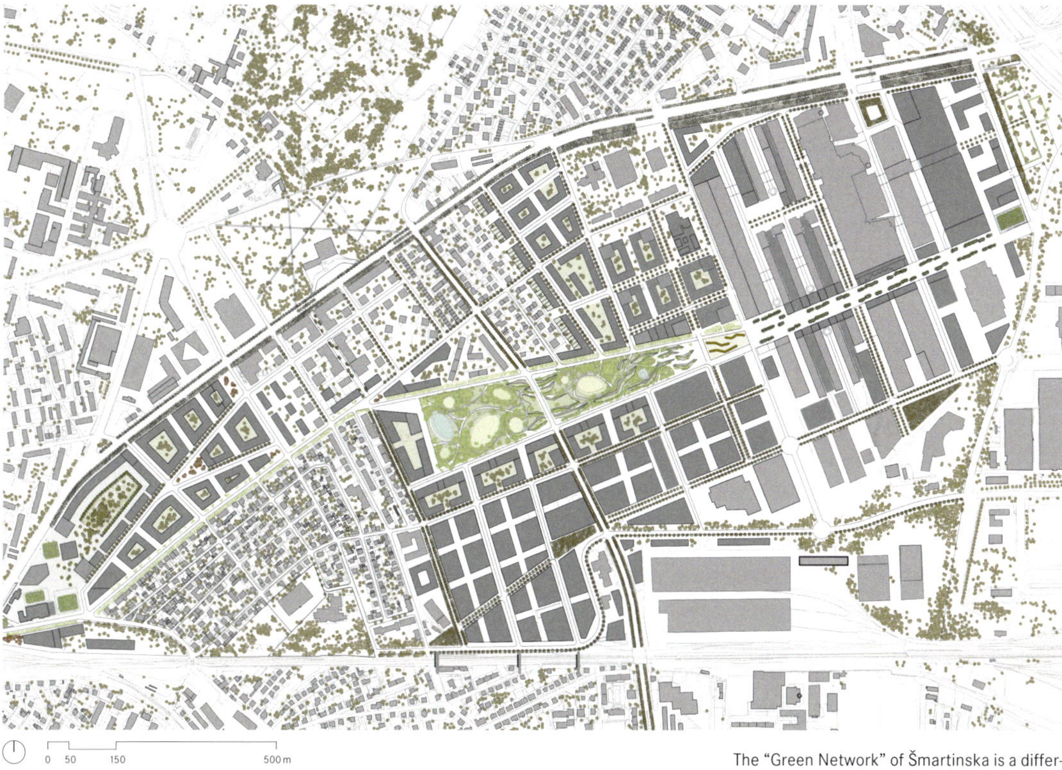

The "Green Network" of Šmartinska is a differentiated system of "Lifelines" running west to east and north to south, and a surrounding green girdle. The backbone of the Šmartinska district is Kavčičeva ulica–the boulevard to the north of it. The newly established connection links the site with the city center and is basically designed for pedestrian and public transport flows.

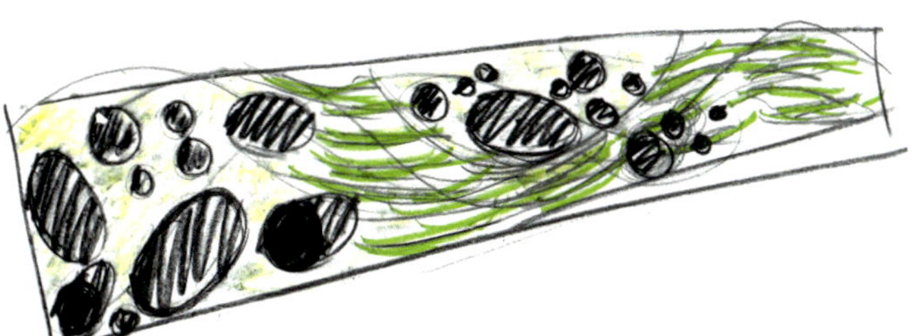

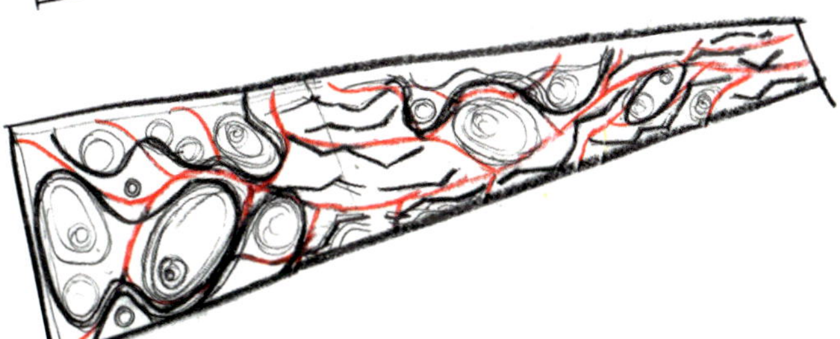

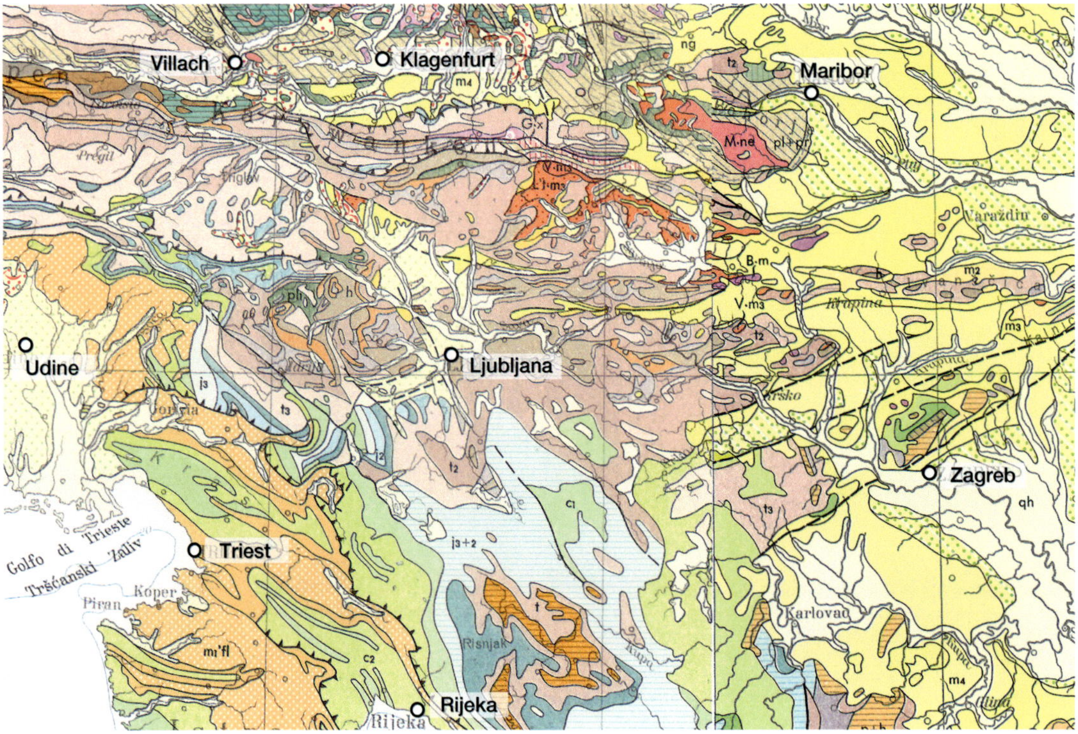

Slovenia: Geology

Ljubljana at the intersection of various geological features

Šmartinska, Ljubljana, SI
The Landscape Beneath the City

Karst is the umbrella term for topographic structures that are created by processes of dissolution and deposition of soluble rocks, mainly limestone. The structures, which on the surface are often confined to the local terrain or region and generally manifest as fallow areas that are difficult to use, typically contrast with a subterranean system of caves that links up to a much wider underground network.

Nude karst

Covered karst

Soft karren

Doline

Sharp karren

Potje

Grinded karren

Cave

Constant surface flow
Occasional surface flow
Ponor
Karst spring
Established groundwater connection
Surface distribution
Alleged karst distribution system
Flood zone of the karst field
Surface at an altitude above 700 m
Surface at an altitude between 600 and 700 m
Surface at an altitude of up to 600 m
50 Karst field with altitude indicated
Collapsed
Big water pit

Ljubljanica river basin

The river Ljubljanica is the continuation of several karst rivers that flow from the Prezid Karst Field (Slovene: Prezidsko polje) to Vrhnika on the surface and underground in caves. Thus, the river is poetically said to have seven names: Trbuhovica, Obrh, Stržen, Rak, Pivka, Unica, and Ljubljanica.

Postojna cave, 1910

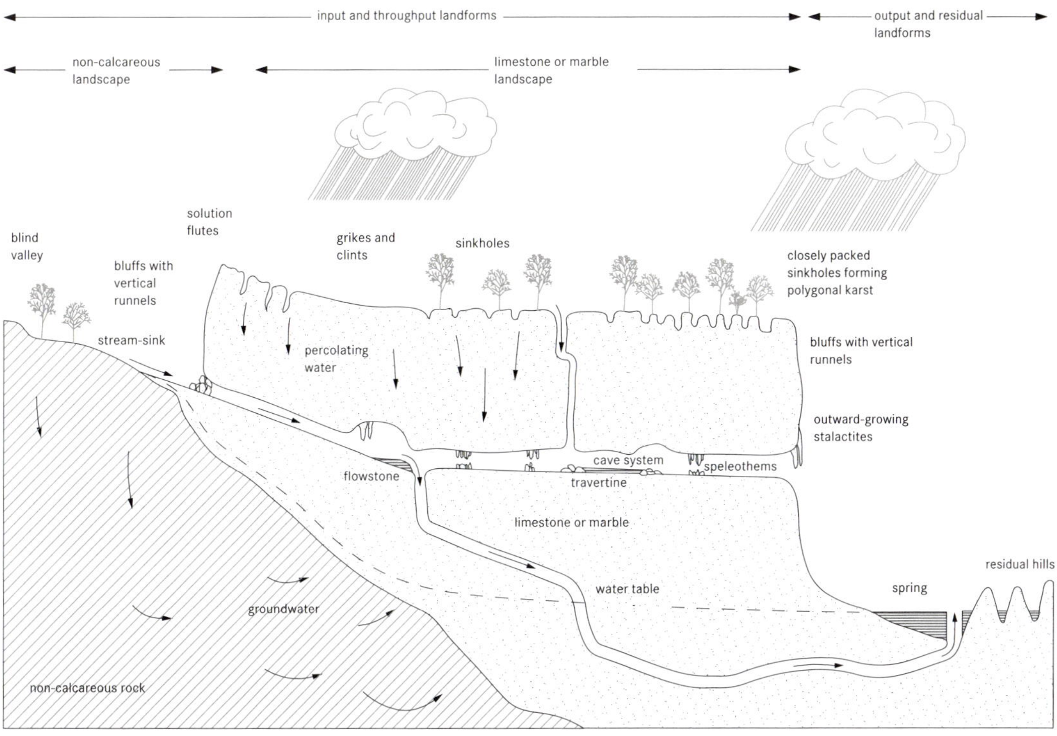

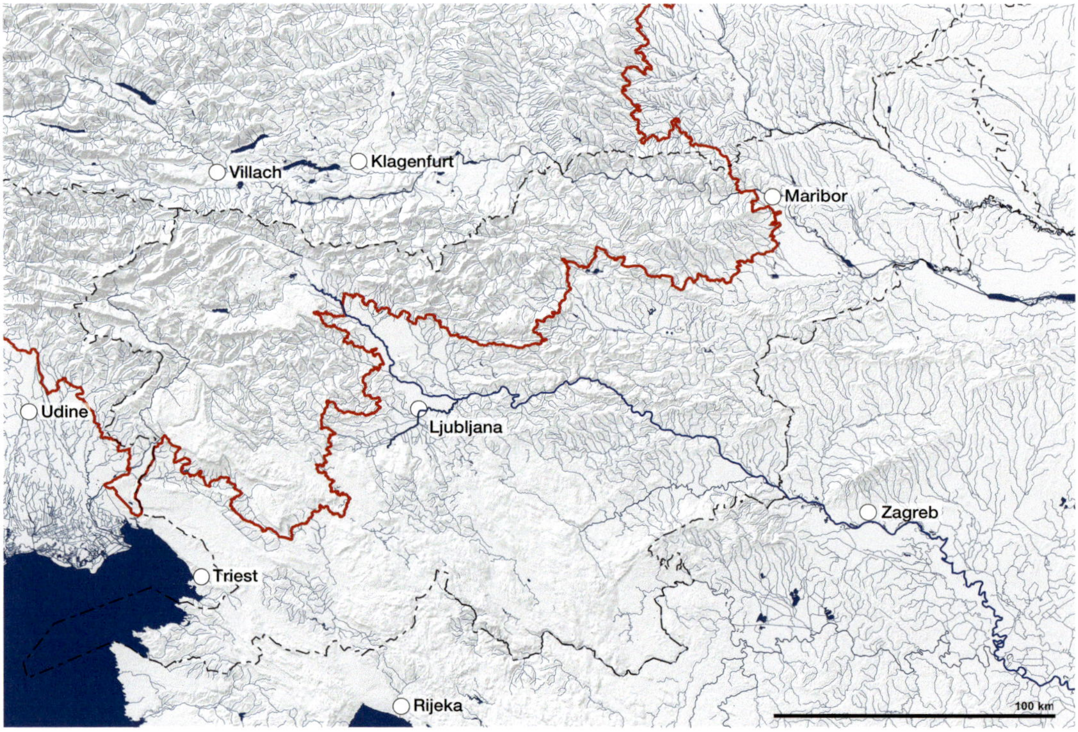

Slovenia: Watercourses

Course of the river as it progresses
from the landscape into the city

Šmartinska, Ljubljana, SI
The Landscape Beneath the City

Water sequencing in the park:
1 Still water on stone
2 Water flowing underneath the stone
3 Water coming up and disappearing between the cracks

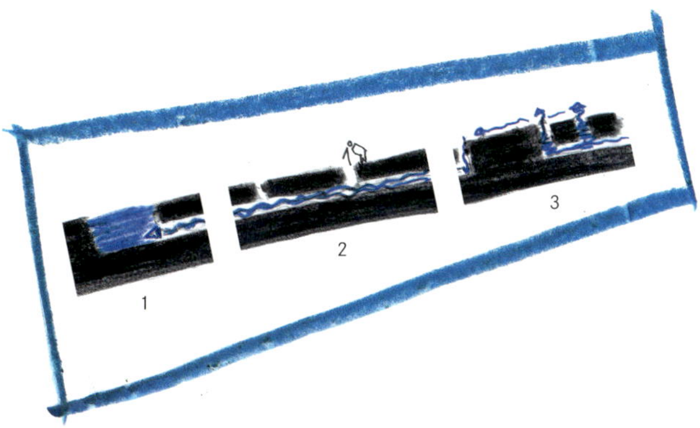

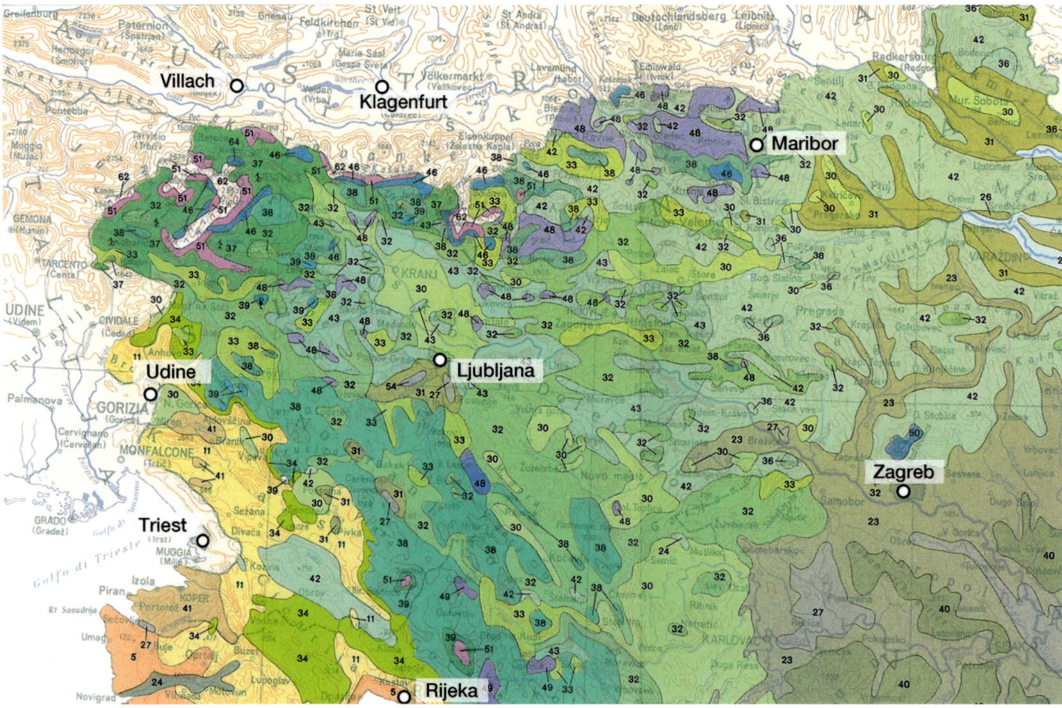

Slovenia: Vegetation

Ljubljana at the intersection of various vegetation zones.

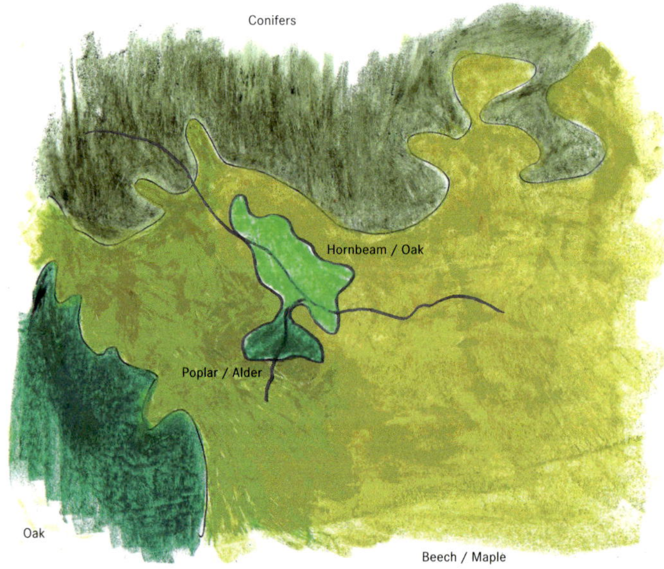

Šmartinska, Ljubljana, SI
The Landscape Beneath the City

Karst creates different site conditions, reflected by the presence of different forest types and tree species.

Vegetation scheme

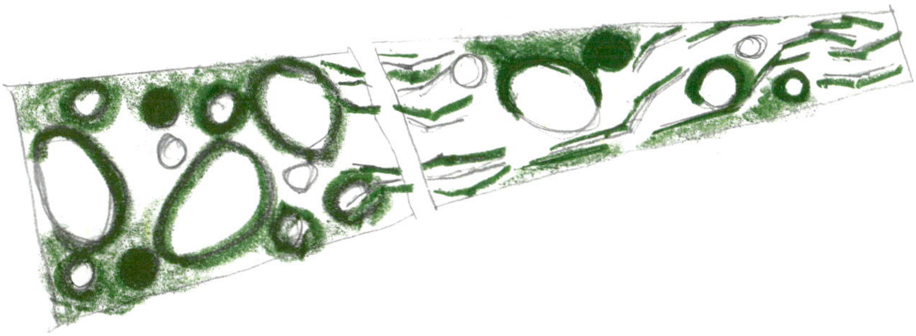

Aerial photographs showing how vegetation adapts to karst formations

Vegetation types

Meadows with single trees

Open dolines

Wood densifications marking the dolines

Clearings marking the dolines

Rims of trees around the dolines

Vegetation along/ between rockbelts

Metaphor: Gradient of soft and hard landscapes

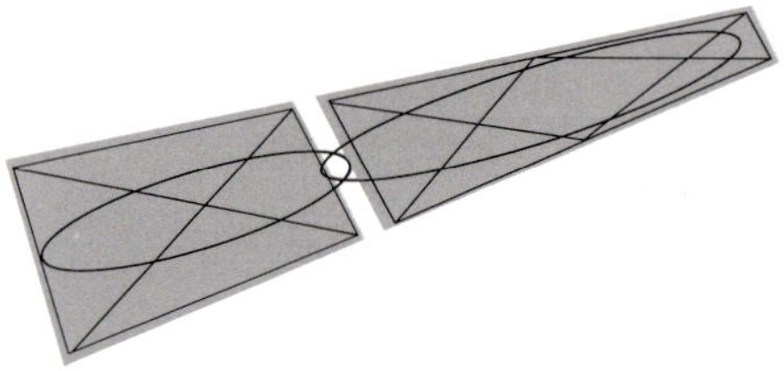

Choreography: Edge trail, loop trail, cross connections

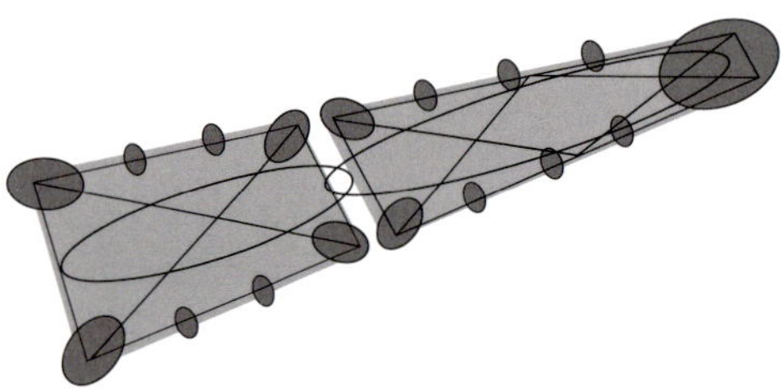

Threshold: Main and side entrances

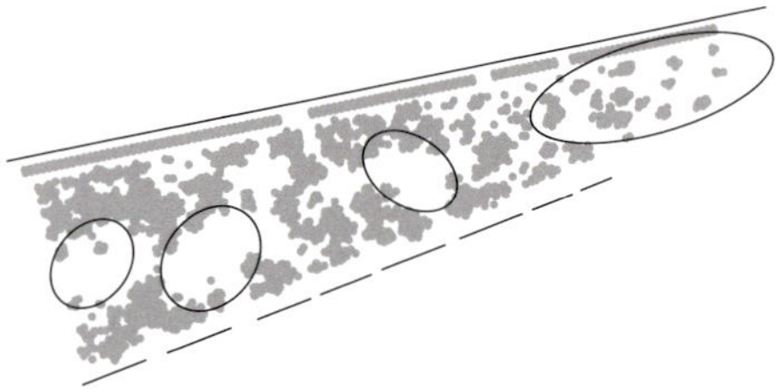

Vegetation: Dense tree planting and open spaces

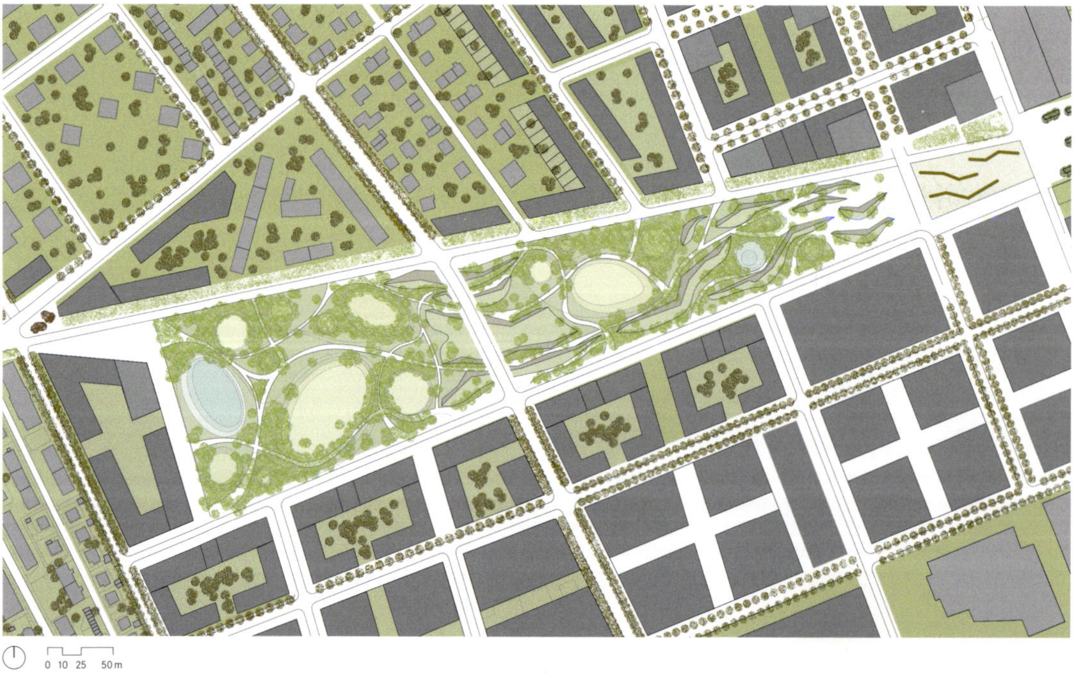

0 10 25 50 m

“The massive **remodeling of the contours of the Earth** can only be represented using complex digital models. The anthropogenic transformation of the world’s topography is more significant than the ‘natural’ erosion that is caused, in particular, by water and wind. Perhaps we’d rather not know, because then we’d stop trusting the ground we stand on. But ultimately we are responsible for these changes, and we need to ask what we are trying to achieve in refashioning the Earth’s surface.” (gv)

Drägerwerk, Lübeck, DE
Erratic Giants

Client:
Drägerwerk AG & Co. KGaA

Cooperation:
Architecture:
Goetz & Hootz Architects, Munich

Design/construction:
2005–2006/2007–2008

Type and size:
Park/Courtyard, 4 ha

Status:
Realized

They are called *Düvelstein* or *Devil's Stone* (location: Grosskönigsförde, weight: 180 t, material: Småland granite),[1] *Mövenstein* or *Möves' Stone* (location: Travemünde, 80 t, Bornholm hammer granite),[2] *Alter Schwede* or *Old Swede* (location: Hamburg, 217 t, Växjö granite)[3], or *Buskam* (location: Rügen, 1600 t, Bornholm hammer granite)[4]: glacial erratic boulders whose names mostly date from a time when the geological inconsistency with the site of the find could not yet be scientifically explained and was, therefore, ascribed to the Devil or mystical giants, who were supposed to have hurled these gigantic boulders to their current location–particularly aimed at objectionable churches, which they seem to have missed though. And although the extent of the glaciers has been scientifically proven since the nineteenth century and the origin of each boulder can now be accurately established by mineralogical analyses, the sight of these erratics is still amazing.

The migration of these erratic boulders, the transport of such huge rocks of up to several thousand tons over literally hundreds of kilometers, is not a local phenomenon but can be found all over the world wherever landscapes were formed by glaciers–whether deposited visibly on the ground or localizable by earth sonar in deep soil layers. The design of the ensemble of research, development and administration buildings of the company links the campus to these glacial relicts and their migration: giant monoliths ostensibly floating on water, standing upright, or resting in a grove create unexpected images and vistas. Like many other erratics found in North German landscapes, these specimens originally come from Sweden. Transported over thousands of years on or in the flowing ice of a glacier mass to be finally deposited at their current location, a field owned by the Dräger family near Lübeck and a gravel quarry on the Danish island of Fyn, they made the last part of their journey in a mere few days on an SLT or heavy-duty tractor unit.

The courtyards also contain references to the local geology: not in the form of a landscape shaped by glacial processes, but as brick surfacing made of fired clay. *Transformation and compaction (diagenesis) of a geological layer by heat.* The bricks are laid unevenly with a few millimeters' variation in height creating a surface relief, accentuated by precipitation and retaining rainwater. *Deposits over time.* The familiar material from the local building tradition is juxtaposed against something foreign: the distinct growth patterns of North American swamp or bald cypresses (*Taxodium distichum*), Chilean monkey puzzle trees or pines (*Araucaria araucana*) and Japanese weeping larches (*Larix kaempferi pendula*), which we mostly know from the front gardens of suburban neighborhoods, turn these small groups of trees into autonomous objects placed in courtyards only open to the sky. Like the erratic boulders they, too, are travelers brought from faraway countries to the Hanseatic city. (lr)

1 Frank Rudolph, *Geologie erleben in Schleswig-Holstein* [Experience Geology in Schleswig-Holstein], Kiel 2011.
2 www.ln-online.de/Lokales/Luebeck/Moevenstein-Bergung-teurer-als-erwartet, accessed March 29, 2019.
3 www.hamburg.de/geotourismus-geologie/144844/alter-schwede-altona.html, accessed March 29, 2019.
4 Ingrid Schmidt, *Hünengrab und Opferstein: Bodendenkmale auf der Insel Rügen* [Megalithic Tomb and Sacrificial Stone: Geological Monuments on the Island of Rügen], Rostock 2001, 42.

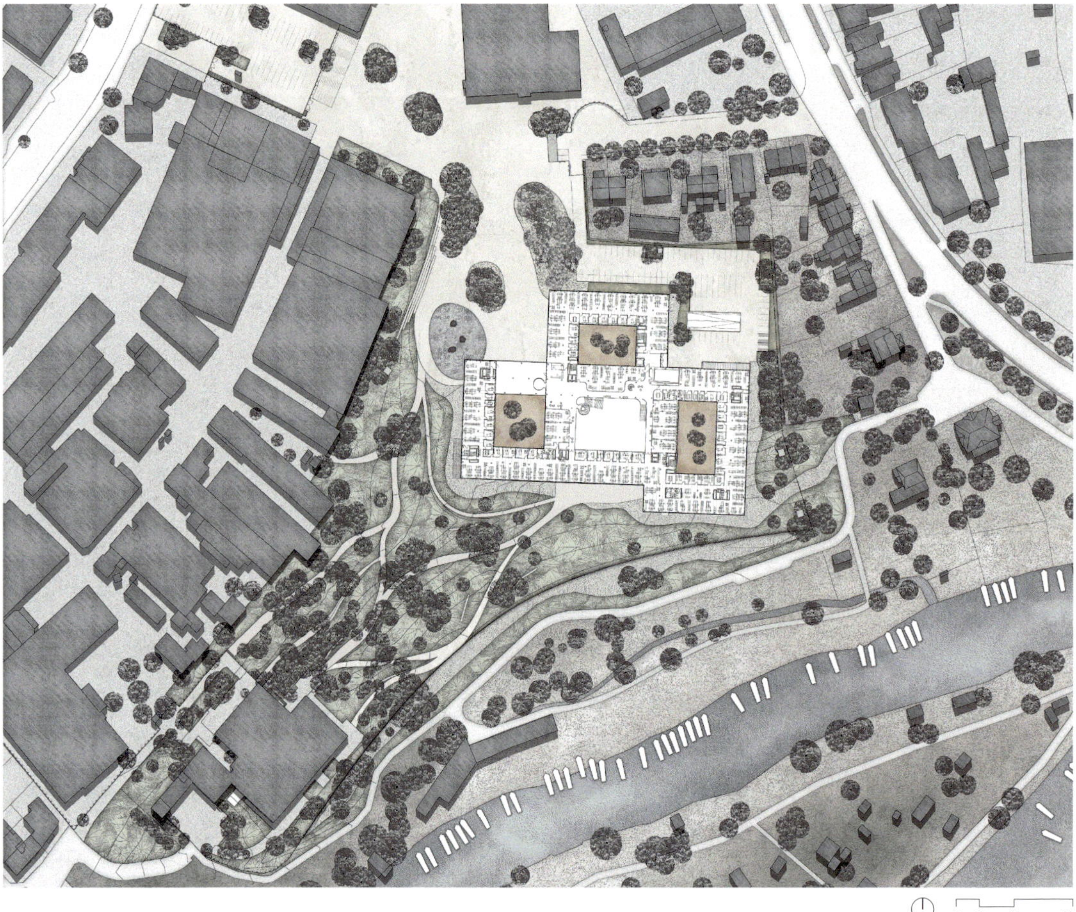

A road cutting through the site was abandoned to allow the new company headquarters to be built. The site includes a spacious campus with a square, park, and several courtyards that mediate between the dense city fabric and the urban landscape of the Trave River. The site has been historically anchored in the Lübeck area, drawing on familiar elements from the landscape and local building traditions, which also respects the Dräger family's desire for a restrained appearance.

Map of Europe showing the extent of glacier systems at the peak of the last Ice Age, 1881

Glacial depositions: Over time glaciers transport boulders across very long distances.

1 Brash and sediments accumulate in front of the glacier.
2 The glacier advances and compresses the sediments, giving rise to floes and folds, with the supraglacial moraine (sm) above.
3 Following the glacier melt, the ground moraine (gm), supraglacial moraine, and terminal moraine are left behind.

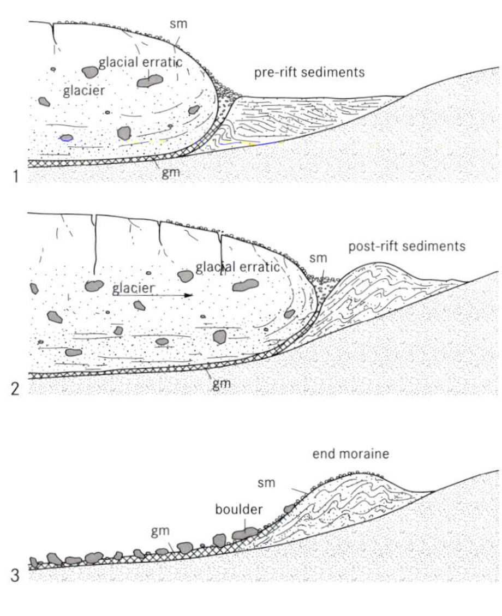

Drägerwerk, Lübeck, DE
Erratic Giants

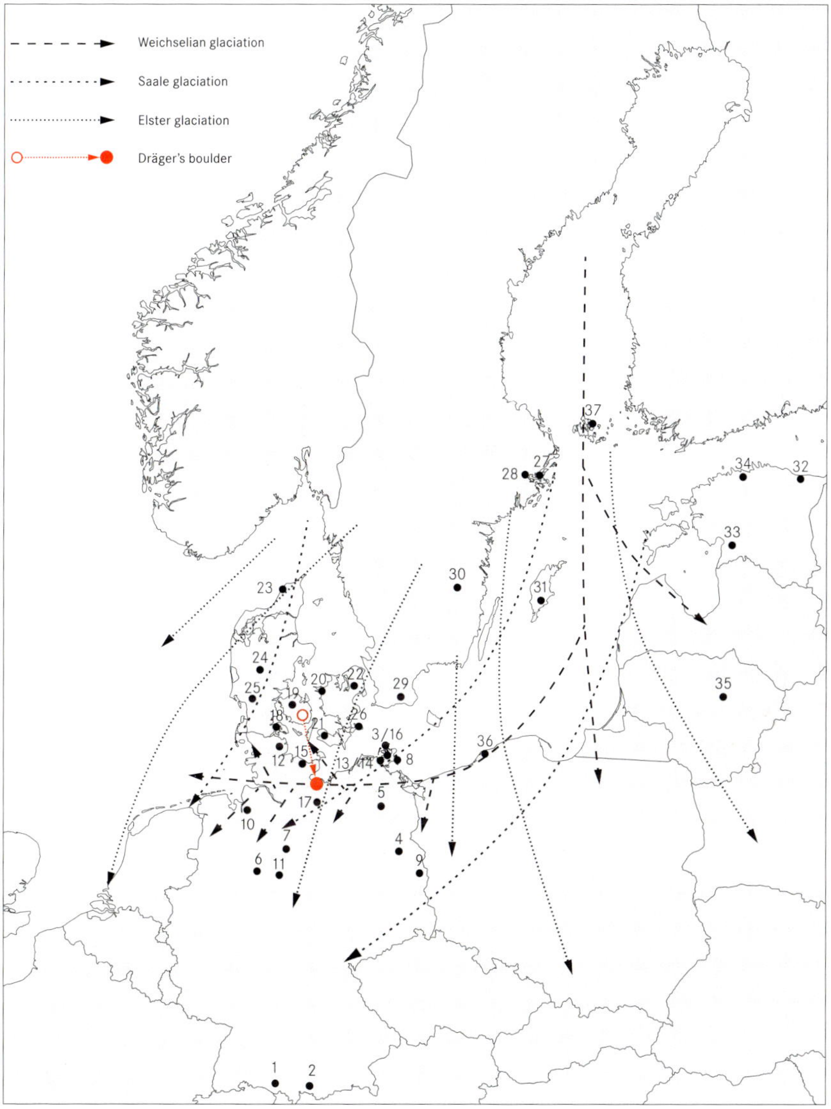

Germany:
1 Erratischer Block
2 Dengelstein
3 Markgrafenstein
4 Buskam
5 Grosser Stein
6 Grosser Stein von Tonnenheide
7 Giebichenstein
8 Der grosse Stein bei Nardevitz
9 Kobbelner Stein
10 Alter Schwede
11 Johannissteine bei Lage
12 Düvelstein von Grosskönigsförde
13 Siebenschneiderstein
14 Schwanenstein von Lohme
15 Wandhoff-Findling
16 Klein Hegoland
17 Grosser Stein in Ventschau

Denmark:
18 Barsten
19 Dammestenen
20 Dyrestenen
21 Høvængestenen
22 Hvissingestenen
23 Janum Kjøt
24 Mørupstenen
25 Tirslundstein
26 Sjælland

Sweden:
27 Blockhusuddens
28 Gustav III
29 Klövasten von Glemminge
30 Runkesten bei Vimmerby
31 Bastustainen

Baltic states:
32 Ehalkivi
33 Matsekivi
34 Majakivi
35 Puntukas
36 Grosser Stein von Tychow
37 Hamborggardstenen

Localization of boulders weighing more than 100 metric tons in northern Central Europe. The arrows represent a reconstruction of the different directions in which ice advanced during the last three glacial periods based on indicator stones.

Underground boulders can only be detected using ground-penetrating radar.

Reconstruction of a geo-sonar image.

Drägerwerk, Lübeck, DE
Erratic Giants

Moved gradually over thousands of years by the flow and thrust of the glaciers, this boulder could only be lifted and moved to its destination with the help of several large machines and transporters.

Drägerwerk, Lübeck, DE
Erratic Giants

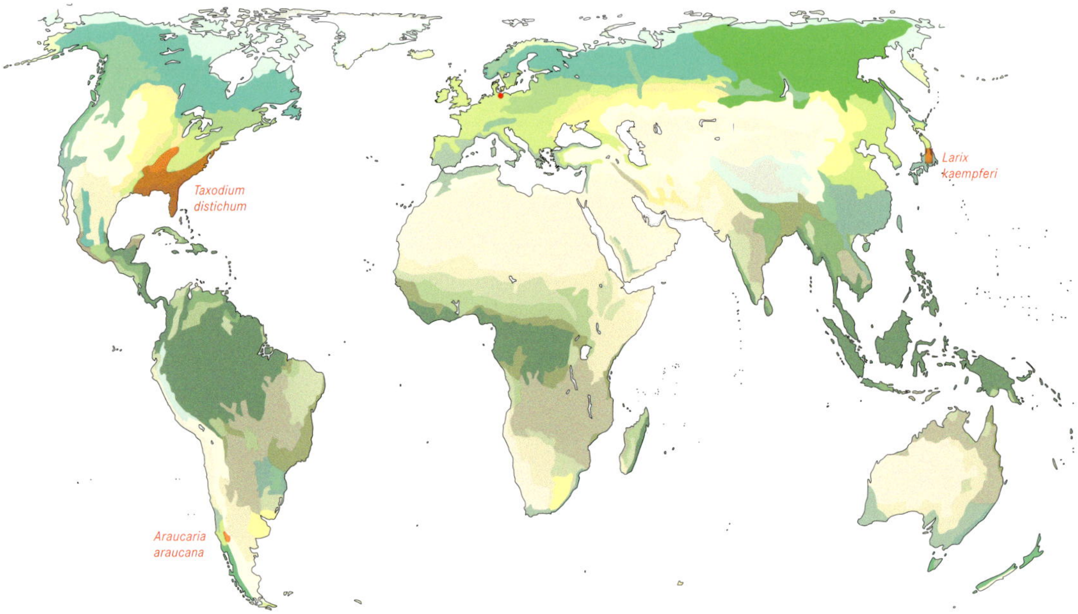

Tree species from comparable climatic zones on three different continents populate the courtyards like travelers from faraway lands.

Tropical zone
- Thorn savannahs, formations of thorny scrub and succulents
- Dry savannahs
- Dry forests and cerrados
- Wet savannahs
- Monsoon forests
- Tropical semi-deciduous rain forests
- Tropical indeciduous rain forests

Subtropical zone
- Sclerophyllous vegetation
- Subtropical rain forests
- Deciduous tree steppes
- Transition and black earth steppes (prairie)
- Dry steppes
- Semi-desert and desert

Temperate zone
- Evergreen coniferous forests
- Deciduous coniferous forests
- Temperate rain forests
- Mountain coniferous forests
- Broad-leaved and mixed forests
- Deciduous broad-leaved forests

Polar zone
- Inland ice, glacier
- Cold desert
- Tundra, alpine tundra and grasslands
- Subpolar meadows and deciduous plants

“We are becoming ever more alienated from the body of knowledge accumulated by the natural sciences over many generations. **Are these trees native?** I have always been surprised by this question. The ginkgo from southwest China is a tree that was the subject of a poetic description by Goethe way back when. Why should it suddenly be excluded now? **Are these plants poisonous?** This is another exaggerated form of alienation. In the end everything is poisonous, it’s just a matter of dosage. But who in their right mind eats three kilos of *Cornus sanguinea* (dogwood) seeds? These berries are so bitter that you’re definitely not going to eat a second one, and yet the lethal dose for humans is measured in kilograms.” (gv)

Géographie des plantes équinoxales, illustration in *Essai sur la géographie des plantes* by Alexander von Humboldt and Aimé Bonpland, Paris 1805

Trachycarpus fortunei
Invasive Plants

Günther Vogt

A Sense of Wonder
A hotel by the lake: a typical scene in the Swiss tourist landscape. The horizontally cut rows of chestnut trees along the water edge create space for an urban promenade. A large building behind it is divided into three approximately equal volumes and represents the beginning of a new era of tourism in Lucerne. A row of tree trunks, lined up as if on a boulevard with the usual geometric tree pits, flanks the approach road. There is not a leaf or frond in sight. It is November, and the slender treetops have been tightly wrapped. Only abstract conical shapes can be seen, a peculiar spectacle to look at, especially in contrast to the chestnuts in the background. Later on, in spring, the trees

View from the entrance of the Hotel Schweizerhof in the direction of the Rigi and the Vierwaldstättersee, Lucerne, winter 2018

will be released from their protective sleeves, but the sense of strangeness will persist for a while. Whether sheathed or unsheathed, the plants seem to be "stabled" in the manner of a menagerie, to create–for a short season–a public space with a dense but lively atmosphere and provide a stage on which the bourgeois life of the city can be enacted.

Originally, the palm trees were moved to and fro between two climatic zones depending on the season. In winter, they were placed in large pots and housed in the mild warmth of the greenhouse in the hotel backyard, the orangery, or the brightly lit lobby. In summer, they migrated to the hotel

Promenade in front of the Hotel Schweizerhof, ca. 1910

Interior of the Kursaal in Lucerne, built ca. 1882

driveway: a grand welcoming gesture to guests and tourists upon their arrival, at the same time evoking a longing for southern climes on this northern flank of the Alps.

From Travelers to Tourists

The Grand Tour was a kind of initiation rite for the British upper classes. The first travel reports focused on the city culture and the aristocratic courts and villas in the countryside. For a long time, crossing the Alps was considered a necessary evil. It was only toward the end of the eighteenth century that the context of comprehensive social, economic, and political changes led to a complete reinterpretation of the Alps. The frightful mountains turned into a beautiful landscape. In this constructed scenery, the threatening mountains formed the inaccessible backdrop, with an idyllic landscape in the foreground. The golden age of alpinism in the second half of the nineteenth century and the exploration of the Alps by the British marked another turning point in the perception of the landscape. Travel became more

Departing from London, a typical Grand Tour itinerary in the nineteenth century would often include Paris and Geneva, before crossing the Alps to Italy. There, travelers would visit some of the most renowned Italian cities, such as Turin, Florence, Rome, and Naples. They would then head back north through Austria, Germany, Belgium, and the Netherlands.

democratic, and "travelers" became "tourists." It was no longer just the fascination with strange beauty and sublime panoramas that was the main focus of interest. The tourist urbanization of the mountains was also driven by the desire to view the archaic way of life pursued by the inhabitants of the Alps, which no longer merely represented one of the numerous staging posts on the journey south but mutated into a destination in their own right. The South became the unfulfilled promise of an imaginary paradise.

Map of the world showing the extent of the British Empire in 1886 and its associated trading routes. Plant hunters–also called botanical explorers–would participate in the trips to discover and bring back new species.

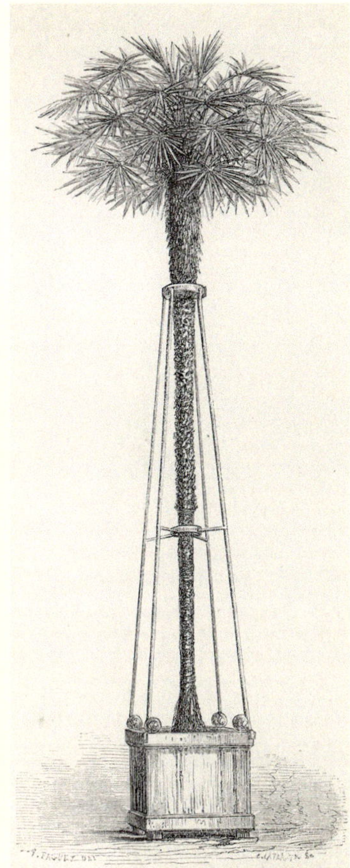

Fig. 8 —Fan-palm at the entrance of the Amphitheatre at the Jardin des Plantes.

The plants were transported with care and then exhibited in glasshouses, such as the Palm House at the Royal Botanic Garden in Kew or the Jardin des Plantes in Paris.

Reality and Idea

The palm trees in the foreground, the lake and chestnut trees in the middle ground, and, in the background, the peaks of the snow-capped central Swiss Alps brightly illuminated at dawn and dusk: the landscape as a stage for a world of one's imagination. The scenery recalls the beginnings of the English landscape garden, when painters conceived ideal landscapes and–despite lacking any technical understanding of what was involved–actually created the profession of landscape architect. Their depictions later became models for actual gardens, such as Stourhead, Blenheim Palace, and Stowe House. Active in the same period, plant hunters operated quite differently. Wealthy

1. Hyphaene thebaica *Mart.* (Dumpalme): *a* Fruchtstand, *b* Frucht durchschnitten. 2. Lodoicea Sechella
a männlicher Blütenkolben, *b* Fruchtkolben, *c* Frucht, *d* desgl. von unten mit den drei Keimlöchern, *e*
Blütenkolben, *d* weibliche Blüten, *e* Fruchtstand, *f* Einzelfrucht (Dattel). 5. Calamus rotang W.
c weibliche Blüte, *d* Frucht (Kokosnuſs) geöffnet. 7. M

llennufs); *a* männlicher Blütenkolben, *b* weibliche Blüte, *c* Frucht. 3. Elaeïs guineensis *Jacq.* (Ölpalme);
chellar 4. Phoenix dactylifera *L.* (Dattelpalme); *a* männlicher Blütenkolben, *b* männliche Blüte, *c* weiblicher
er Rohr); *a* Blattscheide. 6. Cocos nucifera *L.* (Kokospalme); *a* Zweig des Blütenkolbens, *b* männliche,
ifera *Mart.* (Weinpalme); *a* männlicher Blütenstand, *b* Frucht.

CHAMÆROPS FORTUNEI *Hook*

♄ *Chine* *presque rustique.*

< Scientific illustration of *Chamaerops Fortunei,* now called *Trachycarpus fortunei,* pictured in the book *Flore des serres et des jardins de l'Europe* by Louis van Houtte, published in 1877

The native and introduced range of *Trachycarpus fortunei,* as per Gian-Reto Walther et al., "Palms Tracking Climate Change," *Global Ecology and Biogeography* 16, no. 6 (November 2007).

garden owners or scientific associations sent explorers from London to the then colonies of Senegambia or India with the aim of transporting new plants to England in order to cultivate and study them in botanical gardens and, later, introduce them into horticulture. They were excerpts from real landscapes that existed on the other side of the world, while alluding to the borders of the largest colonial empire in the history of mankind.

Trachycarpus fortunei, the Chinese windmill palm, named after Scottish plant hunter and gardener Robert Fortune, is the species of palm that is also found in Lucerne. Originally native to the mountain forests of India, Nepal, Bhutan, Myanmar, Vietnam, and southern China, where it lives at heights of up to 2,400 meters above sea level,[1] the plant is known colloquially as the *Tessinerpalme* or Ticino palm in the Alpine regions.

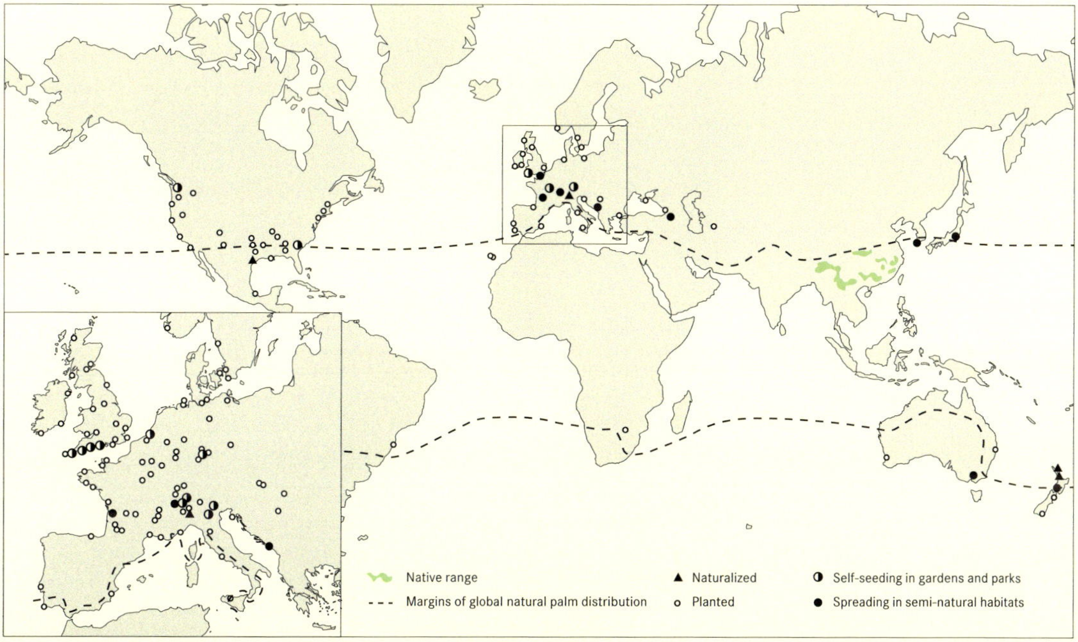

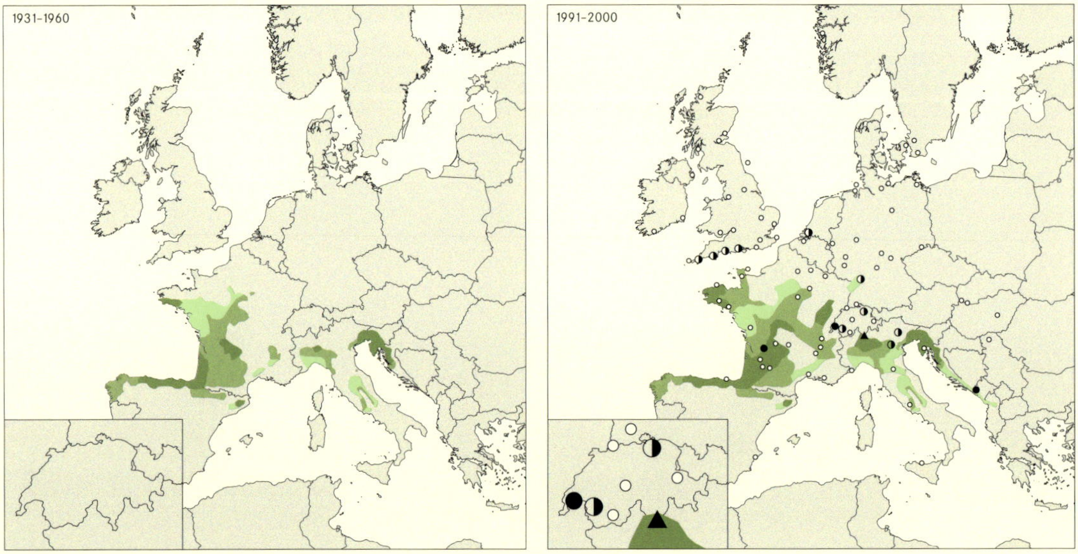

Climate suitability for *Trachycarpus fortunei* "Dark shades of [green] denote better conditions for establishment and growth [...] than light shades due to the direct effect of climate on net assimilation and respiration [...]. The insets show that in southern Switzerland the conditions became suitable for *Trachycarpus* palms only in the latter period [1991–2000]." Walther et al.

Biotopes and Habitats

Originally, the palm was introduced as an ornamental with high frost resistance and planted in the Canton of Ticino and in gardens and parks within areas enjoying clement conditions north of the Alps. The microclimate of some lake landscapes in the north–high levels of insolation on the adjacent hills and mountains due to the reflection of sun rays on the water, coupled with warm winds from the south–ensures moderate temperatures. In the south it is the higher average annual temperature and the generally milder climate in winter that allow such palms to be cultivated even without winter protection.

The once exotic palm trees have by now become a natural part of the Ticino landscape–garden fugitives that have found congenial habitats in the forest undergrowth, at the edge of woodlands, or along shady paths. The continuous rise of the annual mean temperature is creating a new, constantly expanding habitat for the palms outside of gardens. The exotic specimens are becoming invasive, and have now been put on a black list of non-native species that have been officially attested to have a negative effect on the economy, the health of humans, livestock, and plants, local biodiversity, and ecosystem services.[2] The consequent call to eradicate the plant from the landscape seems hopeless given the circumstances. The alien morphology of palm trees, the verticality of leafless trunks, is thus set to create a new type of landscape in the near future. The foreign is becoming familiar.

1 "Trachycarpus fortunei," *Botanischer Garten der Universität Basel,* accessed March 28, 2019, https://botgarten.unibas.ch/arten/trachycarpus_fortunei/index.php.
2 Bundesamt für Umwelt (BAFU), ed., *Strategie der Schweiz zu invasiven gebietsfremden Arten* (Bern: BAFU, 2016), 4, www.bafu.admin.ch/gebietsfremde-arten.

The *Trachycarpus fortunei* finds its habitat in the specific biotope of Ticino, with its altitude, climate, soil and exposure. In Switzerland's southern canton, the first exotic specimens were observed in the forest about fifty years ago. Today, palm trees have become so common in the region that they are regarded as "native." Photograph: Valle Maggia, Ticino, July 2019.

Klosterplatz, Einsiedeln, CH
The Square within the Square

Klosterplatz Einsiedeln, which is edged by the abbey and cathedral churches and the prestigious facades of the adjacent buildings, is the largest ecclesiastical square north of the Alps. As an important place of arrival and gathering, it refers to the Europe-wide network of pilgrim routes that have been etched into the landscape over time. In contrast, the adjoining pastures and the paths trodden by locals, which have been worn into the paved areas through centuries of use, is indicative of the simple village and its choreography of everyday life. Although the connection between monastery and village–between the sacred and the profane–has increasingly dissolved over recent decades, a few targeted topographic interventions have renewed the role of the square as a mediator between these worlds.

Client:
Kloster Einsiedeln and Bezirk Einsiedeln

Cooperation:
Architecture:
Romero Schaefle Partner, Zurich

Design/construction:
2008–2019/2011–2022

Type and size:
Courtyard/Square, 2 ha

Status:
Partly realized

In 1775 Goethe described the Einsiedeln Abbey as an imposing architectural manifestation of the Christian faith in the midst of a vast landscape located far from large urban centers: “We now saw, rising in a dreary treeless vale, the splendid church and the monastery, surrounded by a neat-looking colony, with its wide and stately precincts for the suitable accommodation of so large and varied an assembly of guests.”[1] The place must have seemed much more remote to Meinrad, a monk from the Reichenau monastery, 940 years earlier,[2] when he withdrew to the “gloomy forest” in the high valley between Lake Zurich and Lake Lucerne–back then the Swiss equivalent, as it were, of the Palestinian desert, to which the first hermits had repaired in the third century to devote themselves to God in the solitude of perpetual prayer.

Meinrad’s death marked the actual historical beginning of Einsiedeln Abbey which, in turn, led to the foundation of further monasteries as it sent out monks to help expand a landscape steeped in religion as a territory of faith; not identical with the territories of the cities but overlapped by them and pursuing quite similar objectives: the extension of their sphere of influence and the securing of the livelihood of a particular community.

Part of a Continental Network

Over the centuries, site-development systems serving economic, cultural, military, and ritual needs were inscribed into the landscape and consolidated by the establishment of infrastructures. Einsiedeln’s location north of the Alps also made it an important center and a point of intersection in the network of pilgrims’ routes–to Jerusalem, Rome, and Santiago de Compostela–that spanned the entire continent. This network was also used to disseminate the knowledge of the time and, especially in the early centuries, to transport a large number of familiar and extraneous plants to and fro between the monastery gardens of Europe. The mighty western red cedars in the abbey’s Abtelhof still bear witness to this tradition.

Klosterplatz is evidence of the dense overlapping of religious and secular territories. The square, which was created when the site was reconstructed in the eighteenth century, was anchored in both worlds as a connecting link between monastery and village: in the mundane sphere, it was a commons belonging to the local population, while in the realm of the sacred it was a fitting threshold to the mighty monastery church, a worthy place of reception for pilgrims and, on holy days, a place of gathering and procession. In recent decades, however, there has been a significant shift in this finely adjusted balance between the two worlds.

The Square within the Square

The concept behind the remodeling of Klosterplatz is geared to the urban design of its eighteenth-century arcades. With the help of some few interventions, these arcades are to underline the importance of the monastery forecourt as a central and prestigious meeting place. In line with the baroque design defining the square, the existing convex stairs between the arcades, which lead up to the abbey church, are supplemented by a concave stairway and continued down to the square. A short series of steps below the Marienbrunnen or Lady Fountain complete the oval suggested by the arcades and, thus, define a “square within the square.”

Based on the concept of the Piazza del Campo in Siena, the paved surface slopes down toward the fountain in trapezoids set at a slight angle to one another. The paving, consisting of simple rows of split river pebbles–debris from the once torrential Sihl River that reflect the regional geology–is being replaced. Although the paving stones will no longer evoke the nearby river, at least the color of the surfacing will once again define the square. The fine network of everyday and ritual paths, which has been worn into the paving by centuries of use, will also partly disappear. The course of the individual paths has, however, been recorded and reconstructed on the basis of historical photographs. Future choreographies of daily life and liturgy will give rise to a new network of tracks set in stone. (lr)

1 Johann Wolfgang von Goethe, *Poetry and Truth: From My Own Life*, trans. Minna Steele Smith (London: George Bell & Sons, 1908), 267.
2 Ida Lüthold-Minder, *Madonna im finstern Wald: Aus der Wallfahrtsgeschichte Unserer Lieben Frau von Einsiedeln* (Einsiedeln: Wendelinsverlag, 1973), 12.

The monastery consists of a church, a school, workshops, and stables. It is located above the village and surrounded by the pasturage and forest belonging to the monastery. The center of the complex is the Klosterplatz, the monastery square.

The Way of Saint James is a system of roads and trails across Europe. Since the High Middle Ages, everyone taking the route has had the same goal: the alleged tomb of the Apostle James in Santiago de Compostela in Spain.

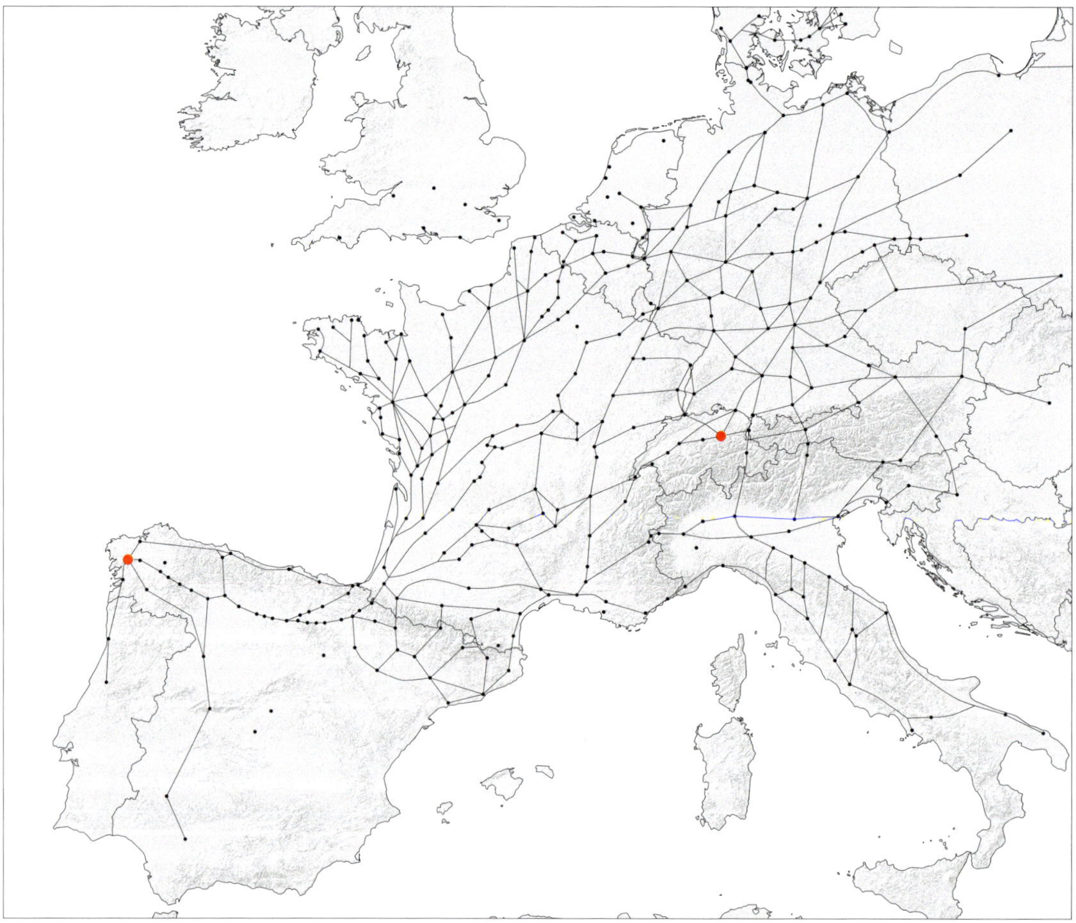

Klosterplatz, Einsiedeln, CH

The Square within the Square

The Upper Sihl Valley before it was flooded to create the artificial Sihl Lake, 1910

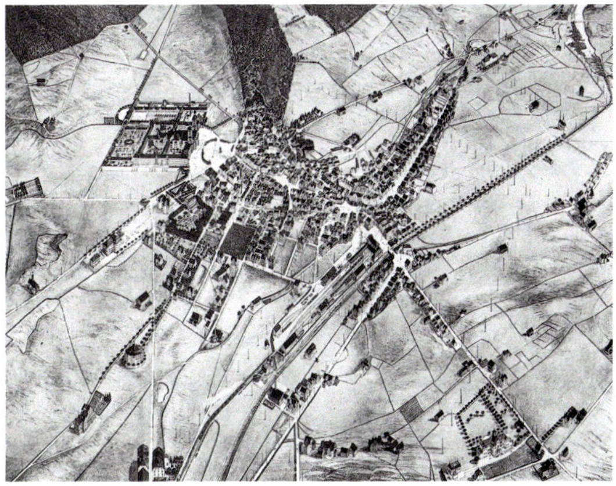

The historical pilgrimage trails and the access routes to the village begin to overlap, 1912.

Switzerland at the heart of the network of pilgrim paths: monastery complex and routes, mapping from 2018

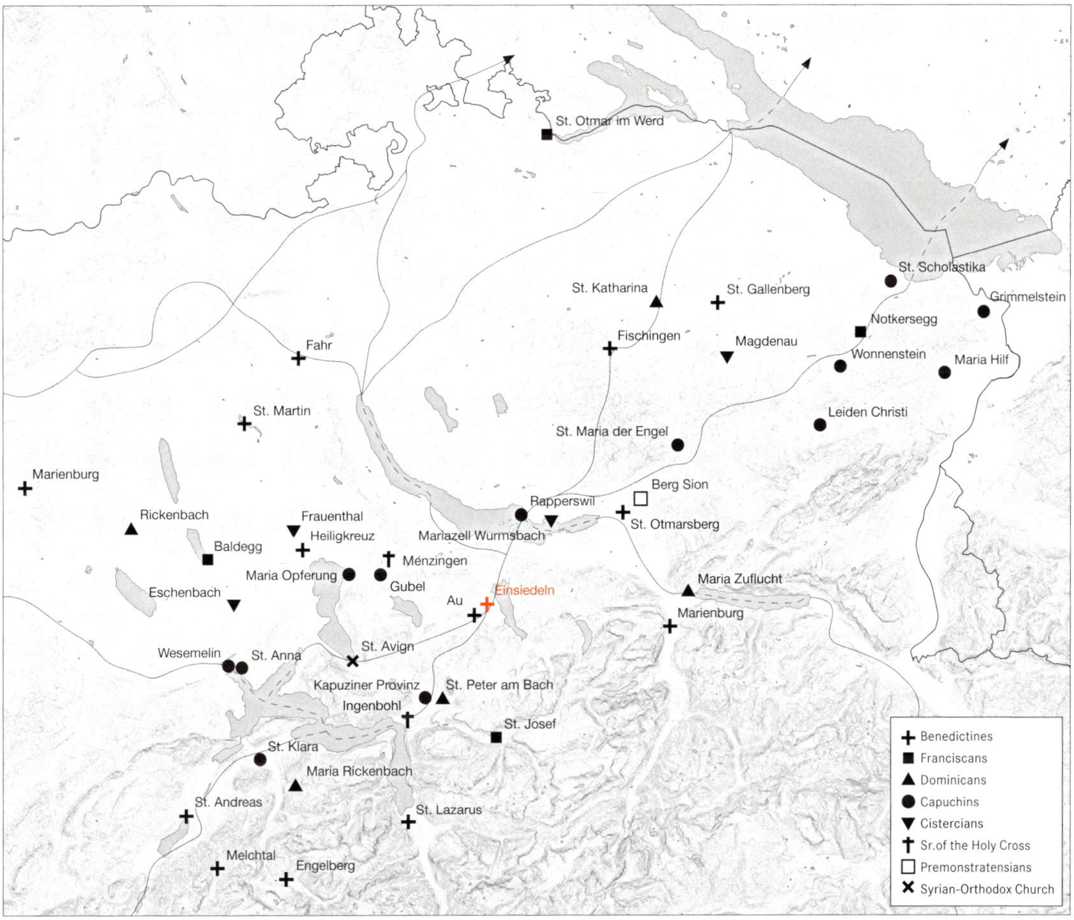

The Klosterplatz mediates between the secular and religious worlds.

The square as a stage, with the arcades and monastery facades as backdrop

Klosterplatz, Einsiedeln, CH
The Square within the Square

The staged choreography of everyday life: the paths have been engraved in the paved surface by centuries of use.

Before the dynamic flow of the rivers had been slowed by reservoirs and power stations, these waterways regularly transported large quantities of bedload from the adjacent mountain regions. The material could then be scooped up on the riverbanks and sorted according to size and suitability. The individual stones were split and set in place with the broken side facing upward. The river stones show a tremendous variety according to their geological provenance. It was only with the advent of road and rail systems, with the possibility they offered of transporting materials over long distances, that the more regular paving made of quarry stones gained in importance and superseded the paving made of river gravel.

Klosterplatz, Einsiedeln, CH
The Square within the Square

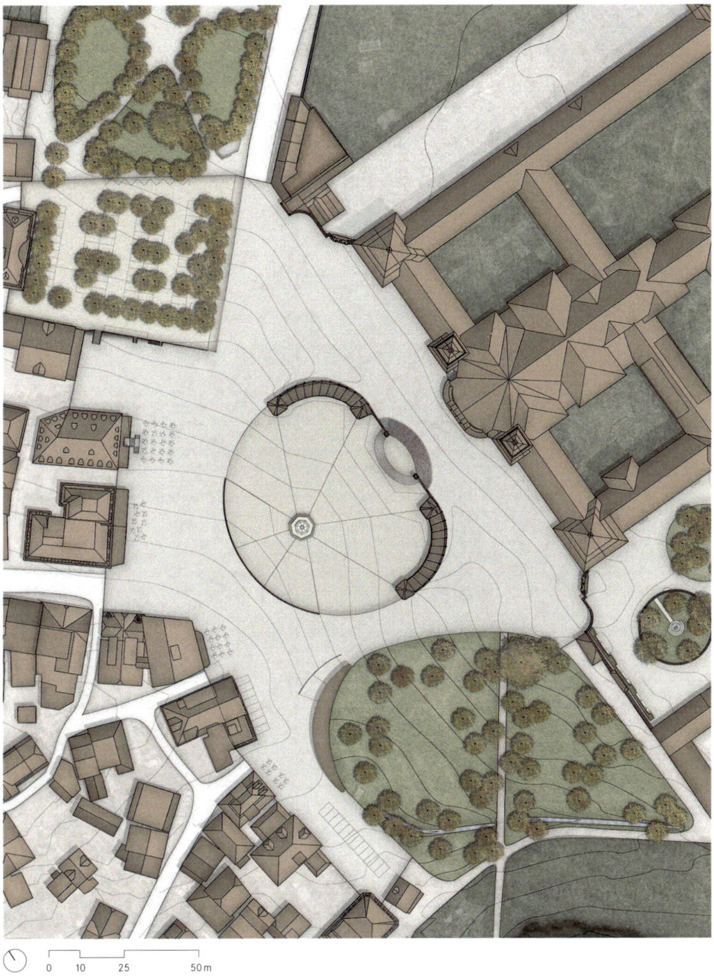

The Klosterplatz plays a key role within the ensemble. Not only is it the most important hub for visitors, but its sloping topography also amplifies the sense of perspective when viewing the monastery. As access to the church, the new square within the square is clearly assigned to the monastery. It resembles an inlay in the larger area of the square as a whole, which establishes the overall relationship between the monastery and the village.

Surrounded by meadows, the monastery rises above the village located on the level below. In the background, the horizon is defined by the forest.

Klosterplatz, Einsiedeln, CH
The Square within the Square

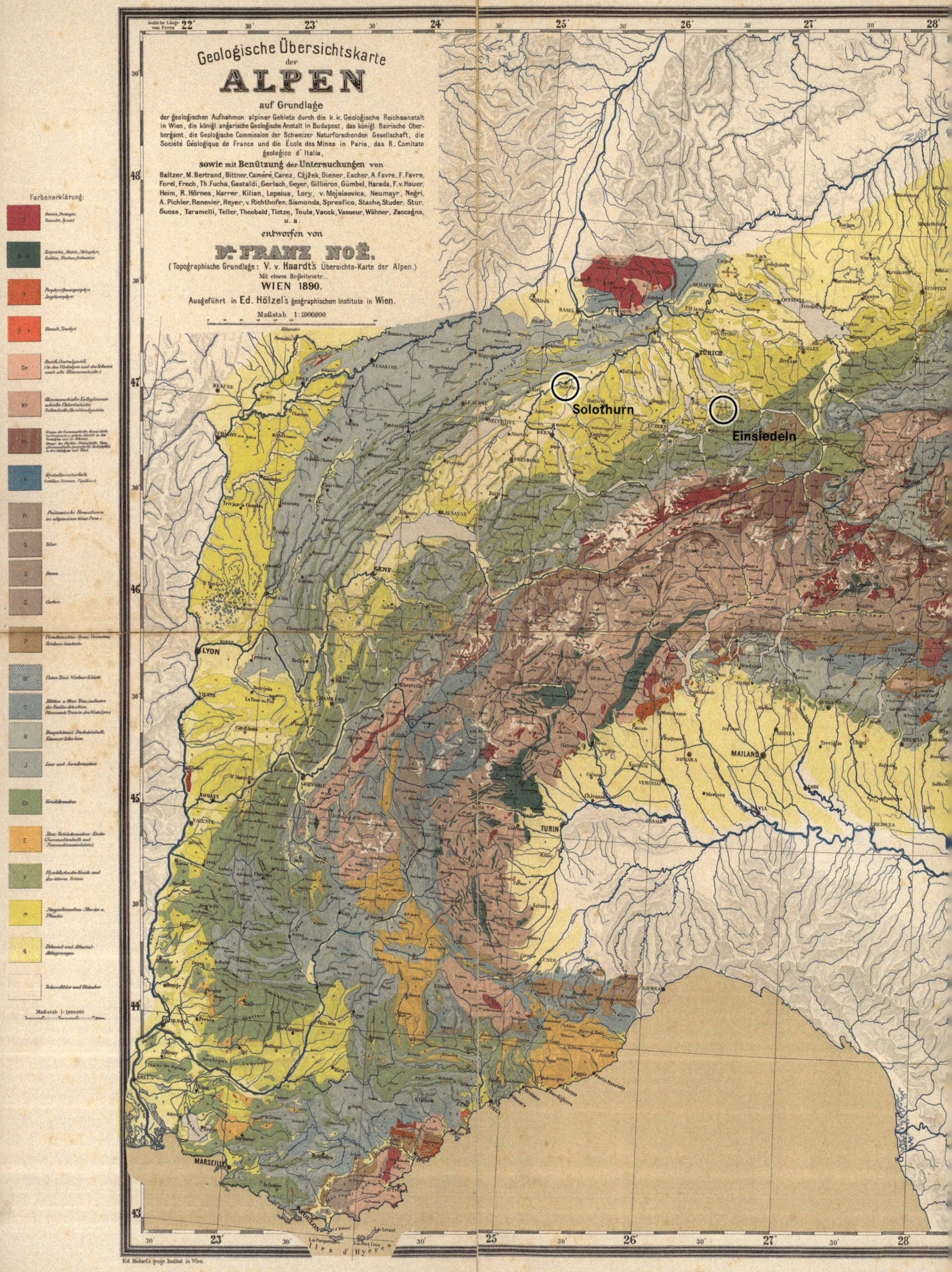
Geologische Übersichtskarte
der
ALPEN
auf Grundlage
der geologischen Aufnahmen alpiner Gebiete durch die k. k. Geologische Reichsanstalt in Wien, die königl. ungarische Geologische Anstalt in Budapest, das königl. Bairische Oberbergamt, die Geologische Commission der Schweizer Naturforschenden Gesellschaft, die Société Géologique de France und die École des Mines in Paris, das R. Comitato geologico d'Italia,
sowie mit Benützung der Untersuchungen von
Baltzer, M. Bertrand, Bittner, Caméré, Carez, Cžjžek, Diener, Escher, A. Favre, F. Favre, Forel, Frech, Th. Fuchs, Gastaldi, Gerlach, Geyer, Gilliéron, Gümbel, Harada, F. v. Hauer, Heim, R. Hörnes, Karrer, Kilian, Lepsius, Lory, v. Mojsisovics, Neumayr, Negri, A. Pichler, Renevier, Reyer, v. Richthofen, Sismonda, Spreafico, Stache, Studer, Stur, Suess, Taramelli, Teller, Theobald, Tietze, Toula, Vacek, Vasseur, Wähner, Zaccagna, u. a.
entworfen von
Dr. FRANZ NOË.
(Topographische Grundlage: V. v. Haardt's Übersichts-Karte der Alpen.)
Mit einem Begleitworte.
WIEN 1890.
Ausgeführt in Ed. Hölzel's geographischem Institute in Wien.
Maßstab 1:1000000
Farbenerklärung:
Solothurn
Einsiedeln
ZÜRICH
LUZERN
BASEL
GENF
LAUSANNE
LYON
GRENOBLE
TURIN
MAILAND
NOVARA
MARSEILLE
Iles d'Hyères
Ed. Hölzel's geogr. Institut in Wien.

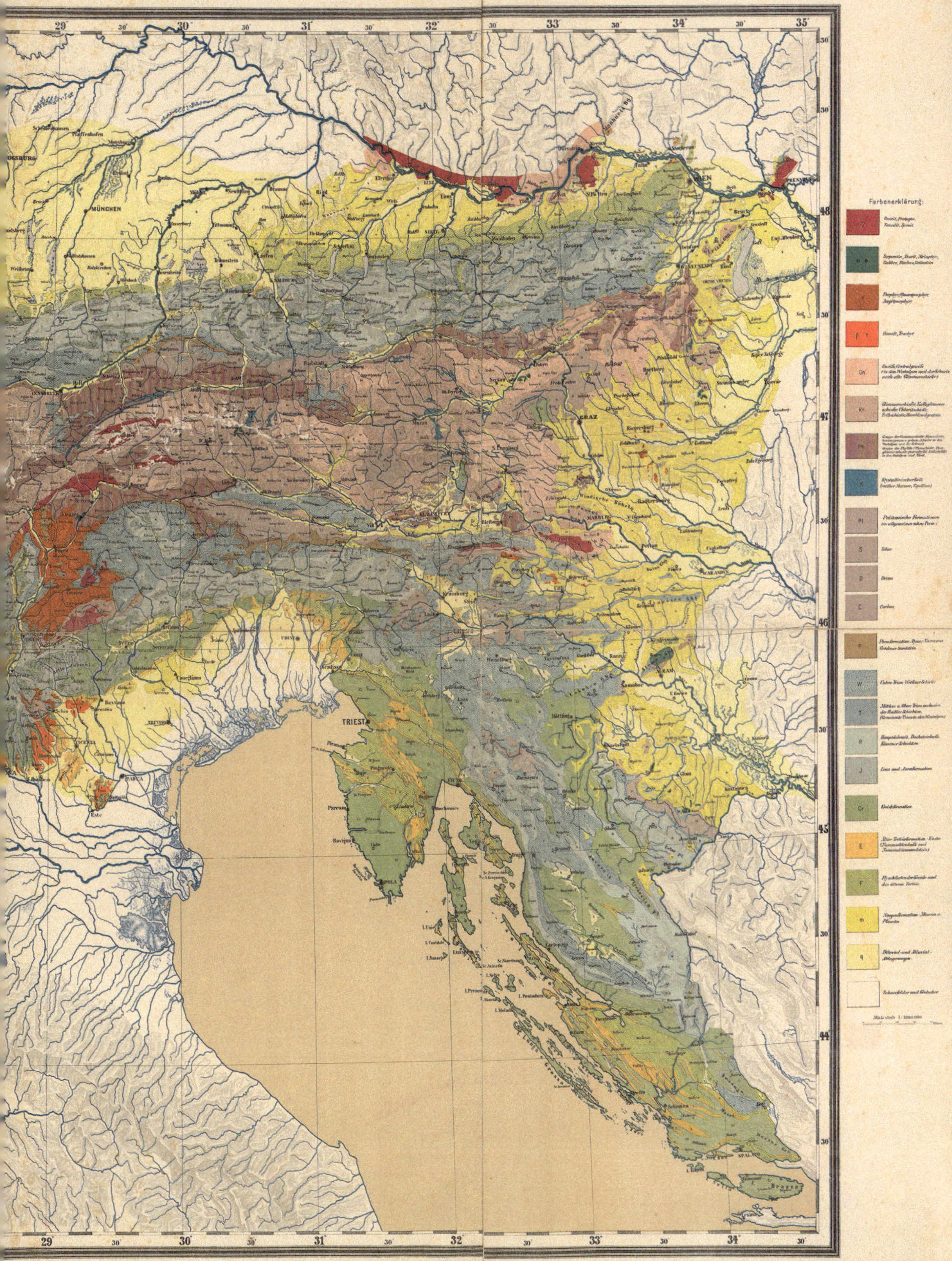

Farbenerklärung:
Basalt, Trachyt
Silur
Devon
Carbon
Kreideformation
Lias und Juraformation
Schneefelder und Gletscher
Maßstab 1: 1000000
MÜNCHEN
GRAZ
TRIEST
WIEN

Wasserstadt, Solothurn, CH
Views and Vistas

The reclamation of soil and removal of refuse involved in cleaning up Solothurn's "Stadtmist"–a waste dump with a volume of up to 360,000 tonnes that was in operation from 1925 till 1976[1]–is on much the same scale as the processes that formed the landscape of the Aare. The river landscape and its evolution serve as a model for an artificial river loop, on the banks of which the new settlement is to be developed. At the same time, the site is closely intertwined with the surrounding cultural landscape.

Client:
Ivo Bracher–Bonainvest AG, Wasserstadt AG

Cooperation:
Master plan: Herzog & de Meuron, Basel

Design:
2006–2007, 2011

Type and size:
Park, 37.5 ha (incl. bodies of water)

Status:
On hold

The same as the first settlement of Solothurn founded here–a Roman *vicus* on a green meadow on the banks of the Aare–the Wasserstadt Solothurn or Solothurn Water City project can also be seen as the founding of a new city. As such, it indicates a possible strategy of housing development in the Swiss Midlands. Instead of advocating a random expansion without local specificity, the new estate emerges from the open space and creates specific sites and places directly referring to the landscape and to readable boundaries. The project originally had a different form: structured around district borders and property boundaries, its appearance suggested a marina on the Aare. The qualities and potentials of the site were first brought to light by a detailed study of the landform between the Alps and the Jura. An analysis of scientific maps made it possible to precisely describe the site-specific vegetation, the karst formations created by geomorphological processes, and the hydrological energy of the river. In addition, field trips made it possible to identify, photographically document and cartographically record the old military observation points, which now serve as scenic vantage points for tourists.

The Quarter

The basic structure of the quarter follows the artificially created river loop, whose pronounced curve traces the earlier course of the originally meandering river. A promenade along the bank with bathing areas and steps leading down to the water form the public backbone of the estate. Running parallel to this are the primary access routes that frame this dense development designed for the highly varied inhabitants of the quarter. Between them is a fine network of squares and greened streets and paths that link the entire neighborhood to the surrounding landscape–the Witi or "expanse" in the local dialect. Hedges line the paths, border the squares, and clearly define the relationship between private and public spaces. The variety of open-space typologies and the diverse uses of the buildings help establish concise urban elements and policies that go beyond any suburban uniformity.

The Island

The history of the river loop can best be understood by viewing its formation as having been caused by a "geological obstacle." The dramatic staging of the island, raised in layers by reintroducing excavated material, accords with the principles of the English landscape park. Coming from the bridge, the only path leads to a lower-lying depression, which is partially flooded when water levels are high, and then proceeds further uphill. The very process of ascending, with the slowly emerging views of the city's steeples and the landscape features of the surrounding area, thereupon shifts one's point of view outward. Just before the path reaches the top of the hill, it unexpectedly veers away from the summit and into a grotto that seems to have been eroded from the calcareous rock over millions of years.

The vegetation is geared to the seminatural surrounding locations. The overall appearance is determined by different species organized according to altitude: whereas the foot of the hill is dominated by small, densely clustered stands of alder, willow, and birch, the ascent is characterized, firstly, by loose groupings of oak and then by mixed woodland consisting of ash and beech. In contrast, the positions of the trees are based on pictures showing the historical park of Drottningholm. However, the organizing principle can only be discerned from higher vantage points. The trees are grouped in concentric ellipses around the high point of the island, creating spaces of varying depth and density reminiscent of an arboretum.

The grotto–which consists of a concrete shell and washed formwork composed of loose gravel–not only illustrates a geomorphological process controlled by anthropogenic sedimentation and erosion but also refers to the local karst rock with its washed-out dolines or sinkholes and miniature glaciers. The grotto also acts as a vantage point directing one's gaze back to the Jura landscape to which it refers–thus, the erstwhile observation posts become today's park follies. (lr)

1 "Haus- und Gewerbemüll: Feldreben, Muttenz, La Pila, Hauterive (FR), Stadtmist Solothurn," Bundesamt für Umwelt (BAFU), last modified February 19, 2019, www.bafu.admin.ch/bafu/de/home/themen/altlasten/fachinformationen/altlastenbearbeitung/grosse-sanierungen/feldreben–muttenz–la-pila–hauterive–fr—stadtmist-solothurn.html.

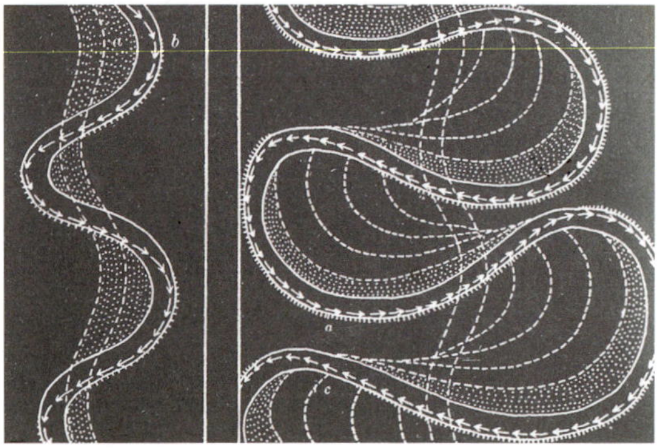

Büren an der Aare, high water, 1944

Riverbank erosion leads to the formation of so-called *oxbow meanders.* Old river channels can turn into bodies of standing water when disconnected from the principal river.

Meanders: oxbows are formed in rivers with minimal bed slope and low flow velocity. Their shape is influenced by a variety of factors: the quantity of fine-grained bedload they carry, the composition of the soil in situ, and the geology of the site. The two flanks of the river are characterized by a steep undercut bank and a flat point bar, which are a key part of the formation process and of the concept devised for Solothurn. The north bank of the settlement, stabilized by walls, demonstrates the idea of the undercut bank, while the flat banks of the point bar mark the edges of the island.

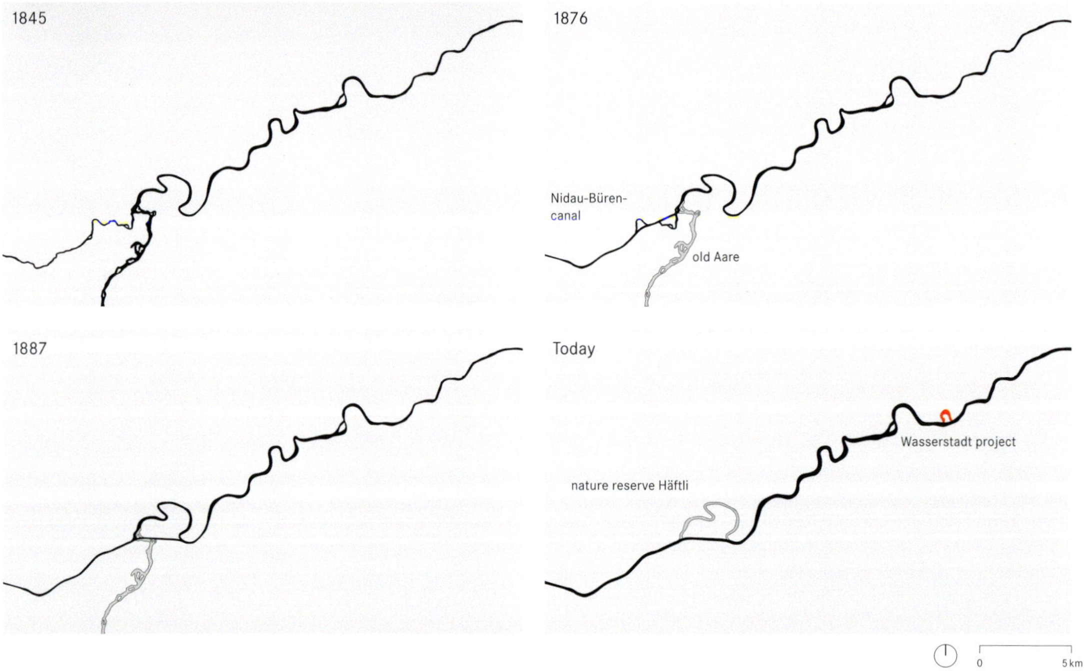

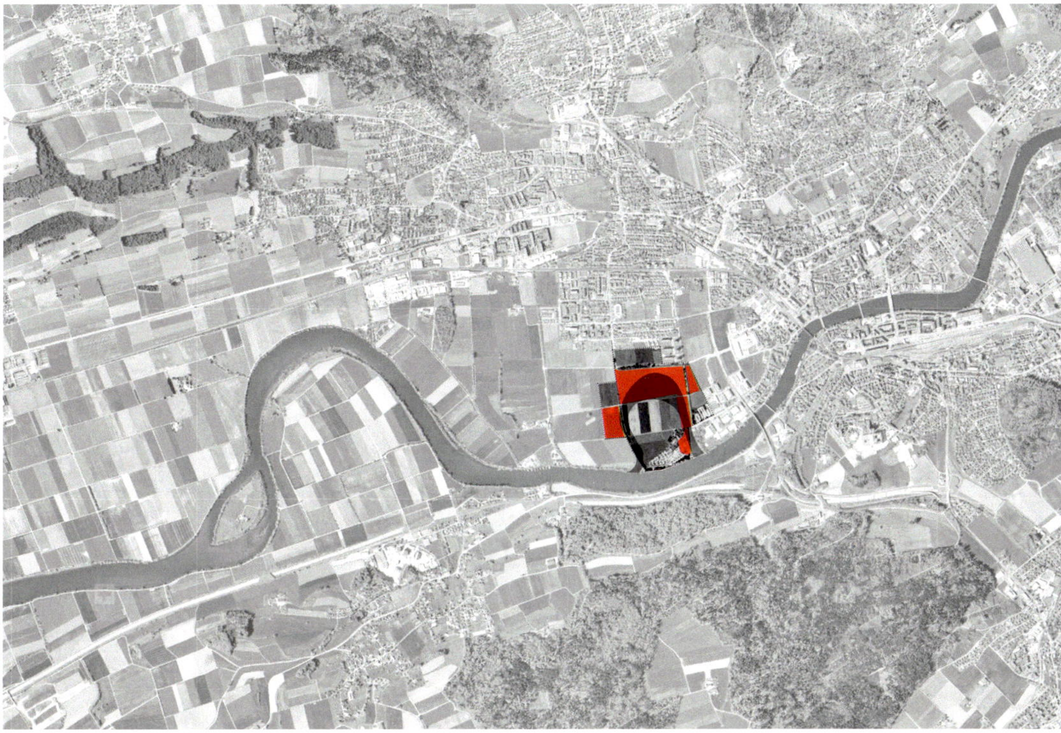

The old landfill site
■ contaminated soil (750,000 m³)

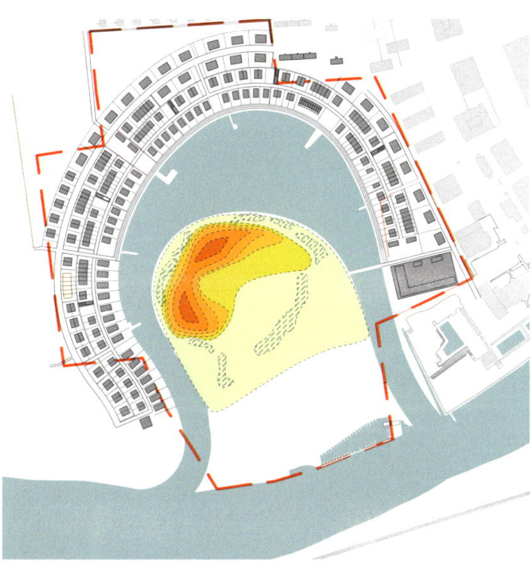

	Removal of contaminated soil	366,250 m³
	Excavated soil of the new Aare bow	239,365 m³
	Material for new quarter	-131,770 m³
	Remaining material	Σ 107,595 m³
(yellow)	Landfill of the entire island i.m. 0.5 m	46,000 m³
(orange)	Additional topography on the island	83,000 m³
		Σ 129,000 m³
	Deficit	Σ -21,405 m³
(hatched)	Excavated soil for wetlands in the Auen forests	

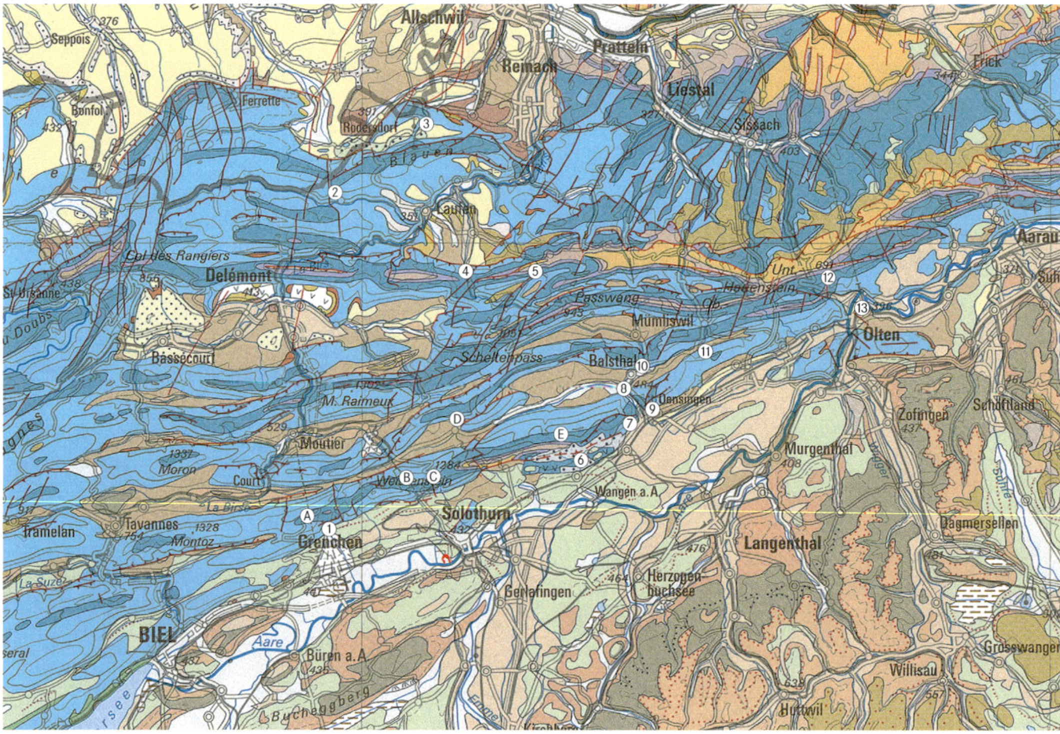

Outer alpine palaeozoic and mesozoic sediments

Late Jurassic/Malm Middle Jurassic/Dogger Early Jurassic/Lias

Castles
1 Ruin castle Grenchen
2 Ruin Blauenstein
3 Ruin Sternenberg
4 Castle Thierstein
5 Ruin Gilgenberg
6 Castle Bipp
7 Middle Erlinsburg
8 Ruin Alt-Falkenstein
9 Castle Neu-Bechburg
10 Ruin Neu-Falkenstein
11 Ruin Alt-Bechburg
12 Ruin Froburg
13 Ruin Chienberg

Dolines/Caves
A Dolines on the Obergrenchenberg
B Nidlenloch
C Dolines on the Weissenstein
D Bäreloch, Gitziloch, Tunnelhöhle
E Dolines on the Hinteregg

Field trip in the Jura: The phenomena and characteristics of the karst on the neighboring slopes of the Jura and the castles and mansions dotting the landscape are points of reference shaping the concept of Wasserstadt Solothurn.

So-called dolines or sinkholes on Mount Weissenstein

Gitziloch, north of Solothurn

View of and from the ruins of Neu-Falkenstein Castle

Wasserstadt, Solothurn, CH
Views and Vistas

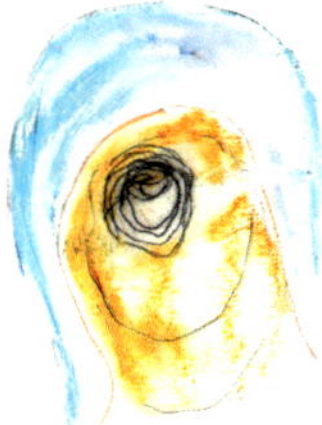

Saint Peter's Island on Lake Biel/Bienne. Colored outline etching by Johann Joseph Hartmann, 1788

Views of the military observation posts and tourist overlooks on the southern flank of the Jura are incorporated into the scenography of the park.

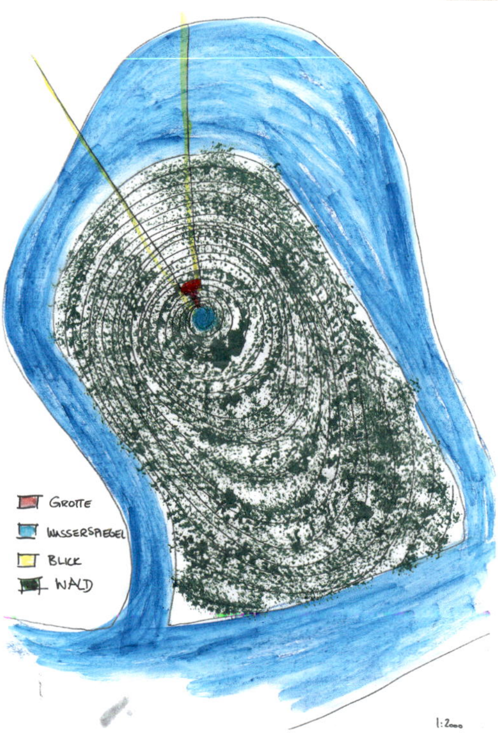

Wasserstadt, Solothurn, CH

Views and Vistas

The vegetation includes the birches characteristic of river sediments, the alders and willows of the floodplain, the oak and ash trees of the Jura slopes, and the beech and silver fir of the plateaux. The concept for this is geared to the strategies of historical parks: the interaction of baroque elements and English-style principles in Drottningholm Park leads to a constantly changing series of impressions, shifting between linear rows of trees and loose clumps, between order and “wilderness.”

Bottomland softwood forest–more humid locations
ca. 4.5 ha

Bottomland hardwood forest–drier locations
ca. 10.1 ha

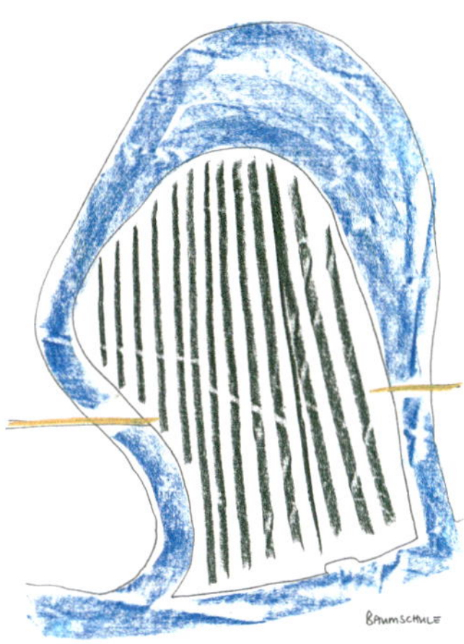

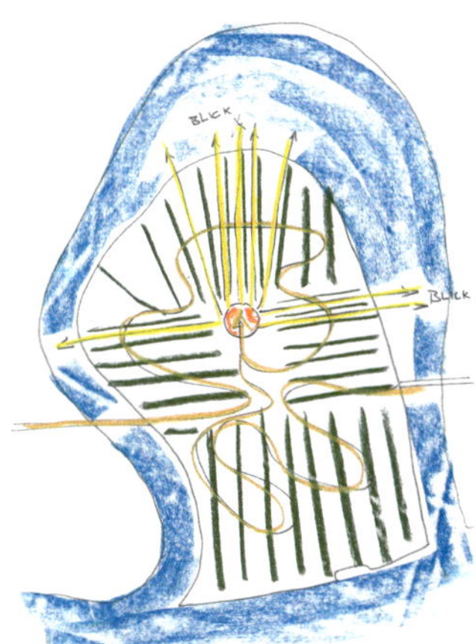

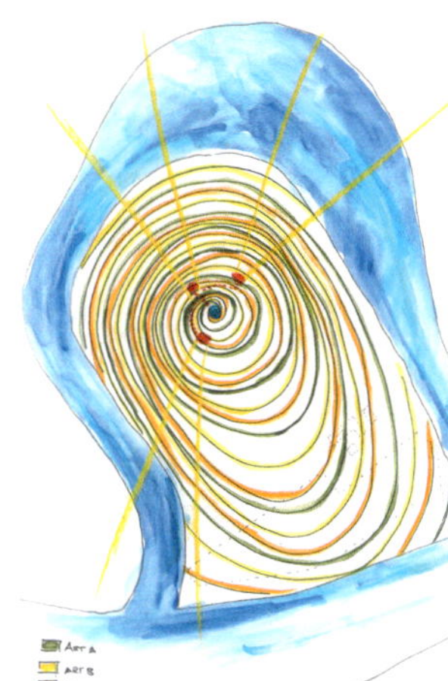

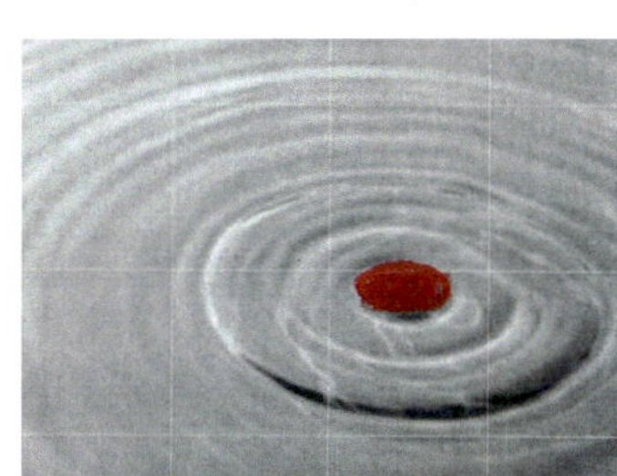

CARTE DE LA VÉGÉTATION DE LA SUISSE.

PUBLIÉE PAR LA COMMISSION PHYTOGÉOGRAPHIQUE DE LA SOCIÉTÉ HELVÉTIQUE DES SCIENCES NATURELLES EN 1949
SUBVENTIONNÉE PAR LA FONDATION Dr JOACHIM DE GIACOMI DE LA SOC. HELV. DES SC. NAT. ET LA FONDATION AMREIN-TROLLER, GLETSCHERGARTEN LUCERNE
LEVÉE ET RÉDACTION PAR EMIL SCHMID

1 : 200 000

BLATT NR. 1
BERN-NEUCHÂTEL-BASEL-AARAU

VEGETATIONSKARTE DER SCHWEIZ.

HERAUSGEGEBEN VON DER PFLANZENGEOGRAPHISCHEN KOMMISSION DER SCHWEIZ. NATURFORSCHENDEN GESELLSCHAFT, IM JAHRE 1949.
MIT UNTERSTÜTZUNG DURCH DIE STIFTUNG Dr. JOACHIM DE GIACOMI DER SCHWEIZ. NATURFORSCH. GESELLSCHAFT UND DIE STIFTUNG AMREIN-TROLLER, GLETSCHERGARTEN, LUZERN
AUFNAHMEN UND BEARBEITUNG VON EMIL SCHMID.

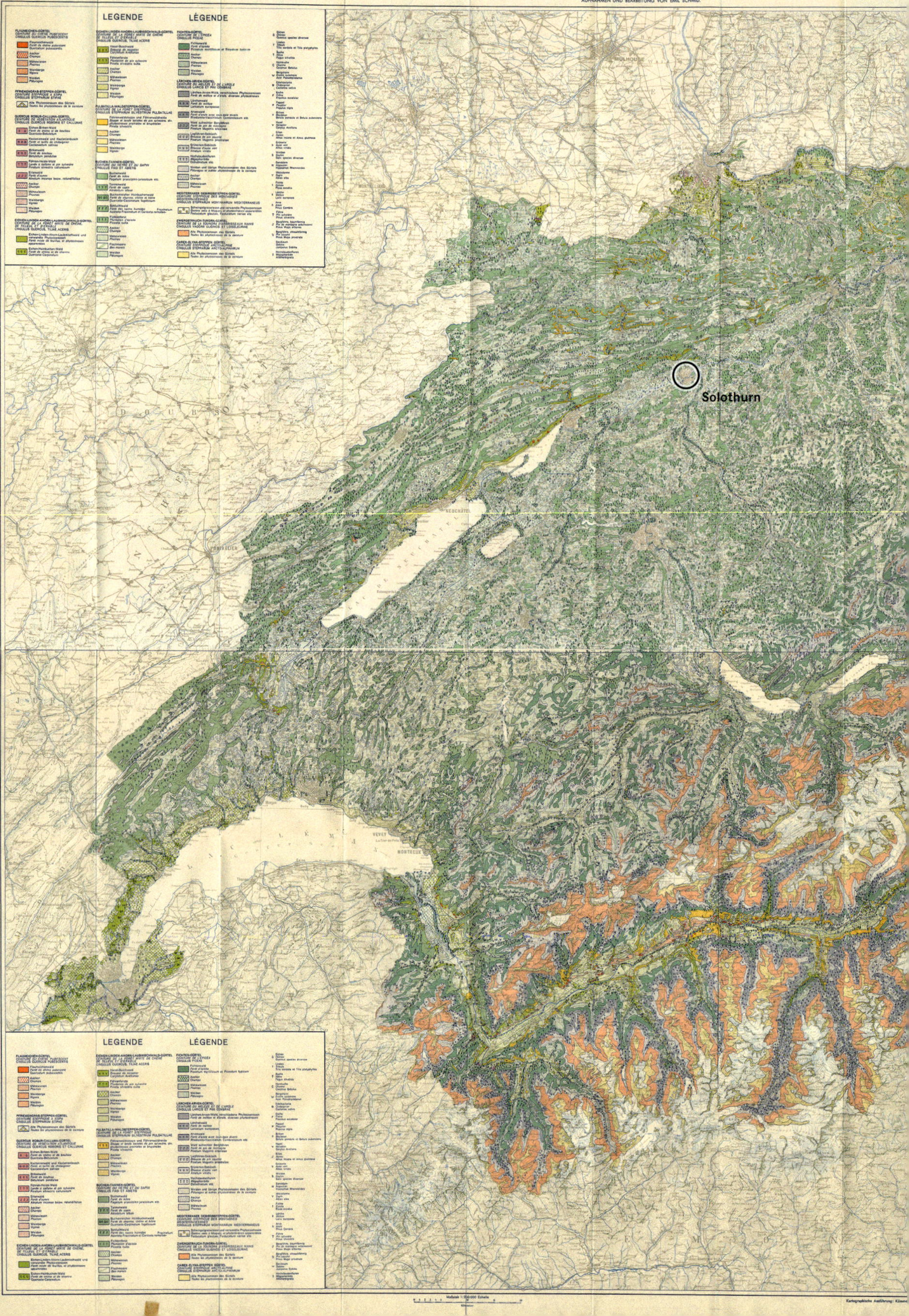

VEGETATIONSKARTE DER SCHWEIZ.

HERAUSGEGEBEN VON DER PFLANZENGEOGRAPHISCHEN KOMMISSION DER SCHWEIZ. NATURFORSCHENDEN GESELLSCHAFT.

AUFNAHMEN UND BEARBEITUNG VON EMIL SCHMID.

1 : 200 000

BLATT NR. 2

LUZERN- ZÜRICH- ST. GALLEN- CHUR

CARTE DE LA VÉGÉTATION DE LA SUISSE.

PUBLIÉE PAR LA COMMISSION PHYTOGÉOGRAPHIQUE DE LA SOCIÉTÉ HELVÉTIQUE DES SCIENCES NATURELLES.

LEVÉE ET RÉDACTION PAR EMIL SCHMID.

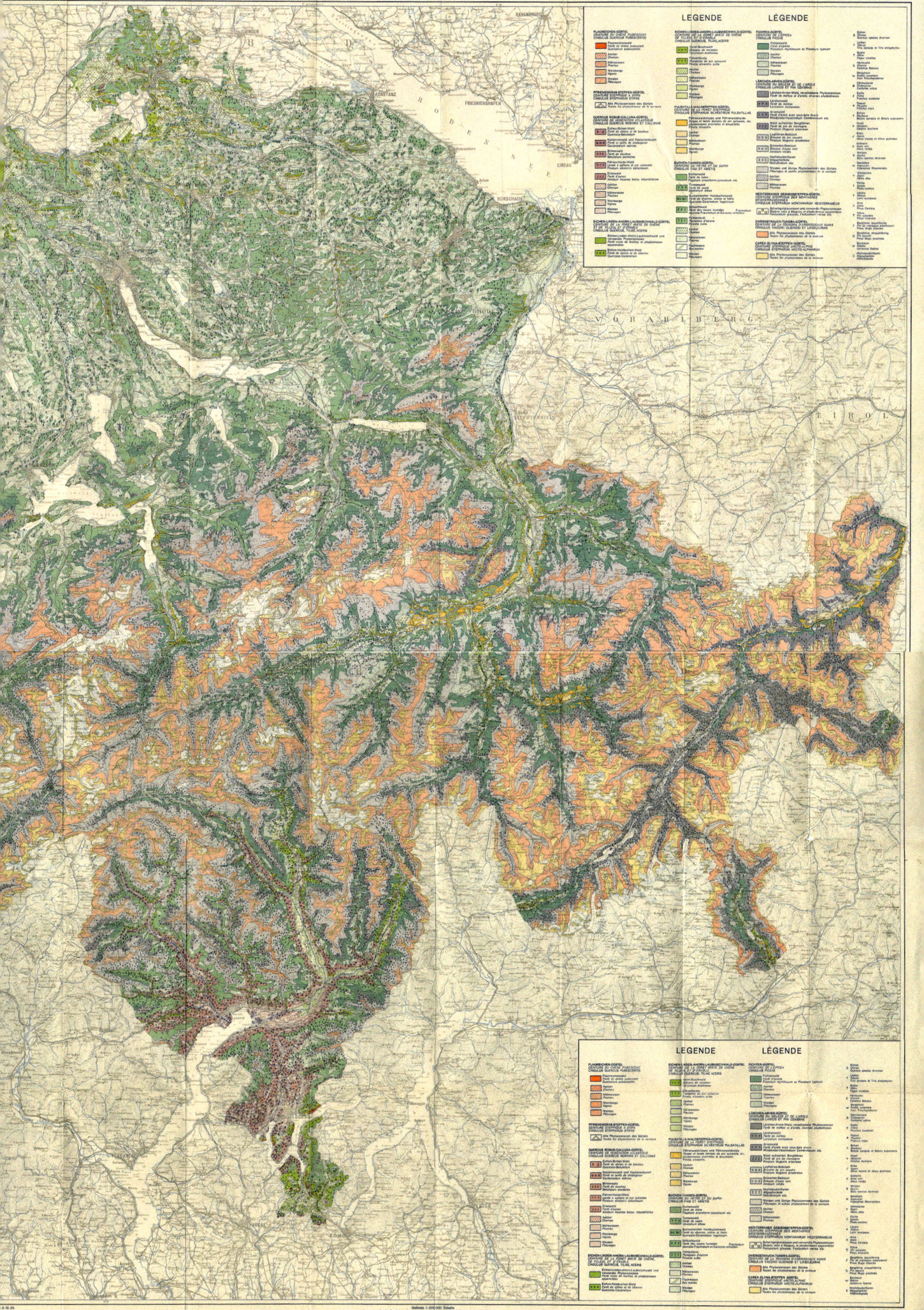

Kartographische Ausführung: Kümmerly & Frey, Bern.

Along the banks of the river, the diversity of the open-space typologies used is clearly evident: the promenade of the settlement provides direct access to the Aare, which can be reached via jetties and flights of steps. To ensure the view of the water from the living rooms and gardens of the multifamily buildings should also be guaranteed in the long term, tree species such as plane trees have been selected which are suited for this purpose in terms of their height and growth form. Owing to the river dynamics and flow rates, the shoreline of the island has to be designed in such a way that the velocity of flow is not significantly reduced and the exchange of water in the Aare loop does not drop too low. Most of the bank area is to be designed so as to extend and compensate for the valuable banks of the Aare. Accordingly, the shoreline will be developed along the lines of a river landscape with shallow expanses of water, silted areas, and zones of residual water, along with the associated vegetation. Beyond the high point of the bank, lower-lying areas will be excavated in sections that will be fed by the water table or flooded at high water and remain as residual water areas once the floodwaters retreat.

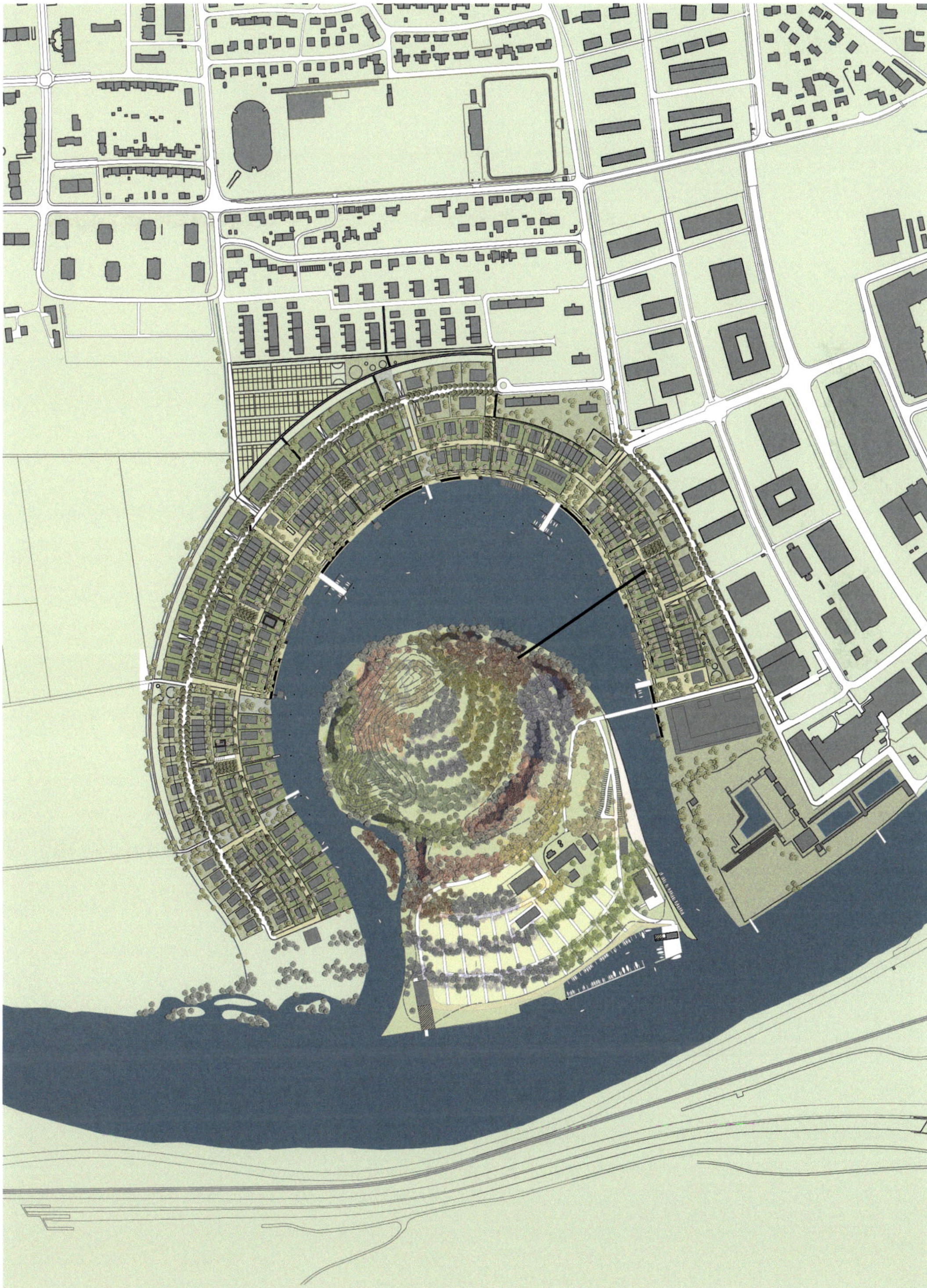

0
50
150
500 m

Landscape in Mutation

August 16, 2019, Büro Vogt Landschaft, Berlin

Günther Vogt: You've realized several projects with Julian Charrière, an artist I have known for a long time and with whom I work to this day. What is it that fascinates you about his work?

Dehlia Hannah: I came across Julian Charrière's work rather by chance. I encountered *Tropisme* at the Armory Show in New York in 2017 and it caught my attention because, at the time, I was working on a book called *A Year Without a Winter* (Columbia University Press, 2018). The project began as a collection of science fiction stories commissioned on the 200th anniversary of the publication of *Frankenstein, Or: The Modern Prometheus* (1818)–a novel written during a global climate cooling crisis–and grew into a transmedia thought experiment in imagining futures brought about by climate change. I was interested in how contemporary art and literature could capture the sense of wonder, horror, and beauty that a year without a winter might bring. When I talked with people about this project, their first response was often to envision endless summer, a wonderful holiday from seasons as we know them. In Phoenix, Arizona, where I was living, orange trees now flower three times a year instead of the usual twice a year. Of course, nothing looks and smells as beautiful as blossoming, dark-green orange trees. But if you think about it more carefully, this delightful scent carries an ambience of horror, for it quite directly reveals the irreversible change of our living conditions caused by climate change. *Tropisme* captured something of this type of revaluation. In the work, frost is a treasure, rather than the signal of the end of the growing season for the plant it encases. I imagined that, in a warmed world, ice would become more precious than a flower. Two weeks later, I met Julian for the first time in Antarctica as part of the Antarctic Biennale, the beginning of an exciting cooperation. *Tropisme* became the cover of *A Year Without a Winter.*

> VIII, *Tropisme*

Günther Vogt: Both the beauty of the ice and the beauty of the plant are very fragile and transient. For them to exist, specific conditions have to apply; conditions that are mutually exclusive. In Julian Charrière's work, the plant, once killed, only develops a new aesthetic because it is completely sheathed and covered by ice. For this to survive however, requires an external source of energy. It's this very act of inversion that I deem most interesting. In fact, it probably constitutes the very poetry of the work. Besides, I think it is quite amazing with how much interest in and commitment to scientific research these young artists grapple with "nature" or "landscape," including–in addition to Julian Charrière–Andreas Greiner, and Julius von Bismarck; all of whom have studied with Olafur Eliasson, by the way. I don't think they were much concerned with political issues such as regarding climate change but actually with landscape itself, its historical but also its current cultural and social significance. And if art is interested in such a subject matter, it also implies that there is a certain deficiency, whether in theory or research, in professional practice or in society's handling of landscape. I still remember that, in the 1980s, a lot of artists started to design furniture. These efforts were a direct reaction to the shortfalls of professional design.

Dehlia Hannah: That's interesting. One thing you mentioned makes me reconsider the work. I wonder whether it is truly about landscape or rather about architecture instead? There's an initial attraction to the plant itself, which pushes into the foreground. But the vitrine could also be read as a building, a small air-conditioned high-rise, within which a tiny microclimate is formed to sustain an organism. It's a bit like a miniature skyscraper that, like many buildings in Phoenix, Arizona, keeps you freezing cold in the summer–a model of the energy-intensive logic of climate control. For all intents and purposes, *Tropisme* is a microcosm of our future architectures and cities. They will likely function more independently from their surroundings and the direct conditions of the external environment. It will, therefore, require a great deal of energy to create the interior conditions.

Günther Vogt: Your description is a close match to reality. There are, after all, numerous examples of entire cities and even landscapes inside buildings. I'm thinking of these huge halls that make it possible to ski all year round. There are quite a lot of them in Europe, too. Or the *Mall of the World* project in Dubai. The plan is to build the world's biggest shopping center under a glass roof that can be closed during the hottest months of the year. To a much lesser extent, air-conditioning plants will work in the same sense. All these technical devices and installations enable us to regulate interior climates. In fact, humans get used to such conditions quickly. The fact that public buildings, shopping malls, or even restaurants are somewhat air-conditioned during the summer months has by now become standard in Europe, too. I became aware of this once again when I spent some time in Los Angeles for an exhibition and a podium discussion last year. Inside the building, where the event took place, the temperature was a mere 20°C. Outside however, the thermometer climbed to 32°C. I attempted to explain to the other participants in the discussion that I did not consider this very cold interior room to be comfortable but a downright luxury instead. For I consider luxury to be whatever I do not truly need, including all expenditures that go beyond anything needful or meaningful. A lot of heat is generated in the otherwise already hot outside space to create cool conditions inside. And this, although it would be perfectly acceptable. Basically, this is an absurd situation.

> p. 314, *Environment[al]*

Dehlia Hannah: Your explanations show very nicely that we should also consider the environment in which we live and work. When I moved from New York to Europe, I was quite surprised that there was no integrated air-conditioning in buildings. That's why I consider it crucial to introduce the cultural dimension into the debate about climate change mitigation and adaptation. Adaptation doesn't only mean developing better walls, tighter windows, or more efficient technical plants. It may also mean modifying one's everyday habits, even fashion choices: for example, putting on a jacket in winter and not requiring professionals to wear a wool suit to work in summer. We should consider changes in our lifestyle that might seem as radical in the social sphere as pumping aerosols into the stratosphere to reflect the sun–thereby turning the blue sky whitish, and potentially causing severe weather pattern disruptions and drought in some parts of the world. If such geoengineering proposals seem utterly crazy, would it really be crazier to shut down the fossil fuel–burning power plants and severely restrict energy consumption on the scale that is needed to reign in carbon emissions and slow climate warming? There would be major economic consequences, and certain familiar ways of life would have to be abandoned. Still, I see a certain potential

The Blue Fossil Entropic Stories

Julian Charrière, 2013

The Blue Fossil Entropic Stories is the photographic trace of an expedition the artist undertook in 2013, traveling to Iceland to climb an iceberg in the Arctic Ocean and melt the frozen water beneath his feet with a gas torch for eight hours. Like an absurd, quixotic hero, Julian Charrière confronts the elements in a seemingly hopeless battle–human time against geological time. It is a battle to which global warming is only the prelude. What remains of this perilous endeavor are three photographs of arresting beauty, a kind of contemporary version of Caspar David Friedrich's *Wanderer above the Sea of Fog* (1817–18), and a questioning of our relation to nature as inherited from the Romantics through the medium of ecological thinking.

in what could be called social and political engineering, even though that term has gained a bad reputation in the last century. It's not just a matter of how to design or equip a certain space–whether it's a built environment or the whole planet–but above all how you behave in it, how you live in it and, thus, influence your environs.

Günther Vogt: The creation of artificial atmospheres has long ceased to be limited to interiors intended for people. Examples include these immense server farms, which require huge amounts of energy or, for instance, the worldwide seed vault on Svalbard in Norway, which was built for the conservation but also the protection of species and the variety and diversity of crop plants. In the event of a disaster, these seeds would be donated to the affected areas. The facility resembles an underground bunker. It is installed about 130 meters below ground and makes use of permafrost conditions. A refrigeration compressor cools the already icy ambient air to a constant –18°C. I consider this seed bank a kind of Noah's Ark in which, it is true, not all the plants of our world will find their place. This becomes quite obvious if you consider, for example, the diversity of potatoes in Peru. For practical reasons, the most diverse potatoes are planted on terraces at different altitudes. For if it rains a lot within a given season at the lower levels, and the harvest suffers, conditions at the upper levels may be better and help avoid a total crop failure. The whole thing works as an integral system, so to say.

> p. 374, *Skolkovo*

Dehlia Hannah: There's something a bit fantastical about the seed bank. The irony of its flooding, because of the melting permafrost in 2017, demonstrates on the scale of an entire building what's wrong with the concept of the seed vault to begin with, namely that you can preserve a seed, but if you don't preserve the context in which it grows then you are basically reducing the plant to its DNA. I'm sure that the seeds are archived along with rich descriptions of their native environments. But really, in order to preserve world's biodiversity, you would need to create a bank of all of the landscapes and ecosystems in which all the species thrive. An environment bank for all those seeds would be the entire world.

Günther Vogt: This would be necessary to preserve the plants integrally. But there is another dimension we will have to take into account. When I explain to students, during a guided tour of Kew Gardens, one of the largest botanical gardens in the world, that the experts have arrived with their examination of all existing herbaria at a moment in the early 1930s, you can imagine the huge variety of plants discovered during all these expeditions. So, you see, there are still a lot of plants in these herbaria that have not yet been identified or described. And if we change or destroy these ecosystems, we will also destroy all these creatures that we do not even know yet. I think this is quite a new development.

< p. 68, *Trachycarpus fortunei*

Dehlia Hannah: I agree. There's an idea that all you need to do if you're going to go ahead and destroy most of an ecosystem is to first pick out the important elements, put them in a box and ship them home, preserved in formaldehyde or frozen in a box. This is a kind of absurd–but it's also an expression of the collector's anxiety: you know you are destroying something, but you want to save it at the same time. You can't save the fish once you take it out of the water. The frenzy of collecting occurs alongside the frenzy of destruction. In addition to this attempt to preserve things by separating them from their environment and making every effort to store them under certain conditions, there is also the attempt to keep entire landscapes alive by means of technical installations. We haven't talked about this yet.

Günther Vogt: These experiments are not only about preserving an object, but also about preserving complex ecosystems. Of course, the fact that the installations necessary for this purpose are often located in the "most beautiful" and protected landscapes leads to conflicts. Different interests have to be weighed in a sociopolitical discourse and the question is whether the aesthetic value of a landscape should be given more weight than, for example, the touristic or the productive aspects. In the Engadine, a project is currently being developed in which a so-called *Schneiseil* or snow rope is used to artificially snow the glacier in summer in order to protect it from melting any further. The aim is not only to preserve the image of the glacier for tourists, but also to preserve it as a water supply, for the glacier releases its

< p. 28, *Pyramides de Terre*

water into the watercourses during the summer heat periods. Of course, this has not only local implications that are existential in dry mountain regions, but also large-scale effects. This question is also highlighted by scientific studies investigating the construction of new dams in the Alps. These dams would additionally ensure the water storage of glaciers in the future. However, all these measures will not be able to solve the thawing of the ice in the Alps and the problems associated with the dissolution of permafrost. In Switzerland, forecasts are being drawn up that predict the complete disappearance of winter tourism within a few years. The white peaks of the mountains will disappear. But instead, the bare rock will be reflected in the newly formed glacial lakes.

Dehlia Hannah: This Alpine landscape is a territory on which a whole aesthetic vocabulary was developed in the eighteenth century. These glaciers were not beloved by the Swiss, who lived in their shadows, dependent upon them for their livelihoods, fearful of floods and avalanches. Rather it was travelers on the Grand Tour from England who, only gradually, came to love the sublime glory of the huge mountains through which they had to pass en route to see Roman antiquities further south. These aesthetic categories will be hard to give up, but as you say, the landscapes upon which they were invented will change quite radically in the near future. I'm very interested in this question of how artists and poets transform our perception of landscape. A project that I worked on with Julian (*An Invitation to Disappear,* 2018) began during a trip to Mount Tambora, in Indonesia, a volcano that erupted in 1815 and caused the whole world to cool—and even a tragic flood of the glacial Lac de Mauvoisin in the Alps. What we confronted there was a landscape of vast palm-oil plantations, which became the subject of the film. Even as sites of ecological catastrophe—deforestation, burning of pristine habitats, loss of biodiversity—these are the landscapes of the twenty-first century. They may be the ground on which new aesthetic conceptions of nature or environment are born, categories that reflect our complex ecological and political entanglement within these environments.

Günther Vogt: What is considered a "beautiful" landscape is always very closely linked to the cultural, economic, and political developments of a society. The Lake District in the northwest of England is a landscape that can be regarded as exemplary for these mechanisms and processes. Its morphology was shaped by the activities of glaciers, and its numerous lakes were subsequently formed within the characteristic trough valleys. This landscape was visited early on by explorers and only discovered by a wider public toward the end of the eighteenth century. This has, above all, to do with the many wars in continental Europe and the associated restriction of any travel activity. Railway construction later led to a renewed expansion of tourism. Today, this landscape is one of the fifteen national parks of the United Kingdom and has been included in the UNESCO World Heritage List. Literature played an important role in its recoding from an unproductive farming area into a tourist hotspot. As, for instance, in *The Alps,* a poem by Albrecht von Haller, or the epistolary novel *The New Héloïse (Letters of Two Lovers Who Live in a Small Town at the Foot of the Alps)* by Jean-Jacques Rousseau, the Alps became popular not only in England but everywhere in Europe. In his travel report, Thomas Gray described the town as part of his Grand Tour. He was later followed by William Wordsworth and other authors from the Lake Poets circle.

> p. 132, *Alps*

Dehlia Hannah: It's worth considering whether it is legitimate or necessary for a society to intervene in landscapes that have been constructed over centuries in order to restore, or even create a new ecological function, perhaps even in ways that could completely transform their appearance. From farming to landscape architecture, this is already something that's considered acceptable and familiar, but what about on a global scale that would require very significant changes to current built environments and land used to grow food? Can you imagine, for example, planting new forests or specially engineered crops to sequester carbon on a very large scale, the scale that would be needed to change the course of climate change? I've been following geoengineering research, and there are proposals of this sort out there. Some of the ideas sound quite outrageous. For example, two years ago, one of my colleagues, Hilairy Hartnett, an oceanographer, published an article that attracted a lot of attention. Her team suggested installing pumps around the Arctic to pump up seawater from underneath the ice and spray it onto the surface so that it could thicken the ice pack ("Arctic Ice Management," *Earth's Future* 5, no. 1: 107–27). More recently, a paper was published about creating an artificial snowstorm to close the rift in the West Antarctic shelf ice (J. Feldmann, A. Levermann, and M. Mengel, "Stabilizing the West Antarctic Ice Sheet by Surface Mass Deposition," *Science Advances* 5, no. 7 [2019]). The lead author was the first to say that the proposal might be unbelievable, absurd even–yet this kind of speculative research reflects the scale of the problem. Even though I don't think there will be any quick and miraculous solutions, I'm interested in geoengineering because the field acknowledges the seriousness of the issue.

Günther Vogt: Personally, I have my doubts about such purely technological measures. While they can lead to local improvements in certain areas, they also have people believe that the failures of the past can easily be corrected by some technical intervention. These expensive solutions also mean that they will not be available to everyone. Today, 20 million people from the world's poorest countries are already fleeing the effects of global warming. And their number will increase in the next few years, not least as a result of fights for our finite and precious resources. We shall have to begin and understand climate change as a phenomenon that affects all of us and start to discuss the values and standards of our world. And this is indeed new. Recent studies show that, unlike preindustrial climate fluctuations, the current warming of the climate is taking place all over the world–simultaneously and very rapidly.

Dehlia Hannah: That's a huge problem, no doubt. But I also think that in the last few decades the general public has become aware of these global relationships. We are seeing more and more images, forecasts, diagrams, and descriptions of these systems and their interaction. We have become aware that rising CO_2 emissions affect not only air temperature but also ocean temperatures and acidity.

The problem is that certain vested interests, whether for political or economical reasons, are still opposed to these findings and work against them. I recently attended a conference on regional climate modeling at the American National Center for Atmospheric Research. Improving regional weather and climate forecasting is important because it effects crop yields, home insurance, etc. Refining the climate models over smaller regions is yielding good results, but I noticed that the physical scientists always bracketed off a percentage, maybe 20 percent, that would vary based on human behavior–and that they handed off to the social scientists and policy makers. We are really the wild card in the equation. Humans are much less predictable than glaciers or CO_2 molecules. People act individually, in groups and in unevenly distributed centers of power. Our strange, irrational dynamics are hard to fit into the models. And as Brexit shows quite clearly, sometimes people try to opt out of the whole system. Some people are escapists: they disassociate themselves, want to fly into space or live on Mars. But we can't do that now, and in any case, it won't be a "solution" for the many. Speaking of literary influences, this is the lesson of Kim Stanley Robinson's *Mars Triology.* We may be able to decide not to belong to a specific political system, but we cannot possibly wriggle out of the existing geophysical dynamics.

Another very interesting artwork in this context is *Public Smog* (2004–2009), by Amy Balkin. For this project, she manipulated California's CO_2 trading markets (which have subsequently collapsed) in order to create a "clean air public park" in the atmosphere. Her illustrations show a white cube floating above cities like Los Angeles and Bejing, within a dark, smoggy sky. The size of the park is meant to vary according to the amount of emission rights purchased, the duration of the contract, and seasonal fluctuations in air quality. Ultimately, it is a critique of carbon trading markets. The images are ironic. Of course, a box of air cannot be scrubbed clean and anchored in one place. Pollutants in the air, the ocean, waterways, cannot be limited locally. You can try to get the European Union, for example, to act, but you cannot steer El Niño or the Polar Vortex, or keep the Atlantic winds from stalling–a condition that led to another record-breaking heat wave in Europe this summer. The effects of pollution and climate change travel beyond political borders and economic instruments. They are global issues.

Günther Vogt: The description of Amy Balkin's work reminds me of the geodesic domes by Buckminster Fuller. His proposals ranged from small buildings to entire pavilions for world exhibitions to the roofing of Midtown Manhattan. A huge dome with a diameter of 3 kilometers and a height of 1.6 kilometers would have provided the opportunity to regulate the weather and control air pollution. And here we are again at the beginning of our conversation. Fuller always underpinned the solutions he proposed with precise cost-benefit analyses. For him, the challenge was to reach the maximum with as few resources as possible. He considered this principle the fundamental condition to survive on our planet. How limited these resources are, how fragile and vulnerable our planet really is, became visible for the first time for all people with the so-called Earthrise picture taken on December 24, 1968. The picture was taken from lunar orbit by astronaut William Anders, during the Apollo 8 mission headed by astronaut Frank Borman, when they saw the blue-white crescent rising from the window of the spaceship. The image subsequently became an icon of the global environmental movement. For the first time, there was talk of worldwide measures to protect the climate and biodiversity, combined with the hope that humanity would move closer together in the future to find joint solutions to these problems. In his book *Earthrise,* historian Robert Poole states that Apollo 8 consisted of an official and an unofficial mission. In addition to the nature of the Moon and flight details that needed to be clarified, the question arose as to man's position in the universe. During this expedition the Moon was searched for and Earth was found.

> X, *We Are All Astronauts*

Canis lupus
The Return of Wilderness

Amalia Bonsack
Thomas Kissling

Johann Elias Ridinger, *Ein umher streichender Wolff: Vor felsigem Umfeld,* 1740

Comeback

The wolf is back. Regularly, headlines reporting the predator's presence make the front page of European newspapers, often accompanied by sensational amateur shots of a lone animal wandering near a village or town. While such news is no longer a surprise to many readers, in many cases it still triggers a frisson of fear and excitement. Wolves do not usually harm humans, but in popular culture–from the werewolf myths that can be traced as far back as ancient Greece to the tales of Perrault and Grimm–the predator has long been a symbol of wildness and danger. In the sixteenth century, it was described by the Swiss scientist Conrad Gessner, today considered one of the founders of modern zoology, as "a predatory, harmful and greedy animal that is universally hated and from which almost everyone flees in abhorrence."[1] This marked the beginning of a continent-wide eradication, with wolves systematically shot, captured, and poisoned, so that they were practically extinct in most parts of Europe by the end of the nineteenth century.

Peter Paul Rubens, *The Wolf and Fox Hunt,* 1616. At the time, wolf persecution was in full swing in Europe.

The predator's mediatized comeback reflects a phenomenon that started in the mid-twentieth century on European territory and affects all large carnivores: wolves, along with lynxes and bears, which were all once widespread throughout the continent but disappeared as a result of deforestation and intensive hunting, have indeed undergone a large-scale recovery owing to a combination of favorable conditions.[2] After World War II, industrial and economic development led to a large rural-urban migration, resulting in the abandonment of acres of farmland. This depopulation made way for the recovery of forest cover and its wild herbivore populations, forming a suitable habitat for large predators. In addition, a shift in attitudes toward environmental issues and wildlife conservation since the mid-twentieth century has resulted in a diminution in hunting and culls. This trend was emphasized by political measures, with large conservation campaigns that contributed to the recovery of wildlife, such as the 1979 Bern Convention on the Conservation of European Wildlife and Natural Habitats, which listed *Canis lupus* as a strictly protected species.[3] In many cases, wild prey was actively reintroduced, while in some cases large predators needed active assistance to recover–such as the lynx and the bear, which were relocated from Slovenia and Slovakia to the Alps.[4]

Distribution of large carnivores in Europe in 2011. From left to right: brown bears, Eurasian lynx and gray wolves. Darker cells indicate areas of permanent occurrence, lighter ones indicate areas of sporadic occurrence. Lines indicate boundaries between populations.

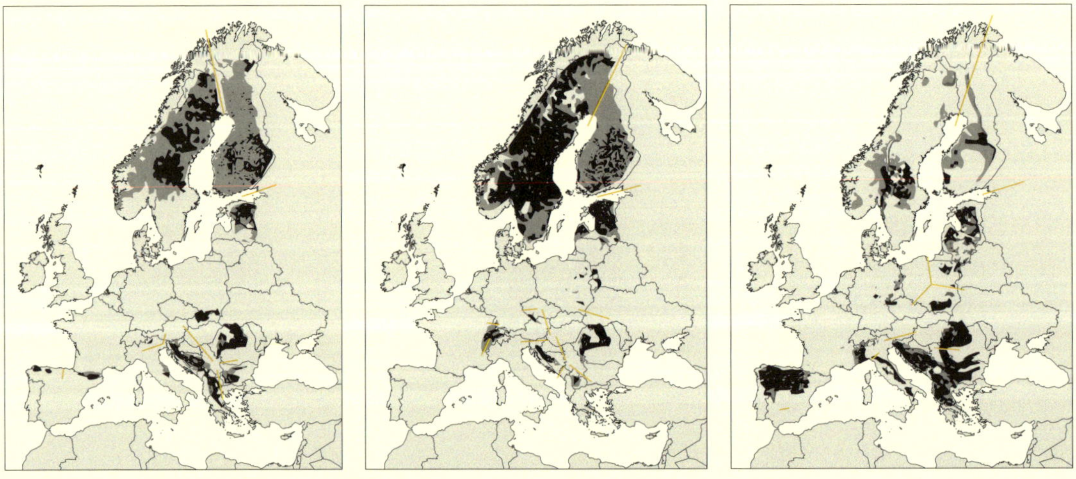

Distribution of wolf populations in Europe and evolution trends (as of 2013)

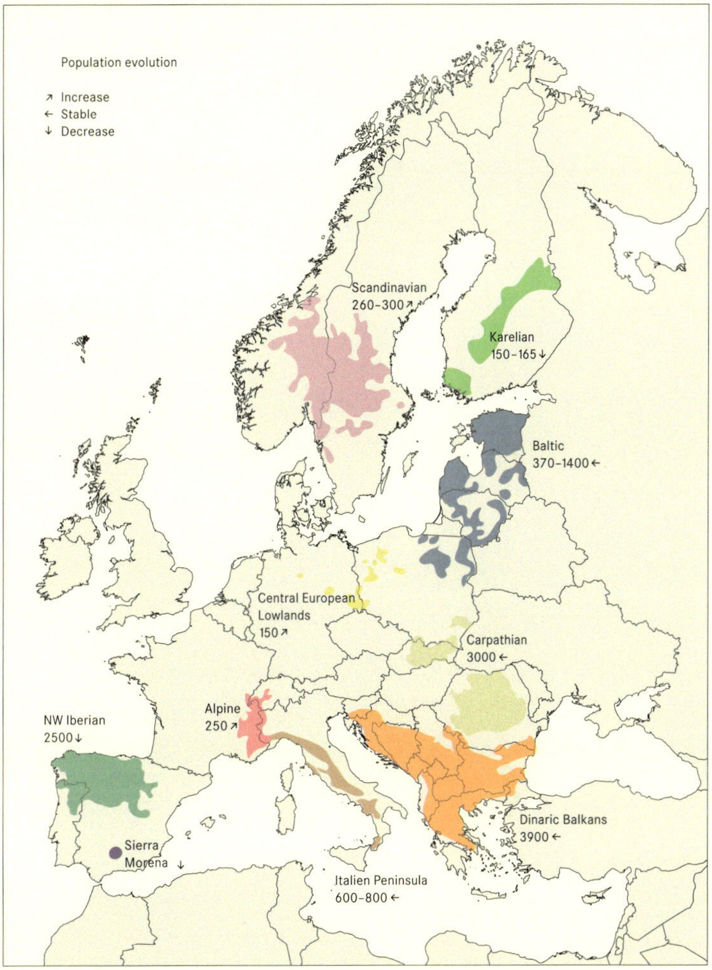

Approximate range distributions of Italian wolves in 1900, 1973, and 1994

Migration Routes

The wolf, however, was never reintroduced in Europe. Thanks to their high levels of biological resilience and their ability to disperse over very large distances in all environments, they were able to naturally recolonize large portions of their territory. Currently, approximately twelve thousand wolves are distributed in eleven genetic populations over the highly heterogeneous European landscape:[5] they can be found "in such diverse habitat as wheat fields in central Spain, alpine meadows in the Alps, forests in Scandinavia, or village outskirts in Italy and Romania."[6] In the Alps, gradual depopulation of agrarian areas led to the renaturalization of acres of hills and mountains, which reverted to a suitable

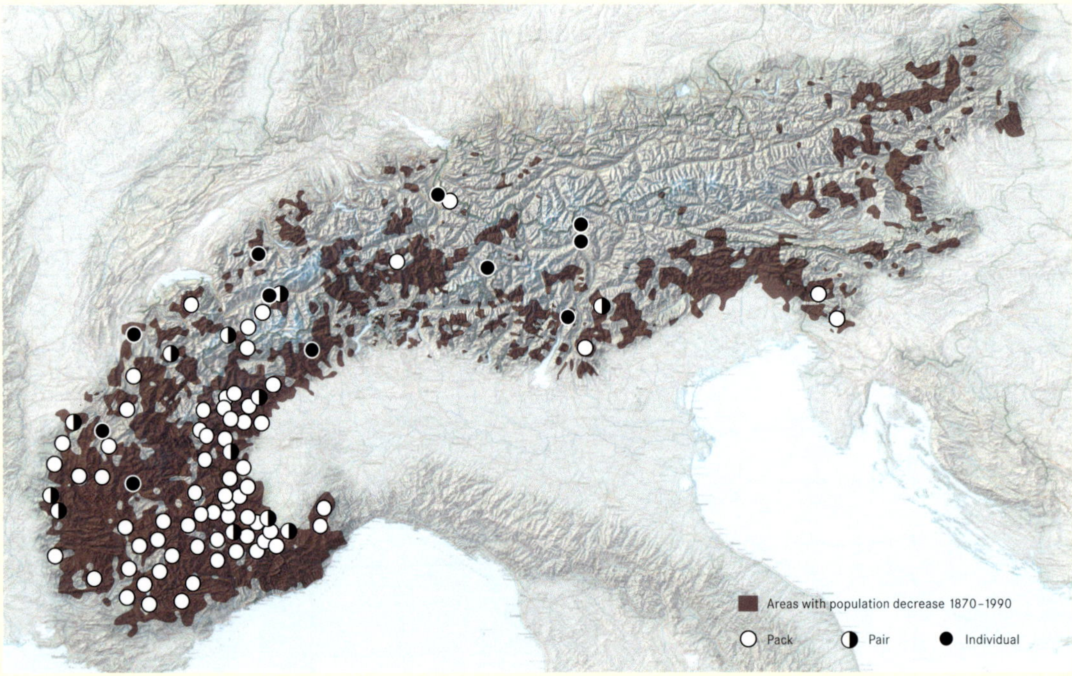

Distribution of wolves in the Alps, 2017–2018. The data is overlaid on a map showing the population decline between 1870 and 1990, from *Switzerland: An Urban Portrait* (Basel, 2005).

habitat for the wild ungulate population and their predators. The Alpine wolf's comeback originated in the Italian Apennines, where it became a protected species in 1972. At the time, a small and isolated population of about a hundred individuals had survived in the Abruzzi mountains,[7] feeding on farm animals and waste owing to a lack of wild prey. Thanks to their protected status, the population was able to recover and slowly started making its way northward following the routes of depopulation and renaturalization. By 1987 isolated wolves had reached the Alps, and the first Alpine pack was spotted in the French Parc du Mercantour in 1992. Today, the Alpine population represents close to a hundred packs, whose territory spreads across the borders of France, Italy, Switzerland, and Slovenia.[8]

“Any time I see Alpine meadows being cut right by the wayside, **it makes me think of a park.** Wild haymaking is something that has fascinated English tourists for centuries, and it has also been responsible for the dissemination of many Alpine flowers. So agriculture and landscape gardening are sometimes very closely connected.” (gv)

16-bits color sample:

hand selection of colors:

The color of the landscape:
The Gotthard Post by Rudolf Koller, 1873

Thanks to tracking technologies, the wolves' routes can be precisely mapped. What monitoring reveals is that their spread is not only happening in remote areas such as nature reserves but that they also often move along the edge of urbanized areas. Indeed, the animal that is an all but unique symbol of "untouched wilderness" can also get along quite well without it. As a habitat generalist, it can biologically adapt to various ecosystems–even in landscapes dominated by humans, where it finds plenty of opportunities to retreat. We are thus increasingly seeing wolves approaching metropolitan areas, where they settle in nearby parks, reserves, or forests, such as the estate of Castel di Guido near Rome or the Forêt de Rambouillet near Paris. In these protected areas, where hunting is not allowed and where wild prey is abundant, they experience less pressure from humans and find easy access to food.[9]

Tracking wolf routes in Switzerland: the map shows the topography (shaded), protected areas (green), and built fabric (dark grey).

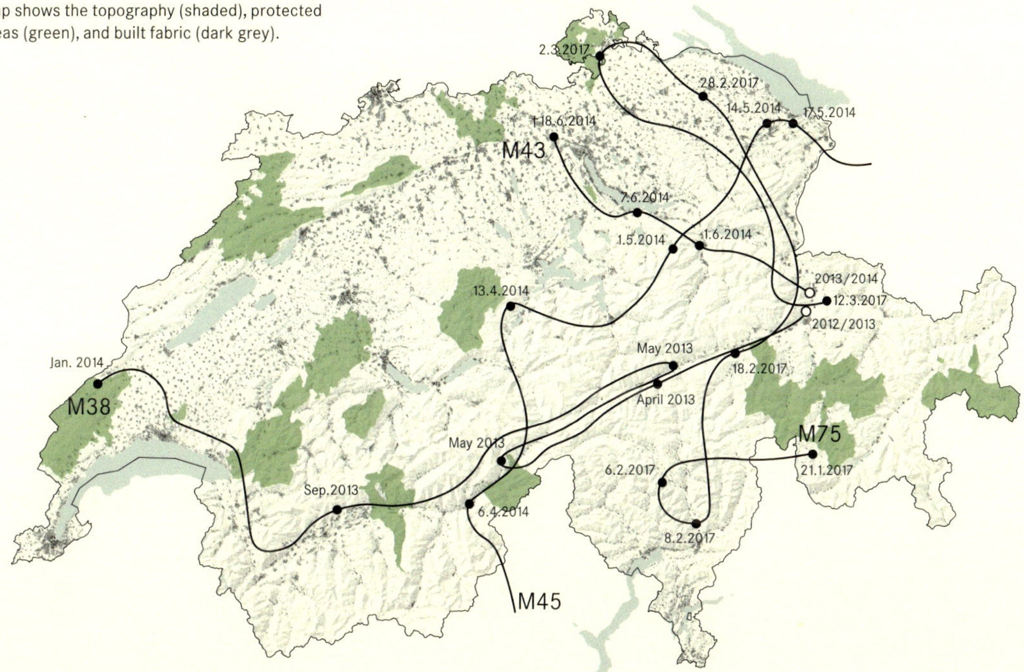

Eurasian wolf

Italian wolf

Steppe wolf

Russian wolf

Buffalo wolf

Mexican wolf

Recently, wolves have started to settle in nature reserves within the metropolitan region of Rome–the city that was mythically founded by Romulus and Remus after being bred by a she-wolf.

Controlled Wilderness

This increasing proximity to our cities reflects the inevitable coexistence of humans and large predators in a European landscape that has been managed by humans for millennia. In this context, the question of wolf conservation is a source of social conflict, and it has become the symbol of wider political divisions between agrarian and urban populations.[10] On the plus side, wolves are seen by urbanites as the romantic icon of wilderness and untouched "nature." Some of their defenders also believe that wolves can play a role as part of a balanced, sustainable ecosystem: in the Calanda park in Eastern Switzerland, where the forest is under protection, their predation helps control wild ungulate populations, thus preventing too many tree seedlings from being eaten.[11] On the minus side, farmers see wolves as a threat to their livestock and, by extension, as a threat to the centuries-old model of pastoral agriculture. Wolves kill

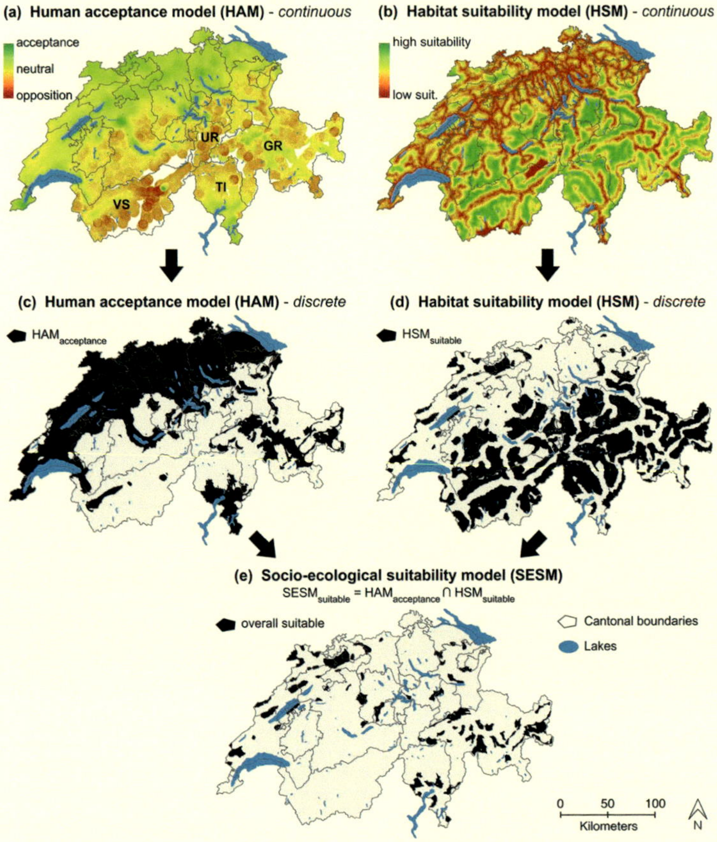

Dominik M. Behr, Arpat Ozgul, and Gabriele Cozzi, "Combining Human Acceptance and Habitat Suitability in a Unified Socio-ecological Suitability Model: A Case Study of the Wolf in Switzerland," *Journal of Applied Ecology* 54, no. 6 (December 2017)

thousands of sheep every year in Europe, requiring the implementation of electrified fences and guard dogs–which, in many countries, are financially subsidized by the government–in addition to livestock compensation programs. All over Europe, we are thus witnessing a rising tide of hostility and large protests against the animal's return, while in Switzerland anti-wolf initiatives have sparked debates on Swiss identity and how territory can be shared. In fact, the issue of "wolf management" has become an integral part of the political agenda.[12] In the relatively small European territory, the spread of large carnivores does not respect national boundaries, and their regulation must be dealt with at an international level. Since it was listed as a protected species in the 1979 Bern Convention, further protection measures have been imposed on European states, which include the continuous monitoring of the population and regular reporting to the European Commission.

In this context of a landscape that is inevitably dominated, managed, and increasingly regulated by humans, the need for new forms of sustainable coexistence may call, in the first place, for a redefinition of the very notion of "wilderness": not as a state of nature, but as an ongoing cultural construct that changes over time and requires continuous social debate.[13]

1 "Der Wolff ist ein rauberisches, schädliches und frässiges Thier, wird fast von allen anderen gehasst und geflohen." Quoted in Conrad Gessner, *Allgemeines Thierbuch* (Zurich, 1583).
2 See Luigi Boitani and John D. C. Linnell, "Bringing Large Mammals Back: Large Carnivores in Europe," in *Rewilding European Landscapes,* ed. H. M. Pereira and L. M. Navarro (New York: Springer International, 2015).
3 See Council of Europe, "Strictly Protected Fauna Species," Appendix II, *Convention on the Conservation of European Wildlife and Natural Habitats,* Bern, September 19, 1979.
4 See Boitani and Linnell, "Bringing Large Mammals Back."
5 See Maris Hindrikson, Jaanus Remm, Malgorzata Pilot et al., "Wolf Population Genetics in Europe: A Systematic Review, Meta-analysis and Suggestions for Conservation and Management," *Biological Reviews* 92, no. 3 (2017): 1601–29.
6 Luigi Boitani and Paolo Ciucci, "Wolf Management across Europe: Species Conservation without Boundaries," in *A New Era for Wolves and People: Wolf Recovery, Human Attitudes, and Policy,* ed. M. Musiani, L. Boitani, and P. Paquet (Calgary: University of Calgary Press, 2009), 24.
7 See Gruppe Wolf Schweiz GWS, "Die Geschichte des Wolfes in der Schweiz," *Gruppe Wolf Schweiz GWS,* accessed September 20, 2019, https://www.gruppe-wolf.ch/index.php?page=4&subpage=1.
8 See "Wolfsbestand im Alpenraum 2017–18: Definitive Zahlen," *Gruppe Wolf Schweiz GWS,* November 3, 2018, https://www.gruppe-wolf.ch/index.php?page=2&newspage=3&item=220.
9 See Kut de Swaaf, "Lupus im Schatten der Grossstadt," *Neue Zürcher Zeitung NZZ,* April 2, 2018, 54.
10 See Dominik M. Behr, Arpat Ozgul, and Gabriele Cozzi, "Combining Human Acceptance and Habitat Suitability in a Unified Socio-ecological Suitability Model: A Case Study of the Wolf in Switzerland," *Journal of Applied Ecology* 54, no. 6 (February 2017).
11 See "Das Wolfsrudel am Calanda ist gut für den Wald," *Watson,* September 5, 2017, https://www.watson.ch/wissen/schweiz/874479475-das-wolfsrudel-am-calanda-ist-gut-fuer-den-wald.
12 See Boitani and Ciucci, "Wolf Management across Europe."
13 See Patrick Kupper, *Wildnis schaffen: Eine transnationale Geschichte des Schweizerischen Nationalparks,* Nationalpark-Forschung in der Schweiz 97 (Bern: Haupt, 2012), 295.

Map of protected sites in Europe. About 1,121,500 km²–or 25.6 percent of EU 28 territory–are protected under Natura 2000 or national designations or some combination of the two.

Alps
A Unifying Cultural Landscape in the Center of the Continent

Thomas Kissling
Amalia Bonsack

The Alps are not a static structural fabric but a dynamic and sensitive organism. Having emerged from complex geological processes that began with the collision and partial obduction of the two continents Proto-Africa and Proto-Europe,[1] geomorphological processes subsequently formed the characteristic relief of the Alps and, thus, created the specific and fundamental conditions for the development of Alpine culture. In a close interaction with the continent–albeit with repeated breaks–a unique space was formed over thousands of years which, today, includes eight nations and in which five national languages as well as a multitude of subtly differentiated dialects are spoken.[2] With climate change, a global shaping force is now beginning to comprehensively transform the landscape of the Alps, with far-reaching effects. And not only for the Alps themselves.

The village of Soglio (Bregaglia, Switzerland) with the reformed church of San Lorenzo and nearby chestnut groves, alpine pastures, and gardens (picture taken between 1910 and 1930)

Creating Conditions

It has always been a characteristic of Alpine culture that people have to directly deal with the climatic, topographical, and hydrological givens and against the “forces of nature” in order to successfully embed themselves in a place and secure not only their own existence but also that of a larger community. Albeit it is true that every human culture is based on the specific effort required to erect settlements and maintain economic activity. The mountains, however, require much more of an effort than, for example, the cities of the Swiss Central Plateau or the countless settlements in the Po plain north of Milan.[3] Besides, the small-scale topographical structure of the Alps not only leads to specific, local solutions but, at the same time, to the creation of collective patterns in the cultivation of the landscape. Specific forms of community have been constituted in order to negotiate competing claims for use based on a collectively defined regulatory and to ensure a sustainable use of natural resources. This principle is impressively spatialized by the type of commons.

Already the first agrarian societies transformed existing “nature” in a profound way for the purpose of food production. The practices of transformation and reclamation brought about comprehensive ecological, economic, and social changes[4]—changes that have always represented a considerable cultural achievement and contrast with the descriptions of Roman writers who, some 2000 years ago, fixed the image of the Alps as *montes horribiles* in literature. This depiction dominated European cultural history until the beginning of the eighteenth century and is based on the experiences of some urban scholars crossing the Alps. In this process, the possibilities to use the site that were limited due to its topographical and pedological conditions and the lack of major cultural centers were unjustifiably associated with the Alps as a whole. Thus, the town dwellers’ traditional view of this cultural landscape had relatively little to do with reality, since the urban lifestyle was used as a yardstick for evaluation and people’s prevalent fear of nature was projected onto the Alps.[5]

The frightful Alps: *Lawine* (Avalanche) by David Herrliberger, copperplate engraving, 1765

1 See Marco Herwegh, “Alpenbildung,” *Institut für Geologie,* accessed September 21, 2019, https://www.geo.unibe.ch/ueber_uns/oeffentlichkeitsarbeit/videos/alpenbildung/index_ger.html.
2 See Eurac Research, “Language groups throughout the territory of the Alpine Convention” (Bozen: Eurac Research, 2010).
3 See Roger Diener, Jacques Herzog, Marcel Meili, Pierre de Meuron, and Christian Schmid, *Switzerland: An Urban Portrait* (Basel: Birkhäuser, 2013), 888
4 See Werner Bätzing, *Die Alpen: Geschichte und Zukunft einer europäischen Kulturlandschaft* (Munich: C. H. Beck, 2005), 44.
5 Ibid., 13ff.

Hannibal Crossing the Alps into Italy, woodcut from *The Illustrated History of the World for the English People,* ca. 1881–1884

Integration

The Alps articulate a topographical obstacle requiring a precisely calculable amount of energy for its crossing and appropriation. Early Roman explorations show that the Alps have never been a completely isolated region, but have always been part of the economic and cultural development of Europe. Already about 100,000 years ago, at the time of the last interglacial period, the first people probably crossed the landscape as hunter gatherers on the tracks of game.[6] Later, farmers and their cattle followed in their footsteps, because not only the daily fodder, but also a much-needed supply of hay for winter grows at higher altitudes. The "migrating" vegetable garden, which was just as much a part of this nomadic culture as the versatile tools or adapted clothing also typical for early pilgrims, proved to be fundamental to their self-sustaining way of life. In addition to a long stick, which not only provided support in impassable terrain but was also suitable to defend oneself against wild animals, their equipment included a bag and a sleeveless coat to use as protection against wind and weather and as a blanket for the night. For centuries, a fine network of paths and roads was continuously inscribed into the land. These infrastructures always directly interacted with the terrain. Crosscuts, embankments, and safety structures were planned and executed under the premise of the smallest necessary intervention in order to save manpower, but above all material.

6 See Walter Ammann, Othmar Buser and Usch Vollenwyder, "Lawinen in der Geschichte," in *Lawinen* (Basel: Birkhäuser, 1997), 13–42.

Intensification and Concentration

One of the elements of this intensive appropriation was the spatial proximity to the important early habitats of the Riviera, Provence, the Rhone Valley, and the peripheral areas of the Po Valley.[7] This situation is unique in the world. Other high mountain ranges are usually far away from urban centers or—where geographical proximity exists, as in the case of the Japanese Alps—only in sparsely populated or largely unused regions.[8] The functional relationship between the Alps and the rest of Europe has been intensified by the continuous expansion of infrastructure. A look at the Alps as a whole shows that, for a long time, the most important innovations and developments in Europe were adopted in a delayed and weakened form here. Only between 1970 and 1980 did this continuity break off. For the first time, the population of the Alps grew faster than that of Europe as a whole, though the character of the Alps as a peripheral region remained unchanged. Yet, a differentiated analysis focusing on the development of the smallest administrative unit, the municipality, reveals that the radical break in the development of the Alps already began with industrialization. The ensuing concentration of modern exploitation caused spatial disparities to emerge and people began to withdraw from the area for the first time in the history of the Alps.[9] This moment also represents a turning point in the history of perception: with the emergence of modern natural sciences, the achievements of the Enlightenment and the Industrial Revolution, "nature" was no longer deemed to be threatening. Shivering at the view of these "terrible" mountains gave way to the enjoyment of looking at their beautiful landscape. The new landscape ideal drew its compositional power from the contrast between an idyllic foreground and the threatening natural landscape with its glaciers, waterfalls, and bizarre rock formations in the background.[10] In the second half of the nineteenth century, a further break in the perception of the landscape was brought about by the exploration of the Alps by the English. Traveling became accessible to a broader section of the

The Alps are reframed: from *montes horribiles* into a beautiful landscape. The novel *Julie, or the New Héloïse: Letters of Two Lovers Who Live in a Small Town at the Foot of the Alps* by Jean-Jacques Rousseau (1761) plays an important mediating role in this process. Like the poem *The Alps* (1729) by Albrecht von Haller, the work thrives on the contrast embedded in civilization between an immoral society and sacred nature.

7 See Bätzing, *Die Alpen*, 44.
8 See "Das größte Problem sehe ich darin, dass die Alpen verschwinden," *Aurora*, accessed September 21, 2019, http://www.aurora-magazin.at/gesellschaft/interview_baetzing_2_frm.htm.
9 See Bätzing, *Die Alpen*, 314–17.
10 Ibid., 14.

In the course of industrialization, cities grew at a rapid pace, and there was a drastic decline in living conditions: *Manchester from Kersal Moor* by William Wyld, 1857.

Distance and engagement: an idyllic pastoral landscape in the foreground and the threatening, hostile mountains in the background–*Leukerbad* by Caspar Wolf, 1774/77

population, and the travelers developed into tourists–the birth of modern tourism.[11]

Fragmentation

As a result of industrialization, the contrast between an intensive and an extensive use of the Alpine landscape has become increasingly differentiated. Easily accessible valleys and peripheral areas are closely integrated into the urban networks of metropolises outside the Alps and, among other things, transformed into attractive settlement areas. This is increasingly the case where a city train of the metropolitan regions, an S-Bahn network, extends into the Alpine region, such as is the case in Zurich and in Munich.[12] Besides, the construction of highways and railway lines through tunnels and over long bridges enables long distances and topographical obstacles to be overcome in the shortest possible time and without great effort. These infrastructures do not only partially exclude the landscape, but treat its resistance as a minor aspect and, thus, change the geography of the Alps in a profound way. In addition to efficient transit traffic, this favors the emergence of urban hotspots that gear their economic structure entirely to tourism. Alpine resorts create monofunctional leisure landscapes that operate cyclically and are intensively used by a national and international public during the peak season. Mid-season, these locations are mainly used regionally and locally, while in the off season their use comes to an almost complete standstill.[13] The intensive development of the landscape, which also includes the construction of large energy infrastructures, often deeply subsoil interventions, represents a new era in the–mainly underground–exploitation of the Alps. This urbanization of the subsurface is accompanied by an unprecedented amount of artificial movements of earth, which are leading to a significant transformation of the visible landscape.[14]

On the one hand, a decrease and concentration of agricultural land use and, thus, a decline in landscape conservation can be observed. On the other hand, people are migrating from the remote

11 See Jon Mathieu, *The Alps: An Environmental History,* trans. Rose Hadshar (Cambridge: Polity Press, 2019), 93–96.
12 See Manfred Perlik, "Alpine Gentrifizierung: Multilokales Wohnen zwischen Landschaftsliebe und Prestige," *Werk, Bauen + Wohnen,* no. 9 (2011), 36–41.
13 See Diener et al., *Switzerland,* 900.
14 See Bundesamt für Statistik (BFS), *Materialaufwand der Schweiz, Umweltstatistik Schweiz Nr. 14* (Neuchâtel: Office fédéral de la statistique, 2008), 6; Heinz Ehrbar, Alex Sala, and Raphael Wick, *Vortriebe am Gotthard-Basistunnel, Erfahrungen und Lehren aus der Sicht des Bauherrn,* Swiss Tunnel Congress 2012 (Zurich: FGU, 2012), 114; Monika Dittrich et al., *Green Economies Around the World? Implications of Resource Use for Development and the Environment* (Vienna: Sustainable Europe Research Institute, 2012), 22.

Alpine Roads III

Christian Vogt, 2018

MCMXXI

regions of the Alps, mainly due to a lack of educational opportunities and future prospects, especially for the younger population. This also accelerates the aging of the communities and mainly affects the Southern and Western Alps, where depopulation is already largely complete.[15] Abandoned and slowly decaying villages are left behind. In Italy, there are already thousands of such *borghi fantasma*, in which the rural structure which for centuries formed the economic basis for the existence of the village community, has completely dissolved.[16]

Subsequently, the vegetation continuously reconquers its original territory. The traces of human civilization are covered by new growth, and the varied cultural landscape of the Alps slowly but inexorably changes. Large predators such as the wolf, who long ago made way for humans, return to their ancestral habitats. These animals mainly migrate along the border between the "new wilderness" and more urban areas, benefiting from their resilience and adaptability. Today, they hunt wild prey and livestock; tomorrow, they will collect civilization waste. However, the return of the wolf is not limited to the Alps or the large-scale landscapes of Scandinavia, the Baltic States, the Iberian Peninsula, the Balkans, or the Appennines.[17] Sporadically, wolf packs even settle at the edge of European metropolises such as Paris, Berlin, and Rome. While the urban population primarily considers the presence of wolves an enrichment of the fauna, the people living in the affected landscapes see them as a threat with negative effects on agriculture and wild prey populations.[18]

As agricultural use wanes, large areas of the Alps are subject to abandonment and reforestation. The aerial photographs of a section of the Val Mesolcina (Switzerland) allow a comparison between the years 1963 and 2005. While any remaining agricultural practices are increasingly concentrated on the valley floor, the forest is reclaiming its traditional territory, particularly on its steep flanks.

15 See "Abwanderung als einzige Perspektive?" *CIPRA,* accessed September 21, 2019, https://www.cipra.org/de/news/1147.

16 Marc Zollinger, "In Italien gibt es Tausende von Geisterdörfern – jetzt kehrt Leben zurück an Orte, die jahrzehntelang von der Zivilisation unberührt blieben," *Neue Zürcher Zeitung,* July 28, 2019, https://www.nzz.ch/panorama/in-italien-gibt-es-tausende-von-geisterdoerfern-jetzt-kehrt-leben-zurueck-an-orte-die-jahrzehntelang-von-der-zivilisation-unberuehrt-blieben-ld.1496802.

17 Petra Kaczensky, Guillaume Chapron, Manuela von Arx, et al., eds., *Status, Management and Distribution of Large Carnivores–Bear, Lynx, Wolf & Wolverine–in Europe* (n.p., 2013).

18 See Georg Jürg Brosi and Adrian Arquint, "Das Calandarudel, Einblicke in den wenig spektakulären Wolfsalltag," in *Wolf: Eine Annäherung,* ed. Klaus Robin and Britta Allgöwer (Lucerne: Verein Freunde des Natur-Museums Luzern, 2018), 37–43.

According to the International Union for Conservation of Nature (IUCN), the Swiss National Park, which was established in the Engadine in 1914, is a category 1a reserve–a wilderness area with the highest level of protection. The landscape has evolved for more than a century without any significant human intervention: Arve in Val Mingèr ca. 1920 and 2012, © Schweizerischer Nationalpark.

Constructing Wilderness

The very first "wilderness park" in the Alps was established in 1914 by some natural scientists in the Lower Engadine. The selected perimeter, which today covers an area of 17,000 hectares, was a collection of intensively used pastures and forests. When this national park was founded, it was by no means a matter of simply enclosing part of the already existing "nature" but of transforming a man-made landscape. To this end, a new use was added, whose "management" was however not handled by locals but by specialists from distant urban centers. The creation of a space that offered the opportunity to scientifically study the process of creation of "original nature" was quite different from the then prevalent and popular idea of a national park, an idea that had already been realized in the US, where attempts were made to preserve grandiose landscapes and, at the same time, create a large variety of recreational opportunities for visitors.[19]

Although the Swiss National Park later advanced to become a global prototype of a scientific national park, its radical concept–which, in fact, meant the exclusion of all other uses–could no longer be implemented in Switzerland. Thus, in the course of the Confederations' new policy for parks, further categories were created which, in addition to the preservation of the cultural and natural landscape, strive to promote a sustainable regional development and sensitize the local population and visitors for ecological, cultural, historical, and economic features.[20] While the regional nature parks and the nature adventure parks impose only a minimum of restrictions on the local population, much stricter restrictions apply to the core zones of national parks to the benefit of nature conservation. For instance, visitors to the parks may not step outside the designated paths. The main reason why the most recent large projects to create new national parks in Switzerland were rejected by society was the fear that others would determine one's own habitat and doubts as to their sustainable economic viability.[21]

19 See Patrick Kupper, *Wildnis schaffen: Eine transnationale Geschichte des Schweizerischen Nationalparks* (Bern: Haupt, 2012), 9–22.

20 See "Pärke von nationaler Bedeutung," *Bundesamt für Umwelt BAFU,* accessed September 21, 2019, https://www.bafu.admin.ch/bafu/de/home/themen/landschaft/fachinformationen/landschaftsqualitaet-erhalten-und-entwickeln/landschaften-von-nationaler-bedeutung/paerke-von-nationaler-bedeutung.html.

21 See Peter Jankovsky, "Adieu, neuer Nationalpark," *Neue Zürcher Zeitung,* June 30, 2018, https://www.nzz.ch/schweiz/adieu-neuer-nationalpark-ld.1398907.

Migrating Landscapes

While the park as an instrument for interregional, municipal, cantonal, and transnational cooperation aims at stable economic, ecological, and social structures, climate change thoroughly changes the conditions of the Alpine environment. In the last 120 years, the temperature in the Alps has risen by almost 2°C. This is almost twice as much as the global average.[22] Looking at the vegetation, the consequences are clearly visible. In principle, three possible reactions of the mountain flora to the changed conditions can be identified. Besides a migration to corresponding climates–which is reflected, for example, by the fact that the tree line is shifting to higher altitudes–some persistency may also emerge. If neither option is possible, the plants will die out.[23] At the same time, plants from outside the Alps immigrate, and exotic species that were originally cultivated in parks and gardens penetrate the local forests, thus changing the composition of plant species and communities. This process can be observed above all in the Southern Alps, but also in climatically favored areas north of the Alps.

The effects of the temperature change become even more obvious with the melting of the glaciers. According to different model calculations, the glaciers will largely disappear in the coming decades.[24] Along with them, their storage function, which is important for the water balance, especially in dry seasons, on a local to continental scale will no longer be available.[25] The retreat of ice also changes the conditions and processes at the now newly exposed surface of the earth. New landscapes, characterized by rocks and debris, are emerging and partially overgrown with sparse pioneer vegetation, which will develop into a closed and dense forest within a few decades. In addition, smaller and larger lakes will form "in the overdeepening of the glacier beds, characteristic of glacier erosion":[26] 500 to 600 of them on the territory of Switzerland itself.[27] This brings with it new natural hazards and, at the same time, changes our perception of the mountains. The beautiful and sublime Alps, which have stood solidly and upright for millennia and

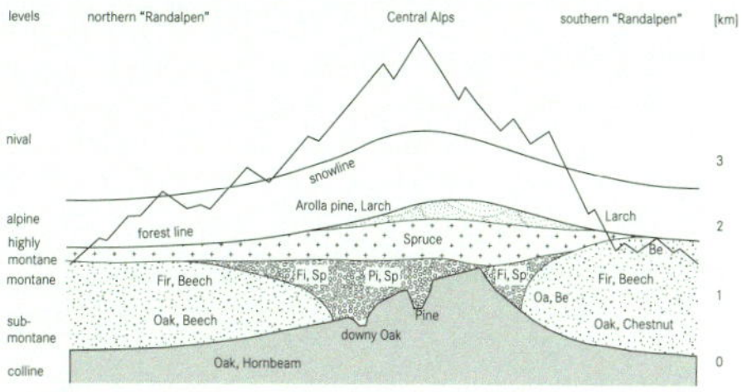

Landscape ecology of the Alps at different altitudes: vegetation profile from north to south. The increase in temperature changes the conditions completely, with the individual vegetation zones shifting to higher altitudes.

22 "Klimawandel: Warum die Alpen besonders betroffen sind," *CIPRA,* accessed September 21, 2019, https://www.cipra.org/de/cipra/international/projekte/abgeschlossen/cc-alps/ueber-ccalps/klimawandel-alpen.

23 Bundesministerium für Umwelt, Naturschutz und Reaktorensicherheit (BMU), *Klimawandel in den Alpen: Fakten, Folgen, Anpassung* (Berlin: BMU, 2008).

24 See Andreas Linsbauer, Frank Paul, Horst Machgut, and Wilfried Haeberli, "Comparing Three Different Methods to Model Scenarios of Future Glacier Change in the Swiss Alps," *Annals of Glaciology* 54, no. 63 (2013), 241–53.

25 See "Studio Meili Vogt Conzett," accessed September 21, 2019, https://meili.arch.ethz.ch.

26 Wilfried Haeberli, "Schwindendes Eis, neue Landschaften und veränderte Naturgefahren," in *Die Natur kennt keine Katastrophen,* ed. Gianni Paravicini and Claudio Wiesmann (Lucerne: Edizioni Periferia, 2016), 177–89.

27 Katharina Bueß, "Prof. Wilfried Haeberli über die Zukunft der Alpen," *Planet Wissen,* February 9, 2016, https://www.planet-wissen.de/natur/klima/gletscher/pwieprofdrwilfriedhaeberliueberdiezukunftderalpen100.html.

New landscapes: Trift Lake near Gadmen (Canton of Bern, Switzerland) was created by the retreat of the Trift glacier and is growing larger year by year. The idea of constructing a dam is currently being examined, a project that would flood the newly ice-free valley including the lake. In the future, the power plant is expected to produce electricity for up to 30,000 households.

seem to resist unshakably, reveal their fragility. "This reinterpretation in the broad social understanding begins in 1987 with devastating floods in the entire Alpine region and an unprecedented amount of damage. Since then, this picture has been reinforced by the extent and frequency of landslides, debris flows, and rockfalls, and is consolidated in collective memory to form a further, powerful picture."[28] The cause of the destabilization of the rock can be found in the continuous dissolution of the permafrost which, in the Alps, occupies an area three times as large as that of the glaciers currently existing, predominantly above the forest line.[29]

Common Ground

Given these circumstances, the question of what specific effort has to be made to create stable living conditions in the mountains applies in a fundamentally new manner. Corresponding adjustments are in full swing or have already been implemented; additional hazardous zones are being identified and the construction of elaborate protective structures, snow-making systems, and glacier covers is continually advanced.[30] In some places, the measures are assuming obscure forms. On the Jungfraujoch, the urban crystallization point in the Bernese Alps at an altitude of 3,466 meters above sea level, visited daily by almost 3,000 visitors,[31] the mountain is partially cooled from the inside to prevent the threatening destabilization of the summit.[32] These purely palliative measures primarily focus on the economically potent regions of the Alps and increasingly accentuate the contrast between the intensive and extensive use of space.

At the same time, new fields of activity are opening up with a view to a more global context and the involvement of local residents. The Alps are full of central resources. "This concerns renewable energies, fresh water, mineral resources, biological resources, and protection against natural hazards that extend far beyond the Alpine region. [...] At the same time, only an orientation of the Alpine economy toward the large customer markets out-

28 Paul Messerli, "Vom Alpenbild zur Alpenpolitik im Werk von Werner Bätzing," in *Leben in den Alpen: Verstädterung, Entsiedlung und neue Aufwertungen,* ed. Tobias Chilla (Bern: Haupt, 2014), 260.
29 See Haeberli, "Schwindendes Eis," 180–86.
30 See Boris Previšiç, "Tiefgreifender Strukturwandel: Kulturen der Alpen angesichts der sich anbahnenden Klimakatastrophe," *swissfuture, Magazin für Zukunftsmonitoring, Zukunft der Alpen* (February 2019); 23.
31 See "1,067 Millionen Gäste auf dem Top of Europe," *Jungfrau: Top of Europe,* accessed September 21, 2019, https://www.jungfrau.ch/de-ch/unternehmen/news/1067-millionen-gaeste-auf-dem-top-of-europe-6637/.
32 Hans Peter Jost, "Permafrost: Der unsichtbare Kitt," *Iniziativa da las Alps,* September 20, 2018, https://www.alpeninitiative.ch/echo_151_3_permafrost/.

side the Alps can secure an economic future for the Alpine regions."[33] This can only be realized based on the principles of cooperation. As in the case of the early agricultural communities in the Alpine region, the exchange will have to be based on a jointly negotiated and sustainable use. This makes it possible to deal responsibly and carefully with the resource of the Alpine landscape without insisting on traditional images and ideas, but rather by actively creating new images and meanings.

Jungfrau Railway, Jungfraujoch Station: Completed in 1912, the landmark engineering feat enabled passengers to travel for the first time to the top of the Jungfrau on an electrically powered train. Most of the line runs right through the rock, with a few stops and lookout points, for example at the "Eigerwand" station on the north face of the Eiger.

The Sphinx research station, named after the crag of the same name. A vertical lift conveys visitors up through the 108-meter-high shaft to the observatory.

33 Messerli, "Vom Alpenbild zur Alpenpolitik," 267.

Ovis gmelini
Creation of a Cultural Landscape

Lars Ruge

The Italian shepherd Luigino Balzan and his flock on the road bends of Brocon pass, Veneto, March 2008

Time-Wrought Change

When you walk through a heathland, you get this creepy feeling that something is missing, that there is no steady dynamic or change–precisely those elements, that is, that define "landscapes," apart from extreme cases characterized by sand or ice. Everything seems static, as if there were no growth or seasons. The sole exception is the period in August and September when the heather (*Calluna vulgaris*) blooms and the heath takes on the appearance of a single, intensely purple carpet. Two factors are primarily responsible for this apparent stasis: a lack of nutrients and the great mass of sheep.

A European Landscape

In northwestern Germany, stands of treeless dwarf shrubs on poor sandy soils are referred to as heaths, whereas in southern Germany, they are calcareous grasslands in mountainous and hilly regions, and in the eastern part of Central Europe they are sparse pine forests found in sandy plains. In every case, they were once common lands or communal pastures.[1] Originally, the heath was thus more a legal term than a landscape one, and on the European continent it was the product of millennia of human cultivation. Locally, there are some naturally occurring heaths–for example, in the coastal regions of Norway, Ireland, Scotland, or France, as well as in boglands and the mountains–but only on a small scale.

The first heaths emerged during the Bronze Age and the Roman Imperial period in places where forests were used as pastures for livestock. Felling trees for use as construction material and firewood, as well as slash-and-burn methods to increase the amount of pastureland, led to a widespread depletion of the soil. Later, beginning in the tenth century

Valley basin at Totengrund near Wilsede, Lüneburg Heath

"Heathlands covered vast areas of the west European landscape during the nineteenth century. Today, less than 20% of the old cultural landscape still exists." P. E. Kaland, "Heathlands: Land-Use, Ecology and Vegetation History as a Source for Archaeological Interpretations," in *Northern Worlds: Landscapes, Interactions and Dynamics,* ed. H. C. Gullov (Odense, 2014).

AD, soils were further deprived of nutrients by plaggen cultivation, and the heathlands once again expanded. The fertile upper soil horizon was removed from large areas of land to be used as fuel, bedding, or to fill in small fields for the cultivation of grains. The depleted and typically acidic mineral soils that were left behind were the point of departure for an initial succession of pioneer plants, among them the robust heather. Aided by slash-and-burn methods, their heat-resistant seeds survived in the ground and were thus able to quickly colonize open areas. The seeds of other grasses, herbs, and trees first had to reestablish themselves as migrant species, though with time they did represent serious competition for the heather. In many locations, sheep have stood in the way of further development beyond this early stage of succession, preventing encroachment by bushes and trees for thousands of years.

Rambling Sheep

Very few animals are so hardy that they can thrive on the meager diet provided by the heaths. Even among sheep, there are few species that are adapted to life in these barren landscapes and able to digest such high volumes of crude fiber. Beginning with the Armenian mouflon, sheep have accompanied humans for more than nine thousand years. If, in sedentary agriculture, they were primarily used for meat, milk, and wool production by subsistence farmers, the tradition of nomadic pastoralism or transhumance emerged as early as Neolithic times. Shepherds moved

Ovis orientalis, the mouflon of southwestern Eurasia, is the wild form of the domestic species *Ovis aries.* Its domestication, about 10,000 years ago, on the slopes of the mountainous arc from southeastern Turkey to southern Iran, marked the beginning of the Neolithic revolution, when humans turned from hunting to breeding livestock.

> *Ovis aries* (domestic sheep) in *Die Säugthiere in Abbildungen nach der Natur, mit Beschreibungen* by Johann Christian Daniel Schreber (1739–1810)

CCLXXXIX.
Ovis Aries Linn.
brachyura islandica

CCXC
A
Ovis Aries Linn.
leptura
Mas cornutus

CCXC
B
Ovis Aries Linn.
leptura
Femina

CCXCI.
A.
Ovis Aries Linn.
Strepsiceros. a.

CCXCI.
B.
Ovis Aries Linn.
Strepsiceros b.

CCXCIV.
C.
Ovis Aries Linn.
guineensis

CCXCIII
Ovis Aries Linn.

CCXCIV.
A.
Ovis Aries Linn.
guineensis.
a.

CCXCIV.
B.
Ovis Aries Linn.
guineensis.
b.

herds of sheep from summer to winter pastures across the high mountains of the Alps, Pyrenees, and Carpathians without creating paddocks to be alternately utilized as farmland and pasture.[2] They took advantage of the varying types of fodder available in different climates and at different altitudes. There was only a limited amount of open or thinly forested land that could be used as pasture. During the Roman period, the European landscape was still dominated by dense forests. Owing to the small amount of feed with sufficient nutrients available in barren locations, constant movement and large pasturelands were needed to ensure that the sheep had an adequate diet.

Historical transhumance routes of the Vlach shepherds in central and southeastern Europe

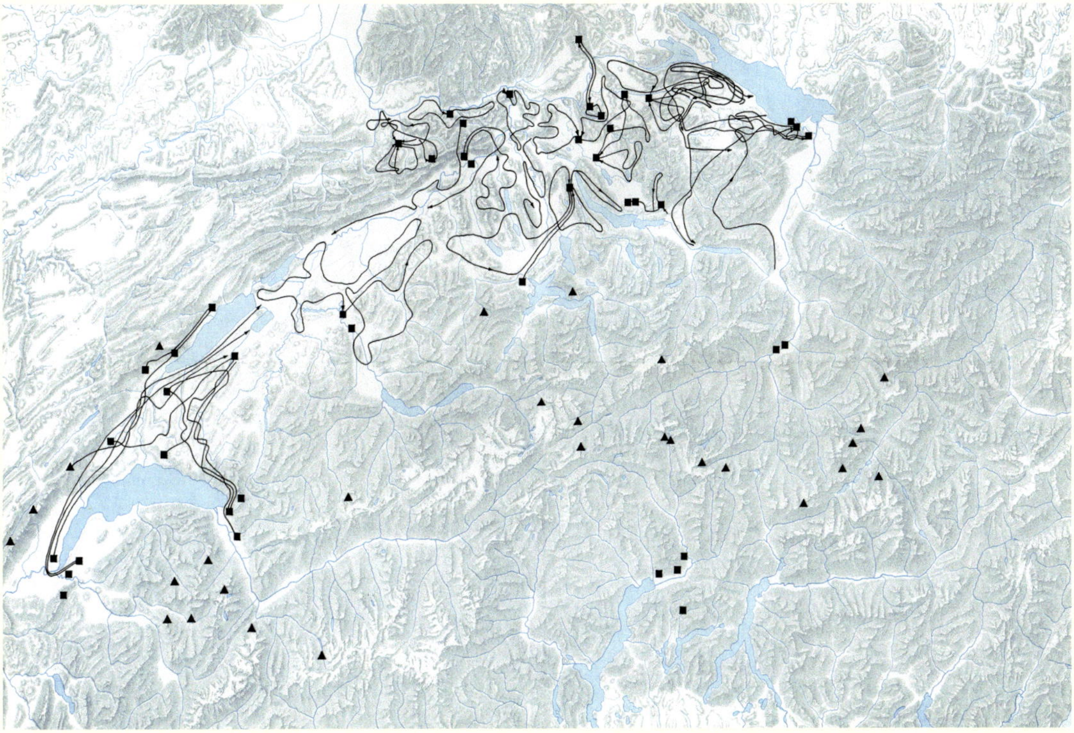

Summer pastures (triangles), spring and autumn pastures (squares), and the winter migrations of Swiss transhumance (arrows), 1969

While there are still many subcategories of "transhumance" that are based on the migration of animals over short distances either across lowland areas or between different altitudes, pastures are for the most part fenced in, and in winter the animals are housed in stalls. The transhumance of large herds of sheep over long distances is also still practiced locally. However, the migration has often been supplemented or, in some cases, replaced entirely by road or rail transport.

Sheep and Culture

While sheep are now primarily transported by truck, the millennia-old network of paths and tracks created by herds of sheep has inscribed itself in the European continent. Many of these paths were later used by pilgrims to journey to religious sites in southern Europe and the Middle East. Beyond this purely functional overlapping of nomadic pasturelands and religious landscapes, sheep are also of central importance in a cultural and religious sense. Germanic peoples saw the animals as bearers of light, and in Christianity they stand for innocence and fertility, while the symbol of the shepherd and his herd represents the pastor and his congregation. In the Greek mythological figure of Pan, the pastoral poetry of the Renaissance, and baroque and neoclassical painting, the shepherd and his herd are a recurring motif, culminating in the ideal of the shepherd king who is concerned above all with the welfare of his herd or people. This concept, as well as the idealized pastoral landscape of Arcadia–in reality a remote, largely infertile karst landscape supporting heather–served as a model for one of the most important epochs in the history of garden art, in which the English garden was regarded as part of the tradition of a communal life free of

Jan van Eyck, *Adoration of the Lamb,* 1432

feudal obligations and class differences. In these gardens, aristocrats often enacted a simple life as farmers and shepherds–a kind of political fantasy without societal constraints. The sheep appears in documents of this period–be it in paintings, texts, or music–in a dual role: as a metaphor for an ideal community and as creator of the gentle, open landscapes encountered in books and paintings.

Thomas Cole, *The Course of Empire: The Arcadian or Pastoral State,* 1834

Joseph Mallord William Turner, *Pope's Villa at Twickenham,* 1808

"Eichhalde in the Great Lauter Valley near Buttenhausen (Swabian Jura, Baden-Württemberg) in 1936 (above) and 1997 (below). Clearly recognizable are the effects of using and abandoning the land. Since grazing stopped, the open sheep pasture has become overgrown with bushes and woodland has established itself." Peter Poschlod, *Geschichte der Kulturlandschaft* (Stuttgart, 2015).

Symbiosis

Under current circumstances, the survival of this specific form of landscape cannot be guaranteed. The harsh working life of the shepherd and the decreased demand for such products as wool and meat have led to the gradual disappearance of the tradition of nomadic shepherding. But it is above all economic factors that are responsible for this ongoing negative trend. Shepherding now ranks as one of the least profitable activities in the European agrarian economy, and this has direct consequences for the heath. For without sheep these vast landscapes, which are bound to the animals in a uniquely symbiotic relationship, cannot be maintained much longer. In the foreseeable future, this will inevitably lead to their complete loss.

1 Christoph Leuschner and Heinz Ellenberg, "Dwarf Shrub Heaths and Nardus Grasslands," in *Vegetation Ecology of Central Europe,* vol. 2, *Ecology of Central European Non-Forest Vegetation: Coastal to Alpine, Natural to Man-Made Habitats,* trans. Laura Sutcliffe (Cham: Springer, 2018), 435–94.

2 Hans Boesch, "Nomadismus, Transhumance und Alpwirtschaft," *Die Alpen* 27 (1951): 202–7.

Future hotspots of land abandonment in Europe 2010–2030: overlay of different scenarios based on three EU studies; source: IEEP 2010

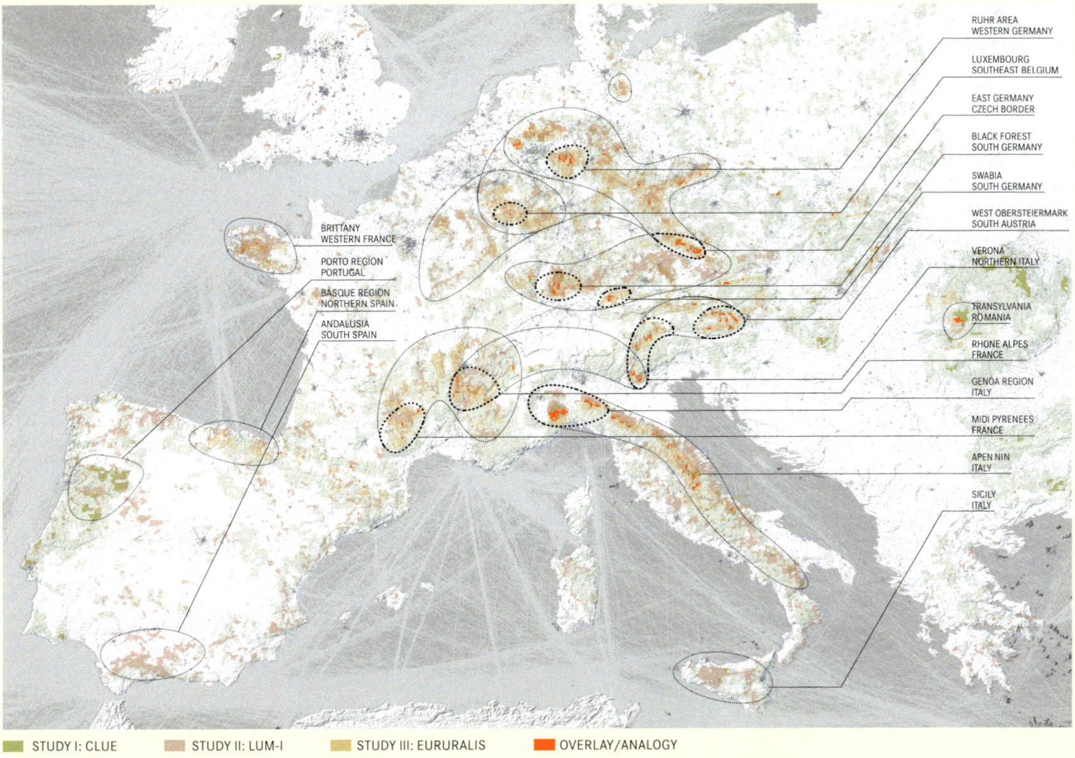

Kvadrat Headquarters, Ebeltoft, DK
Your Glacial Expectations

In the rambling meadows, five oval mirrors form a series ranging from a perfect circle to ever more elongated ellipses, whose proportions vary according to the observer's position. They reflect the ever-changing sky above and the beholder's own gaze as if in the frozen surfaces of glacial ice pits. A piece of the grand Danish sky, uncontrollable nature in itself, is transposed into the cultivated, man-made landscape, now lying there as a clipping of its former self within the countryside. The mirrors refer to the shaping forces of the glacier and the phenomenon of kettle ice: the frozen remains of the melting glacier, which survived over thousands of years, covered and protected by sediments, before finally manifesting as small ponds.

This blurring of the boundaries between above and below, inside and outside, finds resonance in the landscape's melding of "wilderness" and garden. Boulders could be leftovers of the last Ice Age or precisely arranged as park scenery. The dense, clearly delineated groups of trees, planted on slight elevations, may appear to be cultivated gardens from a distance. Up close, they are in fact slices of untamed "wilderness." Although one might expect to be allowed to enter the wild groves, fences deny access. They are Gardens of Eden–that stay enclosed.

Client:
Kvadrat A/S, Ebeltoft

Cooperation:
Art:
Olafur Eliasson, Berlin
Architecture:
Poulsen & Partnere, Aarhus

Design/construction:
2008–2011/2011–2012

Type and size:
Park, 6 ha

Status:
Realized

This metaphor also applies to the sheep, which maintain the broad expanses of the heath landscape by eating up the tree seedlings. Like the artificial relics of a glacial landscape, they blur the boundary between cultivation and "nature" and, in this Nordic park, restore ancient models of a Mediterranean pastoral landscape. (lr)

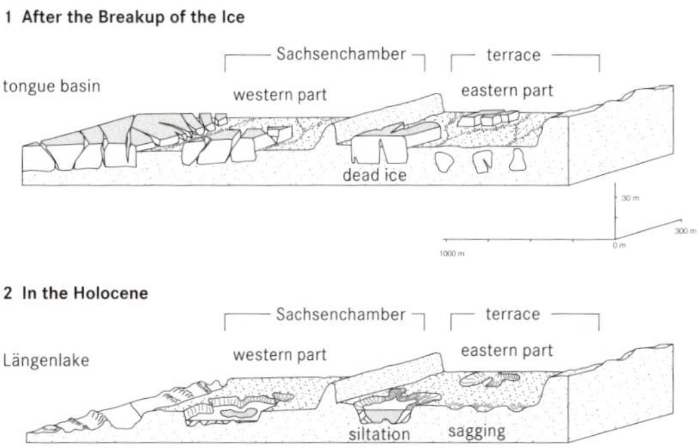

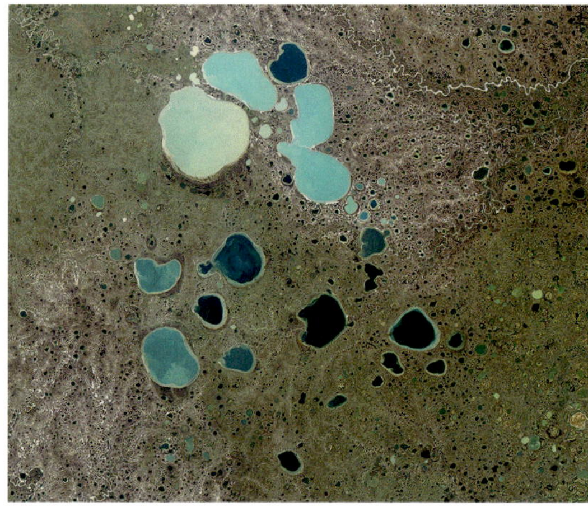

Kettle or dead-ice holes are formed during the melting of the ice cap, as isolated ice blocks are covered by glacio-fluvial material. When these blocks of residual ice eventually melt, dead-ice holes are left behind. Such depressions can vary in size from a few meters to over a kilometer across. Today, many contain lakes or ponds.

The morning small cloud series

Olafur Eliasson, 2006

The nine photographs that make up *The morning small cloud series*, 2006, reveal the passage of time through the gradual emergence of a wispy arced cloud in front of a treeless hill in Iceland. Over the years, Danish Icelandic artist Olafur Eliasson has continually returned to Iceland to capture aspects of its landscape with his camera. The ambitious, ongoing venture–almost cartographical in scope–has resulted in approximately eighty photo series to date and an abundance of individual photographs of glaciers, waterfalls, rivers, volcanoes, and caves. Far from simply documenting the terrain, the images urge us to reflect on our relationship to nature, the physical space in which we exist, and the body's felt motion through space–central concerns in Eliasson's broad œuvre.

1 HIGH WEALD

FORMATION

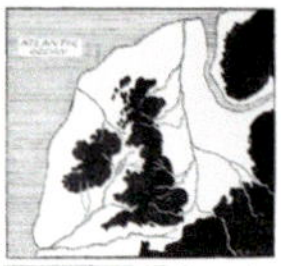

ANCIENT FOREST OF ANDERIDA

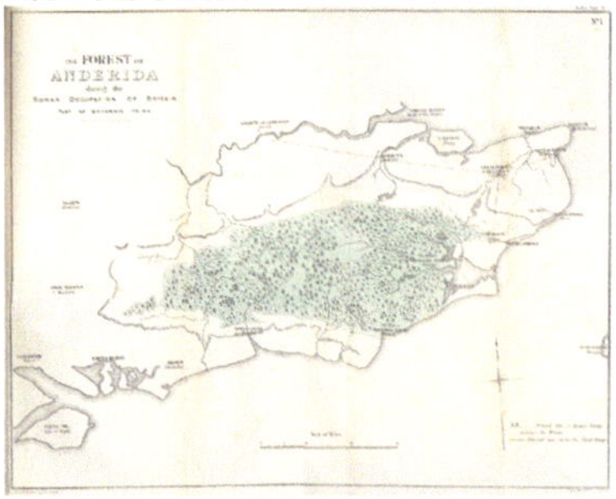

GEOLOGY

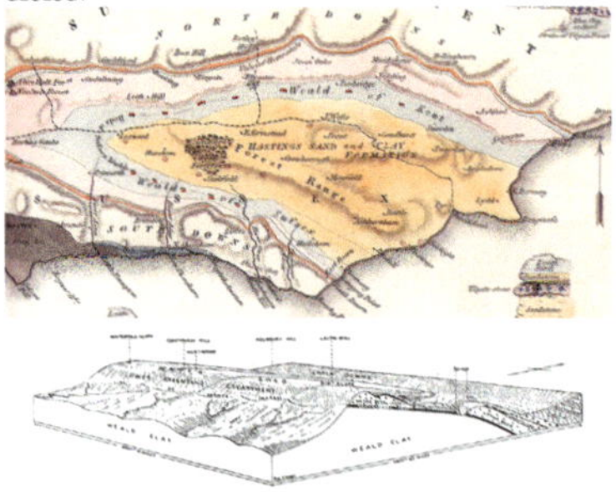

2 GREAT DIXTER

GARDEN PLAN

C. LLOYD: MEADOWS

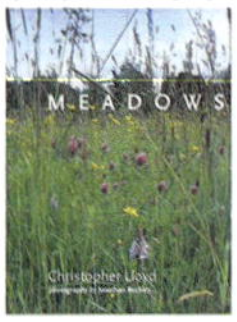

10 ROMNEY MARSH

ROMNEY SHEEP

WATER COURSES

LAND RECLAMATION

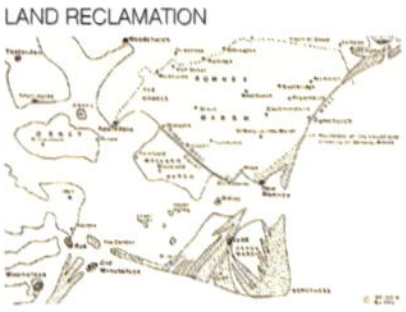

WILDLIFE

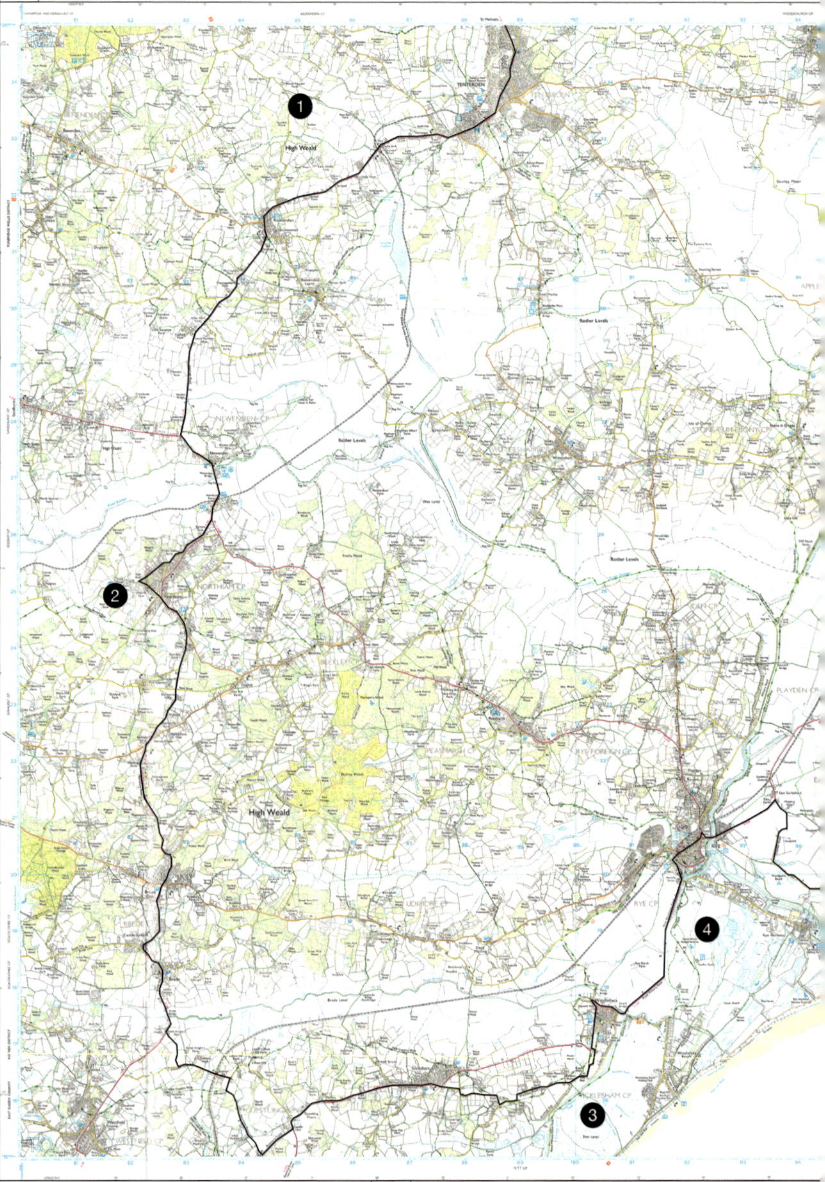

3 PETT LEVEL

SUMBERGED FOREST

TIDES - THU 20 SEP 2018

THE ROYAL ANNE

4 CAMBER CASTLE

1785

FORTIFICATIONS IN SOUTH EAST UK

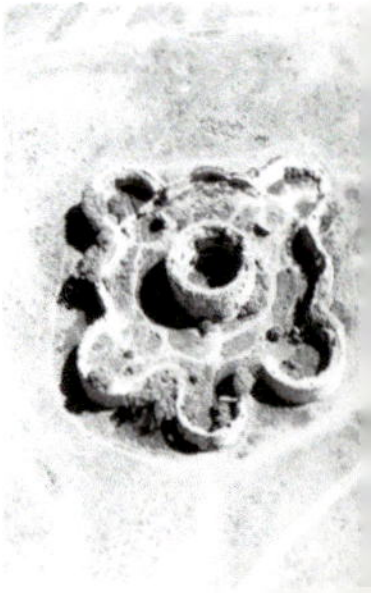

“The pleasure we get from walking is inextricably linked to the knowledge we have as individuals. **Field trips** are an important part of our everyday engagement with the landscape. A while back, I was out and about in the rain in the French Jura and decided that, as far as I’m concerned, good weather is overrated. A rainy landscape is richer, more nuanced than a scene bathed in bright sunlight. **Walking,** with or without a specific intention, also constitutes an unmediated or fortuitous way of reading the landscape.” (gv)

Inventory

A1–A5 Orientation
B1–B15 Sample extraction
C1–C13 Measurement/Analysis
D1–D5 Optics/Photo/Film
E1–E25 Drawing material
F1–F12 Gear
G1 Transport

The Traveling Architect: The cabinet designed by Case Studio Vogt contains the material required to go on a field trip.

TURF FARMING

TURF FARMS IN UK

LOLLIUM PERENNE

PRODUCTION LANDSCAPE

MACHINERY

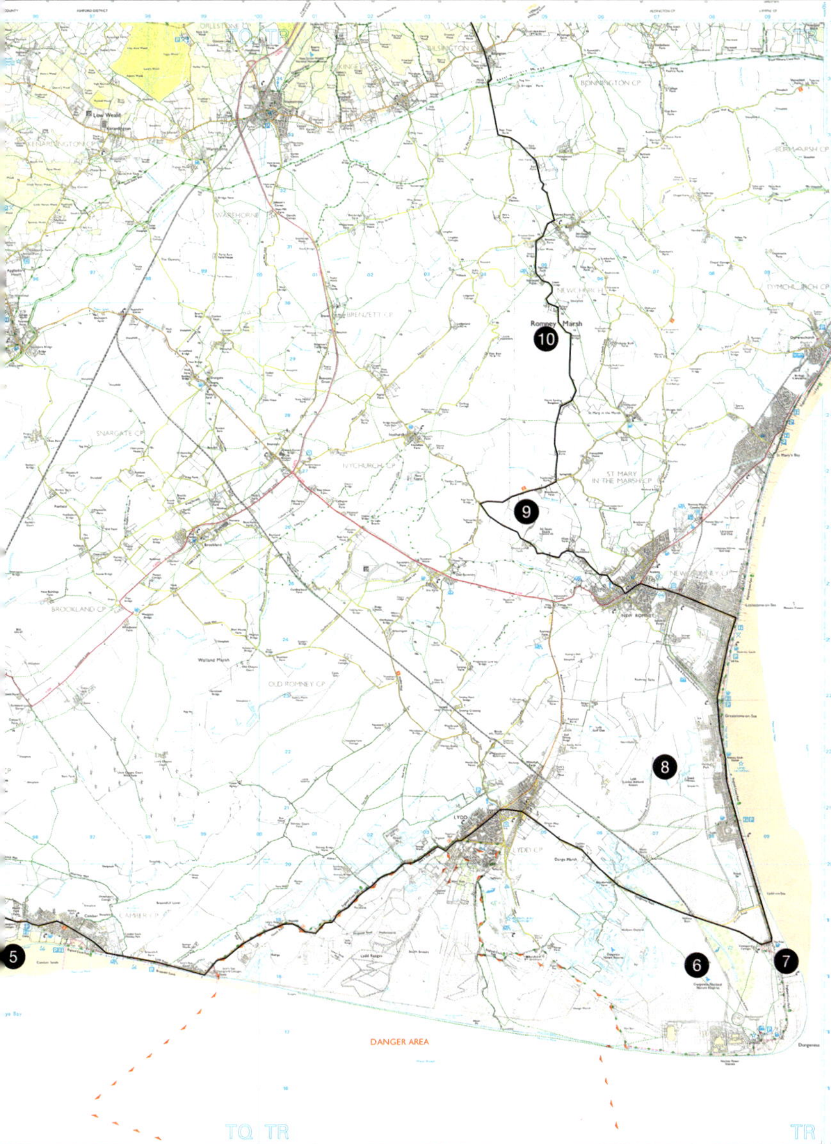

DENGE SOUND MIRRORS 8

1924 - LISTENING DISC SYSTEMS

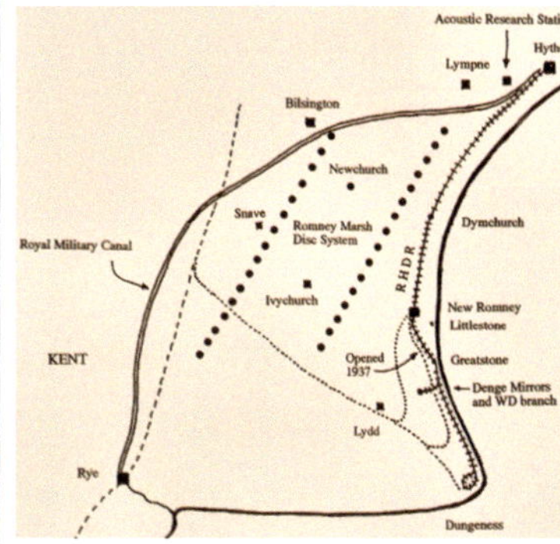

PROSPECT COTTAGE 7

DEREK JARMAN'S DIARY

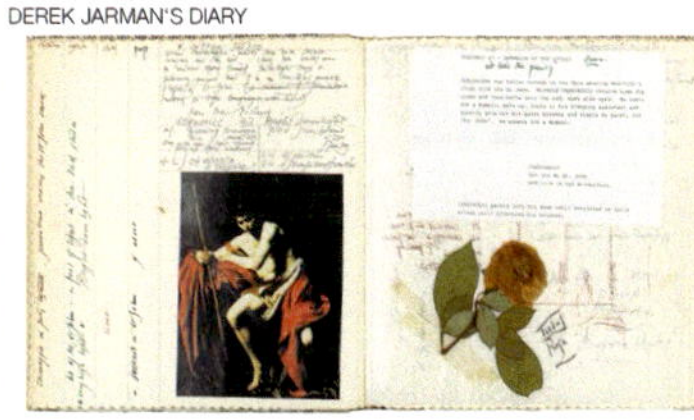

GARDEN SPECIES

CAMBER SANDS

SAND DUNES FORMATION

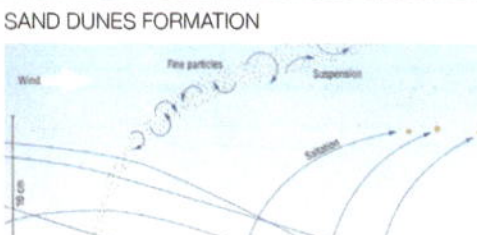

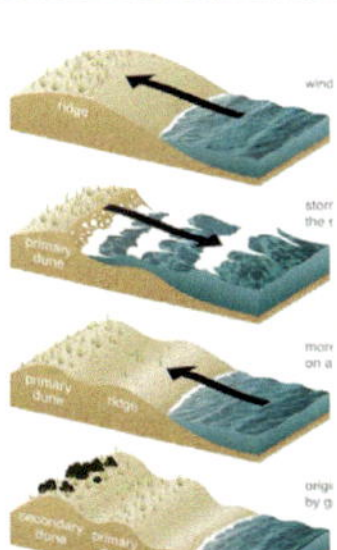

DUNGENESS 6

SHINGLE

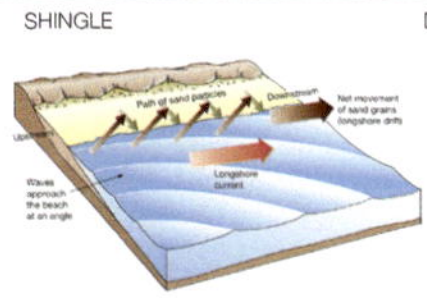

DUNGENESS FORMATION

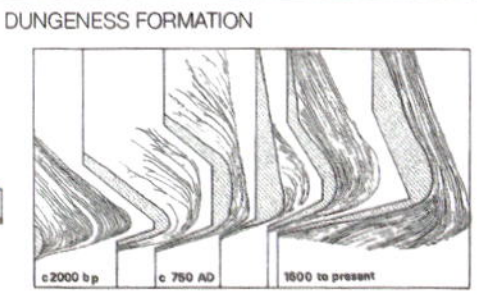

POWER STATION

NUCLEAR FISHIN'

A GIANT nuclear power station has switched itself off twice because it has caught fish from the English Channel. Now the station at Dungeness, Kent, is testing ways of stopping sprats being sucked in through the deep-seawater intake of its cooling system. Possible methods include acoustic, ultrasonic and infra-red devices.

Lolium perenne
Copy Paste Paradise

Amalia Bonsack
Thomas Kissling

Field Trip

Driving in the flat expanses of Romney Marsh, on the coast between Kent and East Sussex, scenes of sheep grazing freely under the cloudy sky constitute a typically English setting. The region is famous for its local breed, the Romney–generally referred to as Kent sheep by local farmers–a long-wool variety that has been exported as far afield as New Zealand since the nineteenth century. In these vast wetlands–which emerged from the sea in Roman times, partly by natural accretion and partly by a process of diking and reclamation–the Romney sheep has become the preferred breed owing to its ability to feed in wet situations.[1]

On this September day, the sheep's light-beige fleece matches the color of the tall grass they are grazing: it has been a particularly dry summer. After a few kilometers' drive, however, one cannot help but notice that this pastured landscape is interrupted by extensive areas where no sheep are to be seen, only perfect carpet-like surfaces of close-cropped green grass, stretching over extensive fields. If, since the 1950s, a widespread conversion to arable land has taken place in the area,[2] which is particularly well suited to crop farming owing to the productive loams formed from alluvial deposits,[3] what we see here is a more recent phenomenon. Over the past decades, Romney Marsh–with its favorable climate, irrigation network, and soil conditions–has also become a prime site for turf growing in the UK, one of the world's largest national markets behind

<< Field trip to Romney Marsh, September 2018

< Albrecht Dürer, *Great Piece of Turf,* 1503

Watercourses on Romney Marsh form a dense network of drainage ditches.

the United States. And while in the United Kingdom turf production is still referred to as "farming," the processes and machines that are used seem rather industrial, as evidenced by the gigantic mowers at work in the fields and the rolls of freshly cropped sod stacked by the roadside. In the distance, the twin-row harvester does not resemble the usual agricultural machinery. It peels off the grass with a 1.5–2 cm root layer, rolls it up, and transports it to the rear of the harvester via a conveyor belt. We would later find out that the machine is capable of harvesting up to fifty rolls a minute, which will be vacuum cooled before being delivered to the buyer's home, less than forty-eight hours after harvesting. Dictated by the logics of efficiency, the roll's format–1 m^2–is the basic unit of this unusual but somehow familiar landscape.

Field trip to Romney Marsh, September 2018: Romney sheep grazing near Rye and harvesting at Grasslands Ltd., New Romney

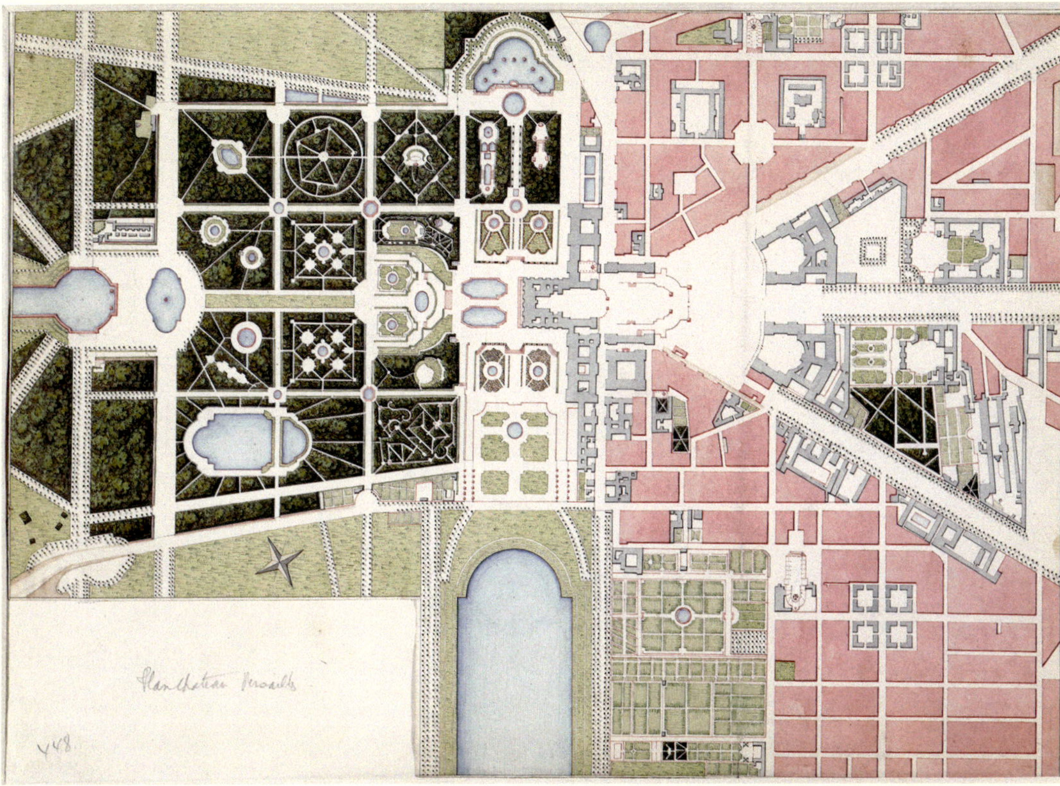

Plan of the city, the gardens and the castle of Versailles around 1770. Situated on the main axis, the *tapis vert* or Allée royale slopes downward to the Bassin d'Apollon, underlining the perspective from the Palais.

Green Boundary

The appearance of the lawn, as a managed green space used for aesthetic or recreational purposes, has its roots in Western European gardening. Throughout their history, lawns have been used to convey a sense of control over nature and have formed a boundary between cultivated and wild landscape.[4]

In the seventeenth century, the principles of imposing order over nature were formalized in the *jardin à la française,* the major gardening style of the time in Europe. As part of a strict composition based on perspective and symmetry, elaborate *parterres*–or planting beds–containing ornamental design were laid out in geometric patterns. Usually separated by gravel paths, these parterres were destined to be seen from above, such as the monumental *tapis vert* at Versailles, a 335 m long alley of turf which marked the *grande*

The design of ha-has, which included a turfed incline sloping downward to a retaining wall, gave the impression of a continuous rolling lawn while providing boundaries for grazing livestock.

Aske Hall, with parkland attributed to Capability Brown

perspective of the château. This green carpet, comprising various grass species which were regularly trimmed, is often considered to be the first large-scale ornamental lawn. Designed by André Le Nôtre, the gardens of Versailles became the archetype of French rationality.

When the English landscape park supplanted the French formal garden as the main style in Europe in the eighteenth century, the lawn would again become one of its central features. As part of the strategy of evoking an idyllic pastoral landscape, the use of extended grass surfaces dissolved the visual boundaries between the estate property and the cultivated or wild landscape. In this context, the sunken fence–or ha-ha–was an ingenious trick to create the illusion of a horizon unimpeded by fences, at a time when grazing animals were still used to keep the grass short. It was in the later expressions of the style, developed by Lancelot "Capability" Brown, that the smooth undulating surfaces of lawn would truly become the icon of the English landscape. While the lawn was still somewhat bound to the regional climate–with its mild winter, moderate temperatures, and high humidity–it soon came to be exported worldwide. Together with the increasing popularity of sports and the playing surfaces associated with them–bowling greens, golf courses, lawn tennis courts–turf met with a particular success in the newly colonized America, where seeds imported from Europe would soon replace the territory's native vegetation.[5]

Levittown, built between 1948 and 1952, was the first American suburb with a preestablished lawn, which residents were required to keep up. Newsletters promoting the importance of a neat, weed-free, and closely mown lawn were sent to all homeowners, along with lawn-care advice on how to attain this ideal.

Suburbia

In North America, the spread of the lawn went hand in hand with the suburbanization process that took place in the wake of nineteenth-century industrialization.[6] City beautification campaigns involved the transformation of the old commons into "greens," public areas characterized by landscaped lawns, trees, shrubbery, and water–all features derived from the grounds of English country estates. Eventually, the lawn migrated from the suburbs' civic center into privately owned properties. As promoters described the suburbs as "reservoirs of clean air and healthy home environments,"[7] a well-maintained front lawn was the visible status symbol of the new middle class.

The advent of the lawnmower, invented in the 1830s by Edwin Budding, was probably one of the most decisive factors in democratizing the lawn. While earlier forms of lawn needed to be maintained by grazing animals, such as sheep or deer, or by labor-intensive methods, the lawnmower allowed homeowners to maintain close-cut grass without additional help: the perfect lawn was finally available and affordable for every average city dweller. The maintenance of the neat homogeneous surface brought along with it a set of weekly routines, and fertilizing, watering, and mowing thus became the common Sunday activity from April to October.

Compilation of some of Dan Graham's photographs of New Jersey, between 1966 and 2006

The Garden of Paradise, ca. 1410

The introduction of setback regulations, which required all homes to have a given distance between the built structure and the sidewalk, also played a major role in establishing the lawn as a key feature of suburbia:[8] while the backyard is an intimate space of privacy, the front lawn is an object of prestige, formulating the boundary between the private property and the street. It has become a global metaphor for the garden itself and stands for the individual dream of life in the countryside, one's own "natural paradise" as a counterworld to the city. Yet, rather than expressing individuality, the conformity of the well-maintained green lawn often contributes to the normative aesthetics of the suburban landscape and its monotony.

Industrial Landscapes

The homogeneity of intensive suburbanization is mirrored in the monocultures required to produce sod at an industrial scale, spreading over extended areas. According to a study mapping irrigated lawns in the United States, the surface of cultivated turf grasses amounts to 163,800 km^2, "an area three times larger than that of any other irrigated crop."[9] Most of the sod is grown in the southern part of the country, thus requiring large quantities of already scarce water resources. The industry, which has been estimated to turn over 40 million dollars in the USA alone[10]–is heavily reliant on the use of petrochemicals, fertilizers, and pesticides,

ALMINDELIG RAJGRÆS, LOLIUM PERENNE.

leading to serious ecological issues such as pollution, the disturbance of ecosystems, and increased health risks.

Industrialization also applies to the microcosm, where the phytosociological difference between the lawn and its meadow counterpart becomes apparent. The variety of native grasses, herbs, and flowers comprising the meadow–providing food and habitat for a rich ecosystem–has been lost in profit to the efficiency of a standardized seed mixture with optimized resistance and a minimum of seasonal variation. From the fourteen thousand grass species that are to be found worldwide, just a few are part of the official seed mixture, strictly regulated to meet quality standards.[11] Independent of climate and soil conditions, the same uniformly green lawn can be found anywhere, as a high-tech product of mass consumption–far from the lush, diverse, and exuberant garden of paradise.

1 "Romney Marsh," *Romney Marsh: The Fifth Continent,* accessed August 18, 2019, https://theromneymarsh.net/romneymarsh.
2 Hadrian Cook, "Boom, Slump and Intervention: Changing Agricultural Landscapes on Romney Marsh, 1790 to 1990," in *Romney Marsh: Persistence and Change in a Coastal Lowland,* ed. Martyn Waller, Elizabeth Edwards, and Luke Barber (Sevenoaks: Romney Marsh Research Trust, 2010), 155–83.
3 "National Character Area Profile: 123. Romney Marshes," Natural England (NE 499), 2013, http://publications.naturalengland.org.uk/publication/5701066775592960.
4 See F. Herbert Bormann, Diana Balmori, and Gordon T. Geballe, *Redesigning the American Lawn: A Search for Environmental Harmony* (New Haven, CT: Yale University Press, 1993).
5 See Virginia Scott Jenkins, *The Lawn: A History of an American Obsession* (Washington: Smithsonian Books, 1994).
6 See Bormann, Balmori, and Geballe, *Redesigning the American Lawn,* 22.
7 Ibid.
8 Ted Steinberg, "Lawn and Landscape in World Context, 1945–2000," in "American West," *OAH Magazine of History* 19, no. 6 (November 2005): 62–68.
9 Cristina Milesi and Steven W. Running, "Mapping and Modeling the Biogeochemical Cycling of Turf Grasses in the United States," *Environmental Management* 36, no. 3 (2005): 426–38.
10 James M. Breuninger, Mark S. Welterlen, Bruce J. Augustin, Van Cline, and Kevin Morris, "The Turfgrass Industry" in *Turfgrass: Biology, Use, and Management,* ed. John C. Stier, Brian P. Horgan, and Stacy A. Bonos, Agronomy Monograph 56 (Madison, WI: American Society of Agronomy, Crop Science Society of America, and Soil Science Society of America, 2013), 37–103.
11 "Wiesen und Rasen: Ansaat bis zur Wiesenpflege," *Natur im Garten* (February 2014).

< *Lolium perenne* is one of the main grass species composing the *Regel-Saatgut-Mischung,* the German guideline on the standard mixing ratio of seeds in horticulture and landscaping.

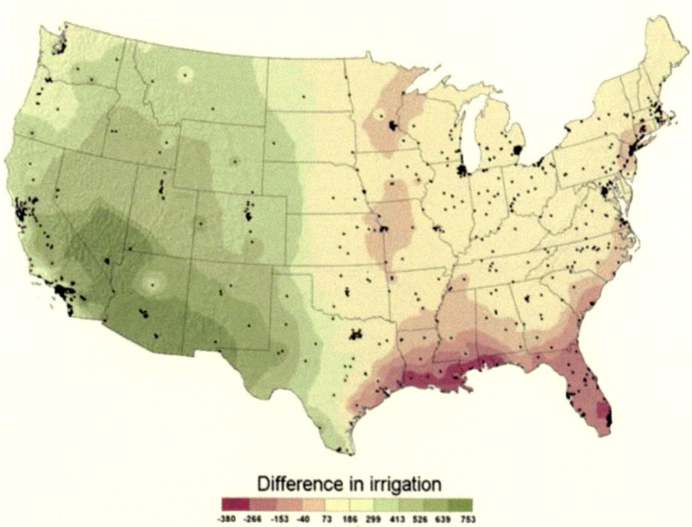

In this study conducted by NASA, "relating turf grass area to an estimate of fractional impervious surface area, it was calculated that potentially 163,800 km^2 of land are cultivated with turf grasses in the continental United States, an area three times larger than that of any irrigated crop." According to the researchers, managing this surface as a well-maintained lawn "would require up to 695 to 900 liters of water per person per day." C. Milesi et al. (2005)

Metropolitan Museum of Art, New York
In the Foreground of the Background

(N 40°46'46", W 73°57'48") The Metropolitan Museum of Art, whose neoclassical longitudinal facade runs parallel to Fifth Avenue, is the only prestigious building actually within Central Park. *The building on the street and in the park. A mansion with park.* Its exhibitions showcase art from all over the world and from many different periods. Walking through the museum is like strolling through a park. High culture alternates with the culture of the everyday, like a cabinet of curiosities. In between, there are also many bizarre, if not outright frivolous exhibits.

The temporary exhibition on the museum roof is a suburban garden equipped with hedges, a lawn, flagstones, and chairs. *A garden above the park.* Dan Graham's S-shaped mirror wall together with the ivy hedges create a spatial center that reflects, doubles, and dissolves as you enter. A familiar motif in baroque gardens blends with the hedge of the gardens of single-family homes, aristocracy with everyday culture. The only element balancing the constant change in reference levels is the uniform horizon of the framing hedge.

Standing in the garden, one can see the tree canopy of Central Park in the middle distance, and beyond the Manhattan skyline one can vaguely discern the vast expanse of New Jersey's suburban gardens. The local horizon–the hedges–enters into dialogue with the world of metropolitan skyscrapers with their reflective, glittering facades. *An image within an image or a garden within a garden.* (gv)

Client:
Metropolitan Museum of Art, New York, The Roof Garden Commission

Cooperation:
Art:
Dan Graham, New York

Design/construction:
2014

Type and size:
Roof garden, 735 m²

Status:
Realized

Green Belt
London's Common Ground

Martijn Slob
Alexandra Savtchenko-Belskaia

For as long as cities have been religious and administrative centers–magnets for commerce and culture distinct from the rural regions and wilderness beyond–they have been intimately linked with, and dependent on, the urban hinterland. Cultivated fields, gardens, and even extramural markets have been vital to the economy of cities, providing goods, services, and clean air to the urban areas they surround. However, the idea of a "greenbelt"–defined broadly as "an area of open land around a city, on which building is restricted"[1]–is the product of a more recent and specific cultural context. As a reaction to the rapid growth of cities following industrialization, the history of this idea is coextensive with that of town planning as a modern discipline. An urban strategy and universal planning tool, rather than a type of landscape, the greenbelt controls urban sprawl by fixing city limits.[2] In London, this narrow definition does not yet reflect the greenbelt's potential as an immeasurable resource and an integral part of the urban territory.

Ambrogio Lorenzetti, *Effects of Good Government in the Countryside,* 1338–1339

Greenbelts in Europe

The figure of the greenbelt is common in Europe. Cities like London, Paris, Milan, and many others have one. But while they all consist of open space that prevents urban sprawl and safeguards urban hinterland, they often vary in size, use, governance, character, and many other aspects. The economic, political, and environmental conditions that led to their creation were distinct in each place, and greenbelt planning–prominent after World War II–affected cities in different ways.[3]

Some of the very first forms of annular open spaces originated in continental Europe. Built in place of medieval walls and fortifications, they were often promenades and gardens that both separated historic towns from new developments and provided important links between the outlying suburbs and the urban core. Vienna's Ringstrasse, for example, replaced the old city walls in 1856 and became a vital organ and intrinsic part of the industrialized city.[4] It became one of the most important urban developments of the Industrial Age and an inspiration to early proponents of urban planning in both North America and the UK.

While these first forms of annular green spaces were still relatively narrow and integrated within the built fabric, the notion of a "greenbelt" proper refers rather to larger-scale areas surrounding the outer limits of the city. Vienna's green belt, which today comprises about half of the city, is one of the oldest and most successful in Europe. Its development began in 1872, as a result of a successful campaign to rescue the Wienerwald forest from being sold by the state to replenish its coffers. Today it is composed of five metropolitan landscapes, each with its own history, qualities, and land use.

However, greenbelts are not always considered part of the city. The Parco Agricolo Sud Milano (Rural Park South Milan) was established in the 1990s to mitigate environmental damage caused by postwar building and unchecked development. In Paris, the term *ceinture verte* was first used in the 1920s to describe an area of thriving fruit, vegetable, and flower farming, while today it is an almost

1 "Green belt," *Lexico*, accessed February 11, 2019, https://en.oxforddictionaries.com/definition/green_belt.
2 See Marco Amati, "Green Belts: A Twentieth-Century Planning Experiment," in Amati, ed., *Urban Green Belts in the Twenty-first Century* (New York: Routledge, 2016), 1.
3 Ibid.
4 See Meinhard Breiling and Gisa Ruland, "The Vienna Green Belt: From Localised Protection to a Regional Concept" in Amati, ed., *Urban Green Belts in the Twenty-first Century*, 169.

European greenbelts can vary in size, governance, and use. From left to right: London, Paris, Milan, Vienna, Munich, Frankfurt, and Cologne.

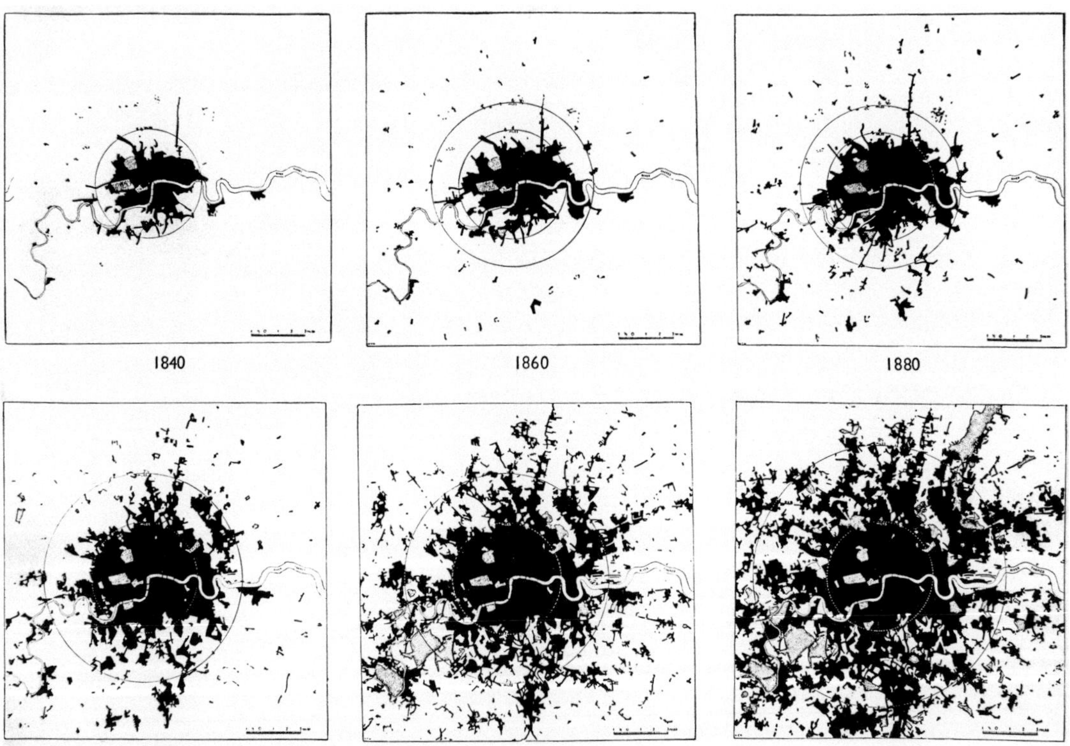

Growth of London between 1840 and 1929, from Sir Patrick Abercrombie's Greater London Plan, showing London's pattern of expansion and Abercrombie's design for concentric circles, each with a specific "urban-rural designation"

continuous chain of parks and woods, and a robust regional planning strategy for the preservation of woodland and farmland around the central urban area.[5] As urban expansion continues, new comparative studies of greenbelts are being carried out around the world in an effort to understand the important role they can play for cities in the future.

Industrialization and Urbanization

Early precedents for greenbelts originate in continental Europe, but the idea for a "Metropolitan Green Belt," as it is now known, was born at the turn of the twentieth century in the UK. Until the Industrial Revolution, the development of London was largely influenced by food. How food came in and where it was sold shaped the city.[6] However, at the beginning of the nineteenth century, the first effects of industrialization began to be felt. The arrival of the railway and motorized transport changed London's patterns of habitation and the rate at which it was expanding. Progressive entrepreneurs with an interest in social regeneration first began to speak about linking existing suburban parks and open spaces with "broad sylvan avenues"[7] as a means to emulate cities like Boston, where annular parks added important green spaces to the increasingly congested urban fabric.

In this context, reformers and early planners began to advance the idea of a "green girdle" as part of a drive for the social regeneration and amelioration of a city where millions were living in poor and overcrowded conditions. To the question of how to restore the people to the land, they replied with "a master key"[8]–the central tenet of what became the modern planning discipline. In his book *Garden Cities of To-morrow: A Peaceful Path to Real Reform* (1898), Ebenezer Howard laid out proposals for the ideal city: circular, with annular rings divided according to land use, and emanating from a central park to a productive, accessible landscape of fruit farms, forests, cattle pastures, large farms, and artesian wells, where "always preserving a belt of country round our cities would be ever kept in mind."[9] This, along with a rigidly regu-

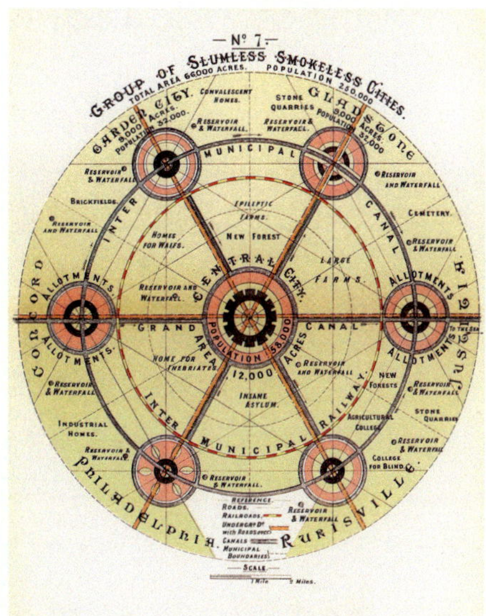

Diagram for a "Group of Slumless Smokeless Cities" by Ebenezer Howard from *To-morrow: A Peaceful Path to Real Reform,* 1898

5 See Nicolas Laruelle and Corinne Legenne, "The Paris-Ile-de-France ceinture verte," in Amati, *Urban Green Belts in the Twenty-First Century,* 227–41.
6 See Carolyn Steel, *Hungry City* (London: Vintage, 2013), 118.
7 Lord Meath, "The Green Girdle around London," *The Sphere* 6, no. 64 (1901).
8 Ebenezer Howard, *Garden Cities of To-morrow: A Peaceful Path to Real Reform,* 2nd ed. (London: Swan Sonnenschein & Co, 1902), 13.
9 Ibid., 142.

lated land-use policy, would provide citizens with proximity to nature, recreation, and fresh air–health being the foundation of physical strength, psychological resilience, and "moral" integrity. The project was a social experiment with a business plan that garnered an influential following.

Metropolitan Green Belt

In 1927 the Greater London Regional Planning Committee first proposed that an agricultural belt should separate London from satellite developments. In 1933 a "green girdle" was proposed. Although not implemented, it was followed by a scheme for local authorities to buy land "to provide a reserve supply of open spaces and of recreational areas and to establish a green belt or girdle of open lands [...] as readily accessible from the completely urbanised area of London as practicable."[10] In 1938 the Green Belt Act was passed to preserve the acquired land permanently and legally, and a public campaign followed that imbued the Green Belt with a bucolic and national character, instilling a positive attitude toward preservation.

In 1944 Patrick Abercrombie's monumental *Greater London Plan* included an analysis of London's growth and a proposal for a Metropolitan Green Belt that would be six miles (9.6 km) wide–much larger than anything that had come before. In the wake of gross postwar overcrowding and destruction, the aims of this plan were explicit: to restrict urban growth, redistribute the population, and provide the city with a large-scale recreational green infrastructure. Rational analysis and scientific method were the cornerstone of the planning discipline, and the normative geography thus established became embedded in government policy.

In 1947 the UK government nationalized development rights,[11] and in 1955 a government circular defined the official purpose and function of green belts in England: "to check the growth of a large built-up area [...] prevent the merging of two neighbouring towns, or [...] preserve the special character of a town."[12] By then, all mention of amenity, agriculture, or recreation was omitted, so

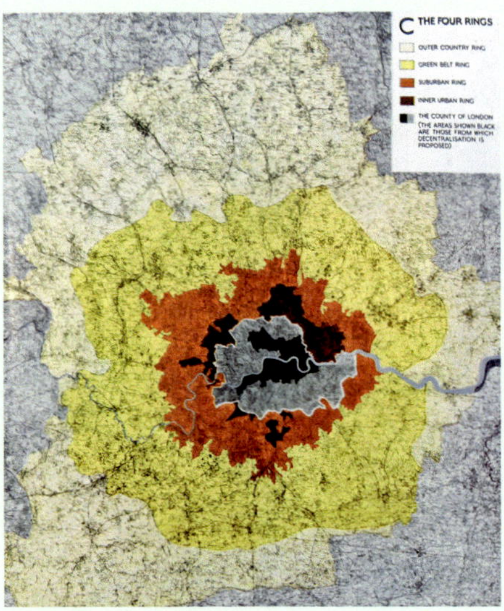

Patrick Abercrombie's proposed structure of Greater London with four concentric rings: inner urban, suburban, greenbelt ring, and outer country ring, from the Greater London Plan, 1944

10 See David Thomas, "London's Green Belt: The Evolution of an Idea" *Ekistics* 17, no. 100 (March 1964): 178.
11 See Amati, "Green Belts," 4.
12 Thomas, "London's Green Belt," 180.

Ruxley Corner
Industrial Estate
SNACK BAR
BAGUETTES, ROLLS, BURGERS,
SANDWICHES, HOT & COLD DRINKS
EDMUNDSON
ELECTRICAL LTD
MOTOR CONTROL GEAR
5

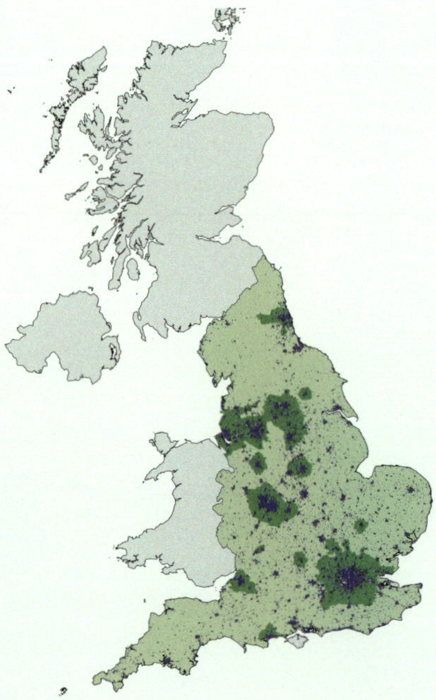

Greenbelts cover around 12.5 percent of England's land area.

that the greenbelt became an instrument designed solely to limit sprawl.

Unknown Territory

Today, the Metropolitan Green Belt (MGB) is a statutory greenbelt around London, comprising parts of Greater London and the six adjoining counties. It covers an area of approximately 514,000 ha (about three times larger than that of London itself), extends up to 40 miles (64 km) from central London, and falls under the jurisdiction of sixty-nine different local authorities.[13] It is a complex conglomerate of landscapes that vary in use, value, character, and quality and are influenced by local, regional, and national dynamics.

However, the policy defining the MGB does not currently reflect this variety, nor the qualities of the landscape. A strong presumption against building is an explicit aspect of the Metropolitan Green Belt, but it comes with numerous exceptions such as industrial estates, agricultural infrastructure, sports facilities, and preexisting suburban developments. Much of it is private and subject to local rather than regional consent, making it difficult to regulate consistently and preserve the land for public use and access. The effect is that large sections of the Green Belt are unknown to urban dwellers, and its potential as a new type of urban landscape remains remote for many. Meanwhile, its parking lots and wastelands tend to be more visible to those driving through it than its wealth of nature reserves, reservoirs, and farmland. The Green Belt's territory remains–to a large extent–invisible, and therefore unknown and vulnerable to external pressure.

Within the current designation, Greater London and the Green Belt are separate entities, overlapping only in parts. Even the term "green," as used in common parlance, seems to suggest the antithesis of the city. This binary opposition offers a limited perspective on the complexity of the relationship between these territories. Even though London's hinterland is no longer able to cater to all the city's needs–and the products and services that

13 See Ministry of Housing, Communities & Local Government, "Local Planning Authority Green Belt: England 2017/18," Planning: Statistical Release, October 4, 2018.

supply London come from all over the world–there is still an intense and strongly interdependent relationship between London and the area surrounding it. Historically, food production has been the predominant form of productive land use in the Green Belt, and two-thirds of it is still in agricultural use.[14] A variety of large-scale farms, greenhouses, allotment gardens, city farms, and community gardens, ranging in scale from a few square meters to hundreds of hectares, all contribute to local food production. While it can only make a modest contribution to London's food demand, production in the Green Belt is significant and offers benefits at multiple levels. On an environmental level, it reduces transportation needs due to its proximity to consumers. On a social level, it offers urban dwellers exposure to the production of their food, encouraging a greater understanding and appreciation of existing resources, the origins of these resources, and the processes of production–thus fostering a closer connection between the city and its hinterland.

14 See "About London's Green Belt," *London Green Belt Council: Protecting London's Green Belt,* accessed June 2, 2019, https://londongreenbeltcouncil.org.uk/about-londons-green-belt/.

An Urban Resource

Even though it is possibly one of the most studied peri-urban landscapes in Europe, much about the London Metropolitan Green Belt remains unknown because there is a lack of concerted knowledge "about its economy, its spatial character, or its value(s)" as a territory.[15] Its governance and accessibility are fragmented, while connectivity to the city is limited, rendering much of it irrelevant for the inner urban dweller. If the Green Belt is to become a real resource in an ever-growing megacity, its landscape should be qualitatively assessed–not as unbuilt land alone but as a territory in its own right, and as an integral part of London's urban system.

The principles of ecology as a holistic, open-ended science studying the relationships of organisms to one another and to their environments can provide a valuable lens through which to read the greenbelt and a solid basis for a systemic understanding of such landscapes.[16] The city

15 Jonathan Manns, *Green Sprawl: Our Current Affection for a Preservation Myth?* (London: The London Society, 2014), 23.
16 See Jusuck Koh, *Ecological Reasoning and Architectural Imagination* (Wagenigen: Wagenigen University, 2004).

Map showing the proportion of the Metropolitan
Green Belt with public access and amount of greenbelt
land considered to be within the Greater London Area

PRIVATE PROPERTY
NO PUBLIC VEHICULAR
OR
PEDESTRIAN RIGHT OF WAY
NO PUBLIC VEHICULAR
OR
PEDESTRIAN RIGHT OF WAY

depends on the Green Belt as a vital recreational and productive resource, while the economy of the Green Belt depends on the city as its main marketplace. Beyond goods and services, the Green Belt is an important environmental resource for London, providing the metropolis with fresh air and water, while supporting a rich ecosystem. Finally, it can be a space for collective use and social interaction, operating at a scale that responds to the size of the metropolis. As such, the Green Belt has the potential to establish a new form of commonly used and regulated space, fully integrated in London's urban system.

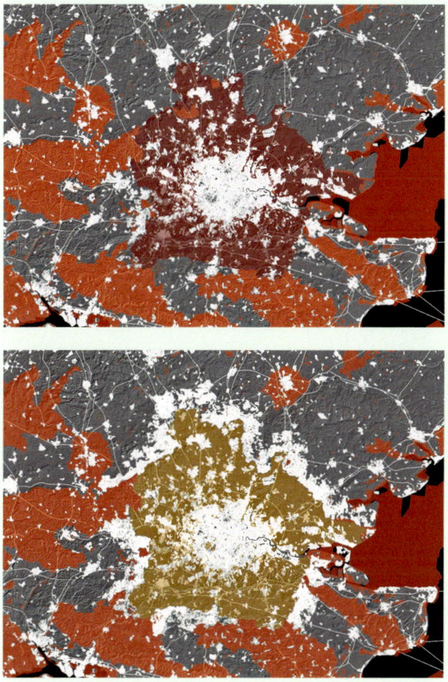

London Metropolitan Green Belt (MGB), a forecast hypothesis for 2100. The city is expected to grow as an urban belt around the MGB, which will act as a trigger for densification. Research by the Chair of Prof. Günther Vogt at the ETH Zurich.

Rectory Farm, London
Time and Scale

In combining mineral extraction, commercial activity, production, and recreation, Rectory Farm sets an innovative example of layered multifunctional intensive land use, providing a new urban park of local and regional significance within the London Green Belt. The design of the new park is driven by the management of landscape and its natural resources and the complexity of laying out a park above a large-scale underground structure in multiple phases.

Client:
Formal Investments, Cheltenham

Cooperation:
Architecture and master plan:
Carmody Groarke, London
Civil and structural engineering:
ARUP, London
Planning consultant:
DP9, London
Project management:
Gleeds, London

Design/construction:
2011–ongoing

Type and size:
Park, 44 ha

Status:
Ongoing

Landscape Types

- Thames floodplain
- Tributary valleys
- Gravel terraces
- Clay plateau
- Clay ridges
- High heaths and commons
- Chalk dip slopes

Rectory Farm is a new 44 ha park built on former farmland in Hounslow, West London. Located within the Metropolitan Green Belt, the site forms part of London's strategic open space network and the All London Green Grid, an extensive system of green and open spaces integrated within the Blue Ribbon Network of rivers and waterways. On a metropolitan scale, the park reinforces strategic green infrastructure, enhancing the biodiversity of the Crane Valley, and forming a gateway into the Colne Valley Regional Park through cycling and pedestrian connections. On a local scale, it is a park dedicated to neighboring communities which are deficient in public open space.

The land is currently inaccessible to the public and lies derelict, as it is unviable for farming owing to its size and concerns over food safety. Under its surface lie large amounts of valuable gravel and sand, and the site has been identified as a strategic supply of building materials for London. The proposed design combines these interests with the needs of the adjacent neighborhoods, by integrating industrial-scale mineral extraction with the creation of a new public park. The design strategy is based on the gradual transformation of the site over several years into a publicly accessible park built over an active gravel quarry. In order to mitigate the negative impacts of long-term open-pit mining, the park will be built on a large concrete slab cast on pile foundations, allowing it to be open to the public while mining continues underground–making it effectively the largest roof garden in the world. Following the extraction of minerals, the space underneath the park will be transformed into a large underground warehouse, strategically located in close proximity to Heathrow, one of the world's busiest airports.

The principles that govern the park's spatial design are driven by the existing landscape, on the one hand, and by the technical possibilities and complexities of building above a large-scale underground structure on the other. These include the management of water and soil, planting strategies, loading capacities, and buildups over the concrete slab, as well as the logistics of constructing in multiple phases. And while the park design will change throughout the ongoing design and construction process, it is the nature of the site–its hydrology, regional ecological connections, and natural resources–that ultimately provides a set of opportunities and constraints governing its development.

While the construction of new buildings within Green Belt land contradicts local and national policy, the proposal for Rectory Farm has been accepted by the local planning authority, as it delivers a new publicly accessible park of local and regional importance that actively contributes to the objectives of the London Plan on a site that would otherwise remain derelict and inaccessible. The park enhances the Green Belt's accessibility and provides different uses for its residents and visitors.

The project lets mining, recreation, and commercial activity coexist in time and space, and as such it establishes an innovative precedent for multifunctional intensive land use and natural resource management in a dense urban environment. (ms)

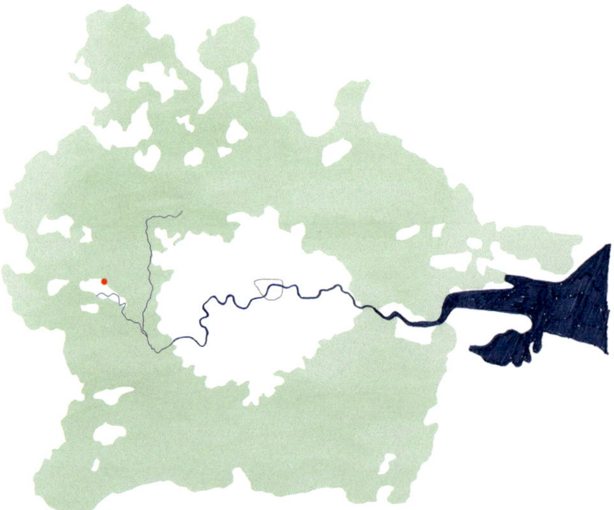

Rectory Farm is located at the inner edge of the London Green Belt, positioned in between two residential neighborhoods and part of the regional landscape of the Crane Valley. While the site is currently inaccessible and unused, the new proposals will transform the former tract of farmland into a new urban park, that can be compared in size to some of London's larger parks.

Rectory Farm

(A) Hanworth Park

(B) Syon Park

(C) Gunnersbury Park

(D) Clapham Common

(E) Primrose Hill

(F) Regents Park

(G) Green Park and St. James Park

(H) Victoria Park

(I) Greenwich Park

(J) Bushy Park

The new park is simultaneously part of the built urban fabric and of the regional network of parklands.

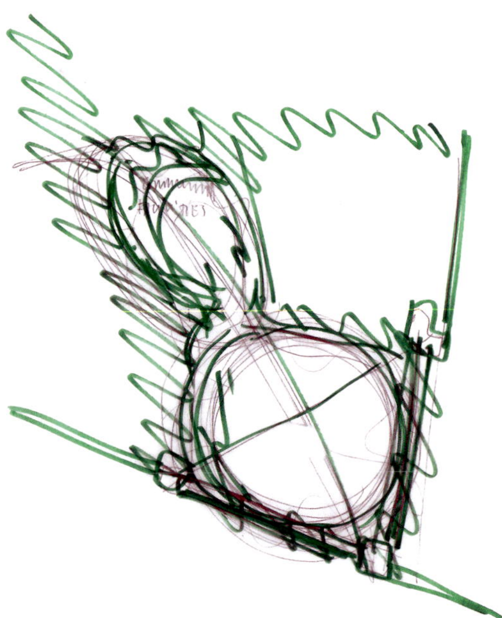

Rectory Farm, London

Time and Scale

As part of important regional "green infrastructure" consisting of the Crane River Valley, the Hounslow Loop, and the London Green Belt the new park makes a significant contribution to the urban ecosystem. For people living in the adjacent neighborhoods, where public open space is scarce, the park is a vital addition. The entrances and pedestrian networks in the park link directly into the surrounding urban fabric, connecting neighborhoods that are currently "turning their backs" to the site.

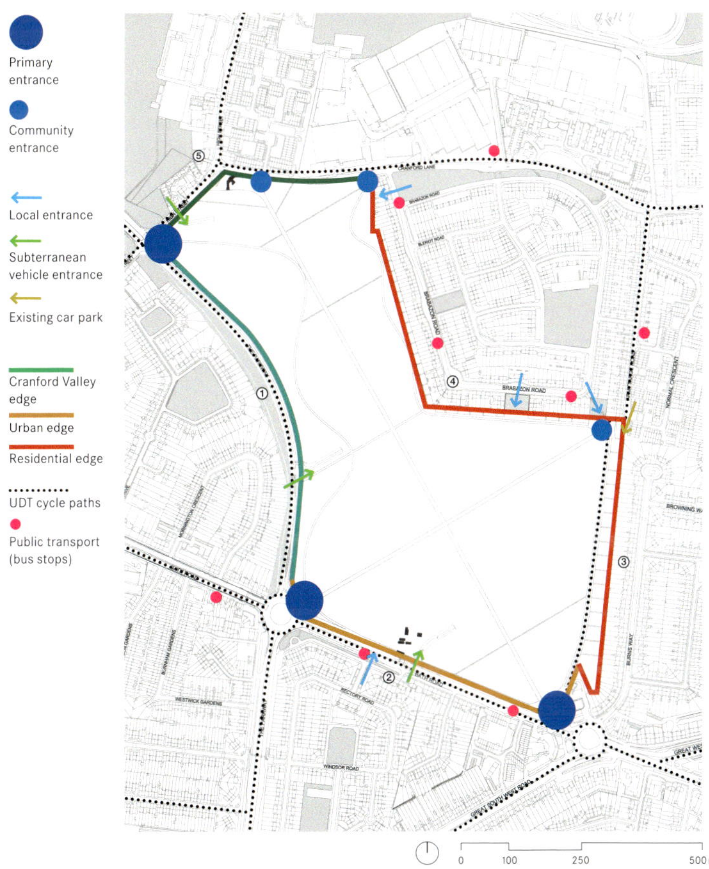

The dense woodland belts are a continuation of the planting in the Crane Valley. In the center of the park, open fields with rich meadows serve as amenity lawns and sports fields. The edges to the south and east allow for productive land use, including allotment gardens, small orchards, and community gardens.

Woodland Activity Area (1.6 ha)
- Informal playgrounds
- Fitness equipment
- Climbing equipment

Community Facilities (1.7 ha)
- Park management
- Community center
- Change rooms / Toilets

Playground (0.2 ha)
- Formal and informal playgrounds

Recreational Area (4.6 ha)
- Formal sport fields

Topographical Woodlands (5.1 ha)
- Wetland / Natural areas
- Cross-country / Off-road activities

Productive Landscape (12.1 ha)
- Meadows
- Agroforestry / Temporary tree nurseries

Amenity Lawn Area (10.7 ha)
- Informal sport fields
- Picnic areas
- Recreation

Community Gardens (2.9 ha)
- Urban farming
- Garden allotments
- Orchards

Existing car park (0.2 ha)

Proposed car park (0.05 ha)

Dense woodland belt planting

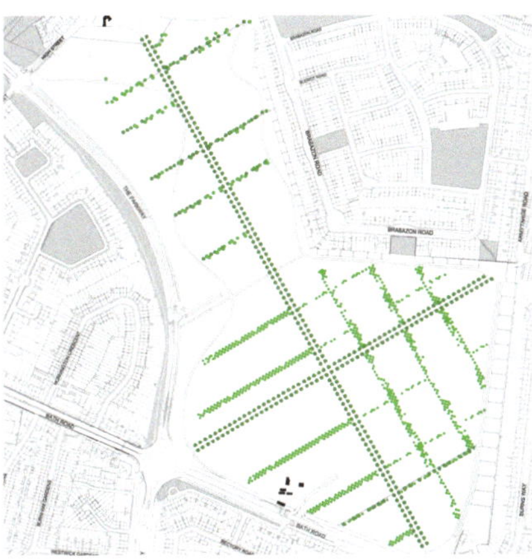

Open fields in the center of the park

Defining a clear urban edge to the park

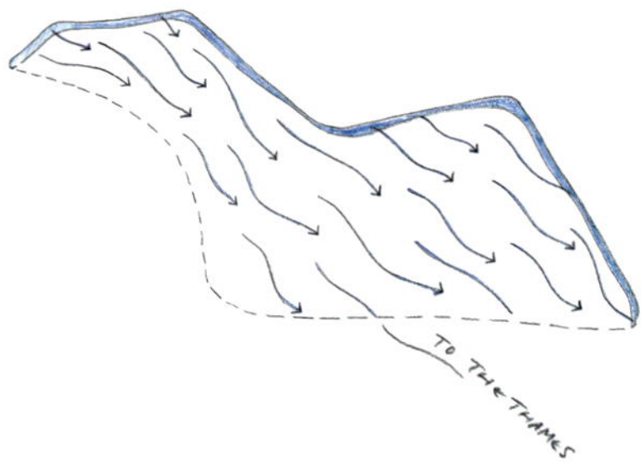

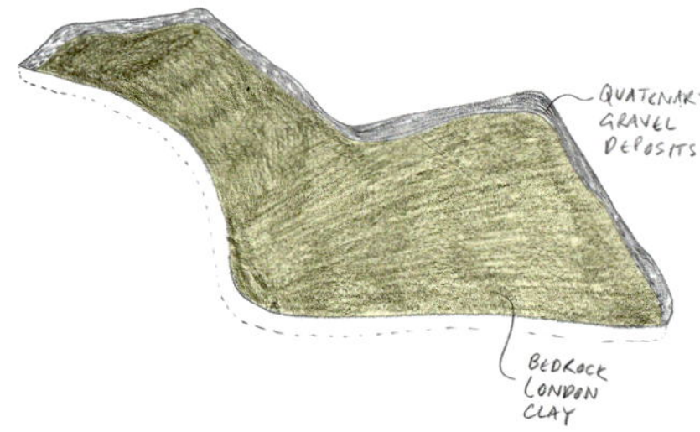

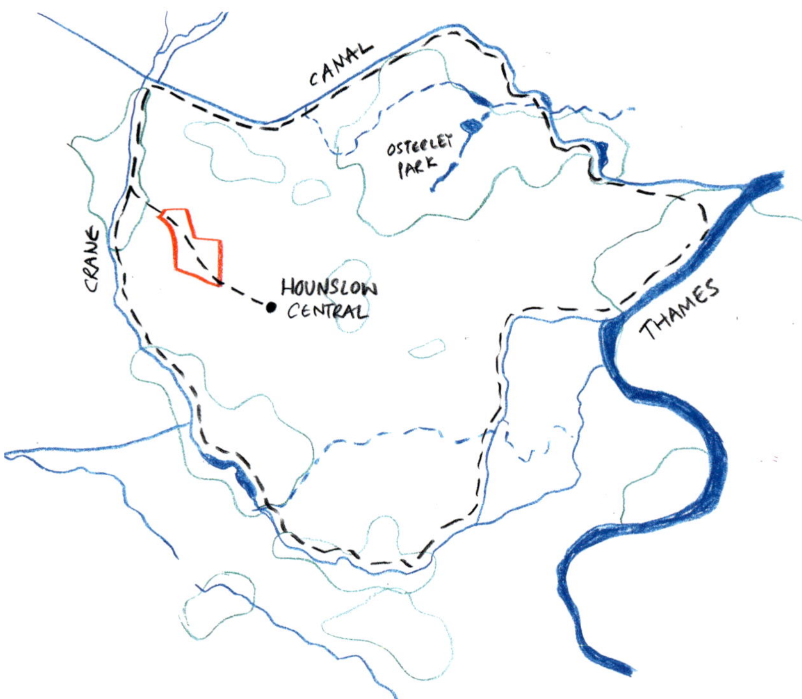

The project is predominantly driven by the management of the landscape and its natural resources: the aim is to extract minerals, while creating minimal disturbance to the surrounding neighborhood and making a meaningful contribution to the existing ecological and hydrological networks.

Rectory Farm, London
Time and Scale

The new park will be built atop a large underground warehouse. Prior to the warehouse being built, the minerals below the surface–mostly gravel and sand–will be quarried and transported off-site. To minimize disturbance to the surrounding neighborhood, the quarrying will happen below a concrete slab, with the park above it open to the public.

Construction and extraction process:
1 Existing landscape
2 Removal of topsoil, creation of piles, casting of ground slab
3 Development of park in tandem with gravel extraction
4 Construction of warehouse building beneath the park

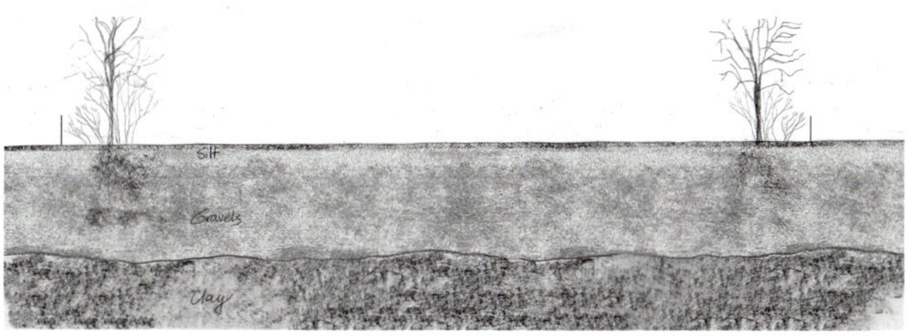

1

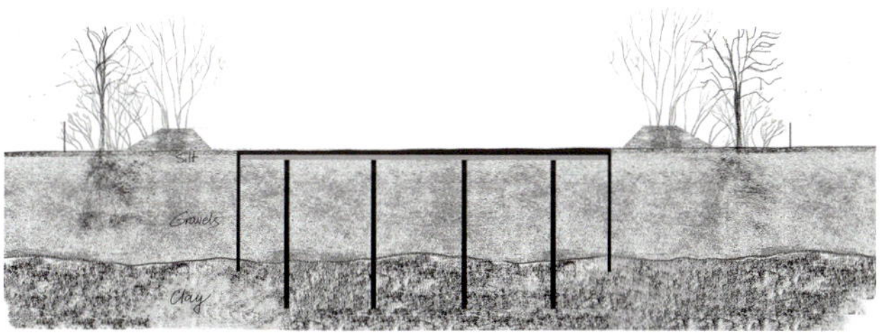

2

3

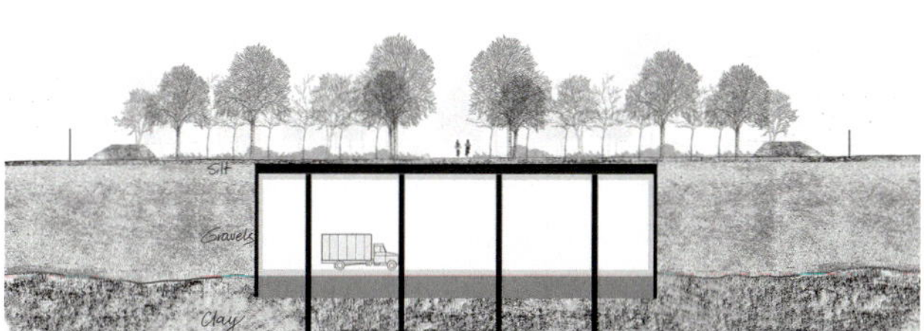

4

Landscape Construction Phase 1
Underground Construction Phase 1
The north of the site is hoarded off to enable work to be undertaken to extract the gravel. Topsoil is removed from this area for perimeter berms and stored for future landscaping across the park. Preliminary planting installed.

Landscape Construction Phase 2
Underground Construction Phase 1
Earthen berms created from excavated gravel, clays, and topsoil form a buffer zone between Bath Road and the Parkway. A small area is hoarded off to begin constructing the vehicle access ramp.

"Day One"
The northwest hoarded-off area is returned to the park. Following the installation of paths, perimeter fencing, and planting, the public gains access to the park. Recreational activities are developed in the north of the park.

Landscape Construction Phase 3
Underground Construction Phase 2
Gravel extraction and basement construction continue to progress underground. After the completion of the subterranean cells, the landscape is reinstated and enhanced. The public retains access to the park during construction.

Landscape Construction Phase 4
Underground Construction Phase 2

Landscape Construction Phase 5
Underground Construction Phase 3

Landscape Construction Phase 6
Underground Construction Phase 3
The final phase of construction begins in the southern tip of the site, and the park progresses toward its final stage.

Landscape Completed
All construction phases are complete. The park is fully developed in the final master-plan phase.

While the mining of gravel and sand and the construction of the underground warehouse will take place in multiple construction phases, the park will be open to the public as soon as the first part of the ground floor slab has been cast and the first park phase is built.

Rectory Farm, London
Time and Scale

The final result is a project where the above-ground park and the underground building are fully developed in tandem and where the design above ground influences the possibilities below ground and vice versa. As such, the structure of the underground building is clearly visible in the planting structure and networks of the park above.

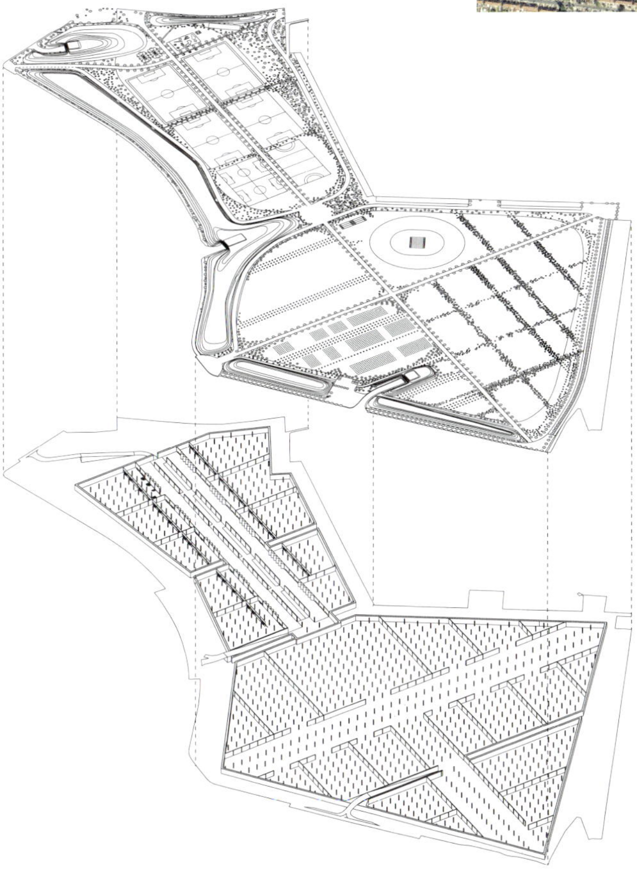

Yorkstone
Surface and Interface

Alexandra Savtchenko-Belskaia

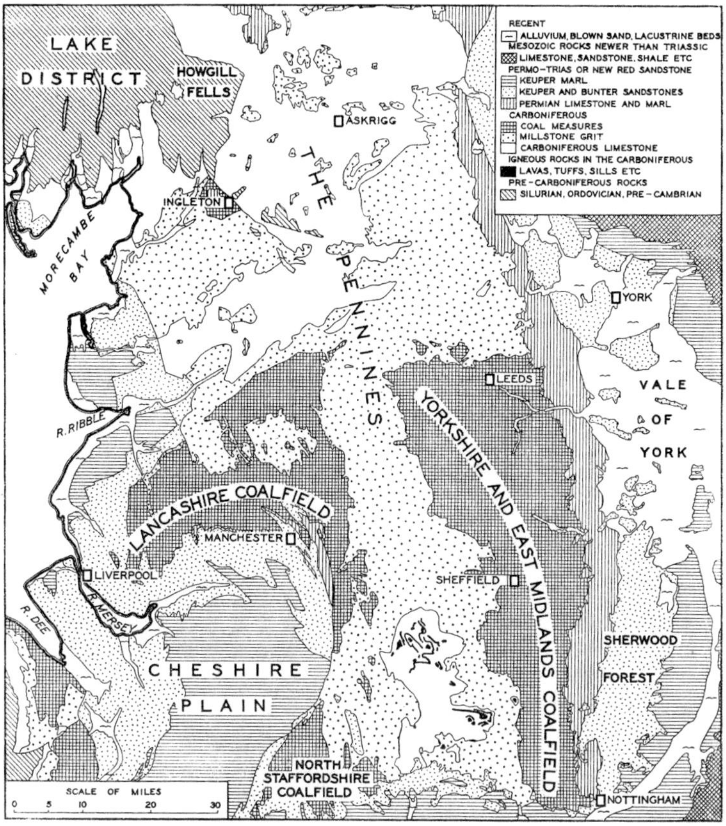

< First geological map of England, Wales, and part of Scotland by William Smith, 1815

Geological map of the Pennines

The Pennine Anticline

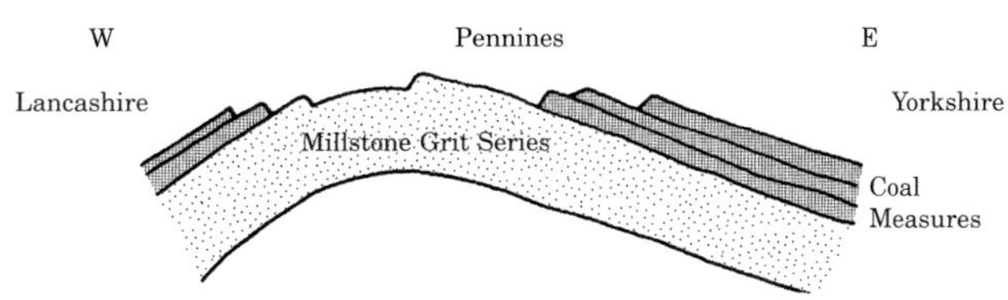

The Backbone of England

Yorkshire sandstone began to form in northern England about 320 million years ago, during the Upper Carboniferous, when an ancient mighty river washed sands and grit into the great delta that covered half of Yorkshire.[1] These sediments were compacted and cemented into stone, and 40 million years later, they were pushed up and gradually eroded, forming what we know today as the Pennine Hills. Due to its richness in natural features and resources, the region has been exploited by humans for energy and materials for thousands of years. The value of local stone was understood by the Romans, who used it, among other things, to build the foundations of the city of York. During the Middle Ages, a growing number of churches, monastic complexes, castles, and halls created higher demand for the stone. However, it wasn't until the nineteenth century that the industry really burgeoned.

The invention of the steam engine, together with Land Inclosure Acts–which required the enclosure of moorlands by thousands of kilometers of drystone walls–led to the proliferation of quarrying all over the region. The Pennine

Traces of medieval quarries, such as these grassed-over hills and hollows, remain visible in the Yorkshire Dales. As early as 1257, sandstone was quarried here to make mill-stones–hence the name Millstone Grit. During the eighteenth century, workings expanded into "delve-holes" or digging places to meet the growing demand for drystone walls for the enclosures.

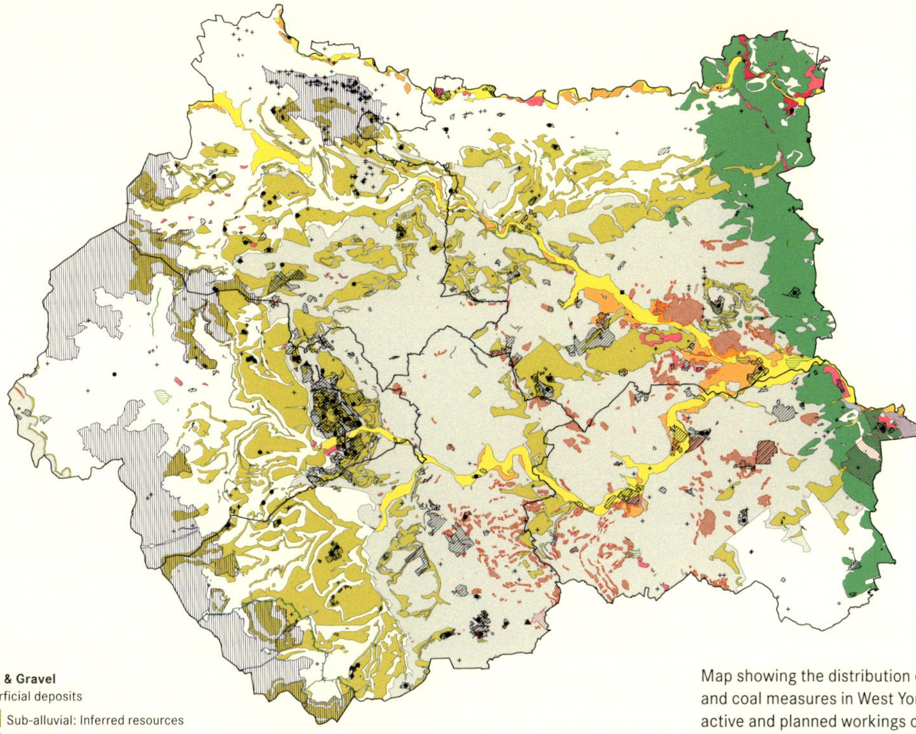

Map showing the distribution of sandstone and coal measures in West Yorkshire, with active and planned workings concentrated around the sandstone deposits. Although quantities of crushed rock extracted from the Yorkshire Dales have declined since 2008, approximately 2.6 million tons are still extracted each year.

CP19/070 Modified British Geological Survey "Minerals of West Yorkshire Map" © UKRI 2019

Hills, often called "the Backbone of England," hence provided the supply of building stone that stoked urbanization during the Industrial Revolution. Vast quantities of dimension sandstone[2] began to be transported by canal and rail to feed the expansion of towns and cities. At the height of production, in 1937, there were 242 large-scale commercial quarries in operation.[3] After World War II, extraction went into rapid decline and demand has since waned due to the emergence of artificial building materials. Nevertheless, "Yorkstone" is still much used in London and many other British cities, and to this day West Yorkshire has the largest concentration of sandstone quarries in the country.[4]

London's Common Ground

While the character of a place is often determined by local building materials, London, unlike Paris, has no indigenous building stone. After the Great Fire of 1666, the city's preferred building material changed from timber to brick, which was more durable and widely available thanks to London's underlying layers of clay. As natural stone needed to be brought in from further afield, its use was restricted to prestigious buildings and street paving. Since the nineteenth century, as mainline railways made haulage viable, Yorkstone came into wider use, and streets and squares began to be paved in sandstone from the north.

After the Great Fire of 1666 destroyed much of medieval London, new buildings were built mostly of bricks from local London clay. These distinctively yellow soft bricks became known as "London stock." Streets continued to be paved in wood or granite cobbles until the invention of the steam engine made transport of stone slabs viable.

In London, Yorkstone paving acquired a distinctive and symbolic appearance. As a subtle reminder of English common ground, its presence provides solidity and a notion of permanence, fostering a sense of belonging and a connection to place across time. Through its frequency of use, it has become a material so recognizable that it has come to define the city's character. Simultaneously distinguished and commonplace, Yorkstone is thus suitable as a signifier of "publicness." For this reason, as well as its reputation for durability and good quality, it is specified by both Central

Due to its physical properties, Yorkstone is known as a strong and durable paving stone. Composed of sand-sized particles of quartz and feldspar cemented by silica–densely compacted and merged into one another–it can carry heavy loads and tolerate the effects of weathering.

Traditional paving in London is laid in stone flags. Large slabs of 900 × 600 mm are common, although older slabs of larger or random-length slabs can also be found. Variations in color, texture, or paving direction often indicate differences in age, levels of maintenance, and, of course, in the specific type of stone used–effectively revealing otherwise invisible boundaries within the city.

London planning authorities–Westminster City Council and the City of London Corporation–as the preeminent stone of choice for public spaces.[5] As the city's main paving material, Yorkstone becomes a subtle agent of consistency, providing coherence within the dense patchwork of the London metropolis.

Nevertheless, small differences in specification and treatment reveal a latent aspect of urban life. They let us discern boundaries between varieties, finishes, and levels of maintenance, revealing London's characteristically complex, controversial relationship between truly public space and space which is publicly accessible but privately owned.

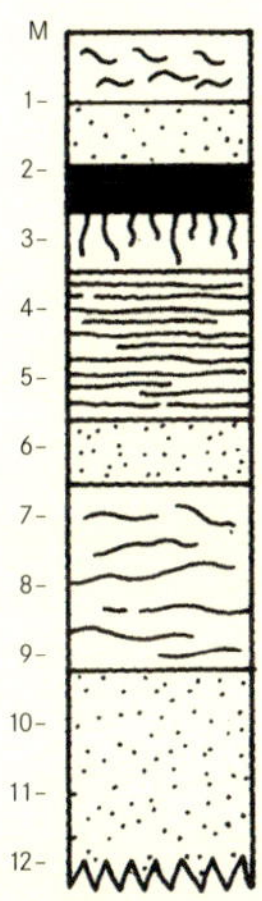

Soil and peat	Overburden
Silica stone	Refractory stone for lining furnaces
Coal	Mixed with good coal and used for a steam crane
Fireclay	Pipes and bricks
Flags	Poor quality flagstones for crazy paving
Sandstone	Good quality construction stone
Rag	Poorly bedded sandstone, used in field walls
Sandstone	Good quality construction stone

< London Yorkstone paving palette; smooth-sawn specimen from near Bank station in East London, and rough-cut pavers from Hampstead in the northwest. Yorkstone is typically buff-colored, with cooler or warmer tones. Dark specks and swirls in the stone indicate coal debris. Often reddish swirls called Liesegang Rings can also be distinguished. These come from the oxidized iron as it moves in solution during the burial and compaction of sediments. When freshly quarried, sandstone can even range from gray-green or pale yellow to variegated brown, purple, and red depending on the composition at different sources and the weathering of iron minerals.

Sandstone is usually "bedded" or laid down in layers (beds) with breaks above and below called bedding planes, which represent periods when deposition ceased. Many of the Millstone Grit sandstones have preserved within them a series of low-angled beds and bedding planes known as cross-bedding. These formed as sandbanks on the inside bend of a meandering river channel where water velocity was lower and finer sediment was deposited. Millstone Grit is tough, but its bedding and jointing presents useful lines of weakness for extraction. Each bed tends to provide stones used for specific purposes.

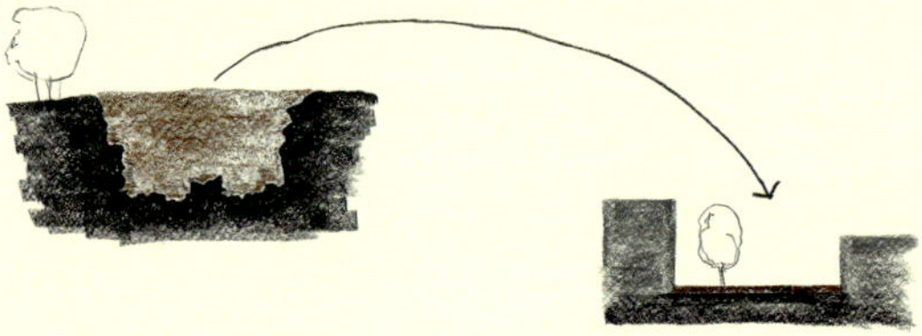

In this sense, Yorkshire stone in London acquires a contextual and subtle communicative value that transcends its provenance.

The Landscape Left Behind

Back in Yorkshire, the underground landscape at the source of the stone has been irreversibly altered by continuous extraction. On the surface, while ancient quarries are now grassed over or have been reclaimed by woodland, many pits from the height of production lie abandoned or have been turned into landfill. More recently, quarry sites are being "restored" to their prior landform through the regrading of overburden. Discarded stone and shale are compacted to refill the pit, and sub- and topsoil are reshaped uniformly to create the required contours, while hedgerows, shrubs, and trees are planted to restore biodiversity. The reinstated topography is made to appear seamlessly continuous with millennia of geomorphological change, but it is fundamentally artificial. If we look very closely, discrepancies emerge as discontinuous contours, strange earthworks, artificial cliffs, and seemingly sudden outcroppings. These altered topographies change existing habitats and affect ecosystems. Artificial cliffs become nesting places for different bird species, while plants grow in places where sheep and rabbits cannot graze them. Other species thrive or fail because of altered soil or hydrological conditions, leading to displacement for some and opportunities for others. In some cases, larger industrial-scale quarries leave an even more remarkable imprint in the landscape. Turned into nature reserves, water reservoirs, car parks, or off-road motor sport tracks, the new topography becomes a recreation ground for urban dwellers.

Ultimately, whether obvious or discrete, traces of extraction in the landscape are always readable and irreversible. While it supplies the raw construction material for the urban fabric, the landscape we observe today is inevitably engendered by what is built in the city. As a resource, it thus becomes an integral part of a widely urbanized territory, where city and landscape function in codependency rather than as separate entities.

1 N. Aitkenhead et al., *The Pennines and Adjacent Areas,* 4th ed., British Regional Geology (Nottingham: British Geological Survey, 2002).
2 Dimension stone is natural stone or rock that has been selected and finished. It is the finished product that leaves the quarry after it has been trimmed, cut, drilled, and ground to specific sizes.
3 A. Chivers et al., *Rocks and Landscapes of Huddersfield* (Huddersfield: Huddersfield Geology Group, 1998), 23.
4 Aitkenhead, *The Pennines and Adjacent Areas,* 154.
5 As per reports from City of London and City of Westminster: *City Public Realm: People, Places, Projects; Technical Manual* (London: City of London, Department of the Built Environment, 2016), and *Westminster Way: Public Realm Strategy; Design Principles and Practice* (London: City of Westminster City Planning Built Environment, 2011).

A man-made hill and the artificial curves of a restored quarry and nature reserve at Johnsons Wellfield in Huddersfield

Tate Modern, London
The Layers of the Landscape

Client:
Tate Modern, London

Cooperation:
Architecture:
Herzog & de Meuron, Basel

Design/construction:
2010–2015/2015–2016

Type and size:
Square, 1.38 ha

Status:
Realized

The addition of a new building south of the existing Tate Modern reshuffled the space around the museum. As a whole, the proposed landscape unites the varied existing and new elements across the site, while emphasizing their spatial differences. Four areas are defined, corresponding to the four sides of the building as an ensemble, clearly linked yet distinct in character.

The landscape design intends to engage visitors in a narrative of the site's geographic setting and industrial history. While on the northern, riverbank side, this duality is materialized in a dense urban forest of birch trees–a species which typically grows on industrial wastelands, often close to rivers–the southern design refers to this industrial past while revealing the site's underlying geology.

These aspects are embodied within the materiality and form of the two main structuring elements: the robust character of the "oil tank wall"–an aboveground representation of the existing underground oil tanks–contrasts with the curvilinear embankment wall, a long, inclined and racked structure with an undulating profile. The locally sourced flint stones cast within the aggregate concrete mix reflect the sedimentation layers of the Thames River Basin.

This translation of physical properties of the landscape's layers into a built artifact involved a slow, painstaking, and complex process of almost alchemical experimentation in order to obtain the desired materiality, texture, and color. The crafting process involved a series of 1:1 experiments in composition, layering, exposure, sequence, and pouring method, resulting in a measured concrete methodology that was scaled up to an industrial process on-site.

In the built project, the embankment wall was replaced with a planted spine and the oil tank wall appears as an additional geological layer in the city of London. Forming large circular terraces, in the manner of either a stone dike erected against the tide or a landscape sculpted by water, it provides the southern landscape with a local horizon and mediates between the scale of the building and the scale of the city. (lb)

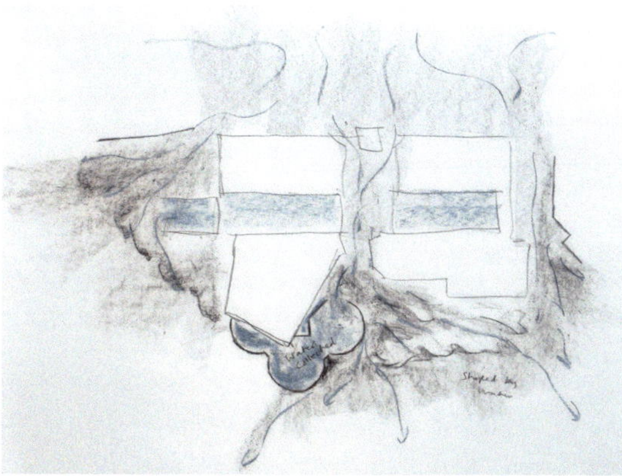

Pencil sketch suggesting the relationship between the Thames's tidal movements, the site, the flow of the river, and people

London Basin with the River Thames from its source to the city with deposits indicated

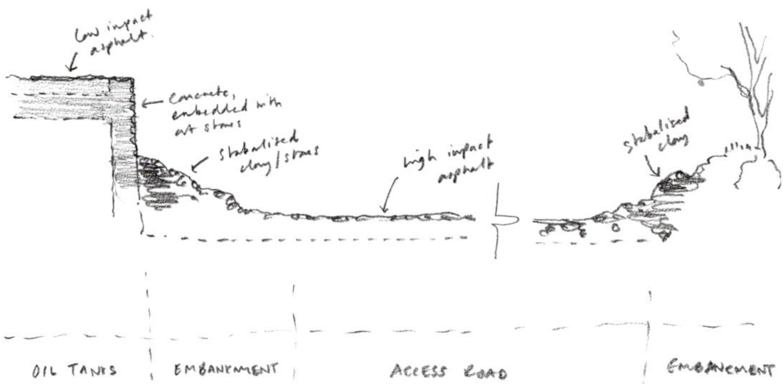

Section showing the relationship between hard and soft landscapes, depicted as a flow channel, echoing the profile of the riverbed

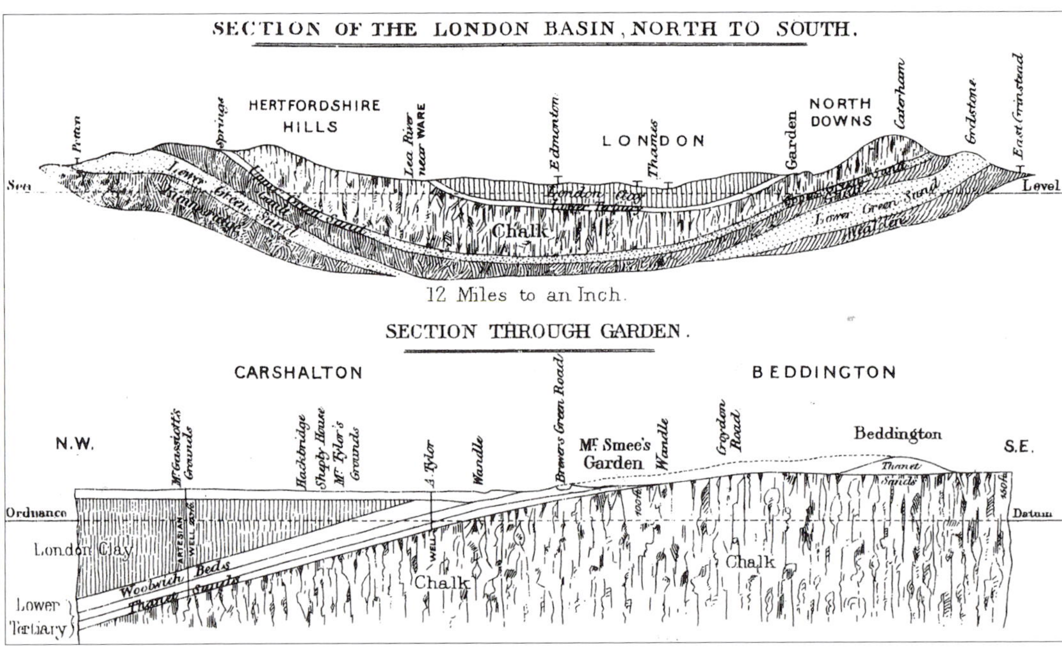

A geological sectional map of the London Basin, from *My Garden: Its Plan and Culture* by Alfred Smee, 1872. Smee's book is probably the largest and most exhaustive account of any single garden. The diagram shows how chalk runs beneath the whole London area, rising to the surface again in Hertfordshire and Surrey. *(Courtesy: Royal Horticultural Society)*

Oil tank section

Embankment and south lawn section

In the design process, mock-ups of both walls were built, in order to test at full scale the proposed materials, construction techniques, and visual appearance of the walls. For the oil tank wall, extensive tests on grain size, color, and concrete mixes were undertaken before the final composition was determined. The concrete components included flint and sand from the Thames Valley, Portland and white cement, and pigments from different oxides.

Oil tank wall concept, and exposed finish study

maylim

The mock-ups for the embankment wall were constructed in the studio space using a buff-colored aggregate-rich concrete mix, containing a matrix of flint stones. Two surface finishes were tested in the process: a worked finish, consisting of concrete poured in layers and hand worked, and a sand mold (pictured here), in which stones were placed before pouring the concrete.

>> In the built project, the embankment wall was replaced by a mounded spine planted with birch trees, an extension of the landscape to the north, which was developed by Vogt in the 2000s. The sinuous movement of the wall's design was preserved. Together with the topography of the lawn, its dynamic draws visitors toward the main south entrance and the oil tank square.

“Conversation thrives on people being present and direct, on thinking that is unmediated and ideas coming into alignment. It takes place in time, on a particular day and in a particular place. A **design-based culture of dialogue** also means conducting discussions with a certain detachment from the subject, the landscape.” (gv)

After the Party Is Over
Urban Big Events

August 8, 2019, Paris

Günther Vogt: With the Tate Modern, which opened in 2000, the city of London got a museum that can keep pace with the large museums in Paris or New York. Originally designed for two million visitors a year, the museum is now one of the world's most frequently visited venues of modern art. The same as the original building, Herzog & de Meuron were also responsible for the design and realization of the much-needed extension, which was added when you were the director of the museum. The Tate Modern has, however, not only changed the reception of art throughout Europe, it has also sparked the transformation of the Bankside into a booming district, an aspect of the Tate Modern that debates about this institution often only mention in passing.

< p. 226, *Tate Modern*

Chris Dercon: The fact that recent urban developments around the Tate Modern were triggered by the construction of the museum is not realized by many. This has a lot to do with the enormous effect of the Turbine Hall. This huge popular space has completely overshadowed the perception of what happened outside. However, to me the surroundings of Tate Modern lacked a visionary master plan. I have been told that there was one though and that the built environment is based on it, but it was never really clear to me. Today, I can see–and some newspapers such as *The Guardian* have described this very aptly–that the neighborhood of the Tate Modern has become a puzzle. Quite opportunistic and confusing as it's not clear what's private and what's public.

Günther Vogt: There is also the question as to whether the Turbine Hall is a public or a private space. For the museum is closed at night after all. During the day, however, the constellation works incredibly well. I am reading the space in the sense of Dan Graham, who describes the museum as a garden, and the garden as a museum. But that has also to do with its use and which artists are there. In the meantime, the Turbine Hall has become an incredibly strong symbol of the city and works similarly as, for instance, the Eiffel Tower, the Arc de Triomphe, or the Louvre here in Paris. The problem of the environment is, of course, based on neo-liberal urban planning. In London, urban-planning decisions are completely

< p. 182, *Metropolitan Museum of Art*

determined by the economy, and the city–the administration, but also the political authorities–is too weak to send a clear signal. Only the Tate itself could make a difference. But the Tate is not in charge of urban development.

Chris Dercon: The problems in the vicinity also become visible if you look from the upper parts of the extension, which was designed as a kind of observatory. The effect is that you can watch from nearly every angle into the apartments of the neighbors. Already after a few weeks, there were the first tensions with the neighbors, for the people who visited the observatory did not only look into their apartments but also took pictures. I've discussed this interesting aspect time and again. For me, these are intriguing art installations, as there are apartments that are not lived in, but they are not completely empty either. They are objects of pure investment, fitted with high-end designer fixtures. In the very end, there was a lawsuit, and the dividing line between public and private has been drawn in a legally unassailable manner. Of course, the public terrain is increasingly interfering with the private one, and the private one with the public terrain. The debate as to whether such an additional observatory is even necessary, however, is only seriously held because of the dramatic incident that occurred in the summer of 2019, when a six-year-old child was pushed off the observation platform. Aren't there already enough viewing opportunities in our big cities, even though I understand the cultural and commercial logic behind it all? It is highly regrettable that a tragic event such as this is necessary to ensure that this issue is addressed at all.

But you're absolutely right, it also has to do with the capacity for different uses. When we talk about the outdoor spaces of the Tate Modern, it's interesting to note that the northern side, the square on the Thames fulfills its function very well. This urban landscape or townscape is a successful continuation of the Turbine Hall. Almost as a kind of echo or of positive/negative in the sense of a sculpture. It not only enters into a dialogue with the river, but is also very naturally connected to the walkway along the Thames. The smaller parts offer various seating arrangements, and there is also room for a temporary appropriation, for example, by food trucks or installations. I feel that people are by now accepting this place and are very happy to use it, ut it took quite some time. On the southern side, such not yet the case as people still have to find their way th ugh this mineral landscape, which is actually quite fragil s to the possibilities of its appropriation and use. Today, it i o longer sufficient to say that there is a public space whi you can use whenever and however you want. One eds other signs and more differentiated interventions or plementations. At the same time, increased securit easures are needed in view of today's virtually never-e g state of alert. In Paris, we have to take specially t d dogs into the budget of every event. And metal and c ete barriers have become an inherent part of an landscape of our time.

> p. 270, *Les Jardins de la Tour Eiffel*

Günther Vogt: It has to be said though that this place to the south of the Tate Modern assumes a different function within the ensemble. I recently attended the opening of Olafur Eliasson's exhibition *In Real Life.* It was a very sunny day and the many thousands of visitors were not only in the Turbine Hall but also and above all on this square. Within the scope of a large event, this part acts much like an extension of the interior.

> p. 290, *Limestone*
< p. 216, *Yorkstone*

And at this point, of course, we should also talk about the cultural dimension. Here in Paris, the city is mineral and London is also completely overbuilt , but for the English a public space is above all "green." If you like, it is actually the landscape that creates the public space for them. You have to work within this context. Many people today have an incredibly rich experience of many cities around the world through tourism and project these ideas onto the place where they live. Globalization may work at the level of architecture or art but not if we look into landscape or the public space. For the cultural and social context, but also the climatic conditions are very decisive when we deal with vegetation, for instance.

Chris Dercon: That's a difficulty, but on the other hand I learned in Paris that it doesn't take much, no huge areas. It can also be a small square, with one or two trees. We live in the Marais on Square Sainte Croix de la Brétonnerie, between the BHV Marais, Rue du Temple, and Rue des

Archives, in the midst of a project by Groupe Galeries Lafayette, who has renovated and remodeled the entire quarter. Lafayette and Citynove development company have commissioned various architects, who have never before done large-scale commercial architecture–such as Jamie Fobert, Office Kersten Geers David Van Severen, and landscape architect Bas Smets–to develop buildings for mixed uses around small interior courtyards and plan them for commercial and cultural functions. Eataly, a gastronomical enterprise, is also involved, for which artist Martin Boyce has realized a huge glass ceiling. OMA has even designed an experimental art center called Lafayette Anticipations, which also houses artisan workshops that recall the industrial past of the Marais. It's all composed of small, flexible spaces, which quite naturally merge into one another. The entire district seems to work quite well and the most diverse public appropriates it as their own. In other words, landscape in an urban sense does not necessarily have to be large. And for me, there is an important difference between size and scale. Size is one thing, but I've found that, for example, Belgian architects do a lot of work that primarily deals with scale.

Günther Vogt: Your descriptions made me smile for, at the moment, a lot of new professors from Belgium are joining the Department of Architecture at ETH Zurich. I think one of the reasons is that both Swiss as well as Belgian architecture has cultivated a remarkably careful approach to the city and that there is a certain kinship. However, there is also the difference of really big cities in Belgium, such as Brussels or Antwerp, of which there are none in Switzerland. This has a lot to do with the history of the country, with colonialism, and also the industrial past of Belgium. When it comes to intervening in these structures, a suitable level of intervention has to be found. You've got to ask what should be preserved, what should be renewed, etc. The experience of how such an approach can be practiced in large cities is something that our Belgian colleagues contribute to.

Chris Dercon: That's interesting, because in my conversations with Rem Koolhaas on his most recent project, *Countryside,* which has little to do with classical landscape architecture, I took interest in the origins of young Belgian architects, designers, and landscape architects and the topics they are working on. Their work is not just about bigger cities as Antwerp or Brussels. There are second and third cities that are equally interesting. People often made fun of the fact that the lights on Belgian highways are always on–as if the day never ends. This shows that we perceive the smaller cities, for example, Kortrijk, Ghent, and Bruges, as a dense network that enables an intensive exchange. Basically, Belgium is a good example of *countryside* according to Koolhaas for he never said: we have to go back to green fields and dense forests. Or: we'll go to the Alps. The point is that, today, an urbanized form of landscape tends to take place between actual cities and thus a new form of urbanity is coming into being. A given with which architect Leo Van Broeck, who is overseeing architecture in Flanders, also works. And here, of course, new concepts of landscaping play a crucial role. One not only works with the ostensibly original landscape, but also with these landscapes that have been massively interfered with. Landscapes which might also include industry and other infrastructure. Young Belgian architects are currently working with exciting ideas for the space between urban poles.

However, in France everything focuses on Paris. It's only now that people are beginning to take an interest in the urban and cultural developments in second- and third-tier cities such as Montpellier or Angers. After the uprising of the yellow-jackets movement, the *gilets jaunes,* people suddenly and constantly talk about *le territoire.* But to date, few are courageous enough to deal with this the way one does in Germany, Switzerland, or Belgium. The roundabouts (*rond-points*) and tollbooths (*péages*)–and there are thousands of them in France–are, basically, the urban landscapes in which the *gilets jaunes* began to give form to their actions. These are strong symbols of mobility, even social mobility. In this context, we have to ask again: where does the public sphere end and where does the private one begin? When Emmanuel Macron decided on that very Monday evening during the fire of Notre-Dame, to talk to Bernard Arnault and François Pinault about donating tons of money for the repair, this sounded like a salvation for the severely damaged Notre-Dame at first. But I wonder: will those politicians and institutions responsible for the many monuments outside

Paris want to procure money in a similar way? It could be that Macron's action might also have a by-effect: those who pay will probably also want to determine the conditions and how things should look?

Günther Vogt: What you describe, we have also studied with Jacques Herzog and Pierre de Meuron at Studio Basel and asked ourselves whether the city can be thought of from the landscape. This change of perspective would give landscape a central role in Switzerland's large-scale planning and create the possibility to elaborate alternative strategies and future visions for dealing with the urban development of the country by looking at undeveloped areas. The resulting publication, *achtung: die Landschaft,* alludes to *achtung: die Schweiz* published by Max Frisch, Lucius Burckhardt, and Markus Kutter, which had already warned in 1955 against the increasing urban sprawl of the country and called for a new and controlled urban development in the form of densely populated settlements.

> p. 450, *Agenti Climatici*

But of course, when we talk about scale, we also have to discuss the very large scale not only of a landscape, but also of a city. Just recently, together with OMA, we won a competition in Milan for the redevelopment of two former railway yards. The city wants to reactivate these huge brownfields at today's city perimeter. Two landscape elements form the core of the project: on one side the forest, which is able to cool the warm winds from the southwest and purify them of toxic particles, and on the other side a system of watercourses as a filter and landscape-shaping element. Or another example: I have been invited to a summer workshop in Piacenza near Milan. The organizer wants a poster with a statement on the role and function of landscape in the city—and we show a map of Paris with new "green corridors." In the big cities it gets increasingly hot in summer. In the future, a supply of fresh air, which can flow into the city from the landscape, will be very important. I'm not so sure whether there will be trees within these "green corridors" though. Meadows would be much more suitable because their flow resistance is much lower. And then there is the dimension of the interventions by Georges Eugène Haussmann who, in the nineteenth century, had aisles cut into the thicket of houses to ventilate, unify, and beautify the city.

> p. 336, *Bois*

What concerns us is, therefore, the question of the proper scale of an intervention. In addition to a very large intervention, a smaller scale is also a way of tackling the problems of a city. One example of this is the flood prevention in Copenhagen, which is part of a comprehensive climate adaptation plan of the city. Among other measures, small retention volumes are built at strategic positions within the city, to minimize the risk of flooding in case of heavy rainfalls. The plan is like a model that, theoretically, can be transposed to other cities. However, in order to achieve something by such small interventions, a unifying superordinate system is needed. Or a kind of social contract in which we agree to assume our responsibility as citizens and to do something against the problems as far as we can. The main thing is to change our daily behavior, be it when using the traffic infrastructure or our consumption of drinking water, etc. For only when united, even the supposedly weak can be strong. I don't know, though, whether we still have time enough to react in this way to today's major and acute problems.

Chris Dercon: I totally agree with you on that. I am currently working in Paris and the heat this summer was nearly unbearable. We don't have enough "green spaces." The revitalization of the Seine as proposed by Anne Hidalgo, the mayor of Paris, does not solve the problem by itself, for the water does not cool down the surroundings sufficiently. And the huge *Grand Paris* project primarily focuses on establishing a built-up and ultra-dense urban perimeter around the city. We need a strong green belt though, parts of which already exist: think of the beautiful forests, parks, gardens, and terraces of Île-de-France. But few habitants of the city center know or enjoy these places, although the public-transport connections are not bad at all. Have you ever been to the Musée national de la Renaissance in Écouen, at the Château de Malmaison, in Saint-Germain-en-Laye or Montfort-l'Amaury? These are wonderful places with a lot of scenery.

> p. 346, *Grand Paris Sud*

< p. 190, *Green Belt*

On the other hand, Berlin, where we lived before, is relatively fresh. Important in this context are the large "green spaces" inside the city, such as the Tempelhof site–which was used as an inner-city airport between 1923 and 2008–but of course also the enormous forests around Berlin. An ecologist explained to me that the highways leading out of the woods toward the city help transport cooler air into the city, especially at night. However, we should not reduce the Tempelhof site to a mere added value in terms of the urban climate. Besides, this place is also a public resource of the city. And when I talk about landscape in this context and about the possibility to reread and appropriate these spaces in a different manner, I think about a large-scale dance event that was initiated at Volksbühne Berlin during my directorship, realized by French choreographer Boris Charmatz. Thousands of people took part and danced on the asphalt of the former airport right next to the highway.

Günther Vogt: What you describe using the example of Berlin is a truly central issue because I am of the opinion that the discussion about traffic is still influenced by too many ideologies. It's important to deal with this issue in as unbiased a way as possible. That is, to enter the debate without a fixed, preconceived opinion to try and understand the problem in all its complexity and its many layers while, at the same time, recognize its inherent possibilities. If we consider the large European cities, we can see that the huge infrastructures that connect parts of the city or cities with each other also and at the same time separate the space. But this is not bad per se. In Lisbon, for instance, we are investigating new forms of parks in the metropolitan area. They are located between railway tracks and highways and interspersed by neighborhood streets and country roads; there are sewage-treatment plants, landfills, and brownfields but also sports and leisure facilities. A right hullabaloo. In-between, there are informal farms run by immigrants from the Cape Verde islands. They produce vegetables, sell them on the markets in the city and, thus, establish their own economy. Of course, you might say that all this is already semi-private and illegal to boot. But it is also extremely lively and regulates itself above all else. These are self-organized communities that have established a type of coexistence, even though an unstable one.

Chris Dercon: If you drive into the city from Charles de Gaulle Airport, there are traffic junctions that are often occupied by refugees and immigrants. But you can't treat human beings in such way, studying them as anthropologists do and stating that this a great example of self-organization. We've got to consider the future and, for example, plan temporary living environments around cities. Temporary homes, where people can live between three, six or nine months, will be relevant for every large city in the future.

Günther Vogt: We are currently also looking at the phenomenon of temporary cities in the context of a research project in the Alpine region. Temporary settlements have often been realized in connection with the construction of large infrastructure projects, such as when a dam or tunnel was built. Many workers, including those from Italy, had to be safely housed for several years. Frequently, prefabricated wooden buildings, originally manufactured for the military, were used for this purpose. Today, these shelters are made of metal and equipped with quite some modern amenities, though the principle of prefabrication and their thinking in modular systems have remained. For now, I can see that many university departments of architecture are assigning temporary cities as design tasks. Quite often, the results are very well-designed objects. But when we think about such settlements, we must not forget that these are large structures, which we should be able to consolidate and which, in a best-case scenario, should enter into a productive dialogue with the city. This is all about the organization of our living together and the necessity of central functions: a space dedicated to culture, not necessarily a mosque or a church, but maybe a school and all these social infrastructures plus some simple residential housing.

Chris Dercon: This could also be an approach when we think about the problem of *shrinking cities*. During my time in Berlin, I realized that there are indeed small villages for instance in Brandenburg that are practically empty but where there is now an influx of people who want to use such villages differently: tech nerds, artists, sympathizers of "green politics," young families, etc. You can see the same developments in Italy or Spain. Many small towns and villages are half empty or even completely abandoned. However, you can consider these places as landscapes that can be used for alternative purposes, for example, for schools, small industries, cultural events, tourism, or sports. Of course, I also think of the large number of new immigrants. You can already see today that interesting research institutes and innovation centers are often located outside big cities.

> p. 374, *Skolkovo*

Günther Vogt: One of the reasons why these huge European regions were abandoned is the lack of even the most minimal infrastructures. I do not just mean the transport infrastructure. Of course, physical access is a central issue, and the question is as to how a place can or should be connected to the next larger city. Besides, also needed are digital infrastructures, access to basic health-care facilities, shopping facilities, training facilities, jobs, and, of course, cultural facilities. It is not necessarily a matter of erecting new architectures, but rather of remodeling and converting already existing ones and introducing new uses to enable a community to continue living in a specific place in the future. For what also dissolves along with the emigration from the villages and smaller towns is the actual village community and, along with it, the collective cultivation and care of the agricultural landscape, which for many people and for countless centuries formed the basis of their existence.

There are quite some attempts to reanimate such peripheral regions with *big events*. In the Alps, in Turin, for instance, where the 2006 Winter Olympics took place. In the short term, it is true, the respective billions of investments led to a boom in the construction and hotel industries. In the middle or long run, however, such events are far from sustainable. Quite some buildings are demolished once the games are over as they are only purposed for temporary use. Besides, the already known destinations are brought to the fore by advertisements. And while, actually, only a few indoor events took place in Turin itself, the city was able to use them to market their destination. Most competitions were actually held in the Susa and Chisone Valleys. After the games, these places had to deal with large and expensive facilities that were no longer needed. That's why, in recent years, all other candidacies in the Alps have failed, with the sole exception of Milan's bid for 2026. On the one hand, because the IOC, the International Olympic Committee, has given preference to other and more influential candidates

Still Water (The River Thames, for Example)

V

Roni Horn, 1999

Still Water (The River Thames, for Example), 1999, was originally conceived as a hybrid form: a ribbon of images of water accompanied by a ribbon of footnotes about water–text, images, and viewer triangulated in the form of an installation. It can be configured as a surround in one room or as a path flowing through many rooms.

> The notes may address the viewer: *"What are you thinking about? Are you paying attention to the numbers? Maybe you won't read all of these footnotes. Maybe you'll get tired and walk away. (But there are more–more pictures, more footnotes, behind you or down the hall or in another room.)"*
>
> Or they may speculate on water and water's relationship to other things: *"This is an image of water. When you look at it, as you are probably doing now, you are looking at paper, and there is no necessary relationship between the two. Yet the paper floats the image of water or facilitates it, and you see before you a water without wetness. As with all images, you imagine what you're looking at and in doing so grasp it."*
>
> Or speculate on the viewer's relationship to water *"What do you know about water? When you talk about water, what is it you're really talking about?"*
>
> *"Water receives you, affirms you, shows you who you are. And all the near-imperceptible qualities that are water tease you with their ambiguity."*

The work in its entirety consists of fifteen 30½ × 41½ in. (77.5 × 105.4 cm) footnoted photographs of the River Thames. Excerpts from *Still Water* are presented here–the text is reproduced in these images as it appears in the individual plates.

1 What do you know about water? When you talk about water, what is it you're really talking about?

2 What do you know about water? Isn't that part of what water is, that you never really know what it is?

3 What do you know about water? That it's everywhere, so familiar-seeming and yet so elusive (a kind of everything without definition), never quite graspable, even as an ice cube?

4 What do you know about water? Only that it's everywhere differently?

5 Do you remember the young Parisian woman I mentioned earlier? They found a suicide note in her hotel room addressed to her sister. (It was written in French.) The note referred in detail to her problems, including her bad teeth. (She thought they protruded too much.) [6]

6 Police said this surprised them since, in their judgment, she did not have buck teeth.

7 (See pudding?)

8 Water brings the distant near, as with these patterns on the surface propagated by unseen forces from somewhere out there. (Elaborate and strange, what are they?—passing irregularities?)

9 Water brings the distant near, as with these patterns on the surface propagated by unseen forces from somewhere out there. (Is this the moon, or a little something arriving from your home?)

10 Water brings the distant near, bits of sound: sighs, gurgles, sucks, almost voices, connecting you with some other place, some other time, an experience from far away or long ago.

11 I don't know if you've had this experience but occasionally when I'm watching the water I hear snippets from various songs drifting up from the river. (Sometimes I even recognize the voice.)

12 I doubt you've had this experience but last night when I was watching the water "I Say a Little Prayer" wafted up from the river. (It came along in a faster tempo than the version I remembered.) "The moment I wake up . . . make up . . . wondering what dress to wear, I say a little prayer . . . . This is my prayer . . . . I say a little prayer . . . . This is my prayer . . . . Answer my prayer. . . ." [13] But it was so brief, a wisp really, almost nothing. (Maybe I didn't really hear it.)

13 From "I Say a Little Prayer," written by Burt Bacharach and Hal David in 1967. Version referred to was recorded by Aretha Franklin in 1968.

14 When you go down to the river you're killing two birds with one stone: you stand there and you go places.

15 (Is this a wave?) [16]

16 (Maybe a wave of sorts but also a soft place to lay myself down, tuck myself in.)

17 Are you wondering why I'm not talking about the Ganges? Or the Yangtze? Or even the Mississippi?

18 This is an image of water. When you look at it, as you are probably doing now, you are looking at paper, and there is no necessary relationship between the two. Yet the paper floats the

image of water or facilita
without wetness. As with
looking at and in doing

19 When you look at th
imagine jumping in?

20 When you look at th
paper is? How soft and s

21 A sprinkle of little nu
possibly endless sequence
the river. They connect y
they locate in the water.
you are connected to thi

efore you a water
gine what you're

hers) do you

how smooth the
't jump in.)

r. They run in a
you read this, to
d particular points
is only an image,
ven all water, but at

first perhaps only this water, in a moment, as it happens, that passed not too long ago.

22 This footnote (and all the others) gives confluence to this spot on the paper (twenty-one inches down and seven inches over), to this undulation in the water, to this greenish color of the ink deployed to image the water, to the idea of water, all water, to the sensual surface of this paper, to the moment when you happened upon this number, and to you in that moment.

23 The Thames is me.

24 Here you are at footnote 24, and even though there's no real beginning to this installation you must have started somewhere. It's possible you started here, at footnote 24. That means you'll have to go on awhile longer and then you'll know what I'm talking about.

25 What about this footnote? Do you like it? I could have moved it over an inch or two but that might have changed its content.

26 Are you following the footnotes in their proper order, or are you just picking out the ones you like?

27 (Did you notice how the numbers are floating on the paper but they're not moving?)

28 (Did you notice how the numbers are floating in the water but they're still not moving?)

29 (Did you notice how the numbers are lodged in the image, fixed like trigonometric points on a map?)

30 This litter of numbers on the photograph is a constellation composing the view.

31 This litter of numbers on the photograph disrupts and annoys like rubbish floating on the water.

32 This litter of numbers on the photograph breaks up the view, punctuating the image of water with little digits. These digits, a small part of a larger corpus, enter by unseen logics into the flow of the river.

33 This litter of numbers on the photograph is a floating arithmetic, a set of aquatic digits to view by.

34 Are these aquatic digits a new fish in the river?

35 They say the river is cleaner now, that ten years ago it was even blacker. (But what about this undulation, this strange irregularity?)

36 Do you know this ditty?

"Blah, blah, blah, your hair,
Blah, blah, blah, your eyes;
Blah, blah, blah, blah, care,
Blah, blah, blah, blah, skies." 37

37 From the song "Blah, Blah, Blah," by Ira Gershwin, 1931."

38 (Sometimes you hear "blah, blah, blah" coming from the river. It might not be from "Blah, Blah, Blah," but it sounds like it; only the "eyes" and "skies" shift among lies, whys, guise, sighs, and sighs.)

39 (This wave reminds me of a wave I saw when I was a kid—it was on my bed.)

40 What is water?

41 What do you know about water? (Only that it's everywhere differently?)

1 What do you know about water? When you talk about water, what is it you're really talking about?

2 What do you know about water? Isn't that part of what water is, that you never really know what it is?

3 What do you know about water? That it's everywhere, so familiar-seeming and yet so elusive (a kind of everything without definition), never quite graspable, even as an ice cube?

4 What do you know about water? Only that it's everywhere differently?

5 Do you remember the young Parisian woman I mentioned earlier? They found a suicide note in her hotel room addressed to her sister. (It was written in French.) The note referred in detail to her problems, including her bad teeth. (She thought they protruded too much.) [6]

6 Police said this surprised them since, in their judgment, she did not have buck teeth.

7 (See pudding?)

8 Water brings the distant near, as with these patterns on the surface propagated by unseen forces from somewhere out there. (Elaborate and strange, what are they?—passing irregularities?)

9 Water brings the distant near, as with these patterns on the surface propagated by unseen forces from somewhere out there. (Is this the moon, or a little something arriving from your home?)

10 Water brings the distant near, bits of sound: sighs, gurgles, sucks, almost voices, connecting you with some other place, some other time, an experience from far away or long ago.

11 I don't know if you've had this experience but occasionally when I'm watching the water I hear snippets from various songs drifting up from the river. (Sometimes I even recognize the voice.)

12 I doubt you've had this experience but last night when I was watching the water "I Say a Little Prayer" wafted up from the river. (It came along in a faster tempo than the version I remembered.) "The moment I wake up ... make up ... wondering what dress to wear, I say a little prayer ... This is my prayer ... I say a little prayer ... This is my prayer ... Answer my prayer...."[13] But it was so brief, a wisp really, almost nothing. (Maybe I didn't really hear it.)

13 From "I Say a Little Prayer," written by Burt Bacharach and Hal David in 1967. Version referred to was recorded by Aretha Franklin in 1968.

14 When you go down to the river you're killing two birds with one stone: you stand there and you go places.

15 (Is this a wave?) [16]

16 (Maybe a wave of sorts but also a soft place to lay myself down, tuck myself in.)

17 Are you wondering why I'm not talking about the Ganges? Or the Yangtze? Or even the Mississippi?

18 This is an image of water. When you look at it, as you are probably doing now, you are looking at paper, and there is no necessary relationship between the two. Yet the paper floats the image of water or facilitates it, and you see before you a water without wetness. As with all images, you imagine what you're looking at and in doing so grasp it.

19 When you look at this image (and the others) do you imagine jumping in?

20 When you look at this image do you see how smooth the paper is? How soft and sensual? (But you can't jump in.)

21 A sprinkle of little numbers over the water. They run in a possibly endless sequence connecting you, as you read this, to the river. They connect you to the various and particular points they locate in the water. And even though it is only an image, you are connected to this water and maybe even all water, but at first perhaps only this water, in a moment, as it happens, that passed not too long ago.

22 This footnote (and all the others) gives confluence to this spot on the paper (twenty-one inches down and seven inches over), to this undulation in the water, to this greenish color of the ink deployed to image the water, to the idea of water, all water, to the sensual surface of this paper, to the moment when you happened upon this number, and to you in that moment.

23 The Thames is me.

24 Here you are at footnote 24, and even though there's no real beginning to this installation you must have started somewhere. It's possible you started here, at footnote 24. That means you'll have to go on awhile longer and then you'll know what I'm talking about.

25 What about this footnote? Do you like it? I could have moved it over an inch or two but that might have changed its content.

26 Are you following the footnotes in their proper order, or are you just picking out the ones you like?

27 (Did you notice how the numbers are floating on the paper but they're not moving?)

28 (Did you notice how the numbers are floating in the water but they're still not moving?)

29 (Did you notice how the numbers are lodged in the image, fixed like trigonometric points on a map?)

30 This litter of numbers on the photograph is a constellation composing the view.

31 This litter of numbers on the photograph disrupts and annoys like rubbish floating on the water.

32 This litter of numbers on the photograph breaks up the view, punctuating the image of water with little digits. These digits, a small part of a larger corpus, enter by unseen logics into the flow of the river.

33 This litter of numbers on the photograph is a floating arithmetic, a set of aquatic digits to view by.

34 Are these aquatic digits a new fish in the river?

35 They say the river is cleaner now, that ten years ago it was even blacker. (But what about this undulation, this strange irregularity?)

36 Do you know this ditty?
"Blah, blah, blah, your hair,
Blah, blah, blah, your eyes;
Blah, blah, blah, blah, care,
Blah, blah, blah, blah, skies." [37]

37 From the song "Blah, Blah, Blah," by Ira Gershwin, 1931.[38]

38 (Sometimes you hear "blah, blah, blah" coming from the river. It might not be from "Blah, Blah, Blah," but it sounds like it; only the "eyes" and "skies" shift among lies, whys, guise, sighs, and sighs.)

39 (This wave reminds me of a wave I saw when I was a kid—it was on my bed.)

40 What is water?

41 What do you know about water? (Only that it's everywhere differently?)

previous spread

1 Darkness reflects the sun. Blackness reflects nothing.

2 Darkness reflects the sun. Blackness reflects nothing. ("Between grief and nothing, I will take grief."[3])

3 From the novel *The Wild Palms*, by William Faulkner, 1939.

4 From out here near the quieter currents you can see fibers of light stretching out on the river's surface.[5] Moving still and swiftly among the dark water, amorphous white energy elongating describes only the surface of this blackness—the beginning of something that cannot be seen.

5 Have you ever noticed how light reflections on the water sometimes look like camouflage?

6 Attracted by the lights upon this liquid blackness, you wade in among them, flowing with them briefly and submerging; from underneath maybe they will appear as constellations in the darkness. Other constellations than the ones you've grown accustomed to. Constellations from some other place, unseen until now.

7 You can't tell from looking at it how treacherous the water actually is. I mean you can't see what's going on with the currents; the river runs fast and tidal reversals work up strong undercurrents. But you sense it: the complexity, the threat, the difference. It's part of the river's attraction, part of its darkness.

8 Sometimes, in a quiet area, the water is tremulous and tender: an easier entrance beguiling you.

9 Crumbs of whitish froth float on the water. They cluster in formations that are not affected by the river's movement, in formations that linger too long.

10 The water is black here, but it isn't really visible. You feel it, but you can't see it. It takes the breath out of you not being able to see it, point to it, touch it or just say it. But that's black.

11 Imagine combining black with water: two equals. One unchangeable, the other wholly corruptible.

12 Going into water is going into yourself. Water is a mirror. But even in black water there's a reflection, though a degraded one. You don't have to witness yourself in black water.

13 And what about juvenile water—immature water, young water? Water that's never seen the light of day. Juvenile water emerging from within the earth, arriving at the surface. All I can think to say is, "Hello."

14 Your reflection uncouples in this water. It drifts away from you. As you stand there on the bank or bridge, helpless, watching your reflection float downstream and disappear, you may wonder what forces black water gathers. But instinctively you already know they must be closer to witchcraft than geometry.[15]

15 "Best witchcraft is geometry."[16]

16 See poem No. 1158 by Emily Dickinson, 1870.

17 There was an article in the newspaper some time ago about a young man jumping off a bridge. He strapped his bicycle, a black Phantom, to his chest and jumped in. (It took six months to identify the body.)[18]

18 Isn't that what you'd expect? Isn't that what you'd be after—to lose your identity? The Thames looks like a solvent for identity, doesn't it?

19 The river is a drain.

20 In winter the darkness in the water deepens, and the river's flow seems to accelerate.

21 In winter the Thames is so drab, the darkness of the water is palpable. Close your eyes and you feel the darkness wafting up from the river: dank, clammy, close.

22 In winter the sky is low and the water is mobbed by clouds. The atmosphere becomes an extension of the river. Its water saturates your view. Its water silently permeates the streets and homes of London, and you live in the river.

23 Boatmen talk about seeing jumpers often—actually seeing people jump—from London Bridge, Hungerford, Tower, Blackfriars, Waterloo, Westminster, Vauxhall. Too many to remember. They're common, jumpers—another form of traffic.

24 A boatman described the tendency of jumpers to stand on the parapet of the bridge and stare down at the water for a while and then let go—face down into the river.

25 It will be cold, stunning. Cramp you up and make you stop breathing—make your heart attack. And then you enter a place that is not visible. But that's an act of faith—you just have to believe it's there.

26 It will be cold, stunning. When you enter the water it's shocking and you breathe fast, so fast euphoria comes, only briefly, but lightening everything up as you pass down and on.

27 It will be cold, stunning. When you enter the water it's shocking, and you breathe deep (you can't stop yourself) and you breathe the water in and you let go.

28 It will be cold. Even in the summer the water is cold; it lingers on—the cold of unabating darkness.

29 In some places when I look out across the river I see crumbs of something or other floating on the surface. The water's reflections are speckled with them. (Mine are, too.)

30 The English have a penchant for dismembering their murder victims. I doubt there's a period of London history free from the heads, limbs, and vital organs found in the Thames or washed up on its banks. Last week police found intestines and a leg (they didn't say if it was right or left). Over near Silvertown—intestines and one leg.

31 Yesterday I read in the evening paper: "On the night of July 8th a man walking on the foreshore at Lower Pool stumbled on a human head." The body it belonged to was found in pieces over the following weeks, a leg here, a hand there. It took one month but police found all the parts including the torso. (More river traffic.)

32 Body parts (victims of murder), corpses (suicides—mostly jumpers), sewage (human waste), heavy metals (lead, mercury, cadmium, for example). Herons and cormorants lighten up the look, but not much—and only briefly.

33 (The Thames is us.)

34 What is the darkness in the Thames?[35]

35 "... It had become a place of darkness. But there was in it one river, especially, ... that you could see on the map, resembling an immense snake uncoiled, with its head in the sea, its body at rest ... and its tail lost in the depths of the land."[36 & 37]

36 See *Heart of Darkness*, written in 1898–99 by Joseph Conrad. Viking Press edition, *The Portable Conrad*, New York, 1947: 497.

37 (Are you wondering if I'm talking about the Ganges? Or the Yangtze? Or even the Congo?[36])

following spread

1 Darkness reflects the sun. Blackness reflects nothing.

2 Darkness reflects the sun. Blackness reflects nothing. ("Between grief and nothing, I will take grief."[3])

3 From the novel *The Wild Palms*, by William Faulkner, 1939.

4 From out here near the quieter currents you can see fibers of light stretching out on the river's surface.[5] Moving still and swiftly among the dark water, amorphous white energy elongating describes only the surface of this blackness—the beginning of something that cannot be seen.

5 Have you ever noticed how light reflections on the water sometimes look like camouflage?

6 Attracted by the lights upon this liquid blackness, you wade in among them, flowing with them briefly and submerging; from underneath maybe they will appear as constellations in the darkness. Other constellations than the ones you've grown accustomed to. Constellations from some other place, unseen until now.

7 You can't tell from looking at it how treacherous the water actually is. I mean you can't see what's going on with the currents; the river runs fast and tidal reversals work up strong undercurrents. But you sense it: the complexity, the threat, the difference. It's part of the river's attraction, part of its darkness.

8 Sometimes, in a quiet area, the water is tremulous and tender: an easier entrance beguiling you.

9 Crumbs of whitish froth float on the water. They cluster in formations that are not affected by the river's movement, in formations that linger too long.

10 The water is black here, but it isn't really visible. You feel it, but you can't see it. It takes the breath out of you not being able to see it, point to it, touch it or just say it. But that's black.

11 Imagine combining black with water: two equals. One unchangeable, the other wholly corruptible.

12 Going into water is going into yourself. Water is a mirror. But even in black water there's a reflection, though a degraded one. You don't have to witness yourself in black water.

13 And what about juvenile water—immature water, young water? Water that's never seen the light of day. Juvenile water emerging from within the earth, arriving at the surface. All I can think to say is, "Hello."

14 Your reflection uncouples in this water. It drifts away from you. As you stand there on the bank or bridge, helpless, watching your reflection float downstream and disappear, you may wonder what forces black water gathers. But instinctively you already know they must be closer to witchcraft than geometry.[15]

15 "Best witchcraft is geometry."[16]

16 See poem No. 1158 by Emily Dickinson, 1870.

17 There was an article in the newspaper some time ago about a young man jumping off a bridge. He strapped his bicycle, a black Phantom, to his chest and jumped in. (It took six months to identify the body.)[18]

18 Isn't that what you'd … to lose your identity? Th… tity, doesn't it?

19 The river is a drain.

20 In winter the darknes… flow seems to accelerate.

21 In winter the Thames… palpable. Close your eyes… from the river: dank, cla…

what you'd be after—
like a solvent for iden-

eepens, and the river's

darkness of the water is
darkness wafting up

22 In winter the sky is low and the water is mobbed by clouds. The atmosphere becomes an extension of the river. Its water saturates your view. Its water silently permeates the streets and homes of London, and you live in the river.

23 Boatmen talk about seeing jumpers often—actually seeing people jump—from London Bridge, Hungerford, Tower, Blackfriars, Waterloo, Westminster, Vauxhall. Too many to remember. They're common, jumpers—another form of traffic.

24 A boatman described the tendency of jumpers to stand on the parapet of the bridge and stare down at the water for a while and then let go—face down into the river.

25 It will be cold, stunning. Cramp you up and make you stop breathing—make your heart attack. And then you enter a place that is not visible. But that's an act of faith—you just have to believe it's there.

26 It will be cold, stunning. When you enter the water it's shocking and you breathe fast, so fast euphoria comes, only briefly, but lightening everything up as you pass down and on.

27 It will be cold, stunning. When you enter the water it's shocking, and you breathe deep (you can't stop yourself) and you breathe the water in and you let go.

28 It will be cold. Even in the summer the water is cold; it lingers on—the cold of unabating darkness.

29 In some places when I look out across the river I see crumbs of something or other floating on the surface. The water's reflections are speckled with them. (Mine are, too.)

30 The English have a penchant for dismembering their murder victims. I doubt there's a period of London history free from the heads, limbs, and vital organs found in the Thames or washed up on its banks. Last week police found intestines and a leg (they didn't say if it was right or left). Over near Silvertown—intestines and one leg.

31 Yesterday I read in the evening paper: "On the night of July 8th a man walking on the foreshore at Lower Pool stumbled on a human head." The body it belonged to was found in pieces over the following weeks, a leg here, a hand there. It took one month but police found all the parts including the torso. (More river traffic.)

32 Body parts (victims of murder), corpses (suicides—mostly jumpers), sewage (human waste), heavy metals (lead, mercury, cadmium, for example). Herons and cormorants lighten up the look, but not much—and only briefly.

33 (The Thames is us.)

34 What is the darkness in the Thames?[35]

35 "... It had become a place of darkness. But there was in it one river, especially, ... that you could see on the map, resembling an immense snake uncoiled, with its head in the sea, its body at rest ... and its tail lost in the depths of the land."[36 + 37]

36 See *Heart of Darkness*, written in 1898–99 by Joseph Conrad. Viking Press edition, *The Portable Conrad*, New York, 1947: 497.

37 (Are you wondering if I'm talking about the Ganges? Or the Yangtze? Or even the Congo?[36])

[1] What do you know about water? When you talk about water, what is it you're really talking about?

[2] What do you know about water? Isn't that part of what water is, that you never really know what it is?

[3] What do you know about water? That it's everywhere, so familiar-seeming and yet so elusive (a kind of everything without definition), never quite graspable, even as an ice cube?

[4] What do you know about water? Only that it's everywhere differently?

[5] You say water is troubled or calm. You say water is rough and restless. You say water is disturbed. You say water is quiet. Water is serene and sometimes clear, it might be pure and then it is brilliant. Water is heavy; that's a fact. Water is often calm, even placid. Water is still and then it might be deep as well. Water is cold or hot, chilly or tepid. You say water is brash or brisk, sometimes crisp. You say water is soft and hard. You say water irritates and lubricates. You say water is foul. You say water is fresh. You say water is tranquil and languorous. You say water is sweet.

[6] What is water?

[7] You say it's a river. I can believe that. But when you say it's water, I get suspicious.[8]

[8] Is the Thames a case of mistaken identity?

[9] Have you ever noticed how light camouflages water?

[10] Have you ever noticed how rarely water looks like water?

[11] What does water look like?[12]

[12] See military camouflage. For example: "Polish Presidential," "Italian Woodland," "San Marco Mediterranean," "Indonesian Spot," and "Belgian Jigsaw" patterns.

[13] Have you ever noticed how reflections on the water at night make water look more watery?

[14] From out here near the quieter currents you can see fibers of light stretching out on the river's surface. Moving still and swiftly among the dark water, amorphous white energy elongating describes only the surface of this blackness—the beginning of something that cannot be seen.

[15] You can't see the blackness at night—only the darkness. It's only during the day that you can see the blackness. That's when you know it's not a reflection.

[16] In the quieter spots near the shore, the surface of the water is quilted and soft. (Doesn't the water look soft here?)

[17] In the rain or under a grey sky, in a weather that imparts little light, water is water less simply.

[18] Sometimes you can hear the water. But you can't really hear the difference.

[19] Every now and then, mostly at night, I hear splashes and plops—but I never see anything. (Do you ever really know what's going on in the river?)

[20] "A Rat surrendered here."[21]

[21] See poem No. 1340 by Emily Dickinson, 1870.

[22] Did you see *Blow-Up*?[23] and the rustling of the bus just watching—wandering bushes was dark. The river

[23] A film directed by Mic on the short-story "Blow-

[24] The sound of the bush sound of the flagpoles in *I* the poles, a row of them, a something.

[25] A film directed by Mic

…er the park scene?—
And the camera—
…? The sound of the
…at sound.

…oni in 1966 based
…tázar.

…minds me of the
…opes banging against
…npty parking lot or

…oni in 1962.

26 I don't know if you've had this experience but occasionally when I'm watching the water I hear snippets from various songs drifting up from the river. (Sometimes I even recognize the voice.)

27 I doubt you've had this experience but last night when I was watching the water "Ain't No Way" wafted up from the river, slow and endless, more or less as I remembered it: "Ain't no way . . . just ain't no way, no way . . . it ain't no way, baby . . . sure ain't no way . . . just ain't no way . . . ain't no way, baby . . . (for me to love you)."[28] It was so brief, I probably just imagined it.

28 From "Ain't No Way," written by Carolyn Franklin, 1968. Version referred to was recorded by Aretha Franklin in 1968.

29 Is water unclear? I mean you might say it's cloudy and that it's not clear. You might say it's dirty or impure or turbid or roiled, but would you say it's unclear? It seems to me that water is always clear even when it's filthy. Isn't this the basic notion of water? Isn't this what we cling to?

30 (The Thames is us.)

31 I remember an incident where a man drowned himself in front of his lover. It was quite sensational, more like a movie. The story goes that the couple was walking across Westminster Bridge late one summer night when the man turned to his boyfriend and said, "I love you," and then without warning jumped over the parapet into the river. The man ran over and looked down into the water. He could hear his name called from under the bridge but he couldn't see his boyfriend. Finally he caught sight of his face, as he emerged from underneath the bridge and just when the current caught him and pulled him under. Do you remember it? Probably not. (I thought it sounded familiar somehow.)

32 (Drowning is a more common suicide here than in the States. In the States it's mostly shooting. Maybe it's because you can't get guns here. But maybe it's also the quality of the water. It must be, because foreigners come to drown themselves in it.)

33 There was another incident recently: a guy was thrown into the river by his friends. (On a lark—they were just having a little fun.) The guy grabbed onto the first thing that came along —it turned out that the first thing to come along was a corpse.

34 The way things happen on a river you really have to keep your eyes open. I'm always afraid I'm going to miss something.

35 A witness says he saw one person jump (it was late at night) and two people come out the other side. (They still haven't found the bodies.)

36 Every now and then, mostly at night, I hear splashes and plops—but I never see anything. (Do you ever really know what's going on on the river?)

37 (What are you doing down by the river?)

38 Are you wondering if I'm talking about the Ganges? Or the Yangtze? Or even the Mississippi?

39 Aren't these shapeless, changing shapes surprising? So intricate, so elaborate, so brief; these treasures in their brevity are especially rare.

40 In the light, isn't water water more simply?

41 But what does water look like?

42 Is this water?

1 What do you know about water? When you talk about water, what is it you're really talking about?

2 What do you know about water? Isn't that part of what water is, that you never really know what it is?

3 What do you know about water? That it's everywhere, so familiar-seeming and yet so elusive (a kind of everything without definition), never quite graspable, even as an ice cube?

4 What do you know about water? Only that it's everywhere differently?

5 You say water is troubled or calm. You say water is rough and restless. You say water is disturbed. You say water is quiet. Water is serene and sometimes clear, it might be pure and then it is brilliant. Water is heavy; that's a fact. Water is often calm, even placid. Water is still and then it might be deep as well. Water is cold or hot, chilly or tepid. You say water is brash or brisk, sometimes crisp. You say water is soft and hard. You say water irritates and lubricates. You say water is foul. You say water is fresh. You say water is tranquil and languorous. You say water is sweet.

6 What is water?

7 You say it's a river. I can believe that. But when you say it's water, I get suspicious.[8]

8 Is the Thames a case of mistaken identity?

9 Have you ever noticed how light camouflages water?

10 Have you ever noticed how rarely water looks like water?

11 What does water look like?[12]

12 See military camouflage. For example: "Polish Presidential," "Italian Woodland," "San Marco Mediterranean," "Indonesian Spot," and "Belgian Jigsaw" patterns.

13 Have you ever noticed how reflections on the water at night make water look more watery?

14 From out here near the quieter currents you can see fibers of light stretching out on the river's surface. Moving still and swiftly among the dark water, amorphous white energy elongating describes only the surface of this blackness—the beginning of something that cannot be seen.

15 You can't see the blackness at night—only the darkness. It's only during the day that you can see the blackness. That's when you know it's not a reflection.

16 In the quieter spots near the shore, the surface of the water is quilted and soft. (Doesn't the water look soft here?)

17 In the rain or under a grey sky, in a weather that imparts little light, water is water less simply.

18 Sometimes you can hear the water. But you can't really hear the difference.

19 Every now and then, mostly at night, I hear splashes and plops—but I never see anything. (Do you ever really know what's going on in the river?)

20 "A Rat surrendered here."[21]

21 See poem No. 1340 by Emily Dickinson, 1870.

22 Did you see *Blow-Up*?[23] Do you remember the park scene?— and the rustling of the bushes in the wind? And the camera—just watching—wandering over the clearing? The sound of the bushes was dark. The river reminds me of that sound.

23 A film directed by Michelangelo Antonioni in 1966 based on the short-story "Blow-Up" by Julio Cortázar.

24 The sound of the bushes in *Blow-Up* reminds me of the sound of the flagpoles in *Eclipse*[25]—of the ropes banging against the poles, a row of them, at night—in an empty parking lot or something.

25 A film directed by Michelangelo Antonioni in 1962.

26 I don't know if you've had this experience but occasionally when I'm watching the water I hear snippets from various songs drifting up from the river. (Sometimes I even recognize the voice.)

27 I doubt you've had this experience but last night when I was watching the water "Ain't No Way" wafted up from the river, slow and endless, more or less as I remembered it: "Ain't no way ... just ain't no way, no way ... it ain't no way, baby ... sure ain't no way ... just ain't no way ... ain't no way, baby ... (for me to love you)."[28] It was so brief, I probably just imagined it.

28 From "Ain't No Way," written by Carolyn Franklin, 1968. Version referred to was recorded by Aretha Franklin in 1968.

29 Is water unclear? I mean you might say it's cloudy and that it's not clear. You might say it's dirty or impure or turbid or roiled, but would you say it's unclear? It seems to me that water is always clear even when it's filthy. Isn't this the basic notion of water? Isn't this what we cling to?

30 (The Thames is us.)

31 I remember an incident where a man drowned himself in front of his lover. It was quite sensational, more like a movie. The story goes that the couple was walking across Westminster Bridge late one summer night when the man turned to his boyfriend and said, "I love you," and then without warning jumped over the parapet into the river. The man ran over and looked down into the water. He could hear his name called from under the bridge but he couldn't see his boyfriend. Finally he caught sight of his face, as he emerged from underneath the bridge and just when the current caught him and pulled him under. Do you remember it? Probably not. (I thought it sounded familiar somehow.)

32 (Drowning is a more common suicide here than in the States. In the States it's mostly shooting. Maybe it's because you can't get guns here. But maybe it's also the quality of the water. It must be, because foreigners come to drown themselves in it.)

33 There was another incident recently: a guy was thrown into the river by his friends. (On a lark—they were just having a little fun.) The guy grabbed onto the first thing that came along—it turned out that the first thing to come along was a corpse.

34 The way things happen on a river you really have to keep your eyes open. I'm always afraid I'm going to miss something.

35 A witness says he saw one person jump (it was late at night) and two people come out the other side. (They still haven't found the bodies.)

36 Every now and then, mostly at night, I hear splashes and plops—but I never see anything. (Do you ever really know what's going on on the river?)

37 (What are you doing down by the river?)

38 Are you wondering if I'm talking about the Ganges? Or the Yangtze? Or even the Mississippi?

39 Aren't these shapeless, changing shapes surprising? So intricate, so elaborate, so brief; these treasures in their brevity are especially rare.

40 In the light, isn't water water more simply?

41 But what does water look like?

42 Is this water?

previous spread

1 In the waiting room of a doctor's office some years ago I overheard a mother talking about how her kids were afraid of it. If they couldn't see into it, they wouldn't go into it. It's like being dismembered. When you wade into this dark fluid, a kind of milk without nurture, you disappear.

2 Disappearance: that's why suicides are attracted to it. It's also why children fear it (see preceding footnote). It's a soft entrance to simply not being here. When I imagine the river, it's something I can enter, something that will surround me, take me away from here. But then the pain of it is less imaginable, too. Less than violence or chemistry.

3 Sometimes when I look at the river I can see into it slightly. Not very far, not more than an inch or two, but it gives the feeling that the water is occupied almost to the exact volume of the river with something other than water—perhaps another water.

4 Thinking about water is thinking about the future—or just a future. My future—yours. It's a personal thing—especially now. It makes sense that children fear water they can't see into (see footnote no. 1). And then, too, doesn't it make sense for someone who can't imagine a future to be attracted to it, to this semblance of water, to this other water?

5 It is night. The darkness of the water reflects the darkness of the sky. But when daylight comes again the water will remain dark, cutting everything in it off from everything beyond it.

6 The water is opaque. It is comforting to imagine that once you are in it, you won't be visible any longer and you won't see anything, either—relief from the unending demands of simple sight.

7 The color of the water changes constantly. Half of it is the sky.

8 The color of the water changes constantly. Half of it is khaki: with all the colors in it, though none are visible, and the whole of it nondescript. And anyway, you wouldn't really see it once you were under. It suits me—beige; it suits me—it isn't a color, it's like white that way—but without distinction. Beige is a form of mediocrity. White is important; maybe a labyrinth of sorts—that makes it a wager for life.

9 Sometimes you use the word white when you mean clear. White water seems to be OK—vital. So you might have white water. But there isn't much of that here. Anyway, what really matters is that once you get in, never mind the currents, nobody can see you. Once you're in there, once you go under, nobody can see you. It's not like a blanket, because nobody will know you're under there. You displace but you're so small, it's inconsequential. Can't see your shape, can't see you move. Don't know if it will be quiet, but no one can see you. You need to know you are invisible. And if it's not wholly silent it will be before long.

10 White water—that's for amusement.

11 There was a story in the newspaper not long ago about a drunk falling into the river one night and dying a few days later. Something to do with rats, they said. But a story like this makes me think of the virulence of the water itself. It's no act of imagination to associate this outcome with its appearance. Maybe there are some really sick rats in this water. But I'm thinking that the water itself is becoming diseased.[12]

12 See Chapter 1, "On the Look Out," in the novel *Our Mutual Friend*, by Charles Dickens, 1865.[13]

13 So maybe it's less diseased than it was 135 years ago, but falling in is still a terrifying prospect.

14 Wade into invisibility, a personal forever. An invisibility that is close enough to instantaneous. Invisible until the body goes limp. Then it will wash up somewhere and become visible again, impersonally visible.

15 The river is lulling and comforting and constant. The color is curious. And it will be cover. You need cover.

16 This morning, just after midnight, a figure was seen to jump from the parapet of Hungerford Bridge. Witnesses on a boat below heard a "plop" off the bow but saw nothing.

17 You say it's a river. I can believe that. But when you say it's water, I get suspicious.[18]

18 Is the Thames a case of mistaken identity?

19 Looking at an image like this you may never get to the idea of water at all.

20 Looking at an image like this, if you get to the idea of water at all, then you'll have to wonder what water really is.

21 This water is not clear, pure, odorless, or colorless.[22] I venture that it is not tasteless either, but I don't know for certain. This water doesn't quite glisten. I have questioned its viscosity often. Walking along the river or watching from the bridges I've wondered: "Doesn't it seem a bit thick here, or here?"

22 See the definition of water in *The American Heritage Dictionary*.

23 Have you ever looked at the river and had the idea that the water is sticky?

24 Have you noticed how rarely water looks like water?

25 What does water look like?

26 There's nothing ambiguous about this color. The problem is believing that it's water. Maybe you think the photograph wasn't exposed properly, that it's too dark? But what about the leaves floating on the surface—they're not too dark. You might think that leaves, even dead ones, would add a touch of the pastoral to the view. But instead they only confirm the blackness of the water.

27 I'm certain the river has gelatinous moments too quick for the eye to see.

28 Water receives you, affirms you, shows you who you are. And all the near-imperceptible qualities that are water tease you with their ambiguity.

29 A middle-aged man was found in the river last week. £3,000 in notes were taped to his stomach along with instructions for his funeral.

30 The Thames has *the* highest rate of suicides of any urban river. Maybe it's not the highest but it's close. It doesn't really matter because even if it doesn't, it *looks* like it does.

31 It's not a river to *attempt* suicide in; it's too treacherous. Once you're in there, odds are you're gone. That's what makes it so appealing. That and the fact that it's opaque. And the fact that getting in is so easy. It's a practical, possibly even efficient choice—but that's just speculation.

32 Hidden by the dark. It's only night and that will pass. But the blackness of the water won't pass. The blackness and the water pass by but they never go away.

33 Black is a place. I don't know what it's like, can't see it, but I know it's there. You can go there—though it's not fixed in location. Black travels well, it's inert, incorruptible—like gold. And no matter where it is, it's always the same. You never know much about it, it doesn't give much away (that's the idea of black); you just have to go there. Black is where you can suspend your faith.

34 Black water is black milk.

following spread

1 In the waiting room of a doctor's office some years ago I overheard a mother talking about how her kids were afraid of it. If they couldn't see into it, they wouldn't go into it. It's like being dismembered. When you wade into this dark fluid, a kind of milk without nurture, you disappear.

2 Disappearance: that's why suicides are attracted to it. It's also why children fear it (see preceding footnote). It's a soft entrance to simply not being here. When I imagine the river, it's something I can enter, something that will surround me, take me away from here. But then the pain of it is less imaginable, too. Less than violence or chemistry.

3 Sometimes when I look at the river I can see into it slightly. Not very far, not more than an inch or two, but it gives the feeling that the water is occupied almost to the exact volume of the river with something other than water—perhaps another water.

4 Thinking about water is thinking about the future—or just a future. My future—yours. It's a personal thing—especially now. It makes sense that children fear water they can't see into (see footnote no. 1). And then, too, doesn't it make sense for someone who can't imagine a future to be attracted to it, to this semblance of water, to this other water?

5 It is night. The darkness of the water reflects the darkness of the sky. But when daylight comes again the water will remain dark, cutting everything in it off from everything beyond it.

6 The water is opaque. It is comforting to imagine that once you are in it, you won't be visible any longer and you won't see anything, either—relief from the unending demands of simple sight.

7 The color of the water changes constantly. Half of it is the sky.

8 The color of the water changes constantly. Half of it is khaki: with all the colors in it, though none are visible, and the whole of it nondescript. And anyway, you wouldn't really see it once you were under. It suits me—beige; it suits me—it isn't a color, it's like white that way—but without distinction. Beige is a form of mediocrity. White is important: maybe a labyrinth of sorts—that makes it a wager for life.

9 Sometimes you use the word white when you mean clear. White water seems to be OK—vital. So you might have white water. But there isn't much of that here. Anyway, what really matters is that once you get in, never mind the currents, nobody can see you. Once you're in there, once you go under, nobody can see you. It's not like a blanket, because nobody will know you're under there. You displace but you're so small, it's inconsequential. Can't see your shape, can't see you move. Don't know if it will be quiet, but no one can see you. You need to know you are invisible. And if it's not wholly silent it will be before long.

10 White water—that's for amusement.

11 There was a story in the newspaper not long ago about a drunk falling into the river one night and dying a few days later. Something to do with rats, they said. But a story like this makes me think of the virulence of the water itself. It's no act of imagination to associate this outcome with its appearance. Maybe there are some really sick rats in this water. But I'm thinking that the water itself is becoming diseased.[12]

12 See Chapter 1, "On the Look Out," in the novel *Our Mutual Friend*, by Charles Dickens, 1865.[13]

13 So maybe it's less disea
falling in is still a terrifyin

14 Wade into invisibility,
is close enough to instant
limp. Then it will wash up
impersonally visible.

15 The river is lulling and
curious. And it will be co

16 This morning, just afte
from the parapet of Hunge
below heard a "plop" off t

35 years ago, but

: An invisibility that
until the body goes
become visible again.

constant. The color is
er.

are was seen to jump
tnesses on a boat
nothing.

17 You say it's a river. I can believe that. But when you say it's water, I get suspicious."

18 Is the Thames a case of mistaken identity?

19 Looking at an image like this you may never get to the idea of water at all.

20 Looking at an image like this, if you get to the idea of water at all, then you'll have to wonder what water really is.

21 This water is not clear, pure, odorless, or colorless." I venture that it's not tasteless either, but I don't know for certain. This water doesn't quite glisten. I have questioned its viscosity often. Walking along the river or watching from the bridges I've wondered: "Doesn't it seem a bit thick here, or here?"

22 See the definition of water in *The American Heritage Dictionary*.

23 Have you ever looked at the river and had the idea that the water is sticky?

24 Have you noticed how rarely water looks like water?

25 What does water look like?

26 There's nothing ambiguous about this color. The problem is believing that it's water. Maybe you think the photograph wasn't exposed properly, that it's too dark? But what about the leaves floating on the surface—they're not too dark. You might think that leaves, even dead ones, would add a touch of the pastoral to the view. But instead they only confirm the blackness of the water.

27 I'm certain the river has gelatinous moments too quick for the eye to see.

28 Water receives you, affirms you, shows you who you are. And all the near-imperceptible qualities that are water tease you with their ambiguity.

29 A middle-aged man was found in the river last week. £3,000 in notes were taped to his chest along with instructions for his funeral.

30 The Thames has the highest rate of suicides of any urban river. Maybe it's not *the* highest but it's close. It doesn't really matter because even if it doesn't, it *looks* like it does.

31 It's not a river to *attempt* suicide in; it's too treacherous. Once you're in there, odds are you're gone. That's what makes it so appealing. That and the fact that it's opaque. And the fact that getting in is so easy. It's a practical, possibly even efficient choice —but that's just speculation.

32 Hidden by the dark. It's only night and that will pass. But the blackness of the water won't pass. The blackness and the water pass by but they never go away.

33 Black is a place. I don't know what it's like, can't see it, but I know it's there. You can go there—though it's not fixed in location. Black travels well, it's inert, incorruptible—like gold. And no matter where it is, it's always the same. You never know much about it, it doesn't give much away (that's the idea of black); you just have to go there. Black is where you can suspend your faith.

34 Black water is black milk.

1 The deserts of our future will be deserts of water.

2 Is this khaki or beige?

3 Is this beige or ochre?

4 Is this ochre or yellow?

5 Is this yellow or green?

6 Is this green or brown?

7 Is this brown or black?

8 Is this black?

9 There's a story (it's true) about a man traveling by tube to Westminster Bridge: handcuffed to a chair. He threw himself in the river with the chair. He was found some days later downstream attached to a stick of wood and a section of naugahyde (almond colored).

10 The color of the water changes constantly. Half of it is the sky.

11 The color of the water (whatever it is) changes constantly. Half of it is khaki: with all the colors in it, though none are visible, and the whole of it nondescript. And anyway, you wouldn't really see it once you were under. But it suits me—beige; it suits me—it isn't a color, it's like white that way—but without distinction. Beige is a form of mediocrity. White is important; maybe a labyrinth of sorts—that makes it a wager for life.

12 Sometimes you use the word white when you mean clear. White water seems to be OK—vital. So you might have white water. But there isn't much of that here. Anyway, what really matters is that once you get in, never mind the currents, nobody can see you. Once you're in there, once you go under, nobody can see you. It's not like a blanket, because nobody will know you're under there. You displace but you're so small, it's inconsequential. Can't see your shape, can't see you move. Don't know if it will be quiet, but no one can see you. You need to know you are invisible. And if it's not wholly silent it will be before long.

13 Black water—is that for amusement?

14 If this paper was water it would be black. Maybe it looks white, but it's definitely not clear.

15 Do you believe that this particular color " (whatever it is) is mainly geology? Just benign muck making the water this foul color. Maybe you can say it's the foulness that attracts body parts and various other items an individual might want to hide, including oneself. And maybe it isn't. Maybe there's some metaphysical reason for the river's special color—some rare spiritual coincidence perhaps. Who knows? Is it filthy-looking water that attracts the wanna-be secrets of humanity, or is it the wanna-be secrets of humanity that sully the water?

16 (Roiled but real.)

17 (This wave reminds me of a wave I saw the other day.)

18 This photograph is an image of a moment on the Thames. It is also a moment similar to other moments of moving water and especially moments of rapidly moving water that were hardly visible. But you extrapolate from your experience, you recognize things you've never actually seen—things that simply weren't visible. (Photographs often portray things unseen or unseeable in a simple sense. Like things that occur too slowly or too quickly.) You recognize things you've never actually seen—even though you may have watched them as you may have watched this river for hours at a time. But you know it's a river, water moving from here to there. You fe
haven't, what you've actu
often takes in real time.

19 When you photograph
restless, liquid reality.

20 When you photograph
essential ways bears no lik

21 When you photograph
about something that has

22 What does water look

en it before. But you
the form a river

it of its form: of its

it an image that in

k in graphic terms
t.

23 See sand? (Especially sand dunes.)

24 See deserts, for example the Gobi or the Sahara.

25 As is often said of photographs, this photograph is a frozen moment. But a frozen moment is no moment at all, it's an oxymoron. So here among a collection of oxymorons, we approach other oxymorons.

26 When I look at water, especially this water, I find myself wondering about it: its mechanics, its poetics, and so on. I wander in my thoughts. I go places. Water is lubricant to other places.

27 Water is lubricant to other places. It dilutes gravity when you're in it; it reduces friction when you're around it. Almost any form of water: rivers, lakes, oceans, even sinks will do. My mind roams freely, breezily near it. My thoughts take me backward and forward; time has no direction near water.

28 Water is lubricant to other places; it catalyzes memory and aspiration. (Time has no direction near water.)

29 Water is lubricant to other places; I use my baths to travel.

30 You know very well this water is filthy. But isn't it strange the way you still go places around it? It's true you go different places than if it was clear—but those places are as alluring as the pastoral variety, don't you think? Or is this the view of a pervert?

31 You know very well this water is filthy. But isn't it strange the way you're still drawn to it? The way you still hang around watching it?

32 I know very well this water is filthy. It's more compelling that way, more unknown.

33 I know very well this water is filthy. And even though I'm told (frequently) that it's much cleaner than it was, I don't believe it. And even if I did, it still looks filthy.

34 What is the darkness in the Thames? Is it you?

35 It is day. The darkness of the water does not reflect the lightness of the sky. And when day comes again the water will remain dark, cutting everything in it off from everything beyond it.

36 Among water? Isn't water a plural form? How could it ever be singular, even in one river? Where did that water come from?

37 This water confuses me. When I'm by the river I wonder: Who am I? Where am I? What is this?

38 (Could be dehydration.)

39 Can the river dissolve your identity just standing near it, just standing nearby and watching it?

40 Confused? Lost? Large expanses of water are like deserts; no landmarks, no differences to distinguish here from there. (If you don't know where you are, can you know who you are?) Just tumult everywhere, endlessly. Tumult modulating into another tumult all over and without end. The change is so constant, so pervasive, so relentless that identity, place, scale—all measure lessen, weaken—eventually disappear. The more time you spend around this water—the more faint your memories of measure become.

1 The deserts of our future will be deserts of water.

2 Is this khaki or beige?

3 Is this beige or ochre?

4 Is this ochre or yellow?

5 Is this yellow or green?

6 Is this green or brown?

7 Is this brown or black?

8 Is this black?

9 There's a story (it's true) about a man traveling by tube to Westminster Bridge handcuffed to a chair. He threw himself in the river with the chair. He was found some days later downstream attached to a stick of wood and a section of naugahyde (almond colored).

10 The color of the water changes constantly. Half of it is the sky.

11 The color of the water (whatever it is) changes constantly. Half of it is khaki: with all the colors in it, though none are visible, and the whole of it nondescript. And anyway, you wouldn't really see it once you were under. But it suits me—beige; it suits me—it isn't a color, it's like white that way—but without distinction. Beige is a form of mediocrity. White is important; maybe a labyrinth of sorts—that makes it a wager for life.

12 Sometimes you use the word white when you mean clear. White water seems to be OK—vital. So you might have white water. But there isn't much of that here. Anyway, what really matters is that once you get in, never mind the currents, nobody can see you. Once you're in there, once you go under, nobody can see you. It's not like a blanket, because nobody will know you're under there. You displace but you're so small, it's inconsequential. Can't see your shape, can't see you move. Don't know if it will be quiet, but no one can see you. You need to know you are invisible. And if it's not wholly silent it will be before long.

13 Black water—is that for amusement?

14 If this paper was water it would be black. Maybe it looks white, but it's definitely not clear.

15 Do you believe that this particular color[16] (whatever it is) is mainly geology? Just benign muck making the water this foul color. Maybe you can say it's the foulness that attracts body parts and various other items an individual might want to hide, including oneself. And maybe it isn't. Maybe there's some metaphysical reason for the river's special color—some rare spiritual coincidence perhaps. Who knows? Is it filthy-looking water that attracts the wanna-be secrets of humanity, or is it the wanna-be secrets of humanity that sully the water?

16 (Roiled but real.)

17 (This wave reminds me of a wave I saw the other day.)

18 This photograph is an image of a moment on the Thames. It is also a moment similar to other moments of moving water and especially moments of rapidly moving water that were hardly visible. But you extrapolate from your experience, you recognize things you've never actually seen—things that simply weren't visible. (Photographs often portray things unseen or unseeable in a simple sense. Like things that occur too slowly or too quickly.) You recognize things you've never actually seen—even though you may have watched them as you may have watched this river for hours at a time. But you know it's a river, water moving from here to there. You feel like you've seen it before. But you haven't, what you've actually seen is a slur: the form a river often takes in real time.

19 When you photograph water you strip it of its form: of its restless, liquid reality.

20 When you photograph water you give it an image that in essential ways bears no likeness to water.

21 When you photograph water you speak in graphic terms about something that has no graphic aspect.

22 What does water look like? [23]

23 See sand? (Especially sand dunes.) [24]

24 See deserts, for example the Gobi or the Sahara.

25 As is often said of photographs, this photograph is a frozen moment. But a frozen moment is no moment at all, it's an oxymoron. So here among a collection of oxymorons, we approach other oxymorons.

26 When I look at water, especially this water, I find myself wondering about it: its mechanics, its poetics, and so on. I wander in my thoughts. I go places. Water is lubricant to other places.

27 Water is lubricant to other places. It dilutes gravity when you're in it; it reduces friction when you're around it. Almost any form of water: rivers, lakes, oceans, even sinks will do. My mind roams freely, breezily near it. My thoughts take me backward and forward; time has no direction near water.

28 Water is lubricant to other places; it catalyzes memory and aspiration. (Time has no direction near water.)

29 Water is lubricant to other places; I use my baths to travel.

30 You know very well this water is filthy. But isn't it strange the way you still go places around it? It's true you go different places than if it was clear—but those places are as alluring as the pastoral variety, don't you think? Or is this the view of a pervert?

31 You know very well this water is filthy. But isn't it strange the way you're still drawn to it? The way you still hang around watching it?

32 I know very well this water is filthy. It's more compelling that way, more unknown.

33 I know very well this water is filthy. And even though I'm told (frequently) that it's much cleaner than it was, I don't believe it. And even if I did, it still looks filthy.

34 What is the darkness in the Thames? Is it you?

35 It is day. The darkness of the water does not reflect the lightness of the sky. And when day comes again the water will remain dark, cutting everything in it off from everything beyond it.

36 Among water? Isn't water a plural form? How could it ever be singular, even in one river? Where did that water come from?

37 This water confuses me. When I'm by the river I wonder: Who am I? Where am I? What is this? [38]

38 (Could be dehydration.)

39 Can the river dissolve your identity just standing near it, just standing nearby and watching it? [40]

40 Confused? Lost? Large expanses of water are like deserts; no landmarks, no differences to distinguish here from there. (If you don't know where you are, can you know who you are?) Just tumult everywhere, endlessly. Tumult modulating into another tumult all over and without end. The change is so constant, so pervasive, so relentless that identity, place, scale—all measure lessen, weaken—eventually disappear. The more time you spend around this water—the more faint your memories of measure become.

previous spread

or because a large part of the population was no longer prepared to accept the huge financial burden and massive interventions in their landscapes. A position paper issued by CIPRA, the International Commission for the Protection of the Alps, clearly illustrates these facts and states that the Winter Olympics in their present form have grown too large for the small-scale organization of the Alpine regions. One possibility suggests that Switzerland should be in charge of the organization, that is, not a place such as St. Moritz or Sion but an entire country that could then benefit from the existing infrastructures and facilities.

Chris Dercon: I'm sure that's correct. But do you think it is too opportunistic to say that it should be possible in Paris, in the context of the upcoming Olympic Games, to push through new large-scale landscaping projects? For instance, take the urgent revitalization of the Champs-Élysées. Today, the lower half of the Champs-Élysées feels like a campsite, the trees no longer have any function and you barely know what is where and why. The borders are occupied by blue cars on an almost daily basis: the Compagnies Républicaines de Sécurité CRS are constantly on-site. But because of the Olympic Games, these problems can finally be addressed. Michel de Certeau has described this procedure as a kind of cultural abuse. And we are currently doing exactly that with the renovation of the Grand Palais and the Palais de la Découverte: these places should once again become a true campus (*îlot*) the way it was planned by Charles Girault. An *îlot* that creates a strong connection to the Champs-Élysées, to its direct neighbor, the Petit Palais, but also the banks of the River Seine, the Hôtel des Invalides and, somewhat farther off, the Eiffel Tower, and the Champ-de-Mars.

The fact that there are extensive underground spaces in Paris with a truly incredible potential, such as that underneath the Hôtel des Invalides—a project that the city of Paris is developing together with Dominique Perrault—is only rendered visible and recognizable by these very processes. All this could also help solve the heat problem in Paris. Of course, this brings us back to London, and here the question is whether life is better following the Summer Olympics of 2012? Who is still talking about the Olympic grounds? And what is left of them?

Günther Vogt: Well, quite a lot has remained. Besides a residential quarter that originally housed the athletes and was designed from the very outset for more people in terms of its subsequent use, an intact network of open spaces, large institutions, and buildings–especially for sports. For instance, the Zaha Hadid Indoor Pool or the stadium, whose capacity was reduced from 80,000 to around 60,000 seats in order to render it "suitable for everyday use." In addition, the transport infrastructure was added that is still in operation and provides an efficient connection to Stratford and the City Airport. As a result, the quarter is now relatively close to the city center and, at the same time, internationally accessible in an optimum manner. There is quite some pressure on the site to further develop it. And the influence on neo-liberal urban development is far stronger for projects developed over such a long period of time as private-sector investments only take place once a certain amount of advance work has been done. In other words, if certain urban-planning or infrastructural impulses have already been set in motion. There is not only the neo-liberal access to the district but also that of the public sector. The London University College is now building a campus on the site, for example. Five museums and a theater are to follow. All of them benefit from these surroundings. For if such a *big event* as the Summer Olympics is held in the city center, I am convinced it can have a positive effect on the city and also generate a certain revival. The context is crucial. It requires a certain amount of urban density all around and the potential to reorient and restructure. Ultimately, the issue is how high the price will be.

> p. 252, *UCL East Campus*

BEAUFORT SCALE

BEAUFORT NUMBER	NAME	MILES PER HOUR	DESCRIPTION
0	calm	less than 1	calm; smoke rises vertically
1	light air	1–3	direction of wind shown by smoke but not by wind vanes
2	light breeze	4–7	wind felt on face; leaves rustle; ordinary vane moved by wind
3	gentle breeze	8–12	leaves and small twigs in constant motion; wind extends light flag
4	moderate breeze	13–18	raises dust and loose paper; small branches are moved
5	fresh breeze	19–24	small trees in leaf begin to sway; crested wavelets form on inland waters
6	strong breeze	25–31	large branches in motion; telegraph wires whistle; umbrellas used with difficulty
7	moderate gale (*or* near gale)	32–38	whole trees in motion; inconvenience in walking against wind
8	fresh gale (*or* gale)	39–46	breaks twigs off trees; generally impedes progress
9	strong gale	47–54	slight structural damage occurs; chimney pots and slates removed
10	whole gale (*or* storm)	55–63	trees uprooted; considerable structural damage occurs
11	storm (*or* violent storm)	64–72	very rarely experienced; accompanied by widespread damage
12	hurricane*	73–136	devastation occurs

*The U.S. uses 74 statute mph as the speed criterion for hurricane.

"Beaufort Scale," from *Merriam-Webster's Ninth New Collegiate Dictionary,* 1983

UCL East Campus, London
Rates of Change

The idea of hosting the 2012 Olympics in London had at its core one of the largest urban regeneration projects to have ever been undertaken in Europe. Indeed, the overarching theme of the Olympic bid was a “lasting legacy of sustainability” for the Lower Lea Valley, an area that, since the decline of industrial production in the 1960s, had become one of the most deprived in the UK. The Olympics intensified the speed and focus of change in the area and catalyzed the initiation of a number of projects at diverse scales, before, during, and after the games. Located within the Queen Elizabeth Olympic Park, the new campus for University College London is one of the many projects still flourishing on the basis of this long-term legacy.

Client:
University College London

Cooperation:
Architecture:
Stanton Williams and Lifschutz Davidson Sandilands, London
Engineering:
AKT/Arup, LLDC, London

Design:
2016–ongoing

Type and size:
Campus, 5.6 ha

Status:
Ongoing

Following World War II, Sir Patrick Abercrombie developed the Greater London Plan for the reconstruction of the city and its surrounding areas. This embedded a vision for the Lea Valley with the aim of turning it into a “green wedge.”

The River Lea is the largest natural tributary of the Thames within the Greater London area. During medieval times, its low-lying fluvial landscape and meandering flood-prone streams became a natural boundary and a marginal landscape. The poor soil and strong westerly winds, its proximity to the Thames, and the energy that could be extracted from its tidal reaches have made its valley an ideal conduit for industry and profit since the seventeenth century. Over time, the site's inherent characteristics and multiple transformations caused by human intervention contributed to a physically fragmented landscape. The confluence of numerous water courses and the presence of extensive regional infrastructure have meant that this vast territory remained relatively underdeveloped up until the second half of the twentieth century.

Early redevelopment plans were articulated when Sir Patrick Abercrombie proposed turning the Lea Valley into a "green wedge" as part of the 1944 Greater London Plan. In 1967, this was realized as the Lea Valley Regional Park. However, the lower valley remained a disjointed part of the city, an apparent rift between the dense urban buildup both to the east and west sides.

In 2005, a new opportunity arose to "stich" the area with the surrounding urban fabric when London was chosen to host the 2012 Olympic and Paralympic games. London's key argument for the selection was the lasting legacy of sustainability that it promised for the Lower Lea Valley. Unprecedented in scale and pace of development, this project was true to Abercrombie's ambition and extended its boundaries south down to the Thames. At the center of the regeneration program was the design of the Legacy Masterplan Framework and of the Queen Elizabeth Olympic Park, both of which aimed to integrate the site's existing features with a complex and fragmented urban fabric.

Once the games were over, the transformation of the Olympic landscape into a livable neighborhood was one of the key challenges involved in establishing the site as part of the wider public realm. The East Village, situated on the doorstep of the Queen Elizabeth Olympic Park, was the first residential legacy, as it became home to more than six thousand new inhabitants after temporarily hosting the athletes during the games. Inscribed in the long-term urban transformations that continue to shape the Lower Lea Valley, the new campus for UCL East is one of the numerous large-scale institutes that are beginning to populate the Queen Elizabeth Olympic Park. (asb/cb)

London at the intersection of national water, railway, and motorway networks

London's sprawling public infrastructure

Lea Valley and the future site of the Olympic Park in 1945

During the Industrial Revolution in Britain, road and railway infrastructures were quickly developed across the country. Situated on a dense area of the network, the Lea Valley developed into a key place for industry and became synonymous with a profusion of chemical and manufacturing industries. After World War II, globalization and the onset of new technologies led to a rapid contraction of manufacturing and related industries. This downturn caused growing imbalances in the capital's economy, as warehouses, factories, and infrastructure closed or were abandoned, turning a once thriving industrial landscape into an "eviscerated agglomeration of post-industrial decay."[1]

1 Tim Marshall, John Glasson and Peter Headicar, *Contemporary Issues in Regional Planning*, New York, 2018.

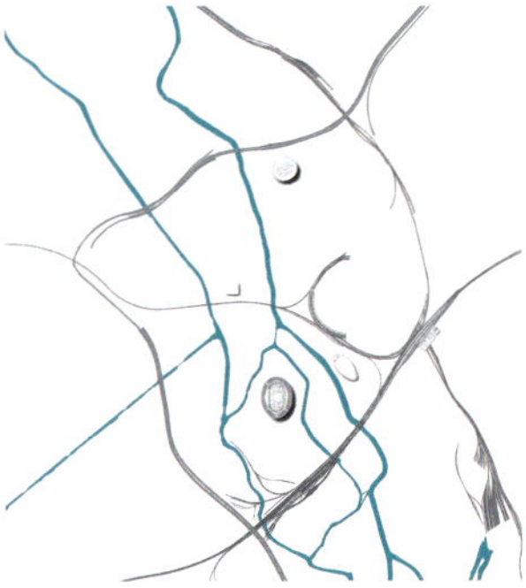

Waterways

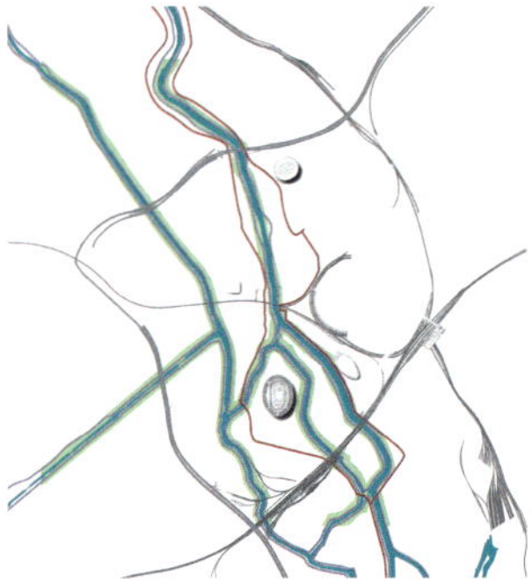

Water promenade, high promenade, and linear park system

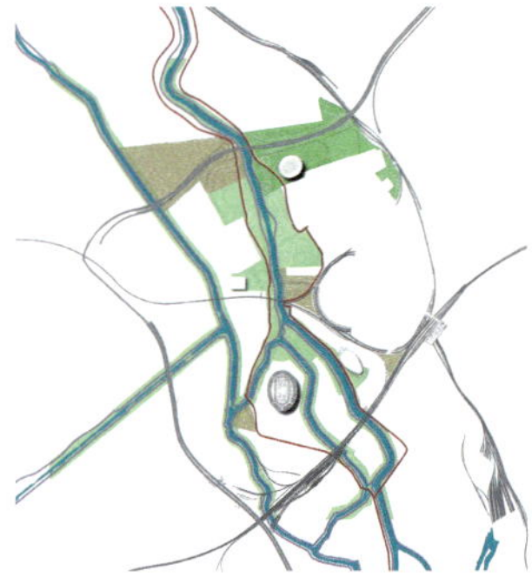

Pocket parks, sports parks, and low-maintenance areas

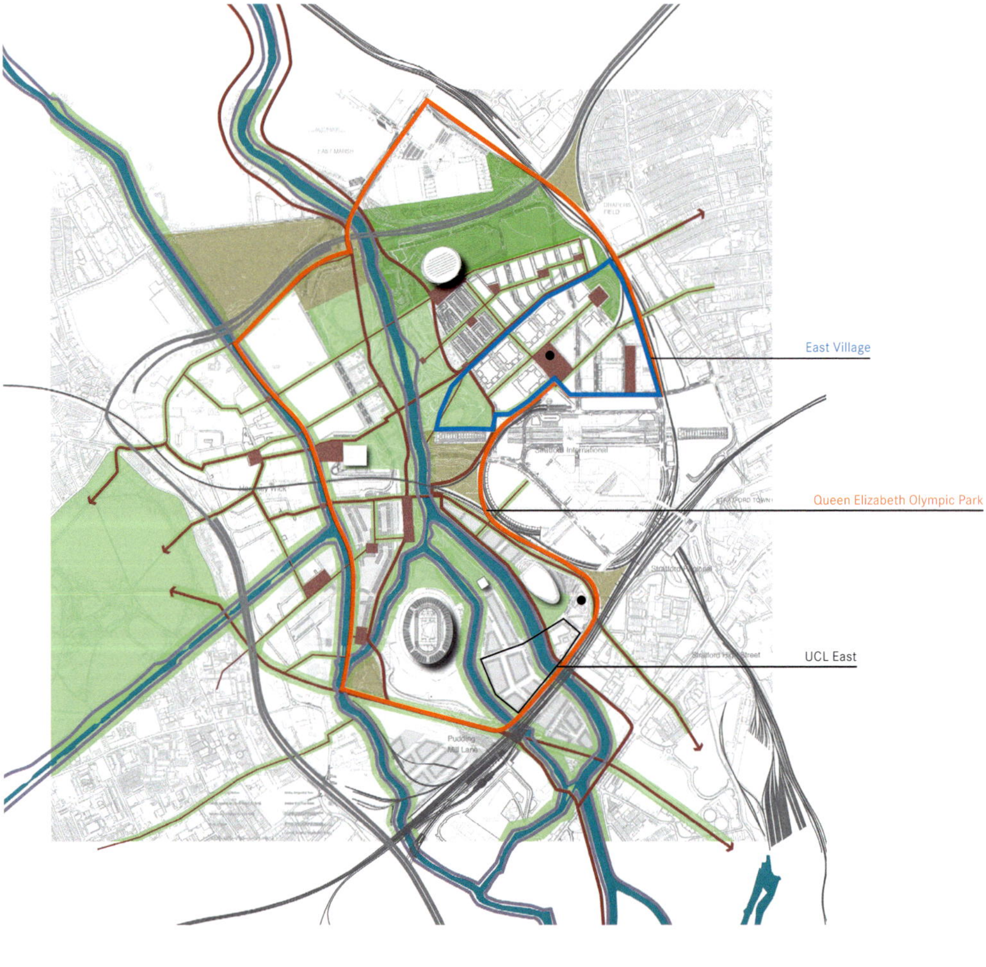

UCL East Campus, London
Rates of Change

The Legacy Masterplan sets out a vision for the entire site and the principles that inform the open space strategy through access, scale, character, use, and urban design. It is based on the existing qualities of the site, combining them with the new elements into a coherent network. As part of the main structuring elements, waterways are integrated and become accessible to the public. The cultural legacy of water sports like rowing establish a framework for the project's development.

The central theme of the Olympic bid was a "lasting legacy of sustainability" for the Lower Lea Valley and the wider Thames Gateway area of East London. It was pitched to the Olympic Committee and the international community as a vehicle for the improvement of life for generations of East Londoners to come. London was the first to take this approach to the master planning of the Games. The immediate program of post-Games transformation was to open up the inward-facing areas and link them up to the local contexts. Part of this involved building new bridges and streets, and then addressing the challenge of adapting such large-scale event infrastructure to the livable, "human" scale of a neighborhood.

Transformation of existing infrastructure for post-Olympic use immediately after the Games includes the removal of temporary venues, the adaptation of the stadium and pool, and the transformation of the "Athletes Village" into the East Village, a neighborhood for nearly 6,000 inhabitants.

Seven years on, as the Queen Elizabeth Olympic Park and surrounding areas continue to develop, we are looking back to see how the neighborhood and its public realm have started to mature. Two walking routes–one along the Lea Valley Park, the other across it through suburban Stratford–provided the basis for a photographic survey investigating how the East Village has integrated into its urban context.

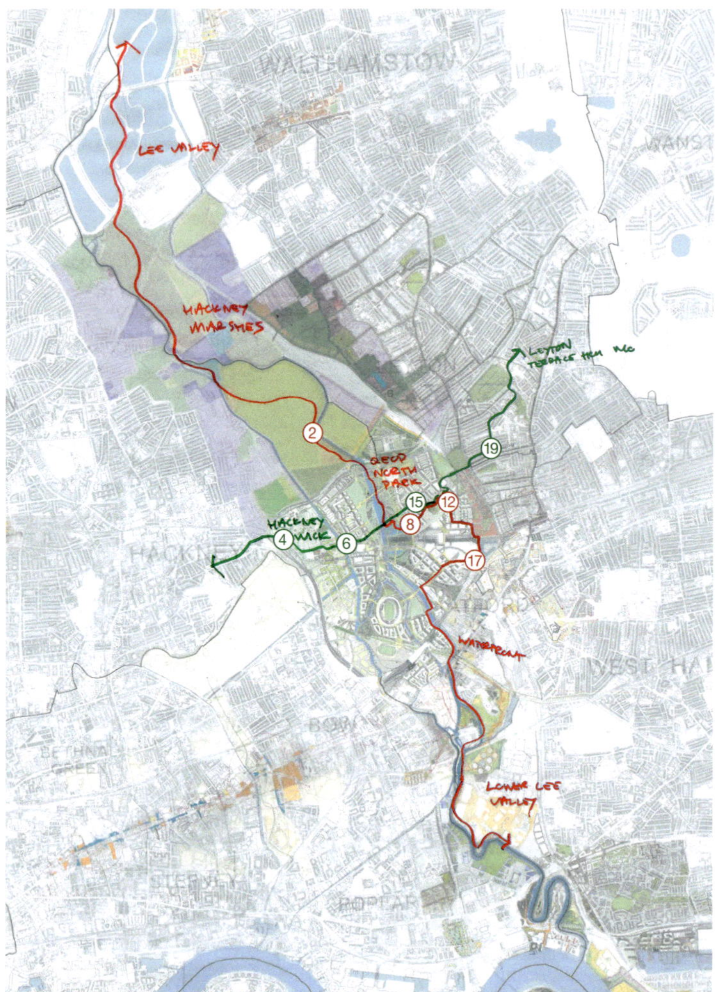

4

2

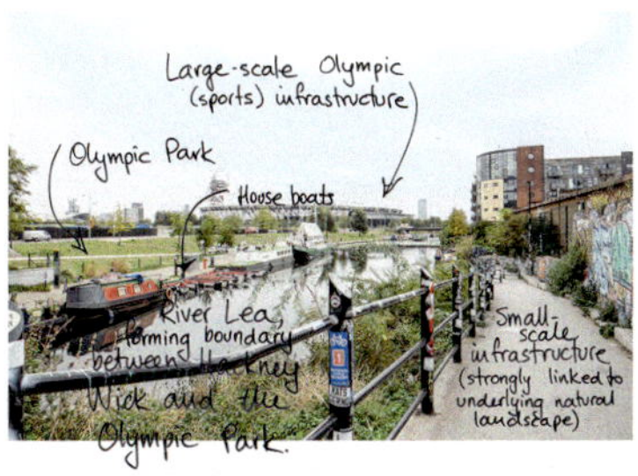

6

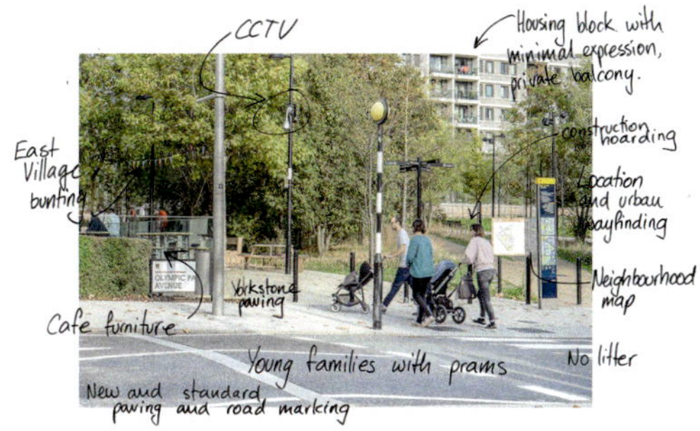

8

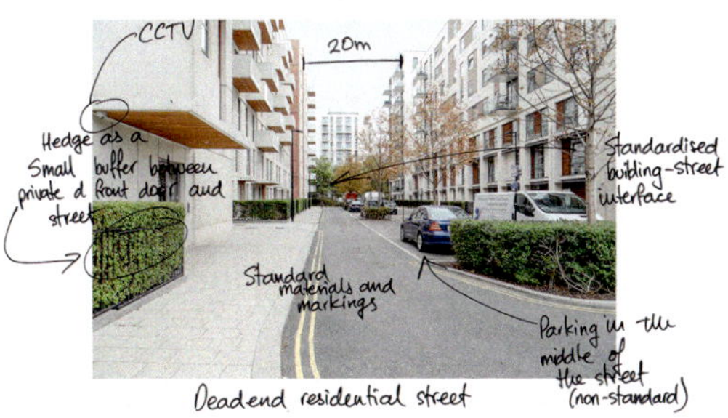

15

12

19

17

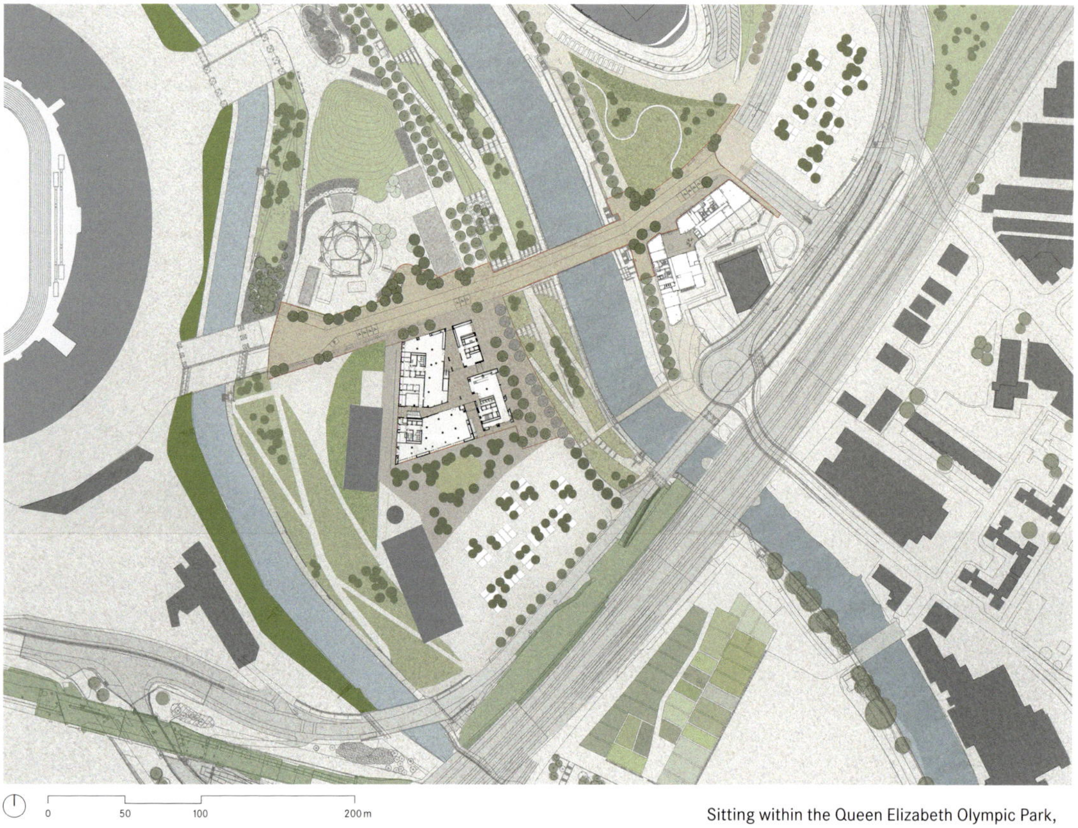

Sitting within the Queen Elizabeth Olympic Park, the campus of UCL East is one of the latest developments within the site. With its strong and prevailing southwest wind, amplified by the river corridors, the site is highly exposed to the elements. With the use of wind mitigation simulations, the planting strategy has been developed to protect the campus from harsh conditions.

Wind mitigation simulations: before and after intervention.

- high exposure
- medium exposure
- low exposure

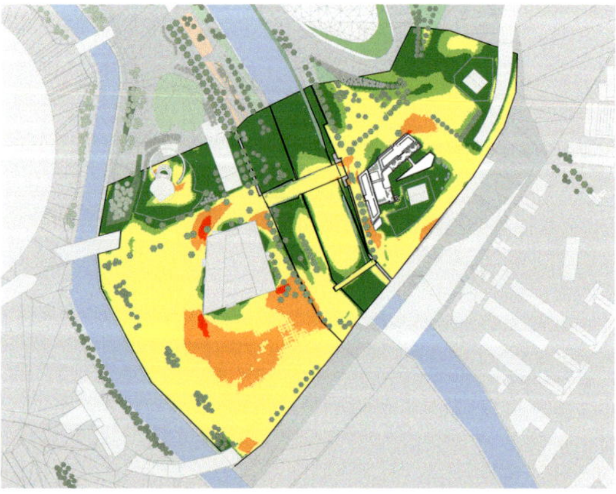

UCL East Campus, London
Rates of Change

With the implementation of large institutions in the area, a new town center is starting to develop in East London. Linked by new transport infrastructures, the Queen Elizabeth Olympic Park is relatively close to the City and very well connected to Stratford and London City Airport.

Olympia Master Plan, Hamburg
Rehabilitating the River

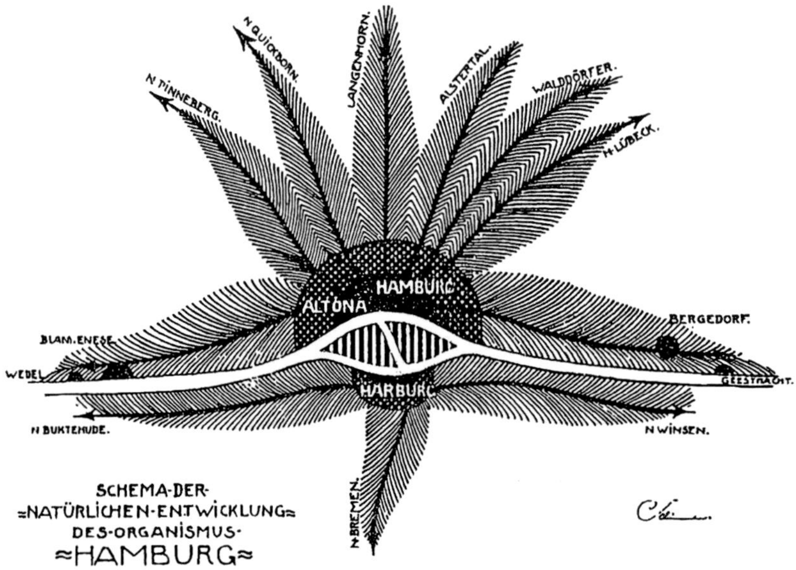

Client:
HafenCity Hamburg GmbH, City Planning Office, Hamburg

Cooperation:
Master plan:
KCAP, Rotterdam
Arup, Berlin
gmp Architekten, Hamburg

Design:
2015

Type and size:
Park/Square/Promenade, 89 ha excl. bodies of water, ca. 125 ha incl. bodies of water

Status:
Not realized

Hamburg is generally seen as the "greenest city" in Germany. This reputation is based on the famous plan by Schumacher and Linne in Hamburg and Oelsner and Tutenberg in neighboring Altona of the early 1920s, with the former as chief planning officers and the latter responsible for the parks and gardens. Their strategy was to create a city-wide network by combining elements of the urban landscape–the merchants' and shipowners' gardens dating back to the sixteenth century and the newly emerging modern building complexes. Since then, this plan has been regularly added to and refined, thereby retaining its validity to this day. Many elements of this network were created in connection with major events in society: starting in the mid-nineteenth century, more or less at the same time as the World Fairs, the tradition of horticultural exhibitions developed into a technical, aesthetic, and social display of the capabilities of horticulture. While the iconographic structures built for these fairs, such as the Crystal Palace in London (1851), the Eiffel Tower in Paris (1889), and the Atomium in Brussels (1958), also shaped the image of the particular city in the wake of the exhibition and became tourist attractions, the parks created for the horticultural exhibitions were generally maintained as public amenities for the citizens. In contrast to Berlin, which hosted three world fairs, the metropolitan region of Hamburg/Altona has so far underscored its reputation as a "green city" with seven horticultural exhibitions. Fischerspark, Donnerspark, Wallanlagen, Planten un Blomen, and Wilhelmsburger Inselpark are just a few of the public parks created between 1869 and 2013 as a result of these exhibitions. Knowledge of this "green tradition" is deeply anchored in the collective memory of the city–just like the port, the river, and the use of clinker brick as a building material. Against this backdrop, in conjunction with the 2024 or 2028 Olympic Games, modern sports infrastructures and a further park were to be created–in addition to a new residential and commercial quarter–as items of lasting value for the city. The plan was to create a park that would have made a "leap across the Elbe" possible and was to have completed the "feather fan" plan of "urban greening" toward the south, connecting Lohsepark and Wilhelmsburger Inselpark.

The new park, which is much smaller than most of Hamburg's major parks, owing to the amount of space available to it, picks up on a central feature of the historical models, with strategically positioned visual axes connecting to the water expanses of the Elbe and the Outer Alster. As you leave the densely built quarter, the view through the park opens up toward the Elbe Valley and expands the scale of the elongated area of open space on the river bank beyond its borders. The passing ships are also part of this setting. Although the fruit and refrigeration center was gradually shifted westward, cargo vessels still ply the Elbe: a reminder of international trade routes and far-distant ports.

When the Hamburg electorate voted against the bid for the Summer Olympics in a referendum on November 29, 2015, the project was suspended. (lr)

1869: International Horticultural Exhibition, Alter Elbpark
The first horticultural exhibition in Hamburg initiated a tradition of creating public parks. Some of the horticultural shows also took place in existing parks–donations from wealthy merchant and shipping families, who bequeathed their family residences to the cities of Altona and Hamburg on the condition that they were to be made permanently accessible to the public.

> Map of Hamburg with its greenbelt and a list of parks dating back to the historical horticultural exhibitions

1897: Wallanlagen

1914: Altona

1953: Planten un Blomen, Jungiuswiesen

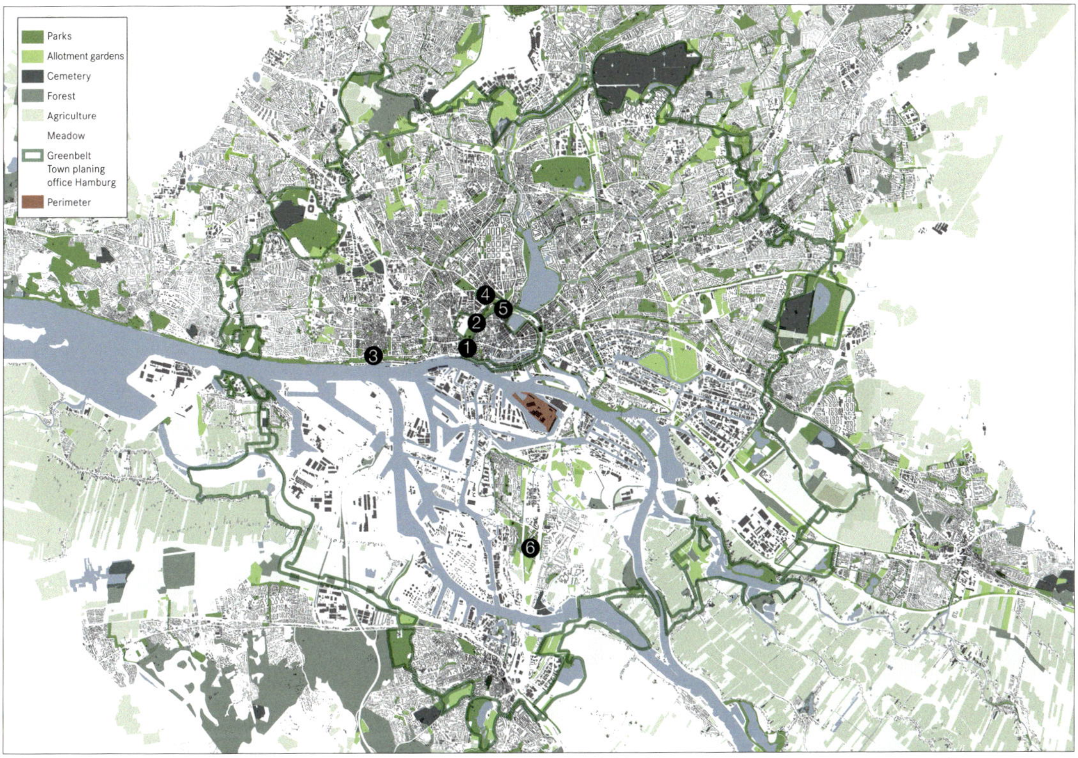

1 Alter Elbpark
2 Wallanlage
3 German Garden Festival / Donnerspark
4 Planten und Blomen
5 Old Botanical Garden
6 Fischers Park

1963: Planten un Blomen, Alter Botanischer Garten, Wallanlagen

1973: Planten und Blomen, Alter Botanischer Garten, Wallanlagen

2013: Elbinsel Wilhelmsburg

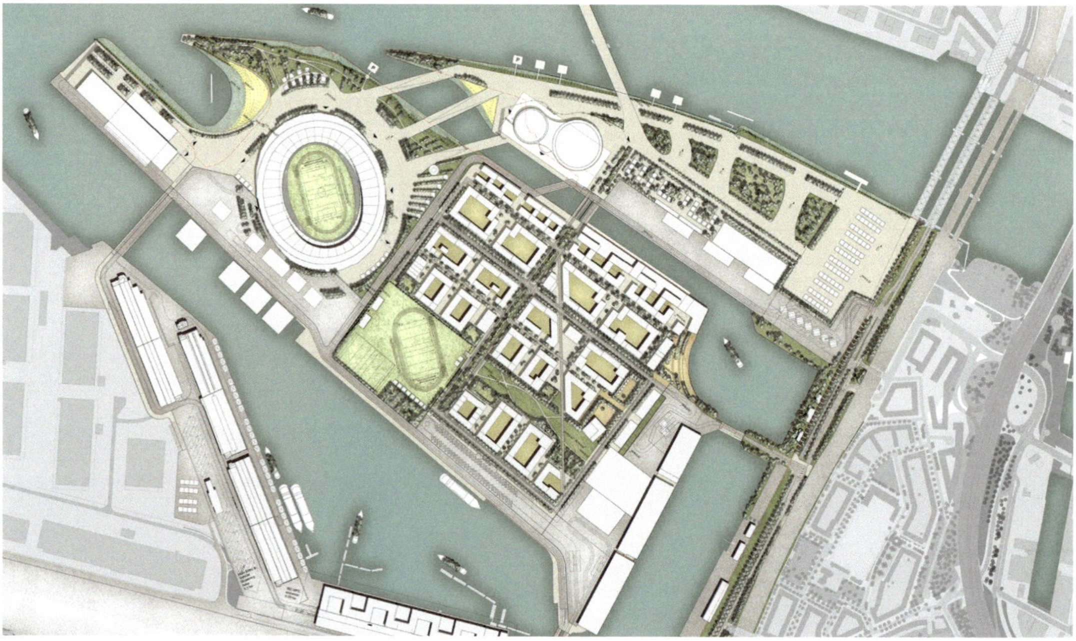

Plan of the Olympic Village for the 2024 Games

Olympia Master Plan, Hamburg
Rehabilitating the River

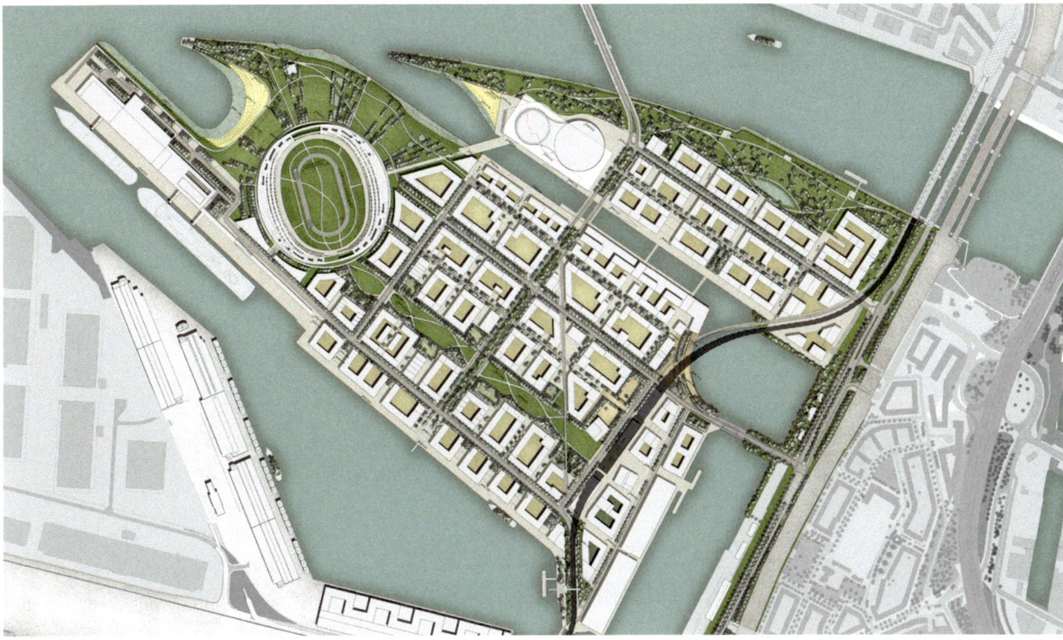

Plan of the post-Games legacy of the Olympic Village

0 50 100 200m

The Olympic Village, where the athletes and their support teams live during the Games, forms the heart of the new quarter, which should provide housing and leisure space for city residents immediately after the Games. The stadium will remain as a symbol of the Olympic Games and also be used for other purposes. The Olympic Hall will be converted into a cruise terminal and the Olympic Swimming Hall will continue as a sports and leisure pool. The basic structure of the urban development will be defined by the harbors, quays, and banks.

Les Jardins de la Tour Eiffel, Paris
Monster in the Garden

With close to seven million visitors a year, the Eiffel Tower is one of the most visited attractions in the world. The recent terror attacks in Paris called for a rethink of the site's security and the fencing off of its surroundings. This new security paradigm became an opportunity to rediscover the gardens that once lay beneath the monument. Indeed, the gardens existed years before the Eiffel Tower was built, as part of the vast ensemble of the Trocadéro–Champs de Mars, stretching from the Colline de Chaillot to the military school on the other side of the Seine. Over time, they changed in layout and composition, so much so that they began to lose their legibility and significance and were gradually forgotten. This journey back into the history of the site was also an opportunity to reflect on the possibility of a historical garden today, as well as notions of preservation, adaptation, and reproduction in landscape architecture.

Client:
DPA – Direction du patrimoine et de l'architecture, Paris
SETE – Société d'exploitation de la Tour Eiffel, Paris

Cooperation:
Architecture:
Dietmar Feichtinger Architectes, Paris

Design/construction:
2016–2017/2017–2018

Type and size:
Public garden, 2 ha

Status:
Realized

From Picturesque *Décor* to Mass Tourism

Since their inception, the grounds of the Eiffel Tower have undergone several transformations. Used successively as a *maraîchage* (a cultivation ground) and a military exercise ground, the site was turned into a garden in 1878 to accompany that year's Universal Exhibition. This original garden acted as the outline for a lasting composition of three main elements: a large clearing with paths for the promenade, two thoroughfares at the edges of the park, and two lateral basins at the lowest points, oriented and articulated to create changing landscape atmospheres. Two picturesque elements completed this *décor:* the grotto and the belvedere, both animated with waterfalls. Throughout the garden's successive transformations, these elements would always provide a sense of continuity.

During the second half of the nineteenth century, the garden evolved from decorative scenery for an exhibition to bourgeois garden, while the rest of the Champ de Mars was transformed into an urban park promenade. The most important change occurred in 1889, when the overall composition was disrupted by the construction of the Eiffel Tower inside the garden. The meeting of the 324 m tall monument with the open expanse of the Champ de Mars brought about the specific sequence known today as "the gardens of the Eiffel Tower," characterized by their relationship in scale and typology to the tower's pillars, rather than to the Trocadéro as a whole. The iron giant, recognized worldwide as the symbol of a city and of a country, rests its massive pillars in a miniature landscape.

From the beginning of the twentieth century, further transformations and the multiplication of built elements began to break up the gardens' rhythm and symmetries. Fragmented and incremental planting gradually obstructed the historical sight axis, and over the years the composition of vegetation became less legible. By 2016, when the city of Paris called for new security measures for the site, the gardens appeared exhausted and trampled. They had become almost invisible to the ever-increasing numbers of visitors and to Parisians alike.

Between Preservation, Reproduction, and Adaptation

The need to fence off the site and shift its points of access for security reasons became an opportunity to reflect generally on the extended perimeter of the grounds, while rediscovering these forgotten gardens. Indeed, despite the many iterations on the original gardens and their subsequent loss of legibility, traces of their original composition by the greatest landscapers and engineers of their time were still visible. With the help of Alphand's written legacy, some of these original features were restored, while new paths were created, allowing visitors to rediscover the architectural events dear to the landscape architects of the time: the grotto, the belvedere, the chimney, the fountain– the subtle play of the excavated *rocaille,* the planted masses and topography that seem to have been there forever. In a carefully designed choreography of interwoven scales, the visitor's focus wanders from the details of this miniature landscape up to the giant iron monument and to its extended urban setting, perceptible through the surrounding transparent walls.

Blurring the boundaries between existing and new, the project does not aim to preserve a static historical object or to formally restore the site to its previous state. Instead, it emphasizes the very notion of continuity and change in the garden, adding a new layer of meaning to the history of the place. (lb)

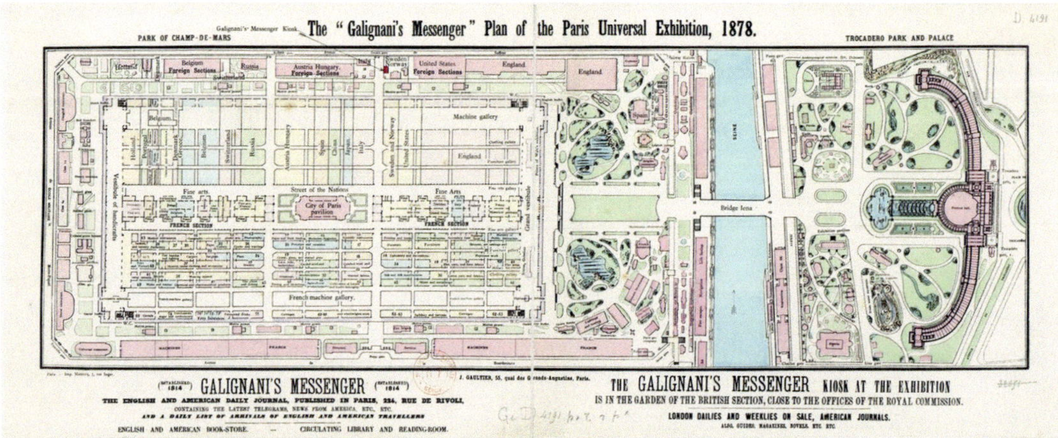

The bourgeois garden
The gardens existed before the construction of the Eiffel Tower, as part of an ensemble designed for the 1878 exhibition, along with the Jardins du Trocadéro. The two bodies of water at the lowest points and the *rocaille* constituted by the grotto and the belvedere have survived to this day.

Monument for the 308

Andreas Greiner, 2016

Monument for a Contemporary Dinosaur

A common broiler chicken of the type ROSS 308 was x-rayed to create a 3-D rendering of its skeleton. For the exhibition *Agency of the Exponent* at the Berlinische Galerie, a 20:1 scaled 3-D print of the chicken's skeleton was created. The resulting monumental sculpture resembles a dinosaur in a natural history museum–except that this animal is not extinct like its prehistoric ancestor, the *Archaeopteryx*.

Today, broilers are bred in staggering numbers with their anatomy manipulated to cater to human meat consumption. The 20:1 enlargement applied for *Monument for the 308* makes this human fingerprint explicit and acknowledges the two species' mutual dependency.

In collaboration with Dr. Markus Lahr,
TH Wildau (ViNN:Lab)

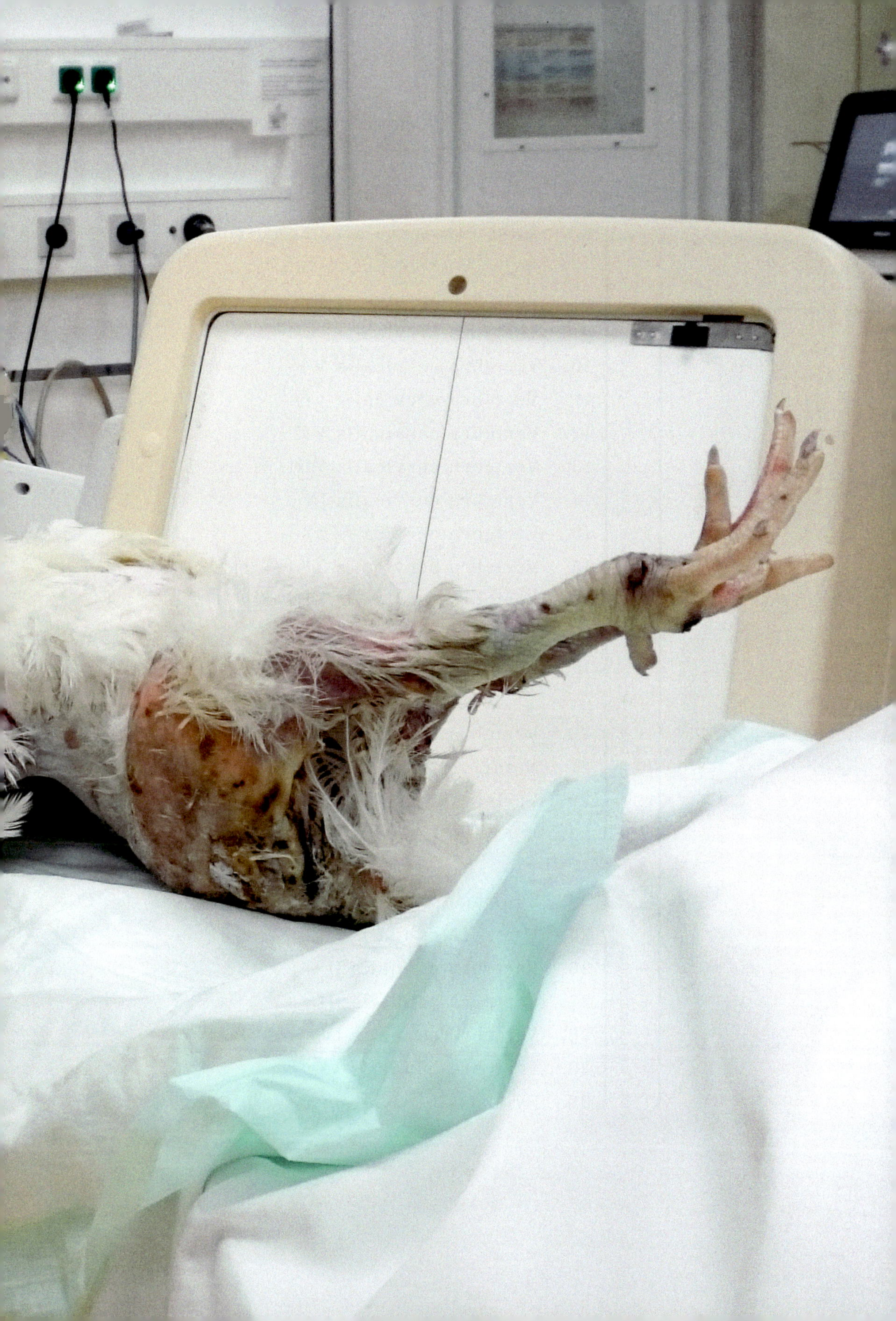

COLUMNA VERTEBRALIS

VERTEBRAE CERVICALES

6. Atlas (Vertebra cervicalis I)
7. Axis (Vertebra cervicalis II)
8. Vertebra cervicalis III
9. Vertebra cervicalis IV
10. Vertebra cervicalis V
11. Vertebra cervicalis VI
12. Vertebra cervicalis VII
13. Vertebra cervicalis VIII
14. Vertebra cervicalis IX
15. Vertebra cervicalis X
16. Vertebra cervicalis XI
17. Vertebra cervicalis XII
18. Vertebra cervicalis XIII
19. Vertebra cervicalis XIV

VERTEBRAE THORACICAE

20. Vertebra thoracalis I
21. Notarium
22. Vertebra thoracalis VI
23. Vertebra thoracalis VII

24. Synsacrum

VERTEBRAE CAUDALES

25. Vertebra caudalis I
26. Vertebra caudalis II
27. Vertebra caudalis III
28. Vertebra caudalis IV
29. Vertebra caudalis V
30. Pygostyl

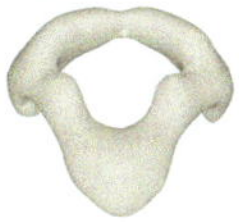

6.

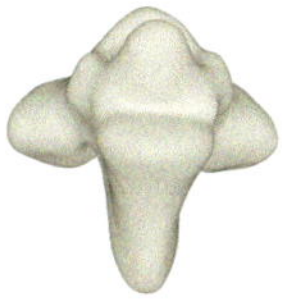

7.

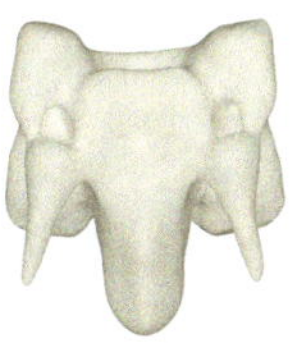

8.

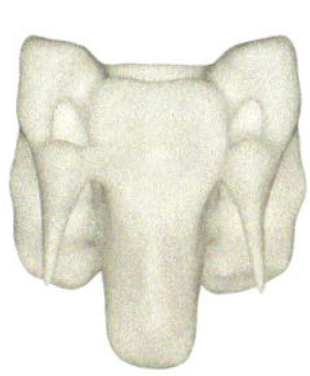

9.

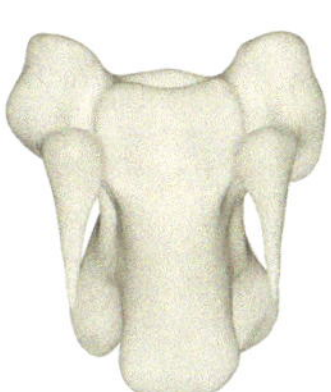

10.

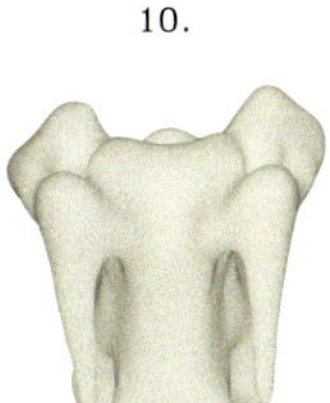

11.

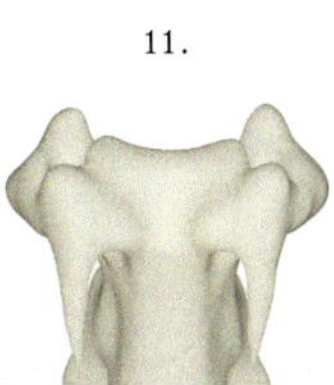

12.

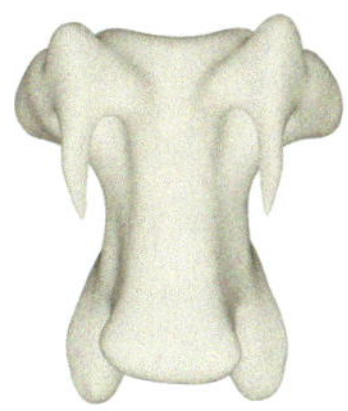

13.

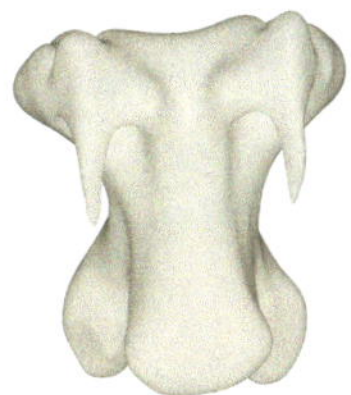

14.

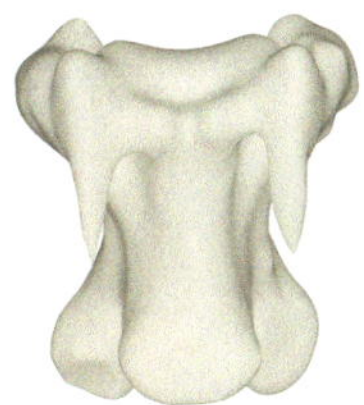

15.

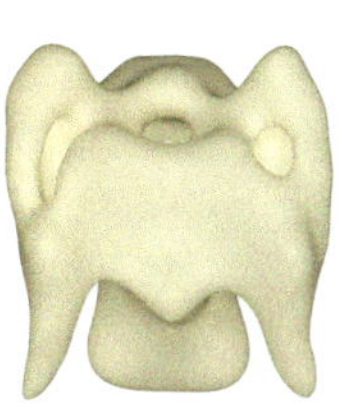

16.

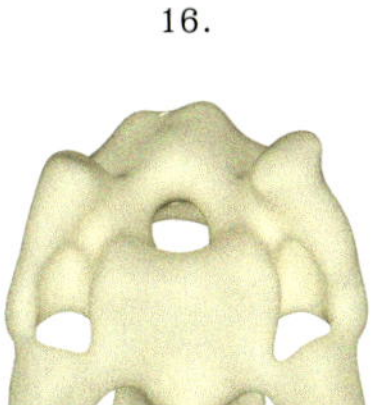

17.

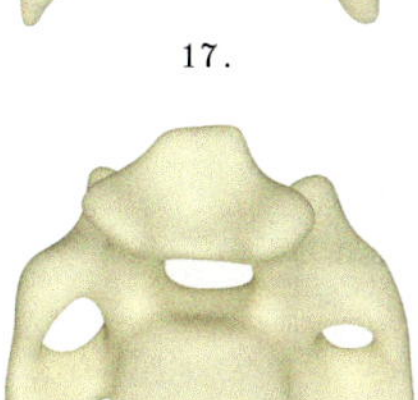

18.

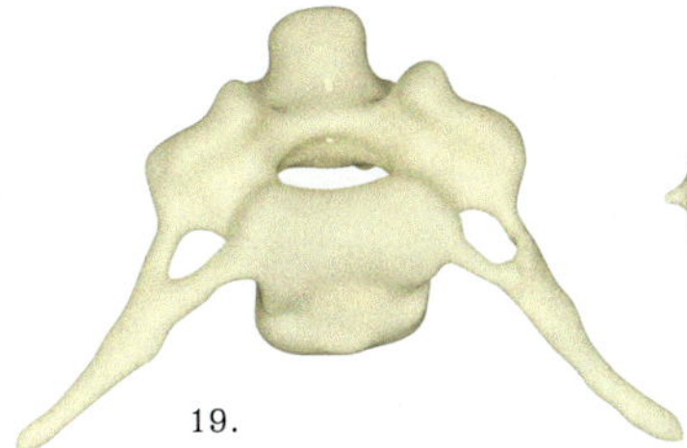

19.

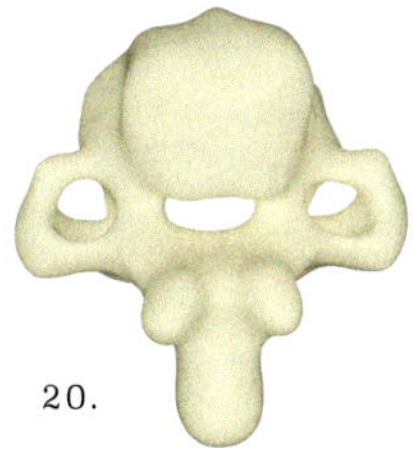

20.

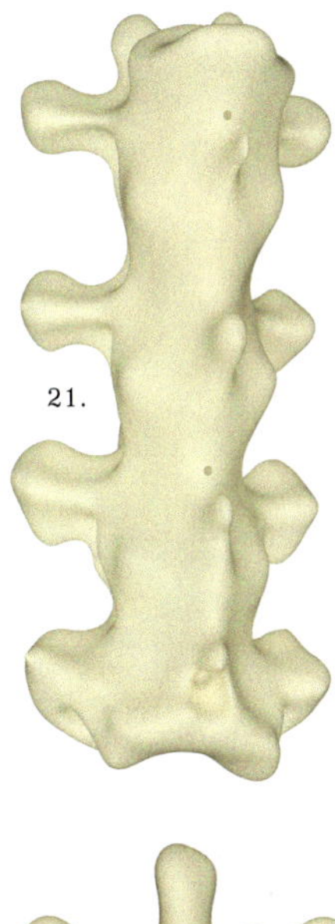

21.

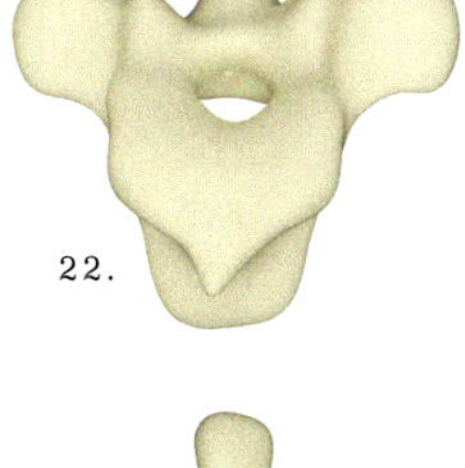

22.

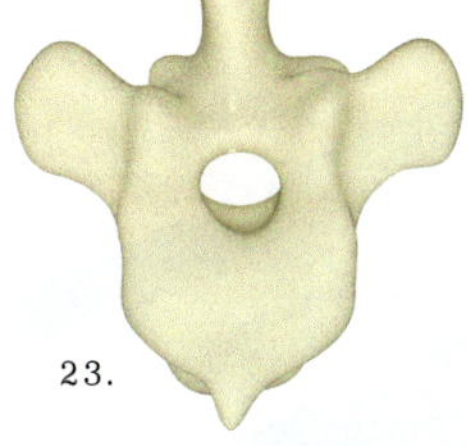

23.

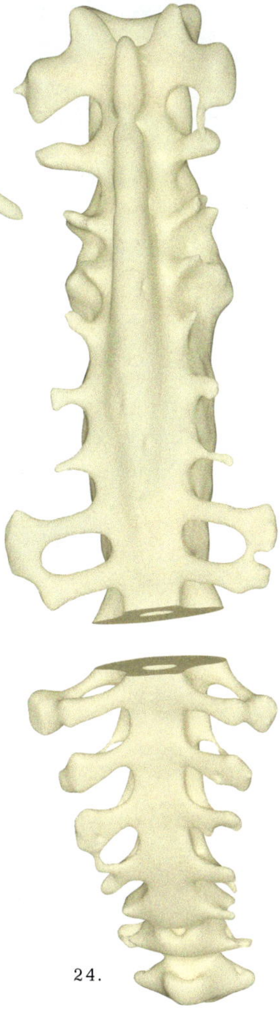

24.

25.

28.

26.

29.

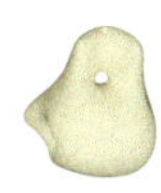

27.

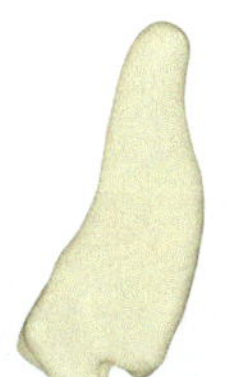

30.

67

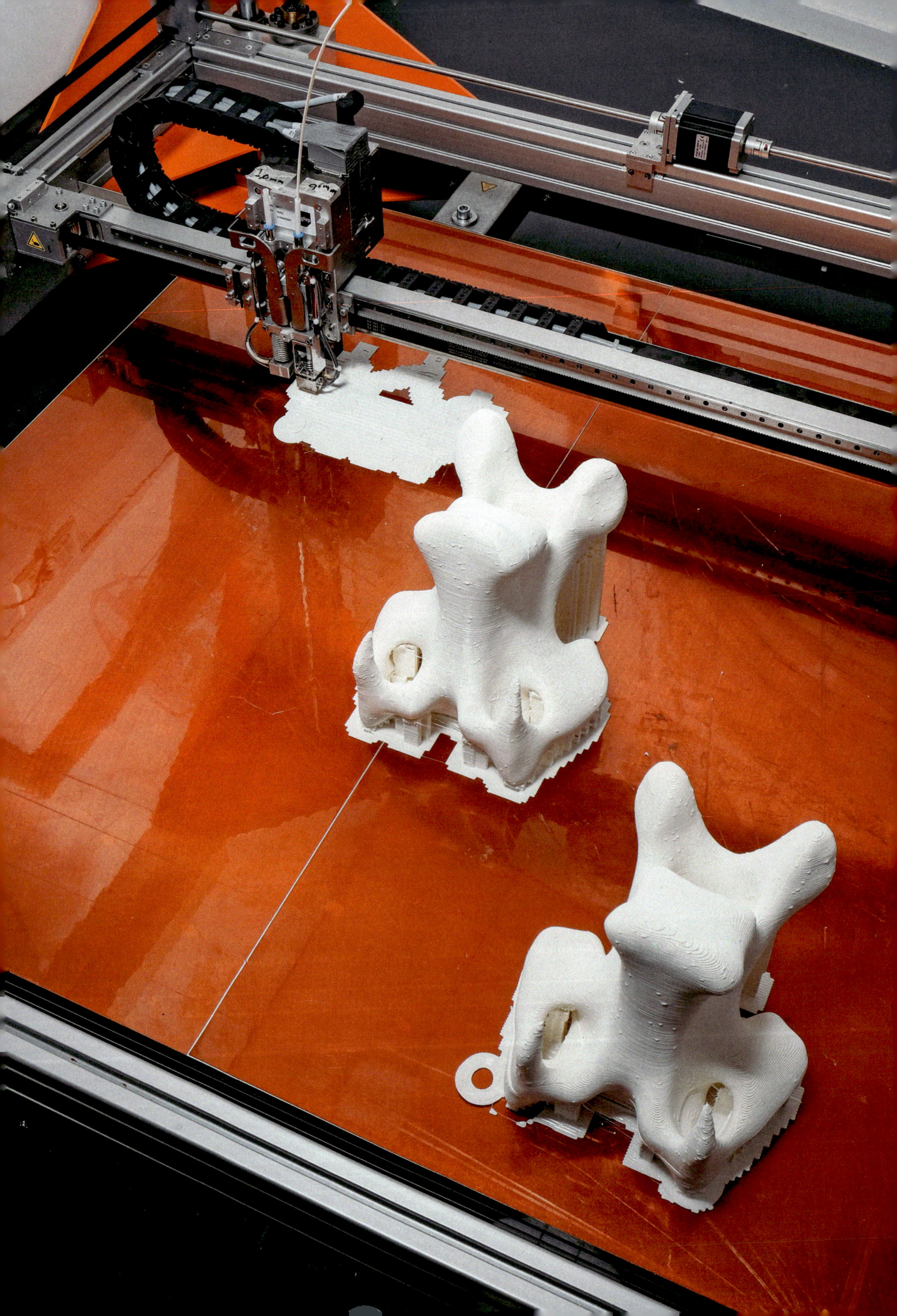

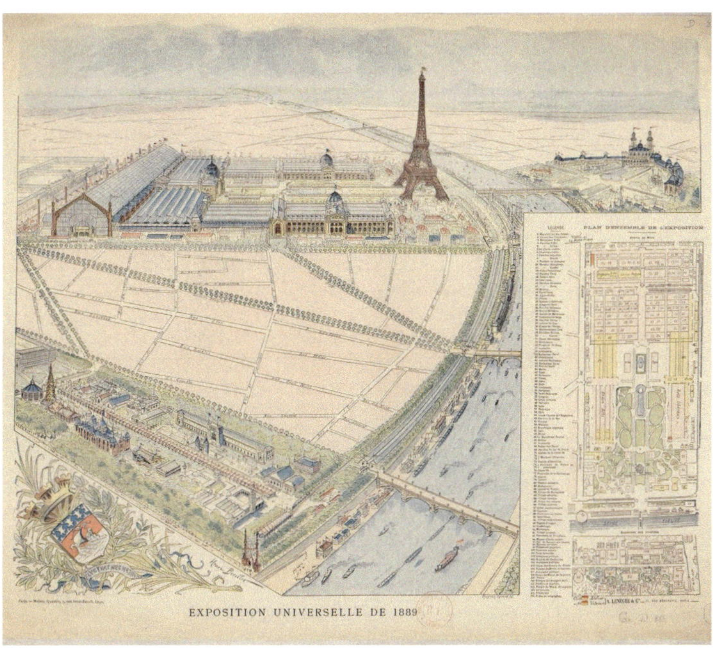

Monster in the garden
The construction of the Eiffel Tower for the 1889 Universal Exhibition disrupts the gardens' composition and visitors' perception of them. The massive pillars of the iron giant collide with the scale of the picturesque gardens below, while blocking oblique views through the space.

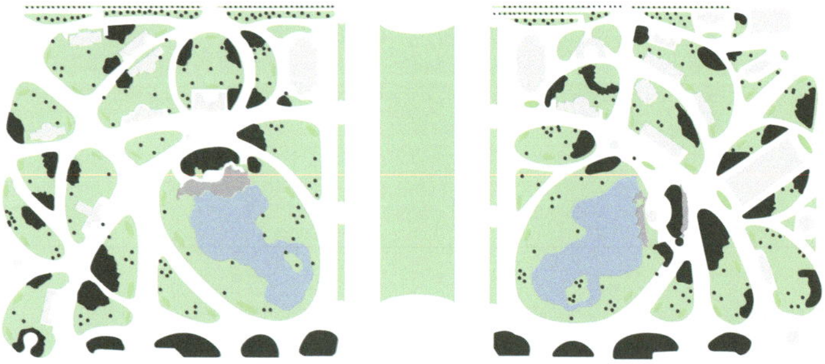

1878: Temporary gardens for the Universal Exhibition–Alphand, Hardy, Viollet-le-Duc
The first iteration of the gardens is created as a backdrop for the Universal Exhibition of 1878. Structured by two main axes, the design consists of a large central parterre, with two bodies of water at the lowest points. Two picturesque elements, the grotto and the belvedere, complete this *décor.*

1882: From decorative garden to bourgeois park–Bartet
Once the Universal Exhibition of 1878 is over, the gardens are transformed into a park for the public. Bartet introduces elliptical paths dedicated to strolling, and structuring plant typologies consisting of a herbaceous layer (for openings and clearing), a shrub layer (to articulate the architectural elements), and groupings of trees.

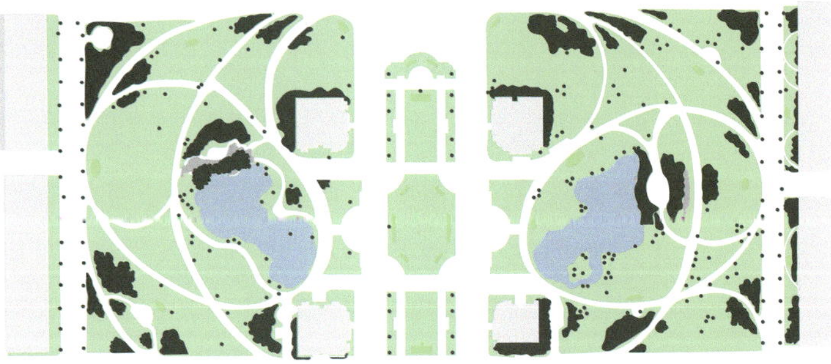

1902: Monster in the garden–Vacherot
With the construction of the Eiffel Tower in 1889, the gardens' composition is disrupted: a square of one hectare is laid out between the pillars, impacting the plantations and pathways below. While the lakes are preserved, the oblique views that defined the initial composition of the garden are blocked. At the same time, the Champ de Mars is transformed into an urban park.

1909: Bridle paths–Forestier
Under Forestier, the gardens are reworked once more and reincorporated into the composition of the Champ de Mars with the introduction of bridle paths (*allées cavalières*). Although they truncate the elliptical paths, Forestier takes care to preserve the principles of the gardens' composition: the axial views and the design of the openings.

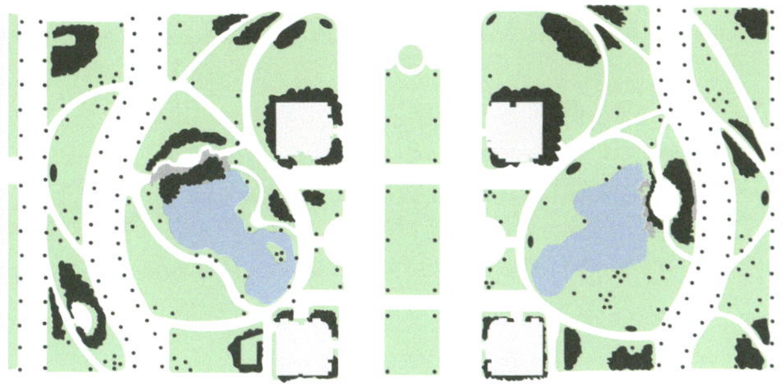

2016: Loss of legibility
The rest of the twentieth century witnesses a series of slow and progressive changes in the gardens' composition, resulting in a loss of legibility. The multiplication of architectural elements gradually erodes the gardens' rhythm and symmetries, while the parterres of the central axis are eventually replaced by a bituminous surface. The exponential number of visitors also contributes to the gardens' degradation. Nevertheless, the lateral parts of the gardens have undergone the least transformations and some of their original qualities persist.

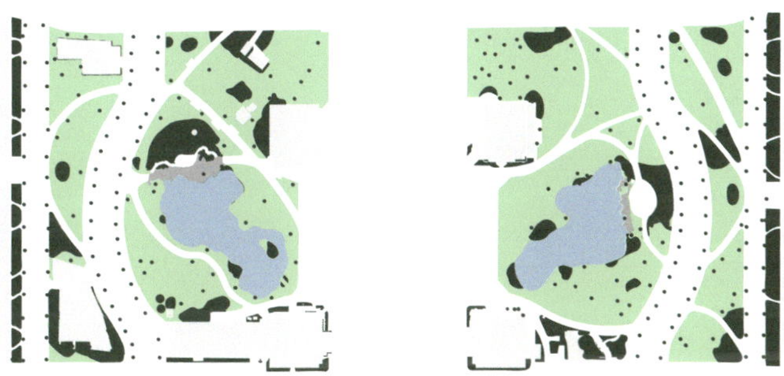

2018: Rediscovering the gardens
New security measures for the site are put in place, shifting access to the tower to the lateral sides. The gardens' composition is clarified: obstructed visual axes are reinstated, and the planting arrangements are restructured. The gardens' cherished features become visible to the *flâneur*, who is once again able to notice their details: paths disappear in the topography, giving an illusion of floating on the lawn, and the waterfalls run once again, their swoosh and spectacle accompanying the promenade. New rockery elements are installed, highlighting the grotto and the belvedere.

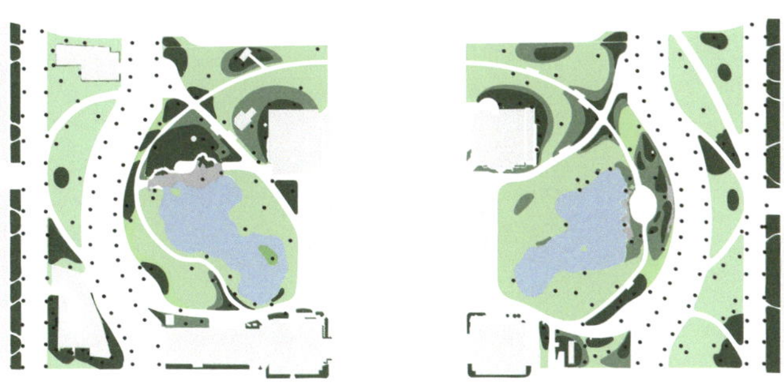

>> **Historical toolkit**
Two key texts, *Parcs et Jardins: Album d'études* by Jules Vacherot (1925) and *Les Promenades de Paris* by Adolphe Alphand (1867–1873), were used to create a toolkit of design strategies inspired directly by the design of the original gardens. These strategies were then adapted to the project's contemporary needs.

a a et un fusain duc d'Anjou *b* (fig. 116) ; ou encore 3 mahonias *a a a* et 2 fusains duc d'Anjou *b b* (fig. 117) ; ou toute autre combinaison analogue.

Fig. 114.

Fig. 115.

Fig. 116.

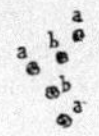

Fig. 117.

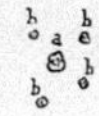

Fig. 118.

Il est à remarquer que les arbustes ne se groupent bien que par 3 ou par 5 et

Fig. 119. — Plantation en décrochement.

qu'on ne peut avantageusement les employer par quatre que pour accompagner un isolé (fig. 118), isolé *a* arbustes d'accompagnement *b b — b b*.

Dans les jardins de ville de peu d'étendue, les parties extérieures d'un massif, c'est-à-dire celles situées du côté du gazon, peuvent, comme nous l'avons vu, en être séparées par une zone fleurie. Dans ce cas, la plantation en bordure du massif se fait régulièrement suivant une courbe, et la zone de fleurs le borde également régulièrement (fig. 120). Nous ne condamnons pas ce procédé ; mais nous n'en préconisons nullement l'emploi et nous préférons, pour avoir de la fleur, la plantation en décrochement, suivant les principes établis plus haut, d'un nombre suffisant de plantes vivaces, de préférence, ou seulement annuelles.

Lorsqu'il s'agit d'un massif divisé en deux par une allée (fig. 121), l'habitude fait qu'on plante des végétaux de bordures des deux côtés de l'allée (*a b* et *a' b'*) constituant ainsi deux massifs distincts *x* et *x'*, coupe *m n* (fig. 122).

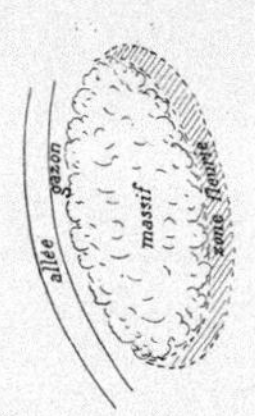

Fig. 120.

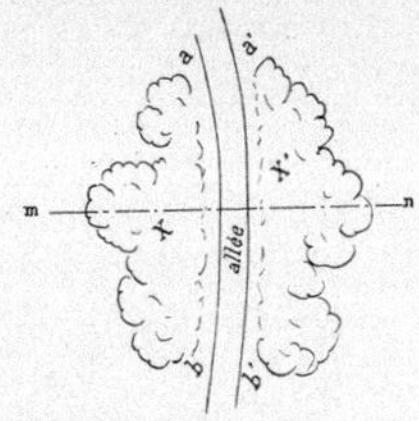

Fig. 121.

A notre avis, c'est un non-sens : les massifs *x* et *x'* doivent être considérés comme deux tronçons d'un seul massif coupé par une allée et, dans ces conditions, on

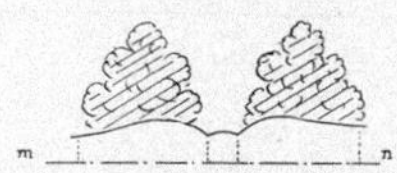

Fig. 122.

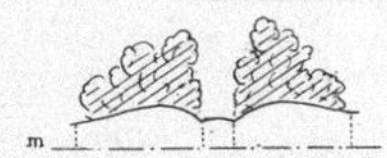

Fig. 123.

doit s'efforcer de lui conserver son mouvement d'ensemble (fig. 123, coupe *m n*) en plantant des végétaux d'intérieur en bordure des deux côtés de l'allée, ainsi que des arbres de première grandeur formant le fond du massif (fig. 124) et en réservant les plantes de bordure pour les côtés extérieurs *a c b* et *a' c' b'* (même figure).

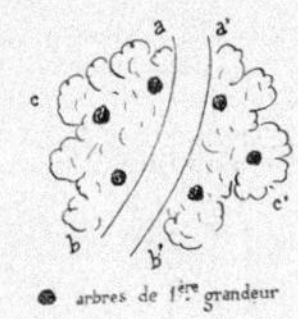

Fig. 124.

12° *Conclusion.* — Les arbres, les arbrisseaux et les arbustes étant les principaux matériaux qui entrent dans la composition des massifs, on doit les employer de façon à en tirer le plus d'avantages possible pour donner aux masses des plantations plus ou moins de profondeur, plus ou moins d'élévation. Ici, elles pourront être irrégulièrement arrondies ; là, plus allongées, plus

travers d'une pelouse ou dans un point de vue, de dissimuler sa présence, du moins pour le promeneur placé à une certaine distance, et d'éviter ainsi d'interrompre, par une coupure trop visible et désagréable, la pelouse ou le point de vue traversé. Il assure de plus l'écoulement rationnel des eaux en formant, par les bordures et par le bombement de l'allée, deux canivaux naturels — en *a* et en *b*

Fig. 372.

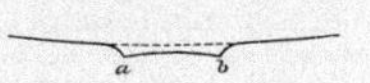

Fig. 373.

(fig. 373) — où se dépose le sable entraîné sans que les eaux se répandent sur le gazon.

L'encaissement a, en outre, l'avantage de limiter par un filet de gazon chaque côté de l'allée, de sorte que, pour le découpage du gazon, le jardinier n'est pas obligé de tracer de nouveau son allée à chaque fois, ce qu'il fait généralement mal. Il n'a qu'à suivre la ligne du filet (fig. 374).

Ce découpage est toujours plus propre que le découpage fait à plat ; il se tient mieux et limite d'une façon plus nette le tracé de l'allée.

La hauteur de bordure fixée par la pratique sur un terrain plat ou peu vallonné varie, sur pelouse, de 0m,17 à 0m,20 et, sur massif, de 0,m40 à 0m60 et même plus suivant l'importance du bombement des terres. Le raccordement de cette bordure

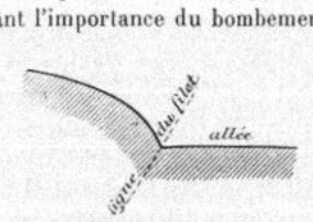

Fig. 374.

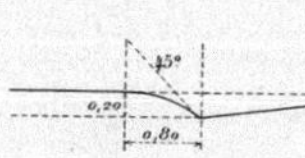

Fig. 375.

entre l'allée et la pelouse doit être fait, ainsi que nous l'avons déjà dit, par une courbe convexe allongée, partant à 45° de la limite de l'allée pour aller se raccorder à 0m,70 ou 1 mètre de là, tangentiellement à la pelouse (fig. 375).

Une allée doit toujours présenter sur son nivellement transversal entre les bordures qui la limitent un léger bombement qui augmente ou diminue suivant que le terrain est plus ou moins horizontal.

e) **Empierrement des allées.** — Les allées carrossables doivent autant que possible être empierrées. On peut s'en dispenser dans les allées d'un domaine ou d'un parc éloignées de l'habitation si le terrain présente, en lui-même, assez de consistance ou si le passage des voitures n'y est qu'accidentel.

L'allée d'arrivée et l'allée desservant les communs, où la circulation est plus active, doivent toujours être empierrées quelle que soit la nature du sol.

Lorsque l'allée empierrée présente une rampe assez forte, il est nécessaire de prendre la précaution de limiter cette allée de chaque côté par un caniveau fait de matériaux plus solides que la route (pavage ou ciment) (voir coupes ci-dessus fig. 376).

Les allées secondaires ne sont habituellement empierrées que dans le cas où les matériaux nécessaires abondent ; ces matériaux doivent alors être autant que possible susceptibles de s'agréger d'eux-mêmes sans nécessiter un cylindrage.

L'assainissement est presque indispensable pour les allées proches de l'habitation, pour celles qui sont les plus fréquentées ou pour les allées d'un petit jardin spécial tel que roseraie, jardin français, jardin de plantes vivaces ou autres et jardin d'orangerie. On peut employer pour cet assainissement les matériaux provenant de la démolition de vieux murs ou de vieilles constructions et, surtout, les

Coupe avec 1/2 caniveau. Coupe avec caniveau.

Fig. 376.

plâtras, les pierres et cailloux trouvés dans les déblais, les vieilles tuiles ou briques cassées, les résidus de cuisson de fours à briques, et, plus particulièrement et de préférence à tout, le mâchefer.

Pour les jardins spéciaux, on peut pousser le luxe jusqu'à créer un revêtement des allées en briques seulement posées sur champ ou à plat, ou disposées et juxtaposées de façon à former des dessins ; on peut aussi faire un dallage en ciment ou en pierre, voire même en marbre, amenant une réminiscence des jardins de la Renaissance italienne ; mais nous croyons nécessaire de limiter l'emploi de ces revêtements spéciaux à ces seuls jardins. Toutefois, ils peuvent encore être utilement employés pour indiquer au promeneur le chemin à suivre à travers une vaste cour d'honneur ou un terre-plein, de façon à lui éviter le contact peu agréable d'une surface gravillonnée destinée au passage des voitures, et nous n'hésitons pas à en conseiller l'usage sur un terrain très glaiseux, pour des cours de service et pour des allées très fréquentées et dans un rayon restreint.

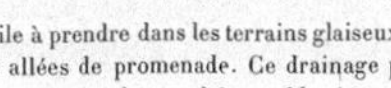

Fig. 377.

Une précaution utile à prendre dans les terrains glaiseux est le drainage, sur leur côté le plus bas, des allées de promenade. Ce drainage peut, dans la plupart des cas, être constitué par une simple tranchée remblayée en pierres roulantes, ayant de 0m,30 de largeur ou davantage, suivant l'importance de l'allée et l'abondance des matériaux, et une profondeur minimum de 0,m40 (fig. 377).

On emploie généralement pour l'empierrement des allées d'un parc des cailloux

Fig. 237. — Roches d'imitation (Bancs de carrière).

le reste de la composition, ce sont eux qui rendent admirables les irrégularités les plus bizarres des mouvements de terrain, les méandres les plus extraordinaires d'un ruisseau ou d'un torrent.

2° *Rochers d'imitation ou artificiels.* — Dans ses diversités de formes et de manière,

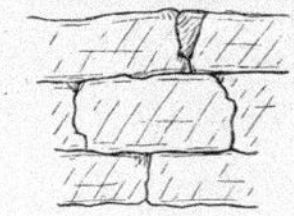

Fig. 238.

Fig. 239.

la nature semble avoir, en toute circonstance, présenté les rochers sous trois aspects qui les distinguent plus particulièrement :

Ils sont en assises horizontales (fig. 234), en assises verticales (fig. 235) et en masses roulées (fig. 236).

Partant de ce principe, on divise les rochers artificiels en trois catégories :

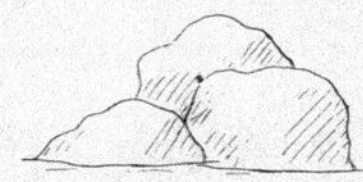

Fig. 240.

1° Rochers dits « bancs de carrière » en assises horizontales (fig. 237, 238 et 241) ;
2° Rochers en assises verticales ou inclinées (fig 239) ;
3° Rochers en blocs détachés ou roulés (fig. 240).

L'emplacement choisi pour un rocher artificiel doit, autant que possible, se rapprocher de l'emplacement qu'il aurait occupé dans la nature.

Il peut devenir obligatoire de relever fortement l'extrémité d'une perspective ou d'un coin de terrain en amenant le rocher à former le soutènement naturel des terres de remblai, tout en paraissant avoir été mis à nu par le déblai (fig. 243).

Il peut aussi servir de soubassement à un réservoir, à un kiosque-abri (fig. 244), à un belvédère ou à une terrasse (fig. 245).

Il peut enfin justifier une chute d'eau, une source, un barrage dans une rivière etc., et même déterminer entièrement le caractère d'un jardin (jardin alpin).

S'il doit laisser échapper une source, il ne faut pas se contenter d'élever à

pouvant cependant se rencontrer au pied de la terrasse. — Ces deux dernières sortes de roches doivent être utilisées de préférence dans les ravins ou émergeant des gazons et des plantations sur les flancs des pentes.

Les bancs en assises verticales peuvent saillir à l'extrémité d'un promontoire

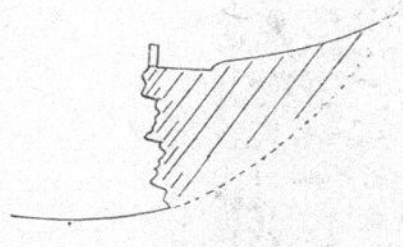

Fig. 245.

Fig. 246 (Schéma).

et servir de support à une construction isolée. Ils peuvent s'employer isolés eux-mêmes en gros blocs comme s'ils sortaient du sol ou avaient été découverts par

Fig. 247 (Schéma).

des déblais : leur présence est toujours admise sur une hauteur, mais jamais dans les points bas.

Les barrages de pièces d'eau ne peuvent être faits logiquement que par des blocs roulés ; on admet difficilement, à moins d'une chute assez élevée, des bancs de carrière ou des assises verticales pour cet usage ; une source ou une chute d'eau peut se frayer un chemin au sommet d'assises horizontales ou même à travers les fentes d'assises verticales, mais un arrêt d'eau dans un courant ne peut se produire que par un soulèvement qui doit toujours être représenté par des blocs roulés.

c) *Plantation des rochers.* — Des rochers sans plantes pour les garnir ne peuvent

Fig. 248. — Un barrage.

Fig. 249. — Plantation de rochers.

être intéressants que d'une façon tout à fait passagère ; des rochers plantés sont, au contraire, constamment intéressants.

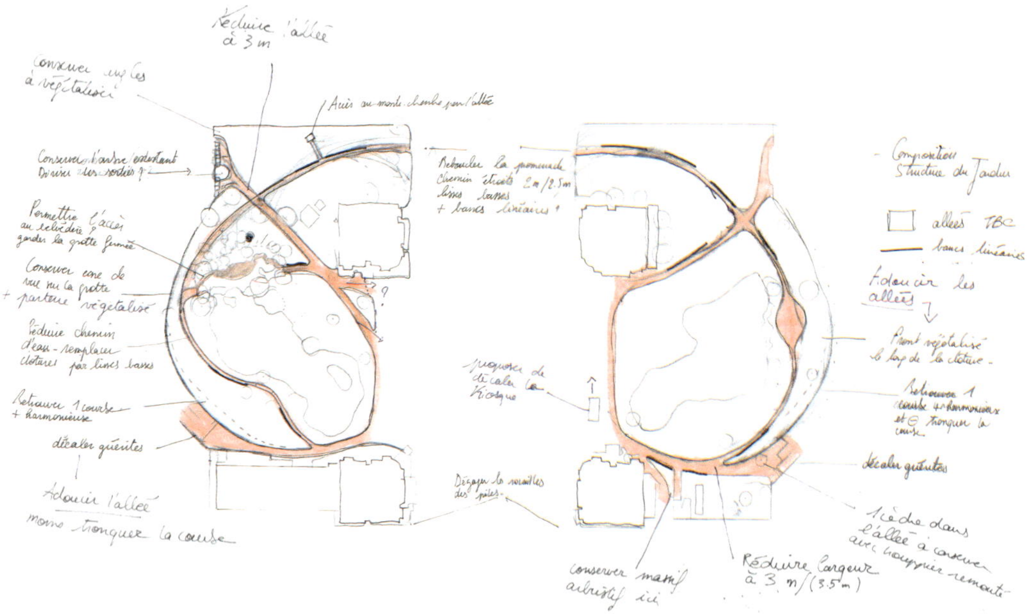

Circulation

The new access points are integrated to stage the arrival to the monument. First, the visitors are gently guided under the linden tree canopy of the curved bridle paths toward the entrances. Once in the garden, they follow the new wide paths curving toward the tower. This progression provides a new experience: the discovery of, first, the gardens and then the tower.

In the garden, two elliptical paths form a new loop enabling a stroll through the forgotten scenic elements, in a reinterpretation of the historical plans. The paths leading to the exit reconnect with the existing rights of way of the bridle paths and encourage the sense of flow toward the Seine.

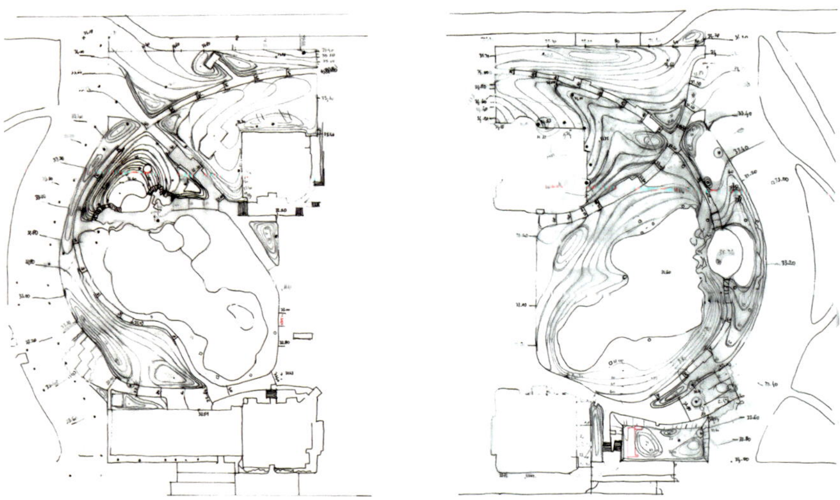

Topography

A sophisticated topography animates the terrain of the gardens in coherence with the existing movement of the site. The entrance paths located at the highest point overlook the gardens, while at the lowest points the concrete edges of the lakes are revealed, their smooth, horizontal surface once again able to reflect the full verticality of the towering monument. A micro-topography enhances the gardens' details: the paths are concealed by *bombés* in the grass, and *corbeilles* planted with flowers are raised on small mounds.

Planting

The planting strategy aims to recover the compositional characteristics of the gardens. The targeted reorganization of plantings reinforces the historical open spaces that form the basic structure of the gardens. The eye is hooked by the diverse mixtures of plants gracefully adjusted to evoke miniature landscapes scenes, from the conifer hill hiding the chimney behind the grotto to *corbeilles*. The latter are a final echo of the elliptic movements of the garden, anchoring the visitor in a picturesque reality that showcases the seasonality of a variety of flowers.

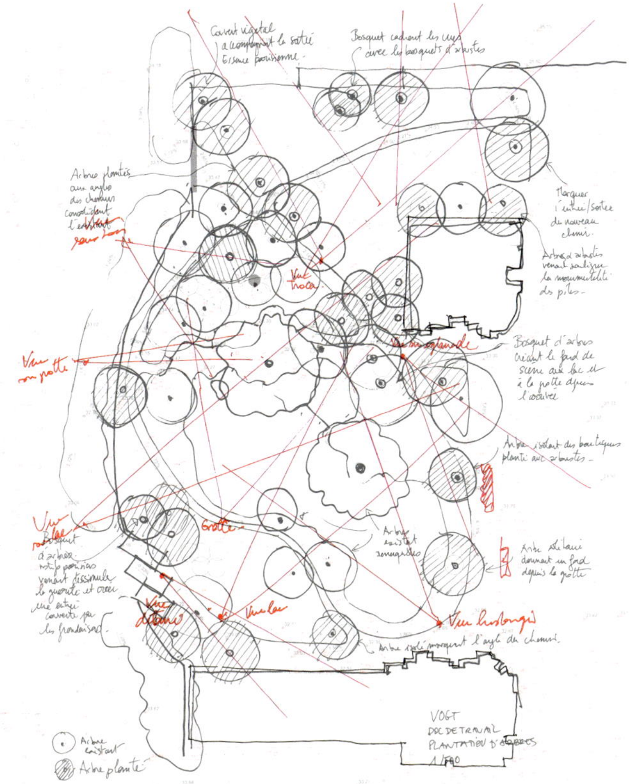

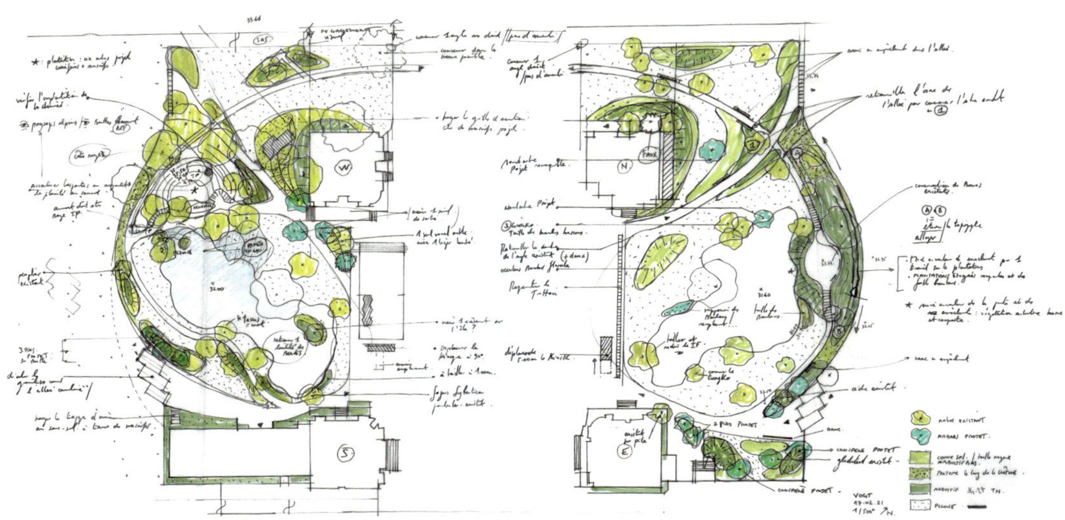

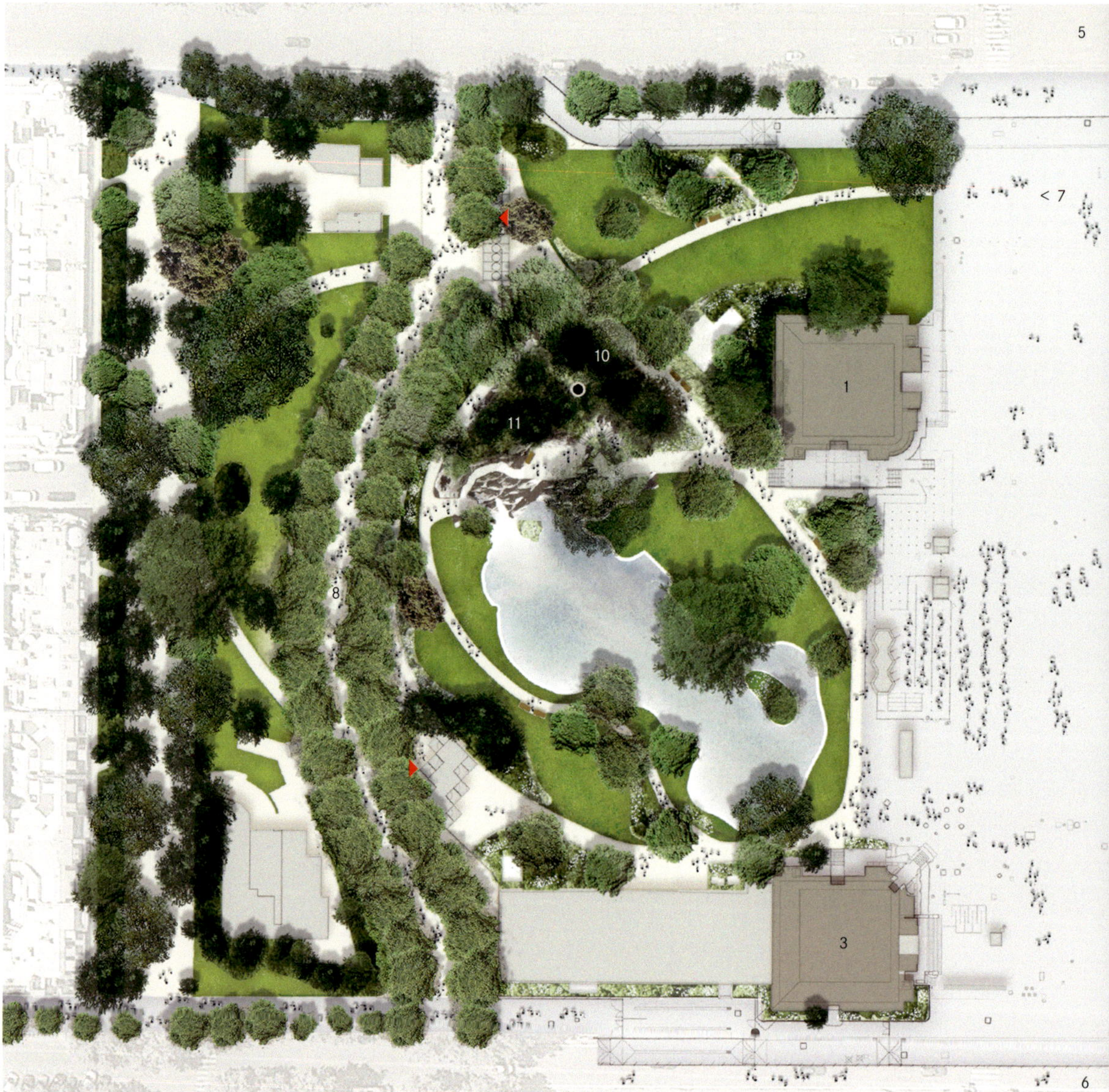

1 West pillar
2 North pillar
3 South pillar
4 East pillar
5 Quai Branly
6 Avenue Gustave Eiffel
7 New interior pathways
8 Allée des Refuzniks
9 Allée Paulhan
10 Chimney
11 Grotto
12 Belvedere

Les Jardins de la Tour Eiffel, Paris
Monster in the Garden

> The belvedere balustrade is constructed in accordance with the historical process used at the time the initial gardens were laid out. Cement is first roughly applied to a wire frame-work constructed on-site. Then a second sculpted layer is carved in carefully to give the balustrade a rustic feel.

New paths work in conjunction with the topography, allowing the gardens to reveal their scenic qualities. Disappearing in a subtle play of leveling, these paths, bordered by cast-iron arches, follow the tradition of bourgeois gardens, inviting the visitor to stroll at leisure.

“The ‘bricoleur’ is adept at performing a large number of diverse tasks; but, unlike the engineer, he does not subordinate each of them to the availability of raw materials and tools conceived and procured for the purpose of the project. His universe of instruments is closed and the rules of his game are always to make do with ‘whatever is at hand’ [. . .].”

Claude Lévi-Strauss, *The Savage Mind*

Limestone
City of Stone

Laure Baretaud
Maria Alexandrescu

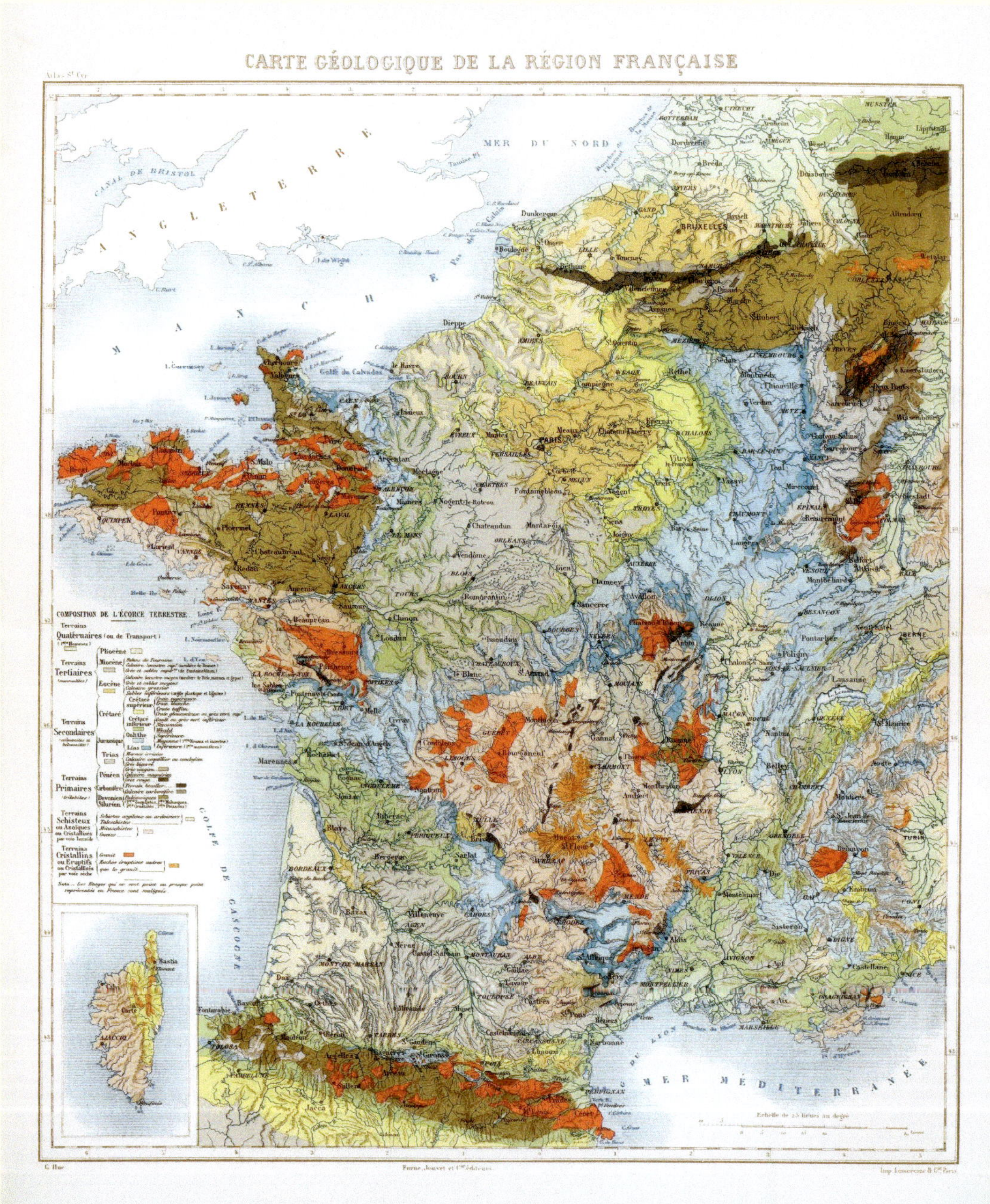

Geological map of the French region from 1882. It illustrates the richness and variety of France's geology: granite in the Alps and Brittany, marble in the Pyrenees, limestone in Jura.

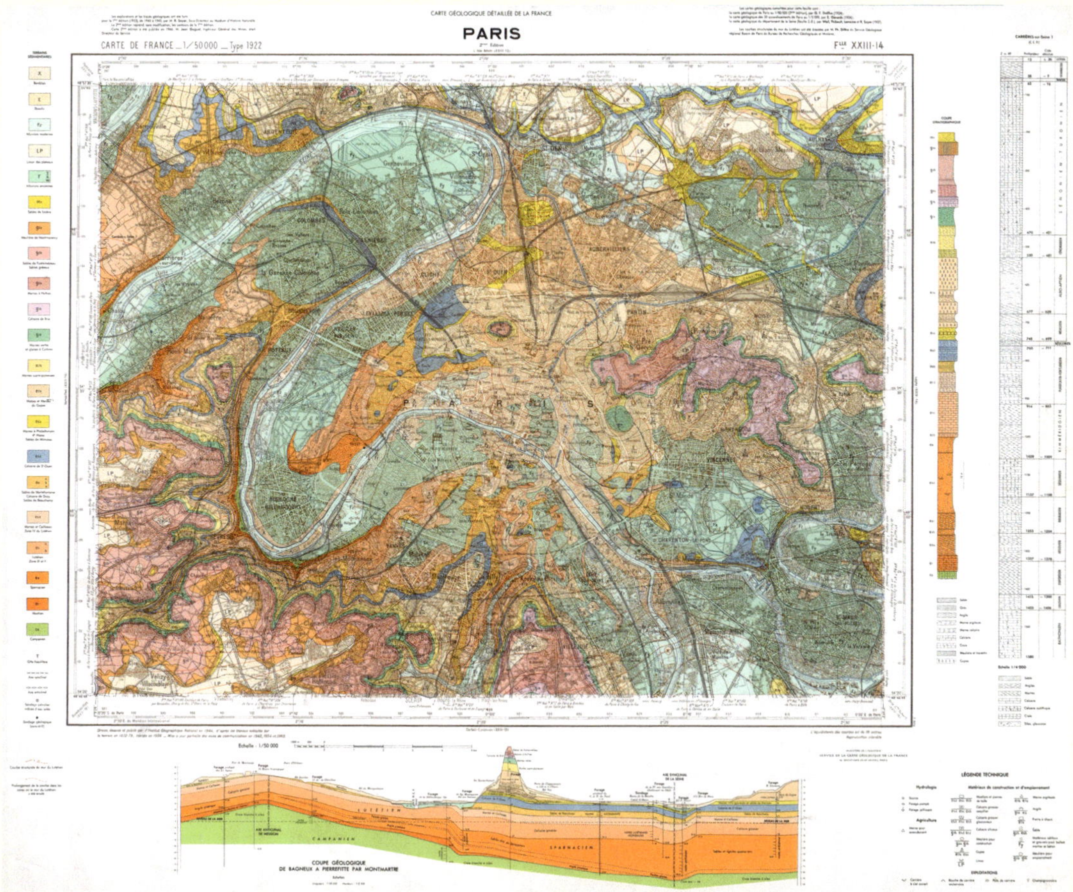

Geological map of Paris, 1966

Lutetia

In France, intense tectonics and volcanic activity, coupled with thousands of years of sedimentation and changing climatic conditions, have resulted in a particularly rich and diverse geological heritage. The terrain is structured by three large ensembles of rocks: igneous rocks, such as blue granite in Brittany, form 12 percent of Metropolitan France, while metamorphic rocks, such as Arudy marble in the Pyrenees, account for 11 percent. The largest share, however, consists of sedimentary rocks, such as the limestone found in Jura and in the Parisian basin, which cover nearly 77 percent of the territory.[1] Unlike the majority of limestone in France, formed from the forests of the Jurassic period,

Illustration of the Carboniferous landscape (358–298 million years ago): the time of great forests formed much of the limestone found in France. The limestone of the Parisian basin, however, was formed during the flooding events of the Eocene (55.6–33.9 million years ago).

Map showing the extent of the sea at the start of the Eocene period, compared with the maritime boundaries today

> Fossils found in Parisian limestone. From the Atlas by Cuvier and Brongniart, 1835.

the limestone of the Parisian basin was formed by the sedimentation of the sea during the tertiary period, giving a different grain and distinct characteristics to the resulting stones.

Approximately forty-five million years ago, during the period called the Eocene, the area stretching between Paris and London was the bottom of a gulf that extended inland all the way from the English Channel. Over the following couple million years, larger geological fluctuations caused the warm tropical sea to recede on three occasions and then return again to the Parisian area. Each subsequent flooding brought in sea creatures and new sediments with shells deposited at the bottom of the sea. When the sea retreated, the basin was engulfed by shallow lakes and marshes, layering in further deposits of sedimentation. This process generated

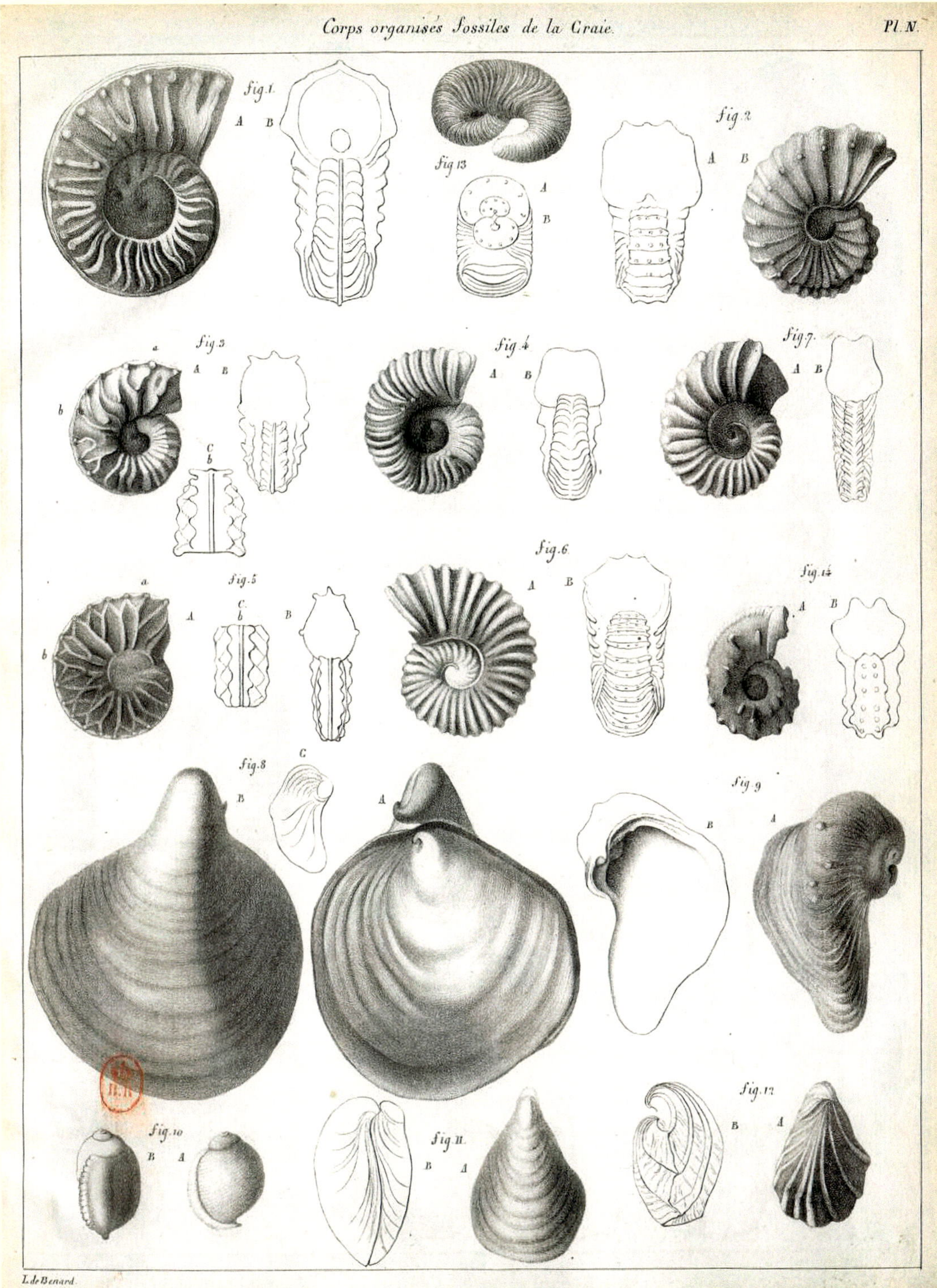
Corps organisés fossiles de la Craie.
Pl. N.
L. de Benard.

the limestone, gypsum, and marl present today. This geological formation, specific to Paris, is called "lutetian," in reference to the Roman name for the city, Lutetia.

As Louis-Laurent Simonin pointed out in his *Histoire de la terre,* "London and Paris lie on the same bed of clay. However, the London Basin emerged from the sea before its Paris counterpart, never to be re-engulfed, whereas the neighboring Paris Basin was immersed and then resurfaced several times, gaining a new sedimentary base on each occasion. It is for this reason that Paris is a city of stone, while London is a city of brick."[2]

Guettard's map of the calcareous basin stretching between England and France, 1746

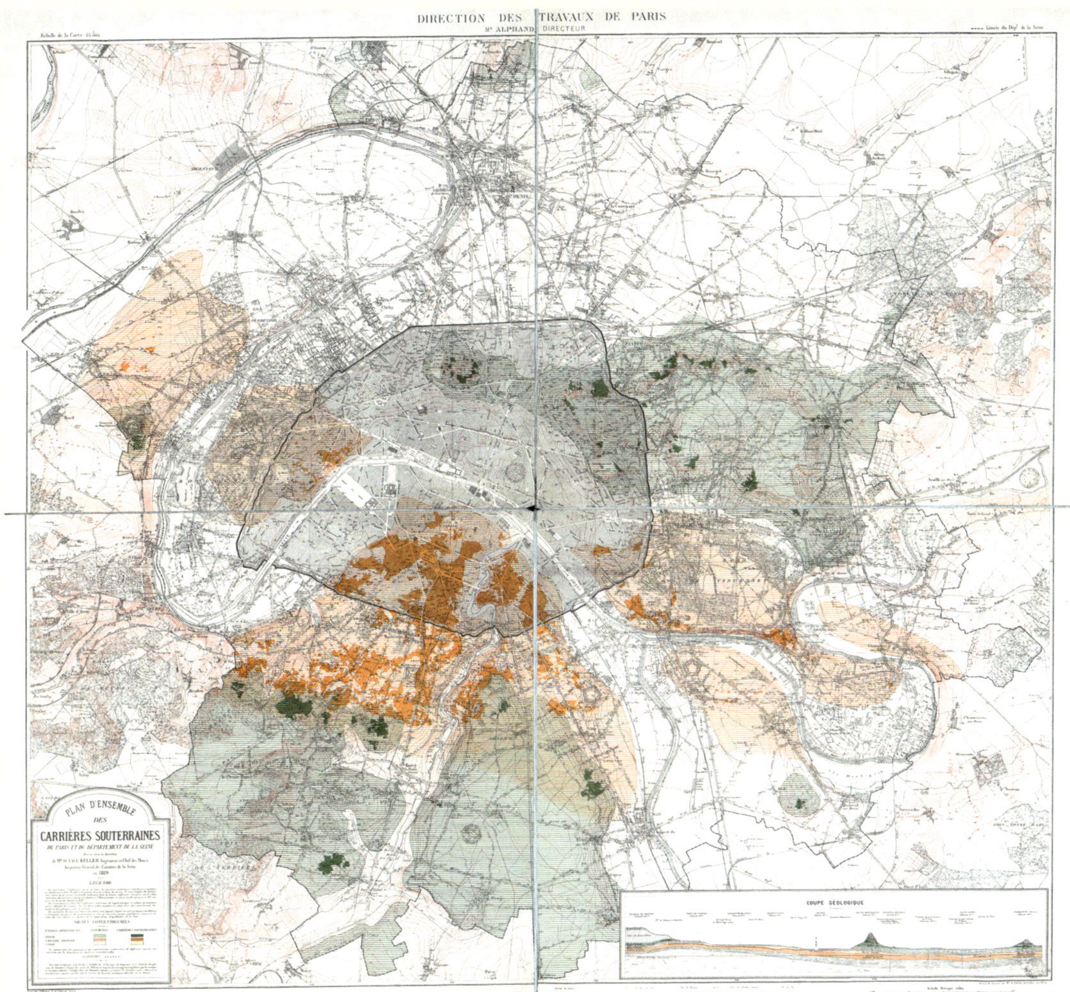

Extent of limestone (orange) and gypsum (green) underground quarries in Paris in 1888, by Octave Keller

Underground Paris

Settlers of the Parisian basin have long used the regular layers of limestone, with an average depth of 45–50 centimeters, and open quarries have existed in the area since Roman times.[3] However, at this time the use of limestone for construction was inconsistent and contingent on specific purposes—other widely available materials such as wood and brick were more commonly used. Due to this, combined with the high built density and the lack of supply infrastructure, the low-laying basin of Paris was thus known up to the nineteenth century as "the city of mud."[4]

Under Louis XIV, there was a growing interest in limestone as part of an increased effort to control and organize the territory's resources. In 1678, the king commissioned his minister of finance, Jean Baptiste Colbert, to survey the mines and quarries that could be used for construction. The aim of this survey was as much to identify the available resources so as to determine the characteristics of the stones, particularly in terms of durability and resistance to erosion. Technical advancements allowed for new underground exploration in the Paris region, and improvements in transportation technologies meant that stone could be brought in from further afield, such as the Oise valley to the north of the capital.

However, it was only in the nineteenth century that the image of Paris as a city of stone arose. Georges Eugène Haussmann's reconstruction of Paris required a durable, readily available, long-lasting material. Limestone was both

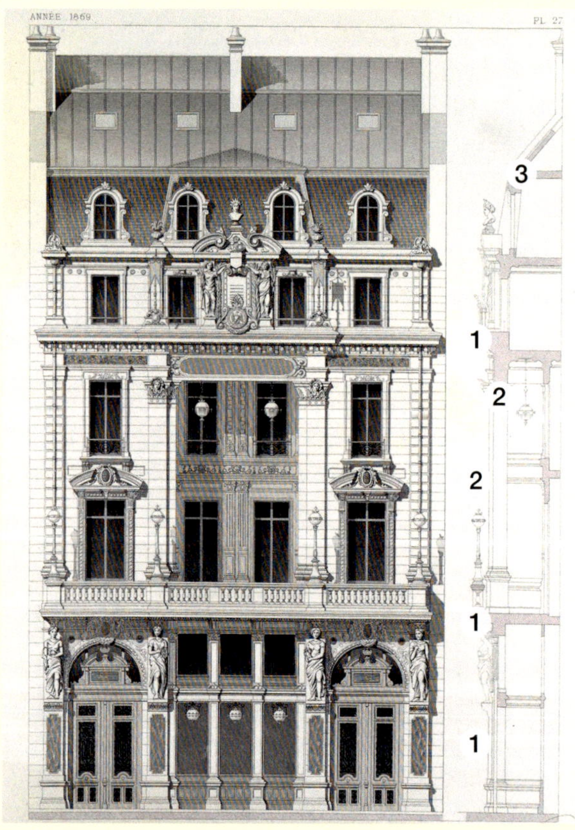

The Parisian Haussmannian facades were systematically built from stone blocks (*pierre de taille*), which formed the entire thickness of the wall. In the facade, the combination of stone types led to polychromatic effects. The use of a particular type of stone was conditioned by the construction and thus reflected its stratification in the ground.
On the lower floors, where the entire load of the building has to be borne and the facade is additionally divided up by large openings, a hard stone, for example from Burgundy (Pierre de Bourgogne), was used (1). Yellow limestone (Pierre de Saint-Maximin) from Paris was mostly used on the main floors (2). Finally, the recessed floors were bricked with clay bricks (3) and protected from the outside by a steep sheet metal or slate roof.
All protruding parts exposed to rain erosion, such as cornices, brackets, or balconies, were made of hard stone.
Source: François Loyer, *Paris XIXe siècle: L'Immeuble et l'espace urbain* (Paris, 1981), 208.

abundant and locally available, and during this time there was a surplus of both capital and labor to support the systematic exploitation of the quarries. This allowed Haussmann to use limestone extensively in his project to transform Paris into the capital city of an empire. This soft material was perfectly suited to the details required by the neoclassical architecture that came together with the rationalization of the city. As a result, Paris's hidden geological underlay was revealed in the urban fabric above ground. Different strata of stones with distinct characteristics were reconfigured to constitute the various parts of the buildings: the most durable layers were used for columns, stairs and sculptures, whereas softer ones were destined for walls and *décors.* Used as the main facade material, the particular characteristics of the Parisian limestone–its durability, its warm beige color, its soft luminosity–thus formed the lasting image of Paris as the City of Light. Meanwhile, gypsum, also widely available in the city's subterranean layers, was applied

While underground quarries left impressive empty voids under the built city (left), some open-cast mining sites were transformed into parks, such as in Buttes-Chaumont (right).

as a thin skin to the raw walls and ceilings inside the houses, producing a homogeneous surface of noble restraint.

While the stones and minerals would consolidate the built fabric, some underground and aboveground quarries were incorporated into the expanding city. This was the case with the so-called Mont Chauve, known today as the Parc des Buttes Chaumont. Home to France's largest gibbet during the Middle Ages, the site was turned into a quarry in the seventeenth century and heavily exploited from the late eighteenth century on for the extraction of marl, clay, and above all gypsum. After the French Revolution, the area was seen as "wild and hideous,"[5] as it had also become home to a garbage dump, sewage pits, and drains. The transformation of this open-cast mining site into one of the main parks of the capital, inaugurated in 1867 for the World Fair, represents the symbol of a new leisure culture for city dwellers. Designed notably by the engineer Jean-Charles Alphand with the gardener Jean-Pierre Barillet-Deschamps, the remnants of the quarry have given the park its dramatic and picturesque landscape. Today, the park remains a popular tourist destination in Paris.

A Globalized Identity

Up to the twentieth century, Paris's geological underlay continued to determine key aspects of the city's appearance. This functional directness, which had its origins in the extraction of the city's immediate geological resources, led from the color of the landscape to the texture of the urban fabric.

In the past, this was a question less of attitude than of availability of resources. Materials were mined locally, and transportation routes and techniques were of major importance. With the surge of globalization, this link has gradually become attenuated, and the connection to the ground has often been lost. As a luxurious export product, Parisian limestone has become a relic, conveying a sense of prestige, with little connection to the geological, technological, and social forces that produced it.

However, in the current context of the *Grand Paris* metropole, materiality could act as a possible anchor in its search for identity. The city's geological richness is a link to its hidden landscape as well as to its history and traditions. The continual presence of limestone–from Hausmannian facades to quarries along the Seine to rubble along the periphery–act as a reminder of the persistence of this physical link to the outer reaches of the city's territory. These reminders hint at ways of future reconnections–not so much a nostalgic return to an archaic landscape but rather a way of anchoring the future of *Grand Paris* in its geographic context. At the same time, responsible and careful use of local resources–

View of Parc des Buttes-Chaumont by Charles Marville, ca. 1877

short transport routes, efficient logistics, direct availability, and control of extraction methods–are likely to play an increasingly important role for the sustainability and resilience of cities in the future.

1 "Le sous-sol en métropole," *Données et études statistiques, République Française,* accessed May 21, 2019, http://www.donnees.statistiques.developpement-durable.gouv.fr/lesessentiels/essentiels/sol-diversite-metropole.htm.
2 Louis-Laurent Simonin, *Histoire de la terre: Origine et métamorphoses du globe; 5e édition augmentée d'un chapitre sur le bassin de Paris; Et d'une introduction à un Cours de géologie* (Paris: J. Hetzel, 1873), 280.
3 Ania Guini-Skliar, "Les carrières parisiennes aux frontières de la ville et de la campagne," *Histoire urbaine* 2, no. 8 (2003): 41–56.
4 "La 'ville de boue.'" Georges-Eugène Haussmann, *Mémoires du Baron Haussmann,* vol. 3, *Grands travaux de Paris* (Paris: Victor-Havard, 1893), 31.
5 Henri de Fontenay, *Boutades d'un promeneur dans Paris* (Paris: A. Laplace, 1867), 102.

Mineral exploitation in northern France, 2015

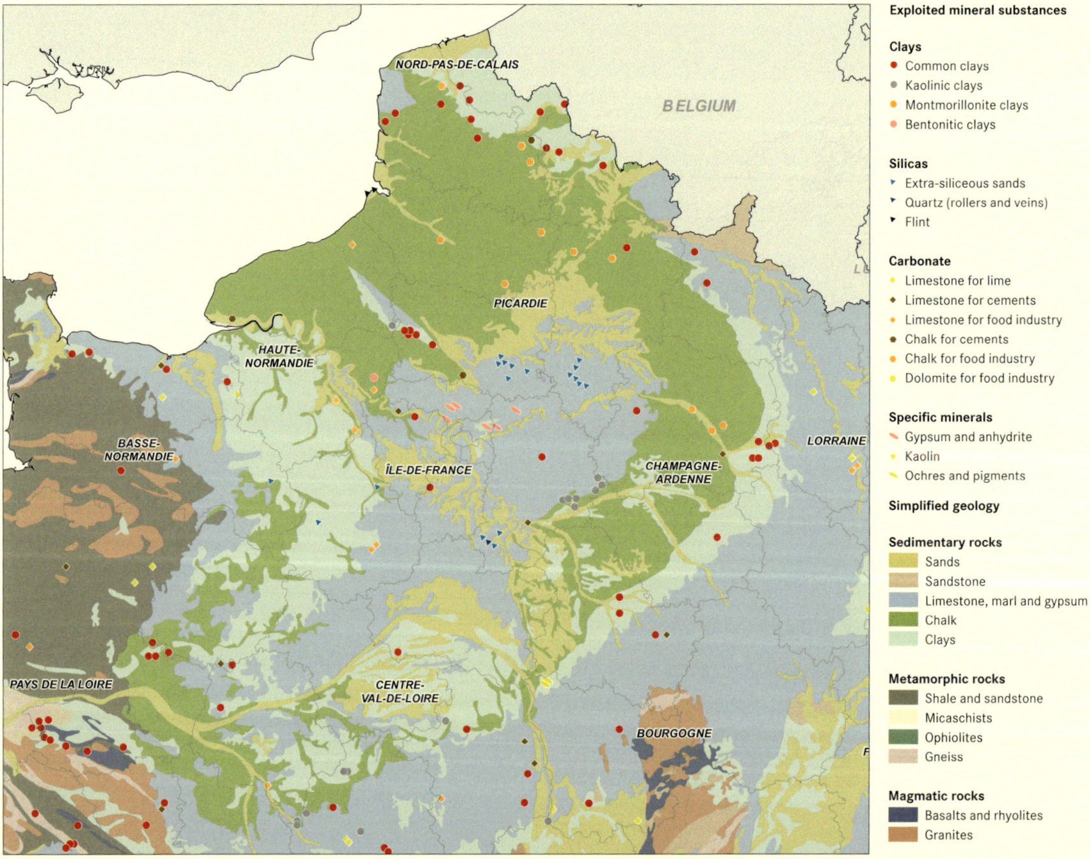

“Generally speaking, when we talk about landscape, our thoughts are geared to the original Arcadian paradise. Walking, perceiving things in sequence, is associated with the process of **reconstructing** a meaningful sense of order in the face of the mishmash of impressions we have accumulated. Even if this image of the land-scape may seem somewhat idyllic to us in today’s urbanized world, the methodological principle of how our **perception** pieces together an image of the landscape from different elements remains valid.” (gv)

Veolia Headquarters, Aubervilliers, FR
Overlooking the City

Client:
Veolia/Icade

Cooperation:
**Architecture:
Dietmar Feichtinger
Architectes, Paris**

Design/construction:
2012–2014/2014–2016

Type and size:
Courtyards, 0.39 ha

Status:
Realized

Veolia's new headquarters are located on the northern edge of Paris, where remnants of an industrial past are in close proximity to an increasing built density. The suburb comprises coarsely juxtaposed warehouses from the textile trade, precarious housing, wasteland, a shopping center, and new offices. Here, the U-shaped building opens out onto the Aubervilliers Basin, an offshoot of the Canal Saint Denis. This strong relationship forms the foundation of the project, linking the interior landscape of the building to an urban horizon.

A succession of courtyards at multiple levels articulate and mediate the scale of the building. Recessed, shaded, and sheltered spaces alternate with the open and dominant high spaces. The play of plant masses, materiality, and topography generates areas that respond to differentiated building programs.

In the courtyards below street level, a small forest of birch, poplar, and pine grows on both sides of the cafeteria pavilion. Gravel paths wind between mounded and hollowed islands, where a vegetation of undergrowth thrives. These gardens are a shaded and quiet inner world where one can get lost, away from the activities of the city.

On the first-floor terrace, in the heart of the building, a sunny clearing overhangs these wooded patios. Surrounding a meandering path, areas of mounded gravel and shade-giving trees provide various types of encounter spaces. The gradual swelling in topography is emphasized by larger boulders which become eroded to a fine grain in the concrete path.

At the end of the sequence–referring to Le Nôtre's terraces in Meudon or Saint-Germain-en-Laye–the belvedere is suspended high up, overlooking the canal. The space is inhabited by a monumental stone bench housing a miniature landscape. Its wide, sinuous curve, embracing the horizon, invites visitors to engage in social interaction or to quietly sit by themselves.

The search for the right stone and the same texture and color shades for each space was at the heart of the realization process. The bench and pavement are crafted from a yellow granite extracted in Portugal and sculpted at the quarry. Its warm hues reflect the color of the river gravel used in the gardens below; they also harmonize with the lines of the facade. Exploiting the evocative power of materiality, the use of granite also bridges the belvedere and its urban horizon, transporting visitors closer to the city in the distance. (lb)

Location of Veolia's headquarters in Aubervilliers, near the border with Paris, and facing an offshoot of the Canal Saint-Denis

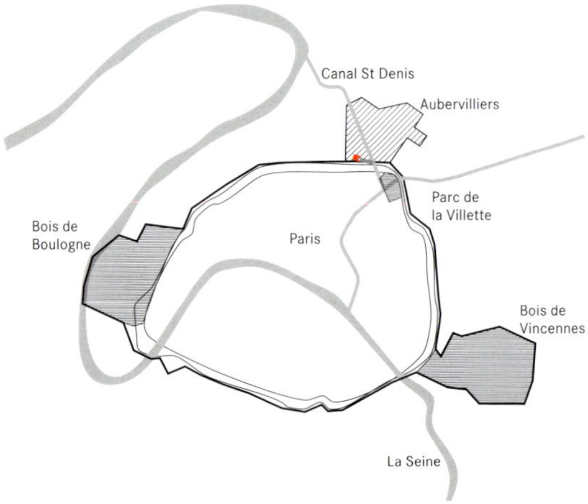

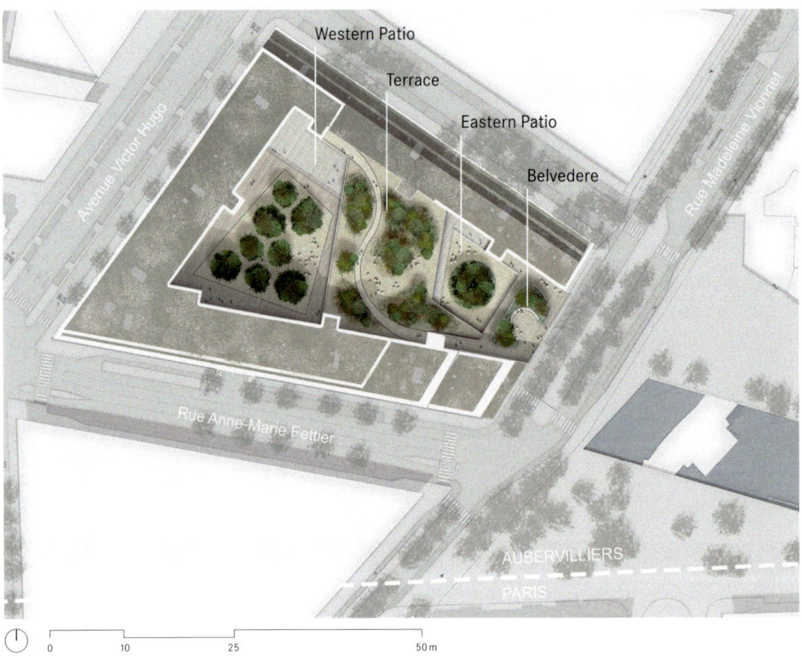

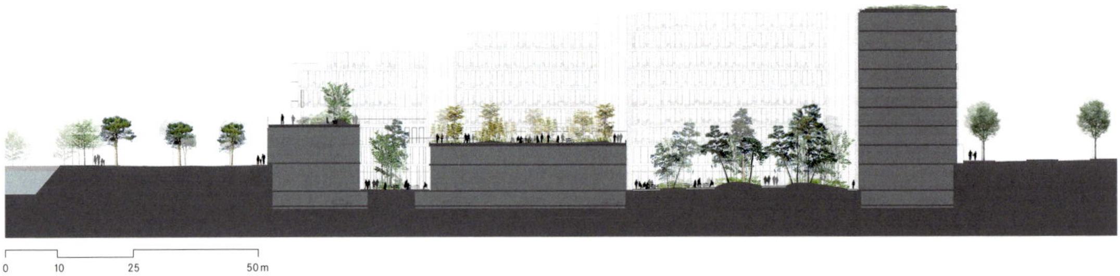

Veolia Headquarters, Aubervilliers, FR
Overlooking the City

Veolia Headquarters, Aubervilliers, FR

Overlooking the City

From above, the courtyards appear to be densely planted woods. As we get closer and enter the space, we perceive a complex landscape that changes with our movements on the sinuous paths. The courtyards are humid places, richly planted crevices within the building.

The terraces have greater exposure to the sun. Here is a drier, mineral landscape with planted stony mounds, where pioneer species emerge out of a gradient of pebbles.

The granite for the belvedere's bench was quarried and carved in Portugal. Each of the bench segments, eighty-two in total, had a unique shape to be carved. First, a rough cut was done by machine, approximating the shape of the stone, then the final form was sculpted and polished by hand. Granite pavers were placed around it in a pattern resonating with its curves.

The tall back of the bench allows for a relatively large tree pit, enabling the dense vegetation to grow and form a protective frame for the terrace, orienting views toward the broader landscape.

WHITES.

Nº	Names.	Colours.	ANIMAL.	VEGETABLE.	MINERAL.
1	Snow White.		Breast of the black headed Gull.	Snow-Drop.	Carara Marble and Calc Sinter.
2	Reddish White.		Egg of Grey Linnet.	Back of the Christmas Rose.	Porcelain Earth.
3	Purplish White.		Junction of the Neck and Back of the Kittiwake Gull.	White Geranium or Stork's Bill.	Arragonite.
4	Yellowish White.		Egret.	Hawthorn Blossom.	Chalk and Tripoli.
5	Orange coloured White.		Breast of White or Screech Owl.	Large Wild Convolvulus.	French Porcelain Clay.
6	Greenish White.		Vent Coverts of Golden crested Wren.	Polyanthus Narcissus.	Calc Sinter.
7	Skimmed milk White.		White of the Human Eyeballs.	Back of the Petals of Blue Hepatica.	Common Opal.
8	Greyish White.		Inside Quill-feathers of the Kittiwake.	White Hamburgh Grapes.	Granular Limestone.

Werner's Nomenclature of Colours: Adapted to Zoology, Botany, Chemistry, Mineralogy, Anatomy, and the Arts by Abraham Gottlob Werner and Patrick Syme, 1814

Environment[al], Los Angeles
Landscape Model Landscape

Client:
Southern California Institute of Architecture (SCI-Arc), Los Angeles

Cooperation:
Curated by Marcelyn Gow and Herwig Baumgartner

Design/construction:
2018

Type and size:
Gallery space, 132 m²

Status:
Realized

Models make it possible for complex systems and concrete landscape phenomena to be visualized. The reconfiguration of their components can create new relationships, leading the viewer into a constructed situation. In the *Environment[al]* exhibition at SCI-Arc in Los Angeles, the gallery space became the stage on which the city's physical appearance and the invisible dynamics that shape its territory could be presented: a model questioning the future of the landscape and its relation to the metropolis.

The landscape of Owens Valley, hundreds of kilometers away from Los Angeles, has played a critical role in the development and prosperity of the city. The history of the region is marked by the discovery of the Los Angeles oil fields and the rapid urbanization that followed, which brought with it a growing need for resources to sustain the population growth. Water was diverted from Owens Lake to slake the city's thirst, and a phantasmagorical, reflective surface emerged as the lake was sucked dry. The remaining layer of salt and dust turned the land into a landscape of uncertainty and environmental disaster. Today, comprehensive measures are being taken by the government to restore this bygone landscape. The pollution levels caused by the desiccated lake are controlled by shallow flooding, managed vegetation, and the use of gravel blankets–an infrastructural landscape shaped by engineering methods desperately trying to bring the lake back to life.

Recontextualized in the gallery space, these mitigation techniques become central aspects of the exhibition. While gravel on the floor–manufactured from urban erosion–provides the ground for future projections, the water from surface flooding functions as a liquid screen. Digital technology transforms the visitor's perception of "nature," allowing static vegetation to travel freely through the air in the form of sound. The exhibition space becomes a platform of experimentation where water, oil, vegetation, infrastructure, and technology are the signifiers of a newly defined history.

Through the integration of disparate spatial and temporal scales, the exhibition seeks to correlate the physical forces at work with the invisible, analog, and digital factors that have shaped and continue to affect the city's relation to the Los Angeles River. A conceptual model enabling us to understand these phenomena is established, whereby the disparate character of the objects on display stimulates new readings which can only become real when experienced physically. Through an expanded notion of scale, these new narratives force the visitor to understand the landscape and its representation as a metaphorical field: a landscape, in a model, in a landscape. (vb)

Location of *Spiral Jetty* by Robert Smithson in relation to the Pacific Railroad which was constructed between 1863 and 1869 to connect the east and west coasts of the United States.

Regional scale and path of the Los Angeles Aqueduct through the desert before reaching Los Angeles.

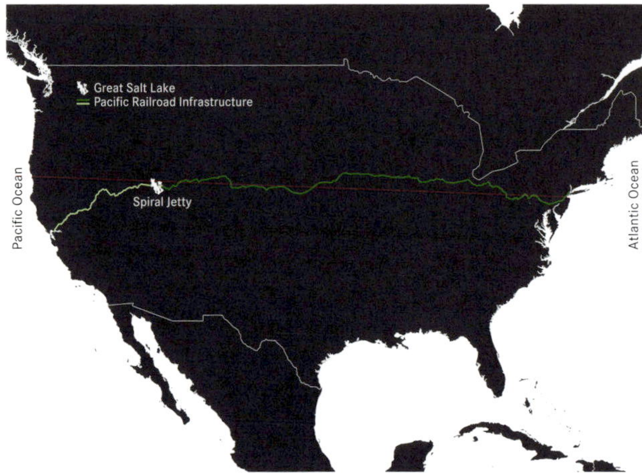

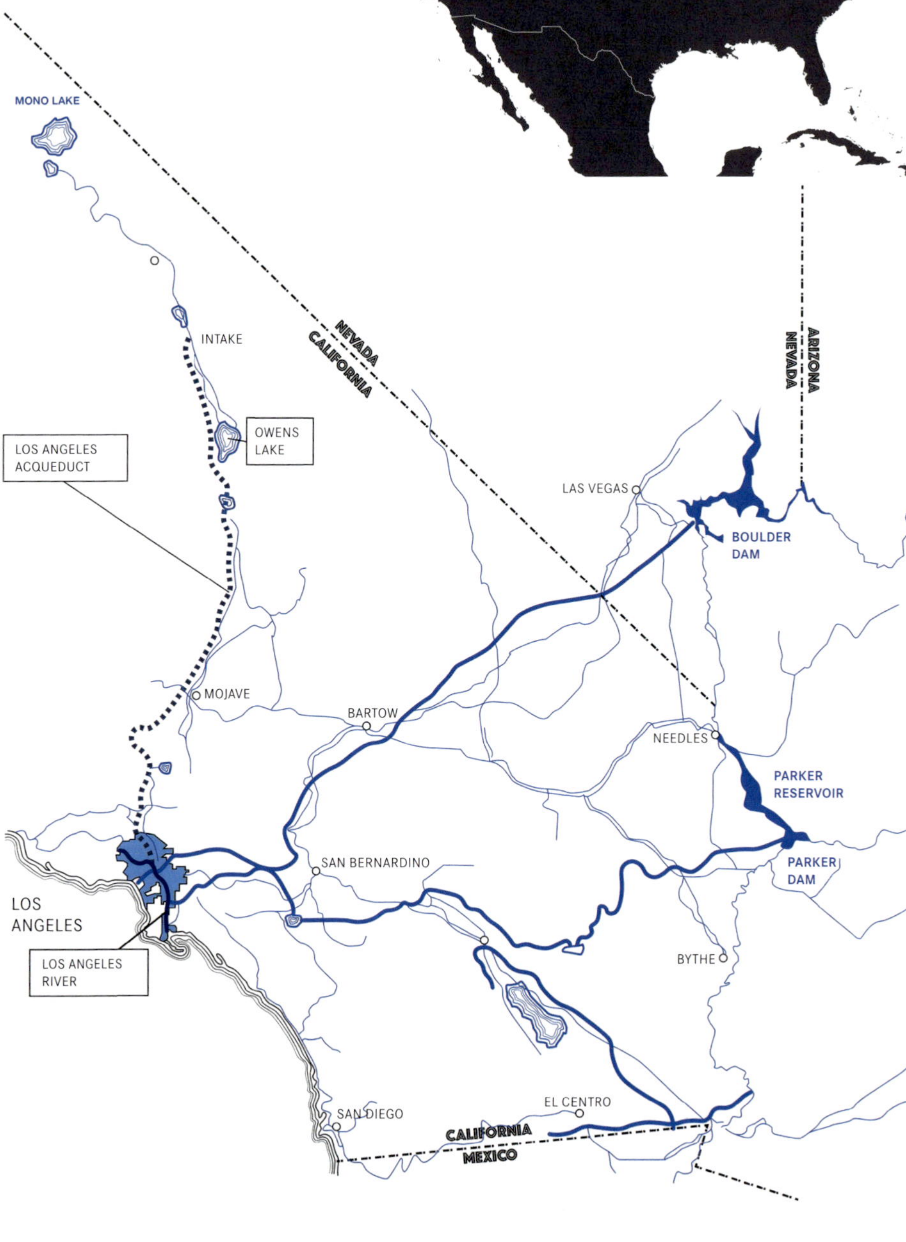

Environment[al], Los Angeles
Landscape Model Landscape

The aim behind the project was to bring the source of the Los Angeles River to the city and to use this rescaling and relocalization to generate a new awareness about the implications of large-scale infrastructure projects and their effect on the landscape, as well as to question our perception of the "natural" and how to use this personal interpretation as a way to construct different kinds of landscapes.

Conceptual reference scales organized around the Los Angeles River from the Owens Valley to the city

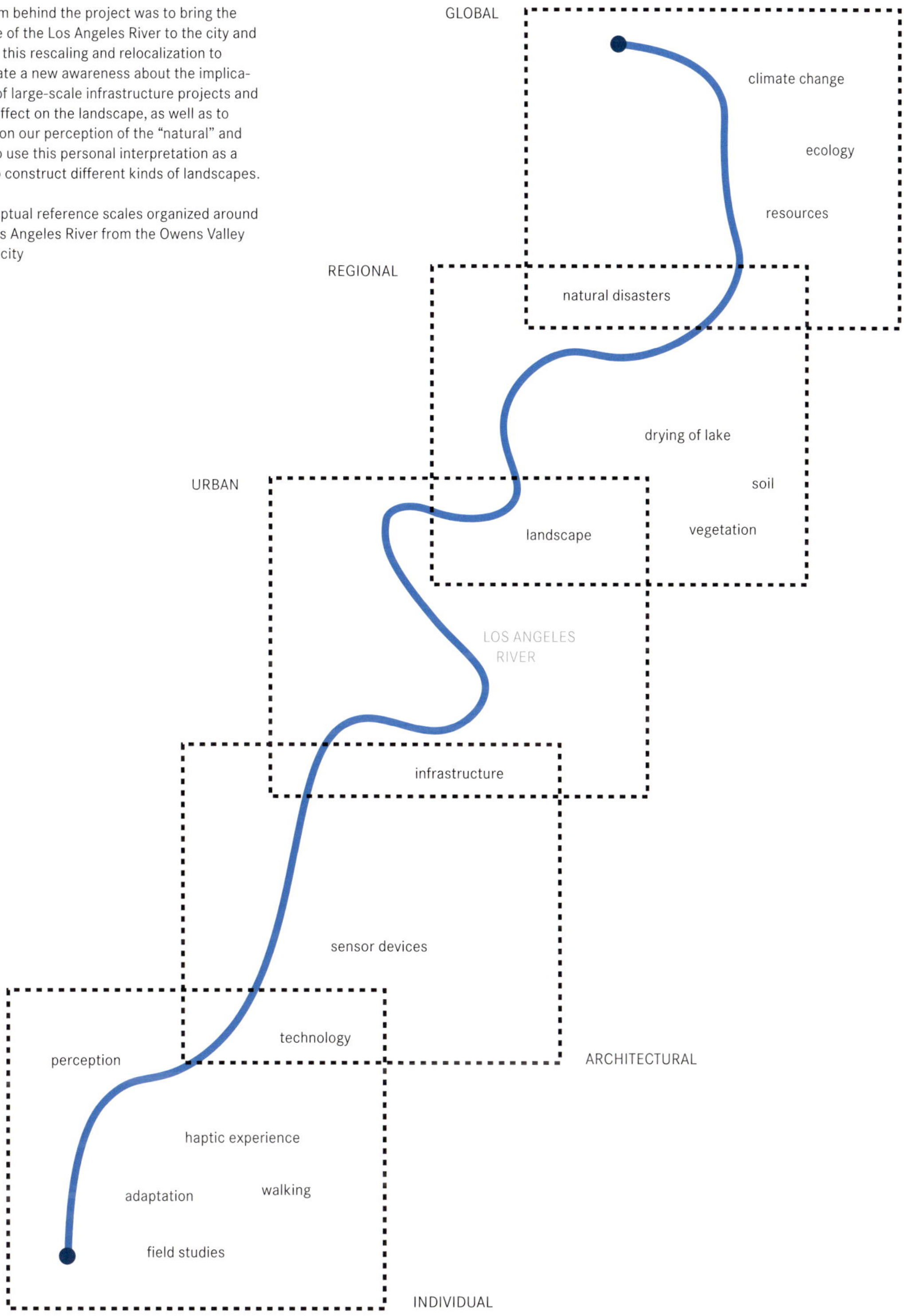

Model showing proposed water regulation of the Los Angeles River

Small streams of shallow water across the Owens Valley

The Los Angeles River during the “rainy” season, around 1938

After pressure from the Inyo County community, the Federal Clean Air Act, and years of courtroom appeals, the aqueduct now allows for 10 percent of its annual flow to go back to Owens Lake.

Between 1902 and 1905, under the leadership of William Mulholland and Frederick Eaton, the Los Angeles Department of Water and Power bought the land rights needed to construct a 356 km conduit linking the Owens Valley with the city.

Aerial view of aqueduct in outer Los Angeles, California

Prehistoric animal remains found at the La Brea Tar Pits–La Brea Tar Pits Museum Fossil Laboratory

Signal Hill Oil Field in Los Angeles, 1930

Hollywood car-chase scene–fictional depictions of the Los Angeles River

Dislocation of the landscape–relocation of vegetation from the Owens Valley to the city

City of Los Angeles, California

Sensor devices were formatted and programmed in order to trigger the sounds recorded previously along the path of the Los Angeles River from Owens Lake to the ocean.

Installing sound devices inside the SCI-Arc Gallery space

Environment[al] exhibition with added sketch of a horizon line in the form of a blinding light. The line was placed at eye level as a symbol of the blinding effects that our quest for energy can have.

The smell of liquid asphalt filled the space, an olfactory reminder of the metamorphosis undergone by organic material in geological time.

Bowls filled with vegetation from the Owens Valley, water from the Los Angeles River, and bitumen from the La Brea Tar Pits. Concept model outlining the basic elements of the exhibition: oil, vegetation, rubble, and water.

Images were projected onto the liquid surfaces of the water, where projects presented by the participants could be seen reflected.

Modulus
Relationship and Scale

May 3, 2019,
Studio Olafur Eliasson, Copenhagen

Günther Vogt: I would like to start our talk by looking at a landscape phenomenon that seems equally fascinating to both of us: waterfalls are not only part of our work, but also important when we think about our perception of landscape. I suppose this has also something to do with our biographies. You grew up in Iceland, while I grew up in the Alps.

Olafur Eliasson: I'd say the most interesting aspect of a waterfall is its movement. What you perceive when water falls is time: if we see a waterfall where the water appears to fall very quickly, it is close and comparatively small but if the water seems to fall slowly, it is a larger waterfall farther away. I've often experienced this myself. In Iceland there are a lot of waterfalls, and I am quite familiar with the scale of the island. Through close observation of this phenomenon, I learned to estimate distances in the landscape quite accurately. There is instance of this that I recall very well: some years ago I sat on the edge of a mountain in Africa and let my legs dangle over a deep gorge. I looked around and enjoyed the spectacular view; the landscape itself was completely unknown to me. Further down the ridge, I eventually noticed a waterfall falling into this enormous abyss. And when I looked at this waterfall, I saw how slowly the water fell, at an incredibly slow pace. This gave me a physical jolt and I reflexively pulled back my legs. I had suddenly become aware of the actual scale of the gorge, of the landscape. The physical proportions of the whole scene hit me like a shock, all because of the falling water. So besides their historical and cultural significance, my interest in waterfalls lies in the fact that one can use them as a kind of introspective tool to scale one's own presence and feel the real, factual situation. This also happens with a river or a small brook, with water in general.

Günther Vogt: I am interested in the possibility of positioning myself in a landscape by introducing a specific scale, too. When I see a waterfall, however, I am less focusing on the speed of the falling water and more on the quantity of water that tumbles down. This very volume then gives me an indication of the catchment area of the waterfall and, thus, of the approximate size of the landscape behind it.

When I now look at the pictures of your four waterfalls in New York [*The New York City Waterfalls,* 2008], they actually look like totally normal waterfalls to me, at least from a distance, so that, at first, I thought there must be a huge landscape behind it. In reality, however, the water is pumped up and there is no landscape in the background but a huge city that resembles a machine. Or let's take the equally temporary installation along the longitudinal axis of the large palace grounds in Versailles [*Waterfall,* 2016]. In order to read this situation, you have to know its history. Louis XIV had the whole landscape drained and huge machines and canal systems built to bring enough water to Versailles. The spectacle was only possible by remodeling the entire landscape around the castle. The waterfall further heightened that situation. And that is where knowledge and perception merge. I think that any perception of a landscape is always connected to our knowledge about it. It is essential to correlate things, for otherwise you merely consume a picture and any perception remains superficial.

If I don't assume however, that everyone thinks as I do, I notice that people who look at waterfalls see quite different things in them. This has to do with the simultaneity of the states of aggregation, namely solid, liquid, and gaseous. The water mixes with oxygen as it falls. The result is spray, and the water turns white. This is like what happens when a spring bubbles up, that is, a kind of "super nature." Humanity's fascination with water is a constant in the history of humankind, not least because it is a changeable element and, therefore, can be interpreted very openly.

Olafur Eliasson: This becomes explicit, for instance, in the Alhambra, where different cultures met and water was used not only as a visual element but also to cool and remove dust from the air. In fact, water produces various sounds and is more of an atmospheric than a spatial ingredient–or at least part of a certain spaciousness.

> p. 410, *Haliç Shipyard*

Günther Vogt: But the Alhambra also is a place where different religions come together. Its shallow pools, for example, which mirror the sky, are from Islam, where there is no image culture. Nevertheless, these reflective pools create the possibility to project images of the sky, clouds, sun, or stars into the garden. This is contrasted by the vertical jet of the fountains. The emphasis of verticality is above all a Christian notion. What fascinates here is the hidden mechanics necessary to shape the water jets. As with the gardens of Versailles, that is. The great stars at the time were the engineers who mastered the intricacies of the water plays.

Olafur Eliasson: Water can also make otherwise relatively minor, incidental phenomena visible. I have often proposed creating a large water surface that would indicate the structure of the wind with its surface. Or consider how flowing water traces the bed of a stream–the waves refer to forms beneath the water's surface that cannot readily be seen from the shore.

I am interested in rendering the invisible–but already present–visible and experienceable; I use the atmospheric aspect as a primary characteristic of space. Atmosphere is often understood as more of a by-product of a successful building. You could however also reverse it and understand atmosphere as a kind of starting point around which everything else is oriented. In retrospect our first collaboration in Bregenz, in 2001, the exhibition *The mediated motion,* was an attempt to perform a gesture with atmosphere as the main aspect, with the claim that the solidity, the very mass of the building, remain in the background. A kind of dissolution or dematerialization. What you could call "the hospitality of space" was somehow secondary. From my point of view, you might, of course, say there has to be a "spatial hospitality" or, rather, an awareness of it for this to work, for in a typical white-cube exhibition space the installation would have worked very differently.

Günther Vogt: I agree. One of the results of that exhibition was, however, that for many years I was invited to give lectures to talk about how atmospherically dense spaces could be created. The example of Bregenz shows that, quite often, much of it already exists on site. You've only got to recognize it: water, fog, color of the earth, etc. All these things are already there, though not in the context of the museum. It's about isolating simple phenomena, rendering them spatially readable and, where necessary, reinforcing them selectively. The difficulty is, rather, to sharpen people's awareness so that these qualities can be recognized at all.

Olafur Eliasson: It is interesting to talk about the limitations of perception and the necessity of becoming more sensitive. I think our abilities and senses allow us to reach a higher degree of perception if we make the effort. We can find answers to things we wouldn't otherwise see. We already read, scan, or explore our environment to a certain extent all the time, something we do both deliberately and compulsively. It can be exhausting to look at an exhibition—unless you refuse to really look and don't really see much anyway. I would add that the realm of perception or, more generally, the question of sensitivity has still been insufficiently studied. And when we think about how to decode perception, it is important to understand that a waterfall is not only an object but also represents a subject that is interested in the falling water—with all their embedded assumptions and the narratives. A waterfall does not wait for you to pass by and activate it by consuming it as a view. It is already active beforehand; it has embarked on its own journey and meets the observer on its path. It is this very meeting that creates the prerequisite of any perception. I, the subject, am not the more important participant in this meeting, the one in the center. I left behind the phenomenological idea that I am sitting on top of the mountain of perception, plucking my favorite flowers, long ago.

I am very interested in this question and would like to make a proposal: the way we experience the world is a system of meetings, comings-together of various interests. I don't want to get too abstract here, but I think this has to do with understanding perception in a larger context. We have entered the

Dominions

Julian Charrière and Andreas Greiner, 2011

Bacterial Map of Germany and Switzerland

For their work *Dominions*, Julian Charrière and Andreas Greiner visited twenty-eight different locations across Germany and Switzerland. At all the stopping points on their route, they placed sterile boxes containing a layer of white nutrition media for microorganisms. After five minutes of exposure, the boxes where sealed again. During this time, some of the airborne microorganisms from the territory—an invisible part of the local landscape—were collected.

Sealed within glass vitrines in the exhibition space, the microbes slowly grew, changing their color, shape, and size; these colonies of mold formed unique topographies—a microbic image of each place. The vitrines were arranged as a bacterial map of the artists' home countries, mirroring the original coordinates and altitudes.

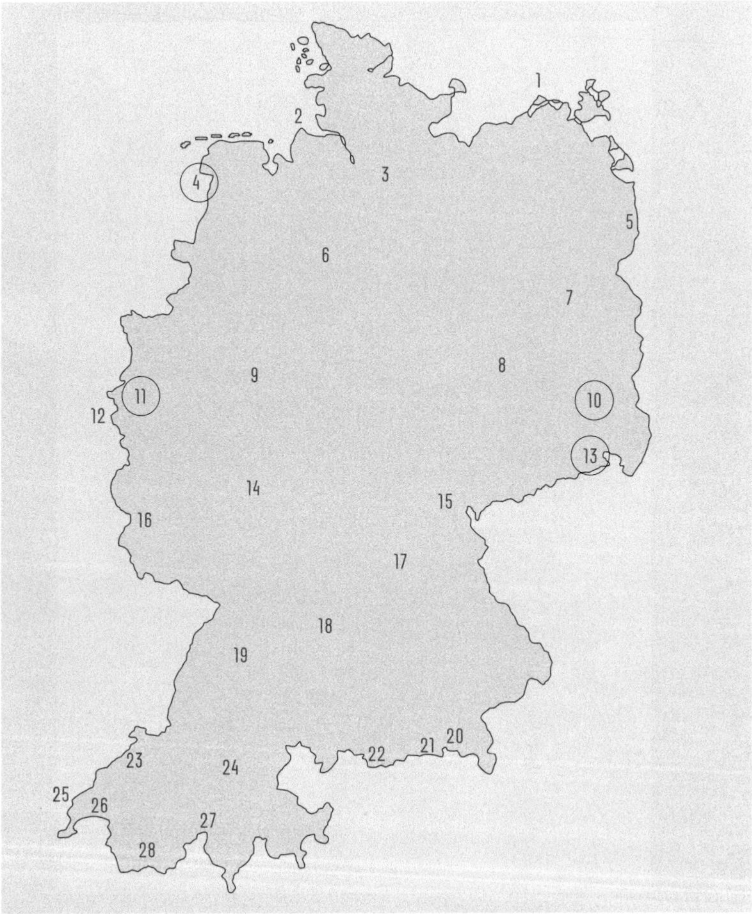

Schwarze Pumpe (10) – Elsdorf Kohlegrube (11)
Elbsandsteingebirge (13) – Greetsiel (4)

Anthropocene; we are an equal part of the system. So when we design a waterfall or an environment or work to create an atmosphere, what we actually do is design part of a system. The exciting thing is that these are cooperative systems. That's why the exhibition in Bregenz is still really significant for me. It wasn't just you and I working together, it was a cultural platform within an architectural structure. There was a community that grew up around the exhibition. It was the combination of all these elements into a larger system that, ultimately, created the exhibition. In retrospect, only a small part of the exhibition is still being talked about. Now we look back and can see that the exhibition actually addressed a series of anthropological issues about ecosystems, issues that touch on human existence as such, but also on questions of atmosphere. I always try to be aware of the potential of systems, when collaborating with the many different people in my studio.

Günther Vogt: What you're saying is consistent with my own experience. During and after the exhibition in Bregenz, what I was most frequently asked about was the invitation card that shows a picture of the Kunsthaus submerged in water by half a meter. Many people criticized it or were simply unable to understand why we were depicting a natural disaster. And when I asked them whether they thought it wasn't more of a cultural than a natural cataclysm, they were initially quite perplexed.

< p. 28, *Pyramides de Terre*

I think that, speaking of the Anthropocene, there are quite a lot of misunderstandings. After all, the term refers to an era in which humankind has become a global geological force. By now we are an important part of the system and, thus, massively influence biological, geological, and atmospheric processes. The problem is that we often exclude ourselves from the overall picture. We see ourselves as customers, authors, or critics but not as part of a whole that we directly influence by our actions. I've also seen that in the exhibition. When people walked through the fog, for example, they thought it was great, but few of them realized that their movement changed the fog and, thus, the space. And I often notice this in the office, too. You often have to explain to your young colleagues that whatever they record will directly affect the place or the city. It is not easy to convey the idea that we shall have to rethink things, away from an object and toward a more systemic context.

Olafur Eliasson: This is indeed the most complicated part of all learning processes. The segmentation of knowledge into individual fields begins very early on. At school math is taught in one room and biology taught elsewhere, and languages are separate, too. Collaboration does not have a high priority. The language used in different fields makes this specialization quite clear: natural sciences, humanities, social sciences–every science has, for centuries, been cultivating its own specific terminology.

When we look at the agendas of architecture and landscape architecture today, we can see that they are very much guided by quests for the most economical solutions. At the same time, any questions are delegated to individual disciplines. The handling of precipitation in cities, for example, is dealt with by hydrologists or hydraulic engineers. But I think there is great potential in working with scientists, mineralogists, and geologists, as well as with architects and engineers. In your work, you have always encouraged and cultivated this coming together. We probably have to accept that the cooperation of the various disciplines is only in its initial phase. I'm very much interested in this situation, in which the singular or individual merges with the plurality or majority and everyone begins to understand and define themselves as part of a whole. And this is really quite unusual, especially in Western culture, where the prioritization of the individual voice has become a status symbol; where, for many years, it was almost considered a loss of identity to be part of a collective or team.

Günther Vogt: In this context, it is important that, in the future, society also learns to comprehensively understand the economic value of a landscape. By this I mean that when I walk, for instance, through the forests here, around Copenhagen, the recreational value of this landscape is taken into account on the one hand, but also the fact that these forests produce fresh air, retain rainwater, and contribute toward the cooling of the city, etc. All this has a value in itself and as long as we do not introduce an economy to cover this, it will be difficult to even talk about it all. We do not evaluate the situation as a whole, but argue, for instance, from a purely ecological perspective. However, we shall need an intermediary, who helps us bring together all disciplines.

Olafur Eliasson: Yes, I agree. But we have to admit that some disciplines are still largely invisible, not only in terms of their internal processes but also in terms of external communication. We can start working together where the opportunities are the most obvious: in the various natural sciences. But philosophy and other humanities can also act across disciplines. It's all about tearing down walls or building bridges–just as this book aims to do. The potential usefulness of collective, collaborative, inclusive ideas has to gain more recognition.

Günther Vogt: You talk about tearing down walls and building bridges. If we deal with landscape, we also have to consider that what we call landscape is always and also a cultural production. The French *paysage,* the English *landscape,* or the German *Landschaft* imply something completely different. It takes a lot of work to establish a common platform in an office in which employees from the most diverse countries work. But it's also exciting, because these very differences open up many possibilities. However, it requires a continuous dialogue in which the different positions are negotiated, some of which have a lot to do with one's own identity.

Today, it cannot always be assumed that these different positions will be approached with a certain openness. Many people are too focused on themselves and do not acknowledge collective work as a real possibility. If we want to work together, we will have to develop a common language to be able to communicate. Otherwise, we may start from completely different premises, although we think we are talking about the same thing. It is not a question of right or wrong, but of trying to understand the world more holistically. Just take our totally Eurocentric view of space; for example, the studio we are currently in, with its red walls and high ceiling. Everything is very Cartesian. But if we try to understand space like the Japanese, then it's not necessarily about what surrounds us, or the object as such, but about the space between things: the *ma* is a multidimensional concept of Japanese culture and also means the space that we now form in our midst. For now, we are not interested in Cartesian space because we talk to each other for a certain time, listen to each other and, thus, form a community. I consider this a truly fascinating model. This example is only a small anecdote, but probably it is one of the main tasks in developing an office to bring such aspects and ways of thinking into the discussion on an ongoing basis.

Olafur Eliasson: Yes, and I think that the role or, if you will, the way the studio works determines the way our collaboration works. There are different aspects that are important: on the one hand, the relationship between "inside" the studio and "outside" in society. It's a matter of creating and maintaining a kind of perforation or permeability. After all, there is the constant danger or even romantic idea of the cultural sector that when you enter your studio, you leave the real world behind. This mythologization is counterproductive for both life and work in the studio.

On the other hand, we have to acknowledge and admit that ours is a studio in which the creative process must be nurtured. We have to promote the unpredictable: disorder, chaos, a kind of unlimited and explorative way of thinking. Trying to directly replicate the outside world would imply also replicating invisible power structures. All these things that we are unable to fully grasp or understand, that is. However, to grasp and reveal such power structures or mechanisms would be a good exercise for, say, design students. Being both open and permeable toward society–although to be too close to the outside world is not good for the studio either. And there is another aspect that I try to cultivate in the studio: the awareness that people are incredibly important. Every single one of us. Everyone is relevant and is coresponsible for the whole–not only for a work of art, but also for the concerns of our society.

Günther Vogt: The concept of a collective or a team is central to our work. We are exclusively working on public spaces which today are subject to many different demands and requirements. That's why it is important that the experiences and opinions of different people are included in our discussions already at a very early stage of the process. To enable this, we often work with analog models or mock-ups. The advantage is that a model allows us to spatialize an idea and present it in a manner comprehensible to all those involved. Everyone can immediately join in the discussion and effortlessly change the model. Neither a plan, nor digital modulations offer this possibility. Therefore, mock-ups are understood by our firm as a design and communication tool. This is also reflected by the fact that such mock-ups are disassembled once the project is completed and the material is used for subsequent projects.

< p. 16, *Campus*
< p. 226, *Tate Modern*

Olafur Eliasson: Our interest in mock-ups is something that unites us both. However, I consider the often-propagated distinction between model and reality to be irrelevant, since a model is an image of reality that can, at the same time, be read as reality. This room here is, basically, a model of our thoughts and ideas as well as those of the architect, Danish artist Jens Ferdinand Willumsen.

Models primarily interest me because of their role in the work process. In the beginning, there is often a thought or a gut feeling that cannot easily be verbalized. This thought is then translated into a first sketch. Subsequently, the idea is separated into several strands of thoughts that may be worked on by various teams. Small-scale models are created, then larger ones–or digital models. Scientists and engineers may be involved at that point; the team will grow. You advance and you retract your steps. You go back and forth. It's only relatively late in the process–when the model is placed in the context of a concrete project–that questions arise like: is this to be red, blue, or green? Do we want to work with wood or metal? Is the object underground, or does it float in the air? The project's creative potential resides not in a specific form or color but in our understanding of the entire network and its causality. The success of the design–whether for a room, a house, an artwork, or a garden–resides in the consequences for its environment.

For me as both a designer and a part of society, the supposedly finished work remains a model, because the moment I say that it is no longer a model, I accept a state that can no longer be changed and, so to speak, discharge myself from any responsibility. And that is inconceivable. At the studio, I always encourage people to focus on developing a sense of *why* we do things more than on how we do them. I consider the ideas of authorship and originality rather controversial, even though they are always being enormously promoted. The need to change that is also one of our responsibilities.

Günther Vogt: Regarding authorship, you address an important question that explicitly arises when we look at today's use of digital media. What is noticeable is a certain nonchalance in dealing with information and knowledge—that is, with pictures, texts, maps, videos, etc.—as to the naming of the authors. At the same time, the rules as to how the material may be handled have become increasingly strict, and the sanctions for infringements drastically increased. Some content is now accessible but not available to just everyone. There are paywalls, or you need to be a member of a network or specific institution in order to work with the material. In fact, I am of the opinion that everything once produced and published may also be used to advance one's own idea. Otherwise, we will lose a huge potential. Nonetheless, the authorship will always have to remain transparent.

Olafur Eliasson: In principle, I agree with you. But against the background of the ongoing process of digitalization, this raises huge questions. In this context, I am interested, on the one hand, in the possibility of visualizing networks and thought processes via directories of literature or atlases, libraries, collections, and so on. In this way, the development and context of a work may be better understood and conclusions drawn about one's own work. The other question touches upon today's open-source culture: of course the potential for people or small organizations with relatively limited resources is exciting. By using publicly accessible data, platforms, and programs, they can develop a lot of power relatively quickly. New opportunities are emerging that, however, are also recognized and used by large companies or institutions to achieve their goals. This destroys smaller, local structures—I am thinking, for example, of workshops that produce furniture, clothes, or printed materials. As a society, we will have to find a way to deal critically with these opportunities since they will—even more strongly than they have so far—influence and determine not only the ways we work but also the ways we communicate and live together.

Bois
Evolution of an Urban Figure

Laure Baretaud
Maria Alexandrescu

In French common parlance, the word *bois* means both "wood," in the sense of a material, and an area of land covered with trees, usually smaller than a forest.[1] Yet the figure of the *bois* cannot be reduced to that of a small forest, as it also involves an identity and practices and uses that bring it closer to that of a park. In the city of Paris, the famous Bois de Boulogne and Bois de Vincennes make for particularly interesting examples. Acting as a hinge between urban and territorial scales, they have evolved in parallel with the development of the city. This transformation occurred both in their form and in their identity and use, from a space of production and resource extraction to a space of leisure and culture.

The Forests of Paris

More than three thousand years ago, the area surrounding Paris–like much of France–was covered by an immense forest.[2] For a long time, what was outside the city limits was conceived of as a world that could escape the laws of society. Forests were seen as a place of wilderness, of mysticism, of liminality, providing refuge for brigands, while also generating tales, myths, and fantasies. In parallel with the exponential growth of cities, these wooded areas quickly turned into a resource, ready to be exploited and controlled by the powerful. As forests were the main source of supply for hunting, heating, furniture making, as well as building and ship construction, woodland management became key to the economic development of nearby villages and towns, and later, of the state.

The exploitation of forests intensified over time, particularly from the sixteenth century on, when the requirement for wood to satisfy the demands of urban growth and naval production increased. The areas of woodland around cities diminished, and while Lyon sought wood in the massifs of Burgundy, and Marseille in the Vivarais Mountains, extending its reach even as far as Corsica, Paris reserved a specific area of supply for itself which stretched beyond its basin. However, levels of production failed to meet demand, and there were significant fears of a shortage.

In the seventeenth century, Jean-Baptiste Colbert's warning to Louis XIV–"France will perish for want of wood"[3]–led to more specific intervention to control the forests. The Minister of Finance launched the so-called "1669 Ordinance," allowing the king to take control of the country's forests with the aim of restoring stocks and exploiting them efficiently to supply the country's needs. Up to that point, there had been no overview of the surface area and perimeter of the forests. During Louis XIV's reign, they were measured and organized in an orderly geometric system. Near Paris, the remains of the immense Forêt de Rouvray became a site of production for the city, and the network of roads traversing it was adapted to cater to the

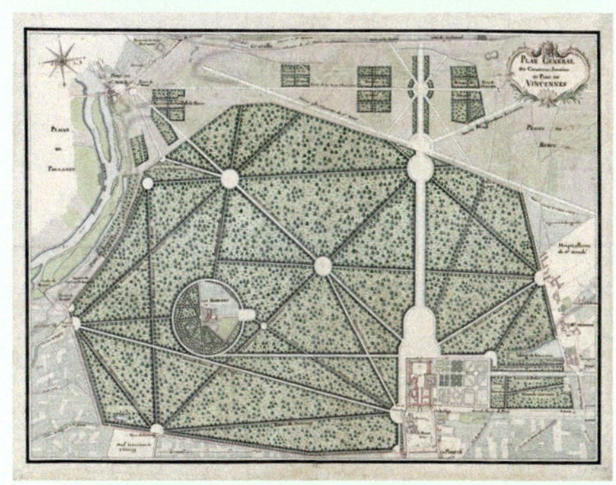

Detail from *Les Très Riches Heures du Duc de Berry,* showing a hunting scene in the Bois de Vincennes in the middle of the fifteenth century, with the château visible in the background

General overview of the Château and Jardins de Vincennes, 1739

1 "Land spanning more than 0.5 hectares with trees higher than 5 meters and a canopy cover of more than 10 percent, or trees able to reach these thresholds in situ. It does not include land that is predominantly under agricultural or urban land use." Food and Agriculture Organization of the United Nations, "FRA 2015: Terms and Definitions," *Forest Resources Assessment Working Paper* 180 (Rome, 2012), 3.

2 See Martine Chalvet, *Une histoire de la forêt* (Paris: Seuil, 2011).

3 Simon Schama, *Landscape and Memory,* 2nd ed. (London: Harper Press, 2004).

logistics of supplying and distributing wood. The alleys cutting through it became wider to facilitate exploitation and to provide visibility while keeping "miscreants" in check. Intersecting axial paths in star configurations were established, and the Bois de Boulogne, to the west of the city, was enclosed by a wall for royal hunts.

By the nineteenth century, the population of Paris had multiplied fifteenfold, from 150,000 in 1650 to 2.3 million in 1880.[4] The increased demand for resources was considerable and the fear of a scarcity of wood exacerbated. While the forest of Fontainebleau to the south of the capital benefited from the support of painters of the Barbizon school, transforming it into a natural artistic reserve, the wooded areas near Paris were depleted and repeatedly damaged by military encampments, deforestation, pasturing, and hunting. At the time, these forests were depicted as desolate and dangerous, as is evident in Comtesse d'Agoult's description of the Bois de Boulogne area:

In the Forest of Fontainebleau, by Jean-Baptiste Camille Corot, ca. 1860. The forest near Paris inspired numerous landscape painters in the mid-nineteenth century, known as the Barbizon school. The movement prompted the protection of the forest as an "artistic reserve," based on the aesthetic qualities of its landscape.

> *"This Bois seemed so far away, so far from Paris, and the road was so long and so gloomy that we rarely went there: it was a matter of state. This place was considered wild: it was associated with images of ambush and murder, as if one had been transported to the days of the troubadours."*[5]

4 See Jérôme Buridant, "Flottage des bois et gestion forestière: L'exemple du Bassin parisien, du XVIe au XIXe siècle," *Revue forestière française* 4 (2006).
5 Marie Catherine Sophie d'Agoult (aka Daniel Stern), *Mémoires, souvenirs et journaux de la Comtesse d'Agoult* (Paris: Mercure de France, 1990), 192.
6 See "La Remise en Valeur des Bois de Boulogne et de Vincennes," *Paris Projet* 18 (October 1978): 6.
7 See Adolphe Alphand, *Les Promenades de Paris* (Paris: Rothschild, 1867–1873).

The *Bois urbain*: Vincennes and Boulogne

The transformation of the *bois* from a derelict geometric and linear forest to a romantic park for the bourgeoisie occurred in conjunction with the surge in urbanization under Napoleon III. In his transformation of the capital, Haussmann chose to include Vincennes and Boulogne as part of a wider strategy of landscape urbanization that was directly related to the Parisian infrastructure.

Both wooded areas–covering 1,800 hectares,[6] an area five times larger than Central Park in New York–were made part of the continuous landscape that organized the city. They were integrated into a system of "promenades," as depicted in *Les Promenades de Paris* by the engineer Adolphe Alphand.[7] These promenades linked key nodes in the city and were flanked by regularized and standardized elements such as lines of trees, along with benches and lighting. Formally, the layout of the city and the forest was reversed: Haussmann simplified and optimized the urban structure with large axial roads linked by star-shaped intersections–in the

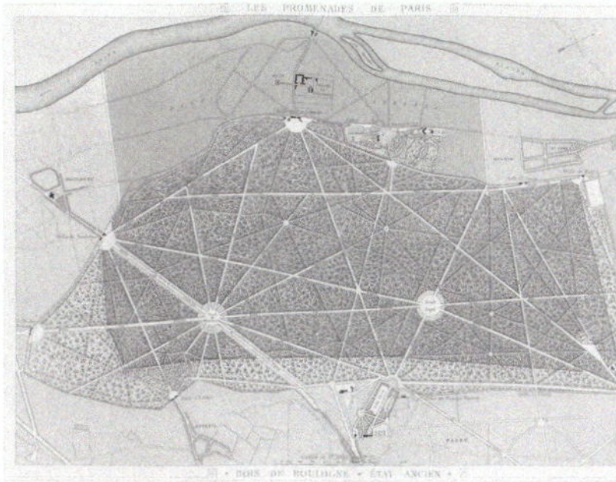

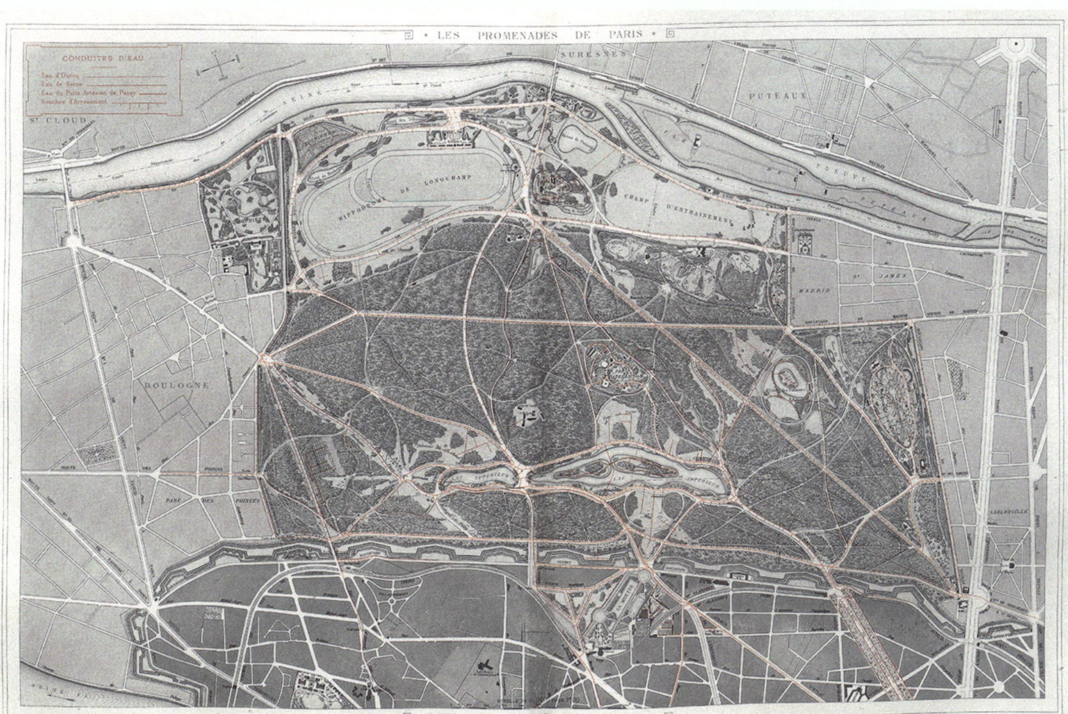

Plan of the Bois de Boulogne, before and after Alphand's intervention. Drawn in red, a new and complex network of underground water pipes supplies the artificial lakes, ponds, and streams in the *bois*, while providing water for irrigation and road cleaning.

Photographs from the *Album du Bois de Boulogne*, taken by Charles Marville between 1858 and 1860

image of royal hunting forests of the seventeenth century. The Parisian woods, on the other hand, became more complex. The transformation of the forest into an urban *bois* relied on various design strategies undertaken by Alphand and his team, in collaboration with the landscape architect Jean-Pierre Barillet-Deschamps and the architect Jean-Antoine-Gabriel Davioud. They adapted the path network by converting existing roads into carriageways, lined by sidewalks planted with lines of trees, while turning other paths into bridleways or meandering curved *allées*. They also developed an invisible underground connection to the city's network of water,[8] in order to feed the new lakes, waterfall, streams, and ponds scattered throughout the park and to provide irrigation. In a mise-en-scène of the landscape, they modified the topography and the groupings of trees to create a contrast between different spaces and establish vistas. In the tradition of English landscapes, picturesque elements such as cascades and grottos were also implemented at specific points.

The urban *bois*, with its romantic character, became a space of enchantment for the bourgeoisie within the city fabric. By becoming an urban park, the former forest lost its productive character to become a *lieu de promenade*, designed to provide pleasure, recreation, excitement, and just enough "wilderness" to remain welcoming to the city dweller. This radical transformation is reflected in the Comtesse d'Agoult's words:

> *"Today, as if at the engineer's whistle, everything is changed. The Bois has come closer, opening on all sides in pleasant aspects.... with gondolas on the lakes, cafés in the cabins, and races on the turf. The revues on the lawns, games, and concerts constantly attract to them a crowd of those with nothing to do."*[9]

8 See APUR and DEVE, "L'Eau dans les bois de Boulogne et de Vincennes: Valorisation de la ressource," April 2013.
9 D'Agoult, *Mémoires, souvenirs et journaux de la Comtesse d'Agoult,* 193.

The Playground of Paris

The creation of the *bois* brought with it a range of amenities such as an outdoor theater, a race course, greenhouses, pavilions, and numerous restaurants, scattered throughout the wooded parcels. Its scale would also allow new types of sports to take place in this picturesque landscape–such as horseback riding, canoeing, or tennis, which were until then restricted to the countryside. The *bois* thus not only provided an area of greenery in direct proximity to Paris but also became a proper recreation ground for the citizens of the capital.

Referring to the Bois de Boulogne as "the Parisian Coney Island," the American journalist Henry Watterson describes it in his memoirs as "literally and absolutely a playground, the playground of the people, and this last Sunday of mine, not fewer than half a million of Parisians were making it their own."[10]

There is, however, a significant difference between the Parisian example and the infamous experience of Coney Island, dissected in Rem Koolhaas's *Delirious New York*.[11] While both were originally destined to counteract urban pressure by providing people with a space for entertainment and pleasure accessible day and night, the attitudes of the two designers toward their respective sites were, quite literally, diametrically opposed. Indeed, by considering Coney Island as an empty canvas–a "magic carpet,"[12] as Koolhaas put it–its promoters turned what was "the nearest zone of virgin nature"[13] to overcrowded Manhattan into a totally artificial ground: "Instead of suspension of urban pressure, it offers intensification."[14] Alphand, on the contrary, was able to anticipate the needs of the expanding city for proximity to "nature" and transformed the decaying forest into an urban park by combining a sense of wilderness with the artificial construction of a picturesque landscape. In order to achieve this, special attention was paid to the inherent qualities of the place, grounding both *bois* in a wider territorial setting. Indeed, Haussmann had insisted that the Bois de Boulogne be attached to the Seine so that the river would constitute its

Press photographs depicting various events in the Bois de Boulogne in the first half of the twentieth century

10 Henry Watterson, *"Marse Henry": An Autobiography* (New York: George H. Doran Company, 1919), 65.
11 Rem Koolhaas, *Delirious New York: A Retroactive Manifesto for Manhattan* (New York: The Monacelli Press, 1994).
12 Ibid., 61.
13 Ibid., 30.
14 Ibid., 33.

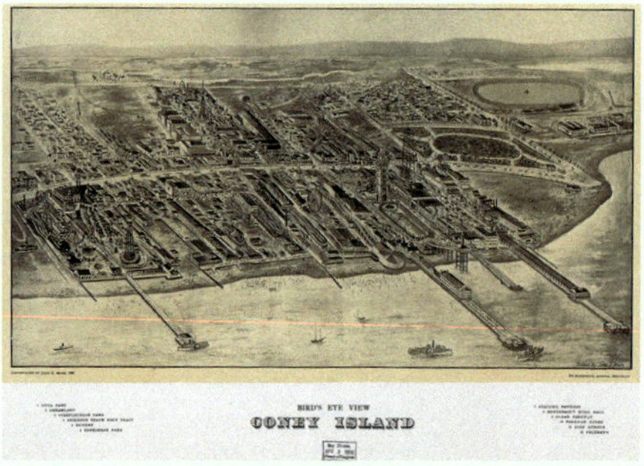

Bird's-eye view of Coney Island, 1906

natural limit,[15] and that the *bois* have openings allowing visual connections with distant landscapes. The quality and specificity of these interventions is thus based on the transformation of the forests into a comprehensive landscape system, tightly interwoven with its urban and territorial surroundings while preserving the essence of the place.

The *Bois* of the Twenty-first Century

Today, the Bois de Vincennes and Bois de Boulogne have been absorbed by urbanization and are considered an integral part of the metropolitan territory of Paris. Throughout the twentieth century, the city's growth has emphasized the need for recreational infrastructure, putting pressure on the picturesque scenery of the *bois*. This has led to bridle paths being transformed into roads with heavy car traffic, along with the multiplication of all sorts of recreational, cultural, and commercial facilities. Further transformations showing a lack of consideration or misunderstanding of the existing qualities–such as the enclosure of some parts by overly dense plantings or the top-down inclusion of new programs disconnected from the site and the privatization of areas for programmed uses–have resulted in a degradation of the image and use of the *bois*. Moreover, as urban society's relationship to "nature" shifted and changed over time, so did the enchantment that the *bois* once sparked in the public imaginary.

In order to respond to the current and future challenges that our cities are facing, such as global warming or the intensification of multiple uses in urbanized landscapes, our vision of the *bois* as a nineteenth-century bourgeois park needs to further evolve. The *bois* envisioned for the twenty-first century should remain a public space, open to all, which can be appropriated by the people and used in many ways. Potential new uses–such as agroforestry–could reconnect city dwellers with their environment in a productive relationship. Furthermore, the *bois* is also a "climatic machine," providing fresh air and water and supporting a habitat for a rich diversity of species.

15 See Georges-Eugène Haussmann, *Mémoires* (Paris: Victor-Harvard, 1890-93).

In the context of the Grand Paris metropolitan development, the figure of the *bois* could be rediscovered as a precious hinge between the inner city and its wider territory. As such, it has the potential to absorb the transformations of the evolving city and to become a structuring element of the urban fabric at the scale of the territory, much as the park and square do at the scale of the city and the neighborhood.

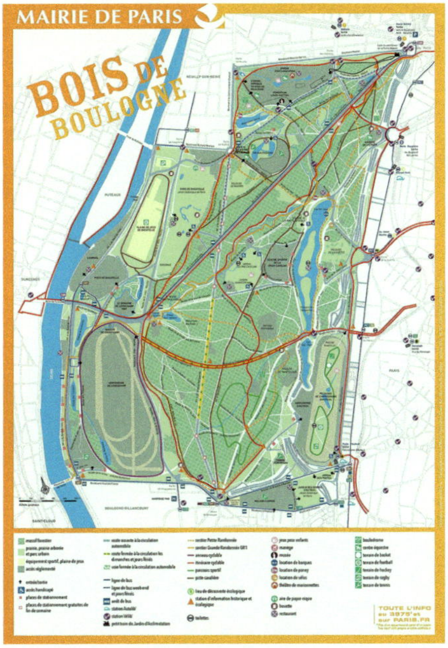

Bois de Boulogne visitors' map, 2014

>> *Plan général de la Ville de Paris, comprenant les Bois de Boulogne et de Vincennes, sous la direction d'Alphand,* 1878, Bibliothèque de l'École des mines de Paris–MINES ParisTech

PLAN DE PARIS
NOUVELLE ÉDITION
ASNIÈRES
CLICHY
COURBEVOIE
LEVALLOIS-PERRET
NEUILLY
PUTEAUX
SURESNES
BOULOGNE
St CLOUD
SÈVRES
ISSY
VANVES
MONTROUGE
MEUDON
CHAMP DE MARS
SEINE
BOIS DE MEUDON

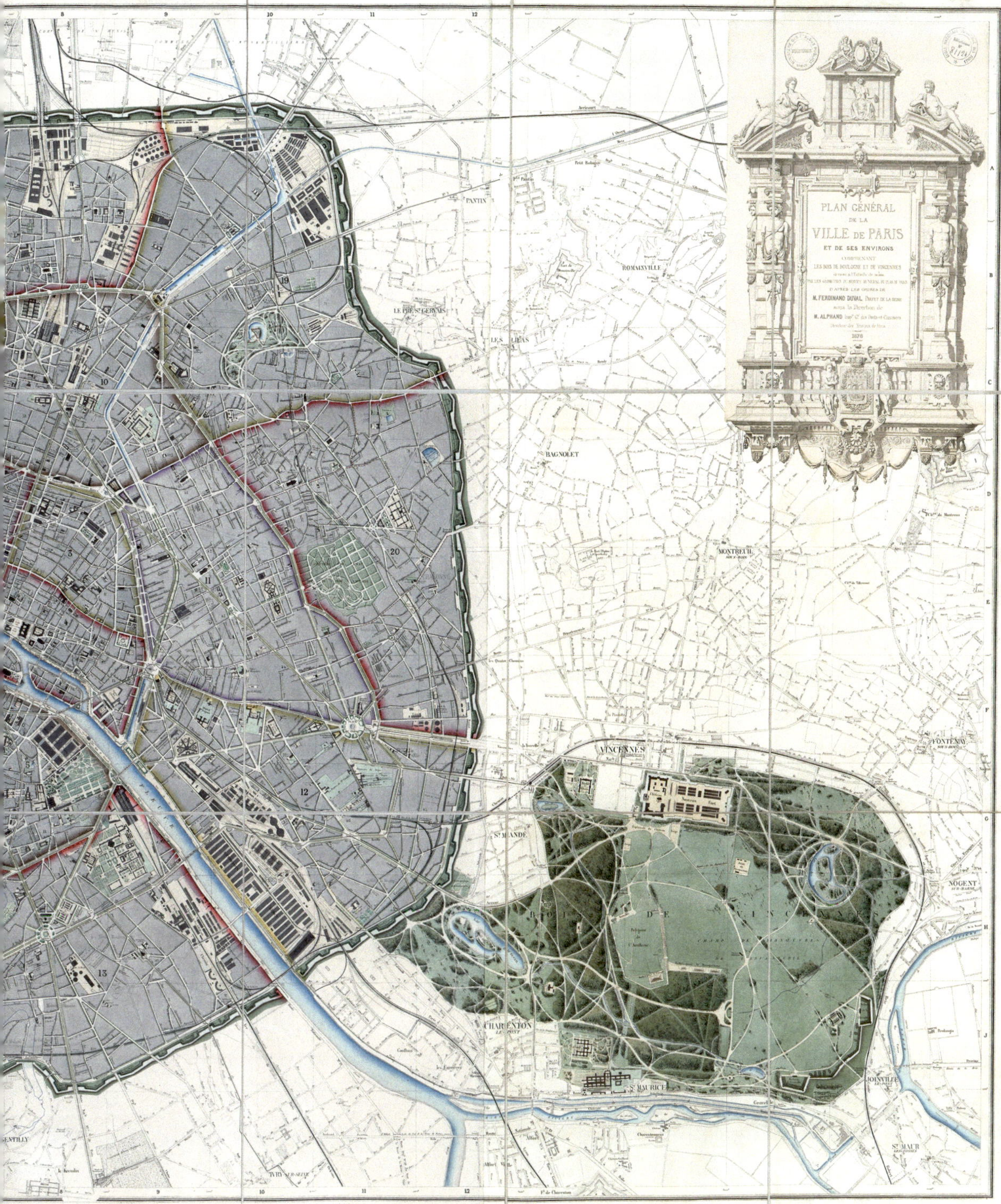

PLAN GÉNÉRAL
DE LA
VILLE DE PARIS
ET DE SES ENVIRONS
COMPRENANT
LES BOIS DE BOULOGNE ET DE VINCENNES
D'APRÈS LES ORDRES DE
M. FERDINAND DUVAL
M. ALPHAND
1878
PANTIN
ROMAINVILLE
LE PRÉ ST GERVAIS
LES LILAS
BAGNOLET
MONTREUIL
VINCENNES
FONTENAY
ST MANDÉ
NOGENT
CHARENTON
ST MAURICE
JOINVILLE
ST MAUR
IVRY
GENTILLY

Grand Paris Sud
Surveying the Territory

In the fragmented landscape of the Parisian suburb, individual elements no longer convey the significance of their larger context. In order to recover the link to the territory and to harness existing potential, adequate planning would imply taking a step back to question a given program or intervention brief and develop a landscape approach to the site. Combining a geographical approach, involving an analysis of the physical and cultural landscape through cartographic surveys, with an on-site examination of the site's characteristics, liberated from a preconceived understanding or anticipated uses, may suggest new programs and new connections, providing additional value to any future development.

Heading out of Paris to the southeast, toward the last ring of suburbs between Paris and the Seine valley, one encounters the site of the former Hippodrome d'Evry, where the sprawling urban fabric of the metropolis meets the hinterland.
At first glance, this area could be any other urban fringe, with its characteristic vocabulary: fences, suburban developments of single-family houses, billboards, warehouses, leftover agricultural fields, and disjointed patches of pristine landscape. These elements float in the territory like an archipelago of isolated events that no longer relate either to one another or to their wider context. Here, cars dominate and movement happens at high speed, offering only glimpses of the fragmented landscape.

Since 2012, a series of projects have been commissioned for the site, first prompted by the planning of the future FFR rugby stadium, an undertaking that was subsequently abandoned. The briefs took a systematic approach, focused on real estate investment, with the site of the former hippodrome viewed as a large "empty" area, ready for the insertion of a new program in order to become financially viable. However, the site's strategic location–as a hinge between the city and its hinterland–was an opportunity to envision new forms of territorial agency, beyond programmatic requirements and site boundaries determined by investors.

While the site of the former hippodrome was continually referred to as "empty" or "marginal," in-depth surveys and mappings encompassing an expanded understanding of the terrain instead unveiled its undeniable beauty. This landscape approach revealed an area still characterized by a great porosity, with open and productive soils–despite the sprawl of urbanization–at whose heart lies a key territorial entity: the Bois de Saint-Eutrope.

Through the surveying work, it became apparent that site specificity based on the presence of abandoned open spaces and agricultural lands can create both the image and framework of the future territory. Within the site's seemingly banal landscape reside unique qualities and the potential to rediscover a sense of territorial coherence. (lb)

The site consisting of the Bois de Saint-Eutrope and the former Hippodrome d'Evry is at the fringe of urbanization and the intersection of four landscape types, as well as part of a network of *bois* and open spaces in the south of Paris.

1 Site
2 Paris
3 The Seine
4 Aqueduct
5 Fôret de Fontainebleau (forest)

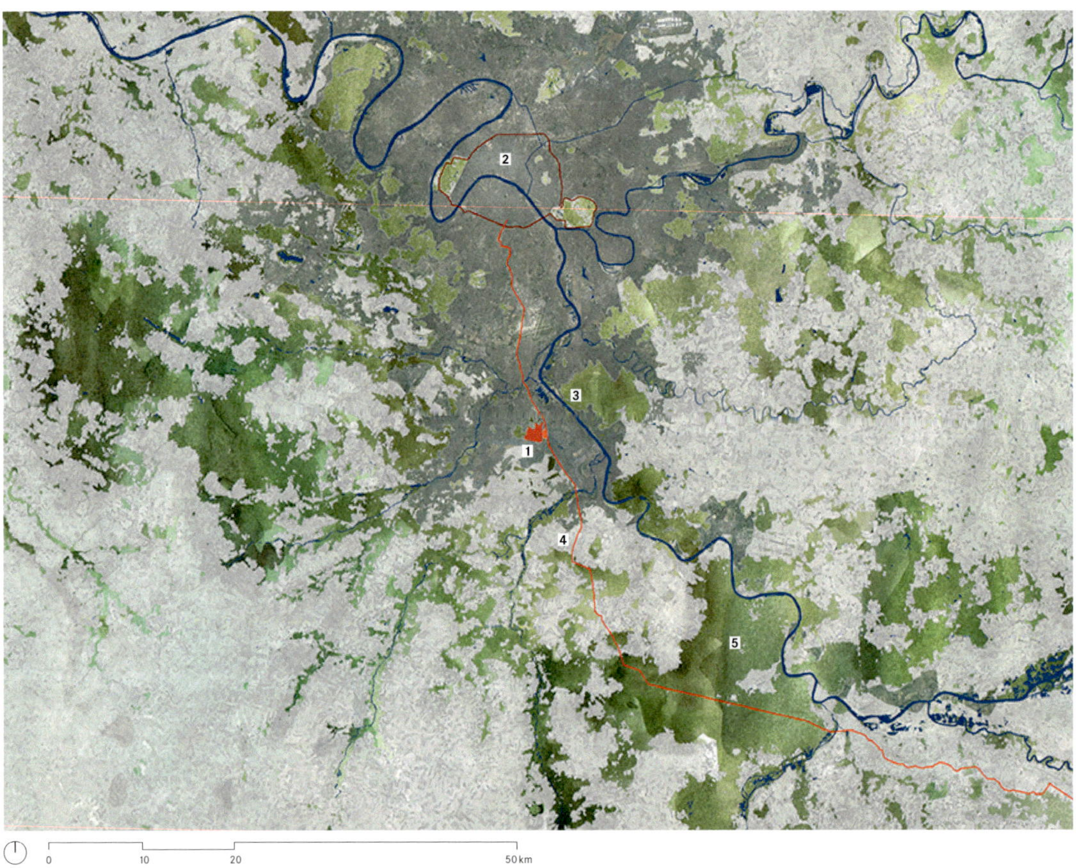

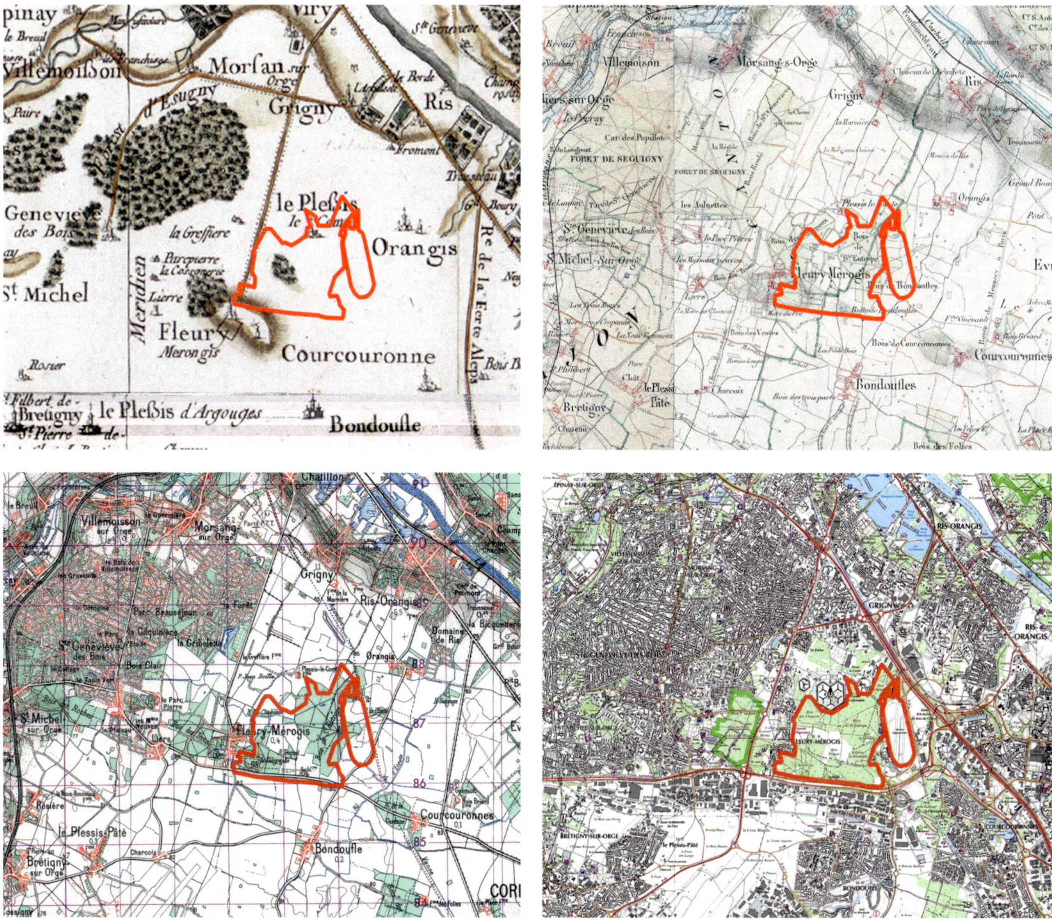

Historical development: 1750, 1850, 1950, 2000

The urbanization of the peripheral environs of Paris led to the loss of open spaces and the gradual isolation of the site. Layers of infrastructure further cut the plateau off from the valley of the Seine.

Within this patchwork of lands uses, the assemblage of Bois de Saint-Eutrope and the old hippodrome form a coherent territorial ensemble and a unique landscape. This strong territorial entity can federate future development and offer new patterns of urbanization.

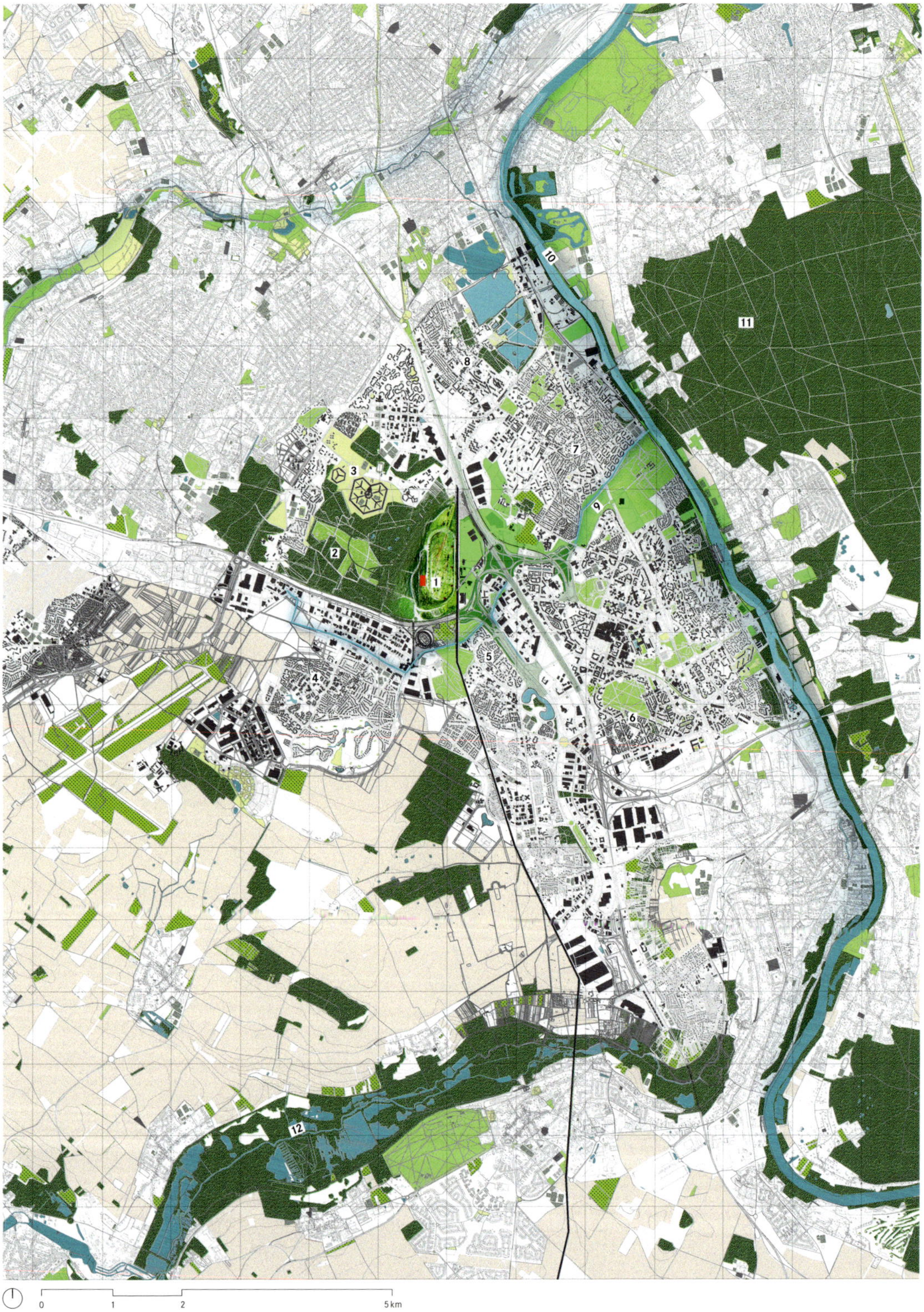
1
2
3
4
5
6
7
8
9
10
11
12
0
1
2
5 km

From the Bois de Saint-Eutrope to the Seine, a succession of residual spaces corresponding to the last open expanses suggests a physical connection and possible ecological continuity between the plateau and the valley.

In the Ile-de-France territorial context, where space is increasingly divided and compartmentalized, the unifying potential of open spaces is important and should be preserved.

1 Racetrack
2 Bois de Saint-Eutrope
3 Fleury-Mérogis
4 Bondoufle
5 Courcouronnes
6 Évry
7 Ris-Orangis
8 Grigny
9 Ru de l'Écoute-S'il-Pleut (brook)
10 The Seine
11 Forêt de Sénart (forest)
12 L'Essonne

1 Prison de Fleury-Mérogis
2 Bois du temple
3 Bois de l'Hôtel-Dieu
4 Passage piéton sous l'A6 (pedestrian passage under the motorway)
5 Jardins familiaux l'Orme Pomponne (allotment gardens)
6 Aqueduc de la Vanne (aqueduct)
7 Route de la Chasse
8 Bois de Saint-Eutrope
9 Maison du directeur (director's house)
10 Anciens terrains usine Lu (former Lu factory grounds)
11 Château
12 Vers la gare (to the train station)
13 Autoroute A6 (highway)
14 Paddock
15 Tour d'observation (observation tower)
16 Bois du kiosque
17 Tribunes
18 Mare (pond)
19 Ancienne voie du petit train (former route of a small train)
20 La Queue de Bondoufle
21 Parking
22 Zone d'activités du Bois de l'épine (mixed-use area)
23 Camp de gens du voyage (travelers' camp)
24 Kart (Go-karts)
25 Francilienne (motorway ring)
26 Jardins familiaux la Garenne (allotment gardens)
27 Zone industrielle de la Marinière (industrial zone)
28 Stade Bobin (stadium)
29 Ru de l'Écoute-S'il-Pleut (brook)

The map reveals the spatial diversity and richness of the former hippodrome, in direct connection with the Bois de Saint-Eutrope. It maps the specific articulation of the hippodrome with architectural elements such as the aqueduct, the gallery, and the former house of the director as well as the specific structure, views, and scales of the site. Most importantly, it reveals the presence of a rich and diverse vegetation.

Grand Paris Sud

Surveying the Territory

1

2

3

4

5

6

7

8

9

Immediately surrounding the lush and diverse ecosystem of the “empty” hippodrome, is located an area of low density, underused commercially and industrially zoned lots. An extended survey captured in photos reveals a landscape of cookie-cutter houses, infrastructures, warehouses, and parking lots designed to be traversed solely by car. At the same time, within this suburban fabric, elements uncovered by the historical study such as the woods and the brook Ru de l’Écoute-s’il-pleut, are reminders that the larger territory still exist beneath the sprawl. The large swath of land–paved over, underused, and mostly empty–is ready to be rediscovered and reimagined.

Project
Modulus

Within the fragmented landscapes of the suburban fringe, the site is located between two river valleys, the Seine and the Orge. At the center is the former racetrack of the Hippodrome d'Evry. Abandoned for more than twenty years, this overgrown plain has developed its own unique characteristics and ecosystem. While the planted vegetation is still visible, the place has become a haven for wildlife, colonized by deer and boar.

1 From the gallery, the plain extends to the horizon marked by the aqueduct. The line of plane trees and poplars marks the course along which the infrastructure runs and the transition into an area of urbanization.

2 & 3 The plain was planted with shrubs and regularly pruned to keep the views open. Once activities relating to the hippodrome had ceased, the vegetation was able to grow freely. The shrubs that were selected for planting often had a horticultural character, and their continued presence is revealed by their bright colors. Their isolation in contrast to the spontaneous vegetation of a park reinforces the strangeness of the composition.

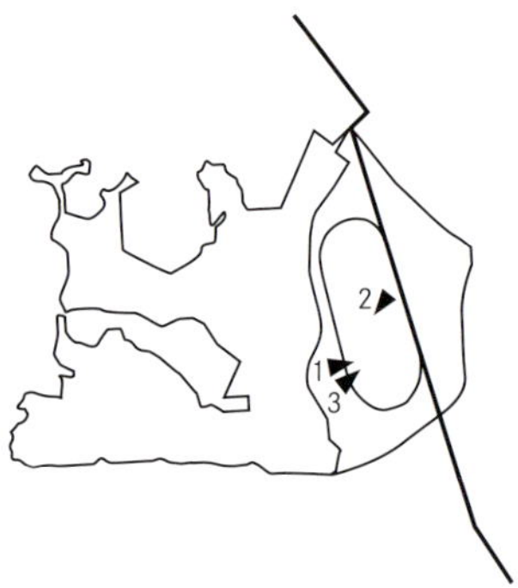

1

2

3

4 This landscape constitutes a unique space with a mixture of artifice, spontaneity, wildness, and scattered architectural elements that is important for the region. The quality and uniqueness of this landscape lies in the scale and openness of the spaces and the poetry that emerges from them.

5 The landscape of the former hippodrome, which is now overgrown, is punctuated by relics of its previous function. The tower that was once used as a platform from which to watch the horse races looks out over what has become a wild plain.

6 There is something elegant and touching about how these architectures have been taken over by "nature." The usual limits are blurred, and we experience a feeling of time frozen and the beginning of a new rhythm of change outside of the human realm.

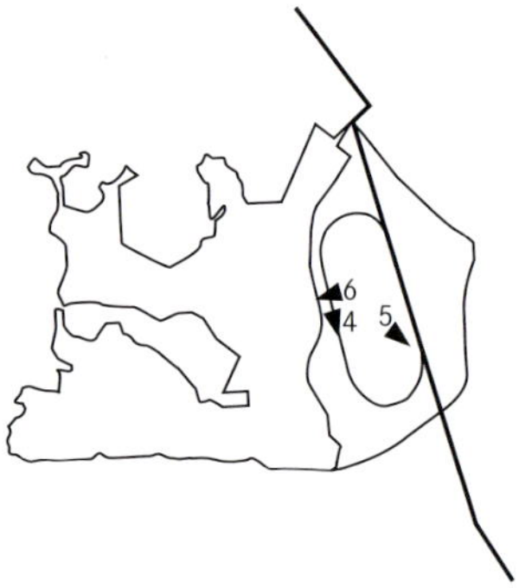

4

5

6

7

8

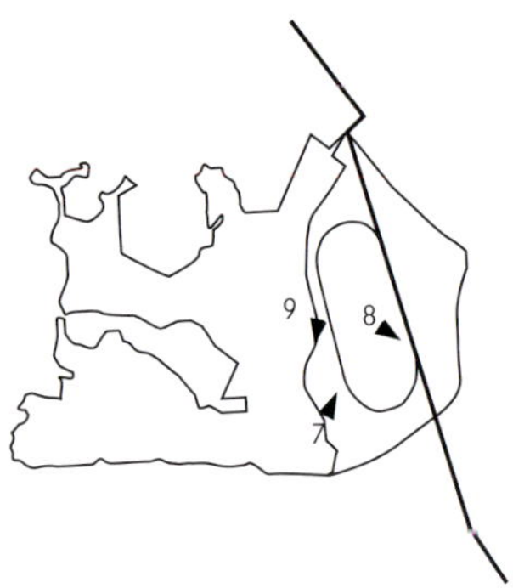

7 & 8 The modern ruins have reversed their roles. The abandoned escalator, once used to speed up movement, only emphasizes the passing of time. The observation tower, which once overlooked the entire racetrack, is now a visual symbol, seen from afar.

9 The racecourse paddock reflects the original and unique architecture of the area. Designed in concentric circles, it welcomed riders and their horses to warm up or relax. It remains a space with a unique atmosphere. Bordered by very high rows of coniferous trees, the sun's rays pierce the curtain of very thin trunks.

9 

10 While the aqueduct effectively cuts through the entire site, its accessible points are not always obvious. Here, it is hidden from the allotment gardens by spontaneous wooded areas.

11 In the center of the *bois,* a large clearing dedicated to agricultural uses mirrors the fields to the south of the site.

12 Behind the aqueduct and its gates lies the abandoned hippodrome, which forms a logical entrance to the plain beyond.

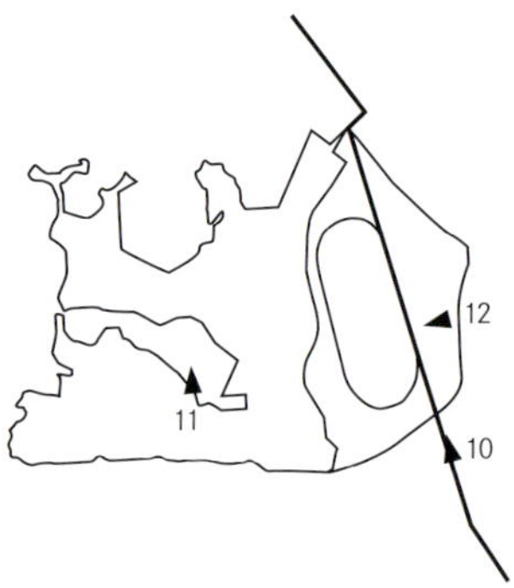

10

11

12

13 The east side of the central plain is structured by the aqueduct of the Vanne and the Loing. The aqueduct is fringed by a magnificent line of plane trees which also act as a landmark. Running toward Paris, one can imagine its development as the "High Line"–of Grand Paris Sud.

14 The presence of the Rue de l'Écoute-S'il-Pleut stretches across the plateau, passing beneath the open plain and through a series of open spaces, which include large agricultural areas and allotment gardens located in the pockets of the infrastructure, suggesting the possibility of a physical east-west connection between the Bois de Saint-Eutrope, the forest of Sénart, and the areas beyond.

15 The quality of the open space makes it possible to read the geography of the territory: the plateau plunges to the east into the Seine valley, while the forest of Sénart on the other side is visible in the distance. It is a place of yearning, a fragile space, subject to the pressures of urbanization.

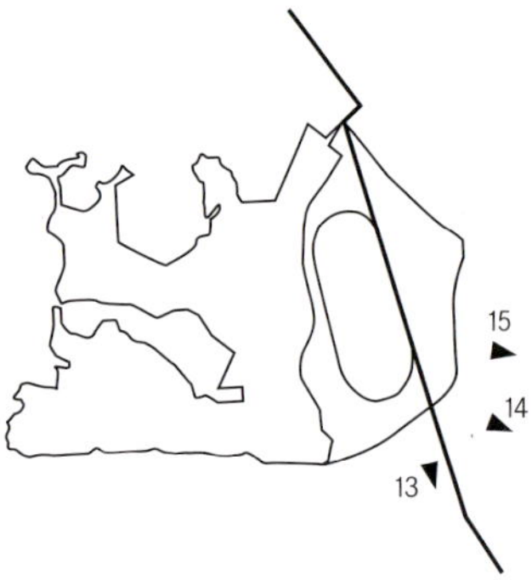

13 

14

15

Fagus sylvatica
On Creating Order in the Forest

Lars Ruge

European beeches, more than 100 years old, form a closed canopy forest that prohibits the emergence of any undergrowth (Schluttenbach, foothills of the Black Forest).

Natural Dynamics

Roman historian Tacitus described the land of the Germanic peoples as *terra, [. . .] aut silvis horrida, aut paludibus foeda*[1]–*their lands, [. . .] consist of dreadful forests and hideous swamps.* At a time when Roman culture had already deforested much of the Mediterranean region in order to obtain wood–mostly for the construction of settlements, infrastructure, military facilities, and ships–as well as to heat their thermal baths, the Germanic peoples generally lived in small settlements within dense forests, worshipping individual trees as divinities. If it were not for the utilization of wood and the clearing of land by humans, Europe would still be a single continuous forest–with the exception of bodies of water and high alpine regions.

The natural climax of forest growth always succeeds a primaeval state, which for its part follows the collapse of existing forest structures–caused, for example, by fires or landslides in forested areas or virgin soils. Depending on the original condition, the duration of the development may vary, but the result is always the same: grass-like structures are succeeded by tall herbaceous vegetation, scrub growth, and the first pioneer trees, which include birches and pines as well as Robinia and *Ailanthus altissima* trees, which are now considered invasive. This is followed by more advanced stages of development, until a self-contained forest is formed in which the European beech tree is frequently able to thrive. Owing to its great tolerance for different conditions, from fresh to dry soils, it is indicative of the potential natural vegetation, manifested in the form of imposing forests with a closed canopy.

The plant succession begins with grasses, shrubs, and bushes, before quick-growing, short-lived tree species establish themselves, culminating in a dense forest. If the forest fails or is logged, the process starts all over again.

The European Beech

As a result of climatic changes, some five thousand years ago the European beech—at that time a neophyte species—replaced the oak as the main tree species in European forests, where it is currently the most prevalent deciduous tree making up some 15 percent of woodland growth.[2] This development can be attributed both to its specific properties and, possibly, to the fact that the foliage and shoots of the European beech are avoided by livestock, and humans used better-tasting leafy trees in forestry and pastoral agriculture for thousands of years. The European beech is presently to be found from southern England to France and northern Spain and across central Europe, stretching all the way to Poland, western Ukraine, and Crimea. The tree can be found as far north as southern Scandinavia and as far south as central Spain, Corsica, Italy, and even on the Balkan Peninsula.

Beech forests in Europe according to altitudinal belts

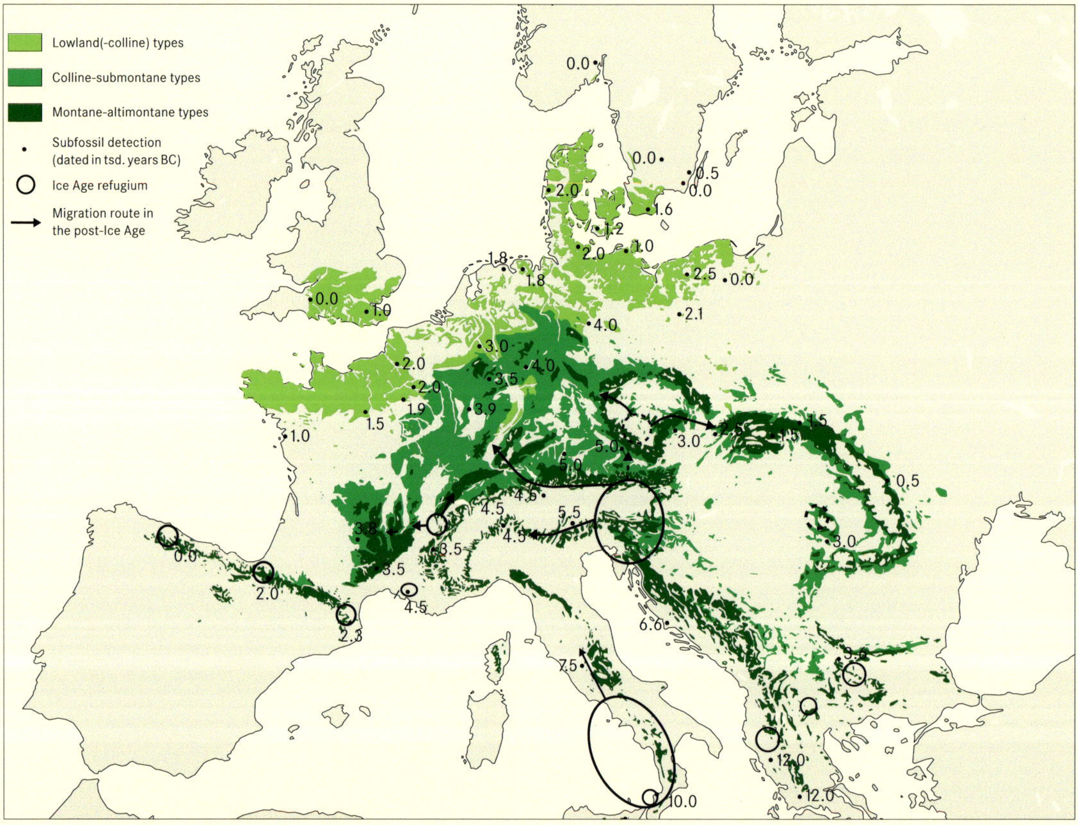

The beech tree has a very broad site amplitude in terms of soil moisture and pH value and is thus much more competitive than other species.

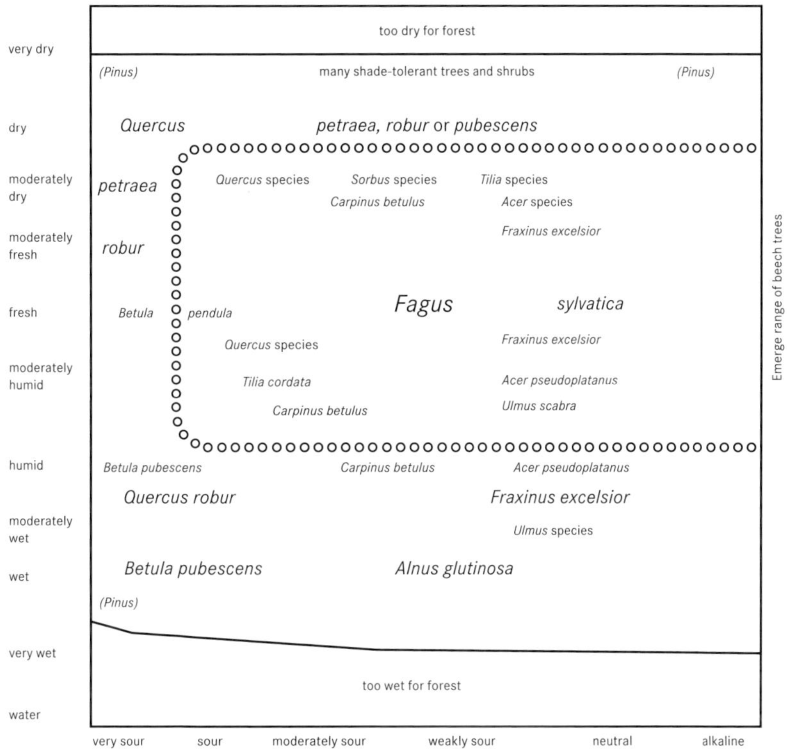

The dominance of the European beech tree can be explained by the fact that it provides a great deal of shade while requiring comparatively little light itself. Owing to its substantial growth, dense foliage, and the robust side branches that manage to efficiently close any gaps, hardly any other tree casts such a deep shadow. These conditions in turn favor the germination of its own seeds. Only the seeds of the horse chestnut, a tree of the same family, thrive equally well. Despite its vigorous growth, the European beech has an extreme tolerance to being pruned: as a result, its reddish-brown foliage, which clings to the tree until new sprouts emerge, characterizes entire landscapes and residential developments in such places as northern Germany, the Netherlands, and Denmark, in the form of clipped hedges. If nowadays the trees are trimmed for the most part in accordance with aesthetic principles, in earlier historical periods agricultural or forest-management uses defined their form, as the goal was to create the best possible conditions for the field crops to thrive and for harvesting.

XXI, 5. 34. Cupuliferae.

160. Fagus silvatica L. **Rotbuche.**

The largest trees are regularly harvested from the forest in order to provide light and space for future generations to develop and to allow trees of all ages to grow. As a rule, there is no prescribed planting pattern: rather, the emphasis is on layering and fostering the concurrency of the different forest stories. Illustration in: *Sylvicultura Oeconomica* by Hans Carl von Carlowitz, Leipzig, 1713.

The Origins of Sustainability

In past centuries, the mighty forests of Europe were used agriculturally in many different ways: originally to a limited extent as pasture for cattle and pigs and as a source of wood and foliage for fuel and animal bedding, and later on a large scale for intensive construction, shipbuilding, and handicrafts. As a result, forest areas were so severely depleted in the Middle Ages that wood became a scarce commodity. The forest ordinance decreed in 1442 in the Bishopric of Speyer was a direct response to this overuse.[3] It regulated the long-term management of forests, based on the principle that the number of trees that were cut down should be equal to or fewer than the number that were replanted, thus ensuring the availability of this raw material for later generations. This goal of maintaining the value of the forests formulated in the fifteenth century led to the stabilization of, and even an increase in forest growth. In 1713, during a new period of wood scarcity, it was invoked by Hans Carl von Carlowitz, who cited it as a basis for the sustainable management of natural resources.[4] His treatises formed the basis for our modern idea of "sustainability," a term that is now used to the point of excess.

Silviculture–Two Strategies

In forestry, diverse tree species are planted, tended, and felled depending on such local factors as water supply, available nutrients, light, exposure, altitude, and soil type, in addition to economic factors and the demand for wood. The density of planting and the mix of species generate

Large-scale timber production to the south of Munich as shown on a map from 1768

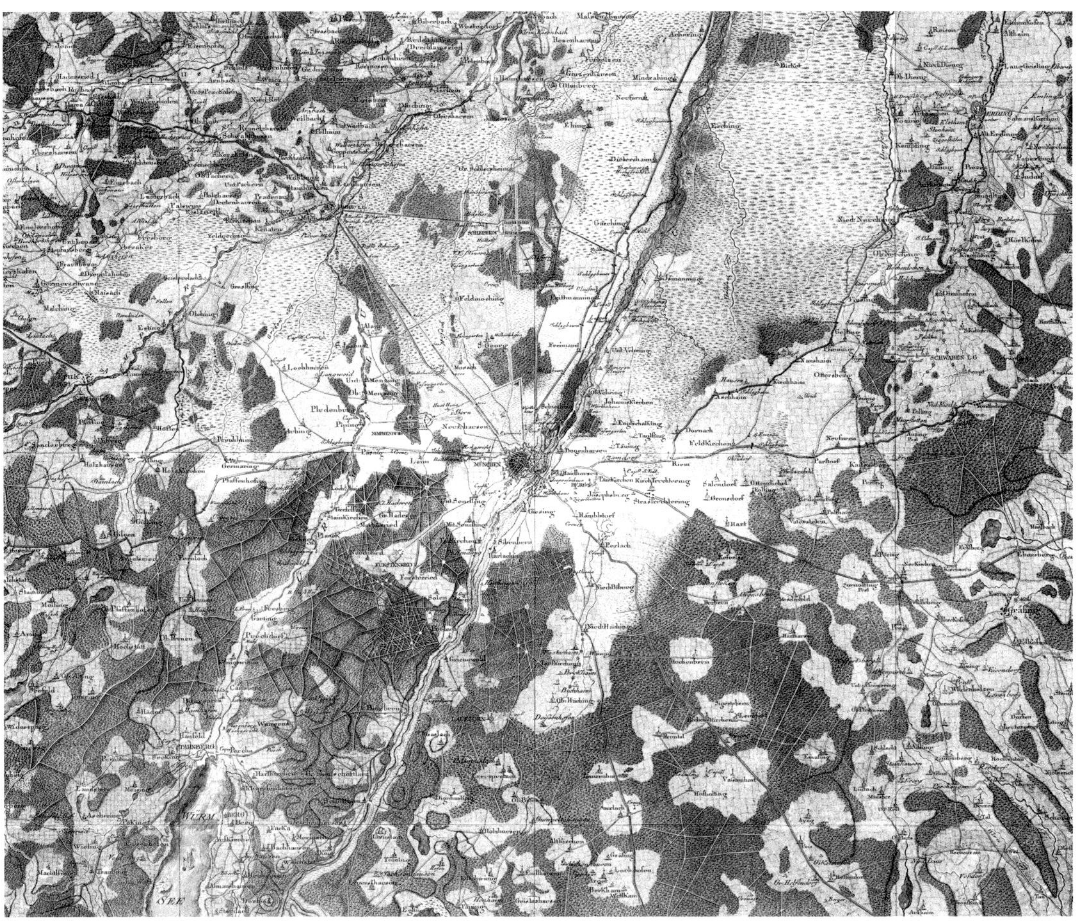

Nursery trees are planted in the Masoala Rainforest Hall at the Zurich Zoo.

competition, regulating growth and allowing the land to be shared by different kinds of fast- and slow-growing species. In the course of the decades, forests are progressively thinned, and wood is extracted.

Nurseries pursue the opposite goal. Here, trees are initially planted close together and subsequently replanted every three years at an ever-increasing distance from one another. The focus is not on competition, elongated growth, or wood mass in a given area but rather on the tree as an optimally cultivated individual. The tools of the disciplines reflect this difference: while in forestry only one part of the tree—the valuable trunk—is of interest after the axe and saw have done their work, in nurseries trees are shaped holistically with pruning knife and shears and harvested along with their roots.

Planting strategies based on the idea of a layered forest

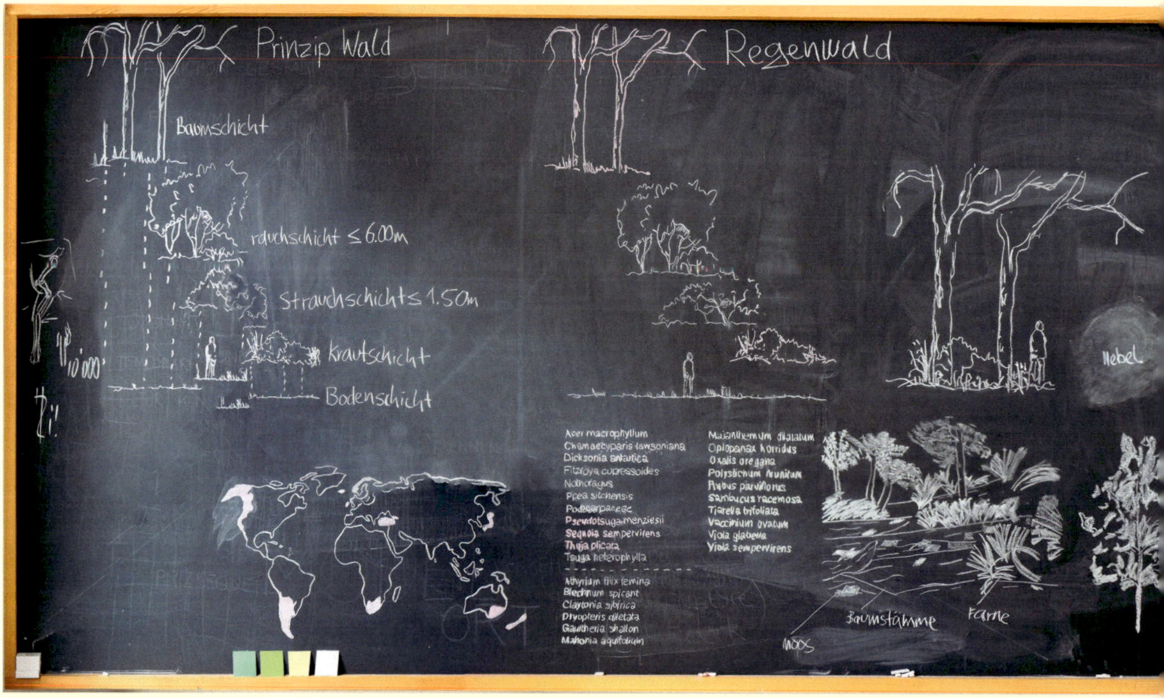

How Does the Forest find Its Way into the City?

In many projects, the question arises as to how the properties of the forest–varying density, volume of vegetation, multiplicity of species, biodiversity–can be reproduced in new residential settlements or parks without interfering with existing woodland, which in many countries is strictly protected by law. The distinct strategies applied by foresters and in nurseries offer a basis for the development of design rules. In combination with the farmer's traditional knowledge regarding the optimal–that is, most productive–distances between plants, and with the models of previous movements in garden art and local variations, plant strategies can be developed that are not merely random. While the average passerby will simply enjoy the varied plant life, an attentive observer will be aware of how the rules that have been applied connect with the individual qualities of various tree species, while at the same time noticing the resulting choreography, the succession of spaces, the variation in vegetation, and the interplay between staged design and natural dynamics.

1 Marcus Nenninger, *Die Römer und der Wald: Untersuchungen zum Umgang mit einem Naturraum am Beispiel der römischen Nordwestprovinze* (Stuttgart: Franz Steiner, 2001), 31.

2 Philippe Della Casa, "Ur- und Frühgeschichte," section 1 of "Wald," *Historisches Lexikon der Schweiz HLS,* April 29, 2017, www.hls-dhs-dss.ch/de/articles/007849/2015-04-29/.

3 See Karl Hasel and Ekkehard Schwartz, *Forstgeschichte: Ein Grundriss für Studium und Praxis* (Remagen-Oberwinter: Kessel, 2002).

4 See Hans Carl von Carlowitz, *Sylvicultura Oeconomica, oder haußwirthliche Nachricht und Naturmäßige Anweisung zur Wilden Baum-Zucht,* 2nd ed. (1732; repr., Remagen-Oberwinter: Kessel, 2009).

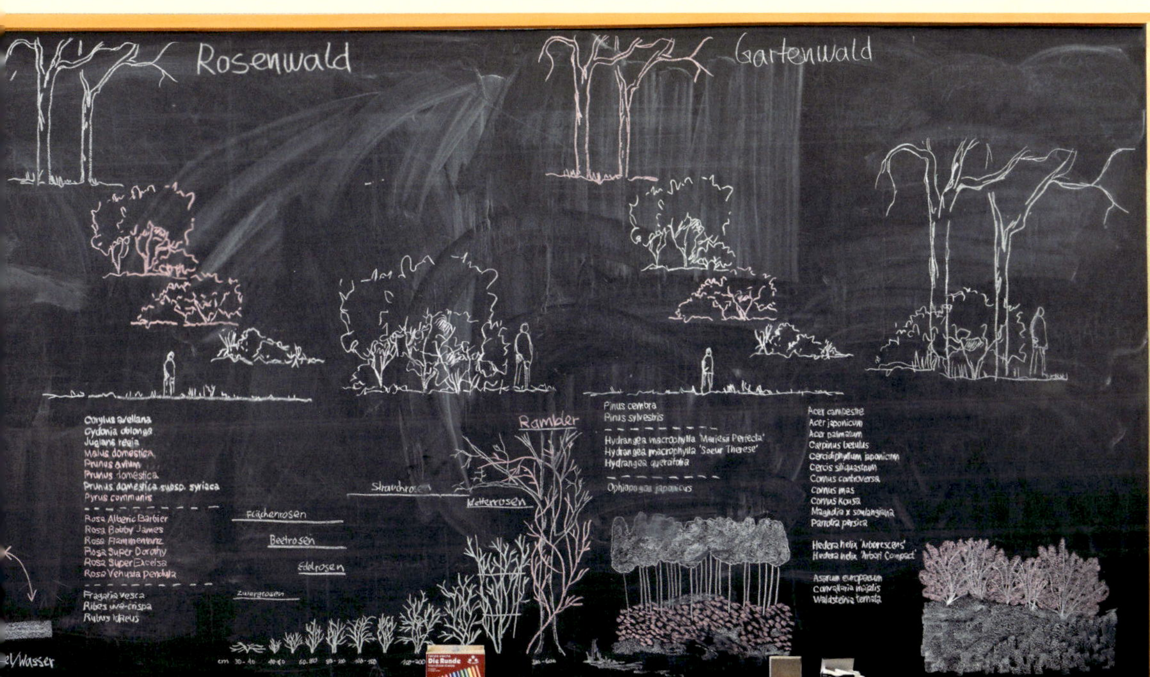

Skolkovo, Moscow
Miniaturized Landscape

Client:
LLC UDPC Skolkovo, Moscow

Cooperation:
Architecture:
Herzog & de Meuron, Basel

Design/construction:
2013–2015/2015–2018

Type and size:
Courtyards/Landscape, 11.2 ha

Status:
Realized

Thermokarst is a geomorphological process associated with the formation of a characteristic landscape created by the thawing of permafrost in Arctic areas and, on a smaller scale, in mountainous areas such as the Himalayas or the Alps. The melting of ground ice is accompanied by the formation of depressions, with irregular surfaces consisting of marshy hollows and small hummocks. These depressions can have a surprising effect on the vegetation: the undermining of the shallow root bed of the trees causes them to tilt at various angles, resulting in so-called drunken forests.

The phenomenon of thermokarst also appears in the courtyards of the new Skolkovo Innovation Center, but in miniaturized form: the floor's differentiated microtopography is covered either with a carpet of perennials and small shrubs or with a usable lawn, depending on the courtyard's function. Individual oblique trees and groups of trees reinforce this dynamic image and are a translation of the archaic, local landscape–a counterpoint to the institute's global alignment and its focus on energy, information, telecommunications, biomedicine, and nuclear technologies.

While the courtyards are an interpretation of this unique formation, the landscape surrounding the buildings is conceived as a spacious forest of birch, aspen, and pine, in reference to the regional vegetation. Overlapping grids and rows of trees generate constant perceptual shifts. While the artificiality of the forest is obvious from a bird's-eye view, only the attentive pedestrian will be aware of its principles: a walk through the forest along its smaller paths reveals the woodland as an area of wild growth, while on the main trails, the regularity of the planting–underlined by the presence of only one species per row–becomes more evident. The species that were selected and their particular characteristics, such as their autumn colors and bark, blur the distinction between the unregulated spread of vegetation and the systematic planting scheme–the concept is based on the strategy of feigning "wilderness" with precision. (lr)

Permafrost is formed in places where the average annual temperature does not go above -1°C. The ground frost can produce patterns such as ice wedges or polygon soils.

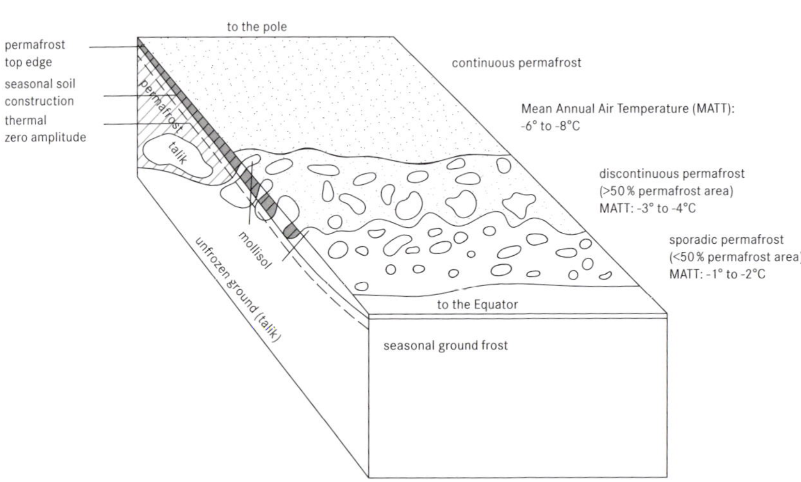

Tropisme

Julian Charrière, 2014–2015

Tropisme consists of a refrigerated showcase in which the artist has deposited plants captured in a sheath of ice–as if time could be stopped, and the plants might be preserved and archived for future use. In this frozen landscape, the vitality of matter is protected exothermically from the forces of entropy and decay. But the organisms also point backward in time, toward the inception of ancient molecular memories. The plants (orchids, cactuses, etc.) are testimony to a geological period–the Cretaceous–which saw the extinction of dinosaurs. The artist thus freezes them like relics from a time whose memory forever escapes us, except perhaps in some residual part of our “reptilian” brain.

Text by Nadim Samman for Galerie Tschudi’s
2016 show, *First Light*

Skolkovo, Moscow

Miniaturized Landscape

The courtyards take up the idea of "drunken" trees and present a transformed version of the phenomenon. The trees lean to the side when the permafrost thaws on the surface and subsides.

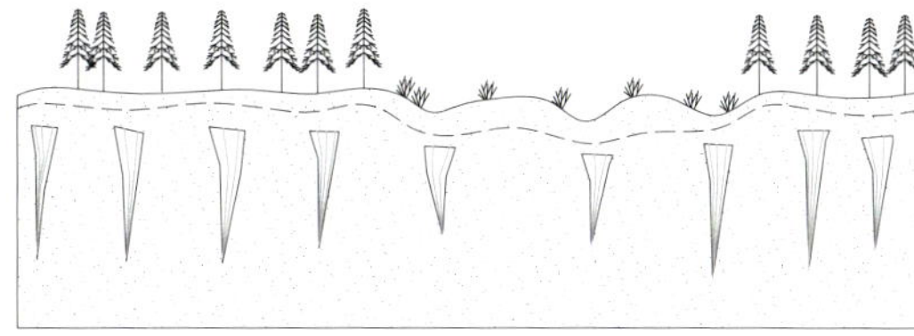

Step 1: Thawing of ice wedges and formation of thermokarst hills

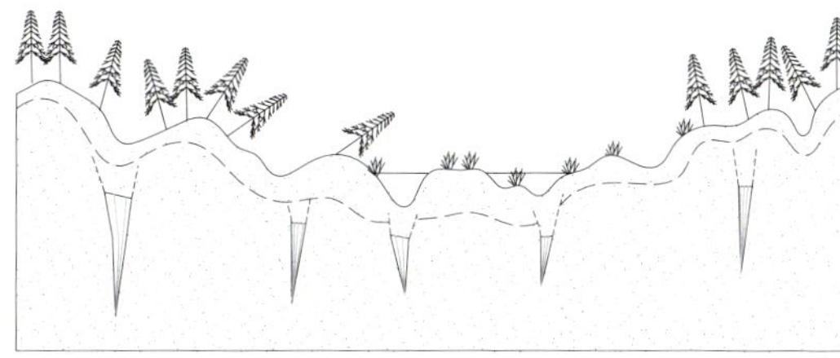

Step 2: Further land subsidence and water accumulation

Icy permafrost with ice wedges

Permafrost surface

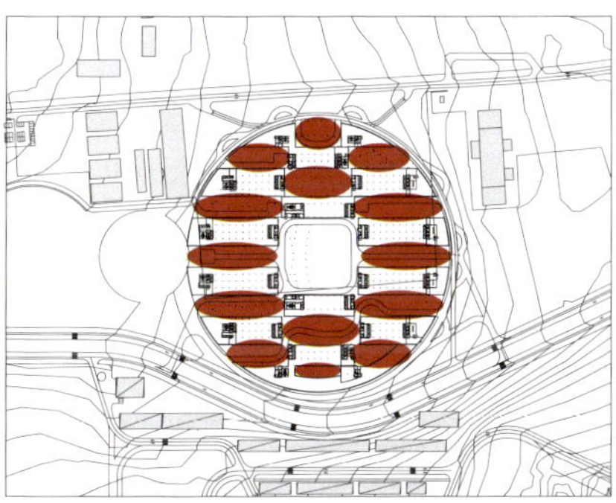

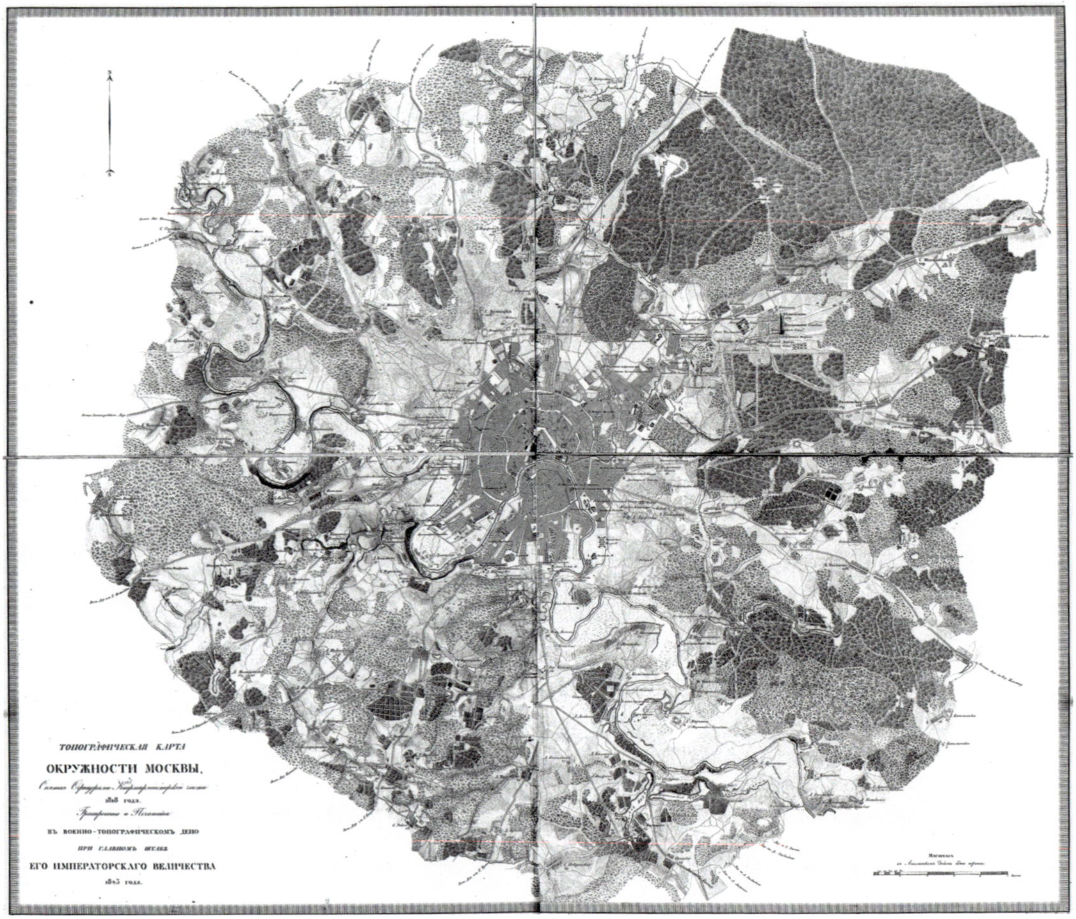

Map of Moscow and its suburbs, 1823

spruce and fir forest

pine forest

birch and aspen forest

mixed-deciduous forest

boreal conifer forest

deciduous forest

Skolkovo, Moscow

Miniaturized Landscape

The artificial wood is based on the principles and strategies used in forestry. From a higher vantage point, the grid system overlaid by the secondary principle of diagonally crossing paths becomes visible. At ground level, this order is only visible when you walk along one of the paths, with each of them flanked by a particular species of tree–however, a look into the woods will reveal it as a "wilderness." Its appearance will change over time due to different degrees of competitive pressure, damage caused by external influences, and forest harvesting. Although the sense of order will relax, the planting principles will persist unchanged.

Badaevskiy Brewery, Moscow
Opushka, the Russian Forest Edge

Located along the Moskva River, the partially dilapidated site of the historic Badaevskiy Brewery is being rehabilitated into a mixed-use public area in central Moscow–with recreational, commercial, and residential facilities. While the heritage buildings of the factory are being restored, a large residential complex is added. It sits lifted 35 meters above ground on a forest of columns. Underneath, at the heart of the development, a 6 ha area is becoming a new neighborhood park for Moscow. Situated atop a 400 m stretch of elevated river embankment, this man-made tract sets the stage for a condensed interpretation of the East European mixed forest. Informed by an understanding of the natural processes that define a forest edge, the park is structured as a succession of layers culminating in an open orchard that recalls Moscow's historic parks and reinforces the collective memory of the city.

Client:
Capital Group, Moscow

Cooperation:
Architecture:
Apex, Moscow
Design Consultant:
Herzog & de Meuron, Basel

Design/construction:
2017–ongoing

Type and size:
Park, 6.1 ha

Status:
Ongoing

The Metropolitan Landscape of Moscow

Moscow is characterized by a high level of complexity and diversity in both indigenous and anthropogenic landscapes. Established in the twelfth century, the city was built on the ancient alluvial terraces of the Moskva river, at the meeting point of three physiographic provinces that defined its shape: the elevated hilly terrain in the southwest, the low-lying flatter landforms in the northeast, and elevated plains in the northwest. Within these, nine individual territorial complexes–specific combinations of topography, hydrology, soil type, and vegetation–converge at the city center. While such a dense array is unique in the Central Russian Plain, this indigenous landscape has over time been transformed by agriculture, infrastructure, and urban buildup, with a tendency toward the reduction of biodiversity. Indeed, even though original woodlands remain at the outskirts of Moscow, urban vegetation is the result of more than eight hundred years of human activity through the cultivation of monastery gardens, large estates, nurseries, or Soviet cooperatives that have become public parks. These parks form part of the collective memory and culture of the living city.

Two Landscape Types as Reference

The project responds to this cultural dimension by integrating two landscape types that bear a literary significance in Russian collective memory: the soft edge of primary succession, affectionately called the *opushka,* and the flowering orchard. In the Russian imagination, the *opushka* carries poetic associative connotations of benign wilderness, softness, abundance, and warmth. In cultivated landscapes, this exuberance is translated into the form of productive orchards. In Moscow, orchards were historically planted near the river's edge, as in Kolomenskoje, where people still collect fruit, or the apple trees planted in the 1950s along Kutuzovsky Avenue, just 4 kilometers away from the site.

Translation into a Layered Design

The "forest edge" provides a layered spatial structure that articulates the relation between existing and new elements–the heritage factory building, the new architecture with its ultimate level of private garden rooftops, and the river bank. At the exterior, the embankment's hard edge is modulated by smaller sun-loving plants and forms the interface with the river. Inside the shaded forest interior, 20 m tall trees merge with the massive columns that lift up the horizontal skyscraper. Gradually, these give way to the *opushka,* where smaller variegated pioneer species and dense ground cover call to mind natural abundance and diversity. Closer to the interior and lower to the ground, undulating soft meadows finally lead into the grassland where clumps of fruit trees change with the seasons and invite genuine biodiversity into the park year-round.

Altogether, over eighty species make up the planting palette of the park. This diversity of vegetation recalls indigenous mixed forests, while the fruit trees bring the visitors into direct engagement with the landscape. The planting scheme is thus central to the project, as it makes tangible the ever-present connection between culturally constructed notions of "nature" and their inherent qualities of biodiversity and vitality, from which cultural significance in turn arises. (asb)

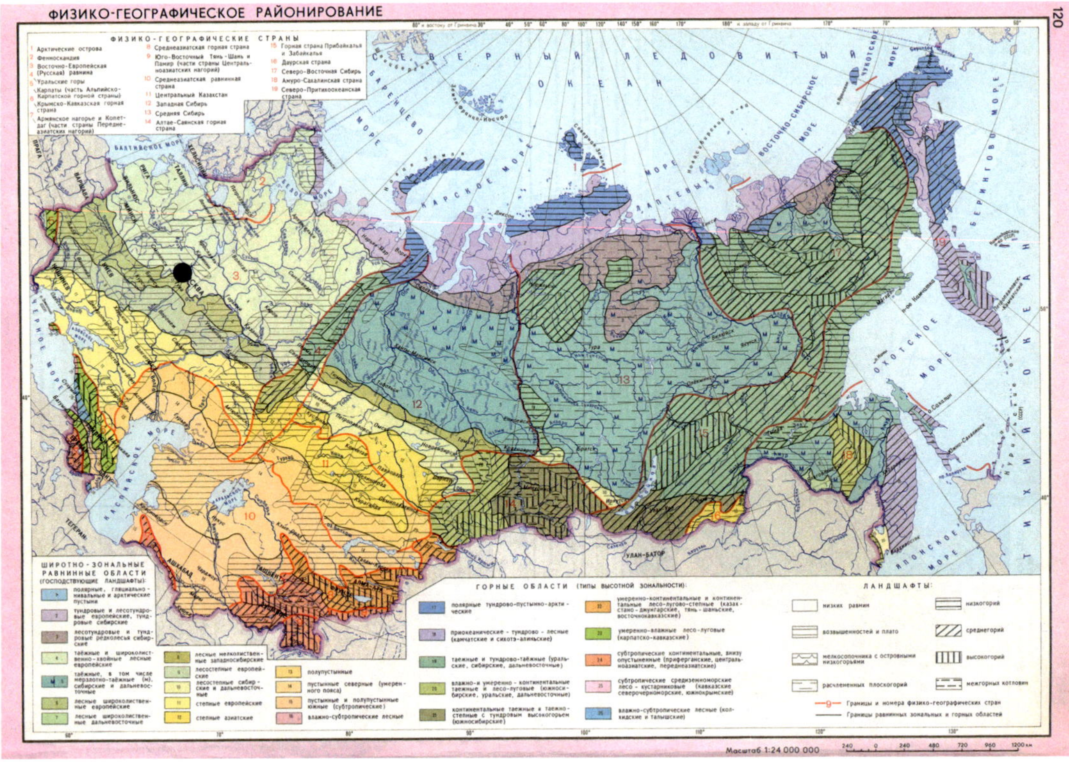

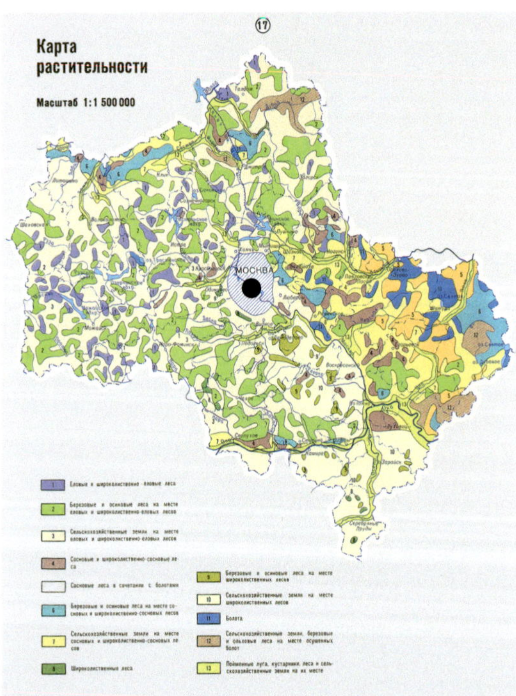

The physiographic makeup of Russia is extremely varied. Vast taiga forests, with predominantly coniferous cover, extend over most of the territory (colored in different shades of green on the map), cool treeless tundra stretches across the northern reaches (purples), temperate steppes and deserts occupy the southern territories (yellows). Moscow is located in the East European (Russian) Plain, near a band of mixed forest of both taiga and broadleaved European forests.

A vegetation map of the Moscow region shows a patchwork of mixed forest types that suggest a varied topography and hydrology and prolonged human occupation. Birch and aspen forests replace pine and spruce as pioneer species in areas affected or altered by human habitation and intervention.

Badaevskiy Brewery, Moscow

Opushka, the Russian Forest Edge

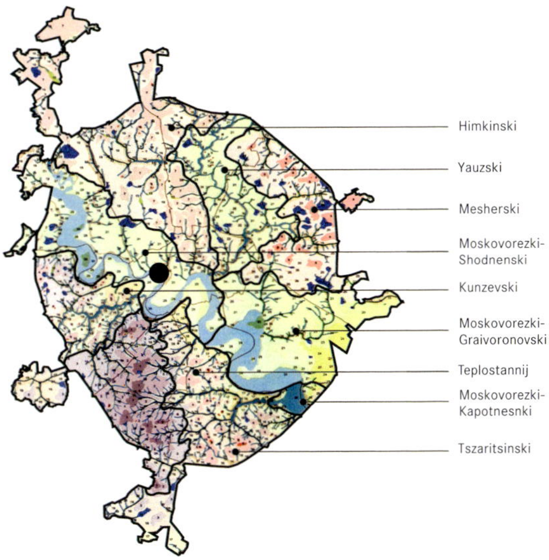

Moscow's indigenous landscape is unique in the Central Russian Plain. The city lies in an ancient alluvial plain, its relief based on a stepped valley of river terraces, channels, glacial hillocks, swampy depressions, and karst forms. It is roughly divided in three morphological zones: an elevated plateau in the east, swampy lowland in the west, and the river plain in the south. Forests vary in composition according to local ground relief, hydrology, soils, and a complex history of agricultural cultivation. Broadleaved species like tilia, elm, oak, and others prevail in the south, while conifers are common in western and eastern parts, where pine, fir, and spruce forests form habitats for rare ground species.[1]

The site is located on the right bank of the river Moskva—an area defined by water-glacial plains and numerous wide streams, where, for a long time, poor sandy soils and weak drainage prevented development.

1 Alexander Shvetsov, "Moscow," in *Plants and Habitats of European Cities*, ed. John G. Kelcey and Norbert Müller (New York: Springer, 2011), 346–47.

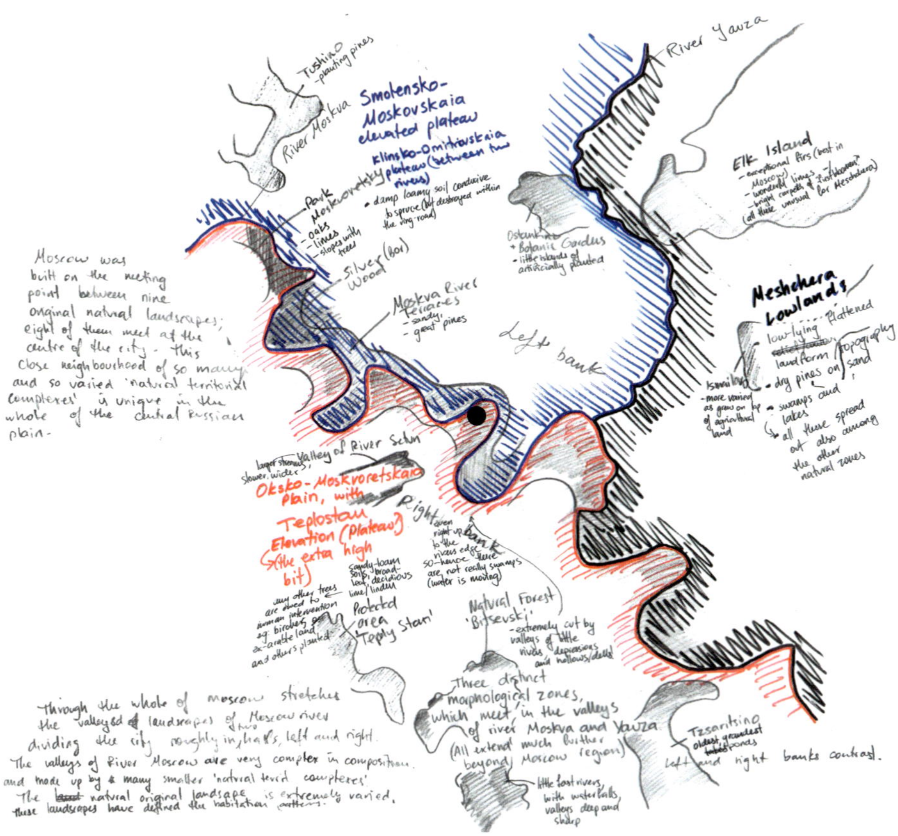

Allotment Apple Plum Cherry Pear Apricot

Over 800 years of human occupation have heavily transformed these indigenous landscapes. Many noble estates and monastery grounds where gardens and orchards were traditionally cultivated are now forest parks and nature reserves. During the Soviet era, imagery related to the vitality and productivity of the land became central to the promotion of the kolkhoz movement.

Picking Apples (1928) by Konstantin Fedorovich Yuon; page from the guide to the "All-Union Agricultural Exhibition" of 1939 in Moscow; still from *How We Live!*, a Soviet film about collective agricultural works near Moscow in 1958; today, fruit and berry picking in the orchards of Kolomenskoe is not advised but popular nonetheless.

< Map of orchards and allotments in Moscow; some historical orchards are protected but many are abandoned or overgrown.

Studies of the forest edge–Diagram of
the structure of ecological forest succession

Ivan Ivanovich Shishkin, *At the Edge of an Oak Forest,* 1882

1 

5 

2 

6 

3 

7 

4 

8 

Section diagrams of the forest edge succession showing various spatial qualities

1 Glade with fruit trees; a small light opening inside the forest, a rest or play area
2 Created edge; an abrupt condition, usually a road or river's edge, a window into the forest interior
3 Forest interior; established dominant species and screened views
4 Forest edge, a sheltered micro-climate with saplings
5 Gradual edge or *opushka*; the most diverse and abundant zone, rich in light-loving plants
6 Meadow and small trees; an open space inviting birds and other animal species
7 Meadow clearing; grassland with high exposure to wind and sun
8 Orchard; flowering fruit trees inviting direct engagement with vegetation

Sketch of woodland interior showing vegetation, building entrances, columns, and playground integrated within the forest edge

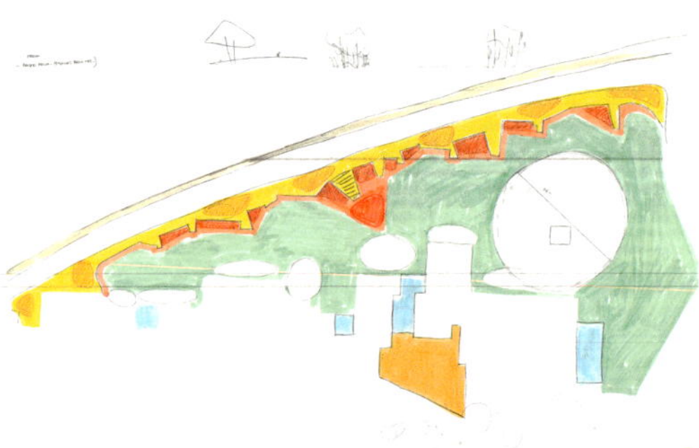

Initial planting concept and interfaces of forest edge layers

Establishing planting zones, refining relationships between forest edge layers and the different plantings

Translation of diagrammatic concept into a tree planting strategy, with development of a variegated forest edge: lawn, meadow with small trees, ground cover and shrubs, hard woodland edge, woodland interior, tree clumps and ground cover, clearing with fruit trees and grassland, and trees in paving

North-south project section showing the layers of made ground, park, building on pillars, and rooftop gardens above

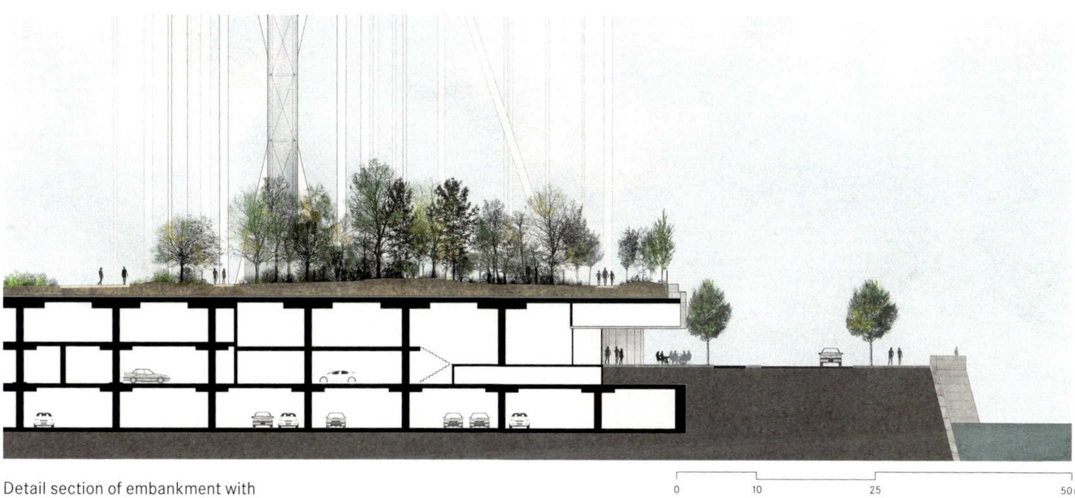

Detail section of embankment with the forest edge spaces

Rooftop plan with private villas and gardens. The planting palette for the rooftop gardens responds to the harsher, more exposed conditions. Species that grow here are reminiscent of the tundra, with resilient shrubs and grasses.

Treetop plan showing the structure of the park and planting. In the north of the site, the exterior edge of the forest corresponds to the hard edge of the embankment, and the soft-edge interior gradually opens to the clearing and the orchard. In the south, a more urban planting pattern defines the boulevard and a public square.

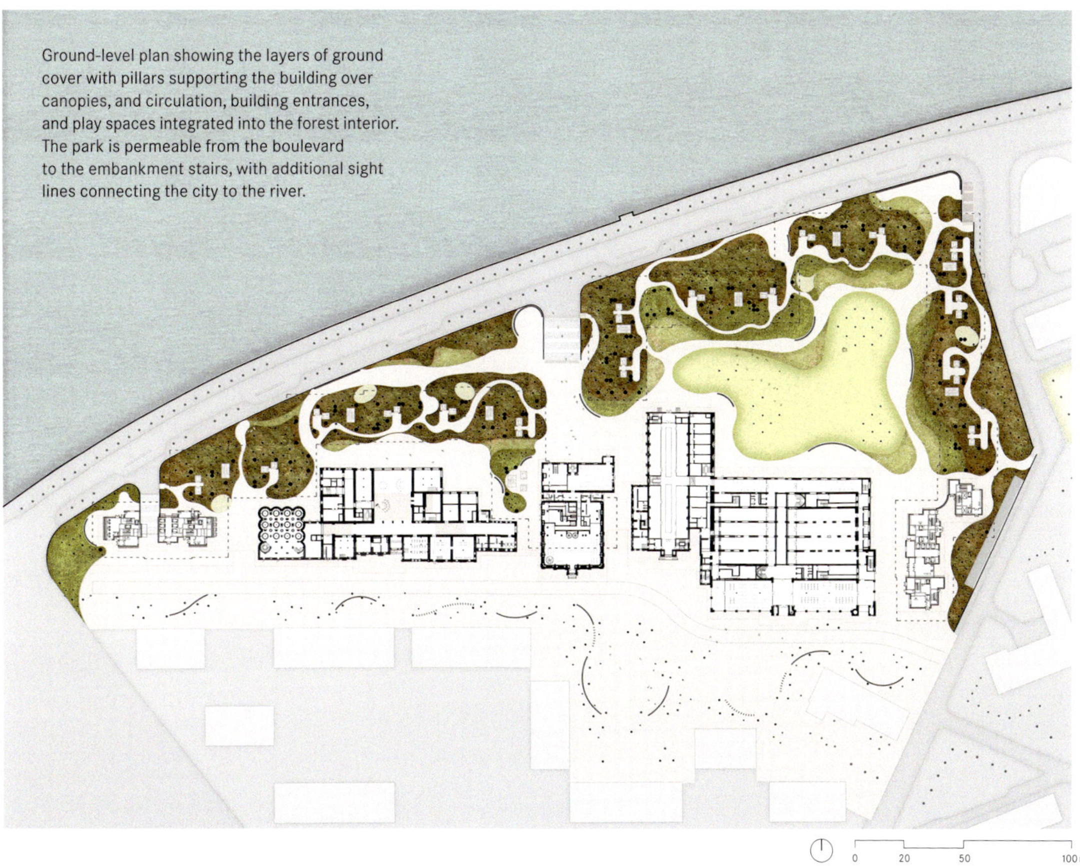

Ground-level plan showing the layers of ground cover with pillars supporting the building over canopies, and circulation, building entrances, and play spaces integrated into the forest interior. The park is permeable from the boulevard to the embankment stairs, with additional sight lines connecting the city to the river.

1

2

3

4

5

6

7

8

9

10

11

12

13

14

15

16

17

18

19

20

21

22

23

24

Woodland interior
1 *Pinus sylvestris*
2 *Larix sibirica*
3 *Quercus rubra*
4 *Larix sibirica*
5 *Tilia cordata*

Soft edge–trees, shrubs, and ground cover
6 *Populus tremula*
7 *Betula pendula*
8 *Populus alba*
9 *Pyrus ussuriensis*
10 *Sorbus aucuparia*
11 *Syringa vulgaris*
12 *Rosa canina*
13 *Sambucus nigra*
14 *Maianthemum bifolium*
15 *Campanula latiloba* "Alba"

Meadow–small trees and grassland species
16 *Crataegus monogyna*
17 *Prunus padus*
18 *Viburnum opulus*
19 *Achillea millefolium*
20 *Galium verum*

Orchard
21 *Malus pumila*
22 *Pyrus ussuriensis*
23 *Prunus tomentosa*
24 *Prunus domestica* var. *Kolonovidnaja*

Planting strategy: Orchards
Fruit trees are usually planted in a grid, depending on the species, to optimize their development and exposure as well as to simplify harvesting. Old orchards may still show signs of a rudimentary grid even if, after decades, a significant number of the trees have died, been removed, or been replenished. Depending on the point of view, the planting may appear loosely organized or strictly planned.

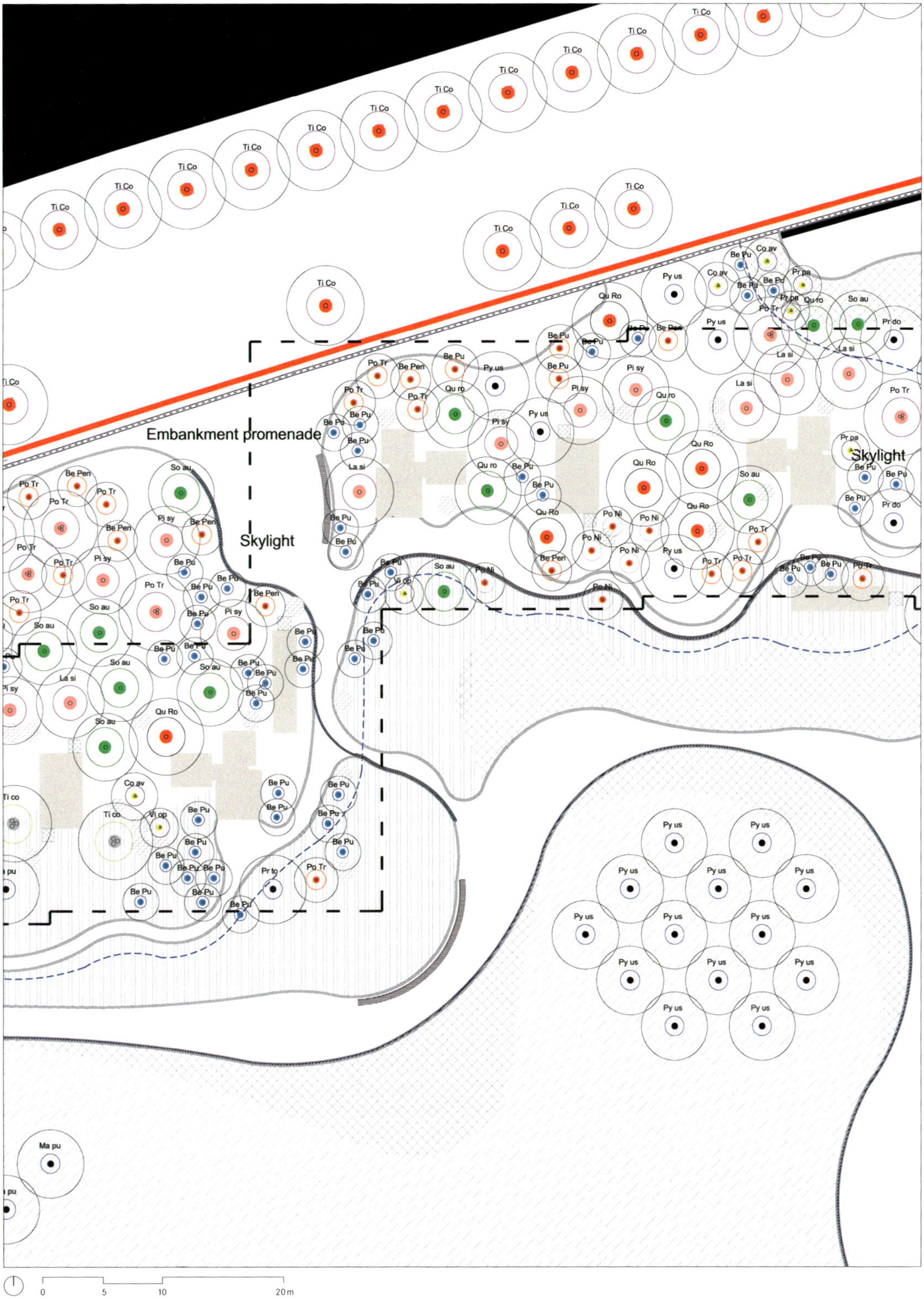
Embankment promenade
Skylight
Skylight
0
5
10
20 m

"The forest is *higher* than man. It may be enclosed and overgrown with all kinds of scrub; it may be hard to penetrate, and still harder to traverse, but its real density, that which makes it a forest, is its foliage; and this is overhead. It is the foliage of single trees linked together which forms a continuous roof; it is the foliage which shuts out the light and throws a universal shadow. [. . .] Another, and no less important, aspect of the forest is its multiple immovability. Every single trunk is rooted in the ground and no menace from outside can move it. Its resistance is absolute; it does not give an inch. It can be felled, but not shifted."

Elias Canetti, *Crowds and Power*

Quercus suber
Landscapes of Controlled Origin

Roland Charles Shaw

A characteristic feature of cork forests is the marking system in white paint that tracks which trees were harvested in which year.

A Mediterranean Ecosystem

Short, gnarled, and coated with a layer of bark up to 30 centimeters thick, the cork oak is a rare anomaly among trees, in that it can withstand the extraction of its bark without dying off. As a result, sparse forests of *Quercus suber* span the coast of the western Mediterranean from southern Italy to Portugal and round to Tunisia, favoring moist winters and scorching summers. Cultivated since ancient Roman times to provide stoppers for wine bottles, much of today's cork also finds its way into the construction industry for use as insulation. But harvesting still follows the tree's rhythm. One must wait at least nine years until the bark has regrown before it is ready to be stripped afresh, and each tree is numbered individually with white paint to indicate which year's harvest it belongs to.

A full third of the world's cork forests are to be found in Portugal,[1] where they form an integral part of a man-made ecosystem, one of the most biodiverse in the world, known as the *montado.* This specific type of cultural landscape takes many years to establish, as neatly described in this Portuguese saying: "Mine are the vineyards, the olive trees my parents', the *montados* my ancestors.'"[2]

Here, a delicate symbiosis has been established between the cork oak, certain butterflies, wildflowers such as the yellow lupin, the Iberian lynx, and the Iberian imperial eagle, the last two of which are indigenous and endangered. Given the often sparse distribution of these oaks, to the northern European eye this is perhaps no forest at all; however, the Portuguese word used to describe it, *florestal,* meaning "forest," is clear on this point.

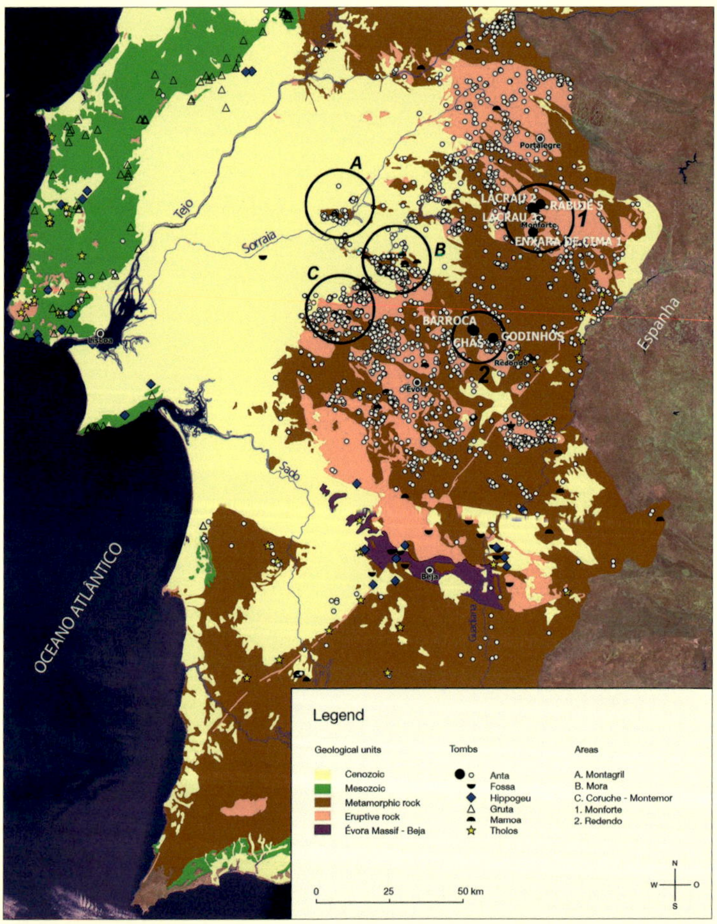

The Iberian Peninsula has one of the highest concentrations of megalithic stone formations in Europe, remnants of a time before the cork oak was intensively planted here, when the region was nonetheless rich with cultural activity.

German archaeologists Vera and Georg Leisner devoted the majority of their careers to surveying Iberian stone formations.

From *Latifundium* to *Monte*

Fossilized fragments of the *Quercus* family have been found in Iberia dating back some ten million years.[3] Between 5000 and 4000 BC, boulders were assembled into megalithic formations that characterize the landscape to this day. These menhirs, dolmens, and cromlechs perhaps mark burial sites or stand in alignment with celestial bodies. Either way, numerous successive generations have inscribed this hilly landscape with instruments of political, religious, and agricultural significance.

Indeed, large-scale agriculture has a long history on the Iberian Peninsula, with remains at São Cucufate near Beja thought to have been at the center of a *latifundium* producing grain for the Roman Empire. At 1,500 hectares, the scale of this operation is worth taking note of. In contrast to the heterogeneous planting here today, *latifundia* tended to be monocultural in nature. Large-scale production of cork came later still, in the early nineteenth century, as part of a new, specifically Iberian, agricultural model.

The Napoleonic invasion of the peninsula left much of its countryside infertile after the Portuguese implemented a scorched earth policy on their own land in order to deplete the enemy's supplies. The *monte,* a municipal acupuncture point that rendered the landscape productive once again after their withdrawal, comprised a constellation of buildings, often arranged along an axis resembling a street that included family cottages and a church. The Portuguese landowner who may previously have owned plantations in an overseas colonial territory now lived on a large, self-sufficient estate together with the farmers who worked the land and their families. *Montes* govern much of today's cork forests even today, particularly along the Spanish border in the Alentejo.

In its size the cork forest bears more resemblance to a latifundium, depicted in this mosaic, than to a typically small Portuguese agricultural holding. Dominus Julius, Bardo National Museum, Tunis

The traditional pilgrimage of Our Lady of Fátima on the main street, forming the backbone of the monte in São Lourenço do Barrocal, ca. 1950.

> The cork oak, after an illustration in *Koehler's Medicinal Plants* by Hermann Adolph Koehler, 1897

Cupuliferae.
Quercus Suber L.

A Protected Terroir

In addition to cork, the *Quercus suber* also produces a nutritious acorn, of which the black Iberian pig is particularly fond. This pig, a breed of *Sus scrofa domesticus* native to Iberia, requires one whole hectare's worth of *montado* to itself to find enough sustenance and is, in turn, an integral part of the ecosystem. Pork is still the most popular type of meat in the world,[4] and this particular pig's meat, fattier than most, enjoys worldwide acclaim for the intensity of its flavor.

Rearing the Iberian pig and cultivating the cork oak tree share certain similarities. In contrast to most of agricultural Europe, these practices have remained immune to industrialization and entail a specific form of labor, only possible by hand, transferred through generations and intimately tied to a particular Iberian cultural landscape: its *terroir,* if you will. While local farmers incise, divide, and extract the cork with the curved blades of specially designed axes, rearing these pigs requires a specific knowledge of their feeding patterns and of the terrain.

Many forests were used as pastures for cattle in earlier centuries. Pigs would search the ground for acorns, while farmers cut the trees at regular intervals to produce firewood. This gave rise to the typical image of the wood pasture or coppice with their low, well-branched trees. This form of pasture management suppresses young growth and leads to open, park-like forests and loose clumps of trees in the open countryside.

> While a variety of pig species exist, it is the *Sus scrofa domesticus,* which includes the Iberian black pig, that has been widely bred in Iberia for its meat.

CCCXXIV. A.
Sus Papuensis Less.

Sus Scrofa Linn.
Aper.

CCCXXIII.
Sus Scrofa Linn.
hispidus.

Sus Scrofa Linn.
Siamensis Buff.

Sus Scrofa Linn.
domesticus.

CCCXXV.
Sus Tajassu Linn.

CCCXXV. B
Sus labiatus.

Sus æthiopicus Pall.

Sus Babirussa Linn.

> Cork bark can either be processed in whole pieces or broken down into smaller chunks to form "composite cork." Further treatments, such as with heat, can generate a broad spectrum of colors.

While cork oak is distributed around the western part of the Mediterranean basin, the production of Iberian ham is concentrated in a specific region between Spain and Portugal.

The cork forests and the black pig are both protected species. Sold as *jamón ibérico,* the production of this meat is tied to a variety of regulations that control what can pass as "authentic" and what cannot. In a similar vein, Portuguese *montados* are protected by mechanisms put in place by both the EU and UNESCO. A certain idea of quality is thus maintained, matched by the high price these products can demand on the market. The cork forest plays a crucial role in retaining water and providing shade, thereby staving off desertification and maintaining the conditions for one of the most diverse habitats in Europe. One can therefore understand attempts to prevent its disappearance, but whether protection categories such as these are healthy for the future development of the countryside remains to be seen.

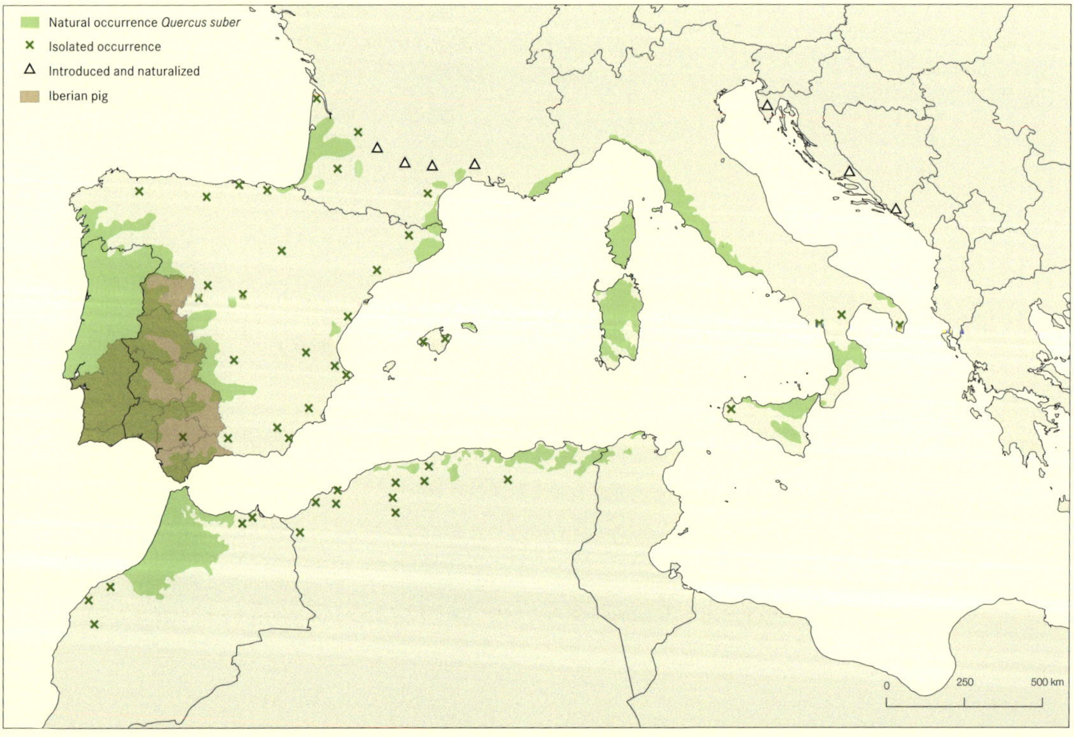

1 APCOR, "Cork Yearbook 18/19," 14, accessed May 3, 2019, http://www.apcor.pt/wp-content/uploads/2018/12/Anuario_APCOR_2018.pdf.
2 "Vinhas minhas, olivais dos meus pais, montados dos meus antepassados." Ana Paula Amendoeira, "... Montados dos meus antepassados," in *Memória Alentejana* 33/34 (2014): 60–61, here 60.
3 "Are Cork Oaks Ancient Trees?," Amorim, accessed April 23, 2019, https://www.amorim.com/en/why-cork/myths-and-facts/Oak-Tree/110/.
4 "Global Meat Production and Consumption Continue to Rise," *Worldwatch Institute,* accessed April 23, 2019, http://www.worldwatch.org/global-meat-production-and-consumption-continue-rise.
5 APCOR, "Cork Yearbook 18/19," 16.

A Landscape of Complexity

In part thanks to unattractive working conditions, a recent generation abandoned the Alentejo for the city, after the Portuguese economy turned its focus to service industries in the 1980s. On the back of recent financial crises, however, the agricultural sector seems once again to be appealing, and the younger generation is returning to the countryside with renewed ambitions. While cork producers invent new markets for their product, expanding into footwear and high-end furniture, previously metropolitan stakeholders are also settling here, including precision engineers and biological researchers.

Aside from producing 100,000 tons of cork a year,[5] the Portuguese landscape continues to transform, accommodating an ever-increasing wave of tourism. Today's *montes* demonstrate a new, multifaceted economic potential. A number of hours' drive from the nearest airport, top-quality restaurants, gyms, local products, and so-called wellness spas are offered, combining a notion of remoteness with a cultural landscape that is still agriculturally productive.

Cork products between handcraft and high tech

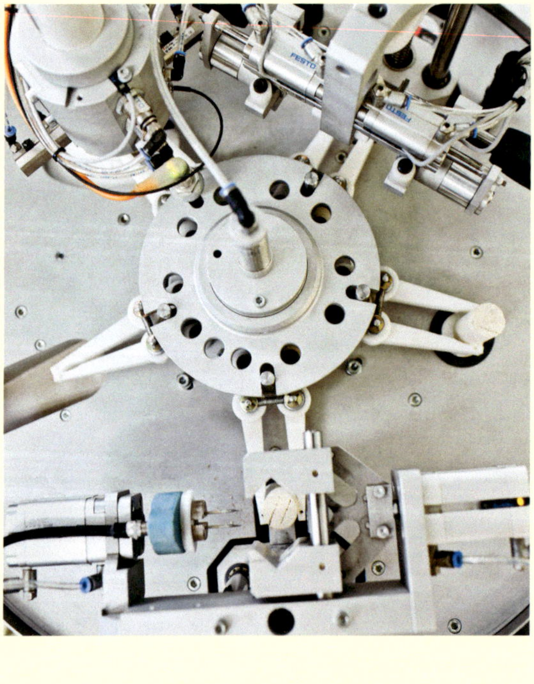

“In the early part of the modern era, we used **binoculars, microscopes,** and other technical equipment to mediate our experience of the landscape. Today, I’m fascinated by the idea of being able to **locate myself** in the landscape without any equipment, tracking the movement of the sun, for instance. If the sun is behind the clouds, the moss on the tree trunks acts like a compass indicating where north is.” (gv)

بچشم شود جمع نو باکهن
شود روح پیاشهر ادربدان

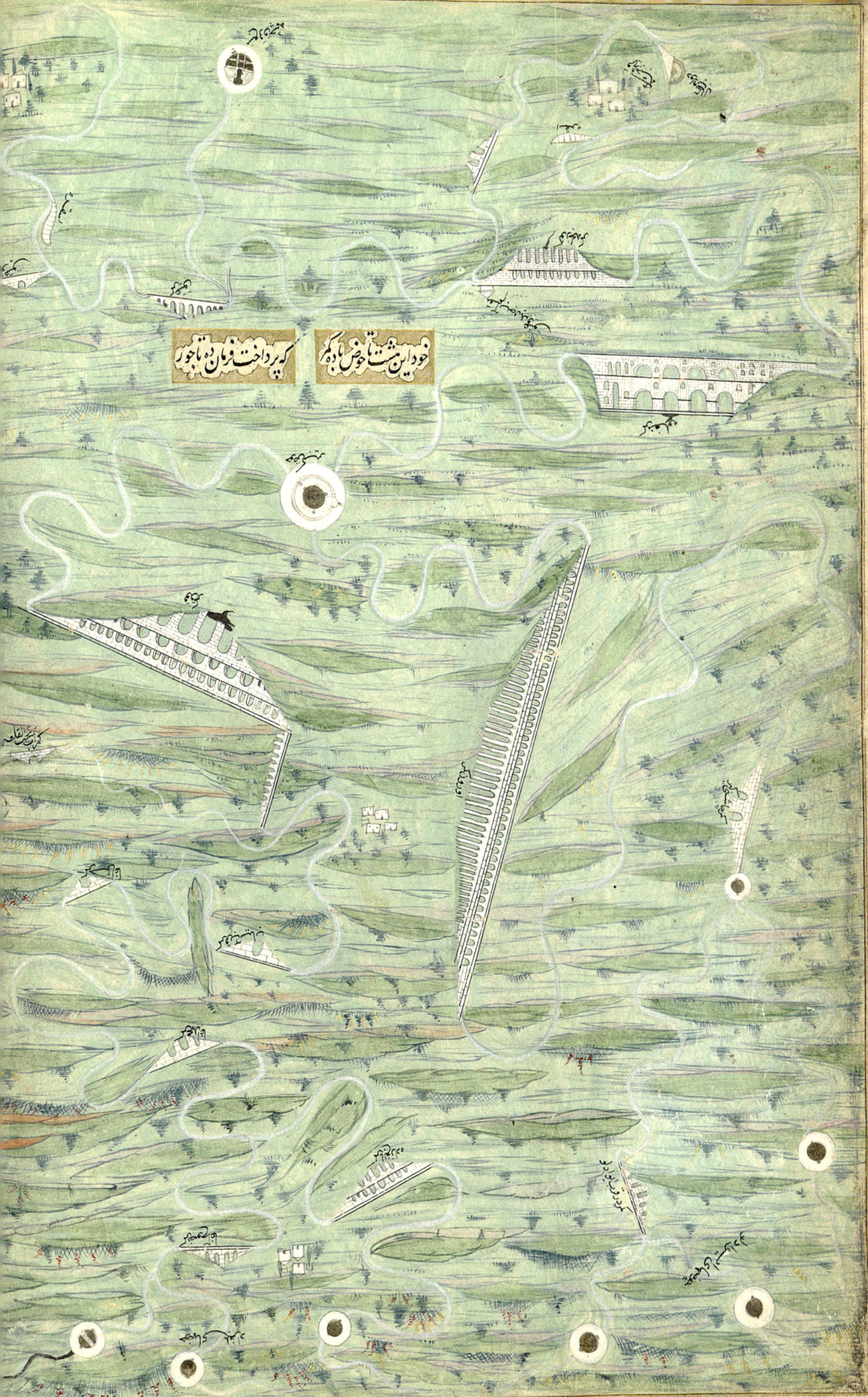

خود این هشت تا حوض با دگر
که پرداخت فرمان ده تاجور

Haliç Shipyard, Istanbul
The Value of the Existing

The task of transforming the shipyard complex, formerly inaccessible to the public, raised questions about the typology and dimensions of the open spaces that form the matrix within which the new district was to be developed. The lack of any local patterns and the very size of the site require it to be considered at the level of the urban landscape: the yardsticks for the master plan were not small neighborhood parks but rather the sea, the straits, and the woodland at one of the most prominent locations within the city.

Client:
Haliç Altın Boynuz Marina Turizm Gayrimenkul İnş. Yat. Tic. A.Ş.

Design:
2014–2015

Type and size:
Master plan, 28 ha

Status:
Not realized

<< Water supply system in the Ottoman period. Istanbul's old town was supplied with water through a complex system of aqueducts and pipes coming from the Belgrad Forest north of the city. Although probably started by the Emperor Hadrian, the main features of this system were built by Mimar Sinan between 1554 and 1563.

Adolphe and Émile Rouargue, *Constantinople,* 1855

Istanbul–like Rome–is almost unique among Europe's metropolises in that the infrastructures that once supplied the city are still in evidence in the surrounding territory. Deposits and fragments relating to more than two thousand years of history document the city's utilization of existing resources and the basic requirements it relied on to support the livelihood and prosperity of a potent urban culture.

Waterways

The forests to the north of Istanbul are of vital importance for the city. They were once used for hunting and to provide wood to build ships and heat the city's numerous thermal baths, while the resulting clearances also freed up land for cultivation. Fresh water for drinking and bathing was collected in reservoirs. It was transported over long distances, sometimes aboveground and sometimes out of sight underground, flowing through caverns and along aqueducts and canals. Once inside the city, the water was then piped back to the surface, often inside very small architectural structures: the kiosks, which were originally designed by rich patrons as places for the poor to collect water, not only symbolize the economic, social, and religious significance of water but also point to the underlying geology and the system of waterways. These are far more than simple elements of the secular infrastructure, appearing to the outside observer today like metaphors in an English landscape park.

Within the city, the water is brought to the surface in kiosks and wells, places that symbolize the important economic, social and religious significance of water.

Plan of the underground water supply network of the city of Istanbul south of the Golden Horn.

The forests north of Istanbul are a central and diverse resource for the city.

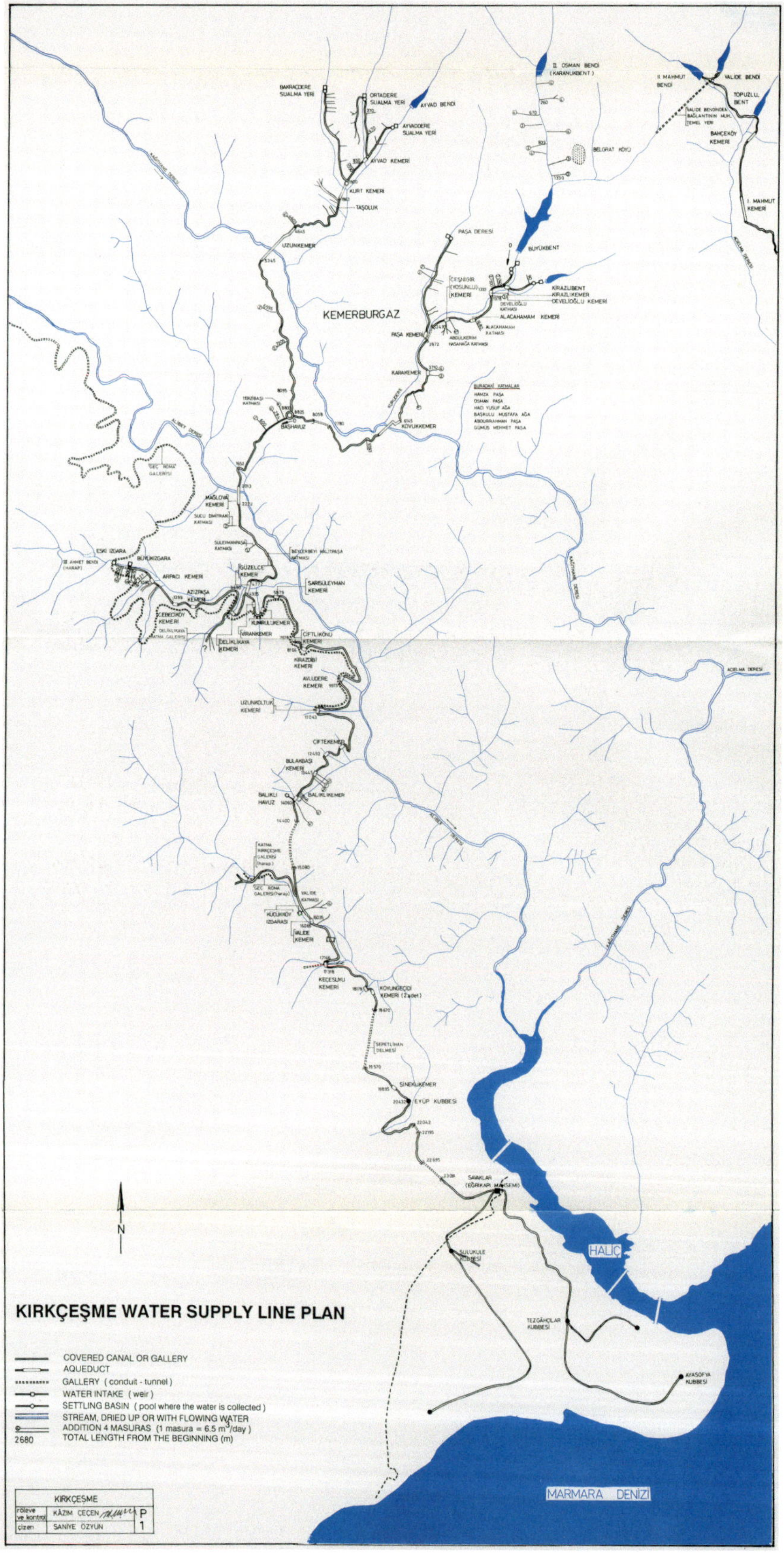
KIRKÇEŞME WATER SUPPLY LINE PLAN
COVERED CANAL OR GALLERY
AQUEDUCT
GALLERY (conduit - tunnel)
WATER INTAKE (weir)
SETTLING BASIN (pool where the water is collected)
STREAM, DRIED UP OR WITH FLOWING WATER
ADDITION 4 MASURAS (1 masura = 6.5 m³/day)
2680 TOTAL LENGTH FROM THE BEGINNING (m)
KIRKÇEŞME
röleve ve kontrol KÂZIM ÇEÇEN
çizen SANİYE ÖZYÜN
P 1
N
KEMERBURGAZ
HALİÇ
MARMARA DENİZİ
AYVAD BENDİ
AYVAD KEMERİ
KURT KEMERİ
TAŞOLUK
UZUNKEMER
PAŞA DERESİ
BÜYÜKBENT
KIRAZLIBENT
DEVELİOĞLU KEMERİ
ALACAHAMAM KEMERİ
PAŞA KEMERİ
KARAKEMER
KOVUKKEMER
BAŞHAVUZ
BELGRAT KÖYÜ
VALİDE BENDİ
TOPUZLU BENT
BAHÇEKÖY KEMERİ
I. MAHMUT KEMERİ
MAĞLOVA KEMERİ
ESKİ IZGARA
BÜYÜKIZGARA
ARPACI KEMERİ
AZİZPAŞA KEMERİ
GÜZELCE KEMERİ
SARISÜLEYMAN KEMERİ
KUMRULUKEMER
ÇİFTLİKÖNÜ KEMERİ
KİRAZDİBİ KEMERİ
AVLUDERE KEMERİ
UZUNKOLTUK KEMERİ
ÇİFTEKEMER
BULAKBAŞI KEMERİ
BALIKLI HAVUZ
BALIKLIKEMER
VALİDE KEMERİ
KEÇESUYU KEMERİ
KÖYUNGEÇİDİ KEMERİ (2 adet)
SİNEKLİKEMER
EYÜP KUBBESİ
SAVAKLAR (EĞRİKAPI MAKSEMİ)
SULUKULE KUBBESİ
TEZGÂHÇILAR KUBBESİ
AYASOFYA KUBBESİ

The Street and the Forest

In addition to the inaccessible gardens and parks belonging to wealthy citizens, which are still largely closed to the general public, the streets and courtyards in Istanbul have traditionally been regarded as public places, much like the city's mosques, cemeteries, and markets, which are often protected by walls and roofs. Given the size of the metropolis, however, there is an overall lack of open space today–a situation that was given widespread exposure in the vast protest movement against the destruction of Gezi Park, Istanbul's first public park.

This has led to people's appropriation of the extensive forest landscapes to the north of the city, which have long been used informally for recreational purposes. New infrastructures are being created and becoming established on a routine basis, though this increase of the city's leisure amenities has not resulted in the area's becoming more accessible to the general public–rather, the primary outcome has been a partial privatization of the space. At the same time, the forests are steadily being enclosed by the expanding city and its new, large-scale infrastructures. This not only poses a threat to the local flora and fauna but also undermines the important function the woodland serves, helping to cool the city and supply it with fresh air.

Openings in the City

While the forests are ultimately being transformed into privatized structures, the timely planning and development of formerly inaccessible areas within the city have created the potential for open spaces with long-term stability. The Haliç shipyards, founded in 1455 by order of Fatih Sultan Mehmet on the site of the former Genoese colony, were among the world's shipyards longest in service.[1] The site is located on the Golden Horn, directly opposite the old center of what was once Constantinople. And although the area is bordered to the north by densely built neighborhoods and a small park, the waterfront was so far inaccessible.

Looking in–Looking Out

The first step in appropriating the disused area was a photographic study of the site. While the maps and aerial images tend to show the large structures and the embedment of the site into the city at the macro level, the subtle nuances in the spatial structure and the peculiarities of the local topography are revealed at the closer range of a pedestrian. The documented walk provided some initial ideas about suitable open-space typologies and how they might function in the new quarter. A long waterfront promenade forms its backbone, supplemented by a multitude of squares, lanes, passages, and gardens. Much of the typology follows local traditions: fountains and kiosks offer free drinking water, while walls create thresholds marking off the squares and gardens as discrete elements. The spaces behind them are freely accessible rather than being kept off-limits.

Based on the idea that the existing structures are respected and integrated into the concept, the master plan formulates an initial proposal for the new urban district, which is to be conceived and developed on the basis of its open spaces. In addition to the material legacy of the site, the intangible aspects of its history–the craftsmanship and knowledge that go into the art of shipbuilding–are also taken up so as to remain legible for future generations in the structure of the open spaces and buildings. (lr)

1 "Haliç tersanesi'nde son durum," *Akdeniz Dünyası Araştırmaları,* November 3, 2014, www.akdenizdunyasi.org/halic-tersanesinde-son-durum.

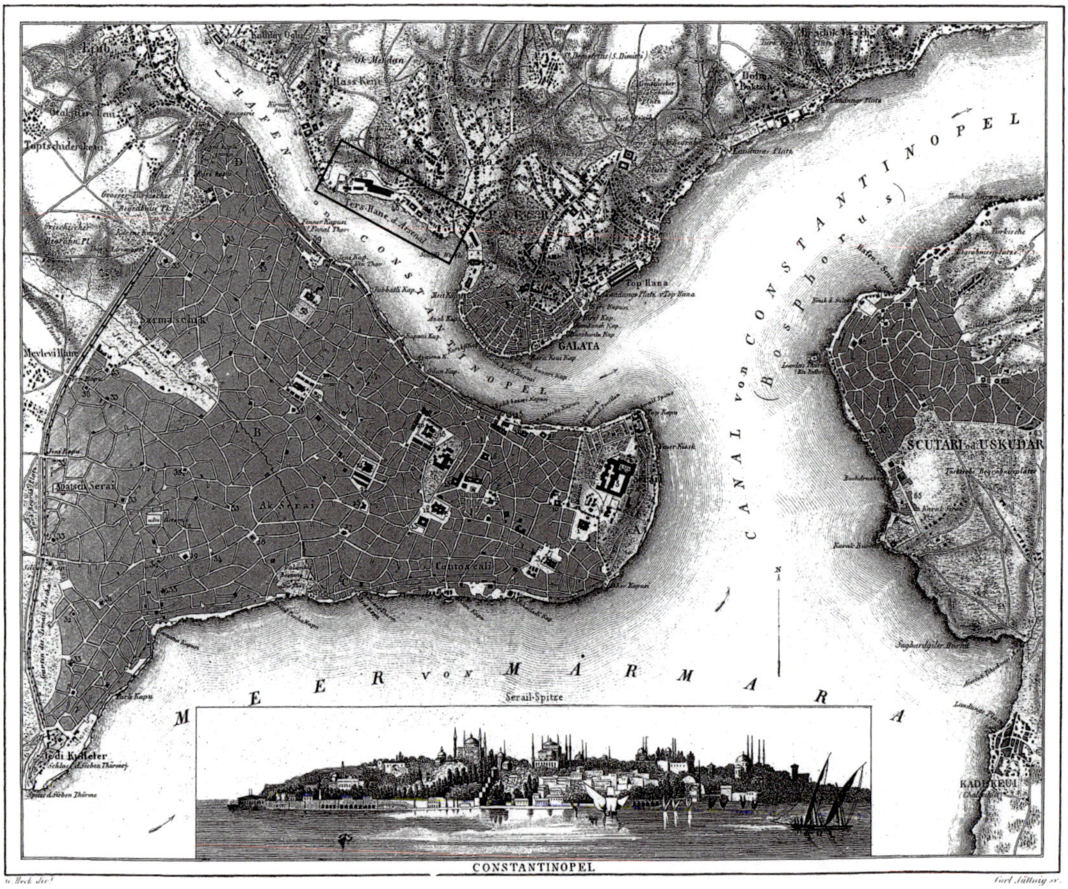

Constantinople around 1850. The Haliç Shipyard is situated on the northern side of the Golden Horn.

Historical enclosure of the site-map drawn by Necip Bey, 1918.

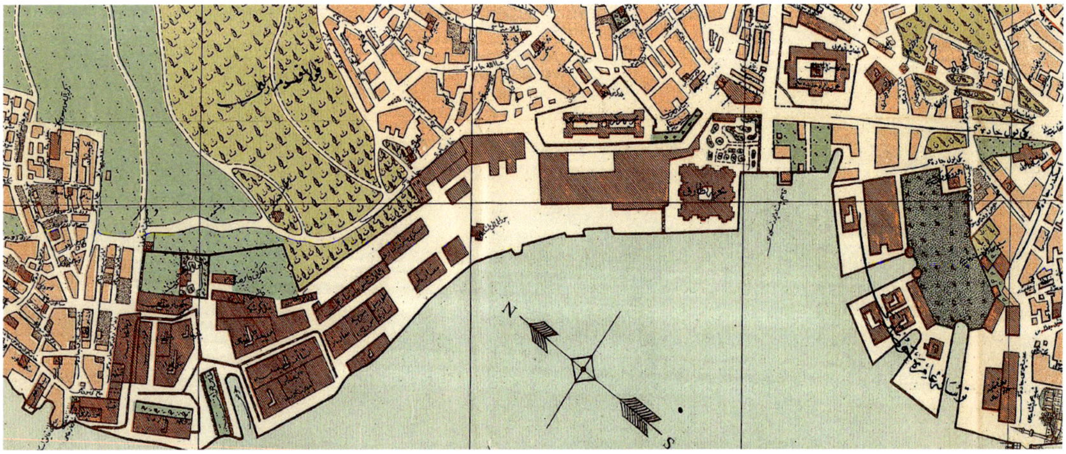

Photographic survey: this series of black-and-white pictures offers a preliminary introduction to the site. The absence of color highlights the key structures, while the sense of approaching on foot gives an idea of the spatial sequencing.

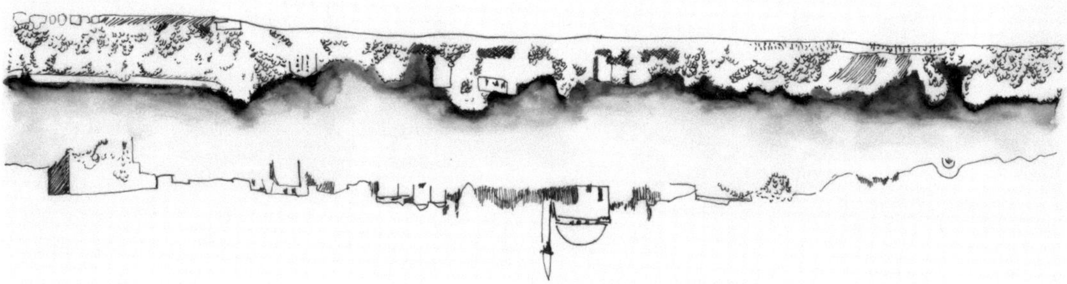

While most sections of Istanbul's river banks have been privatized, the transformation of this area has the potential to enable a range of public uses directly on the water's edge and to make the river accessible once again to the general populace.

Belgrad Forest, Istanbul

Christian Vogt, 2018

MEET LAB
Coffee

HYMER
34 LL 8448

Coca-Cola
Coca-Cola

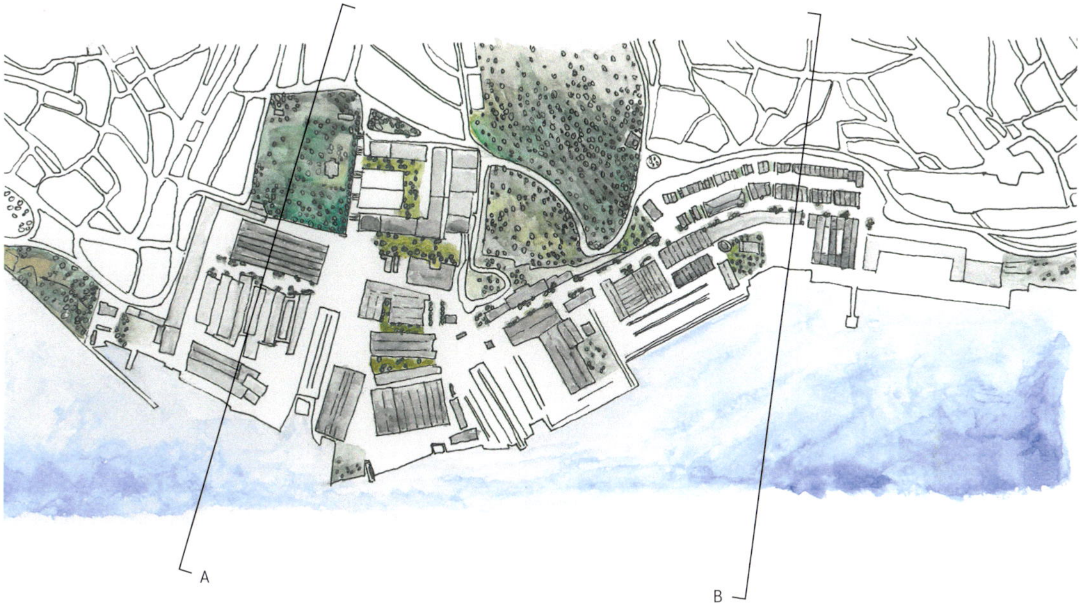

Sections through the bank edge and the inclined terrain. The project creates a connection between the water and the slightly elevated residential areas.

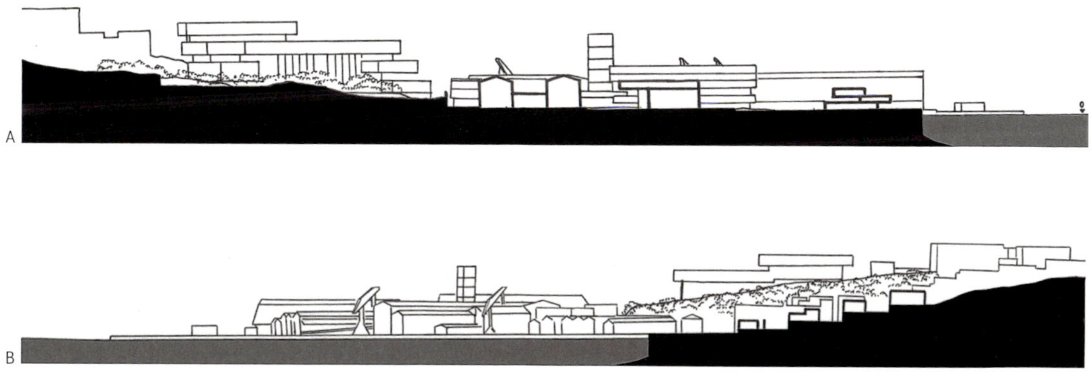

Main Axis: Waterfront Promenade

The waterfront promenade runs right along the water's edge and connects the two parks Içi Yolu and Garanti Bankası. The space is publicly accessible and creates a direct connection to the water. In addition, the linear sequence of the promenade offers a range of distinct waterfront situations to be enjoyed at leisure.

Main Axis: Main Street
The main street is defined by existing and new buildings devoted to different uses, as well as by the vegetation that frames it. It connects some of the site's key public spaces. Adjacent to the imperial gardens, the main square offers a view past the ramps all the way to the water. At the center of the site, the Haliç Terraces are some of the most interesting topographical features, including retaining walls and steps that are viewed as part of the city's industrial heritage.

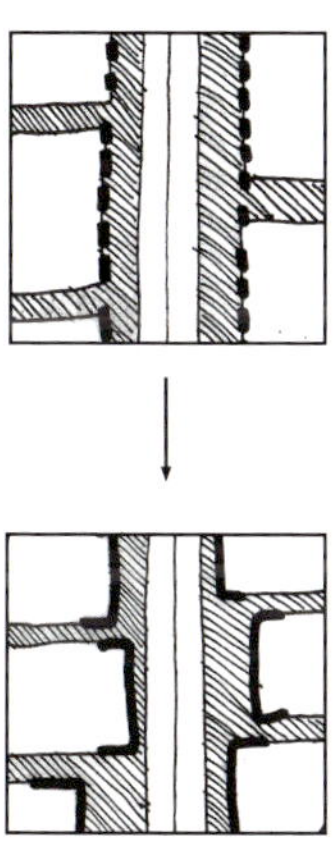

Passages: Primary and Secondary Passages
The passages connect the waterfront promenade to the main street. The entry and exit points are chosen according to the situation and link up to the existing open space network.

The main passages allow a direct and fast connection between the waterfront and the main street. Attached to them are publicly accessible courtyards with dense vegetation.

The secondary passages are of a smaller scale, and their points of entry may be more discrete than is the case with the primary passages. They weave between buildings, finding a path that cuts through the larger busy areas to get to their chosen destination.

Giovanni Paolo Pannini, *Belisarius at the Gate of Constantinople*

Threshold: Boundary and Entry Points
For a long time, the site was not accessible to the general public. The original threshold situation was integrated into the concept, manifesting in the form of gates, walls, ramps or steps.

Haliç Shipyard, Istanbul
The Value of the Existing

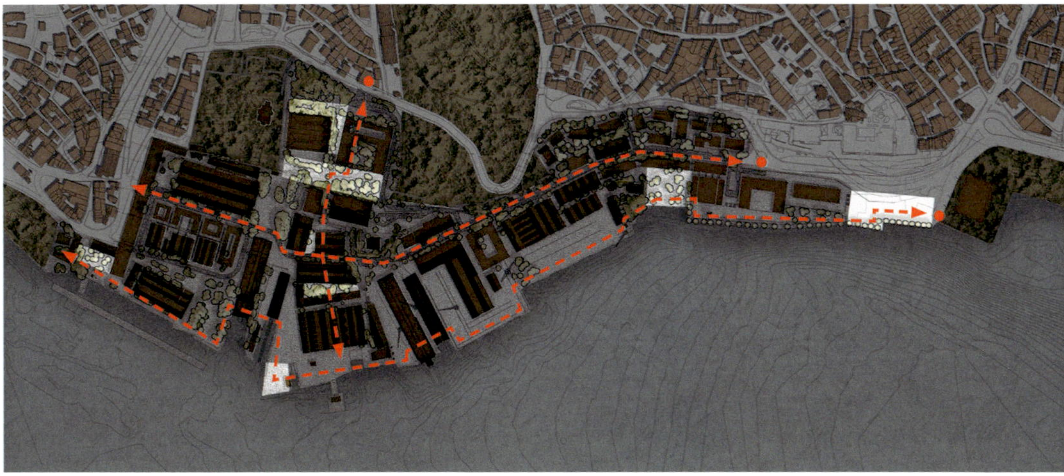

Pockets
The pockets occur throughout the site and vary widely in terms of scale and function. The pockets, enclosed by a wall, are places of respite within the bustling and noisy city.

Columnar Trees
For millennia, the cypress tree (*Cupressus sempervirens*) has been found throughout the Mediterranean region. After the conquest of Constantinople, Mehmed II ordered a garden to be created, at the spot where he had made his first encampment during the siege. At his order, twelve thousand cypresses were planted here in a "checkerboard pattern."

Shade Trees
In the Quranic recital, trees and shade are mentioned as some of the countless blessings of Paradise: "In Paradise, there is a tree under the shadow of which a rider of a fine and swift-footed horse would travel for a hundred years without covering (the distance) completely."(*The Book Pertaining to Paradise; Its Description; Its Bounties and Its Intimates,* Book 40, Hadith 6786)

Fruit Trees
In the imperial gardens, fruits and vegetables were planted for nutritional needs, while other fruit trees, cypresses, and a number of similar plants were cultivated solely for aesthetic purposes and to create heavenly images. During the Ottoman period, although the function, scale, and content of houses would change according to the social hierarchy, most of them would have a garden and courtyard.

Walls
Thresholds are a crucial element in the Ottoman expression of garden culture. Entrance and exit situations are ritualized. In addition, the visual link from the inside to the outside and from the outside to the inside was a defining moment. Walls were often short enough to see over but tall enough to create an internal cohesiveness.

Water
Water was a critical element in the Ottoman garden and had many functions. It operated as a backdrop, a pragmatic or religious necessity, or as an ornamental feature.

Vegetation
Much of our understanding of the planting regimes of the Ottoman period is derived from traveler's accounts, augmented by the analysis of depictions of gardens in miniature painting. They often show garden kiosks, pools, and fountains. A typical planting palette appears to favor a mix of conifers, shade trees, fruit trees, and bulbs. The distribution of the species tends to be less formally ordered than in Islamic garden cultures, most likely because of the absence of the strict irrigation geometries necessary in desert climates.

Droogdokkenpark, Antwerp, BE
Measure and Interval

Client:
City of Antwerp: AG Stadsplanning/AG Vespa

Cooperation:
Architecture: Van Belle & Medina Architects, Antwerp

Design/construction:
2011–2015/2016–ongoing

Type and size:
Park, 15 ha

Status:
Phase one built

The Droogdokkenpark forms the main public space of Antwerp's new Eilandje district, one of the largest urban regeneration areas in the city. Built within the nineteenth-century harbor and along the outer curve of the river Scheldt, it is positioned at the crossroads between the historical city center, the large-scale modern harbor, and the river landscape.

Throughout the site, historical buildings and other port structures reveal the history, of the place embedding the new park in its temporal and spatial setting. Bounded on all sides by water, the site is accessible in four places by crossing existing locks and bridges, articulating moments of arrival and departure. The main entrance into the park from the city is marked by the Belvedere, the transformation of a former harbor infrastructure into a closed hexagon. Once the landmark for ships entering the docks, it is now becoming an orientation and gathering point in the park, offering far-reaching panoramic views over the fluvial landscape, the historical city center, and the modern harbor.

Droogdokkenpark is also part of the master plan for the river quays, which envisages the transformation of more than 6 kilometers of riverfront over a fifteen-year period by improving flood defenses and creating a new public realm along the river. Raising the existing dike and the Belvedere's quay wall by one meter for flood defense has a significant impact on the way the river is experienced.
The required changes in topography are also an opportunity to further emphasize the different spatial qualities of the park: the raised Belvedere, the dike promenade, and the "Green Finger" provide elevated lookout spaces, while the sunken clearing, limiting outward views, is a well-defined space focused on the park's interior.

Through a careful choreography of physical and visual connections, the new landscape weaves itself neatly into its immediate environment and broader setting. This is emphasized by the use of regionally occurring vegetation patterns, selected in response to the habitats that are formed by the new topographical, hydrological, and soil conditions.
A network of cycle and pedestrian routes, as well as carefully planned visual axes, link the different components of the park to one another and help embed it in the city. Derived from the tradition of the English landscape park, the strategy aims to merge the diverse events in the visitor's mind by orchestrating movement and gaze. The articulation between old and new, near and distant, results in a landscape that is profoundly rooted in time and place. (ms)

Droogdokkenpark is located between the nineteenth-century harbor, the river Scheldt, and the modern harbor, forming a pivot point between these distinct landscapes and connecting them visually and physically. The site is located along the outer curve of the river, just north of the historic fortification, an area which would later become the harbor and a key to the city's economy.

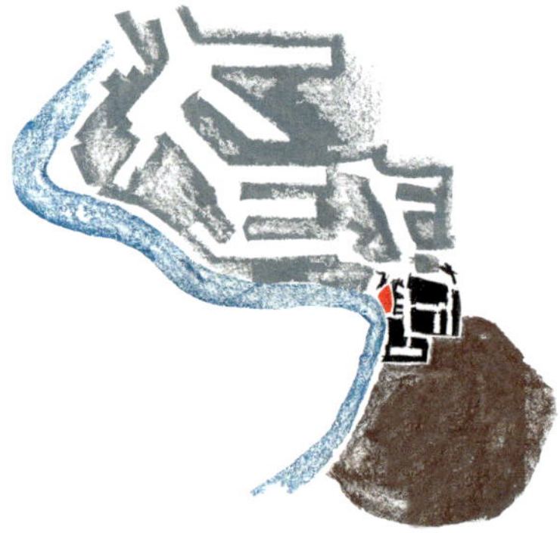

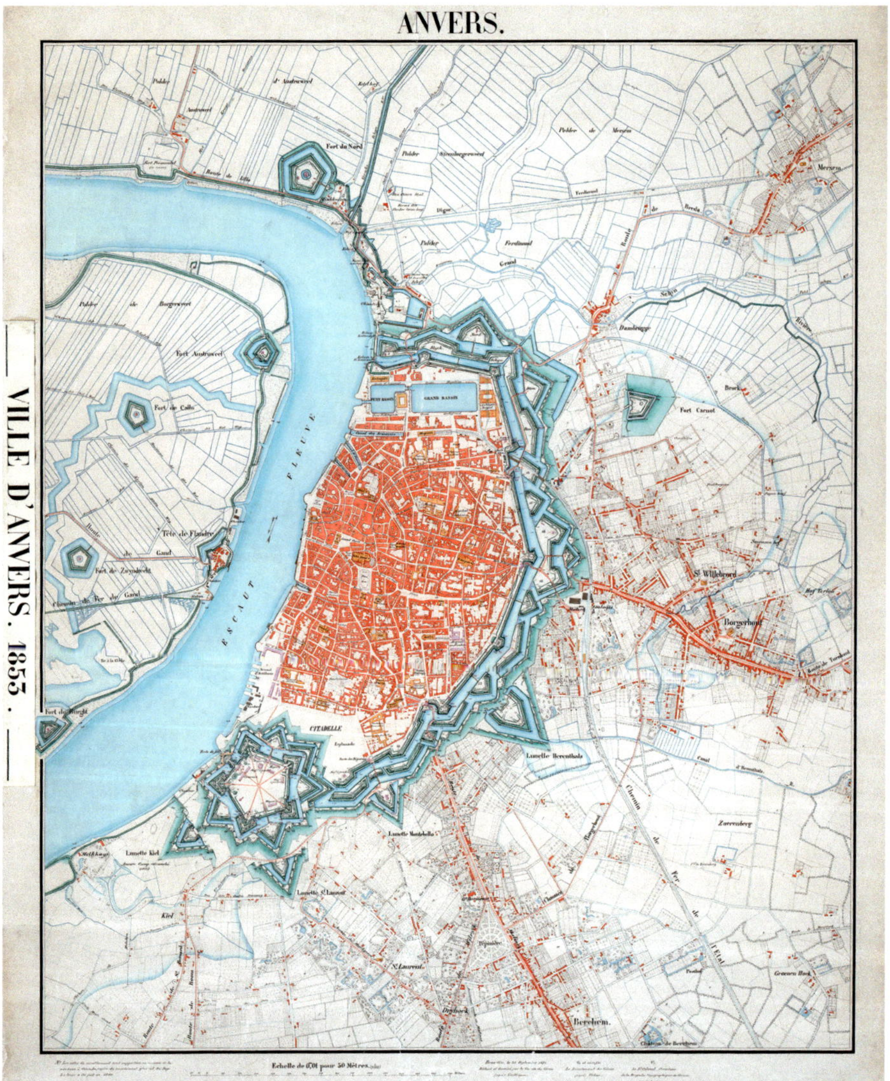

The new park design builds on the qualities of the existing landscape. The wetlands along the river are enlarged and the gradient of the slope to the river reduced to allow new wetland vegetation to establish itself. It also allows visitors to access the wetlands and enjoy this part of the park, which lies outside the protective dike and is in direct contact with the water.

The park interlocks with the old harbor, creating a complementary landscape to the mineral and industrial site.

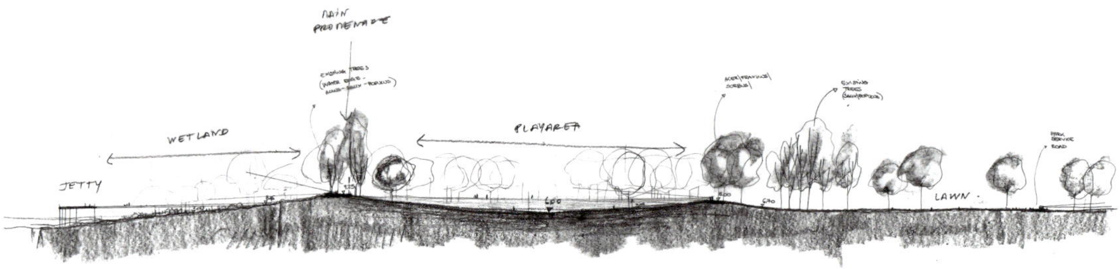

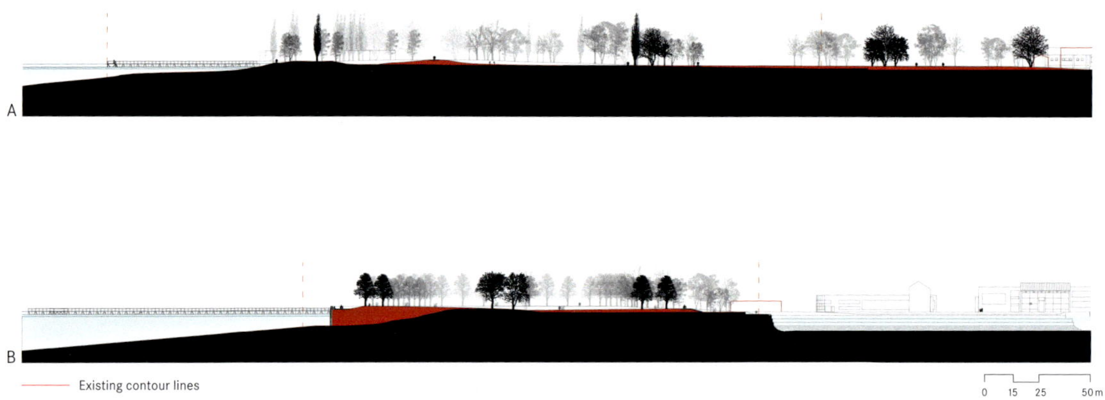

Existing contour lines

Proposed contour lines

Relocated soil to form the new levels

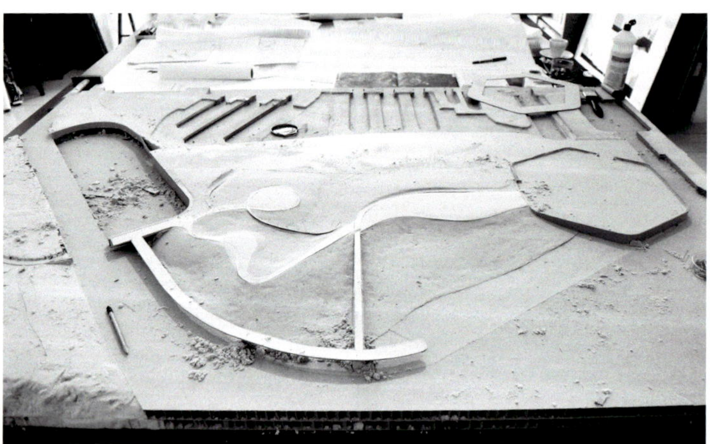

The introduction of a raised dike and quay wall for flood protection creates significant topographical changes to an otherwise flat terrain. These changes further strengthen the spatial variety of the park by creating low-lying areas that are focused on its interior, while the higher areas provide for distant views to the surrounding river, city center, and harbor landscape, emphasizing the park's position as a pivot point.

Droogdokkenpark, Antwerp, BE

Measure and Interval

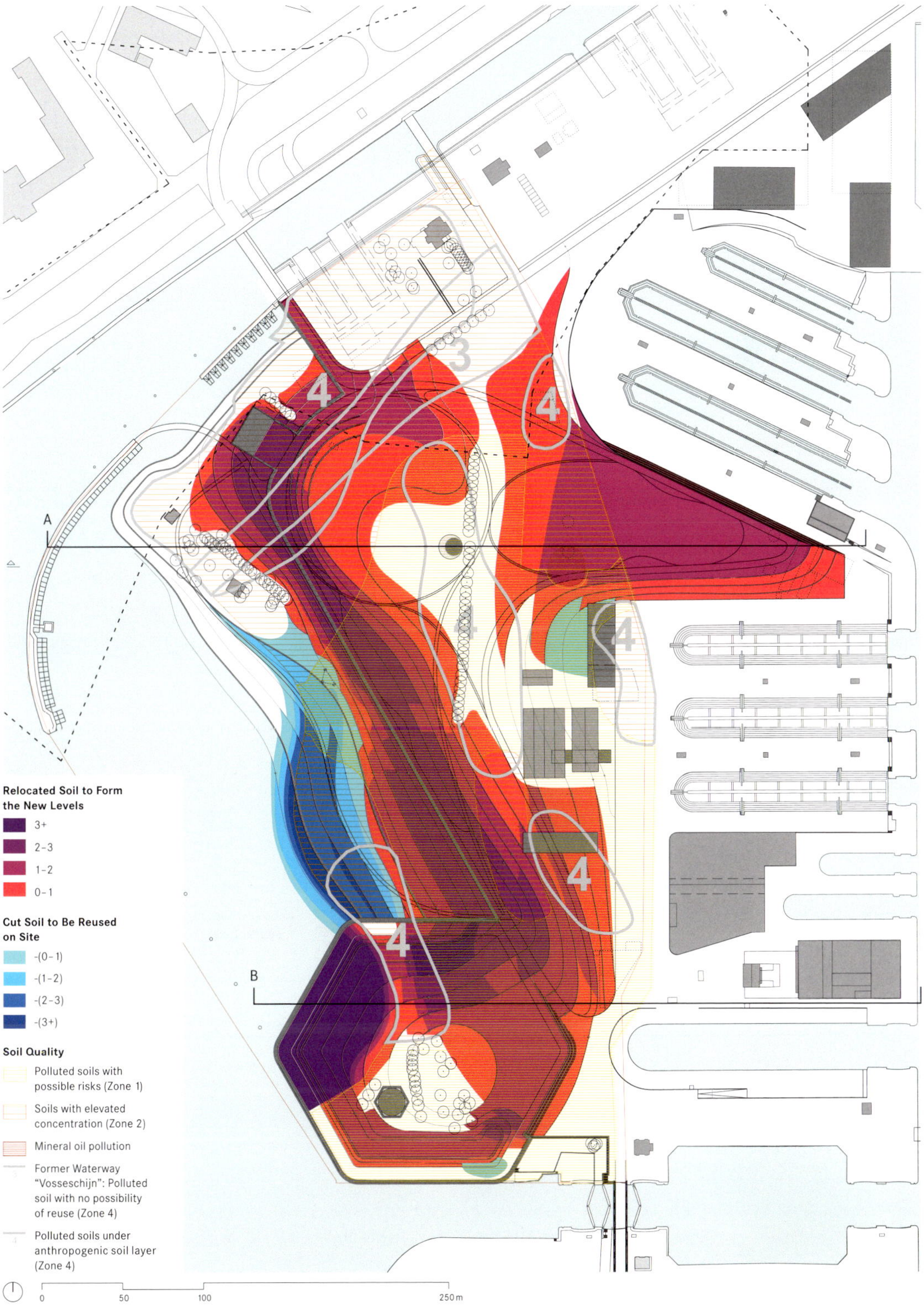

The Belvedere, originally conceived as part of the industrial infrastructure of the old harbor, is transformed into a raised hexagon of parkland. Situated at the entrance of the park, it acts as a threshold as one arrives from the city, while also marking the entrance to Antwerp for ships sailing up the river Scheldt.

Droogdokkenpark, Antwerp, BE

Measure and Interval

A new network of routes integrates the various park components and atmospheres that are created by the new vegetation and topography.

As the dike has become an integrated element of the park with very shallow slopes on either side, the network of pedestrian paths cuts across the flood defense line. This allows visitors to explore the wetlands and experience the river landscape up close.

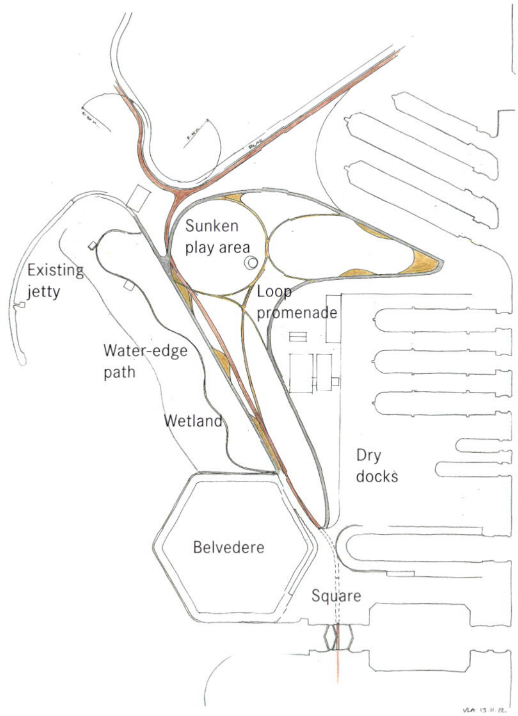

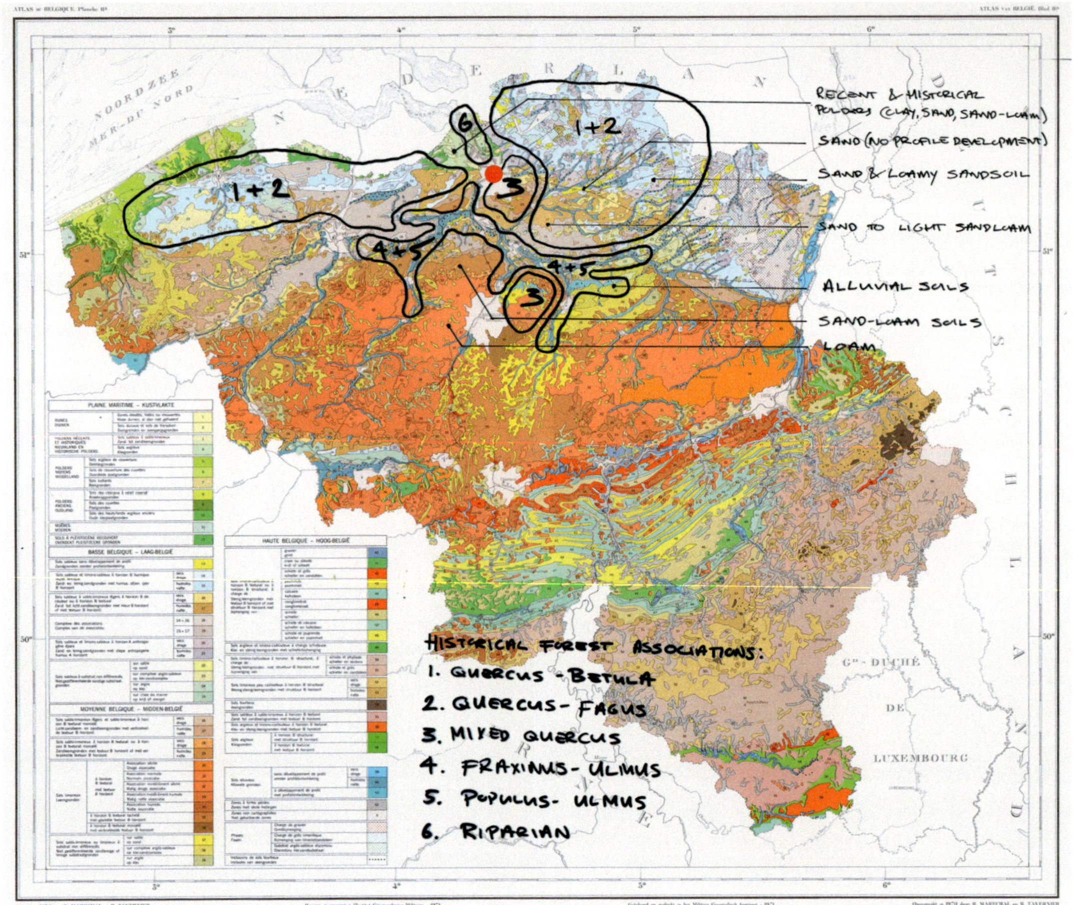

The Antwerp region is situated at the confluence of different soil types and is surrounded by a wide variety of regionally occurring vegetation patterns. An overlay of historical forest associations on Belgium's soil map highlights the direct relationship between soil conditions and vegetation types.

The topographical changes to the park and the resulting hydrological conditions create different ecological niches within the park. The proposed planting palette is a response to these conditions, based on regional vegetation patterns around Antwerp. Woodlands, meadows, and a tidal wetland are created with vegetation native to the region.

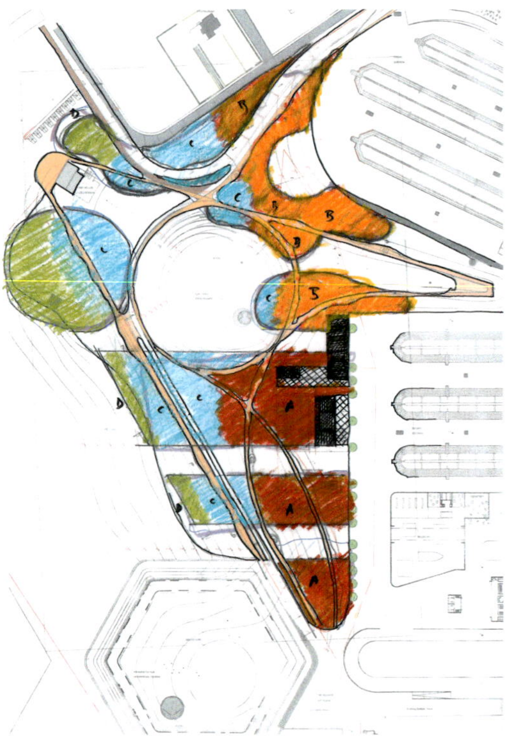

Sketch showing developments of planting scheme
- A: *Quercus-Betula* and *Quercus-Fagus*
- B: Mixed *Quercus*
- C: *Fraxinus-Ulmus* and *Populus-Ulmus*
- D: Riparian

Droogdokkenpark, Antwerp, BE
Measure and Interval

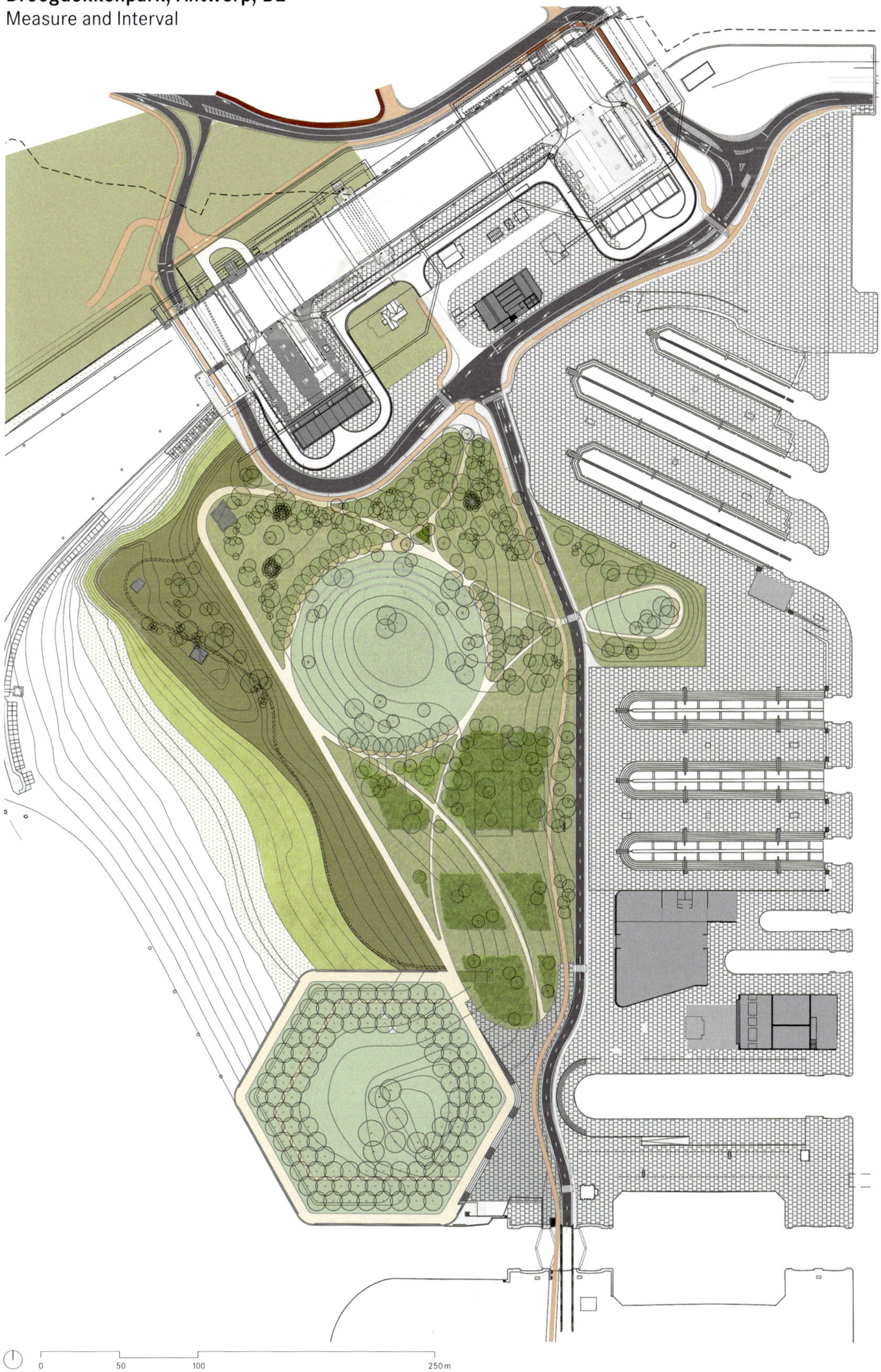

City and Territory

July 30, 2019, Diener & Diener Architects, Studio Basel

Günther Vogt: On your website, there is a text about the design approach of your office. In this programmatic piece of writing you present design as the measuring and embedding of a building task into the societal context of the city. It is, you say, the experience of the city as witness to an immeasurable diversity of activities which forms the basis of your design approach. And you added that "we cannot imagine a design developed with a warning finger, nor do we wish to overhaul each and every memory of the city that is inscribed into its *gestalt* as an artifact. A city that robs itself of its history begins to dissolve itself."—While many other contemporary architects tend to avoid the term *city,* you use it quite explicitly. Where does this awareness come from?

Roger Diener: For me, the city is the first source of all perceptions. Biographical aspects are no doubt key for this. I grew up in town and have practically always lived right in the city. To experience it in its complexity and to try and explore its *gestalt,* I always considered the very prerequisite of designing actual projects. It's only through the analysis and exploration of the existing city that a design can take effect; that it can, so to say, tune into the score. I never experienced this insight as a restriction though; quite the contrary, in fact, it has always opened up new paths. I also saw this during my studies with Luigi Snozzi, who—as a guest lecturer during my first year at ETH Zurich—focused his discourse on architecture almost exclusively on the city.

Günther Vogt: Although Luigi Snozzi, who taught at the same time at ETH Zurich as the sociologist Lucius Burckhardt, always spoke about nature or landscape in this respect. On the one hand, when he described building as a way of changing nature—saying that architecture should never arrange itself with nature but always act against it. On the other hand, when he discussed urban-planning studies and defined a single-family home as something opposed to the city. He located the sole possibility of constructing such a building in relation to the landscape. Thus, his single-family houses can also be seen as an intensive exploration of the Ticino landscape. The most interesting and, at the same time, most highly regarded of his works is, however, his plan for Monte Carasso. On the scale of a small town, not to say a village, he has carried out urban planning projects and realized architecture as if in a laboratory. While he emptied and remodeled the center with its various secular and religious institutions, he defined a building code for the residential quarters that consisted of but a few building laws which put qualitative criteria center stage. In his thirty years of commitment, he thus succeeded in creating an ideal example of modern settlement development that focused on an internal densification. Monte Carasso is, however, a unique case of the local settlement policy, where the rules of architecture are usually and consistently defined by the existing, by public space.

Roger Diener: Monte Carasso is characterized by a physical confrontation with the existing, with the topography and the landscape and, in particular, the solitary buildings that delimit the settlement toward the outside. This is interesting not only as to the rules derived for the city or the buildings, but also as to the claim to organize the entire territory with the help of these very rules. Something that proved to be quite a difficult undertaking though.

Günther Vogt: Indeed, Luigi Snozzi's efforts, but also those of the entire Tendenza, to bring some order into the territory through their interventions and by means of orderly and succinct architectures made of concrete to counteract the spreading mire of developments and, thus, somewhat control the urban sprawl, can largely be judged to have failed. At best, you could speak of a certain aestheticization of space. And if you look at the architectures in the city centers, the difficulties encountered become quite obvious. Of course, there are some attempts to deal as carefully as possible with the grown structure of the city. With their interventions composed of so-called strong forms, which were placed quite self-confidently and at the same time distanced themselves from their surroundings, the Tendenza succeeded in placing singular buildings in the landscape, but not in building houses for the city.

Roger Diener: Luigi Snozzi and other Ticino architects of the Tendenza referred to Aldo Rossi's rationalist theory that the city consists of monuments, districts, squares, and streets. Monuments are defined as important public buildings such as town halls, churches, railway stations, or market halls. Due to their significant design energy, they have elevated these buildings to the status of monuments, which legitimized them as a memorable appearance. Examples include the comparatively modest house for the mayor of Monte Carasso by Snozzi or Mario Botta's much larger and more dominant casino in Campione.

Complex historical and social references were first located in the typology of the buildings. For it is in these typologies that the spatial organization of living and use has consolidated itself over long periods of time into basic patterns—social references, as far as concerns the Tendenza, are mainly based on this. There are older and more recent patterns such as the arcade typology, which some of the significant, rationalist buildings by the Tendenza follow—for example, Aldo Rossi's residential buildings in Gallaratese.

And if you refer to the attempt to limit urban sprawl with buildings, an iconic project is the famous outdoor swimming pool in Bellinzona by the Ticino group of architects around Flora Ruchat. The passageway with the locker rooms underneath was intended as a delimitation of the settlement area which extended from Bellinzona into the Piano de Magadino. Originally, it was intended to extend across the highway to the west side of the Magadino plain. At that time, the architects hoped that a strong architecture and landscape gesture could control the increasingly rapid urban sprawl. As we now know, this has turned out to be an error; architecture is unable to create this boundary, it cannot control structural developments. We have used this insight in our research at ETH Studio Basel, in which we systematically studied structural questions of territorial differentiation in Switzerland. Thus, we were not tempted to seek new answers and concepts by way of architectural projects.

Günther Vogt: There are many contemporary examples that still try to do just that though. However, I would not speak of an iconographic but rather of a spectacular architecture in the case of these buildings–one recognized by every layman. The true spectacle is this incredible waste of space. This becomes obvious when you look at Frank Gehry's private museum building for the Fondation Louis Vuitton in the Bois de Boulogne in Paris or Zaha Hadid's Naples-Afragola station building, which opened in 2017. The notion that individual solitary buildings can be used to repair the city is evident in these architectures. It is hoped that this will have the same effect as the opening of the Guggenheim Museum in the northern Spanish city of Bilbao in 1997. This expressive building stands at the beginning of a development in which not only the old industrial area at the harbor but the entire town was transformed from a formerly industrial city into a cultural city–though with all the negative consequences that are inherent to modern mass tourism. In individual cases such an approach might work, but not as a general recipe. I do not believe architecture can actually have such an effect.

< p. 336, *Bois*

Roger Diener: The buildings you are talking about seem more like huge sculptures than buildings. In my opinion, the architectural *gestalt* always has to be linked to the idea of how to use an edifice, with the very idea of human presence, that is–regardless of whether it is based on a secular or spiritual program. In the expressive, sculptural buildings you mention, this "parable" has dissolved though. This is of even greater concern to me than their excessive dimensions. Contemporary buildings can unfold an extraordinary effect without–in my opinion–having an aggressively spectacular *gestalt.* The first version of the Tate Modern in London, with its calm and balanced urban design, was already highly effective. I quite agree that the kind of *gentrification* that buildings with new cultural programs trigger in formerly disadvantaged urban districts is not completely fair, nor always positive. Affordable space for living and working all of a sudden becomes extremely expensive and an old, grown, social, and economic structure risks to erode.

< p. 226, *Tate Modern*

But it's not just a waste of space, it's also a glut of obstinate architects' fancies. By now almost anything we architects can think up could actually be realized. In Singapore, I noticed the implementation of the craziest fantasies. To me, this city seems like a gigantic mall in which the most colorful brands are demanding attention–for me a highly unpleasant experience of an apparently huge but hermetically sealed space.

The production of buildings has also been characterized by a demanding analysis of the very conditions of production. Manufacturing processes were the basis of a separate type of building. This experience has become much rarer today. If you look at a large building, it's as if it had been built in a single day. There is no longer any stratification of time, on which every traditional house is based–something that is already an inherent part of each and every clay brick that was shaped and fired, and in the walls erected with these very bricks. The aspects we traditionally associate with our experience of architecture threatens to dissolve into spectacular contemporary architecture.

Günther Vogt: The example of Singapore is highly significant. In architecture, a transfer from the original context, for instance Switzerland, may work to some extent–because office towers in Singapore have to meet similar requirements in terms of climate, information technology, development, etc. to office buildings in Zurich or New York. Of course, there are different structural solutions, but in the end, the architectures are relatively similar as to their basic structure. In the case of a landscape it is somewhat more difficult, because what we define as landscape is always a cultural production, too. In a broad sense, this has to do with the environment. That is, not only concerning the altitude, the climatic or topographical condition, but also with the social constellation and the constantly changing conditions of living together in urban space.

Roger Diener: Our understanding of design is also based on the values that you take as a given for the design of landscape architecture–the culture or social constellation you find on site. This includes a basic experience of the European city as such and its development over a very long period of time. We also pursue physical aspects though, such as topography or the climate, which probably determine your work even more than mine. This cannot possibly be separated into individual aspects: the cultural and social dimensions of a specific place have always been linked to geographical and physical factors that–together–form the prerequisite of shaping a place, whether in the landscape or the city.

Actually, in this context I would be interested in knowing what role or significance the history of a place has on the large-scale urban-planning projects that you are currently planning and realizing? After all, these new urban quarters are quite often created on former industrial areas that already have a certain inventory. In architecture, we have meanwhile become very much aware of the connection between local history and the present and try and develop designs aware of this very history in order to, possibly, define the special feature of a new project. I imagine that the contrast between the existing and the new is much less apparent in landscape architecture, because it concerns a slower and much more continuous process that you, thereupon, proceed to steer in a certain direction.

> p. 450, *Agenti Climatici*

Günther Vogt: That's the way it's been until now. But I'd say that in the last four to five years, the climate debate has changed this quite a lot. The demand for native trees, for instance, has almost been washed overboard. Today, it's less a question of the origin of the trees but whether the vegetation will be able to cope with the current and future heat stress. This is associated with the demand to plant trees wherever possible in the city. And this is considered something of an emergency now.

It is interesting to note that this most recent "green movement" in the city has begun with projects that were primarily concerned with aesthetic aspects: green facades, vertical gardens, or greened bridges–all of them projects that are not really very sustainable and lead to a certain segregation within the urban space, as such spaces are often privately owned, with the resulting consequences and conditions as to their accessibility. I think we should no longer discuss these images but develop viable projects for the city instead. The prerequisite for this is that we no longer imagine these interventions as singular objects that only conform to their own standards. A historical example are some of the avenues in Paris planned by Jean-Charles Alphand. These trees grow so well because their root systems are connected belowground. Now, if it is dry in one place and very wet in another, the system simply redistributes the water. Thus, the venue functions as a kind of large organism. Today, we are again resorting to such old methods, not least because the context or the conditions within which we have to act nowadays are changing massively. This requires us to rethink the situation and broaden our view. Not only from the point of view of landscape architecture but also from that of all disciplines and instances involved in planning, controlling, and designing the urban space in the broadest sense. Including architecture, of course.

> p. 506, *Platanus × hispanica*

I often find that only the built part of a quarter or the surrounding area are meant in urban-planning discussions. The "grain" of the building volumes is discussed, the color of the facades or the height of the eaves. We simply need to move to another level of this discussion. The study done by ETH Studio Basel, *Switzerland: An Urban Portrait,* published in 2005, can certainly be read in this sense, though it was often misunderstood as a kind of projection for Switzerland. As a matter of fact, it reflects reality and precisely describes the processes that take place more or less visibly: for instance, the formation of city networks or the existence and expansion of tourist resorts in the Alps.

< p. 132, *Alps*

Roger Diener: It is certainly true that the project exerted a certain influence in Switzerland that still has some impact. In *Switzerland: An Urban Portrait* we were able to introduce a series of terms that were thereupon widely accepted. The language used to discuss urbanized Switzerland and urbanization and urbanity in general has changed accordingly. But the study also directly influenced the country's strategic, political, and administrative planning. This becomes obvious if you look at the Swiss spatial concept published in 2012.

Günther Vogt: What I found quite exciting, seeing that you now talk about the reception of the work, is the view of people who do not look at these spaces from the point of view of planners or researchers. On the one hand, when you published this study, it met with great disapproval by the inhabitants of the so-called Alpine wastelands. They were pretty upset about the fact that people were apparently ready to give up part of the Alps without much ado and cede it to "wilderness." On the other hand, the people living on the edge of "metropolitan regions" and "city networks" did not want to be defined as part of these larger urban units. What became visible was the understanding of an urban versus a rural Switzerland deeply rooted in people's minds. In fact, in your study you have dissolved this distinction; a distinction that has been abolished for quite some time. However, thinking in these absolute categories with all the positive and negative qualities ascribed to them, is still pretty much evident. Thus, for example, if we look at the posters of major distributors advertising products allegedly produced by the type of farmer you still remember from your childhood, operating a farm outside the city on a broad green meadow. Or if we look at the countless folkloric fairs that are becoming more and more popular. The Federal Swiss Wrestling and Alpine Festival in Zug attracted about 420,000 people. In an exemplary manner, the venue mirrored the division into these two worlds. Thus, the Gabentempel or Temple of Gifts was housed in the barns of the bull market located right next to the premium business center, Uptown Zug, an office tower in the center of the city, located directly adjacent to the station with its connection to Zurich and the international Zurich Airport.

< p. 132, *Alps*

< p. 120, *Canis lupus*

Roger Diener: Well, yes, this love of the Alps, this longing for the countryside has probably always existed and, today, is increasingly met by artificial means. Just recently, I noticed a picture of the queue in front of the summit of Mount Everest in a daily newspaper. It was quite phenomenal to see how these urban mechanisms appropriate "nature" in an unsustainable manner. Of course, as you say, this intangible appropriation also plays an important role in the context of new folk festivals. Not only do events take place in urban centers now but fairs and festivals that traditionally take place in the country. For example the *Brünigschwinget,* the Swiss wrestling competition on the Brünig pass in the mountains, that experienced an immense influx of predominantly urban spectators. These events refer to a culture that no longer really exists in this form. You could say they are artificial. But that's not really new, for already starting in the nineteenth century, Swiss wrestling, blowing an alpenhorn, or stone putting were deliberately reconstructed with the aim of consolidating society and the state. All this was also about offering something to the emerging tourist public. The image of an idyllic and agrarian Switzerland, whose inhabitants live in harmony with the surrounding landscape, is a myth that is still and quite deliberately staged today.

The fact that these places outside the urban centers become, for a short time, urban crystallization points, also has to do with the country's development structure. Our *service public* makes even the most remote corners of Switzerland accessible to the general public. In this context, it seems all the more paradoxical that we still find it difficult to accept commuting–for example between Zurich and Basel, although the journey only takes 53 minutes. In larger European cities, this is a normal distance and commuting time between individual city districts.

Günther Vogt: This resistance is, indeed, incredibly pronounced. I think, it has above all to do with the history, the culture, and also the federal structure of the country. It's interesting to note that if you ask a Swiss citizen abroad where he or she is from, you will get a highly detailed answer–for example, Liestal or Pratteln or Oberwil–and not simply "Basel." But if our Italian assistant asks compatriots about their place of origin, they'll say "Milano," for instance. In a first step, the idea is to establish the greatest possible overlap between the person you ask and yourself. Then, once it has been established that the other person also is from Milan or knows the city very well, they will begin to discuss the precise localization and everything connected with it. On our last field trip to Naples, we were told by our local guide that even the cuisine of the different city districts can be distinguished. There is a specific awareness for this difference that, in Naples, has to do, if you like, with an awareness of social class. But also, of course, with the way the city has dealt with the different conditions within its territory: the sea and the port in the south, Vesuvius in the east, and the Phlegraean Fields with their about 40 smaller and larger volcanic craters in the west.

In the course of the centuries, specific patterns and character traits developed not only as to the building structure, but also as to the culture and, thus, in the kitchens. This difference between cities is something you have examined in the study *The Inevitable Specificity of Cities.* The central conclusion is that fundamental constellations of urbanity are difficult to change and that it is equally difficult to implement plans against centuries-old traditions that have developed on territorial premises. As a result and despite globalization, the specificity of cities is maintained and even reinforced.

Roger Diener: We have opposed the hypothesis of "specificity" to the thesis that, in the course of globalization, all cities will become and look more and more similar. Every city has evolved over time under its specific physical, economic, social, and cultural conditions, and has created and cultivated its own identity. These may be material or immaterial characteristics of the shape of a city, which have not only survived, but also shape its permanent process of development. The city thus remains, to put it in a nutshell, integrated in its form. For us planners and architects, this is an interesting and enriching insight and can be an important prerequisite of design. And here we are back again at the conditions of designing in the city, which we spoke about at the beginning.

We Are All Astronauts

X

Julian Charrière, 2013

We Are All Astronauts, whose title is inspired by the writings of Buckminster Fuller, is composed of world globes stripped clean of their geographic information. Choosing globes that date from the period between 1890 and 2011, the artist has sanded away their successive, shifting geopolitical contours using "international sandpaper" created from mineral samples from all the UN-recognized countries–which the artist originally created for his previous work *Monument: Sedimentation of Floating Worlds* (2013). Dust created by the abrasion gently settles beneath the globes, creating new, yet-to-be-defined cartographies. The globes are rendered as useless as their carefully drawn territories in an increasingly globalized world bound less and less by borders.

Agenti Climatici, Milan
Green Milan and Blue Milan

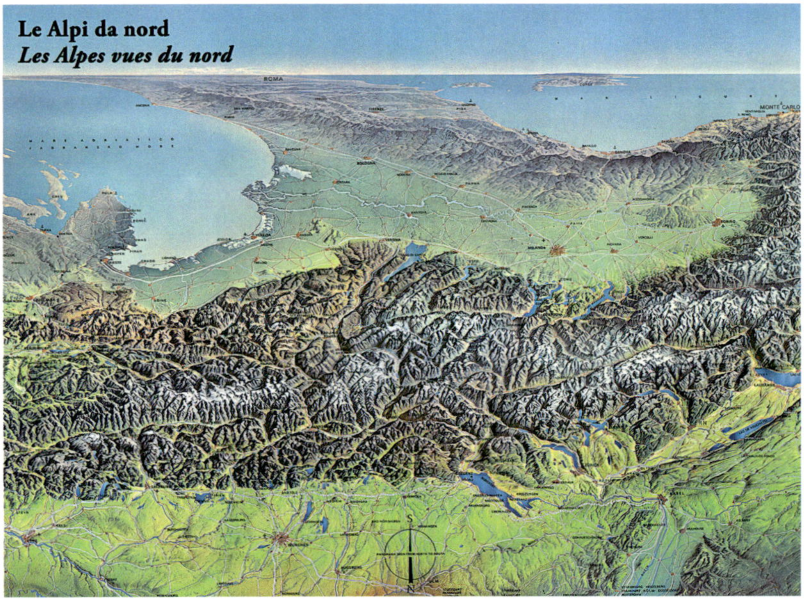

Client:
FS Sistemi Urbani S.r.l., Rome
COIMA SGR S.p.A., Milan

Cooperation:
Architecture:
OMA, Rotterdam
Laboratorio Permanente, Milan

Design:
2018–2019

Type and size:
Urban development/Park, 75 ha

Status:
Ongoing

<< London's street network merges with the contour lines of the Jungfraujoch and the Aletsch glacier. Mapping: Lukas Ryffel, Institute of Landscape Architecture, ETH Zurich.

At first glance, the assignment seems straightforward and limited by local parameters. Two obsolete railyards that were part of Milan's urban expansion in the nineteenth century are to be developed as part of an urban-planning project. Farini–a mixed-use zone situated north of the city center catering to residential, commercial, educational, and cultural needs–is to be closely integrated into the adjoining neighborhood, while San Cristoforo to the southwest is to be transformed into a park for the nearby city districts.

However, in light of the contamination of the old industrial sites and the rapid climatic changes taking place in our cities, the project needs to be viewed on a much larger scale and in more comprehensive terms. The primary task is not simply to create new, attractive urban spaces but to include strategies for decontaminating the water, soil, and air. Steps will also have to be taken to help cool the city in the future. This requires a landscape-based approach, which determines the parameters of the urban-planning concept and the design of the open spaces.

An analysis of the complex landscape structure of the Po region reveals that man has created here, over the space of millenia, a territory that is culturally highly developed and effectively exploited. Today, this space is to a large extent, though not fully, under control. The two defining elements of this landscape are clearly evident in Milan: the forest and the water. A difference in height of a mere few meters separates the city into two parts–the northern area, which is more structured and dry and primarily caters to industry, and the plain to the southeast, which is more humid and chiefly used for agricultural purposes.

Farini–the Forest–Green Milan

In the first phase, the concept is designed to biologically cleanse the contaminated soil over a long period of time. To achieve this, suitable plants are sown and cut back on a regular basis; the clippings and cuttings, which contain concentrated amounts of pollutants, are removed–a process that is to last for decades. The neighborhood park, which is being created in parallel to this, is planned as a forest whose role is shifting away from a farmed resource used for timber production and toward a valuable element of the urban climate with numerous ecological functions. The forest promotes evaporation and helps cool the city; it also binds dust from the air and helps to retain local rainwater and purify it through a process of percolation.

In addition to an extensive system of paths, playgrounds and areas for sports and sunbathing are incorporated into the forest clearings. The planting concept takes into account the state of the nutrient-poor wasteland: in addition to pioneer trees such as robinia and birch, it includes Siberian elms, Japanese pagoda trees, and Chinese gutta-percha trees, which can deal much better with the changing urban climate.

San Cristoforo–the Water–Blue Milan

By integrating generous areas of meadowland, the plain along the canal is transformed into a landscape corridor with a significant impact on the climate in the center of Milan. As meadows are much more efficient than forests at cooling air, a continuous stream of cooler fresh air flows from the surrounding countryside into the center of the city. In addition, the large open spaces are accessible both to Milan residents and to visitors and can be used for many different purposes. The canal (Naviglio Grande) helps to purify the rainwater, while a finely structured network of smaller canals and brooks channels the water from the surrounding urban neighborhoods into the site. At the same time, parts of the main canal become available for leisure activities.

In addition to open-air swimming pools, jetties and facilities for water sports are being built. (lr)

The political unification of Italy consolidated Milan's economic dominance over northern Italy and led to a new era of railroad construction. Milan became a rail hub, and the opening of the tunnels under the Gotthard Massif (1882) and the Simplon Pass (1906) turned it into the most important southern European railway junction for business and passenger traffic.

Map of the railway lines, broken down by use and construction date, 1967

Street map of Milan, 1937, with the largest railway stations of the city marked.

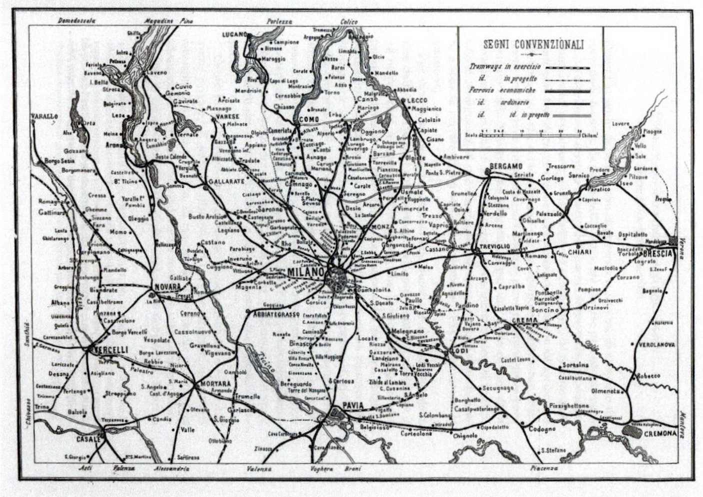

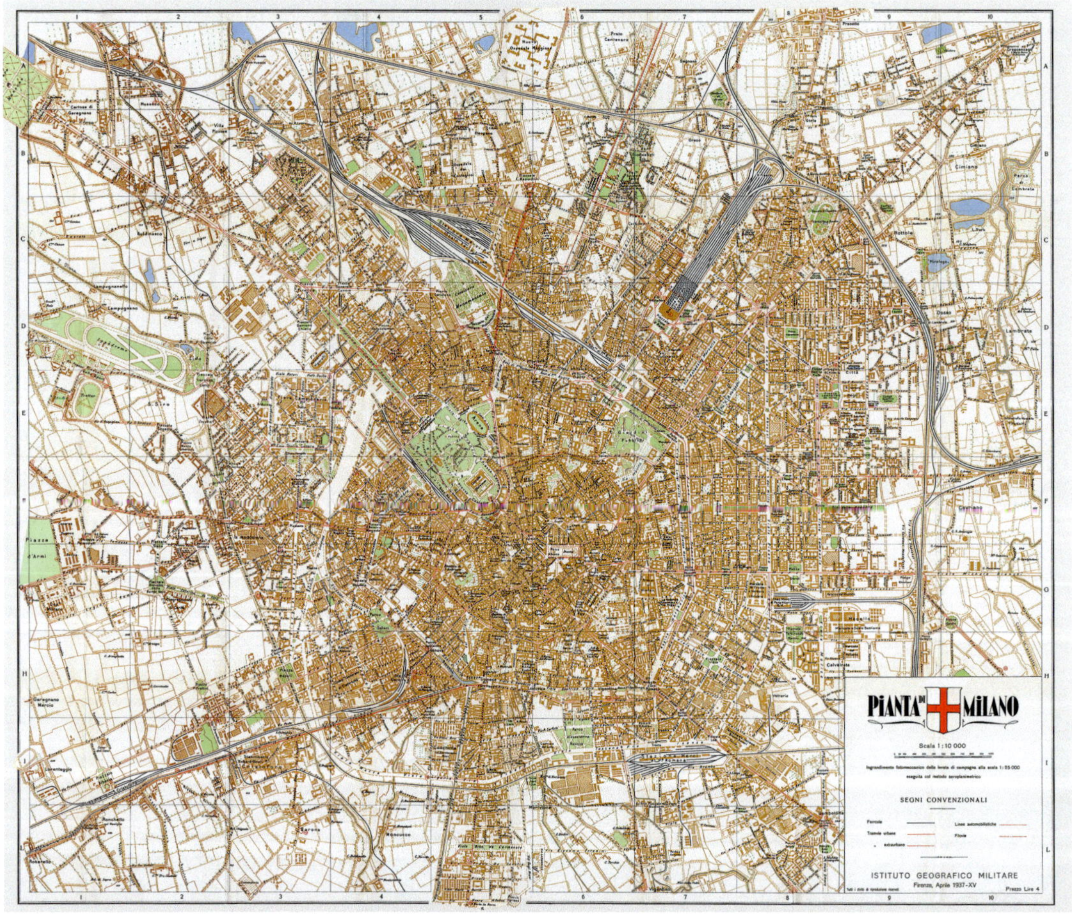

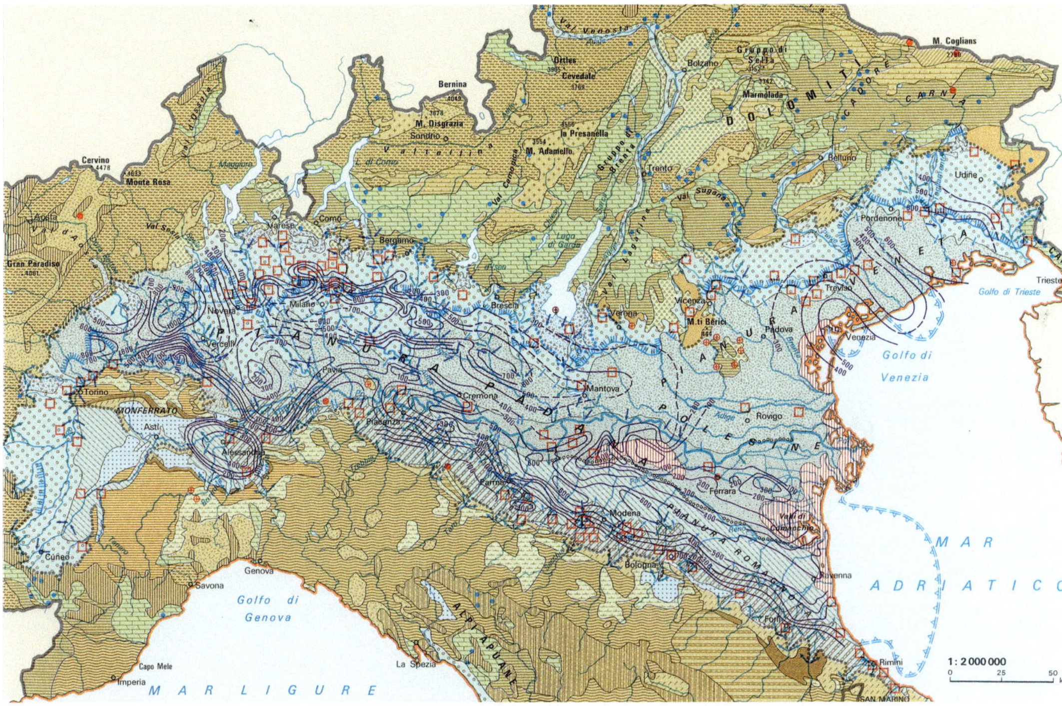

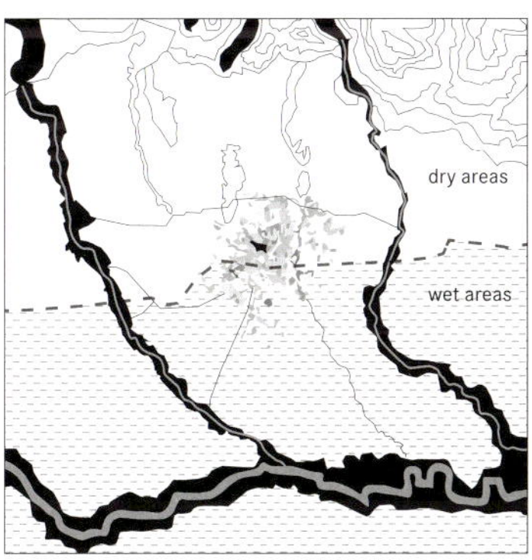

Hydrological situation and soil conditions of the Po plain (*Pianura Padana*): the plain is divided, roughly speaking, into an upper, drier zone (*alta pianura*)–only parts of which are suitable for agricultural production–and a lower, very fertile, and heavily irrigated zone (*bassa pianura*).

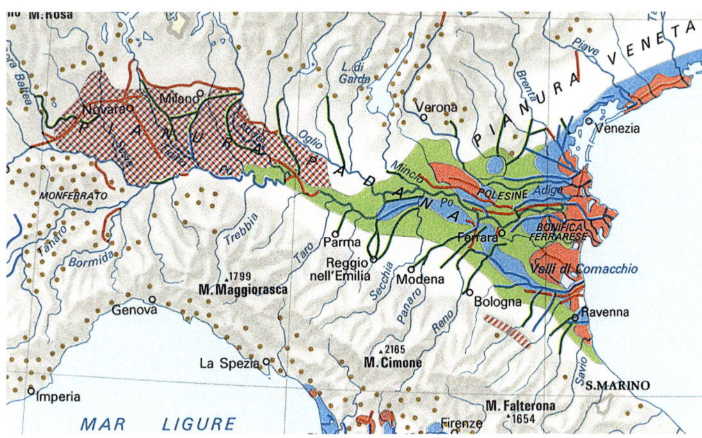

Type of intervention	Time of realization 11th to 15th century	16th to 18th century	19th century
Filling or draining operations	green	blue	red
Work on ground and hillside with notable reshaping of the topography		blue hatched	red hatched
Correction and canalization of the river	green line	blue line	red line

The different phases of drainage (*bonifica*) in the Po plain

Once upon a time, the Po plain was almost completely covered by alluvial forests. Over the centuries, the forested area was greatly diminished by the consistently high level of demand for timber–primarily required by the Republic of Venice to build its huge fleets–and the opening up of large areas to cater to the spread of agriculture. These days, the defining structures most closely resembling a forest are, above all, the fast-growing poplar plantations. Here, three different forms can be distinguished: productive plantations, which mostly supply wood for pulp, cardboard, and paper; protective plantations along riverbanks that prevent erosion and improve water quality; and plantations to preserve the landscape.

Lines of poplars, paths, and irrigation systems separate the fields from one another.

Reforestation at Cinisello Balsamo, in the eastern area of the Parco Nord Milano, initiated in 1983

Cultivated woodland for timber harvesting in the Po Valley

“Robert Smithson was also interested in **infrastructures,** like his landscape designs for the Dallas Fort Worth Regional Airport. Land art is particularly exciting in this context, as it can be viewed both from a bird’s-eye **perspective** and from ground level by someone on foot.” (gv)

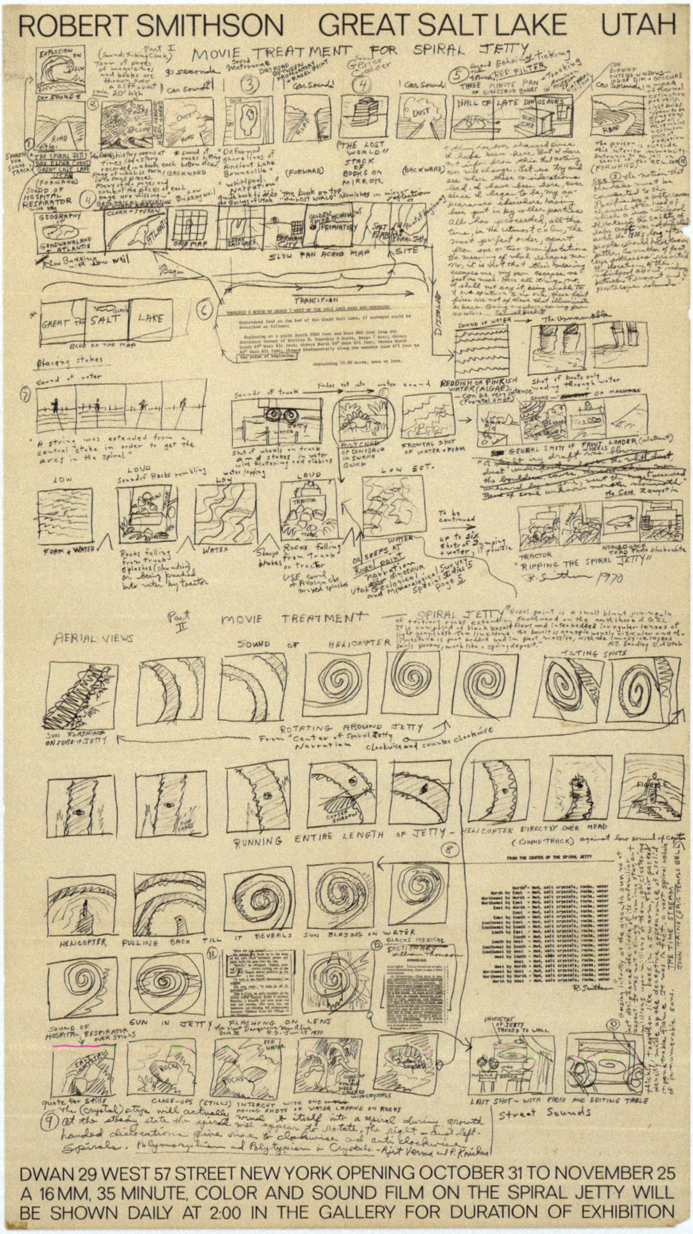

Movie Treatment for Spiral Jetty, Great Salt Lake, Utah, designed by Robert Smithson, 1970

Agenti Climatici, Milan

Green Milan and Blue Milan

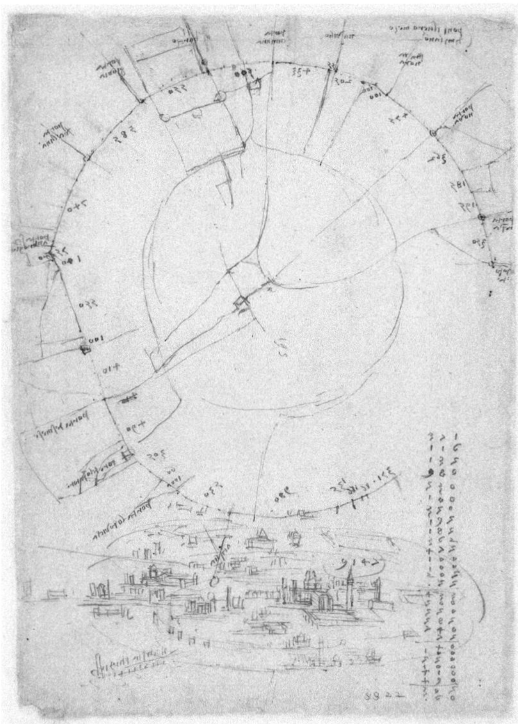

Since ancient times, the densely populated towns and cities of Northern Italy have relied for their development on the water of the Po plain–in particular, its network of canals. The Romans were the first to construct canals, which were initially designed to drain swampland for agricultural cultivation and later used for a controlled irrigation of the land. Between the twelfth and fifteenth centuries, these canals were regulated, and a large number of smaller navigable waterways were added, the so-called *navigli*. In and around Milan, this gave rise to a complex system of canals and locks–designed by Leonardo da Vinci, among others–on which goods could be moved quickly and inexpensively. These goods were transported from northern Europe over the Alpine passes, then conveyed by boat across Lake Maggiore or Lake Como and then on to Milan along the Ticino and Adda rivers. Once in Milan, they could be transported further on the city's canals to the Po and the Adriatic. The city thus became an important transshipment point for European merchandise.

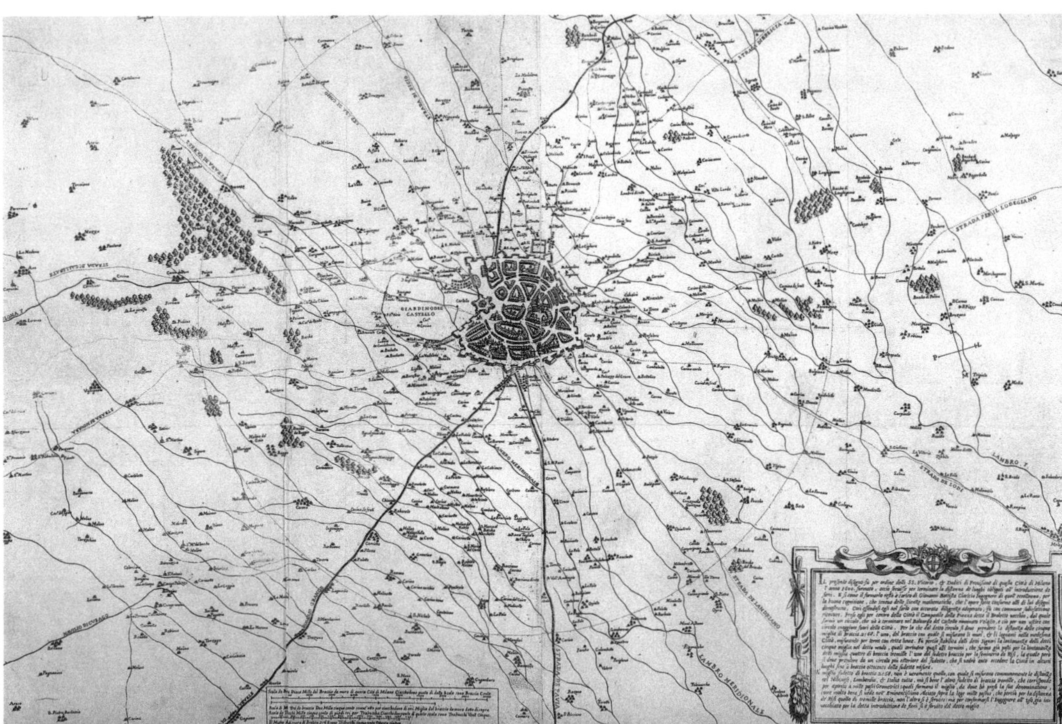

The course of the Po River from its source
to its estuary and the Adriatic

Navigli in the center of the city, 1860

The late nineteenth and early twentieth centuries witnessed the incipient decline of aquatic transportation routes. The *navigli,* which had been incorporated into the metropolitan area with the expansion of the city and the slighting of its fortifications, increasingly were the source of health hazards. At the same time, canal traffic was superseded, firstly by the railroad and later by trucks, as a cheap and fast means of transport. As a result, many of the city's *navigli* were filled in–as were its two rivers, the Olona and Lambro–and covered by roads and train tracks.

The perception of the *navigli* has changed in recent years. Their quality and importance for the city and the tourist trade have been rediscovered, and some canals and harbor basins were rehabilitated in the run-up to Expo 2015. The Naviglio Grande, which runs directly alongside the project area, is the oldest and best-preserved canal of this system and still leads right up to the historic fortifications at Porta Ticinese. It was already used to transport marble for the construction of the *Duomo di Milano,* the Milan Cathedral. The railroad tracks run parallel to the waterways, both relics of what were once the most modern means of transportation of a bygone age.

>> Territorial Scale: Milan at the junction between the Alps and the Po

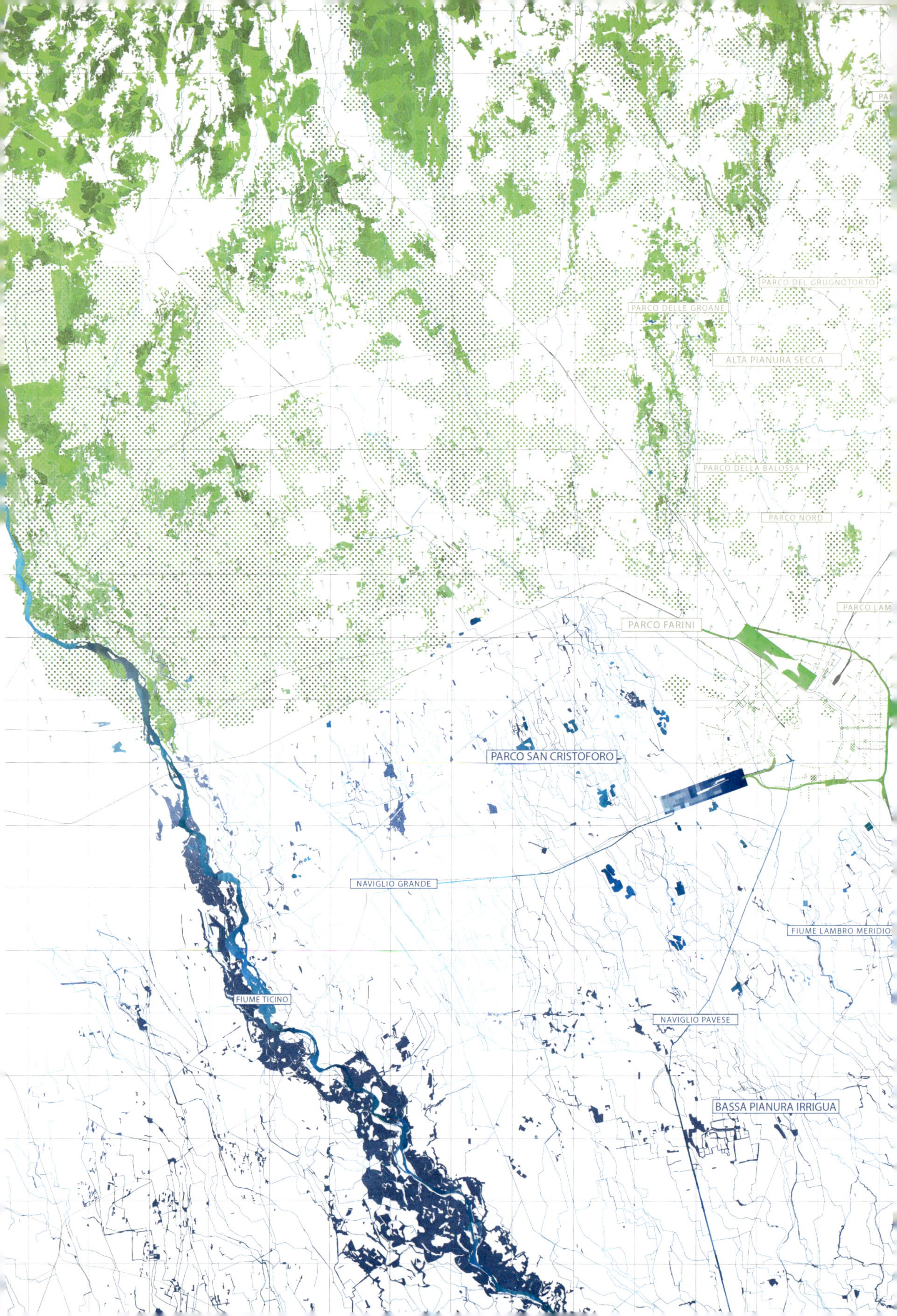
PARCO DEL GRUGNOTORTO
PARCO DELLE GROANE
ALTA PIANURA SECCA
PARCO DELLA BALOSSA
PARCO NORD
PARCO LAM
PARCO FARINI
PARCO SAN CRISTOFORO
NAVIGLIO GRANDE
FIUME LAMBRO MERIDIO
FIUME TICINO
NAVIGLIO PAVESE
BASSA PIANURA IRRIGUA

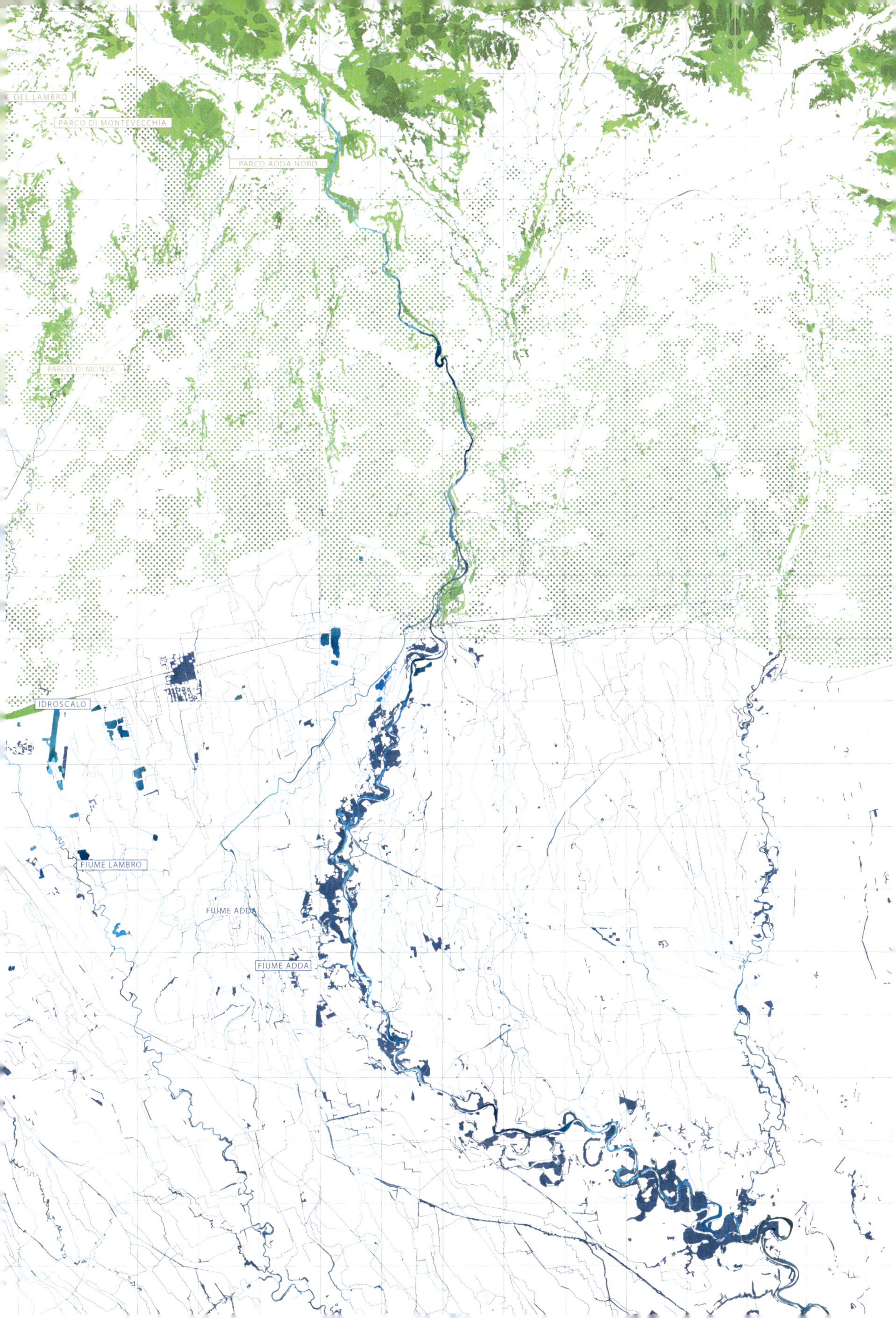

E DEL LAMBRO
PARCO DI MONTEVECCHIA
PARCO ADDA NORD
PARCO DI MONZA
IDROSCALO
FIUME LAMBRO
FIUME ADDA
FIUME ADDA

Apis mellifera
The Honeyscape

Günther Vogt

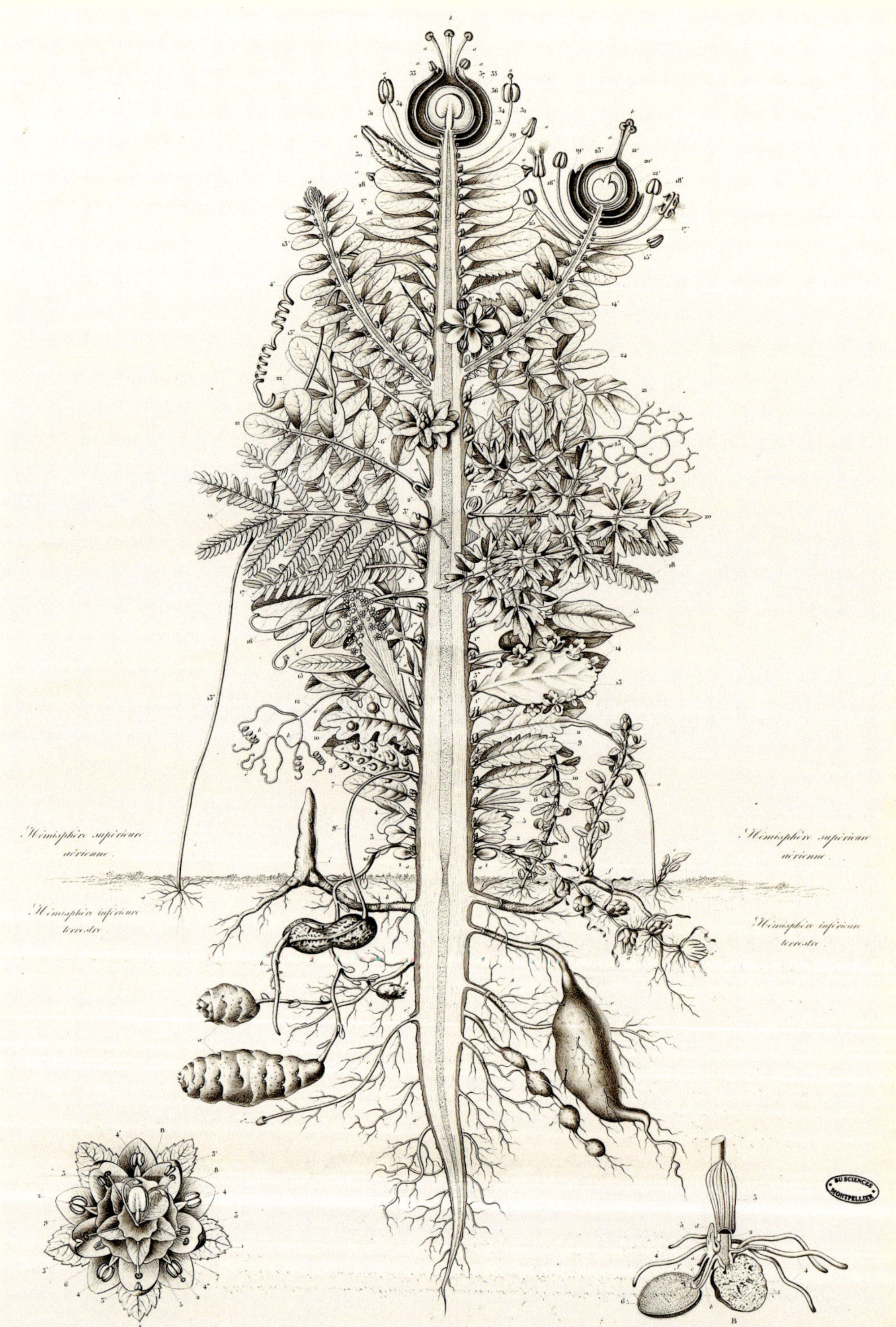

Concentration and Conservation

In the elegy *Die Metamorphose der Pflanzen,* Johann Wolfgang von Goethe not only presented the results of his botanical studies, but also communicated his morphological teaching in a concentrated form. The text, a miniature, proceeds from the description of tiny seeds to the ecology and, even further, to the cosmos of the surrounding landscape: the continuous exchange of light and warmth, water and minerals, leads to a higher level of energy and to more complex organic matter. Two germ layers are followed by more differentiated leaf forms up to the most complex form: the flower. The seeds of the flowering plants contain the most concentrated state of the plant: the oil and the DNA of new life. What Goethe omits however from his descriptions is the pollination of the flowers by bees, other insects, or the wind. After fertilization, the cycle of life begins all over again–an open system that includes the entire environment into the process of reproduction.

< Illustration of Johann Wolfgang von Goethe's primordial plant (*Urpflanze*), Pierre Jean François Turpin, 1837

Beekeeping, Eureka Canyon, Ventura County (California, USA), 1914

Joseph Beuys carried out a similar study, albeit not a literary one. With his installation *Honey Pump at the Workplace,* shown at Documenta 6 in 1977, consisting of an aggregate that pumped 150 kg of honey through a hose system and a tub of 100 kg of margarine continuously stirred by a copper shaft, he established a relationship between the cost of producing the organic matter, social organizations, and the common goals of living together.

Liquid and Solid

Honey is part of the organic world, but has a very long shelf life. It mutates into an almost mineral substance by crystallization. Honey several thousand years old was found as a funerary object in Egypt and testifies to the belief of the ancient royal cultures in eternal life.[1] This precious commodity was produced in apiaries along the Nile in specially developed clay pipes that were combined into large structures and sealed with river mud. The honey was removed, after the bees had been calmed with smoke, filled into special vessels and sealed.

Honeypump at the Workplace, installation by Joseph Beuys at documenta 6 in Kassel, 1977

Areas in ancient Egypt where it is likely that bees were kept and wild honey collected (source: Friedhelm Hoffmann, "Die Imkerei im Alten Ägypten," *Imkerfreund* 49, August 1994). The Egyptians, who were already systematically keeping bees as livestock some five thousand years ago, have maintained the world's oldest tradition of beekeeping, which is still practiced in certain parts today.

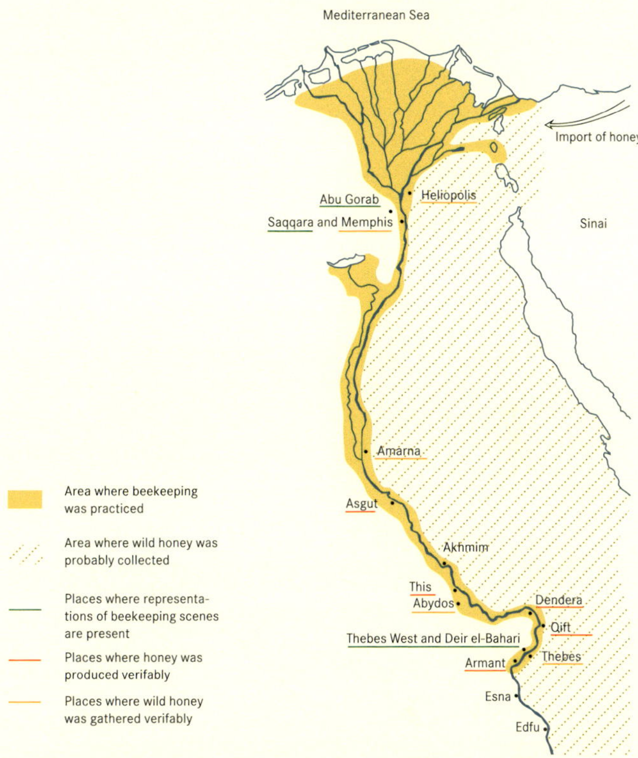

The production of honey is an elaborate and complicated process and begins with the bees gathering the blossom nectar or honeydew. Stored in their honey sacs, they transport the raw material to the hive and pass it to the worker bees. The aim of this transfer is to preserve the honey. For this purpose, bees add endogenous substances such as amino acids, enzymes, and other proteins during the exchange. The worker bees then press the nectar outward, drop by drop, only to gather it up again. This reduces the water content and the slightly thickened nectar is stored in the honeycombs, where more water evaporates. The worker bees in the hive promote this process by fanning with their wings, until the water content is a mere 18 to 20 percent. Now that the honey is finished, it is transported one last time, put into storage cells and covered with a layer of wax. This step marks the potential beginning of the honey harvest, during which any excess honey produced by the bees may be removed.[2]

Benard Fecit

Œconomie Rustique,

Mouches à Miel.

Architecture and Landscape–the Space of Honey

Specific architectures (beehives) suitable for the production of honey have accompanied mankind ever since its cultivation of landscape; different forms were developed over time depending on the location, the size of the bee population, the type of beekeeping and the efficiency of the desired honey production. The nucleus of each hive is the single cell made of wax produced by the bees themselves. In combination with heat and the close conditions of the apiary, the colony of bees produces hexagonal shapes joined in endless repetition. However, the structure inside the beehive is by no means without a hierarchy. The brood cells are located in the center, followed by the combs with stored pollen, while the cells in which the honey is stored are located outside. The structure is based on the logic of the production process and is directly reflected by the vertical forms of modern hives. Complementing the beehive is the landscape: meadows, woods, or intensively cultivated crops of lavender, apple, or lemon. Honey is a concentrate that directly reflects the *terroir* and its climatic, geological, and hydrological conditions, and the terrain and soil of a site. A teaspoon of honey combines the varied colors, textures, flavors, and scents of the landscape.

< "Oeconomie Rustique: Mouches à Miel" illustration from *L'Encyclopédie ou Dictionnaire Raisonné des Sciences, des Arts et des Métiers,* 1762

Apiary, by Isaac Levitan, around 1885

Variety and Uniformity

As varied as the landscapes are the numerous wild bee species with their onomatopoeic names. *Ammobates punctatus* (spotted sand bees), *Hoplitis anthocopoides* (*Echium vulgare* or Viper's Bugloss bees), or *Thyreus orbatus* (Thyreus cuckoo bees) do not live in bigger social units, but as loners (so-called solitary or hermit bees);[3] they occupy small niches in the ecological spectrum. On the other hand, commercial honey producers, who must reach a critical size in order to function profitably, no longer work with "pure" species but with specially bred subspecies. In Switzerland, the *carnica,* the *mellifera,* the *ligustica* and the Buckfast are predominant–all subspecies of the honey bee (*Apis mellifera*) that are considered to be particularly hardworking and gentle.

The taste of the landscape: honey tasting at Günther Vogt's Chair for Landscape Architecture at the ETH Zurich, September 2019

The western honeybee (*Apis mellifera*) is the most common bee species today.

Today's reduced diversity also results from the fact that the breeders have long concentrated on resistant species in order to protect the animals from pest infestation and disease. The acarapiosis that raged in England in the early 1910s led to the almost complete extinction of *Apis mellifera mellifera* (European dark bee). The Buckfast is the result of a crossing of surviving bees with the *Apis mellifera ligustica* (Italian bee) carried out by Brother Adam at Buckfast Abbey in southern England. Based on the findings of Ludwig Armbruster, a zoologist and one of the most important beekeepers of his time, he bred a species which is not only highly efficient, fertile, resistant to disease, and hardy, but also swarms less than other honeybees and thus brings in greater yields.[4]

Austrian ethologist and Nobel laureate Karl von Frisch was one of the first to translate the meaning of the so-called waggle dance. By performing this dance, honey bees share information with other members of the colony about the direction and distance from the hive to diverse resources such as plants, water sources, or new nest-site locations.

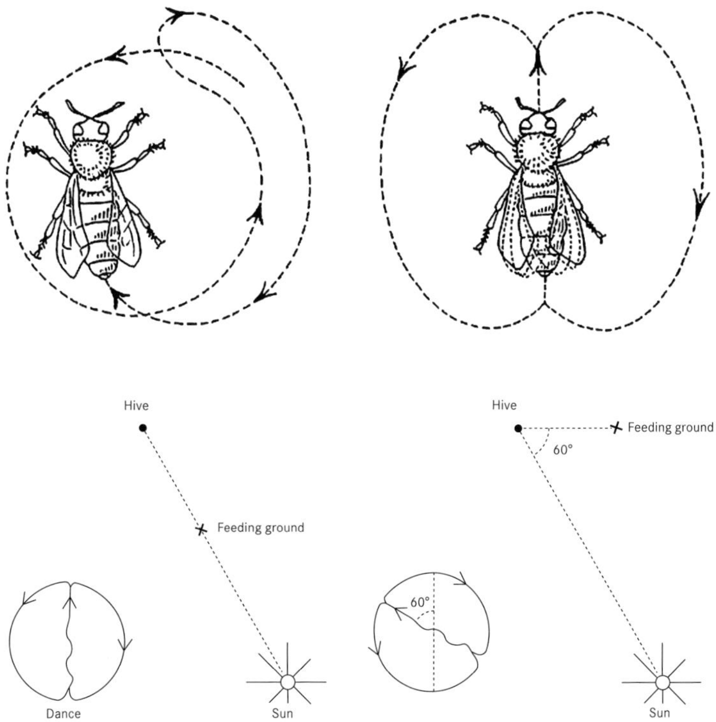

Migration

The starting point of honey production always is the local beehive, whose location, however, often changes depending on the flowering populations of the landscape. The early beehives in Egypt, which could be transported by ship on the Nile, bear witness to this long tradition of nomadic honey production. While the transport of bee colonies is quite fast in most cases, bees need up to half a day to find their way around in the new environment. They navigate according to an “inner map,” which they have to create again and again. The animals fly in circular movements, which are constantly expanded, and in doing so memorize the characteristics of the landscape, taking into account the position of the sun.[5]

In preindustrial times, individual bee colonies were distributed within a limited territory, depending on the season and weather. Later, the expansion of the rail and road infrastructure made it possible to transport large quantities of bees over long distances. The goal of such a large-scale relocation, for example in the United States, is no longer primarily the production of honey. While no bees existed on the American continent before its discovery by Spanish conquerors and flowers were pollinated by other insects,[6] bees are now used to pollinate large areas of the plants cultivated in the plantations, especially in the high season between January and May. Carried out by professional pollinators, the bee thus became an important link in the highly efficient industrial food-production chain.

1 See Birgit Sonja Feierabend, "Biene und Honig im pharaonischen Ägypten: Eine Studie anhand schriftlicher und bildlicher Quellen," diss. Johann Gutenberg-Universität, Mainz 2009, 289ff, https://publications.ub.uni-mainz.de/theses/volltexte/2014/3643/pdf/3643.pdf.

2 See *Honig Wissen,* accessed September 25, 2019, https://honig-wissen.de.

3 See Erwin Scheuchl and Hans Richard Schwenninger, "Kritisches Verzeichnis und aktuelle Checkliste der Wildbienen Deutschlands (Hymenoptera, Anthophila) sowie Anmerkungen zur Gefährdung," *Mitteilungen des Entomologischen Vereins Stuttgart* 50, no. 1 (2015). https://www.zobodat.at/pdf/Mitt-Ent-Ver-Stuttgart_50_2015_0003-0225.pdf.

4 See Bruder Adam, "Meine Betriebsweise als Grundlage meines imkerlichen Erfolges," lecture given on September 4, 1960, accessed September 25, 2019, https://wp.gdeb.eu/wp-content/uploads/2015/11/Vortrag-Kassel.pdf.

5 See "Schadstoff im Körper, Orientierung weg," *Spiegel Online,* March 20, 2014, https://www.spiegel.de/wissenschaft/natur/pestizide-machen-bienen-orientierungslos-a-959820.html.

6 See Dirk Asendorpf, "Wenn das Summen verstummt," *NZZ Folio* (August 2018), https://folio.nzz.ch/2018/august/wenn-das-summen-verstummt.

Pollinator movements in the USA (source: USDA Economic Research Service, 2014)

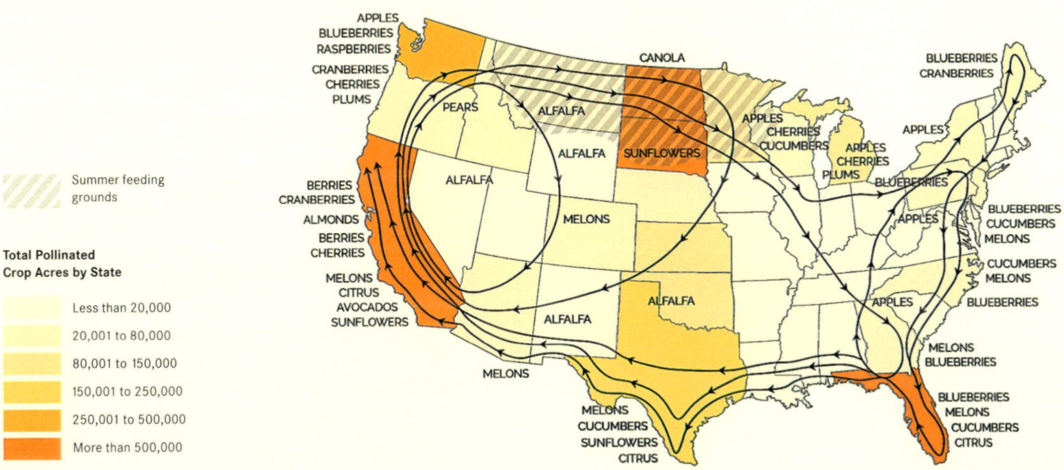

Via Giulia, Rome
Pairi Daeza

A new "Pairi Daeza," or paradise garden, on Rome's Via Giulia, invites locals and visitors to enjoy a lush urban space. Partly neglected, with water basins full of plants, overgrown with old trees and vines, it seems to have been there for centuries, forgotten. It could be an old garden, following the tradition of Roman aristocratic villa gardens, visible on the maps of the city: some of them rediscovered and accessible to local residents and visitors alike. Reminiscent of the quieter areas of the nearby Farnese Gardens or the remote parts of the park at Villa Borghese, this garden has both an internal and an external narrative.

Client:
CAM Edilizia – CAM. S.r.l., Rome

Cooperation:
Architecture:
Diener & Diener Architects, Basel

Design:
2015–2017

Type and size:
Garden, 0.45 ha

Status:
On hold

From the outside, it is an elusive world separated from the busy, hot city, containing the promise of lush vegetation, shade, and quietude. Large tree canopies reach over the wall to the street, while climbers and ramblers seem to be escaping from the garden and create a dialogue with the Farnese Gardens. The tall trees on Via Giulia help restore the street by continuing the line of building facades.

Inside the wall, the garden reveals itself as vibrant and diverse. It is organized on three levels: the *atrio giardino, frutteto,* and *giardino segreto.* The *atrio* is located on the same level as Via Giulia, and its large water basin acts as a central gathering place for the whole neighborhood. The *frutteto* on the intermediate level forms the transition between the *atrio* and the *giardino segreto.* It resembles an ancient *limonaia,* a terraced garden used to grow citrus trees for fruit production and to convey a sense of prestige. Slightly shaded by pine trees, this part refers to the tradition of agricultural fruit cultivation in historical villa gardens. Instead of lemons, the orchard comprises rows of fruiters of different kinds and invites the visitor to pick an apple, sit in the shade, and listen to the gentle sound of water trickling in the fountain. Finally, on the highest part of the site stands the secret garden, where a mix of trees, climbers, and bushes seems to surround ancient ruins. Built partly on a new car park and partly on a 2,000-year-old stable, the garden forms a new layer in the urban geology of Rome. (lr)

The garden walls of Palazzo Farnese, view from Via Giulia

This city garden is built on the ruins of a 2,000-year-old stable. Since then, the constant process of construction and demolition has caused the level of the city to rise by several meters. The project renders another layer in the "geological" history of the metropolis visible.

Via Giulia, Rome

Pairi Daeza

north

0 5 10 15 m

east

0 10 25 50 m

The motif and its elements can be found in many parts of the city: the lush green of the trees and climbers extends beyond the walls of the *hortus conclusus*, leaving its mark not only on the garden but also on the adjacent urban situation.

“The box ball is the perfect shape. It represents the world, a sense of **control over nature.** It is an evergreen. And there is no process of development: it is frozen in a particular shape. Like André Le Nôtre’s park in Versailles, designed for Louis XIV. Voltaire’s *Il faut cultiver notre jardin,* however, has the opposite intention: not the preservation of a form but withdrawal into a private world, a dialogue with oneself that includes the possibility of failure.” (gv)

Villa Lante
Villa Farnese
Villa Gregoriana
Villa d'Este
Villa Adriana
Villa Borghese
Villa Mondragona
Villa Falconieri
Villa Torlonia
Villa Aldobrandini
Villa Grazioli
Castel Gandolfo
© Google Earth

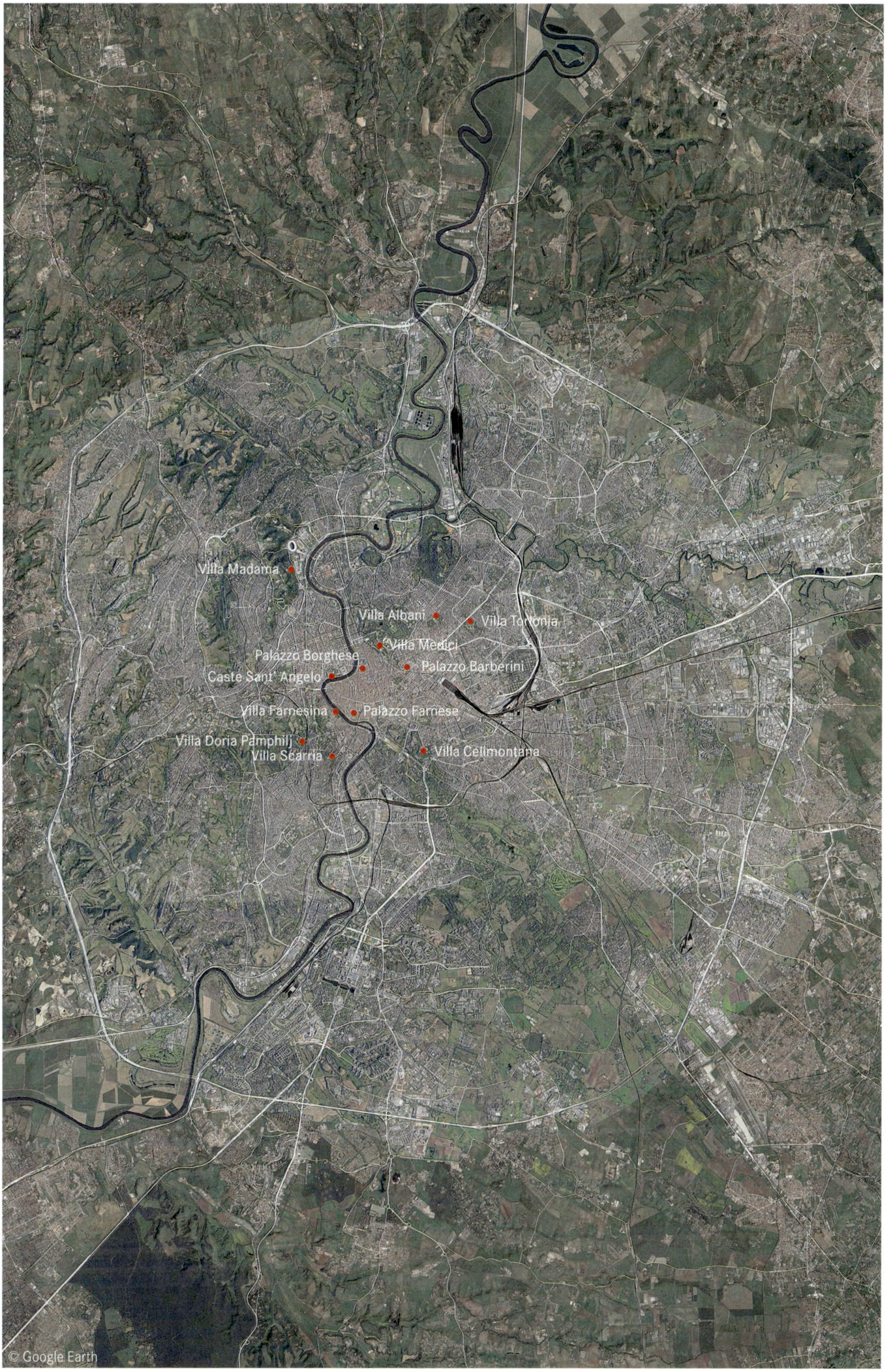

Villa Madama
Villa Albani
Villa Torlonia
Villa Medici
Palazzo Borghese
Palazzo Barberini
Caste Sant' Angelo
Villa Farnesina
Palazzo Farnese
Villa Doria Pamphilj
Villa Scarria
Villa Celimontana
© Google Earth

City Garden
Urban Treasures

Lars Ruge

Gardens have accompanied people through all phases of urbanization, ever since mankind became sedentary. Depending on their meaning and use, repeated migrations from the countryside to the city and vice versa can be identified–occasionally even simultaneous ones, though with different programs or social significance. What has remained the same from the beginning to this day, are the elements characterizing a Garden of Eden: borders, threshold, water, vegetation, metaphor, choreography, and topography–in varying degrees, depending on time and points of view.

<< While early gardens were protected by walls and embedded in the grounds of mosques, monasteries, or ancient latifundia, in courtyards or in the confines of medieval cities, In the Renaissance period they moved out into the countryside. Both types of garden can thus still be found, for example, on the outskirts of Rome and Florence: the gardens of Roman emperors, Catholic clerics, and wealthy merchants occupy wooded slopes and rises in refreshing country surroundings, while their lush counterparts, compressed within the dense urban setting, are secluded behind walls, serving as tiny paradises in the heat and noise of the city.

This Persian miniature features the basic quadripartite structure of a Persian garden with water in the middle. These gardens were called *pairi-daēza,* literally "enclosed space," a term that was later adopted to describe paradise on earth.

From the Landscape into the City

The archetypal garden–a piece of land wrested from nature and clearly demarcated–consists of a delimited agricultural plot to raise vegetables and fruit, protected against predators by a hedge or a wall. Located directly next to the farm and often covered with trees giving it shade, its size has always been in direct proportion to the farmer and his needs and capability. A reflection of the human scale in the landscape.

On the one hand, the gardens found their way "through" town walls that had become useless due to defortification. Formerly built as ramparts, ditches, or walls to protect towns, these massive structures lost their military function in the nineteenth century. Their demolition created the conditions for growing cities such as Hamburg, Frankfurt, or Basel to spread unhindered across the plains. Fruit and vegetable gardens formerly located outside the densely built historic towns, but directly adjacent to the town walls, thus became gardens within the town perimeters: city gardens, that is. Mostly, these were integrated into the public boulevards and parks that were created on the former, now razed ramparts. Their form and function were thereby abolished. However, there are still some gardens, above all in smaller towns, that have retained their original size and use and remain a functional part of the dense urban fabric.

On the other hand, gardens gradually migrated to the cities by the end of the nineteenth and the beginning of the twentieth centuries as part of the garden city and Volkspark movement. In England, cooperative socialist Ebenezer Howard initiated, responding to the housing speculation and bad living conditions rife in the bigger cities, the model of the garden city as a new type of settlement outside the already existing cities. This culminated in Frank Lloyd Wright's vision of Broadacre City in the 1930s, while garden reformer Leberecht Migge stipulated that "everybody should be self-sufficient" and till his own plot of land.[1]

Both visions were based on sufficiently large tracts of land that could be cultivated by a sin-

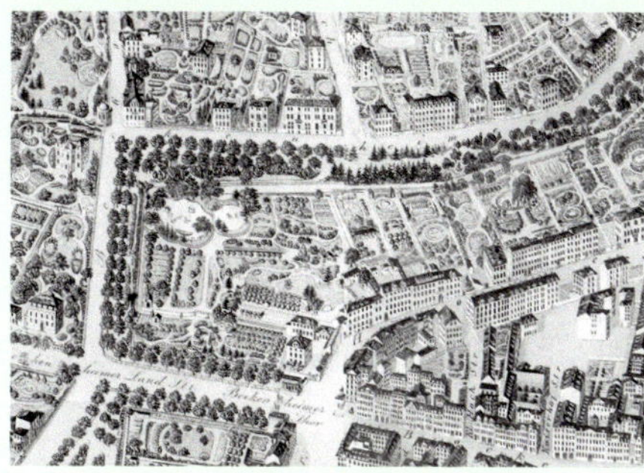

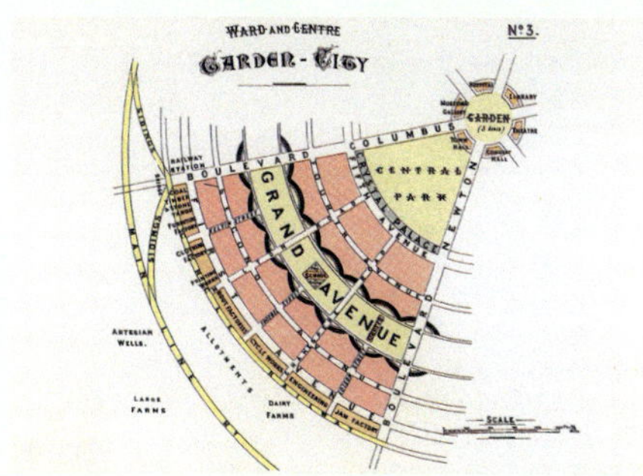

An archetypal garden in the Alps (Grisons, Switzerland)

Gardens in place of the former fortifications in Frankfurt

In his book *To-morrow: A Peaceful Path to Real Reform,* published in 1898, Ebenezer Howard envisioned self-contained communities planned according to a concentric pattern of open spaces and public parks.

1 Sophie von Schwerin, "Jedermann Selbstversorger! Lebensreform und Landschaftsarchitektur," *Tec 21,* August 8, 2017, https://www.espazium.ch/de/aktuelles/jedermann-selbstversorger.

1

2

3

4

Development of the *Schrebergarten* (allotment)

1 The world's first Schreber playground. A simple meadow was leased by Dr. Hauschild in 1864.
2 Children's beds are created around the plot. In 1868 Mr. Gesell laid out children's beds around the play area.
3 The children's beds became family beds. These family beds were inaugurated on June 7, 1869.
4 The family beds became gardens. In 1870 the world's first allotment garden was created.

gle family and fundamentally secured its food supply. An originally rural tradition thus became part of big-city structures.

Paradise Landscapes

On a smaller scale, garden plots laid out and organized in groups had been made available as a social measure ever since the end of the eighteenth century. Landgrave Carl von Hessen's project against hunger and poverty, the so-called *Carlsgärten* in Kappeln on the Schlei of 1798, was followed in the nineteenth century by quite some comparable projects in which municipal plots of land, mostly located on the outskirts of a city, were ceded to the townspeople in exchange for a small lease. The initiators had partially different models and goals: Berlin's workers' gardens, for instance, were developed according to Parisian and Luxembourgian models and subject to strict regulations. The community administered the facilities collectively and organized the way people lived together. The gardens were not only intended to improve the economic situation of the workers, but were also meant to make the families bond and create opportunities for physical and mental recreation. The allotment gardens or *Schrebergärten* by Moritz Schreber, Carl Ernst Bock, Ernst Innozenz Hauschildt, and Heinrich Karl Gesell with their children's and family patches and playgrounds were used both for cultivation and physical exercise, education and children's games. What they all had in common, apart from alleviating poverty and hunger, was the social aspect of the community.

A special form of minimal gardens are the *railway gardens*, which were laid out in various countries by railway employees on their own along the tracks or on unused railway yards. At first merely tolerated, they are regularly leased to this day. As soon as the urban infrastructure spread into their territory, these gardens "migrated" from the centers to the surrounding countryside, and first urban structures and individual visions of paradise emerged alongside the tracks.

Models of Broadacre City by Frank Lloyd Wright, 1934

Allotment gardens between the railway lines with a view of the locomotives and administration buildings at Westhafen in Berlin

The Liz Christy Garden was the first community garden in New York. It was founded in 1973 by local residents and a group of activists known as the Green Guerillas.

Rooftop gardening in London

Community Gardening and Urban Farming

In the 1970s, the Community Gardening Movement emerged in the US in several large cities. A lack of open space and the poor supply of affordable fresh food led to gaps between buildings and wastelands being occupied by local residents and repurposed into community and kitchen gardens.[2] The beginning of *urban gardening* lay in the reversal of the original development: no longer was a piece of land made arable or wilderness transformed into order and cultivated, but a community appropriated parts of an area reserved for building, transformed and farmed it. The transformation of a building plot into "controlled nature" used to cultivate flowers, vegetables, and fruit primarily met a social need, reclaiming a public space in one's own neighborhood.

As part of this urban-farming movement and pursuing similar goals, new forms of urban farms have emerged in London in recent decades, often initiated as community projects. Pig farming in housing estates, quail and ostrich farming in the gardens of terraced houses, beekeeping along the high-speed railway line, distilleries, orchards, and vineyards between logistics halls now characterize an urban, decentral agriculture that produces local food within the M25 motorway ring.[3] The city has turned edible. In contrast, the ubiquitarian vegetable gardens in EUR-pallet demanded in every design brief are often the empty relics of just such movements. In the past, you wrested such a garden from the "wilderness" that you conquered and, later, by fighting against building volumes and speculation: always with the goal to secure one's food supply and establish social cohesion. If individual initiative and the struggle for this small free space are lacking however, the substrate box is degraded just as much as a bench, a swing, or a lamp to a pure furnishing element.

The Garden of the City

Today, there is hardly any urban-planning study, master plan, or actual project in which the proposal of a city garden–a garden in a dense urban context, that is–does not meet with a lack of understanding,

2 Joshua Birky, "The Modern Community Garden Movement in the United States: Its Roots, Its Current Condition and Its Prospects for the Future," MA thesis, University of South Florida, Tampa, 2009, http://scholarcommons.usf.edu/cgi/viewcontent.cgi?article=2859&context=etd.
3 Carole Cadwalladr, "Urban Farms: Can You Source a Complete Meal from Inside the M25?" *The Guardian*, June 20, 2010, https://www.theguardian.com/lifeandstyle/2010/jun/20/urban-farms-local-food.

or at the very least triggers intensive discussions. The idea of a space in the midst of the city surrounded by hedges, walls, or fences is rejected, pictures of single-family houses framed by thuja hedges, flower beds, weed-free lawns, and garden gnomes are sought. Hedges and gardens are perceived as metaphors of "suburbia" and, thus, as a counterbalance to the city. This also shows an interesting change in perception: if for one part of society, the abovementioned suburban scenario is exactly the place where people long to be, a natural paradise as a counter-world to the city, another part wants a direct reference to the wilderness. The "social green" of Migge, Frederick Law Olmsted, or Gottlieb Friedrich Rothpletz seems to have lost its status in the density of today's city.

Rather, a desire for a wilderness in the midst of a city emerges, the proposal of a "dynamic nature" not "squeezed" into the borders of a garden, but allowed to develop freely. At the same time, flexibility of use is always equated with a dynamic situation. Instead of the durability of a slowly maturing garden, open urban spaces are to remain changeable at short notice and spontaneously, too. More like a stage set, in fact: urban life against the backdrop of "wilderness."

The images that are often used to show such a dynamic "urban wilderness" are quite often their perfectly designed and commercialized opposite instead. This wish is not represented by a pioneer or young forest or an overgrown infrastructure and industrial buildings, but a railway viaduct in New York, a vertical facade forest in Milan, or solidly embedded temporary restaurants on the brownfields of Zurich or Berlin.

However, neither suburbia's strategies, nor set pieces of a safe "wilderness" can satisfy the basic, day-to-day need of an urban society for open spaces.

City Garden as a Design Tool

While today's urban development is precisely defined by building laws and standards from its structures to the percentage of its green spaces and the selection of plants, the individual demands of society as to open spaces have become more varied, while long-term predictions regarding future residents and user groups have become more volatile. A city garden introduces a different scale into the city compared to, say, a park. Therefore, it has no significance for the food supply of the entire city but may well fulfill a lot of local functions. Its essence is not based on an already defined design concept or fixed program. A city garden is a strategic design tool for urban-planning developments with long time horizons, where the utilization of buildings–and thus its future users and their demands–may not yet be known. It is conceived as a programmable vessel, whose shell is already embedded in the urban ground plan. Thus, its design retains, based on the definition of its basic elements, a certain degree of flexibility–even without being fully formulated as yet. Conceived on the scale of a neighborhood or entire quarter, a city garden exudes the atmosphere of a private space, but can be used by the public.

Ailanthus trees on the High Line in 2000 before the start of its refurbishment in 2006

Typologically, a city garden is an ambiguous figure, borrowed from the garden in terms of size and design basics, though it can assume the social functions of a community garden or playground, an ornamental garden or an agricultural tract of land. It offers what is often lacking in today's settlement and cities: a defined location and a recognizable content. And thus, it offers continuity and, at the same time, a certain mutability reminiscent of nineteenth-century squares in London. In any case, one thing it may never be is noncommittal, even if this would also be deemed a reflection of today's urban culture.

Postcard, around 1910

Lokstadt, Winterthur, CH
Gardens of the City

The city of Winterthur grew quite significantly as it underwent industrialization. Numerous companies moved in, the majority of them focused on manufacturing machinery and locomotives. With its historic fortifications torn down, the city began to expand into the surrounding countryside. After the economic crisis of the 1930s, when many factories were shut down, the population declined sharply, before enjoying a resurgence in recent years with the construction of the Zurich suburban railway. At the same time, the former industrial sites, which are located in the center of the city and within walking distance of each other, were being transformed into attractive residential locations. The overlapping of architectural and horticultural motifs derived from the industrial culture preserves a clear sense of the historical legacy, while at the same time allowing modern requirements for open spaces to be met.

Client:
Sulzer Immobilien
Implenia AG

Cooperation:
Architecture:
Annette Gigon/Mike Guyer Architekten, Zurich

Design/construction:
2018–2019/2020–2023

Type and size:
Square/Street/Garden, 2.3 ha

Status:
Under construction

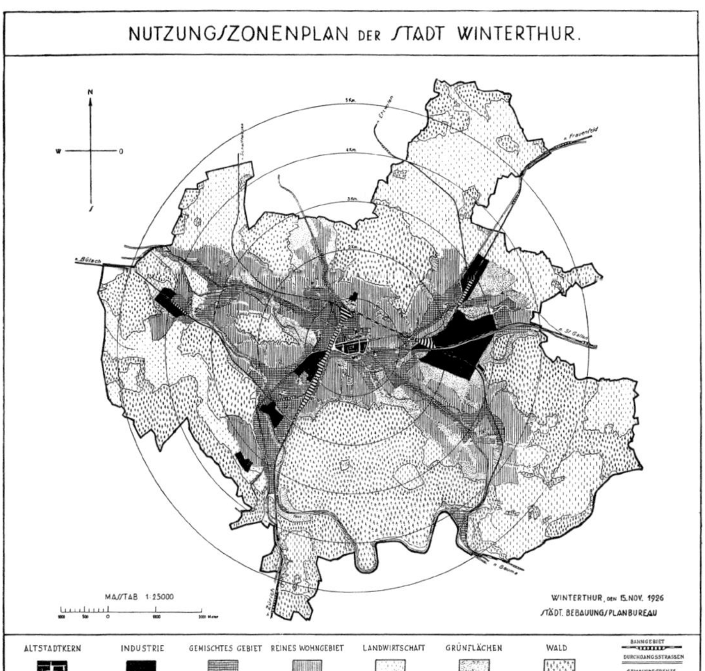

Like the parts of the Sulzer site that have already been transformed, the image of Winterthur's Lokstadt will retain its industrial flair through the preservation of its historical production halls. However, the emphasis will shift with the creation of several hundred apartments, commercial premises, children's daycare centers, and offices. In the future it will no longer be just the working population and students who will use the site–and the open spaces in particular–but mainly parents with children and senior citizens.

Points of Reference

While small-scale squares articulate distinctive points of entry, the figure of the expansive square plays a crucial part in the daily urban experience of residents and visitors alike. Community and commercial uses will overlap. In addition to a playground, the neighborhood will also have a pavilion that can be used as a venue for events. Opening up an area that had previously been off-limits to the public also is of regional significance, creating new connections between the city center and the Tössfeld area southeast of it, as well as between the forests of Ebnet, Brühl, and Herrgottsbüel, which deeply extend into the urban fabric and can easily be reached on foot.

Individuality and Serialization

The dense clustering of structures and the corresponding restrictions on the space between buildings makes mixed use a necessity: the areas must serve a range of different needs, as an access area and a place to meet, a children's playground, a sheltered front garden, an ecological compensation area, and an outdoor space for visitors to enjoy. The classic typologies–square, park, garden, street–cannot fully accommodate all these requirements. As a result, an "ambiguous" figure has been inserted between the typically narrow streets of the area and the garden: the city garden–a type whose basic elements and scale can also be found in the immediate vicinity.

As you walk through Winterthur, you can clearly see the different types of buildings that characterized the cityscape during industrialization: the many small-scale workers' housing estates, directly adjacent to the former factories, and the factory owners' villas on the higher, forested slopes on the periphery. The basic serial design of the workers' house and garden, multiplied to create an entire estate, is the counterpart to the large factory halls, which were also built in series–scales and typologies that are closely intertwined. The standardized dimensions of the gardens are set off by the different uses to which they are put: five meters wide, individual images of paradise, evident from the outside in the variety of fences.

Frame and Infill

Embedded in the street spaces of Lokstadt, we now find the typology of the city garden as an area for communal use. As a connecting design element, the frame provides a clear zoning of the street space. The base made of cut hedges creates a local horizon separating different usages from one another, while also affording a general overview of the space and the ability to monitor it. Trees, outdoor furniture, and other hedge elements that help to frame the space allow specific designs to be implemented to suit the required functions.

The first projects–the Krokodil building and the townhouses–are already under construction and cater to specific functions such as a toddlers' playground, an area for playing *boules,* seating, and gardens for residents, some of whom are advanced in years. They also provide infrastructures such as outdoor restaurants and bicycle stands. As yet, though, work on the urban gardens in the other parts of the neighborhood has gone no further than designating the relevant sites. The program and the concrete design are open and will only be developed in conjunction with the uses specified for the adjacent areas. Of all the cities in Switzerland, Winterthur seems one of the locations best suited to the city garden typology. (lr)

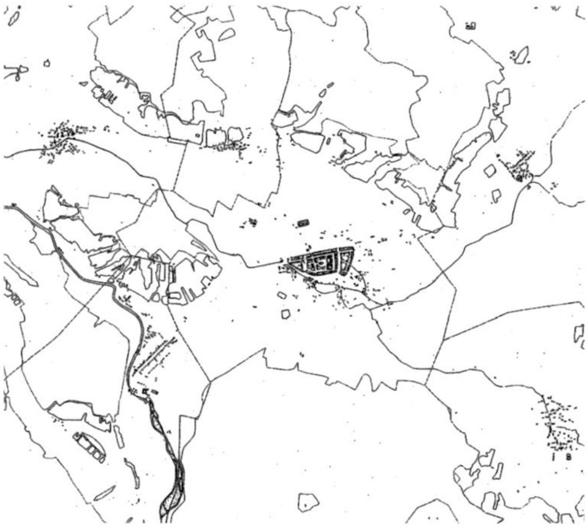

1830: On the eve of the Industrial Revolution

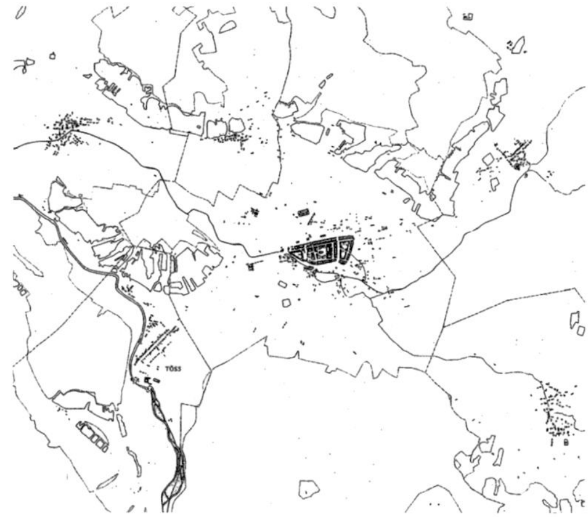

1850: Battle for political supremacy in the canton

1870: Urban development policy, railway construction, and national railway crisis

1890: Development of the industrial and settlement city

1900: Determination of the bourgeoisie for representation

1930: The industrial garden city

Lokstadt, Winterthur, CH

Gardens of the City

The forests on the mountain ranges and along the Töss Valley reach far into the urban fabric and today assume the function of large-scale city parks.

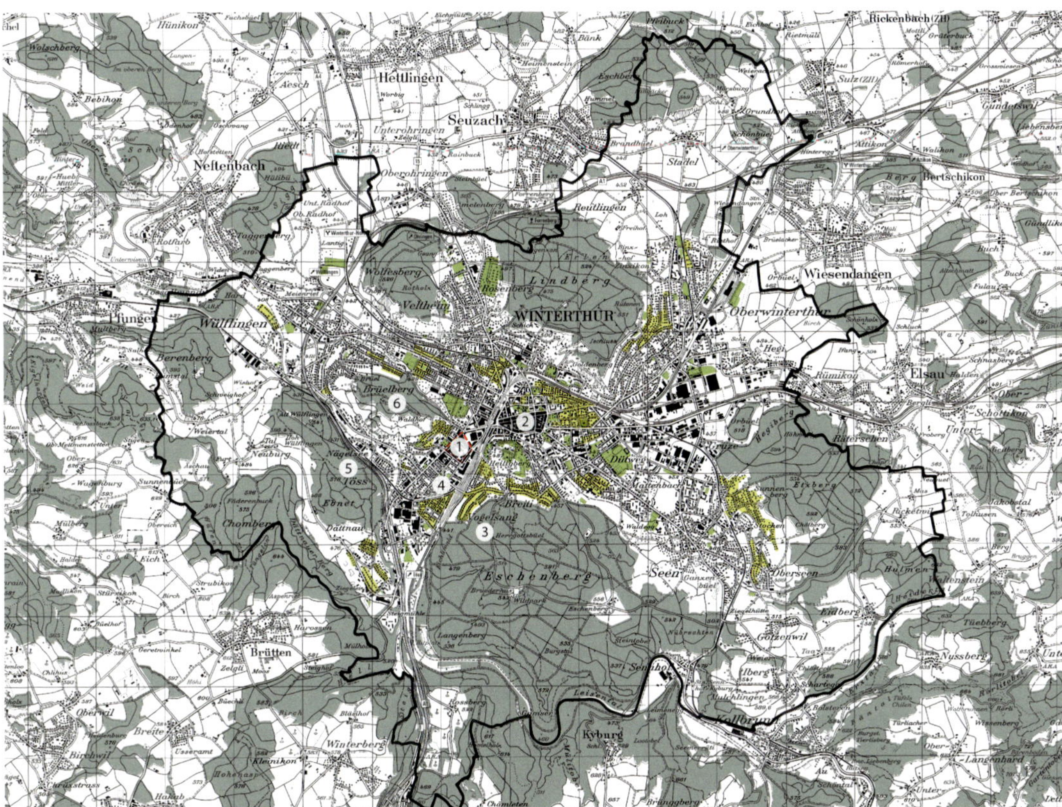

Garden city — Parks — City boundary

1 Lokstadt 2 Historical center 3 Herrgottsbüel 4 Tössfeld 5 Ebnet 6 Brüelberg

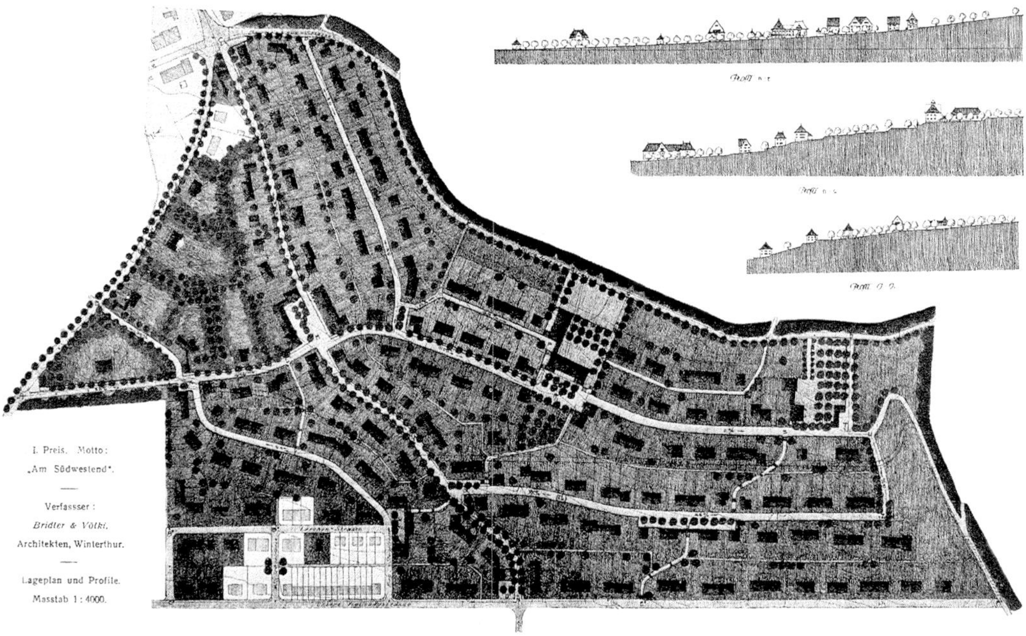

Detached houses, Untere Vogelsangstrasse
Estate built by the GEbW housing association, Ernst Jung, 1891

A "self-help" colony
Franz Scheibler and Adolf Kellermüller, 1925/26. Illustration from Henry Eberlé, *Kleinhäuser: Musterhaus-Aktion des Schweizerischen Verbandes für Wohnungswesen und Wohnungsreform,* Zurich, 1927

The Bleichewiesen residential colony Double duplex houses built by Allgemeine Baugenossenschaft, a housing cooperative, Lebrecht Völki, 1923; view from the east along the garden path

Detached houses, Weberstrasse (west side)
Settlement built by the housing cooperative Heimstätten-Genossenschaft, Hans Bernoulli and Adolf Kellermüller, 1923

Lokstadt, Winterthur, CH
Gardens of the City

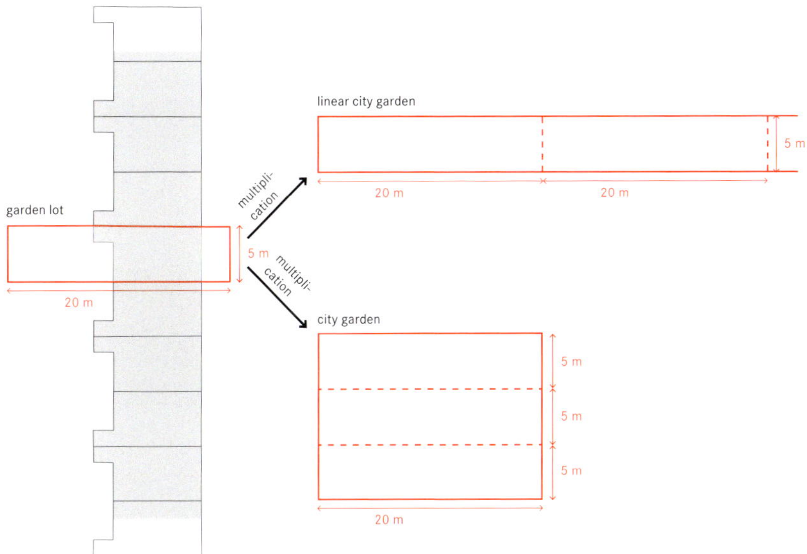

The concept of the *Stadtgarten* ("city garden") is related typologically to the *Arbeitergarten* ("worker's garden") directly adjacent to it: a five-meter-wide, individual image of paradise, evident from the outside thanks to the diversity of the fences. The dimensions of the serial basic motif of a worker's house with garden are adopted and multiplied according to its location in the neighborhood.

Studies on the hedge as a local horizon from a pedestrian's and a bird's-eye perspective

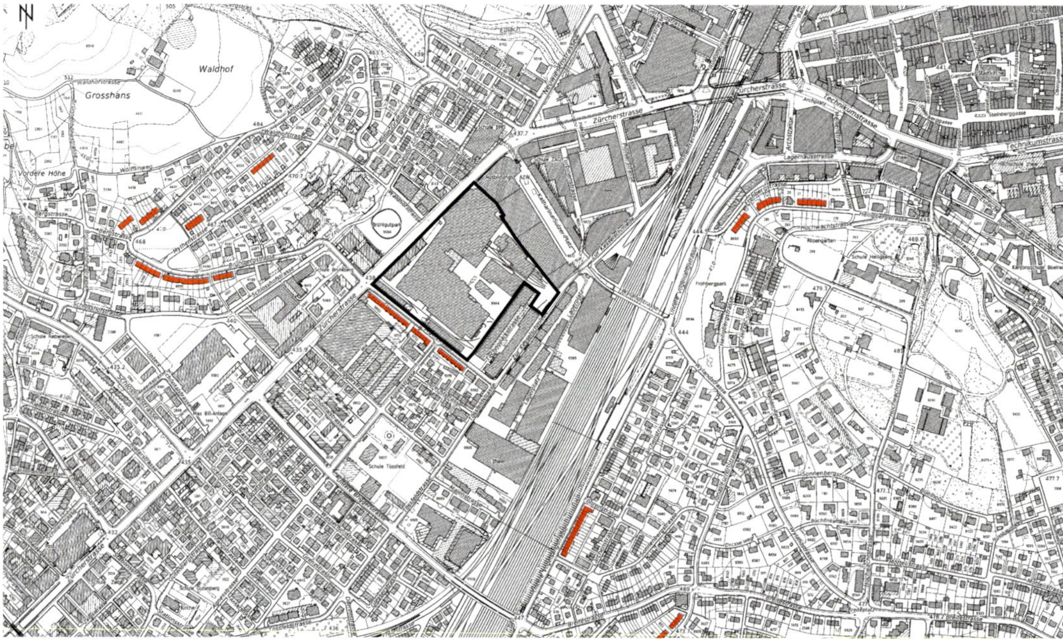

■ Localization of the workers' housing estates around the perimeter

The city garden fulfills a wide spectrum of requirements in the neighborhood. A frame formulated as a hedge defines its basic structure and clearly divides the space into zones without confusing the lane's spatial structure. The city gardens, organized in a tightly clustered sequence, assume various public usages, not only incorporating a children's play area, seating, ornamental or vegetable gardens, and lawns but also providing space for exhibitions and gastronomy.

The area is structured by a variety of clearly defined open-space typologies.

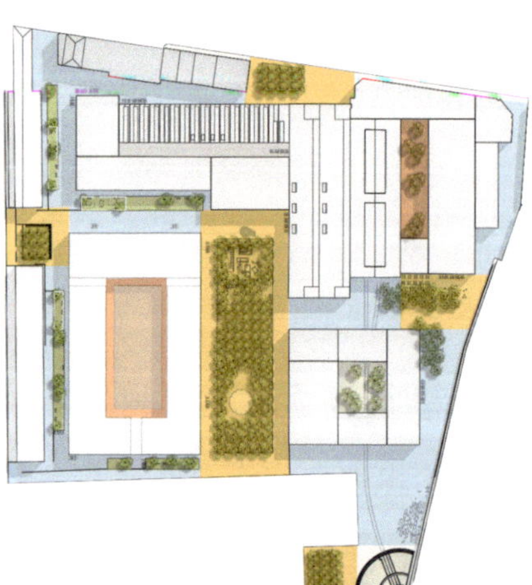

Square	Sulzer Square
	Agnes Square
	Jäger Square
	Züricher Square
	Track Triangle
	Central heating
Courtyard	Residential yard
	Office yard
Street	Industrial alleys
Garden	City gardens

Lokstadt, Winterthur, CH

Gardens of the City

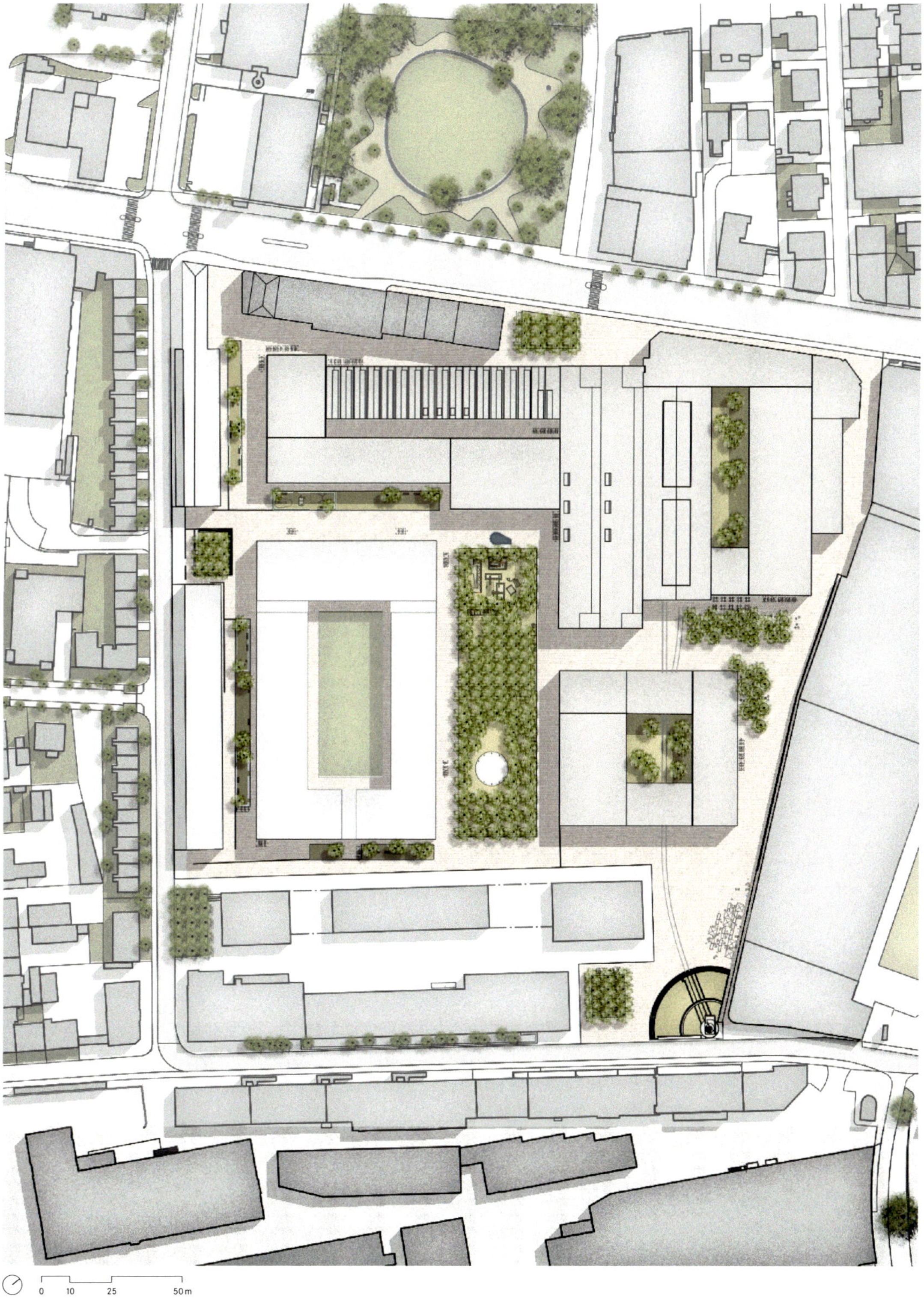

Innovation Park Zurich, Dübendorf, CH
An Airfield Turned City

Client:
Kanton Zürich, Baudirektion (study, reference project)
HRS Real Estate AG, Frauenfeld (development and detailed design)

Cooperation:
Urban planning:
Hosoya Schaefer Architects AG, Zurich (study, reference project)
KCAP, Zurich (development and detailed design)

Design/construction:
2014–2019/2020–2040

Type and size:
Urban development/Campus, 38 ha

Status:
Ongoing

The advent of aviation required suitable sites to be found for the construction of airfields, in Switzerland just as elsewhere. Shortly after 1900, large airports and smaller airfields were built all over Europe on large, flat areas of reed land outside of urban centers that had no agricultural value at the time. One example of this kind of landscape was to be found between Dübendorf and Wangen, northeast of the city of Zurich. From 1910, the marshland was drained and transformed into Dübendorf airfield, which developed into a European air base between the wars. By 1914, the military had begun to make use of the airfield, and since 1949 this has been its sole function. The military will cease operating there in the foreseeable future though.

Although it would be possible for much of the site to continue being used for civil aviation, the areas adjacent to Dübendorf are to be developed into an innovation park with an international focus, linking the research institutes and scientific organizations in the Zurich area with other locations in central Europe. The aim is to create an attractive new part of the city that will be sustainable and future-oriented with many of the qualities of a campus. The site will offer a wide range of opportunities for companies and institutions specializing in research and technology to establish themselves and will benefit from the scenic quality of its open setting, with sweeping views stretching from the plain all the way to the Alps.

The most characteristic feature of the site is the flat landscape, the Dübendorfer Ried wetland, where an underground drainage system has been in operation since 1910. The planning concept preserves the old identity of the open space as an airfield and reed land by making the meadows and water system an integral part of restoring the landscape. This creates a varied and dynamic range of habitats for flora, fauna, and people.

The open spaces of the Innovation Park are planned in a variety of different forms and scales and will enter into the entire campus fabric. Different types of public space will be combined as a means to satisfy the conditions determined by a mixed urban and landscape setting: streets and squares, parks, promenades, and lanes. By incorporating the apron in front of the hangar buildings and the staging area facing Wangenstrasse, the plan also harnesses spatial elements that are specific to this location and its history.

The apron in front of the old hangar buildings forms an important part of the airfield ensemble. This is not only significant in historical terms but also serves as a key link to the *Innovation Village.* For reasons of conservation, it will be preserved as a reference to the existing buildings. As a kind of palimpsest, the dimensions of the old asphalt strip are to be made legible again, and tokens and remnants of it will be preserved. At the same time, larger areas of meadowland will be cut into it, not only as a reminder of how the site looked in the 1920s but also to help meet requirements relating to the microclimate, rainwater management, and biodiversity.

The quality of the campus is essentially defined by the public areas of open space designed to cater to different needs. The specifications for the landscape are adopted and integrated into a concept combining expanse and density, such that the open spaces round off the basic structure of the development plan. For the first time in decades, the spaces at the center of the site will once again be freely accessible–and this creates new opportunities for employees, for Dübendorf, and for the region. (rv)

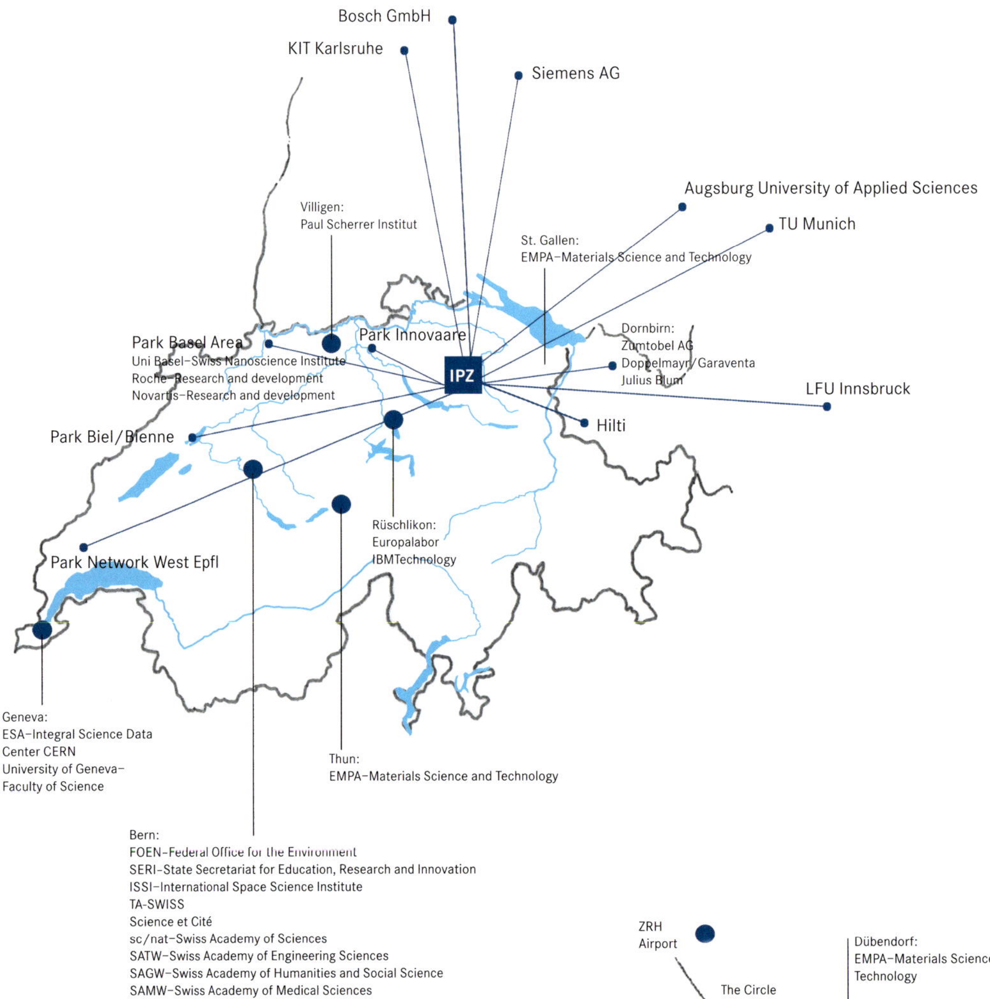

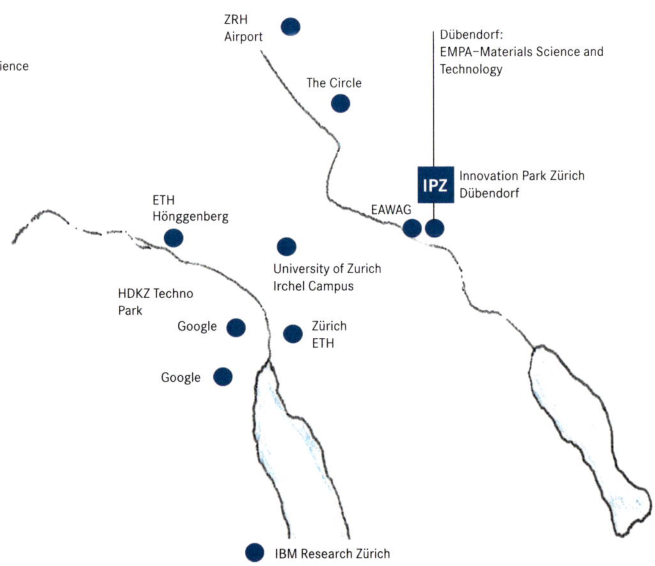

Dübendorf is to become part of a network of research and knowledge centers in the local, regional, and supraregional context.

Innovation Park Zurich, Dübendorf, CH

An Airfield Turned City

The aerial photo shows the complete extent of the former wetland and the present airfield. The first development phase of the Innovation Park is marked in white.

Early photograph of the Dübendorf airfield in what was then a village setting, 1929

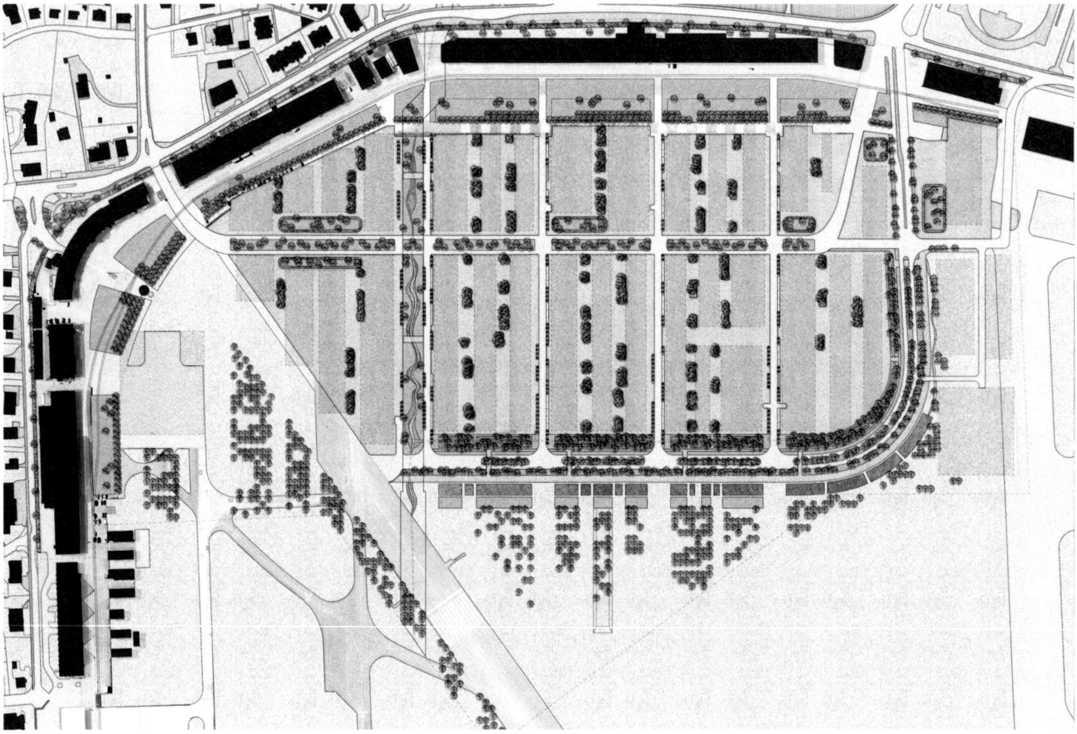

Master plan for the open spaces in the Dübendorf Innovation Park: to the south and west, parts of the airfield will be transformed into a park and connected to the development area via the main parkways. The hierarchical pattern of streets segment the various construction plots. The system of open spaces is rounded off by the restored Chrebsschüsselibach stream and the maneuvering area in front of the landmarked former hangar buildings.

> Variant study for the design of the apron and the zone in front of the heritage hangar buildings, with a combination of different design principles

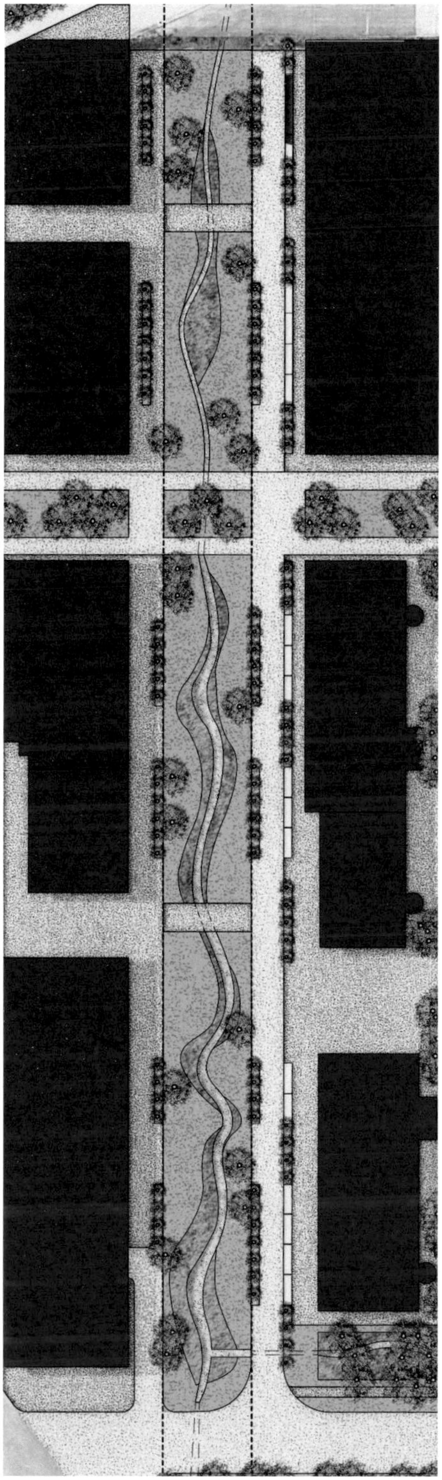

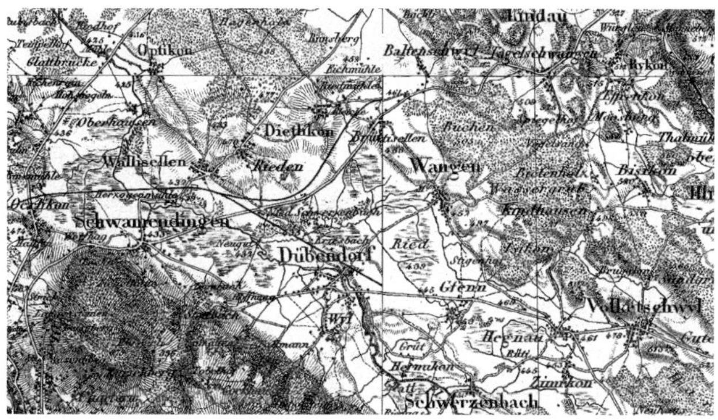

The Chrebsschüsselibach stream is to be exposed and will manifest once more as a shallow brook in a meadowland setting. Owing to the high groundwater level, a rainwater and drainage system with shallow ditches and extensive reservoirs is required.

< Study of the usage density on the largest section of the apron with five hundred people or completely deserted. However, the density of use shown here will almost never be achieved on a routine basis.

Platanus × hispanica
The Engineer's Tree

Lars Ruge

Allée of plane trees near Nîmes,
Southern France

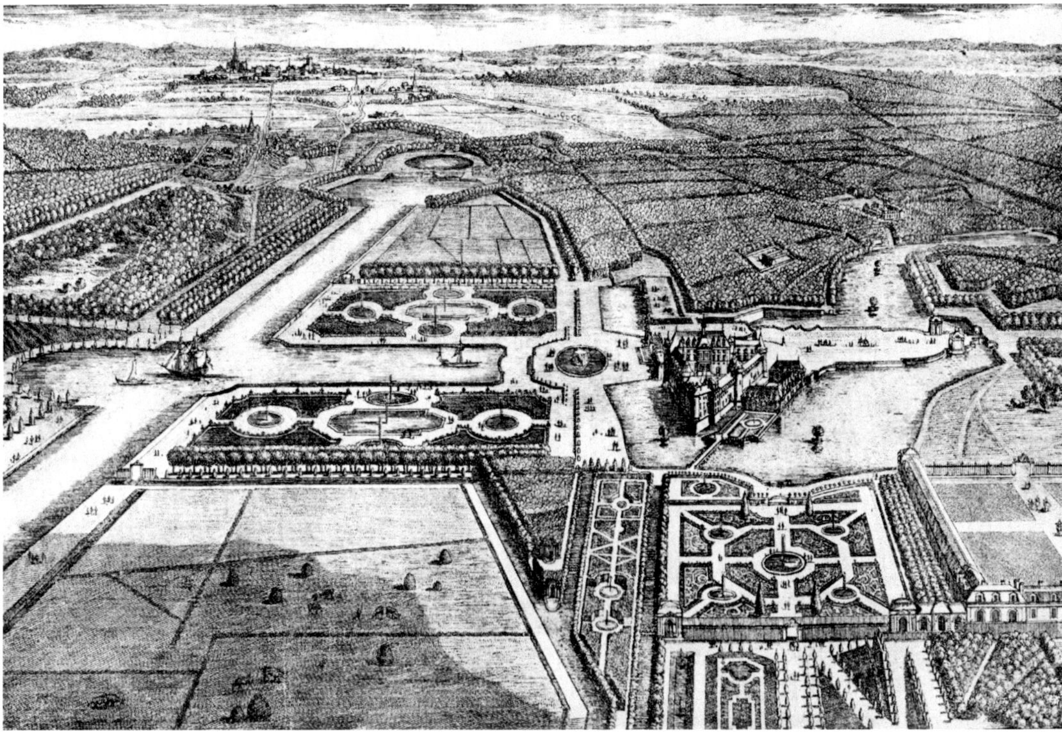

The gardens of the Château de Chantilly, designed by André le Nôtre, in the seventeenth century. The *allées* of the baroque gardens extended beyond their borders, often providing driveways, and thus became a structural element in the design of the road system.

From Garden Cultivation to Urban Culture

Although some few tree-lined streets already existed back in ancient times, the typology of the *allée* (from French *aller,* "to go") became increasingly important in the seventeenth century. Initially laid out in baroque parks outside the city gates to protect pedestrians, they extended the perspective of the park far beyond its borders into the surrounding landscape. A principle which was also applied in France to the then modern *chaussées* (from Latin *calciata via*; designating a road with tamped stones) and adopted by neighboring countries as well. In addition, major infrastructure projects such as the Canal du Midi, which was completed in 1681 and connects Toulouse with the Mediterranean near Sète,[1] contributed to the typological spread of tree-lined roads. While the levees along the canal were initially planted with willows, the subsequent practice was to use plane trees, whose roots penetrated and stabilized the moist ground and whose mighty crowns not only reduced the evaporation of the canal water but also made the towing of the barges more tolerable by providing shade for horses and people.

Napoleon Bonaparte also capitalized on this idea at the beginning of the nineteenth century. He had dense rows of trees planted along the country roads to protect his troops from the blazing sun as they marched across Europe on foot, traversing the continent from north to south and from west to east.

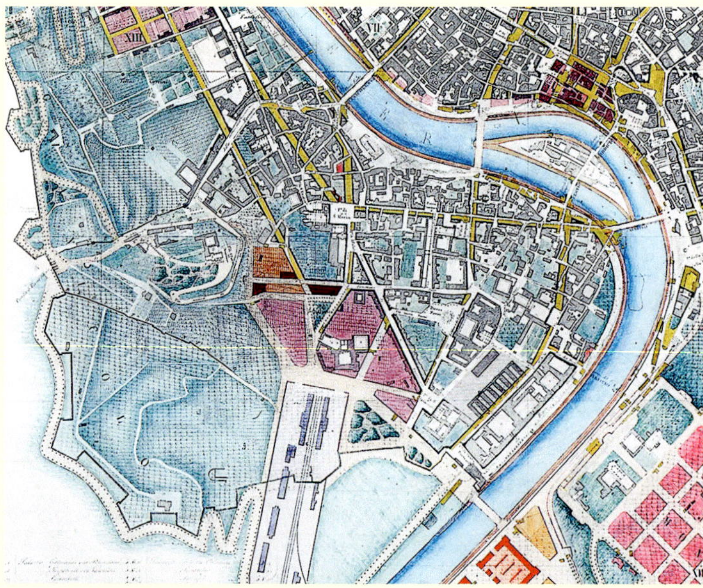

Detail from Rome's regulatory and expansion plan of 1882. Clearly visible on the left edge of the map, *allées* planted with plane trees (called *passeggiate*) replaced the city's old fortifications.

The Canal du Midi and its accompanying plane trees, Southern France

In many places, the *allée* reached to the very edge of the city as old and obsolete fortifications were demolished. The first public open spaces with (in part) regularly spaced trees, organized in the form of boulevards on the outskirts of the city, often still form the core and starting point of public open-space systems, as a ring-shaped structure between the old and new parts of the city; this is the case in Lucca, Basel, Hamburg, Copenhagen/Christianshavn, Bremen, Lübeck, and Frankfurt. In the wake of the radical reconstruction of Europe's metropolises in the nineteenth century, which entailed the demolition of old neighborhoods and the expansion of new districts, the construction of boulevards, and the transformation of rivers and canals into urban waterways, the tree found its way onto the streets of Berlin, Paris, London, Rome, and many other cities. The former transport routes became boulevards catering to city dwellers out for a stroll. The *allée* thus found its way from the countryside into the modern metropolis.

Allées of plane trees in European cities: Passeggiata del Gianicolo in Rome, *allée* in Meudon near Paris, pétanque playing area in Arles, park avenue in London

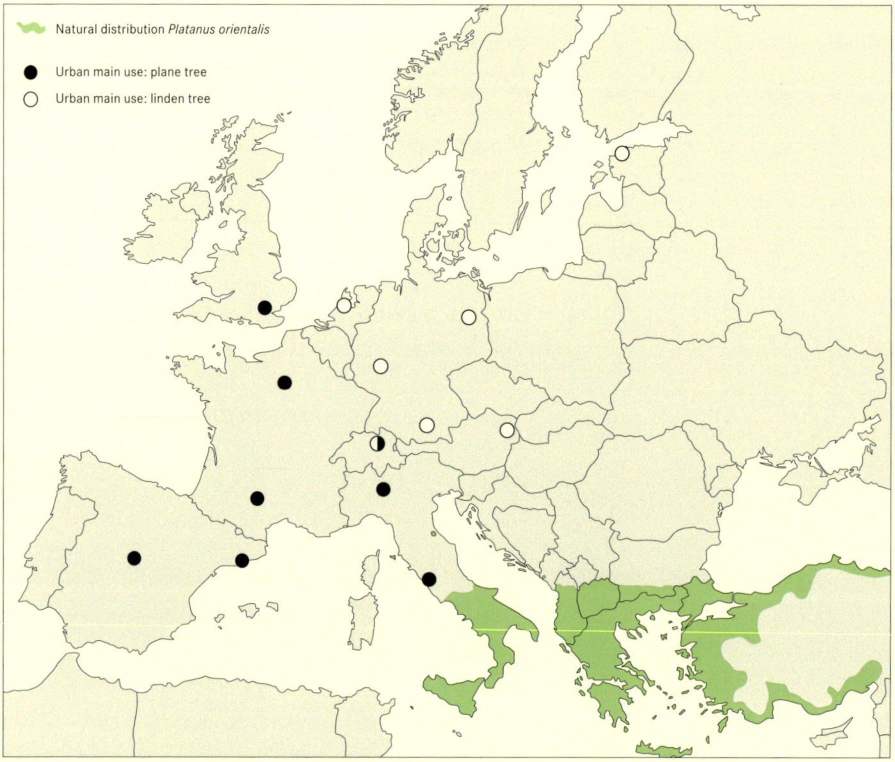

Local Differences

The type of the *allée* can be found in most European cities. However, the choice of tree species reveals a clear split within the continent. While the linden tree (or lime) is the most prevalent tree in northern and eastern European metropolises –more than 35 percent of the trees on Berlin's streets are linden trees,[2] and it is also the commonest or second commonest species in Munich,[3] Hamburg, and Vienna[4]– the Mediterranean and Western European metropolises are dominated by plane trees: in Paris, more than 40 percent of the street trees are plane trees,[5] while in the English capital the "London plane" introduced from Spain is a subspecies. This species also dominates the urban landscapes of Milan, Rome, Barcelona, and Madrid, albeit with local differences: while in Paris, the trees are generally pruned, in London they grow freely, and in Milan or Rome they are hemmed in by parked cars. While many of the European metropolises can be assigned to one of the two traditions, in Zurich there is an evident overlap. Thus, in the fifteenth century, the first public park within the city walls was created in the northern tradition, when fifty-two linden trees were planted on the Lindenhof, giving the site its name.[6] The plane tree came to Zurich under Napoleon's influence. The mighty trees, some of which are more than two hundred years old, dominate the cityscape to this day. The tree is an attendant feature of the linear infrastructure, such as the banks of the Limmat and Sihl rivers, which were originally left in their "natural" state but subsequently lined with plane saplings. It can also be found in many city squares created in the late nineteenth and early twentieth centuries, highlighting their position in the urban space. The cultural and historical significance of both tree species, which have shaped public space since antiquity, becomes evident here in one and the same city.

Les Ponts Jumeaux in Toulouse:
the Lateral, Midi, and Brienne canals

Lindenhof, Zurich, 1504

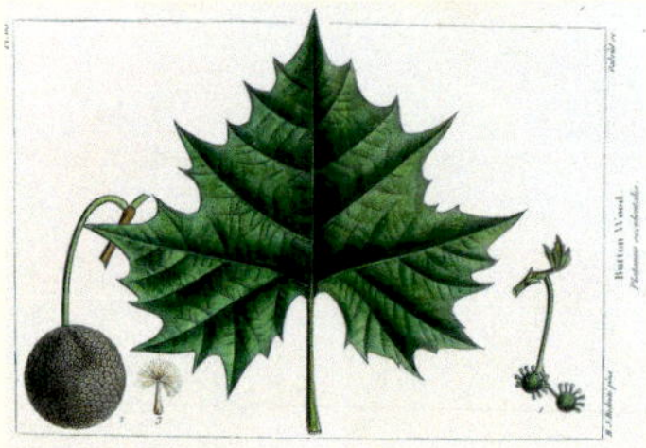

Platanus occidentalis

Platanus orientalis in its native habitat: Vale of Tempe, northern Thessaly (Greece).

Habitat

Depending on their classification, eight to ten species are known in the *Platanus* genus. The Oriental plane (*Platanus orientalis*) has the largest distribution in Europe. In the cities, the predominant specimen is the London plane (*Platanus × hispanica* or *Platanus × acerifolia*), a hybridization of the oriental and occidental species. The former has its origins in the humid gravel plains of the river valleys of Greece, Albania, and Croatia, where the trees constitute their own plant community. The sun-bathed gravel warming its roots and the humidity of the riverine air that cools its crown offer optimal living conditions for the tree, conditions that can also be found in urban situations with paved surfaces and a gravelly substrate. Although the plane tree does not have any outstanding characteristics–with neither a recognizable flower nor a beguiling scent–its special bark with its scaly "plates" and color tones ranging from green or yellow to brown makes each specimen unique during the annual growth spurt and shedding of the old bark.

“Swedish naturalist and collector Gustaf Eisen routinely performed a meticulous examination of certain objects, such as a silver chalice he had discovered in an antique shop in New York, which he believed to be the Holy Grail. Today, it is on show in the Metropolitan Museum of Art. I take an interest in these kinds of speculative approaches, which **unfold a world** based on a single object.” (gv)

View into the collection
of Case Studio Vogt in Zurich

The Street Space of the Future

Haussmann's magnificent Paris avenues still serve as a model for many cities, an example of a consistent and thorough practice of "urban greening." While at the time, the concept worked on the basis of a system of integral city planning, nowadays traffic requirements, a wide range of vested interests and ownership structures, and the increasing relocation of supply infrastructures beneath ground no longer permit the presence of continuous rows of regularly planted trees.

Therefore, new ideas and principles for the design of street spaces are required. This urban planning task involves an exceptional degree of interdisciplinarity, whereby city planners and landscape architects should play a major role as they consider streets to be public spaces that are built and lived in. It is not so much a question of understanding streets as large-scale linear structures as of focusing on local contexts. There are instances in the city of Basel, for example, where the streetscape is characterized by dense clusters of trees consisting in part of different species. Such approaches give definition to small-scale locations and establish connections to the adjoining open spaces.

1 Thomas Veser, "Der Canal du Midi als Meisterleistung des 'Grossen Zeitalters,'" *Neue Zürcher Zeitung,* February 22, 2001, www.nzz.ch/article75C91-1.467604.
2 Senatsverwaltung für Umwelt, Verkehr und Klimaschutz, "Straßen- und Parkbäume: Bestand nach Hauptbaumgattungen," *berlin.de,* accessed March 5, 2019, www.berlin.de/senuvk/umwelt/stadtgruen/stadtbaeume/de/daten_fakten/hauptgattungen/index.shtml.
3 Christian Sebald, "Welche Bäume eine Zukunft in Bayerns Städten haben," *Süddeutsche Zeitung,* August 25, 2017.
4 "The Significance of Roadside Trees and Some Related Data for Vienna," *Weatherpark,* accessed March 5, 2019, https://www.weatherpark.com/roadside-trees.
5 *Der Alltag: Die Platanen,* Arte, April 8, 2017.
6 "Lindenhof," *Stadt Zürich: Tiefbau- und Entsorgungsdepartement,* accessed March 28, 2019, www.stadt-zuerich.ch/ted/de/index/gsz/natur-_und_erlebnisraeume/park-_und_gruenanlagen/lindenhof.html.

Photos by Giuseppe Micciché, Zurich 2018

8 Heads High
Andreas Greiner, 2016

Appearing in various forms and sizes, algae are among the oldest existing species and one of the main contributors to carbon dioxide fixation worldwide. For *8 Heads High,* a scanning electron microscope is utilized to capture a series of single-celled algae. After preparation of the minute subject alga, electrons in the microscope bounce off the surface area, carrying information of its outline, magnified 5,000 times.

The microscope reveals a highly detailed image of a microcosm, which the naked human eye is unable to perceive. In the final image each individual monocellular organism is displayed isolated against a black background, in the style of traditional portraiture. As well as giving each alga a human name, the title of these depicted nonhuman organisms refers to a method of proportion used in human figure drawing.

The series was realized together with the Culture Collection of Algae at the University of Cologne and the Bavarian Polymer Institute at the University of Bayreuth.

Series of Scanning Electron Microscope (SEM)
Images of Various Algae

Peter
synura petersenii

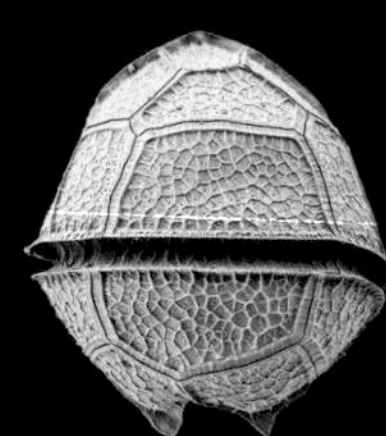

Florian
peridinium bipes

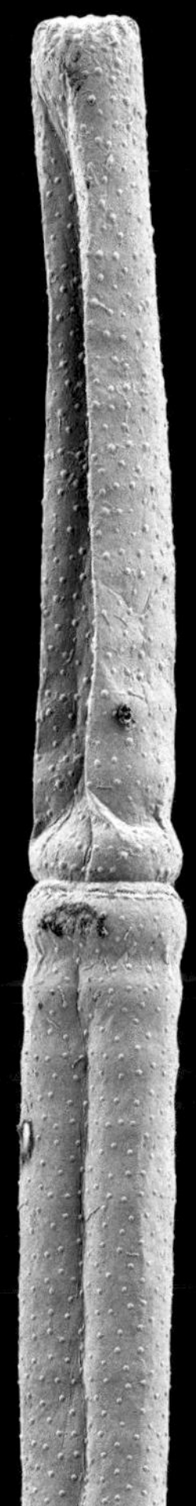

Katarina
pleurotaenium ehrenbergii

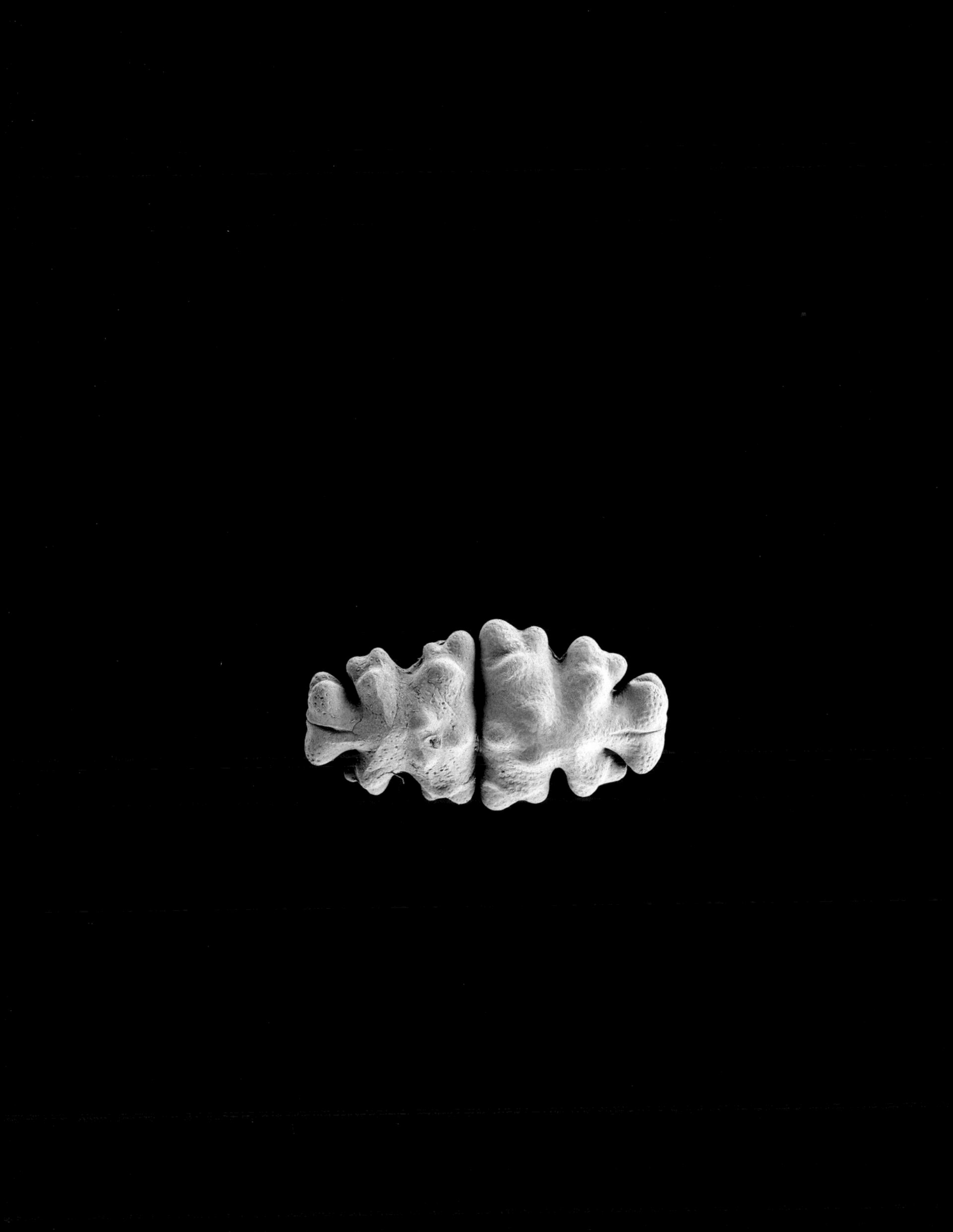

Ulrike
euastrum oblongum

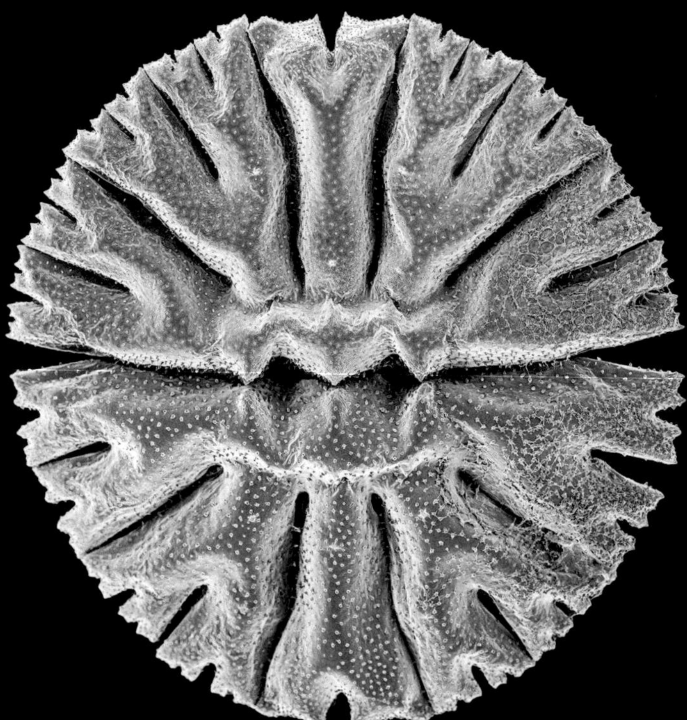

Lena
micrasterias thomasiana

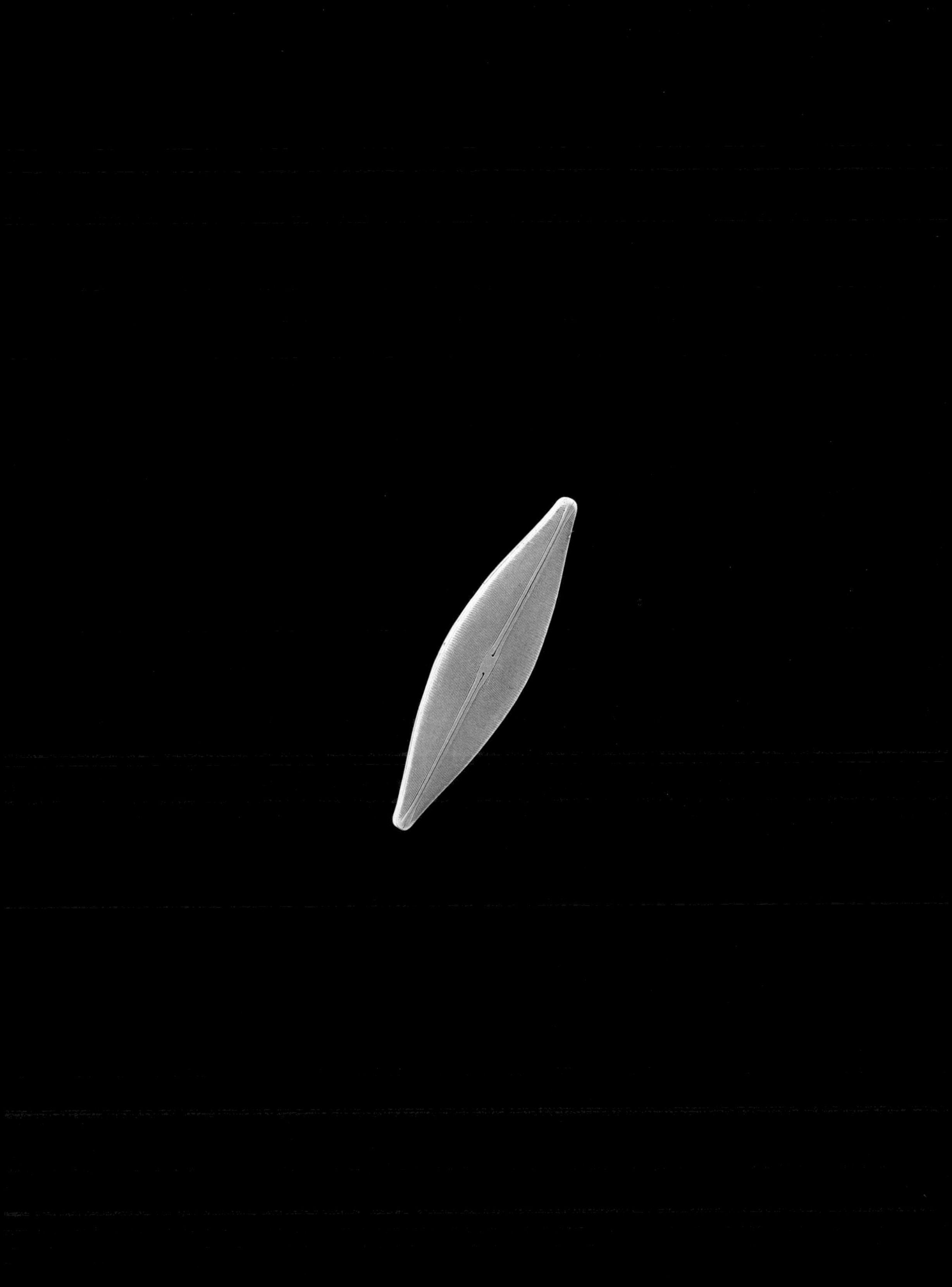

Lisa
craticula sp.

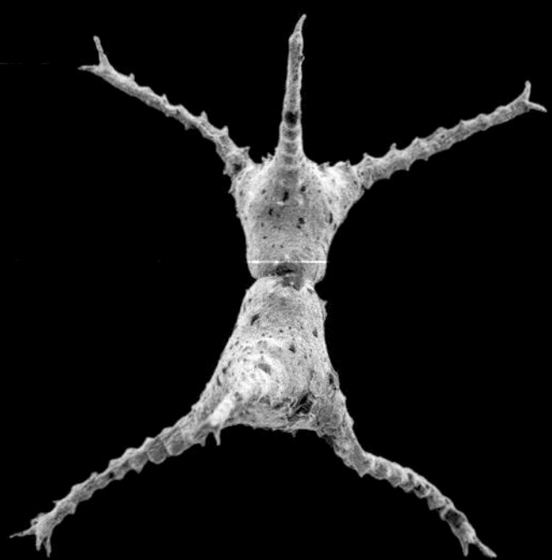

Swiss National Museum, Zurich
The Nature of the City

Client:
Swiss Confederation, Federal Office for Buildings and Logistics FOBL

Cooperation:
Architecture: Christ & Gantenbein Architekten, Basel

Design/construction:
2008–2019/2014–2021

Type and size:
Square, 1.9 ha

Status:
Partly realized

Arriving at Zurich's main station brings you right to the doorstep of its most famous park: the Platzspitz. Once a pasture used as commons and shooting ground, and subsequently a baroque pleasure grove, in the 1980s the park degenerated into notoriety, when it was dubbed "Needle Park," the center of the open drug scene. Since its rehabilitation in 1993, the park has once again been open to the public. The extension of the National Museum has revealed the multifaceted nature of the place and made it visible.

Characteristic of the site are its mighty plane trees, which are some two hundred years old and part of both the riverine landscape and the townscape. While the canopy of their branches projecting over the river evokes images of pristine locations in Croatia's cool river valleys, the plane trees also recall the tradition of tree-lined streets and waterways in Europe's major cities.

Until recently, the most famous of these plane trees represented a special *topos* within the urban space. Located directly at the entrance to the park, it has provided shade to the otherwise rather inconspicuous and simple fountain with its delicate sculpture of Flora for many decades. The figure that passersby bow to while drinking the spring water was protected by the impressive trunk and the overhanging crown, but slowly pushed aside by the tree's vigorous growth–a temporary relationship that had to end after decades of intimate closeness.

This unlikely couple revealed different levels of urban culture: not only the access to free drinking water in public space, but also the play with scales, and, above all, "the nature of the city." This aspect can also be found somewhere else: The clear, greenish water of the Limmat moves sedately in a controlled flow between artificially constructed banks, while, a mere few meters away, the wild Sihl washes brownish-gray sediment in its riverbed through the city whenever it floods. Once, sedimentary river-terrace deposits led to the creation of the Platzspitz: these aggregates, now bound in concrete, have been sanded and compacted to form the surfacing for the museum square.

The rugged urban location complements the large hall of the main station, which is unable to fully compensate for Zurich's lack of a station square. The station concourse is closed at night, and apart from restaurants and cafés, travelers have no benches or chairs to wait on. By contrast, the long, gently curving benches in front of the National Museum offer passersby an opportunity to sit down at the same time, as close to each other or as far apart as they choose. Meanwhile, in summer, groups of visitors, school classes, and teenagers gather on the patches of grass that are set into the mineral square like inlays. As a link between Switzerland's most important international traffic hub and its most popular museum of cultural history, the square is not confined to this parcel of land but is an integral part of the complex, multi-layered urban fabric. (lr)

In the baroque period, the riverbanks were covered from end to end with trees. Remnants of this are still visible today. While the lower-lying banks were primarily lined with plane trees, horse chestnuts were planted on the high banks further away from the groundwater.

The baroque riverbank promenade in Platzspitz park around 1815

Swiss National Museum, Zurich

The Nature of the City

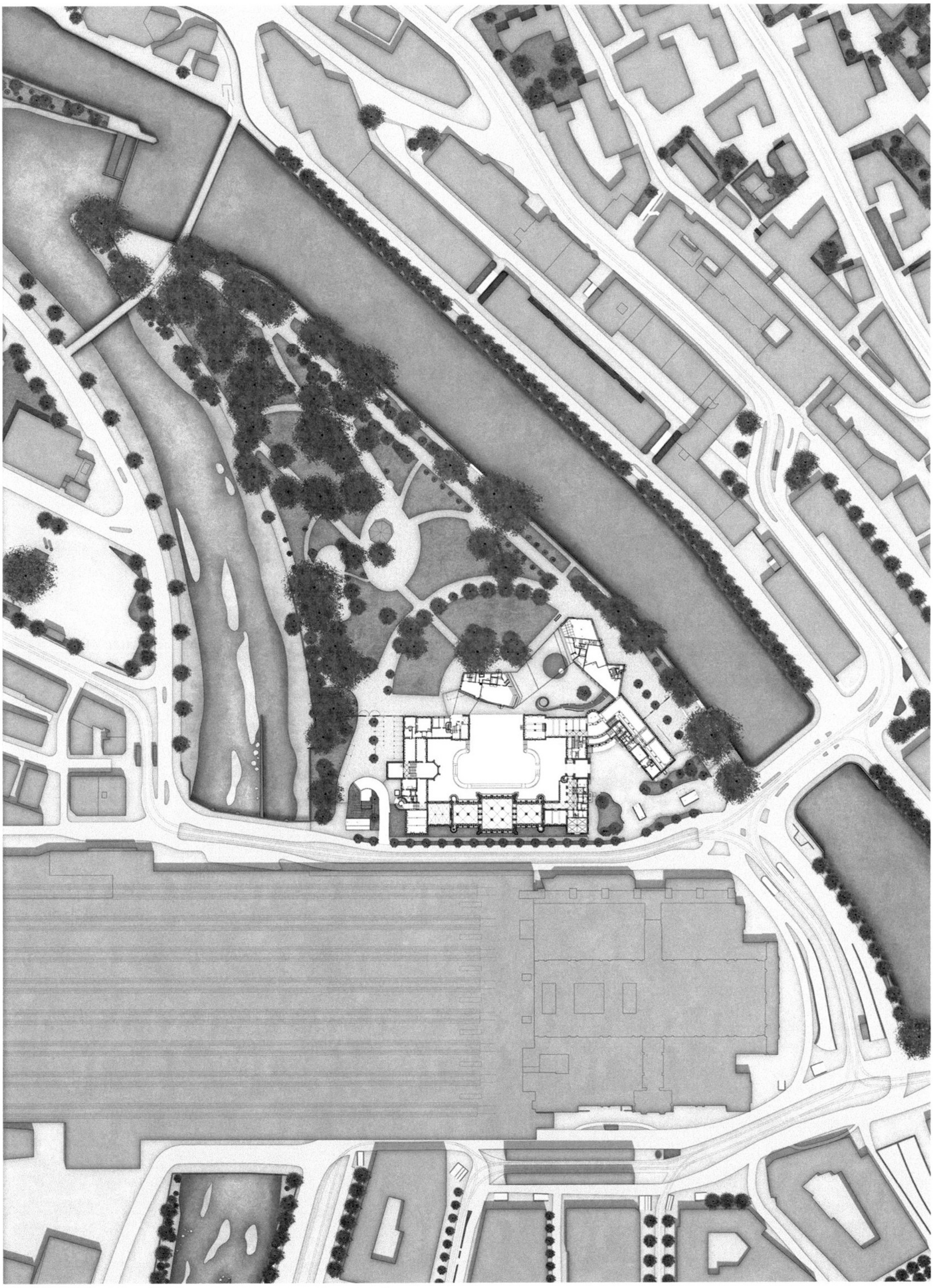

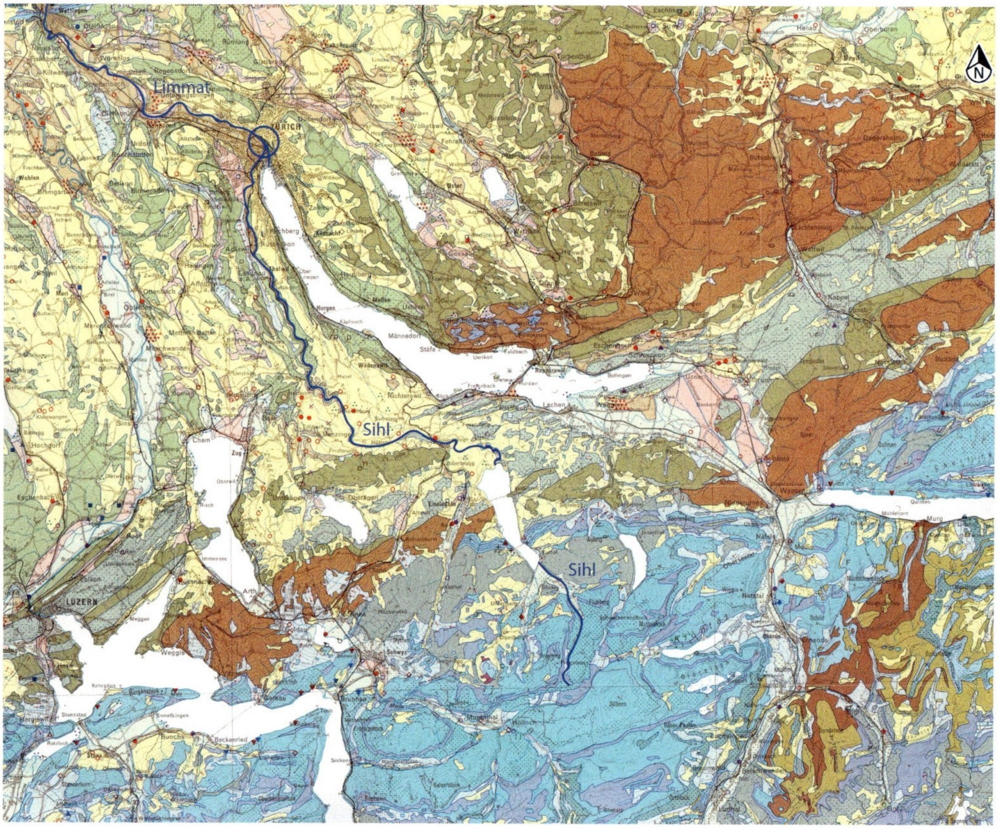

Rock types of the subsoil

The numbers in () indicate the main variation of the QUARTZ CONTENT of the individual rocks in percent. In the case of surface formations, the quartz content varies depending on the river- or glacier-area or on local rock composition.

Loose surface formations

Sands to silts, mostly clayey (loams), often with boulders (ground moraines), or as intermediate mass in fine to coarse debris accumulations (surface moraines)
Silty to silty sands, often clayey, mostly calcareous (loess, loess loam)
Clayey silts to clays with deposits of sand (alluvial loam, lake bottom loam, hanging loam)

Gravel and sand, clean or silty, rarely clayey, sometimes cemented (Ice Age gravel)

Gravel and sand, mostly clean, sometimes with thin clayey or silty coverings (Deposits of today's watercourses)
Extensive scree deposits of the torrents (mostly as debris cone)

Mainly angular debris, coarse to fine (rockfall material, suspended debris)

Larger peat areas
Smaller peat deposits

Marl (15-40), with intercalations of weakly solidified sandstones, sporadicallyfrom conglomerates (marl-rich molasse)
Calcareous, porous sandstones (30-60) abundant to predominantly (sandstone-rich molasse)
More powerful layers of firm sandy mussel breccias (10-35)

Marl (10-25) and slate clays (20-40) with lime, dolomite and sandstone benches, in places with layers of gypsum and anhydrite rocks (Opalinustone, Lias, Keuper, Anhydrite Group in the Jura Mountains)

Ferriferous, mostly lime-free, lean to fat clays (5-30), often together with bean ore (Eocene bean ore formation in the Jura Mountains)

Marl (15-40) with inclusions of more strongly consolidated sandstones, occasionally of conglomerates (marl-rich molasse of the Alpine foothills)
Sandstones (30-60) predominantly, moderately solidified (subalpine molasse sandstone)
Thicker layers of firm sandy shell breccias (10-35)

Conglomerates (25-60), weakly to moderately solidified, always accompanied by sandstone and marl layers (molasse conglomerate)
Abundant to predominant Sandstone and marl layers

Conglomerates to breccias (30-50), arcoses (30-60) and sandstones (50-70), often deep red, strongly solidified, partly slate, sometimes with intercalations of sandy phyllites (25-40), quartz porphyrene (30), spilitene (0-10) and keratophyren (0-10) (conglomerate verrucano, melser sandstone, carbon)

The geological catchment area of the Sihl River

In 1910 large areas of Zurich and parts of the Limmat Valley were flooded–including the Platzspitz park.

Deposits from the Sihl River once created today's Platzspitz park.

Model: gravel islands in the Sihl

Replica: distribution of different-sized gravel particles

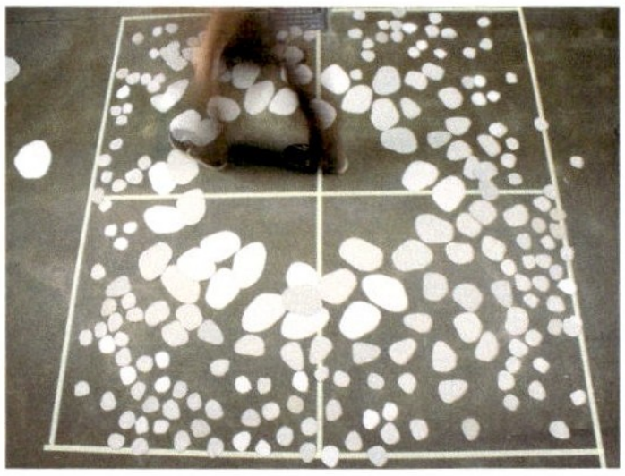

Studies and implementation: inclusions of Sihl gravels indicates deposits along the flow lines.

Swiss National Museum, Zurich

The Nature of the City

Limat Fluß
Sihl Fluß

Zürich - See
Fluss
See
Ost
Nord
Süd
West
ZÜRICH - SEE
Zürich - See

Freilager, Albisrieden, CH
The Other City

A new residential and commercial quarter was created on the site of the Zurich bonded warehouse, a former extraterritorial area of Switzerland for the tax-free storage of goods such as cars, coffee, and carpets. The opening of the complex enabled the construction of public squares, courtyards, and promenades at the transition between the densely built city, the "green neighborhoods," and the wooded slopes of Uetliberg. The formerly closed site has thus become a vital link in the body of the city. The concept behind the outdoor spaces features two overarching themes: up to three meter-tall hedges clearly structure the open space into private and public areas and serve as walls and roofs to accommodate covered parking spots for several hundred bicycles and benches. As a secondary feature, two of the garden courtyards have special playgrounds that are exclusively reserved for children.

Client:
Zürcher Freilager AG, Zurich

Cooperation:
Architecture:
Meili & Peter Architekten, Zurich
Rolf Mühlethaler Architekten, Bern
office haratori GmbH
Zeno Vogel, Mercè Portell, Zurich

Design/construction:
2008–2013/2014–2016

Type and size:
Courtyard/Square/Promenade, 7 ha (entire quarter)

Status:
Realized

<< Zurich's Müllerplan, 1793

Leaps in scale within the urban fabric: the transition between large-scale production and logistics facilities and small-scale residential settlements on the outskirts of Albisrieden

For a family, the delivery of a new household appliance is often a dual cause for joy. Some are thrilled with what is in the package, others are excited about what can be done with the box. For children, it is obvious–even without instructions–that this box is more than just packaging. The cardboard box is commandeered, doors and windows are painted on or cut out, and the children then move in: it is the model of a house. The key here is the shift in scale and responsibility: the size of the house corresponds to the size of the children. Doors and windows can be reached unassisted, and the children are free to arrange things as they want. It is a space for fantasy, one that is inaccessible to adults.

The Freilager largely dispenses with the standard array of classic play elements such as slides, swings, and seesaws, opting instead to transpose the idea of the cardboard box described above, which is duplicated many times over to create an actual little city and village. The children's self-crafted, isolated model is turned into an abstract, precise concrete structure that is both part and prototype of the surrounding city.

Children's City and Village

Embedded in the new district of high-rises and elongated structures, the children's city lies on a single level. Here, the rules governing the surrounding neighborhood also apply, as do the dense clustering of the buildings, the variety of uses, and the articulation enabled by open spaces such as streets and squares–only the scale is different. The concrete buildings are prefabricated, with uniform basic dimensions and doors and windows in identical places. The variety resides only in their positioning in relation to each other. Wooden window and door frames turn the shell structures into simple houses. Residential buildings, school, shop, factory, construction site, and laundry are differentiated by their flooring, walls, and furnishing–for example, a bench with a table or a counter. The grid of the city forms a primary network of streets that adults can also walk through. The playhouses are connected to one another by doors and windows, a secondary system only accessible to children.

Just as the characteristic hedges separate private gardens from common areas, the territories of the buildings in the children's village are marked out by fences, hedges, or even just groups of shrubs. Although the houses appear uniform from the outside, they are not identical: the design of the interior walls with mirrors, plasterwork, or wooden paneling creates different settings. What, for adults, is just play equipment–the model of a building–is real for children and an integral part of their everyday life. Where does the prototype end and the model begin? (lr)

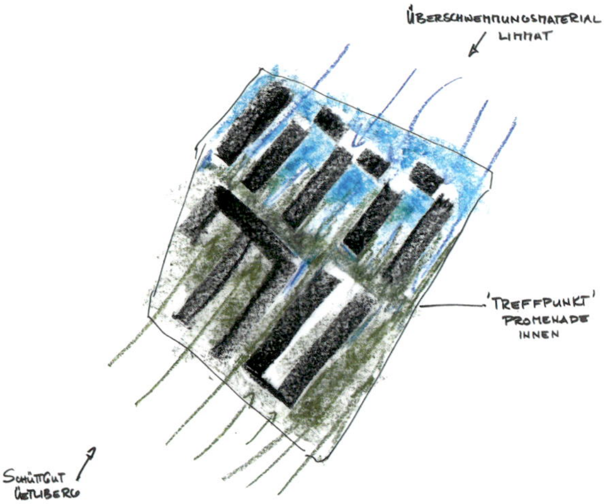

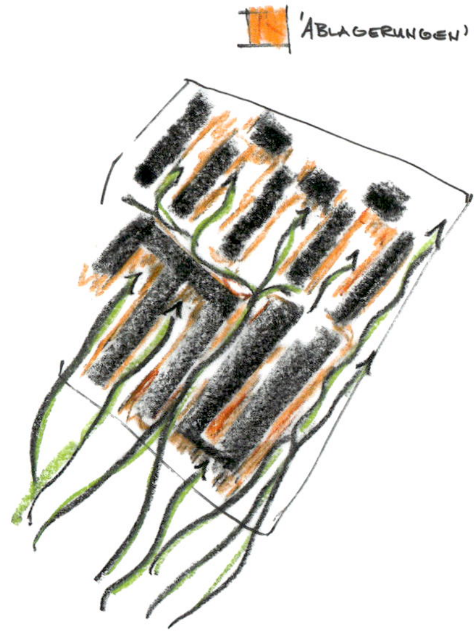

The former bonded-warehouse site acts as a segue from the dense urban fabric to the landscape of the Üetliberg.

Freilager, Albisrieden, CH

The Other City

Sketches of the open-space concept, which incorporate the character of the adjacent urban landscape

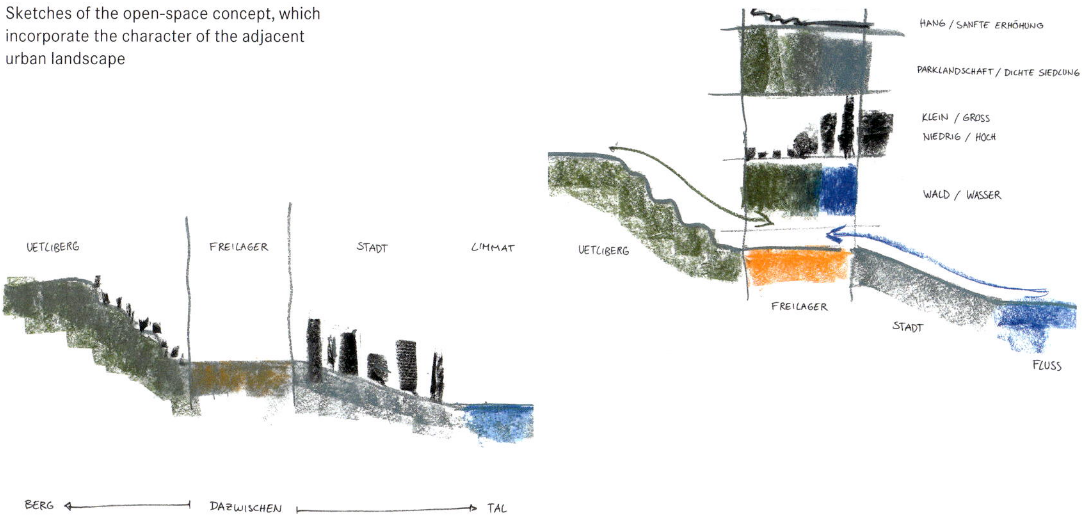

Tree framing, promenade, and courtyards

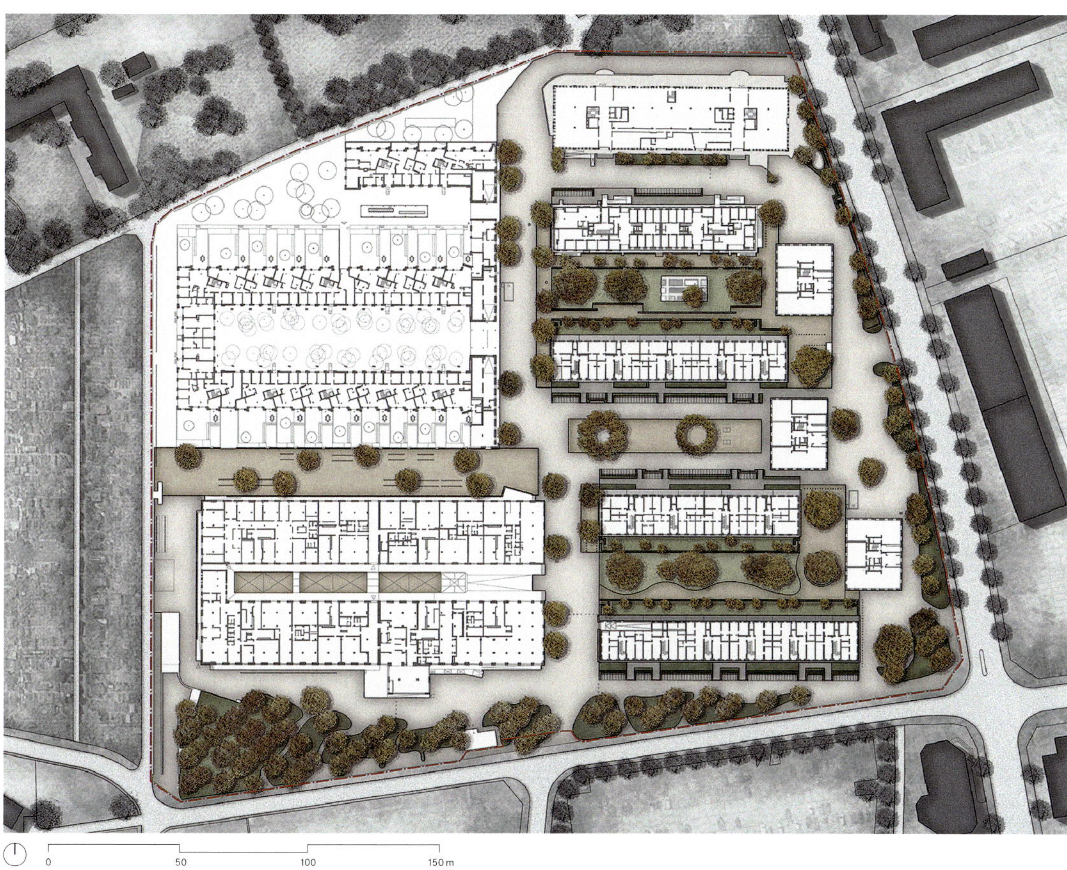

The hedge as a "filter" between private and communal space

The other city: *Children's Games,* a 1560 painting by Pieter Bruegel the Elder, shows ninety-one different games, many simply played on the street in the urban space, or with repurposed everyday objects. The concept draws on this basic idea and creates a framework within which to develop a space for free play. The playhouses serve as "containers," which foster children's creativity.

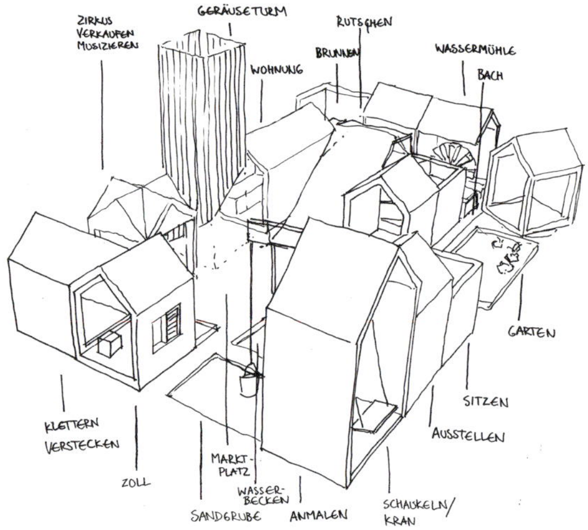

Playhouses of different shapes and sizes made of cardboard were set up for an office party. While the guests moved through the office space, their children immediately commandeered the small-scale "buildings." To start with, they used the houses in a variety of ways and painted them. As they gradually ran out of steam, all the kids retreated into the smallest, gabled house with a ceiling covering it on top.

The design of the houses was inspired by Pompeii with its uniform pattern of entrances, window openings, and narrow spaces.

Miniature and model: the roof of Le Corbusier's *Unité d'Habitation* in Marseille was designed as a miniature landscape to play in. In the background, you can see the mountain ridges around Marseille, on which the children's landscape is modeled.

Tilia cordata
On Fashioning Boundaries

Lars Ruge

Aerial view of a *bocage* landscape in Normandy, 1945: the hedges and hedgerows that are characteristic of this type of landscape indicate the boundaries between agricultural fields and protect against soil erosion.

Local Horizon

A visit to a recently built urban housing development will reveal two current trends: a move away from boundaries and dividing lines, coupled with the attempt to communalize all the open space, including the facade: the playground leads up to the bedroom window, the private seating area borders directly on the public walkway. This eschewal of physical borders is equated with urbanity, even though its main effect has been to create indeterminate spaces and lowered blinds. Such modernist residential developments as the Hufeisensiedlung in Berlin or the Fritz-Schumacher-Siedlung in Hamburg leave a very different impression. These large complexes, comprising similar, often serially built designs, seem at first to be framed by gardens that are also laid out in series. Their outward appearance is characterized as much by hedges, often consisting of a single species and extending for kilometers, as it is by the clinker or concrete of the buildings. These are not the tree-high hedges of aristocratic gardens or the wild shrubbery of cultivated landscapes. Their uniformly trimmed height between 100 and 140 centimeters–applied throughout an entire estate–has introduced a new motif to the garden: that of the local horizon. This ensures two things: it forms a physical border between two plots of land or two different usage areas, while the low-level growth allows for visual connections to be established.

The Hufeisensiedlung ("Horseshoe Estate") in Berlin, built between 1925 and 1933 by architect Bruno Taut and landscape architect Leberecht Migge: the hedges serve to separate public and private space.

How Does the Hedge Come to the City?

The hedge–the Old High German word for which, *hegga,* means “to nurture” or “to enclose”[1]–is a linear growth of trees or shrubs that take well to trimming. For centuries, it has been used in farming to separate culture and nature, to mark out property and to protect livestock and crops from vermin and the wind. A good tolerance of the trimming shears was an essential factor for two reasons: the ability of this species of plant to sprout and regenerate keeps the hedge dense and impenetrable at the base, while the trimmings can be used as animal feed or firewood.

The widespread use of hedges or other structures to mark property boundaries was generally the result of social upheaval. In England, for example, the Enclosure Act–the transformation of communal lands into private parcels–led to the segmentation of what were once large-scale, open landscapes into small plots, divided up by hedges, banks, or walls. The resulting landscape still defines the appearance of large parts of England and prompted similar developments in other regions, including northern Germany.

Similar to the French *bocages,* the hedges in Monmouthshire are the result of a redistribution of the land following the Inclosure Acts initiated in 1604.

Letchworth Garden City (above), designed by Richard Barry Parker and Raymond Unwin, 1903–1905, and Welwyn Garden City (below), designed by Louis de Soissons, 1920

A further development came with the ideas of the garden city movement in England. While well-to-do middle-class mansions were located at a good distance from one another, adequately separated by gardens and large copses, the introduction of small, tightly clustered housing units required new kinds of boundaries to deal with the enforced proximity. The new urban type of garden was like a miniature version of agricultural structures: vegetables and fruit were grown individually on very small plots, and property was demarcated by fences or hedges. It was a trend that spread, in the wake of industrialization, to other countries in Europe and North America.

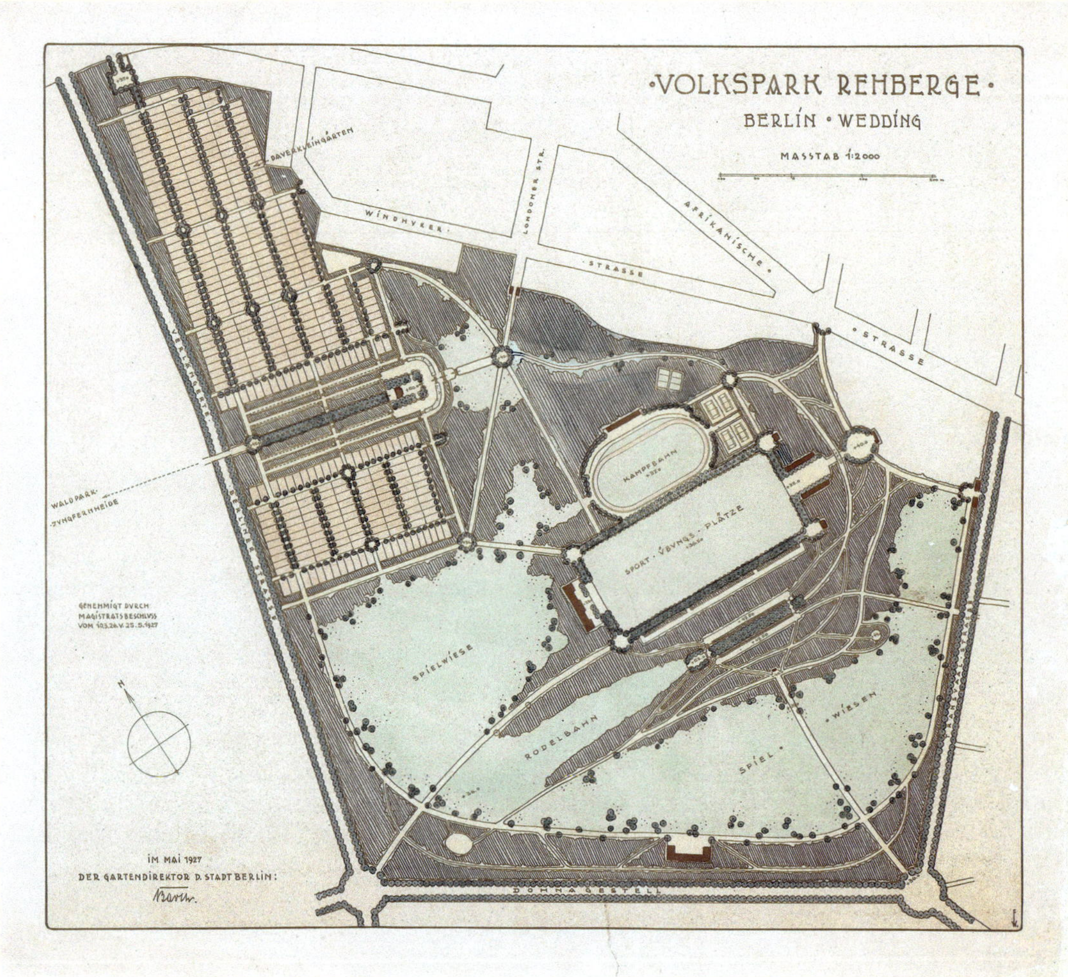

In the Rehberge *Volkspark,* designed by Erwin Barth in 1927, hedges separate different activities.

With the Volkspark movement, the hedge migrated once and for all from the suburbs into the city. The motif of the local horizon was introduced to modernist housing developments and the gardens and communal spaces they incorporated. The hedge now no longer served merely to delineate borders between privately owned plots—for example, in the case of allotments—but was utilized in parks and housing developments to designate discrete zones for gardens, play areas, athletic fields, and outdoor seating.

The Linden, a Tree of the Urban Landscape

In addition to beeches and hornbeams, linden trees were often used to create such a physical barrier. Linden hedges were a common feature of baroque gardens in France, where they were trimmed to the height of a house or often

Hedges need regular trimming to produce the desired shape and height. Their function is both integrative and exclusive: they define spaces (enclosures, entrances, etc.) or create boundaries.

Tab. 207.
TILIA. Off.
Tilia europaea. Bot.
Die Linde.

used as fencing around north German farms–the tree of kings and farmers. Originally from Scandinavia, the plant subsequently spread across Eastern Europe and made it all the way to Spain.[2] In the warmer climatic period between 8000 and 4000 BC, it was among the dominant tree species in European forests.[3] From the earliest age of human history through the nineteenth century, linden forests were used as a source of leaf litter and as forest pastures.[4] The reason for this is their tremendous capacity to put out new shoots, which makes them suited for long-term cultivation. This quality is also evident in rare talus forests. When trees are damaged there by falling rocks, only the linden tree is able to continue to grow in the damaged area, while other species die off. These naturally occurring phenomena, which are characterized by rocks and debris that are regularly warmed by the sun, are comparable to urban locations and the heat radiated by asphalt and stone surfaces, for which the tree species is also well suited. Thus, the linden, which primarily blooms in midsummer, has been wafting the scent of the countryside into the city for centuries.

Linden-tree talus forest in the Klöntal or Klön Valley, created by falling rock. The trees regenerate and continue to grow despite damage to their roots and trunks.

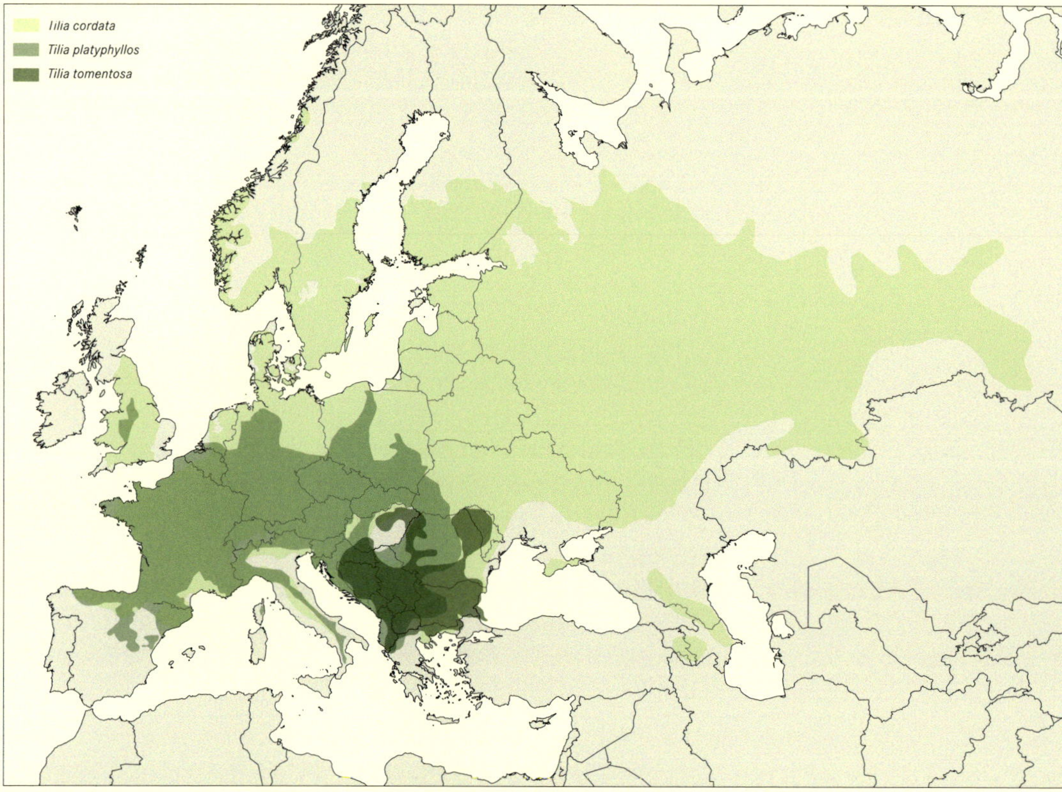

The distribution of linden trees in Europe

Memory and Community

This olfactory aspect is not the only reason why the linden tree is so firmly anchored in the collective memory of residents of German-speaking regions. Even now the "tree of peace" is still prominent in many villages and squares–locations where communities have been gathering in some cases for centuries. One German saying goes: *It takes 300 years to grow, stands for 300 years, and takes 300 years to decay.* In the tree's shadow, justice has been administered and public markets have been held. In its crown, boisterous parties have been celebrated. On its limbs the condemned have been hanged. The linden hedge is thus not only a spatial design element but also refers to the social importance of this tree in communal life and culture.

1 Jacob Grimm and Wilhelm Grimm, *Deutsches Wörterbuch* (Leipzig: Hirzel, 1960).
2 Alexandra Poraszka, "Sagenumwobener Lindenbaum," *Wochen-Zeitung für das Emmental und Entlebuch,* June 10, 2010.
3 Gerhard Stinglwagner, Ilse Haseder, and Reinhold Erlbeck, *Das Kosmos Wald- und Forstlexikon* (Stuttgart: Kosmos, 2001), 560–61.
4 Peter Poschlod, *Geschichte der Kulturlandschaft: Entstehungsursachen und Steuerungsfaktoren der Kulturlandschaft, Lebensraum- und Artenvielfalt in Mitteleuropa* (Stuttgart: Ulmer, 2015), 50.

Border Zone

While a pastoral tradition invoked by the hedge has been lost virtually everywhere, the desire for privacy lives on. And wherever there are property or usage rights at stake, clear boundaries are needed, regardless of whether it is a picket fence that separates us from other people or a rail commuter's demonstratively spread newspaper. The boundary is one of the foundations of neighborliness, a prerequisite for chitchat over the garden fence. Wherever borders are not clearly defined, intermediate spaces emerge–neither public nor entirely private. Yet while I read a book in the privacy of a protected terrace, *boule* is played on a public square. The semipublic space is an urban myth of our time. For just as there are states of aggregation that are solid and liquid but not "semiliquid," the same is, true of space. The reduction of the hedge to a mere design element in suburban areas fails to take this into account. Far more than just a banal stylistic element, the hedge is a helpful means of ensuring regular peace in city neighborhoods.

"Tanzlinde," in Peesten, 1850; a carefully sculptured linden tree, often in the village center, under which people danced on high holidays

Res Publica
Public Space of the City

May 8, 2019, Case Studio Vogt, Zurich

Günther Vogt: Ms. Gentinetta, today we shall talk about public space and its historical and contemporary significance for the city and society. When we are planning and realizing projects, it is important to us to understand public space as a part and, at the same time, the result of a lived everyday reality. How would you describe public space from your own personal point of view?

Katja Gentinetta: As we discuss public space, I would like to make a distinction that I consider important in this context. Personally, I use public space primarily for transit or as a place of "private" encounters: I move from A to B, from home to work or even to the movies and back, or I meet people for eating or drinks, on a garden terrace or the sidewalk in front of a bar. However, as a political philosopher, I am primarily interested in the political dimension of public space, whose origin lies in the *agora,* the square where Greek citizens met to debate politics. It was the single most important site of Athenian Democracy, which reached its apex in the fifth century BC. However, the *agora* was not only a place to debate politics, but also to dispense justice and settle legal disputes. It also served as a market, a place of barter and trade. And it was a place for religious festivals and cultural events. Today, we are far from having such a central space where public life may take place. Rather, the respective functions have become more localized and been relocated to buildings dedicated to their specific purposes, where they are either accessible to the interested public or reserved to specifically authorized persons. Accordingly, public space today has a completely different function and has primarily become a place of transit and only secondarily a meeting place.

Günther Vogt: I would like to pick up one aspect of your description: In European cities, the spaces where public life took place were always very clearly defined. In other words, they were identifiable by and available to people. Individuals knew what could take place in these spaces and were aware of the respective limits set by society. There are quite some examples of this: Let's take a medieval fresco cycle as an example, the *Allegory of Good and Bad Government* by Ambrogio Lorenzetti, painted between 1338

< p. 190, *Green Belt*

and 1339. It shows the city of Siena on one side and the surrounding countryside on the other one. Outside the city walls, food was produced and, inside the city walls, products were traded on the market square. Besides, it also shows political business being dealt with. Today, such a congruence between a built space and its meaning and use is no longer a given, not even in Siena. And here I quite agree with you. This dissolution of spatial determination in the broadest sense tends to turn public space more and more into a space dedicated to movement. This is something we can observe every single day. If we ask ourselves which type of public spaces we are mainly in, nine out of ten are street spaces. Since the beginning of modern times, street spaces belong among the worst designed spaces of European cities. Perhaps we will talk about the specifics of each country later. But in Switzerland, the fact that the Swiss do not want to be urbanites, that is, the fact that their self-image is influenced by an agrarian background and, therefore, by the concept of a village, plays an important role in the planning and design of streets, but also of public spaces in general.

Katja Gentinetta: Taking Paris as an example, where I love to be, I would disagree with you about the streets. Paris boulevards are spacious and lined with trees–creating a network of streets that allow you to traverse the entire city. With their wide *trottoirs* or sidewalks and large *brasseries,* they are an important part of its system of urban open spaces. Historically, however, these avenues were built for the army. Napoléon III, who commissioned city planner Haussmann to create them, however also wanted to prepare the city for the industrial age. The boulevards still retain a high public quality. Then there are the squares and parks: in France these were originally feudal grounds. They were the generous external and, above all, internal grounds of castle complexes and townhouses and exclusively used for private purposes. Today, they are mostly open to the public and an integral part of cities. In Swiss cities, though, such grounds are not only much smaller but also rarer–because we had no aristocracy to build them.

Some Pigeons Are More Equal Than Others

Julius von Bismarck and Julian Charrière, 2012

Some Pigeons Are More Equal Than Others is a collaboration between Julian Charrière and Julius von Bismarck that has been performed and exhibited in Copenhagen, Venice, and Berlin. While engaging the city as a robust spatial ecology of things, perceptions, movements, and constant surprise, *Some Pigeons Are More Equal Than Others* consists of a specially designed pigeon-trapping apparatus, which is installed in public forums. While inside of the machine, pigeons are airbrushed with vibrant, nontoxic dyes before being released back into the urban environments we all share. While the paint is harmless to the pigeons, it destabilizes our perceptions concerning the roles of art, institutions, and urban animals, including humans, when different species interact in public spaces–the space of their rights, and of our everyday lives. Painted pigeons reenter the public sphere as a new species of sorts, challenging those who cocreate the city to reorient their perceptions and renegotiate the terms on which they cohabit.

Günther Vogt: Paris is a highly interesting example, not least seen from the current political perspective. The demonstrations of the *Gilets jaunes,* the yellow vests movement, make visible what Manuel Valls already noted years ago: the problems France faces are rooted in urban-planning problems. The urban fabric of the country which, to this day, is strongly characterized by its centralist structure, has many people who belong to the middle or the lower-middle class depend on their car. Their lives take place in the periphery of the city or in housing estates, many of which were created in modern times and quite often lack any access to public transport. The politically higher echelons are blamed for this massive urban development and the social deficits of the immediate living environment. Therefore, any displeasure about the situation is primarily discharged on the streets in the city centers, first and foremost of course in Paris, identified as the home of the better-off social strata and political elites.

Katja Gentinetta: In France, the streets have traditionally been the place of public political debates. This has been so ever since the French Revolution and is highly symbolic. Thus, it is understandable that not only the Champs-Élysées in Paris, but also the roads and roundabouts in the countryside tend to be places of assembly and protests. Some of the *Gilets jaunes* explicitly refer to this: here, the symbolism is program. In Switzerland, the situation is quite different. On the one hand, we do not need our streets as a political venue because we have ballot boxes. Four times a year, we cast our votes on numerous political issues. Physical protests are virtually nonexistent because voting also fosters a constant political discourse in which politicians have to explain to the people what they are proposing and why.

Things are quite different from a historical perspective, too. The Swiss Republic, which only came into being with the French Revolution, was first and foremost a republic of men. And although its assemblies needed the public space, the main perimeter, that of voting, was reserved to men for a long time. The decisive discussions also took place in restaurants, salons, or back rooms, that is, in more or less private circles. Seen this way, public space in Switzerland has a different political function than in many other countries, especially the surrounding ones. In Germany, this difference became manifest with the protests against the *Stuttgart 21* project, requesting that this historic public space should be preserved.

Günther Vogt: It needs to be noted with regard to the topic of France that, despite massive pressure from the streets, it has not been possible to find a truly plausible answer to the acute social problems either at the political or the urban-planning level. On the contrary, in fact. In the south of Paris, I have seen projects that literally seem to ignore these clear demands. Huge satellite towns are created on the scale of entire city districts, completely geared
< p. 346, *Grand Paris Sud*
to the use of cars–the same as in modern times. In addition to shopping centers and amusement parks, there are several movie theaters that show films for all age groups at the same time. These are places that isolate themselves from their surroundings and are only accessible to a very specific group of people.

Katja Gentinetta: Public space, just like the buildings surrounding it, mirrors the respective society. In France, it is more segregated, as well as social mobility is significantly less pronounced.

Günther Vogt: I think, as planners and designers, we need to clearly position ourselves. We do not operate in an isolated space but, as social and political actors, we also share in the responsibility for current developments. With regard to public space, my position is quite clear: for me, a public space should be accessible twenty-four hours a day and not be subjected to video surveillance. Drinking water should be offered for free, as well as places to sit down, but without
> p. 580, *Kurt-Hackenberg-Platz*
any pressure to consume something. It all sounds pretty easy and obvious. But imagine what the free availability of drinking water would mean. This requirement alone would completely change the world. Or the possibility to sit down somewhere without having to buy anything. Our project for the National Museum in Zurich is a direct response to this
< p. 524, *Swiss National Museum*
demand. The long city benches on which you can sit down while keeping a certain distance from others are a reaction

to the situation existing at the main station. Its main hall is one of the most important public spaces of the city, even though it is closed at night and hosts numerous events that have nothing to do with civil society. However, on the ground floor, there are only 18 seats available to the public.

Katja Gentinetta: This is a highly normative approach. I would like to discuss to what extent it works politically. After all, it is a basic human need to have a home, whether as a house, apartment, or room. A roof over your head that offers protection, a place where you feel safe and to which you can retreat, is the necessary antidote to public space. Nowadays, more and more functions can be shifted into private space; from a home office to online shopping or the delivery of meals, public space is increasingly developing into the aforementioned transit zone or becoming an outright party zone. Accordingly, people behave in a private or even intimate manner in basically public spaces: they isolate themselves acoustically and, where possible, visually, navigate through a crowd listening to music or making phone calls, and barely perceive the outside world. Or revel loudly in the streets and alleys. They hardly notice that they are not only affecting this public space, but other people as well. In other words, public space has increasingly turned into a private one. A place of private use, of private occupation. But let's return to the original question of political philosophy. If you ask how we want to live together, my answer is quite clear: in such a way that we get on well with and alongside one other. And that means: My freedom ends where the freedom of others begins. Today, the inconsiderate use of public space–be it streets, squares, public transport, or even cafés and restaurants–radically challenges this principle. If public space were the programmatic space you postulated–a space in which we meet and exchange ideas, and in which we respect each other–I could agree with your definition. However, it describes an ideal that hardly matches reality.

Günther Vogt: I don't see this as absolutely as you put it. Of course, we live in highly individual situations. This model is the result of postmodernism and also shows that what applies at the age of 30 no longer necessarily prevails at 40. In the course of our work, we experience this every day. For example, when we plan large housing estates, residents often demand a children's playground. However, a mere five years later they oppose it, as it is no longer their own children who are noisy. The problem arises because people rarely have the collective need in mind. They do not act as citizens but focus on their individual needs.

> p. 590, *Volkspark*

And yet. I continue to locate the most important resource of any city in its public space. There are many places where individual demands and the needs of the general public coexist quite easily. Take the so-called Josefwiese in Zurich as an example, that was built as a playground at the interface between a Gründerzeit neighborhood and the former industrial district of Zurich West. The park has a finely tuned system of social agreement that allows for the greatest possible freedom of individual users, but at the same time tolerates it only to the extent that it is compatible with the general public. This mechanism protects the site, so to speak, from a one-sided use and, instead, leads to a very high level of exchange between people. The system has steadily expanded over the years and now represents a socio-cultural production within the city proper. Or let's take the example of a landscape. In her book *Governing the Commons,* Elinor Ostrom describes the problems of collective action given scarce natural resources that are shared. She shows that sustainable management, such as of fish resources in Sri Lanka or high-mountain pastures in Valais, only works if they are subject to an ongoing negotiation process. The local cooperation of those concerned is not only superior to any state control, but also to all forms of privatization.

Katja Gentinetta: Ostrom was inspired by the original cooperation in Valais. The slopes were steep, water scarce, and food and shelter simply had to be organized as a joint endeavor. As I come from Valais, I have known the fascinating *suonen,* the water channels and pipes on the steep slopes since childhood and admire them to this day. Ostrom has laid down some very important conditions for the commons, without which they would not work. A commons needs clearly defined boundaries and an effective exclusion of external, unauthorized persons. There are clear rules regarding the appropriation and provision of resources, which need to be adapted to local conditions. These rules can only be changed by the users themselves, and even then, only by common agreement. In addition, compliance with the rules has to be strictly monitored and violations of the rules have to be sanctioned according to their seriousness. There are fixed mechanisms to resolve conflicts. And: the self-regulation of the community must explicitly be recognized by a higher-level government body. If we were to apply these principles to today's public space, the problems I have mentioned would be obsolete and the norms you postulate could be realized.

Günther Vogt: Rules and compliance with these rules or the sanctioning of any violation are, of course, an inherent part of this mechanism. The Josefwiese project shows this quite clearly as it is very strongly regulated, even stronger, I would say, than other public spaces in the city of Zurich. The decisive factor is, however, that these rules are not imposed from the top down but determined by the users themselves. And especially given today's situation with regard to the regulation of public space, we have to ask how such rules come about and who is involved in the respective decision-making processes. The problem can be illustrated by the aspect of surveillance. If I fly to London and continue from the City Airport to my hotel, later visit a museum, go out for dinner in the evening and return to my hotel, I will be monitored about 300 times by government cameras, but also–and I think this is crucial–by privately owned cameras. This has been the case ever since the 2012 Summer Olympics. This is not really a problem for me, as I am not a criminal up to no good. But it's a bit like nuclear energy. The issue is what else could be done with this technology. Examples in China or Singapore only allow a vague premonition of what is to come. State surveillance in these countries already goes far beyond the public sphere. For instance, if a state like Singapore uses thermal imaging cameras to spy on people in their homes to check whether the smoking ban is being complied with.

< p. 252, *UCL East Campus*

Katja Gentinetta: Sure, but of course the Chinese government would not call this abuse. It corresponds to the party line and its understanding of system, control, and a harmonious society. It is also significant that the Western concept of "civil society"–as the very epitome of an open and committed society–has been translated into Chinese as "civilized society." This renders any further explanation superfluous. And that is also the decisive difference to us: we may participate in decisions on how we want to design our coexistence and, thus, the public space. But in recent times, we have also been subject to more and more surveillance because there were events that claimed human lives–I am talking about the terrorist attacks aimed at the Twin Towers in New York, the attacks in Barcelona, Manchester, Berlin, Nice and, of course, Paris, to name but a few. And because a real threat can be inferred from these events, there is an obvious need for protective measures. In the end, every society–whether bottom-up or top-down, but at least in the context of its policies–will have to decide whether it is going to adopt an excessive intrusion into privacy with more surveillance or run a greater risk for its citizens with less surveillance.

Günther Vogt: The problem is, I think, that both surveillance and state or private control in the broadest sense always proceed from an assumed future abuse and, thereby, hugely determine our dealings with public space. After the 2017 attack, it has become difficult for the city of London to induce enough tourists to once again visit Parliament Square. In our talks with the authorities, two options were offered to solve the problem. Either you build a nine-meter-high wall made of concrete or natural stone, your choice, or you don't do anything at all. So, there is only complete protection or no precautions at all. In the end, an intermediate solution was built: a safety barrier made of steel and concrete. However, this did not prevent a repetition of the attack in 2018. This shows the difficulty in dealing with such measures, which ultimately cause the actions of the authorities and the reactions of the attackers to fuel each other.

By the way, securing such locations is a new area of business with which we are increasingly confronted. In response to the attack in Manchester, access to the Allianz Arena in Munich is to be remodeled. The same question also arises in the case of the Chelsea stadium, whose redevelopment is currently being planned. The garden below the Eiffel Tower is now completely closed off, too. In concrete terms, this

< p. 270, *Les Jardins de la Tour Eiffel*

means that we have surrounded the site with thick glass walls. If someone wants to get onto the Eiffel Tower today, the security checks will take a whole day. All these measures lead to segregation in urban space. And there I see a conflict between the demands that we formulate for a public space and the everyday reality we have to face with our projects. I think it is important to always strive for the best possible solution for a free society, but also to repeatedly raise and address the real problem.

Katja Gentinetta: That's for sure, and ultimately, every society has to decide on the most compatible solution for itself. It is up to it to decide how much freedom and how much security is to prevail in their public space. Ultimately, it is a question of defining the line separating the use and abuse of public space. If serious abuse can be contained by a suitable degree of surveillance and sanctioning, this will, in turn, allow public space to become a place of encounter, exchange, and mutual respect. Ultimately, public space, and how it is used and regulated, mirrors how open or closed a society is, both in a positive and a negative way. Not to mention regarding pleasure. Take Zurich with the new Sechseläutenplatz, where people simply like to sit in the sun and chat. I appreciate even small parks, where people like to sit because they have no terrace and no front yard of their own. But these are idylls and only reflect part of reality.

Günther Vogt: In principle, I agree with you. In large European cities such as Barcelona, London, or Paris, this aspect of "extending living space" into public space is even more essential due to the small spaces available for living. But this, too, reflects only part of reality. And if I take Zurich's example further by looking at the riots taking place during the demonstrations on May 1, which are also part of everyday urban reality in Zurich, it becomes clear that public space must also be able to withstand conflicts. I definitely don't approve of these riots, but in this context it is interesting that although vandalism at football matches or other major events has been lamented for years, no effective countermeasures have as yet been devised. The general public regards the riots in the wake of the rallies on May 1 however as more virulent and generally condemns them much more severely. I think this has to do with the fact that, as a society, it is fundamentally difficult if political opinions manifest themselves publicly in this manner.

Katja Gentinetta: I think this needs to be regarded in more detail. It is a fact that public space takes over part of this valve-type function. On the other hand, it is the great achievement of democracy that it has replaced armed fighting by fighting with words. Whether the public space has to endure such riots is a matter of opinion. After all, as a shopkeeper with shattered windows, my private property would be affected and not just the public space.

Günther Vogt: Here, too, Switzerland is a special case. Theoretically, there have been no more labor demonstrations since the peace treaty of 1937. A compromise was negotiated. Compared to other countries in Europe, these are almost ideal conditions, even if we look at the naturalization process, for example. Of course, there are also negative cases. But the very fact that the people can decide whether or not to admit someone to civil society conveys an idea of how far-reaching the competences and rights of citizens in our country are.

Katja Gentinetta: This is really an archetypal characteristic of Swiss society, which in the words of Ferdinand Tönnies would almost have to be called a *community:* Through the process of naturalization, thus its origin, the community accepts for whom it is prepared to provide, if he or she should be in distress, and if it can expect that person to be equally as willing to contribute his or her share to the care of the community and help in an emergency. Ultimately, this is an expression of solidarity, which always has to be understood as reciprocal.

And in this context I would like to ask you as an landscape architect: Do you think that the way you design public spaces can foster this respectful coexistence based on solidarity or that a bad design could well make this difficult?

Günther Vogt: That's hard to achieve with good design alone. Nevertheless, I think that it is possible to create suitable conditions for it. For this purpose, we always work with different disciplines, with geographers, sociologists, historians, et cetera. But, of course, also with potential users. Because our concept of the city is just one possible view of reality. Our aim is to grasp the place in its larger and more comprehensive context to uncover the different levels of meaning and functional relationships in order to reassess them. To do so, aspects such as centrality are crucial. It is all about the question of how individual elements can be reached via access systems; or the possibilities of adapting individual elements. Physical, temporal, but also mental accessibility is also important. Ultimately, the most diverse people should be able to occupy the places in a variety of ways and, if possible, at the same time, to create a high social density and interaction. Density is therefore a decisive moment that we should not equate with built density. In London, I know absurd examples of skyscrapers, where the bottom 40 meters are not used. Behind the facade is only the raw structure of the building. The privileged owners on the upper floors thus enjoy a free view of the city. The built density is very high, whereas the lived density is extremely low.

Katja Gentinetta: I experience skyscrapers, especially the new ones in Switzerland, quite differently—straight and literally from below. Because of my former job in the immediate vicinity, I witnessed the construction of the Prime Tower in Zurich for years. From the rather shabby periphery via a mammoth construction site with constantly changing pedestrian and traffic routing to the finished plaza—or space, as I would say now. Today, I walk across an open square, flanked by bars, restaurants, and shops that do not exactly invite you to take a stroll, but still provide a space in which to move gladly and safely. Besides, the space is impressive: the building was built high in order to gain free space in the area. For me, this is a very important aspect of the often-criticized densification.

Günther Vogt: In my opinion, the tower together with its immediate surroundings is crucial to make the place work. But much more important is the proximity to the Hardbrücke station, one of the ten largest railway stations in Switzerland in terms of passengers, as well as the direct access to Langstrasse, located within the city's Gründerzeit quarters. Basically, I have nothing against skyscrapers, but they do not solve the real problem. On the one hand, because the higher the buildings–and this has primarily to do with construction and logistics–the more expensive they become, and the more directly this affects the price per square meter and, therefore, the size of the apartments or offices. In their current form, skyscrapers rarely make a significant contribution to an inner development. In the future, it will be interesting to see what the new technological possibilities will achieve. On the other hand, planning in Switzerland is still far too local. You've got to operate within the limits imposed by the administration. Utilizations are separated by zones and spread across the area. However, the historical coexistence of uses and their spatial separation increasingly dissolve. They are replaced by operationalized urban landscapes, which are often used in the catchment areas of major cities for informal recreational and sports purposes. This is a direct result of the inner development and increased mobility radius of people. Just take the Limmat. For the city of Zurich, the river has always been a reservoir of drinking water, a source of energy, a traffic route, a site of swimming baths, a nature reserve, and a flood-control zone. Now the space is being reinterpreted and currently used as a kilometer-long leisure landscape. This overlapping of uses leads to tensions and conflicts.

Katja Gentinetta: What you are describing is that the city reaching out into the countryside and the landscape's being used as a kind of public space. I believe that the need for recreation in the countryside is increasing, especially in the face of densification. From my point of view, this is also an important argument in favor of densification–as long as the landscape is preserved and maintained as a recreational area.

Günther Vogt: If we look at Europe, we see that people are actually more and more frequently moving back into the cities. Preserving and maintaining a landscape for leisure-type purposes, however, is only one aspect of the question, which deals with what happens to the landscape in the course of this process. Many regions from which people migrate lie fallow or run to seed. Part of the Apennines, the Ruhr area, and even huge landscapes in Eastern Europe are quite substantially affected. In the Alps, too, we are seeing a tendency toward wasteland, in addition to the intensively used edges and the well-developed Alpine valleys and tourist hotspots. One of the strategies that have been used in recent years to respond to this is to put the landscape under protection status. Of course, this is a very urban perspective, which was already prevalent when the Swiss National Park was founded in 1914. However, many of these recent initiatives to expand or establish parks have been rejected by the local electorate. This has to do with the fact that a protection status always entails massive restrictions in addition to economic benefits for the people actually living in the affected areas. Besides, the question is: who decides for whom? In addition to local rules that have to be respected, new rules from outside will be necessary. In order to reach a consensus in this situation, a dialogue between the various parties is indispensable.

< p. 132, *Alps*

European Central Bank, Frankfurt a. M., DE

Discovery of a Fluvial Landscape

The new headquarters of the European Central Bank (ECB) in Ostend–a former industrial district of Frankfurt–was built at the point where the banks of the Main River meet the large open spaces of the city's greenbelt. Its position in the urban layout and the dimensions of the site demanded a project scaled to the landscape. The design takes its cue from the most powerful feature of the site, the river, and translates the existing space into an consistent concept for the park: the park incorporates the specific topography of the floodplain with its oxbow lakes and residual water, undercut banks and point bars–yet these elements are not copies of already existing forms but rather objectified and geometrized figures. The design takes one by surprise: the riverbed is dry, while small areas of water appear like islands in the bedload. This sense of the unexpected is reinforced by the vegetation. The combination of local floodplain trees (alder, silver birch, ash) and wetland species from North America (tupelo, tulip tree, swamp cypress, redwood), planted to the south and north of the building, creates an ambiguous view somewhere between a landscape and a park. It nurtures seeds that were brought to Frankfurt by the wind and the river or arrived as “stowaways” on board a ship from faraway countries. Last but not least, there is the perplexing choreography of the site. While the paths of the neighboring public and open spaces are clearly defined by their dimensions and materials, the park can be constantly experienced in new ways–and as there are no paths in the tradition of an English park, this allows for a myriad of other possibilities. To explore the park, you will have to enter the riverine world. (lr)

Client:
European Central Bank (ECB), Frankfurt am Main

Cooperation:
**Architecture:
Coop Himmelb(l)au, Vienna**

Design/construction:
2005–2013

Type and size:
Park, 12 ha

Status:
Realized

Project
Res Publica

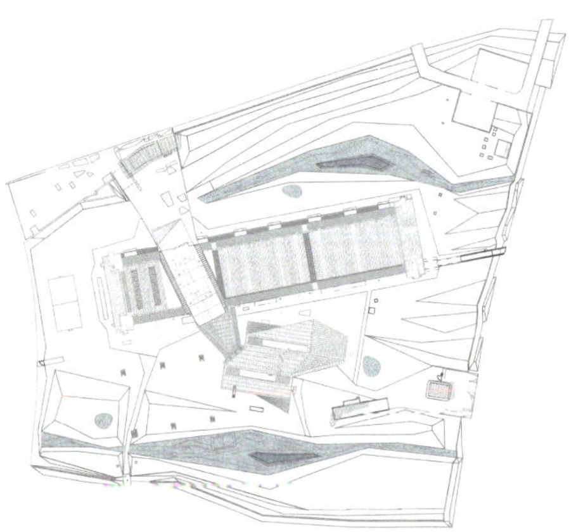

River

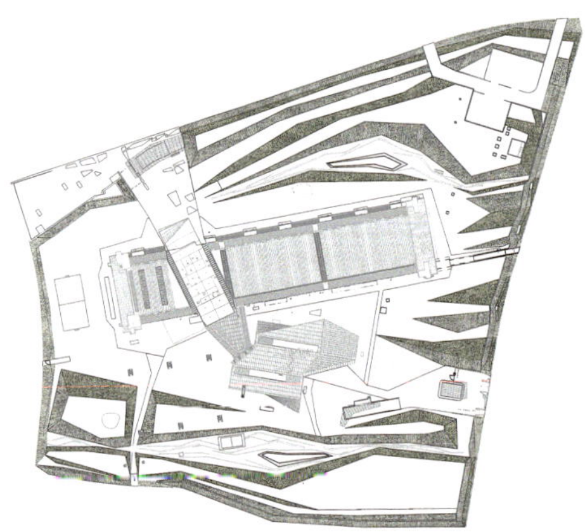

Topography

European Central Bank, Frankfurt a. M., DE
Discovery of a Fluvial Landscape

Over the past three decades, the areas located directly on the Main River have seen a continuous decline in port usage, freeing them up for transformation. On both sides of the river, promenades have been built or added to, and further public spaces have been created in the vicinity of the new housing estates and commercial buildings. Directly adjacent to these open spaces on the river, a site that had previously housed the wholesale market hall, the Grossmarkthalle, was chosen for the headquarters of the European Central Bank.

Vegetation

European Central Bank, Frankfurt a. M., DE
Discovery of a Fluvial Landscape

The defining feature of the park is its stylized river landscape. The image of the banks, gravel islands, and channels is created by unbound and cement-bound gravel with varying gradation and coloring.

Numerous mock-ups at various scales, from hand-made samples to 1:1 details, were used not only to check and refine the density and composition of the aggregates but also to determine the surface treatment, the layering, and the shape of the walls.

Kurt-Hackenberg-Platz, Cologne
Listen, Drink, Savor

Kurt-Hackenberg-Platz is a square located in the center of Cologne. Situated between the Romano-Germanic Museum, the Philharmonie concert hall, and Museum Ludwig with its collection of contemporary art, the former Bishop's Garden with the silhouette of Cologne Cathedral in the background was, for many years, a bleak leftover area in the urban fabric. The new "Garden of Eden" with its sparsely planted Japanese pagoda trees, which are well suited to the city's climate, bears reference to the history of the site, while two elements in the public space indicate its present-day usage: a long stone bench made of local graywacke sandstone that frames the garden and a drinking fountain cast in bronze. And yet when it comes to something as basic as drinking, we are in two minds about it–a sign put in later certified the good quality of the water.

As soon as we bend down to drink, we hear strange noises from beneath the ground. A resonating body with integrated acoustic elements uses the water flowing from the fountain as its "player." In both material and sensory terms, the funnel-like ear trumpet and the water bowl refer to the tradition and craft of bell casting. In the past, drinking places were central meeting points in a city and are embedded as such in our collective memory. Today, however, free access to drinking water is no longer taken for granted. The project is focused, then, not only on reinstilling a sense of how to use this resource with care but also on restoring one of the key functions of any public space. (mb)

Client:
City of Cologne

Design/construction:
2014–2016/2016–2018

Type and size:
City square, 0.36 ha

Status:
Realized

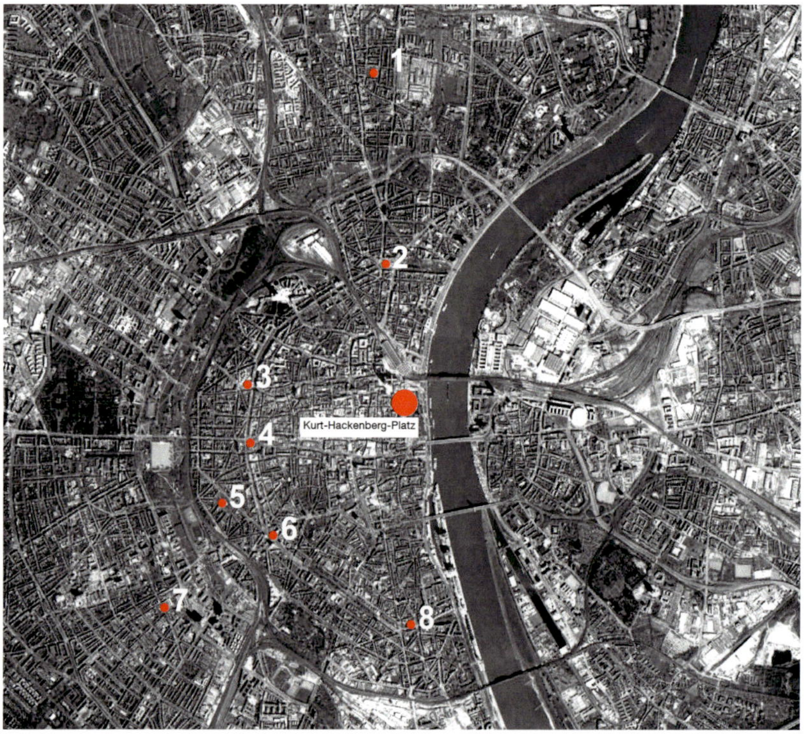

Public squares in the center of Cologne

1 Leipziger Square
2 Ebert Square
3 Friesen Square
4 Rudolf Square
5 Rathenau Square
6 Barbarossa Square
7 De-Noël-Square
8 Chlodwig Square

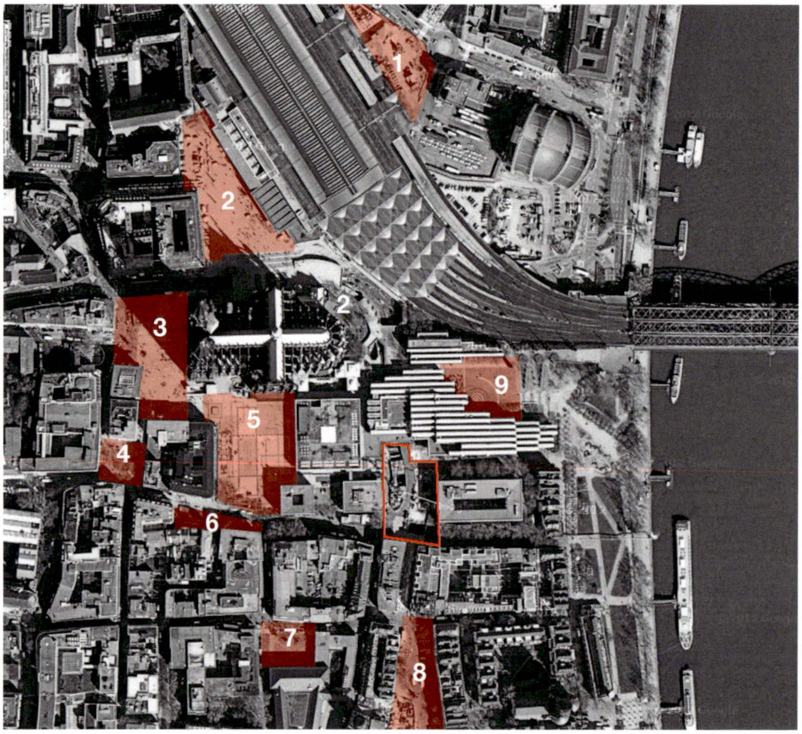

Public squares in the immediate vicinity

1 Breslauer Square
2 Station forecourt
3 Dome cloister
4 Wallraf Square
5 Roncalli Square
6 Heinzelmännchen fountain
7 Theo-Burauen-Square
8 Old market
9 Heinrich-Boll-Square

FOXP2

Marguerite Humeau, 2016

FOXP2, FOXP2, FOXP2. An illuminated FOXP2 sign flashes at the end of a dark entrance hall. Two vectors of varying light lead to the end of the corridor. A *Homo sapiens* breathes. Its voice sings the rain, sings the wind and birds, its throat vibrates, and FOXP2 mutates. The voice then evolves and multiplies. One hundred and eight billion *Homo sapiens* are now singing in chorus. They are the souls of all human beings who have ever lived on planet Earth since the first tribes of *Homo sapiens*, one hundred thousand years ago. They start speaking in an incomprehensible protolanguage.

At the end of this corridor, an opening leads to the luminous horror. We enter the bright, dazzling showroom. An elephant herd is displayed on various platforms, each covered with a pink carpet. The carpet has been dyed with pigments concocted using the chemical components of a human body. The carpet is a body without a soul. The oldest female pachyderm on display knows this is the end. One beast, Enid, shows emotion: tears. Enid is a female engineered to cry out of sadness. Edwina, Amelia, and Antonia are three females, whose larynges have dropped, allowing them to sing in an almost articulated language. Tony is fed with depressant hormone powder. Félicie, in the background, shows signs of self-destruction. Jean is watching the scene with a sense of wonder. The matriarch enters in its last act. Life has evacuated its receptacle. The heartbeat stops. A silence follows. The genetic code resets. The heart starts beating again, FOXP2 starts flashing again.

Casting mold for the drinking fountain jointly developed with Hartmann-Metallbau AG (Saas im Prättigau, CH) and Harms Metallguss GmbH (Oldenburg, DE)

The individual elements of the fountain are made of patinated bronze.

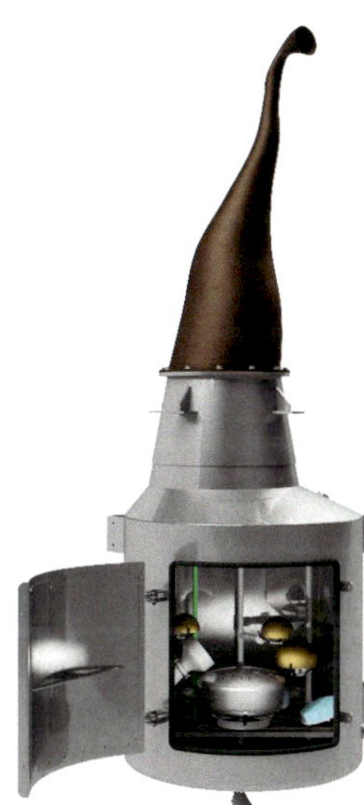

Plan von Treptow

Der Plänterwald
Die Spree
Bullenbruch
Stadtgemeinde Berlin
Eisenbahn
Der Cöllnischen Ackerschaft gehörig
Rehberge
Marienthal
Bärwinkel
Zwiestädter Heide
Separations- u. Abfindungsplan für die Gemeinden Deutsch- u. Böhmisch-Rixdorf
Bienen Garten
Gem. Rixdorf
Gem. Britz
1:6000.

Volkspark
Liberating Rules

Daia Stutz

In the early twentieth century, an intense debate flared up in Germany on the principles governing the function and design of urban public spaces. The resulting reform movement led to a radical break with traditional ideas of landscape-architectural design and gave rise to the development of a new park typology: the so-called *Volkspark*. This featured not only a new stylistic approach but also a new way of planning open spaces, which would be of critical importance for the development of public space in Europe. The idea of the Volkspark would later be ideologically co-opted by the National Socialists and was abruptly abandoned following the outbreak of World War II. And yet the fundamental principles in terms of design, program, and, in particular, a systemic approach to open-space planning are still relevant today.

<< Plan of Treptow, 1895

Large green in Treptower Park in Berlin after the Industrial Exposition, ca. 1900

Light, Air, and Sun: The Volkspark Movement in Germany

In the late nineteenth century, rapidly expanding industrial cities, including Hamburg, Berlin, and Cologne, were faced with increasing social and hygienic problems. In the dense, overpopulated city districts, there were not enough public spaces and those that did exist–for the most part decorative squares and public gardens–primarily served the middle class and were extremely limited in terms of their potential uses. Their symbolic, prestige-oriented design was exclusively derived from aesthetic criteria based on the predominant landscape style. However, the purely ornamental value of these amenities, which had no clear practical usage, was increasingly criticized and condemned as "compensation by reintroducing nature."[1] The founders of the reform movement, among them such well-known landscape architects, city planners, and architects as Martin Wagner, Ludwig Lesser, and Leberecht Migge, advocated a functional, problem-oriented design of public spaces based on architectural and geometric principles and geared unconditionally to the needs of the local residents.[2] Beginning in 1909, the first Volkparks were developed in accordance with the ideological, yet nonetheless pragmatic rubric "light, air, and sun." Neighborhood residents had quick and easy access to them,[3] and they could be used by the general populace not just as a place to stroll in but also as public spaces for games and sports activities. Of central importance was the fact that the grassy areas could be actively used, which had previously not been the norm. In addition to the social ideology, emphasis was placed on the healthful aspects of so-called sanitary greenery,[4] which was intended to promote activities in the fresh air and, thus, to forestall such diseases as tuberculosis. The intended "healing of the public body" did indeed have positive effects, as it provided the foundation for adequate public space and fresh air in many German cities. However, it essentially emerged from a conservative attitude that opposed the modernization of urban society and was closely associated with the emergent idea

1 Annemarie Bucher, "Park," in *Enzyklopädie zum gestalteten Raum,* ed. Vittorio Magnagno Lampugnani, Konstanze Sylva Domhardt, and Rainer Schützeichel (Zurich: gta, 2014), 351–52.
2 Ibid., 352.
3 Leberecht Migge speaks of "stroller distance." Leberecht Migge, *Die Gartenkultur des 20. Jahrhunderts* (Jena: Diederichs, 1913), 31.
4 Martin Wagner, *Das sanitäre Grün der Städte: Ein Beitrag zur Freiflächentheorie* (Berlin: Heymann, 1915), 92.

The aerial view of Hamburg Stadtpark provides a clear picture of how the French and English design vocabulary are superimposed here: straight lines, surfaces, and edges are embedded in a scenic setting characterized by curved or round forms. Below: everyday scene at the Stadtpark lake, which could be used by the public for leisure and recreational activities, ca. 1932

of preserving homeland and nature, which was tinged with a strong sense of idealism and later took on nationalist overtones.[5]

Stylistically, Volkparks are characterized by a design language that is based to varying degrees on clear geometric forms. Toward the end of the nineteenth century, a mix of styles initially emerged that included organic and geometric approaches—for instance, Gustav Meyer's Treptower Park in Berlin, which opened in 1888. In the early twentieth century, the so-called architectural style was increasingly prevalent in Germany. Straight lines and precisely defined areas complemented and increasingly replaced the organic forms traditionally derived from the landscape. In most cases, an existing tract of forest or newly planted group of trees provided the overall natural spatial structure, to which geometrical sports facilities and play areas were integrated. This concept can be clearly seen in Friedrich Bauer's Schillerpark, which was opened in 1913, and Volkspark Jungfernheide, designed by Erwin Barth and completed in 1927, both of which are located in Berlin. However, the Hamburg City Park designed by Fritz Schumacher is considered the best-known example of this park typology. Here, the design principles of both the English landscape park and the French baroque garden coincide and contrast with one another. This Volkspark, which was conceived in 1920 as "a garden not to be walked through but to be taken possession of,"[6] is a prime example of the desire at the time to open up and make active use of urban public spaces. This new style is indeed characterized by high functionality and various opportunities of use. The parks often feature a complex network of paths, shady parkways and graveled areas, and sunny fields, where people can walk, play, or relax on the grass, lakes and ponds, outdoor swimming pools, stages, libraries, play and picnic areas, and restaurants.[7] All the spaces, the entire infrastructure, and even the vegetation in these modest, robustly designed parks serve specific functions—prestige-oriented and decorative elements play a secondary role or are completely absent.

5 See Stefanie Hennecke: "Der deutsche Volkspark zwischen individueller Bedürfnisbefriedigung und ganzheitlicher Gesellschaftsreform: Die Diskussion eines gartenkünstlerischen Reformprojekts im 20. Jahrhundert," in *Gärten und Parks als Lebens- und Erlebnisraum: Funktions- und nutzungsgeschichtliche Aspekte der Gartenkunst in Früher Neuzeit und Moderne,* ed. Stefan Schweizer (Worms: Werner, 2008), 151–64.
6 "Der Stadtpark – ein historisches Gesamtkunstwerk," *Stadtpark Verein Hamburg e.V.,* accessed August 8, 2019, https://stadtparkverein.de/stadtpark/.
7 See Bucher, "Park," 350.

Josefwiese Spielpark in Zurich

In the early twentieth century, the Volkspark movement began to establish itself in Switzerland as well, and one of its first offshoots appeared in Zurich in the form of the Josefwiese park, created in 1916. Based on the plans drawn up by Garden Inspector Gottlieb Friedrich Rothpletz, it occupied the last free plot of land in what was then the city's working-class district. Since its official opening in 1924, the park has been continually adapted to residents' changing needs, most recently in 2008.[8] Although it contains all the typical elements of the classic Volkspark, Josefwiese cannot be compared with the expansive park complexes of large German cities on account of its size. It corresponds instead to the Spielpark ("play park") typology advocated by Hamburg garden reformer Leberecht Migge. These "inner parks" were available to city residents and within walking distance. The goal was to satisfy the populace's "need for unlimited play activities with as much diversity as possible."[9] In contrast to the decorative square, which was designed to convey an overall sense of symbolic prestige, the Spielpark is embedded in the local architectural context and entirely geared to the needs of neighborhood residents. This principle was also applied to Josefwiese. Its extremely simple design was in keeping with the surrounding urban structure, echoing in its design and dimensions the perimeter block construction that was standard in the neighborhood. At the center of the trapezoidal plot of land is a rectangular patch of lawn measuring approximately 120 by 100 meters that was originally framed by a triple row of linden trees, now reduced to a double row.[10] An informal line of slender Lombardy poplars marks the transition between field and play area, while a hedge, some 1.5 meters in height, signals the outer boundaries of the park without creating a visual barrier. The periphery of the park, which is planted with trees, accommodates a kiosk with toilets, a *pétanque* clubhouse, playgrounds and sports fields, benches, and a wading pool. This clear distinction between an outer area conceived for specific uses and a central section open to different activities pro-

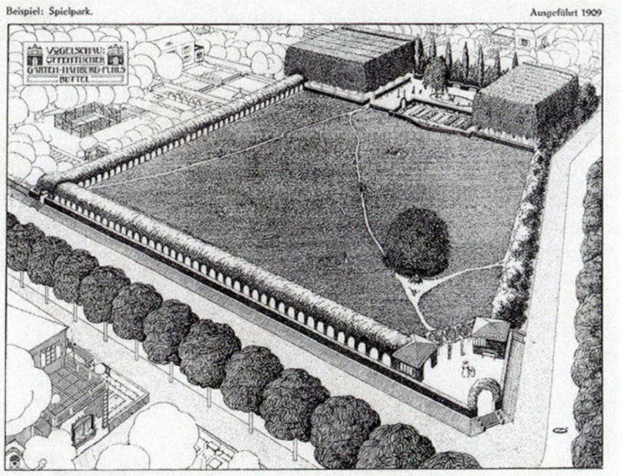

Josefwiese Park in Zurich: periphery with designated playground and seating areas–in the center of the amenity, there is a green that can be used for different activities.

Example of a Spielpark by Leberecht Migge: Wacholder Park, a small, versatile neighborhood park in the northern part of Hamburg, 1909

8 "Josefwiese," *Stadt Zürich: Tiefbau- und Entsorgungs-departement,* accessed April 24, 2019, www.stadt-zuerich.ch/ted/de/index/gsz/natur-_und_erlebnisraeume/park-_und_gruenanlagen/josefwiese.html.
9 Migge, *Die Gartenkultur des 20. Jahrhunderts,* 31.
10 See Johannes Stoffler and Tanja Hirsig, "Garteninspektor Rothpletz (1864–1932) und das städtische Grün in Zürich," *Topiaria Helvetica: Jahrbuch,* Schweizerische Gesellschaft für Gartenkultur (2006): 16.

Josefwiese Park was created on the last free plot in Zurich's old workers' quarter.

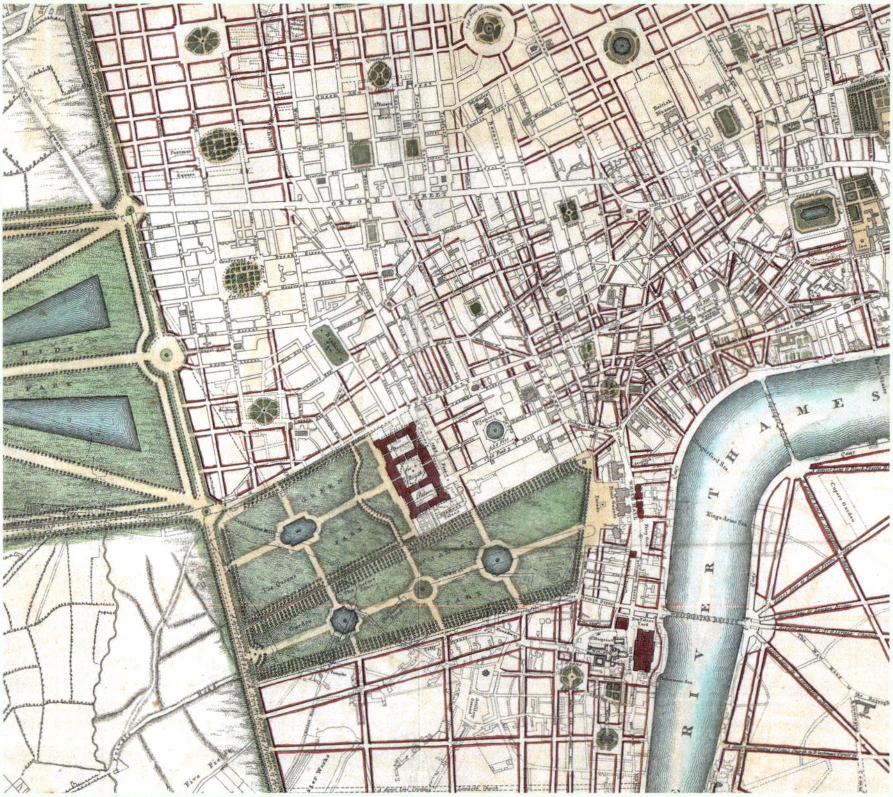

One typology, many options: the squares in London constitute a system of multiple, evenly distributed open spaces within the borough.

vides the park with a clear profile within the urban context and offers considerable diversity and flexibility, allowing the space to be used for a variety of different activities at the same time.

Integral Part Instead of Antithesis to the City

From the perspective of urban development, the Volkspark movement was an important milestone in the evolution of public parks with an integrative social and programmatic approach. The parks' spatial concepts no longer presented a direct counterpoint to the city–as is the case with many types of parks and gardens, such as the English landscape park or the Volksgarten–but were formally and spatially integrated into their immediate urban context. It would appear, however, that it is not so much the design as the planning program that is key here. This is especially evident in the example of the Spielpark. Because these facilities can be appropriated and used without difficulty, they are firmly anchored in the everyday lives of neighborhood residents. The constructed space reflects the lived space. Besides, the local community often exercises across-the-board social supervision, regulating the spaces more effectively than any government restrictions. We may make a pertinent comparison here with an Anglo-Saxon type of public space: the English square. In his conception of Spielparks, Leberecht Migge had originally mentioned the square as a model.[11] These small open spaces interspersed throughout residential neighborhoods in London are also characterized by a simple, clear design and are naturally integrated into the urban setting. However, the basic structure is reversed: the squares consist of a paved rectangular space with an enclosed oval garden in the middle. This garden is typically surrounded by a wrought-iron fence and serves, depending on its size and location, as a private or communal garden for residents, and less frequently as a public neighborhood park. The outer areas–that is, the residual space around the arbored center–are public and open to different uses and, thus, part of street and city life. As is the case with many Spielparks, in English

Hoxton Square and Bedford Square, London: enclosed communal garden; the peripheral areas of the square are public spaces without specific, designated uses.

11 See Migge, *Die Gartenkultur des 20. Jahrhunderts*, 32.

squares the arbored areas are adopted for predefined activities and regulated by a particular group of users, while the spatially open zones can be used and appropriated with greater flexibility. It is precisely this duality of open and specific usage that makes both the Spielpark and English square a model for public spaces that can be deployed in a range of different urban contexts.

Open Spaces–An Urban-Planning Task

The greatest achievement of the Volkspark movement is that it established the planning of public space as a discipline of urban design that defined the "greenification"[12] of the city as a central objective. The roots of this paradigm shift are certainly to be found in the glaring deficits in the existing urban space, but it was also the expression of a *zeitgeist* whose ideological underpinnings can be traced back to Ebenezer Howard's idea of the English garden city. In 1902 Howard proclaimed that cities were to provide adequate public space; his ideas would later form the basis for the development of large-scale greenbelts in many European metropolises. Yet city planners first undertook the overall design and organization of public spaces not in Europe but in the United States, where numerous large-scale park amenities, and ultimately park systems, had already been created in the late nineteenth century in many major cities, among them Chicago, New York, and Boston.[13]

Gottlieb Friedrich Rothpletz also followed an urbanistic approach with a consistent attention to the large scale. His strategy was to bring about a comprehensive transformation of the city(scape), using simple means, and to embed this transformation in the overall urban context. In the case of Josefwiese, he was able to subtly refer to the size and scale of the Alps by planting Scots pines alongside the railway viaduct. However, in addition to creating new public spaces, Rothpletz was primarily interested in upgrading and enhancing the usability of existing facilities and landscape spaces and in making their amenities more accessible. Thus, as president of the Verschönerungsverein (Beautifica-

12 Reinhard Baumeister, *Stadterweiterungen in technischer, baupolizeilicher und wirtschaftlicher Beziehung* (Berlin: Ernst & Korn, 1876), 184–85.
13 See Robert Freestone, "Greenbelts in City and Regional Planning," in *From Garden City to Green City: The Legacy of Ebenezer Howard,* ed. Kermit C. Parsons and David Schuyler (Baltimore: Johns Hopkins University Press, 2002), 67–98; Marco Amati, "Green Belts: A Twentieth-Century Planning Experiment," in *Urban Green Belts in the Twenty-First Century* (Aldershot: Ashgate, 2008), 1–20.
14 See Stoffler and Hirsig, "Garteninspektor Rothpletz," 16–19.

tion Society), hc ensured that the Zurich city woods were systematically opened up to the public. Footpaths, signposts, park benches, fountains, play and viewing areas were all installed in the forests, in essence converting them into city parks.[14] His legacy is a network of numerous public spaces throughout the city of Zurich.

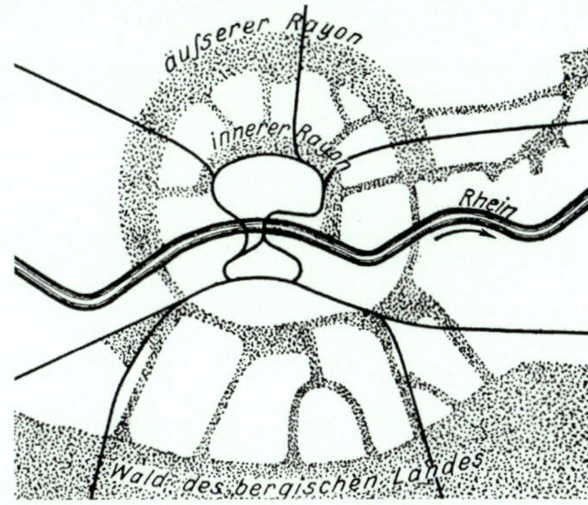

Systemic open-space design on a large scale: Fritz Schumacher's greenbelt system for Cologne of 1920 remains in use to this very day.

Systematic Approach and Urban Context

In view of the current densification of built-up urban spaces, new climatic conditions, and residents' greater mobility, public spaces must now increasingly take on a full range of infrastructural functions in addition to their importance for the health of the city. In order to satisfy these diverse requirements, the systematic approach so essential to the Volkspark movement is once again in the spotlight. In addition to these other factors, increasing privatization, eventification, and surveillance have led to ever more fragmentation–and, consequently, a partial disintegration of public space.

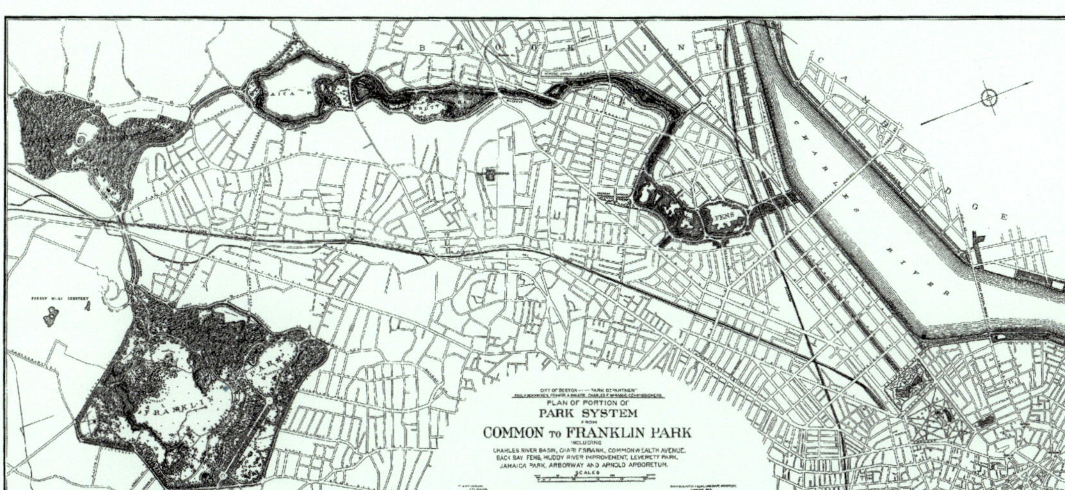

"The Emerald Necklace," the incorporation of new and existing spaces into a chain of parks in Boston–Frederick Law Olmsted, 1894

If we see public space as a part of everyday reality, planners are called on to focus on accessibility and appropriation potentials. These factors can cater to diverse usage needs and are essential for a productive process of exchange. A carefully balanced juxtaposition of open-use and user-determined spaces is essential, which integrate themselves quite naturally into their individual, broadly defined urban context, while extending and enhancing it.

Friedrich Rothpletz's design for Josefwiese Park (1915–1922), with its triple row of linden trees as a spatial enclosure, is modeled on the surrounding perimeter-block development.

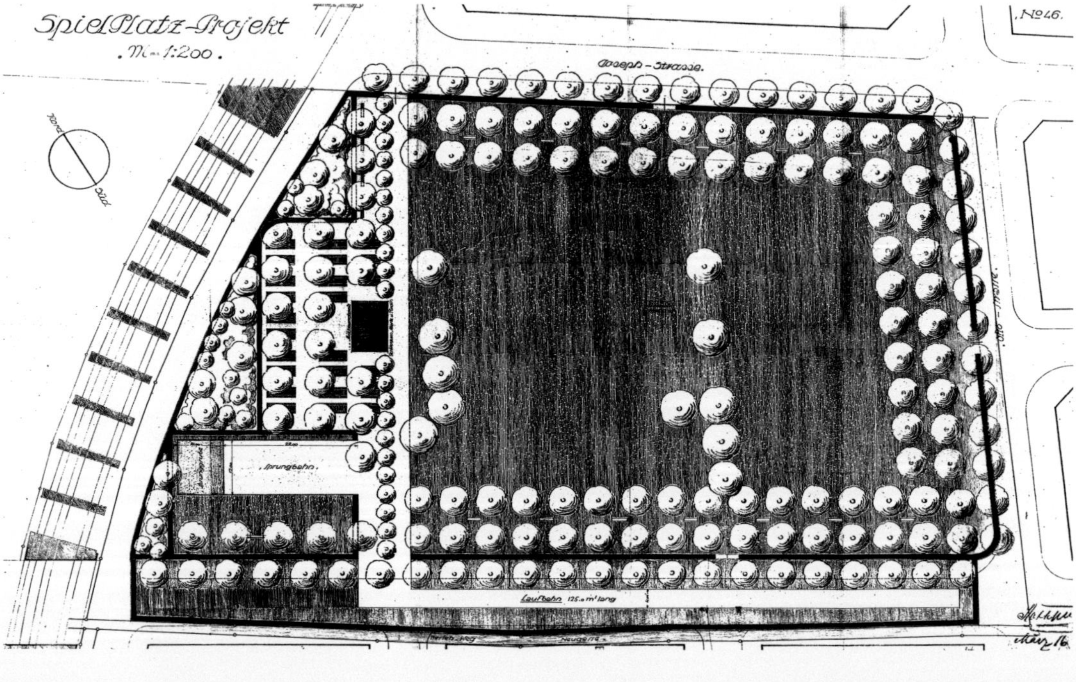

"So, there are countries without space and histories without chronology. Whole cities, planets, continents, universes that are impossible to trace on any map or in any sky, quite simply because they do not belong to any space. Without doubt these cities, continents, planets are born, so to speak, in the heads of men or, more precisely, in the interstices of their words, in the weft of the tales they tell or, if not there, in the placeless place of their dreams, in the empty well of their hearts; in short, wherever the salve of utopia is sought. Yet I believe there are also–in every society–utopias that occupy a precise and real place, a place that can be fixed and measured according to a regular calendar. It is highly probable that every human group, every culture, carves out places that are utopian in the space that it occupies, where it really lives, where it works, and moments that are uchronic in the time it goes about business."

Michel Foucault, *Heterotopias*

Lohsepark, Hamburg
The City's Collective Memory

The city of Hamburg has a rich tradition and many parks created by the Volkspark movement. Today, numerous neighborhoods dating from the early twentieth century can still be clearly recognized, influenced by reformist ideas that advocated more light, air, movement, and education for the populace. According to Alfred Lichtwark, one of the promoters of the Gartenkunst reform movement in Hamburg, every inhabitant ought to have access to public green space within "pram-walking distance" of where they live. This tradition is part of Hamburg's collective memory, which to this day still conditions not only the city's architecture but also the expectations and usage habits of its population. The basic motif of many of the facilities is an open core framed by woodland or allotments: the so-called *Volkswiese* or "people's meadow." In its basic composition, Lohsepark continues the tradition of the Volkspark movement: like Hamburg's Stadtpark or Altona's Volkspark, the park was established "outside the city gates" with an eye to the anticipated process of urban development.

Client:
Hafencity Hamburg GmbH, Hamburg

Design/construction:
2010–2014/2015–2017

Type and size:
Park, 4.7 ha

Status:
Realized

From Water to Water
If you stand in the middle of Lohsepark and turn around in a circle, you will get a sense of the spatial qualities of the area. At both ends, the longitudinal axis of the open space leads to a harbor basin, bringing light, air, and sunshine into the interior of the park. The traditional transition into a *Volkspark* marked by allotment gardens or a stand of trees–not realized due to a lack of space–has been replaced by a terraced shift in levels. As a complement to the line of sight leading from one body of water to another, this represents the second basic motif of the park: the separation into three tiers corresponding to three semantic levels. This stepping of the site not only acts as flood protection, it also acknowledges the history of the site and meets the spatial and programmatic requirements of the new quarter, while keeping the layering of the city legible.

The City Level
The main entrance leads via planted terraces, which act like bastions, projecting into the park as enclosed landmarks. Spatially part of the park, they mediate between the built structures of the city and the actual open space. The honeycomb clinker brickwork used for the retaining walls and parapets of the terraces, was specifically designed in an extended process. Not only does it embed the site in Hamburg's architectural tradition, but its pleated form and perforation break up the monolithic character of the otherwise massive wall.

The Park Level
Lohsepark, with its spacious lawns for games and sunbathing, is 1.5 meters below the level of the streets and promenades and bordered by a rich collection of familiar-looking trees and shrubs. The park features unusual places: the so-called follies. A small grove contains hornbeams grown in quirky shapes; a piece of fenced-off "wilderness" shows how a fragment of landscape evolves without human intervention; and the grotto, with its layering of tamped concrete and various inclusions such as shingle, peat, and even glass, creates an unusual space for children, complementing the other play features in the park.

The Historical Level–A Memorial
Lower still, precisely demarcated by a further drop in level, are the historical sites: the architectural remains of the Hannoversche Bahnhof have their own visual idiom and recall the history of the station as the main starting point for the deportation of Jews, Sinti, and Roma during World War II. Resembling a deeper geological layer, the site lies one meter below the park level and up to three meters below the city level. The details of its history are laid out in full in the planned documentation center, relieving the station itself of the need to serve as a memorial in the didactic sense. In this way, it is possible to dispense with any grand gesture in the design of the site–in favor of the unchanged historical site, supplemented by simple name boards in the form of tables made of glass and concrete. No decorated or demarcated monument; instead, unmediated history as an integral part of the park program. (lr)

The site of the former island of Grasbrook lay outside the city gates until the early nineteenth century. Between the eighteenth and nineteenth centuries, shipwrights and harbor tradesmen settled here. In 2000, the municipality decided to convert this part of the harbor into the so-called "Hafencity," a new urban district–at the same time creating a park in the tradition of Hamburg's Volksparks.

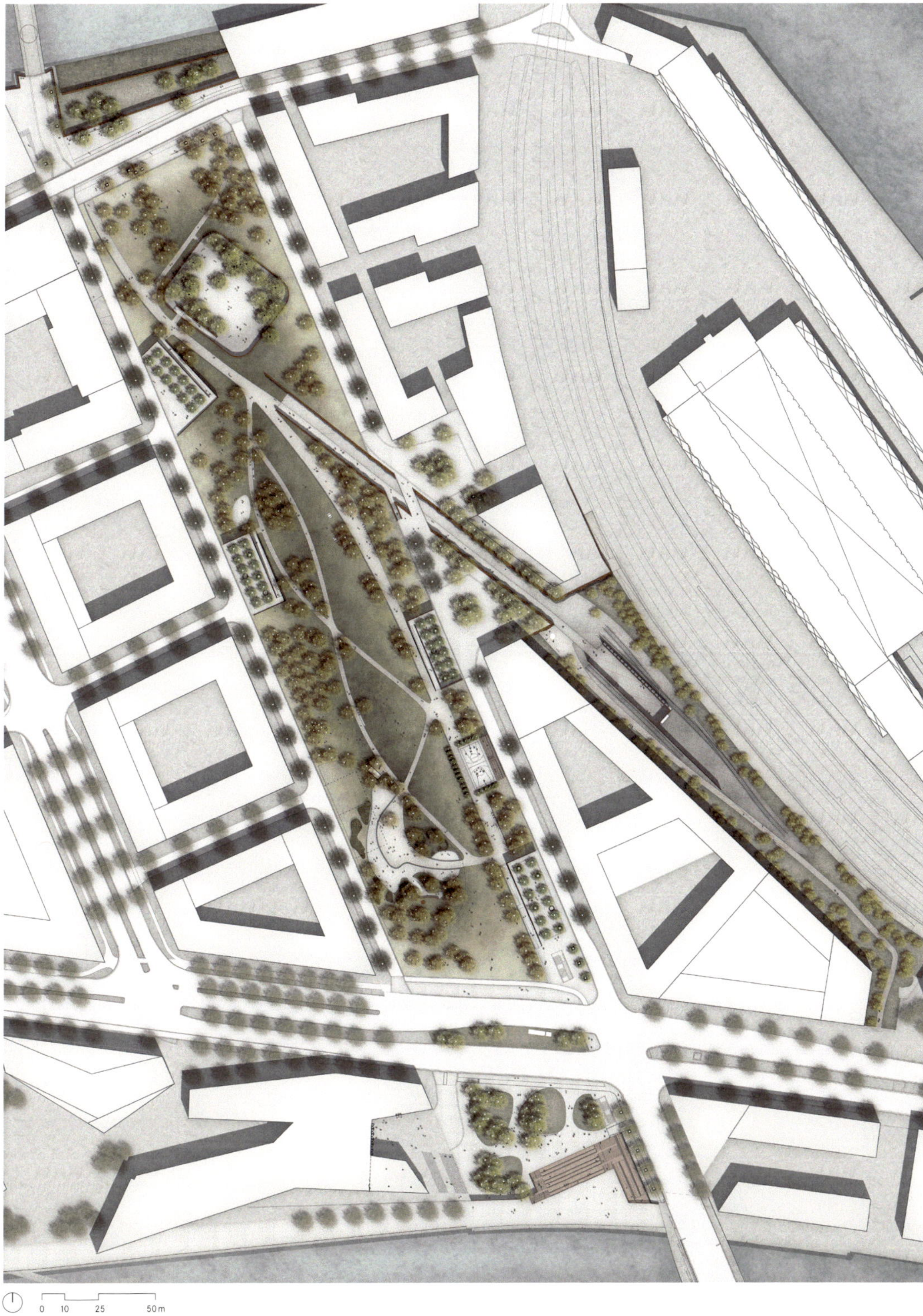
0 10 25 50 m

DER SPIEGEL

1

Clinker brick as a reinterpretation of an old building tradition: A new type of clinker brick was developed for the project that can be stacked to create parapets or retaining walls. Their honeycomb structure also has a decorative effect and is based, like many other walls in Hafencity, on Hamburg's tradition of brick expressionism.

1 Mold, blank, and form studies
2 Color studies with local earth
3 Model study of the bastions

2

3

The Park Level includes follies for visitors to discover, including small fenced gardens in which densely planted hornbeams suggest what would seem to be an area of "wilderness."

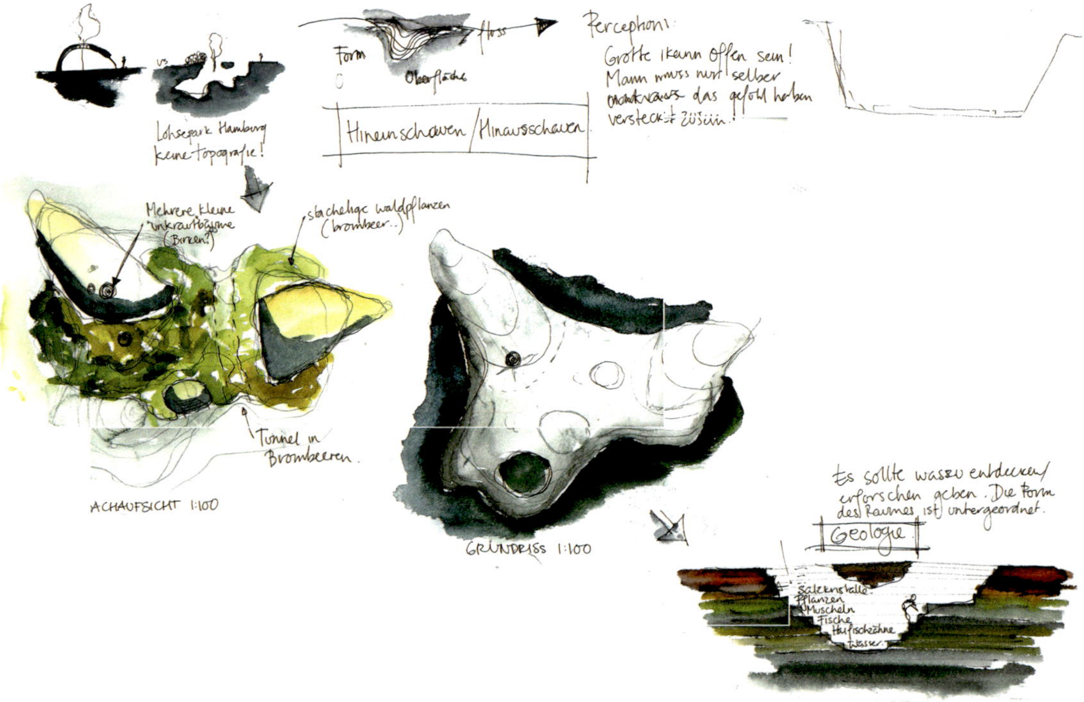
Lohsepark Hamburg
keine Topografie!
Hineinschauen/Hinausschauen
Tunnel in Brombeeren
GRUNDRISS 1:100
Geologie

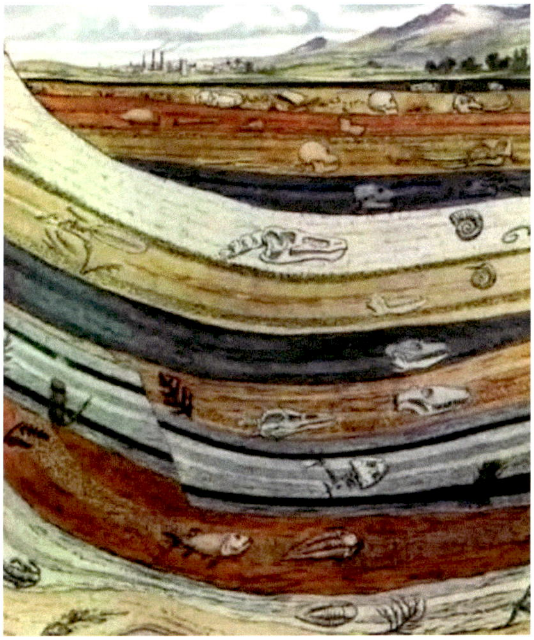

The grotto as a window into a possible geological past

The Historical Level: The site where the Lohsepark now stands once included part of the Hannoversche Bahnhof, the Hanover main station from which more than eight thousand Jews, Sinti, and Roma were deported in the period 1940–1945. The monument to Hanover Station is an integral element of the park.

Lohsepark, Hamburg
The City's Collective Memory

The platform with the historic tracks has been carefully repaired. The spot is defined by a commemorative table and twenty panels bearing the names of the deportees, a dignified memorial to the victims and a reminder of a dark chapter in history. The surrounding area has been designed with birches, robinias, and wild roses: pioneer species that are commonly found on areas of track ballast. The "joint" articulated by folded retaining walls connects the platform of the memorial burdened with history with Lohseplatz as part of the former station forecourt across the park and also creates links to the City Level.

“We do not approach design in the traditional sense by sitting in front of a white sheet of paper and sketching a park or a courtyard. To us, designing is a collective act that involves many partners and is primarily to be understood as a process—starting from a **paradigm** by way of a **physical working model** and, finally, the built land-scape **intended as a model.**” (gv)

A Postscript to the Intention

This book is not based on a predetermined structure. It has grown over time and found its present form in a long process of additions, omissions, and compression. The intention to dispense with a rigid sequence of topics, categories, and chapters and–instead–give priority to an intuitive order is the consequence of the editors' insight that there should be no limits to the principles of curiosity and discovery. Rather, it should be emphasized that the landscape itself is an aggregate whose parts and their interaction we are urged to explore and develop. It is up to the readers to find their way through the book: linearly, thematically, or by random discovery. The collection is consistent but incomplete. It is your task to continue and link the individual parts of the canon thus revealed!

Lars Müller

MODEL, TYPE
AND SCALE

Acknowledgments

Many responded to our call for “complicity”: the numerous authors (see page 2), the interviewees Katja Gentinetta, Dehlia Hannah, Chris Dercon, Roger Diener, and Olafur Eliasson as well as artists Roni Horn, Marguerite Humeau, Julius von Bismarck, Julian Charrière, Olafur Eliasson, Andreas Greiner, Dafi Kühne, and Christian Vogt. In addition, the countless helpers at the ETH Zurich Chair of Landscape Architecture and the offices of VOGT Landschaftsarchitekten: Agnieszka Banach, Lidia Bischoff, Jonas Erni, Claudia Gebert, Maria Silvia Giulietti Cemak, Fabrizio Gramegna, Stella Hauff, Scott Hayworth, Sven Högger, Michelle Ineson, Andraž Keršič, Andreas Klein, Andreas Moroder, Noël Picco, Lukas Ryffel, and Laura Schöngart. All of them have their share in this extraordinary work and we thank them for their zeal and their trust in us. Last but not least, we thank Coralie Berchtold and Amalia Bonsack and the Team of Lars Müller Publishers for their persistence and their faith in our project as well as Network City and Landscape (NSL) of ETH Zurich for their kind support.

Günther Vogt
Thomas Kissling

Editors

Günther Vogt (* 1957) Günther Vogt's training at Gartenbauschule Oeschberg provided the practical basis for his intensive landscape work. His knowledge of vegetation and his skills in cultivation continue to be the very cornerstones of his work. His studies with Peter Erni, Jürg Altherr, and Dieter Kienast at Interkantonales Technikum Rapperswil, combined the disciplines of culture, design, and natural sciences. VOGT Landschaftsarchitekten emerged from the office partnership with Dieter Kienast in 2000. With projects such as the Tate Modern in London, Allianz Arena in Munich, or the Masoala Rainforest Hall at the Zurich Zoo, the firm has achieved international recognition. Its work is characterized by the dialogue established between the various disciplines and its close cooperation with artists. Since 2005, Günther Vogt has been pursuing a combination of teaching, practice, and research with his chair at the Institute of Landscape Architecture at the Swiss Federal Institute of Technology (ETH) in Zurich. As a passionate collector and keen traveler, he is looking for ways to read, interpret, and describe landscapes, and finding answers to questions about future forms of urban coexistence. In 2012, Günther Vogt was awarded the Prix Meret Oppenheim by the Federal Office of Culture. > (gv) on pp. 68, 110, 182, 239, 325, 439, 462, 559

Thomas Kissling (* 1980) studied architecture at the ETH Zurich, having previously trained as a draftsman, and graduated in 2010 under the tutelage of Prof. Wolfgang Schett. He has worked as a research assistant since 2010 and as a research associate at the Chair of Prof. Günther Vogt at the ETH Zurich since 2016. His teaching and research focus on transformation processes in the Alpine landscape and topics relating to design methodology at the interface between digital and analog technology and practice. He is coeditor of the 2015 publication *Landscape as a Cabinet of Curiosities,* which is a compilation of five conversations with Günther Vogt. > (tk) on pp. 120, 132, 172

VOGT

The work of VOGT Landschaftsarchitekten focuses on urban landscapes. The international team of VOGT has been designing, planning, and implementing national and international projects at various scales for twenty years. Its work ranges from small town squares to metropolitan parks and is carried out in cooperation with renowned architecture firms and artists.

VOGT's permanent employees include landscape architects, architects, botanists, and urban planners who contribute their expert knowledge to the development of its multilayered projects. VOGT Landschaftsarchitekten was founded in Zurich in 2000 and expanded to include offices in London (2008), Berlin (2010), and Paris (2019).

Attached to the firm is, moreover, the Case Studio VOGT, as an interface between the practice and the theoretical and investigative studies of Günther Vogt's chair at ETH Zurich. As a platform for exhibitions and debates, the Case Studio also is an instrument for the training and further education of the employees, who play a central role in the corporate culture of VOGT.

Authors

Maria Alexandrescu (* 1989) studied architecture at the University of Waterloo and landscape architecture at the Technical University of Delft, where she graduated *cum laude* in 2015. Since 2016, she has been working with Vogt Landscape London, and since 2019, with Vogt Paysage–Urbanisme Paris. Maria also teaches Design Studio 3 at Oxford Brooks University School of Architecture, exploring themes such as geopolitics and logistics, bodies and (re-)production through specific architectural interventions in urban peripheries.
> (ma) on pp. 290, 336

Laure Baretaud (* 1979) studied geography and urban planning at Paris-IV La Sorbonne and landscape at the Academie Van Bouwkunst in Amsterdam and at the École Nationale Supérieure du Paysage de Versailles, where she graduated with honors in 2007. Before joining Vogt Landscape London in 2013, she worked for both the public and private sector in China, Netherlands, and France. From 2015, she co-led the London office with Martijn Slob while volunteering for the botanical gardens in Kew and Chelsea and taught landscape at Kingston School of Art. In 2019, she opened the French office Vogt Paysage–Urbanisme in Paris. > (lb) on pp. 226, 270, 290, 302, 336, 346

Coralie Berchtold (* 1992) studied architecture at the Swiss Federal Institute of Technology in Lausanne (EPFL) and Zurich (ETHZ). Her diploma thesis focused on public space in Zurich and won the 3rd Heinrich Hatt-Bucher Prize in 2018. After working professionally in various capacities in Switzerland and Tokyo, she is now a freelance architect and collaborates with young architectural firms in Zurich. Since 2018, she has been a research assistant at the Chair of Prof. Günther Vogt at the ETH Zurich, where she has been involved with the publication *Mutation and Morphosis.* > (cb) on p. 252

Amalia Bonsack (* 1991) studied architecture at the Swiss Federal Institute of Technology in Lausanne (EPFL) and Zurich (ETHZ), where she graduated in 2017 having specialized in urban design. She has gained a range of professional experience abroad (USA, Spain, Portugal) and collaborates with various architecture collectives in Switzerland. Since 2018, she has worked as a teaching and research assistant at the Chair of Prof. Günther Vogt at ETH Zurich. Besides her involvement in the publication *Mutation and Morphosis,* she is in charge of the course Territory of the City, which deals with current transformation processes in European metropolitan landscapes. > (ab) on pp. 120, 132, 172

Maren Brakebusch (* 1974) studied landscape architecture at Leibniz University in Hanover. From 1998 to 2002, she was project manager at the Berlin office of Kamel Louafi handling a variety of projects for Expo 2000 and subsequently Deutsche Messe AG. Since 2002, she has managed projects for Vogt Landschaftsarchitekten in Zurich and has run the office there since 2009. In 2014, she became VOGT's overall managing director and a member of the office management team, which she has headed since 2017. Besides giving talks and sitting on various juries, she has had a lectureship at the Potsdam University of Applied Sciences since 2017, where she teaches aspiring architects.
> (mb) on p. 580

Violeta Burckhardt (* 1987) studied architecture at UNAM in Mexico City and urban design at TU Berlin and Tongji University in Shanghai. She currently works for Vogt Landschaftsarchitekten in Zurich, where she designs projects geared to research and practice for the Case Studio. Based on her experience in film and art production, she has curated several cultural events and was invited, as a member of the Vogt team, to help devise the concept for the exhibition *Environment[al].* She is currently developing various exhibition projects investigating the shift in ecosystems caused by human activities. > (vb) on p. 314

Lars Ruge (* 1969) studied landscape architecture at Leibniz University in Hanover after training in arboriculture in Hamburg. From 1998 to 2005, he worked in the office of Landschaftsarchitektur + Ökologie in Darmstadt, where he was primarily involved in new construction projects. In 2005 he moved to VOGT and took over a project team, expanding his areas of responsibility to include urban development, large-scale design projects, strategic planning, and issues relating to the preservation of historical monuments. He is also regularly involved in jury activities, gives lectures, and applies his expertise in an advisory capacity. He has been a member of the office management team since 2009 and has run the Zurich office since 2016. > (lr) on pp. 16, 38, 52, 80, 96, 142, 154, 264, 364, 374, 410, 450, 472, 482, 490, 506, 524, 536, 548, 572, 600

Alexandra Savtchenko-Belskaia (* 1985) is an architect, artist, and writer. After gaining a bachelor of fine arts at the University of Auckland, New Zealand, she codirected the nonprofit gallery Newcall and developed an installation practice focusing on latent cultural narratives within the built environment. Since gaining the AA diploma in 2018, she has continued to deepen her practice through drawing and writing. She is currently landscape architect assistant at Vogt Landscape in London and teaching assistant in the Environmental and Technical Studies program at the Architectural Association London.
> (asb) on pp. 190, 216, 252, 380

Roland Charles Shaw (* 1984) read Oriental Studies (Sanskrit and ancient Greek) at Oxford (St. John's College) and Munich (LMU) universities. In 2014 he completed a diploma in architecture at the Architectural Association in London (AA dipl.), where he was also coeditor of the student magazine *AArchitecture.* He has been an academic assistant at the Chair of Prof. Günther Vogt at the Swiss Federal Institute of Technology Zurich since 2015, where he is responsible for the elective course Urban Food and modules in digital media.
> (rs) on pp. 28, 396

Martijn Slob (* 1982) studied landscape architecture at Wageningen University, where he graduated in 2009 (MSc). He has worked as a landscape architect in New York, Zurich, and London, working on projects of all typologies and scales. He joined Vogt in 2011, initially in the Zurich office before subsequently moving to London. He is currently the head of Vogt Landscape London and a member of the management team.
> (ms) on pp. 190, 202, 426

Daia Stutz (* 1985) studied landscape architecture at the University of Applied Sciences in Rapperswil as well as urban design at the Harvard University Graduate School of Design, where he graduated with distinction. Previously he worked as a project manager at Vogt Landscape Architects in Zurich. In 2013, he joined the Chair of Prof. Günther Vogt at the Swiss Federal Institute of Technology Zurich as a teaching and research assistant. In 2016 he founded his own practice, S2L Landscape Architects, together with Jan Stadelmann. > (ds) on p. 590

Ralf G. Voss (* 1967), grew up in Fischerhude, a village on the North German Plain. After studying landscape architecture in Hanover and Edinburgh, he worked for seven years as a landscape architect in Hamburg and has been with Vogt Landschaftsarchitekten in Zurich since 2003. He supervises projects through all the different phases from the development of the master plan through to its final execution. His work ranges from designing open space for urban planning projects (Olympic Village, London; Šmartinska, Ljubljana; Carlsberg, Copenhagen) to projects with a distinct historical setting (Munich Kunstareal; Private Clinic, Hohenegg; Haliç, Istanbul).
> (rv) on p. 498

Conversation partners

Chris Dercon (* 1958) In 2016, at the end of his tenure as director of Tate Modern in London, Chris published the book *Tate Modern: Building a Museum for the 21st Century* in collaboration with Nicholas Serota. At the helm of the Volksbuehne in Berlin, he developed projects for the former airport site at Tempelhof. As president of the Réunion des Musées Nationaux and the Grand Palais in Paris, he is responsible for the renovation and development of the Grand Palais.
He became director of Museum Boijmans Van Beuningen, Rotterdam, in 1996, working with Robbrecht en Daem on the extension of the museum: while in Rotterdam, he advised Rem Koolhaas's Office for Metropolitan Architecture on museum infrastructures. As director of Haus der Kunst, Munich, from 2003 to 2011, Dercon developed exhibitions of Droog Design, Konstantin Grcic, Herzog & de Meuron, Rem Koolhaas, and Carlo Molino.

Roger Diener (* 1950) studied at the ETH Zurich and the École Polytechnique Fédérale de Lausanne (EPFL), where his teachers included Aldo Rossi and Luigi Snozzi. In 1976 he began working in the office founded by his father, Marcus Diener, which he has been running since 1980. Following a series of guest professorships at EPFL, Harvard University, and universities in Vienna, Amsterdam, and Copenhagen, he was professor of design at EPFL from 1987 to 1989. From 1999 to 2015, he held a professorship at ETH Zurich, where, together with Marcel Meili, Jacques Herzog, and Pierre de Meuron, he taught and published at Studio Basel. From 2005 to 2013 he was a member of the Council for the Preservation of Historic Buildings and Monuments in Berlin. He has been a member of the Swiss Federal Commission for Monument Preservation since 2013 and of the Zurich Commission for Monument Preservation since 2018. Roger Diener has received numerous awards, including the French Grande Médaille d'or d'Architecture, the Prix Meret Oppenheim, and the Heinrich Tessenow Gold Medal.

Olafur Eliasson (* 1967) grew up in Iceland and Denmark. In 1995 he founded Studio Olafur Eliasson in Berlin, which today comprises more than one hundred team members, including craftsmen, architects, archivists, researchers, administrators, cooks, programmers, art historians, and specialized technicians. Since the mid-1990s, Eliasson has realized numerous exhibitions and projects around the world. His projects in public space include *Green river,* realized in various cities between 1998 and 2001; *The New York City Waterfalls,* 2008; and *Ice Watch,* for which Eliasson and geologist Minik Rosing transported massive blocks of glacial ice from Greenland to Copenhagen (2014), Paris (2015), and London (2018) to raise awareness of climate change. In 2012 Eliasson set up the social business Little Sun, and in 2014 he and architect Sebastian Behmann founded Studio Other Spaces, an office for art and architecture.

Katja Gentinetta (* 1968) studied philosophy, history, and German language and literature in Zurich and Paris. She has a doctorate in political philosophy and teaches at the universities of St. Gallen, Zurich, and Lucerne. She has a regular column on business and economics in the *NZZ am Sonntag* and, together with editor in chief Eric Gujer, hosts the TV talk show *NZZ Standpunkte.* She is also one of the regular guests on SRF 1's *Der Philosophische Stammtisch.* Sitting on various boards in both a supervisory and trustee capacity and as a member of the International Committee of the Red Cross (ICRC), she is directly involved in shaping corporate strategy. She has written several books on social and political themes, most recently *Worum es im Kern geht* (2017), in which she addresses the crises we are currently facing. She regularly publishes, lectures, and moderates meetings on important economic, political, and social questions both in Switzerland and abroad.

Dehlia Hannah (* 1978) Ph.D., is a philosopher and curator. She is currently Mads Øvlisen Postdoctoral Fellow in Art and Natural Sciences at the Department of Chemistry and Biosciences at Aalborg University-Copenhagen and affiliated faculty of the School of Earth and Space Exploration at Arizona State University. She holds a Ph.D. in philosophy from Columbia University, with specializations in philosophy of science, aesthetics, and philosophy of nature. Her forthcoming book *Performative Experiments* examines contemporary artworks that take the form of scientific experiments. Her most recent project, *A Year Without a Winter* (Columbia University Press, 2018), reframes contemporary imaginaries of climate crisis by revisiting the literary and environmental aftermaths of the 1815 eruption of Mount Tambora. Past exhibitions include *Placing the Golden Spike: Landscapes of the Anthropocene* (Milwaukee, 2015), *Control: Experiment* (Stockholm, 2016) and *Pareidolia* (Copenhagen, 2017). Her current research examines the role of imaginary places, creatures, and technologies in the history of philosophy.

Artists

Julius von Bismarck (* 1983) currently lives in Berlin. He is a graduate of the Berlin University of the Arts (UDK) and the Institute for Spatial Experiments founded by Olafur Eliasson, who was his teacher until his Master's degree in 2013. Associating visual arts to other fields of research and experimentation, such as physical and social sciences, Julius von Bismarck's artistic practice can take on various forms– from installations to happenings, from sculpture to land art. It is defined by an in-depth and complex exploration of the phenomena of perception or the representation and reconstruction of reality. The artist has had numerous solo shows, including at the Palais de Tokyo in Paris (2019), Kunstpalais Erlangen (2018), Städtische Galerie Wolfsburg (2017), and Kunstverein Göttingen (2015).

Julian Charrière (* 1987) is a French Swiss artist based in Berlin, whose work bridges the realms of environmental science and cultural history. Marshaling performance, sculpture, and photography, his projects often stem from fieldwork in remote locations with acute geophysical identities such as volcanoes, ice fields, and radioactive sites. To date, his work has explored post-romantic constructions of "nature," staging tensions between deep or geological timescales and those relating to mankind. Charrière's approach further reflects upon the mythos of the quest and its objects in a globalized age. Deploying seemingly perennial imagery to contemporary ends, his interventions at the borderline of mysticism and the material encapsulate our fraught relations with place today.

Olafur Eliasson (* 1967) > p. 622

Andreas Greiner (* 1979) graduated from Olafur Eliasson's Institute of Spatial Experiments at the University of Fine Arts in Berlin in 2013. Before embarking on fine arts, his fascination with the human body initially led him to a three-year study of figurative sculpture and then medicine with an emphasis on human anatomy. His creative practice pushes the boundaries of classical parameters in sculpture by incorporating dynamic, natural, and living variables. In cocreation with natural phenomena, unpredictable and volatile moments become part of the artworks. The content of his artistic research focuses on anthropogenic influences on nature's evolution and its change of aesthetics and form. Andreas Greiner often collaborates with scientists and experts from different fields such as (micro-)biologists, physicists, architects, and computer scientists. He is part of the artist collectives A/A and Das Numen.

Roni Horn lives and works in New York City. Her oeuvre focuses on conceptually oriented photography, sculpture, books, and drawing. Since 1975 Horn has traveled extensively in the more remote landscapes of Iceland–these solitary experiences have long been important influences in her life and work. Literature and Horn's prodigious reading have had a similarly profound impact on her work across various media. The sculpture is often paired or doubled, as are the drawings and photographs. Recent solo exhibitions include: Tate Modern; Whitney Museum of American Art; Centre Pompidou; Kunsthalle Bregenz; Kunsthalle Hamburg; Kunsthalle Basel; Fundació Joan Miró, Barcelona; De Pont Foundation, Tilburg; Fondation Beyeler; Glenstone Museum, Potomac, MD; Pinakothek der Moderne, Munich; and the Drawing Institute at the Menil Collection, Houston, TX.

Marguerite Humeau (* 1986) lives and works in London. She received her MA from the Royal College of Art, London, in 2011. Humeau's work stages the crossing of great distances in time and space, transitions between animal and mineral, and encounters between personal desires and natural forces. The work explores the possibility of communication between worlds and the means by which knowledge is generated in the absence of evidence or through the impossibility of reaching the object of investigation. Humeau weaves factual events into speculative narratives, therefore enabling unknown, invisible, extinct forms of life to erupt in grandiose splendor. Combining prehistory, occult biology, and science fiction in a disconcerting spectacle, the works resuscitate the past, conflate subterranean and subcutaneous, all the while updating the quest genre for the information age.

Dafi Kühne (* 1982) is a poster designer and letterpress printer from Glarus and Zurich. In his factory studio in Näfels, he has amassed over 25 tons of letterpress material, with which he produces typographic poster designs using old-fashioned printing technology: traditional lead typesetting, wood type, linocut, laser-cut wood panels, plexiglass, card, molded plastic letters, or pantograph-milled letters. Although some of the technology is distinctly outdated, his posters appear fresh, topical, and visually concise. Kühne has lectured and held teaching positions at universities in Switzerland, Germany, Italy, Great Britain, and the USA. Since 2016 he has offered a two-week workshop in his studio every summer, attended by international design students. His posters have appeared in exhibitions and publications in Switzerland and abroad. In 2016 his first artist's monograph, *True Print,* was published by Lars Müller Publishers.

Christian Vogt (* 1946) Since the late 1960s, Christian Vogt has produced a photographic oeuvre impressive for its creative inventiveness and its unexpected twists. He is a master of the art of photographic haiku and a virtuoso of associative story telling with pictures. To Vogt, photography is never a mere reproduction but always a speculation about the meaning of the story hidden behind the surface, a reflection on the subjectivity of the photographic eye, in the awareness that the actual picture only emerges through the perception of the beholder... (Martin Gasser)

Publications, Exhibitions, Colloquia

Chair of Günther Vogt ETH Zurich

Publications

Simon Kretz and Lukas Kueng, eds., *Urbane Qualitäten: Ein Handbuch am Beispiel der Metropolitanregion* Zürich, research group and author's collective: Marc Angélil, Rebecca Bornhauser, Kees Christiaanse, Maik Hömke, Thomas Kissling, Philipp Klaus, Simon Kretz, Lukas Kueng, Vittorio Magnago Lampugnani, Gabriela Muri-Koller, Rahel Nüssli, Verena Poloni Esquivié, Christian Schmid, Carolin Ting, and Günther Vogt (Zurich: Hochparterre, 2016)

Günther Vogt, *Landscape as a Cabinet of Curiosities: In Search of a Position,* ed. Rebecca Bornhauser and Thomas Kissling (Zurich: Lars Müller Publishers, 2015)

Republic of Common Ground: Un-common News–Un-common Venice, newspaper edited by Rebecca Bornhauser, Nicola Eiffler, Thomas Kissling, and Günther Vogt, Participating Project to the 13th International Architecture Exhibition, La Biennale di Venezia, a project by the Chair of Landscape Architecture Günther Vogt, ETH Zurich and Case Studio VOGT, 2012

Franziska Bark Hagen, *Versuche das Glück im Garten zu finden* (Baden: Lars Müller Publishers, 2011)

Jürgen Krusche, *Strassenräume Berlin Shanghai Tokyo Zürich: Eine foto-ethnografische Untersuchung* (Baden: Lars Müller Publishers, 2011)

Dominique Ghiggi, *Tree Nurseries: Cultivating the Urban Jungle* (Baden: Lars Müller Publishers, 2010)

Jürgen Krusche and Frank Roost, *Tokyo: Die Strasse als gelebter Raum* (Baden: Lars Müller Publishers, 2010)

Exhibitions, Colloquia

Common Water: The Future of an Alpine Resource, NSL Colloquium, ETH Zurich, October 20–21, 2017

The Alps as Common Ground: Position Lyon, exhibition, Case Studio Vogt, Zurich, November 2016

Dreiländerbahn Scuol–Mals–Landeck, discussion forum and exhibition, HTW Chur, September 21–27, 2016

Roma 20–25: New Lifecycles for the Metropolis, Exhibition Contribution *Changing Landscape,* MAXXI–Museo nazionale delle arti del XXI secolo, Rome, December 19, 2015–January 17, 2016

Positions–Metropolitan Milan in Metamorphosis, Istituto Svizzero, Rome, June 26–July 22, 2015

Un-Common Venice, a project by the Chair of Landscape Architecture Günther Vogt ETH Zurich and Case Studio VOGT, Participating Project to the 13th International Architecture Exhibition, La Biennale di Venezia, August 29–November 25, 2012

VOGT

Publications

Günther Vogt, ed., *Wunderlust/Wanderkammer* (Zurich: Lars Müller Publishers, 2016)

Günther Vogt, ed., *Miniature and Panorama: Vogt Landscape Architects; Projects 2000–2012* (Zurich: Lars Müller Publishers, 2012)

Günther Vogt and Marcel Meili, *Fünf Orte in der Schweiz* (Zurich: MMMP, Vogt Landschaftsarchitekten, 2012)

Alice Foxley, *Distance & Engagement: Walking, Thinking and Making Landscapes*; *Vogt Landscape Architects* (Baden: Lars Müller Publishers, 2010)

Günther Vogt, ed., *Miniatur und Panorama: Vogt Landscape Architects; Projects 2000–2006* (Baden: Lars Müller Publishers, 2006)

Exhibitions, Colloquia

Fragile Landscapes, OCiam International Exhibitions, International Comparison of Ideas, Piacenza, August 27–September 12, 2019

Environment[al], exhibition, SCI-Arc, Los Angeles, June 15–August 26, 2018

Dan Graham–with an intervention by Günther Vogt, gta exhibition, ETH Zurich, April 15–June 21, 2015

The Roof Garden Commission: Dan Graham with Günther Vogt, installation on the roof of the Metropolitan Museum of Art, New York, April 29–November 2, 2014

Laubvulkane, part of the exhibition *Parfum – Verpackte Verführung,* Museum Bellerive, Museum für Gestaltung Zürich, December 2, 2011–April 9, 2012

Four Tor Panorama, part of the exhibition *Switzerland: Design for Life,* A Foundation, London, June 19–July 1, 2010

Spiegel Nebel Wind, installation as part of the exhibition *Nature Design: Von Inspiration zu Innovation,* Museum für Gestaltung, Zurich, August 10–December 2, 2007

Magnifying Glass and Binoculars: Miniature and Panorama, exhibition, Aedes Land, Berlin, March 24–June 3, 2007

Smells & Sounds: The Invisible in Public Space, interventions in public space, Zurich, October 2006; Tokyo, October–November 2006

WUNDERKAMM

PALFINGER

Bücherkarton

Image Credits

Unless otherwise indicated, the copyright for the illustrations, plans and photographs is held by Vogt Landschaftsarchitekten AG.

(l) = left
(r) = right
(t) = top
(b) = bottom
(m) = middle

Cover image, embossing: London's street network merges with the contour lines of the Jungfraujoch and the Aletsch glacier. Mapping by Lukas Ryffel, Institute of Landscape Architecture, ETH Zurich
7 Lukas Ryffel, ETH Zürich, 2019
15 © Anne Gabriel-Jürgens
16 Oswald Heer, *Die Urwelt der Schweiz. Zürich: Druck und Verlag von Friedrich Schulthess,* 1883. ETH-Bibliothek Zürich, Rar 1586, http://doi.org/10.3931/e-rara-19962 / Public Domain
18 (t) Source: Bundesamt für Landestopografie, *Der Zuger See vor ca. 15'000 Jahren*
18 (b) Paul Duvigneaud, *La synthèse écologique: populations, communautés, écosystème, biosphère, noosphère,* 1974
19 (t) Photographer unknown
19 (b) Source: Ralph Works Chaney, *Redwoods of the Past* (Berkley: Save-the-Redwoods League, 1947)
25 (t) Photographer unknown, *BioScience,* vol. 37, no. 8
25 (b), 26–7 © Giuseppe Micciché
28 Unknown, *Pyramides d'Euseigne,* ca. 1940, Lausanne: Edition O. Satori, Postcard, 9 × 14 cm, ETH-Bibliothek Zürich, Bildarchiv, PK_012360, Public Domain
30 Julien Seguinot, *Advance and retreat of the Alpine glaciers during the last glacial cycle,* 2018, Videostills, © Julien Seguinot
31 Unknown, *Table sur moraine médianne, M. Forel, glacier du Rhône. Lugeon, Maurice. 30. VIII.1900,* photography, 13 cm × 18 cm, ETH-Bibliothek Zürich, Bildarchiv, Hs_1458-GK-B001-1900-21, Public Domain
32–3 *Geologische Karte der Schweiz,* 1975, © Atlas der Schweiz, Tafel 8
34 Hartmut Leser, *Moränen in und um einen Gletscher, Geomorphologie, Geographisches Seminar,* 2003, © Westermann Gruppe
35 Swissair Photo AG, *Konkordiaplatz, Aletschgletscher,* 1973, photography: transparency positive, colored, 23 × 23 cm, ETH-Bibliothek Zürich Bildarchiv, © CC BY-SA 4.0, Swissair Photo AG
36 (t) Michel Bonvin, *Walter Förderer's Saint Nicolas Church in Hérémence,* © Michel Bonvin
36 (b) Walter Maria Förderer, Eglise Saint-Nicolas, 1967–71, Schweizer Heimatschutz, photo: Sebastian Heeb
37 Swissair Photo AG, *Grande Dixence, Staumauer (Hérémence),* 1977, photography: transparency positive, colored, 23 × 23 cm, ETH-Bibliothek Zürich Bildarchiv, © CC BY-SA 4.0, Swissair Photo AG
38 Unknown, *Laibach und Umbegung aus der Vogelschau,* 1916, Postcard, Public Domain
40 (t) Source: *Surveying and Mapping Authority of the Republic of Slovenia: Ljubljana DEM,* Ljubljana Land cadastre, Ljubljana Topographic data, 2016
40 (b) Source unknown
42 (t) Source unknown
43 (tl) *Žlebiči (Rills),* The Karst living museum, Sežana, © TIC Sežana, photographer: Stojan Gorup
43 (tr) *Kal (pond),* The Karst living museum, Sežana, © TIC Sežana, photographer: Stojan Gorup
44 Iztok Sajko, *River basin of Ljubljanica,* Ivan Gams, *Karst in Slovenia in time and space,* 2004, Založba ZRC, Ljubljana, © ZRC SAZU
45 (t) Maks Šeber, *Razglednica Postojnske jame,* 1910, Postojna, Public Domain
45 (b) Source: Bruce W. Hayward, 2012
46 (t) Source: *Surveying and Mapping Authority of the Republic of Slovenia: Slovenia DEM,* Slovenia Topographic data, 2016
46 (bl) Kotel, Zadnji kraj, 2018, Otok, © Notranjska regional park, photographer: Tine Schein
46 (br) Karst field, 2017, Ponikve pri Preserju, Jana Vidic, © Ljubljansko barje Nature Park
47 (bl) Zoran Leban Trojar, *Keršič,* www.igslovenia.si, © Zoran Leban Trojar
47 (br) Karen Baijens, Ljubljana, 2016, Public Domain
48 (t) Source: *Map of natural potential vegetation of FSR Yugoslavia,* Univerziteta Kiril i Metodjie u Skopju, 1983
52, 55, 60–1, 63–4, 67 © Christian Vogt
56 (t) James Geikie, *Map of Europe showing the extent of the glaciated areas at the climax of the Ice Age,* 1881, Public Domain
56 (b) Karl Gripp, *Glaciologische und geologische Ergebnisse der Hamburgischen Spitzbergen-Expedition 1927* (Hamburg, 1929), 191
57 Source: *Findlinge Europas,* 2019, Wikipedia
58 (t) Unknown, *Geologischer Aufschluss. Moräne bei St. Anna,* Zürich, 1912, photography: paper print, 12 × 17 cm, Zürich, © ETH Bibliothek, Bildarchiv
66 *Géographie des plantes équinoxiales: tableau physique des Andes et pays voisins dressé d'après des observations et des mesures prises sur les lieux depuis le 10e degré de latitude boréale... / par Alexandre de Humboldt et Aimé Bonpland ; esquissé et rédigé par Humboldt, dessiné par Schönbergeret Turpin,* 1805, Bibliothèque nationale de France, département Cartes et plans, GE C-11167
68 (t) Unknown, *Luzern, Schweizerhofquai mit Pilatus,* 1910–1920, Postcard, 10 × 15 cm, ETH-Bibliothek, Bildarchiv, Public Domain
68 (b) SALU F2a/Strassen/Haldenstrasse 4a, © Stadtarchiv Luzern
70 (t) Unknown, *Luzern, Promenade vor dem Hotel Schweizerhof,* before 19.5.1915, Postcard, 10 × 15 cm, ETH-Bibliothek Zürich, Bildarchiv, Public Domain
70 (b) *Innenraum des Kursaals in Luzern,* © Stadtarchiv Luzern, photo: Josef Willmann-Ronca
71 Source: Clement Cruttwell, Europe in Atlas to Cruttwell's Gazetteer, 1799, 35.5 × 40.6 cm, Public Domain
72 J. C. R. Colomb, *Imperial Federation, map of the world showing the extent of the British Empire in 1886,* 1886, 63 × 86 cm, Boston Public Library, Norman B. Leventhal Map Center Collection, Public Domain
73 (l) Decimus Burton and Richard Turner, *Palm House at the Royal Botanic Gardens, Kew,* 1840–48, McGill University Library, Montreal, Canada, Public Domain
73 (r) Louis Figuier, *The Vegetable World: Being a History of Plants, with Their Botanical Descriptions and Peculiar Properties* (London: Cassell, Petter, and Galpin, 1869) © Harold B. Lee Library
74–5 *Brockhaus' Konversations-Lexikon,* vol. 12, 1892, Public Domain
76 Louis Van Houtte, *Flore des serres et des jardins de l'Europe,* vol. 22, 1877, Public Domain
77–8 Source: Gian-Reto Walther et al., *Palms Tracking Climate Change, Global Ecology and Biogeography 16,* 2007
79 Amalia Bonsack, ETH Zürich, 2018
80 Archiv Kloster Einsiedeln, Creative Commons Schweiz CC BY-NC-SA 2.5
82 Thomas Kissling, ETH Zürich, 2018
83 (l) *Sihlhochtal,* 1910, © Karl Hensler, Einsiedeln (Saurer 2002), 146
83 (r) Laurenz Landenberger, *Einsiedeln aus der Vogelperspektive,* 1912, Lithography, 32.8 × 50 cm, Staatsarchiv Schwyz, Quellennachweis (STASZ.SG.CII.4081) © Staatsarchiv Schwyz
83 (b) Source: Susanna Etter, ETH Zürich
84 (t) Pater Sidler/C. Steinauer, Einsiedeln, 1868, © Archiv Kloster Einsiedeln
84 (bl) *Welttheater Einsiedeln 1930,* before 7.9.1930, Postcard, 9 × 14 cm, ETH-Bibliothek Zürich, Bildarchiv, Public Domain, Jean Gaberell
84 (br) *Prozession, Versammlung auf dem Klosterplatz,* ca. 1900, Archiv Kloster Einsiedeln, Creative Commons Schweiz CC BY-NC-SA 2.5
85 (t) *Einsiedeln, Kloster, Etzel,* before 1.6.1918, Postcard, 10 × 15 cm, ETH-Bibliothek Zürich, Bildarchiv, Public Domain, Photoglob AG (Zürich)

85 (b) Klosterplatz an Christi Himmelfahrt, 1977, Archiv Kloster Einsiedeln, © Archiv Kloster Einsiedeln
86 (tl) Archiv Kloster Einsiedeln, Creative Commons Schweiz CC BY-NC-SA 2.5
86 (b) Die geplante Neugestaltung des Hauptplatzes, Graphic: Total Real
89–93 © Christian Vogt
94–5 Franz Noë, *Geologische Übersichtskarte der Alpen. Wien: Ed. Hölzel,* 1890. ETH-Bibliothek Zürich, K 281029, https://doi.org/10.3931/e-rara-22886 / Public Domain
96 © Tourismus Biel Seeland
98 (t) Nachlass Prof. Dr. Robert Müller, *Grosse Überschwemmung,* 1944, II. Juragewässerkorrektion, © ETH-Bibliothek
98 (m) *Diagram of oxbow meanders,* Hyde Collection, Case Western Reserve University © The Jesse Earl Hyde Collection
98 (b) *Entwicklung von Altarm und Altwasser,* source: Stua Köln nach DVWK 1991
99 (t) Source: © CNES, swisstopo, NPOC
100 (t) Source: © swisstopo
101 (t, m) Fabrizio Gramegna and Sven Högger, ETHZ, 2019
101 (bl) Christoph Hurni, *Burgruine Neu Falkenstein,* © Christoph Hurni
101 (br) Fritz O. Schuppisser, *Neu Falkenstein,* 2011, © Fritz O. Schuppisser
102 Fabrizio Gramegna and Sven Högger, ETHZ, 2019
104 (t) J. J. Hartmann, *St. Petersinsel von Süden,* 1811, gouache, 40.7 × 59 cm, © Schweizerische Nationalbibliothek
105 (bl) © Klaus Leidorf
105 (bm) Sten Karling, *Drottningholm Castle,* Fredrik Magnus Piper and the Landscape Garden (Stockholm: Kungl. Akademien för de fria konsterna, 1981)
106–7 Emil Schmid, *Vegetationskarte der Schweiz,* 1942–50, Schweiz. Naturforschende Gesellschaft
108 (m) Unknown, *Ascona,* ca. 1930, Postcard, 10 × 15 cm, ETH-Bibliothek Zürich, Bildarchiv / photograph: Unknown / PK_006365 / Public Domain
120 Etching by J. E. Ridinger, *A wolf in a mountainous landscape,* © Wellcome Collection CC BY
121 Peter Paul Rubens, *Wolf and Fox Hunt,* 1616, 245.4 × 376.2 cm, Metropolitan Museum of Art, New York, Public Domain
122 Source: Guillaume Chapron, *Recovery of large carnivores in Europe's modern human-dominated landscapes,* Chapron et al., *Science,* vol. 346, issue 6216 (2014), 1517–19
123 (r) Source: Petra Kaczensky, Guillaume Chapron, Manuela von Arx, Djuro Huber, Henrik Andrün, and John Linnell, eds., *Status, management and distribution of large carnivores–bear, lynx, wolf & wolverine–in Europe, and LIFE project database (1992–2011),* 2013
123 (l) Source: Ettore Randi, Vittorio Lucchini, Mads Fjeldsø Christensen, Nadia Mucci, Stephan M. Funk, Gaudenz Dolf and Volker Loeschcke, *Mitochondrial DNA Variability in Italian and East European Wolves: Detecting the Consequences of Small Population Size and Hybridization, Conversation Biology* 14, no. 2 (April 2000)
124 Studio Basel: Werner Bätzing et al., *Der sozio-ökonomische Strukturwandel des Alpenraumes im 20. Jahrhundert. Eine Analyse von «Entwicklungstypen» auf Gemeinde-Ebene im Kontext der europäischen Tertiarisierung* (Bern: Geographisches Institut der Universität Bern, 1993)
126 Rudolf Koller, *Die Gotthardpost,* 1873, oil on canvas, 117 × 100 cm, Kunsthaus Zürich, © Kunsthaus Zürich, 1898
127 Source: Gruppe Wolf Schweiz (GWS) and NZZ-Infografik/jok.
128 Falk Nordmann, © Verlag Matthes & Seitz, Berlin
129 Source: © 2000–2017 Michelin Travel Partner, © 2006–2016 TomTom
130 Dominik Behr, *Combining human acceptance and habitat suitability in a unified socio ecological suitability model: a case study of the wolf in Switzerland,* 2017, Universität Zürich © John Wiley and Sons
131 Source: European Environmental Agency, CDDA boundaries 2010
132 Unknown, *Soglio, reformierte Kirche San Lorenzo,* 1910–1930, photography: gelatine silver print, mounted on cardboard, ETH-Bibliothek Zürich, Bildarchiv, Ans_05105-143-AL-FL, Public Domain
133 Photographisches Institut der ETH Zürich, *Schneelawinen, Schneebrüche, Landlawinen genannt, wie sich dieselbige in die Tiefe herabwälzen, alles mitführen und zugrunde richten was sie antreffen, Reproduktion eines Kupferstichs aus: Neue und vollständige Topographie der Eidgenossenschaft von David Herrliberger ; 41,* copperplate printing, 27 × 14 cm, 1931, ETH-Bibliothek Zürich, Bildarchiv, PI_31-D-0011, Public Domain
134 *Hannibal crossing the Alps into Italy,* engraving from the book: *The illustrated history of the world for the English people. From the earliest period to the present time, ancient-mediaeval-modern. With many original high-class engravings,* ca. 1881–84, New York Ward, Lock, Public Domain
135 Oeuvres de J.-J. Rousseau, *Héloïse,* partie iv, p. 191, citoyen de Genève, Paris, 1793–98, engraved by N.A. Monsiaux, Houghton Library, Harvard University
136 (t) William Wyld, *Manchester from Kersal Moor,* 1852, painting, http://forquignon.com/history/global/industrial_revolution/manchester_medium.JPG, https://commons.wikimedia.org/w/index.php?curid=5386960, Public Domain
136 (b) Caspar Wolf, *Loèche-les-Bains,* 1774–1777, oil on canvas, https://commons.wikimedia.org/w/index.php?curid=11494968, Public Domain
137 (t) *Verwaldung im Misox (Graubünden): Luftbilder von Mesocco,* 1963, ETH-Bibliothek Zürich, Bildarchiv/Stiftung Luftbild Schweiz.
137 (b) Luftbilder von Mesocco, 2005, © 2013 swisstopo (JD100042)
138 Hermann Langen, 1920 (t), Fredy Wyder, 2012 (b), © Schweizerischer Nationalpark
139 Source: *Spektrum Akademischer Verlag, Heidelberg*
140 Triftbrücke mit Triftgletscher, image: KWO / photo: Robert Bösch
141 (t) Unknown, *Jungfraubahn in der Station Jungfraujoch,* ca. 1912, photograph: paper print, 12.5 × 17.5 cm, ETH-Bibliothek Zürich, Bildarchiv, Ans_04395, Public Domain
141 (b) Maksym Kozlenko (Maxim75), Sphinx Observatory, 2010, https://commons.wikimedia.org/w/index.php?curid=11355033, CC BY-SA 3.0
142 Giancarlo Rado, *The italian sheperd Luigino Balzan and his flock on the road bends of Brocon pass,* Veneto, 2008, © Giancarlo Rado
143 Paul Schultze Naumburg, *Wilseder Berg, Lüneberger Heide, Landschaft und Städte,* 1965
144 Lüneburger Heide, © heimatsammlung.de
145 Source: Herbert Diemont and Peter Emil Kaland, 2002, © Europäische Union, Eurostat
146 Alfred Brehm, *Mufflon,* in *Brehm's Life of Animals,* 1895, Public Domain
147 Johann Christian Daniel Schreber, *Ovis Aries,* in *Die Säugthiere in Abbildungen nach der Natur, mit Beschreibungen,* 1739–1810, Public Domain
148 Anca and Nicolae-Serban Tanasoca, *Transhumance Ways of the Vlachs Shepherds in the Past,* 2004, Public Domain
149 Rolf Gubler-Gross, *Moderne Transhumanz in der Schweiz,* 1962, © Rolf Gubler-Gross
150 Jan van Eyck, *The Adoration of the Mystic Lamb,* 1432, oil on wood panel, Sint-Baafs Cathedral, © GhentSaint-Bavo's Cathedral, www.lukasweb.be – Art in Flanders
151 (t) Thomas Cole, *The Arcadian or Pastoral State,* 1834, oil on canvas, 100.33 × 161.29 cm, Gift of the New York Gallery of the Fine Arts, negative #6046c, Digital image created by Oppenheimer Editions, © New-York Historical Society
151 (b) Joseph Mallord William Turner, *Pope's Villa at Twickenham,* 1808
152 (t) *Eichhalde im Grossen Lautertal,* 1936, Bothner, © Landesmedienzentrum Baden-Württemberg
152 (b) © Rainer Ressel, 1997
153 Daia Stutz, *Future hotspots of land abandonment in Europe 2010–2030,* ETH Zürich, Source: IEEP 2010

155–7, 158 (b), 159–61 © Iwan Baan
158 (tl) Source: J. Gareis
158 (tr) NASA image/Jesse Allen, *Landsat image of pothole lakes in Siberia,* 2001, Earth Observatory, Wikimedia Commons, Public Domain
166–71 Thomas Kissling, ETH Zürich, 2018
172 Albrecht Dürer, *The Large Piece of Turf (Das große Rasenstück),* 1503, watercolor and opaque color, 40.8 × 31.5 cm, Albertina, Public Domain
173 © Romney Marshes
174 Amalia Bonsack, ETH Zürich, 2018
175 Photo © RMN-Grand Palais (Château de Versailles) / Philipp Bernard
176 (b) George Cuit, *Aske Hall View from the South,* 1769–1980, oil on canvas, Zetland Collection
177 (t) © Ezra Stoller/Esto
177 (b) Richard Wagner
178 © Dan Graham, *Dan Graham's New Jersey* (Zurich: Lars Müller Publisher, 2012)
179 Oberrheinischer Meister, *Paradiesgärtlein,* around 1410/20, mixed techniques on oak, 26.3 × 33.4 cm, Städel, Public Domain
180 Carl Axel Magnus Lindman, *Lolium perenne L.,* 1901, in Billeder af Nordens Flora, 1901, Public Domain
181 Cristina Milesi, *Spatially interpolated differences in irrigation water use between fixed and evapotranspiration driven irrigation,* © Cristina Milesi
183–9 © Hyla Skopitz, *The Photograph Studio,* The Metropolitan Museum of Art. 2014
190 Ambrogio Lorenzetti, *Effects of Good Government in the City,* 1339, Siena, Civic Museum and Mangia Tower, Public Domain
192 (t) European Green Belts, ETH Zürich
192 (b) Patrick Abercrombie, *London Growth. Urban sprawl 1840–1929,* from the *Greater London Plan* published by His Majesty's Stationary Office, 1945, illustrative diagrams, Public Domain
193 Ebenezer Howard, *Group of Slumless Smokeless Cities,* from *To-morrow: A Peaceful Path to Real Reform* (London: Swan Sonnenschein & Co., Ltd., 1898), illustrative diagram, Public Domain
194 Patrick Abercrombie, *Four Rings,* from the *Greater London Plan* published by His Majesty's Stationary Office, 1945, planning map, Public Domain
195 Alexandra Savtchenko-Belskaia, *Business Park in the Green Belt* (t), *Allotments in the Green Belt* (b), photograph, 2018, © Vogt Landschaftsarchitekten AG
196 Extent of Green Belt in the UK, 2018, map, © Crown
197 Alexandra Savtchenko-Belskaia, *Paddock in the Green Belt* (t), *Nature reserve in the Green Belt* (m), *School grounds in the Green Belt* (b), photograph, 2018, © Vogt Landschaftsarchitekten AG
198 Alexandra Savtchenko-Belskaia, *Nursery in the Green Belt,* photograph, 2018, © Vogt Landschaftsarchitekten AG
199 Alan Mace et al., *Land with public access in the whole MGB,* diagram from the report *A 21st Century Metropolitan Green Belt,* by the London School of Economics, 2016; © Crown, map data contains public sector information licensed under the Open Government License v2.0. Sourced from: DCLG 2015, Area of Designated Green Belt Land, London Data Store; GLA 2009, inner and Outer London Boundaries (London Plan Consultation 2009), London Datastore; Historic England 2016, Parks and Gardens; Natural England 2016, Crow Act 2000; Natural England, (2016), Country Parks.
200 Alexandra Savtchenko-Belskaia, *Industrial shed in the Green Belt* (t), *Private road in the Green Belt* (b), photograph, 2018, © Vogt Landschaftsarchitekten AG
201 Roland Shaw, *London Metropolitan Green Belt London 2015/2100,* GIS map, © ETH Zürich
202 Source: Alan Baxter Engineers', *London Natural Signature: London's Seven Landscapes,* 2011, GIS map data, Natural England, © OS Base map Crown copyright, all right reserved Natural England 1000220212011. Open Government Licence v3.0.
204 (b) Greater London Authority, *London Green Grid Accessible Open Space,* 2012, GIS Map data derived from Greenspace Information for Greater London GiGI, © Crown
205–6 (t) Carmody Groarke, *View of site at Rectory Farm,* digital photograph, © Carmody Groarke
207 (t) *Google map aerial view of the Hounslow loop,* © 2019 Google
209 (tr, br) David Iliff, *A Spring Day in Green Park,* London, 2007, © David Iliff, CC BY-SA 3.0
213 (b) Carmody Groarke, *CAD plan study for warehouse layout,* © Carmody Groarke
216 William Smith, *A delineation of Strata of England and Wales,* 1815, map, 2.6 × 1.8 m, Natural History Museum at South Kensington, © The Trustees of the Natural History Museum, London
217 (t) W. Edwards, M.A. and F.M. Trotter, D.Sc., *Geographical sketch map of the Pennines and adjacent areas in the north of England,* 1954, map, 1514 × 1667 pixels, British Regional Geology, The Pennines and Adjacent Areas, © Public Domain /Wikimedia commons
217 (b) Andrea Chivers et al, *The Pennine Anticline,* 1998, sketch, Huddersfield Geology Group, © Alison Tymon
218 (t) Robert White, *Aerial view of shallow hills and hollows near Bolton Castle dating to 1378,* 1985, aerial photograph, © YDNPA (Yorkshire Dales National Park), YDNPA.ANY.228.11, photograph by Robert White Gloucestershire
218 (b) Alexandra Savtchenko-Belskaia, *Drystone walls in Huddersfield,* 2018, photograph, © Vogt Landschaftsarchitekten AG
219 F.M. McEvoy et al., *West Yorkshire Mineral Resource 1:100000,* 2006, map in British Geological Survey Commissioned Report CR/04/172N, published by British Geological Survey, OS Map and British Geological Survey with permission of Ordnance Survey on behalf of Her Majesty's Stationery Office, © Crown
220 (t) Unknown, *The Great Fire of London,* 1975, 27 × 46.3 cm, London, Museum of London, Public Domain
220 (b) Jack London, *The Municipal Dwelling, not far from Leman Street,* black and white photograph, from *People of the Abyss,* 1902: 159, Public Domain
221 (b), 224–5 Alexandra Savtchenko-Belskaia, photograph, © Vogt Landschaftsarchitekten AG
223 (t) *Bedding plane structure of a quarry face, section through Low Edge Quarry,* Magnum, diagram, 1998, © Alison Tymon
223 (b) Alison Quarry, *Digley,* 1998, photograph, © Alison Tymon
228 (b) *Section of the London Basin, North to South,* from Alfred Smee, *My garden: its plan and culture, together with a general description of its geology, botany, and natural history* (London: Bell and Daldy, 1872), © RHS Lindley Collections
230 (tl) Orsett Depot Quarry, near Grays, Essex (1973) BGS (British Geological Survey) London and the Thames Valley, ed. M. G. Sumbler, London, HMSO (Her Majesty's Stationary Office), 1996: 101, © BGS / © HMSO
232–3 Alexandra Savtchenko-Belskaia, © Vogt Landschaftsarchitekten AG
251 *Beaufort Scale,* 9th edition from 1983, *Merriam-Webster's New Collegiate Dictionary* © by Merriam-Webster, Inc., https://www.merriam-webster.com
252 Patrick Abercrombie, *The Lee Valley Green Wedge, Looking South Towards London, with Broxbourne Park in the Foreground* from *Greater London Plan 1944,* Public Domain
254 (b) Satellite image of London, © 2019 Google Maps
255 (t) Google Earth, Lea Valley aerial, 1945 © Google
255 (b) Patrick Abercrombie, *Carpenters Road pre-1944 Stratford* from *Greater London Plan 1944,* Public Domain
257 (ml) *June Radley at no 5 in combined Lea Clubs crew on the Serpentine during the Festival of Britain,* 1951, from Radley, C., *The Radleys of the Lea,* Clive Radley2015, image provided by Clive Radley
257 (bl) *Ye Olde Boat House–the Radleys, original boathouse and cottage beside Lea Bridge Dock,* 1910, from Anderson, D., *Springhill:*

Two Centuries of River Lea Rowing, (Lapesse Publishing, 2014), image provided by Clive Radley
258–9 *Olympic Park Aerial,* © ODA 2008
260 (b) Source: *Changes in the Lower Lea Valley,* map from *A Walk Around Queen Elizabeth Olympic,* a report by the London Legacy Corporation, © London Legacy Development Corporation
261 Alexandra Savtchenko-Belskaia, *Queen Elizabeth Olympic Park Walk,* 2018, © Vogt Landschaftsarchitekten AG
262 (t) AKT II, *UCL East Wind Mitigation digital testing,* © AKT II
263 (t) London Legacy Corporation, *London's New District,* a diagram from the London Legacy Development Corporation report *A Walk Around Queen Elizabeth Olympic Park,* © London Legacy Development Corporation
263 (b) *Aerial view Lower Lea Valley,* © London Legacy Development Corporation
264 Fritz Schumacher, *Siedlungsentwicklung in Hamburg, Federplan,* 1919
266 (t) J. Schöpel, 1869, planographic printing, 43 × 68 cm
266 (bl) Georg Thielen, *Allgemeine Gartenbau Ausstellung Hamburg 1897,* 1897, lithograph, 78 × 55 cm
266 (bm) *Altona 1914,* © Gartendenkmalpflege der Behörde für Stadtentwicklung Hamburg
266 (br) *Internationale Gartenbau Ausstellung Hamburg 1953,* © DBG
267 *Internationale Gartenbau Ausstellung Hamburg,* 1963 (bl), 1973 (bm), *Internationale Gartenschau Hamburg 2013* (br), © DBG
268 (b) Holger Weitzel, *Kleiner Grasbrook,* Hafen Hamburg, 2015, © imageBROKER / Alamy Stock Foto
270 Leon et Levy, *Construction de la Tour Eiffel. Paris, juillet 1888. Détail d'une vue stéréoscopique,* 1888, photograph, Paris, Léon et Lévy, © Léon et Lévy/Roger-Viollet
272 (t) Jules Gaultier and Galignani's messenger, *The "Galignani's Messenger." Plan of the Paris universal Exhibition 1878,* 1878, 87 × 27 cm, Bibliothèque nationale de France, Public Domain
272 (m) Adolphe Block, *Exposition universelle,* 1878, photograph, 11.6 × 18.5 cm, Bibliothèque nationale de France, Public Domain
272 (b) Unknown, *Exposition universelle de 1878 à Paris. Vue vers le pavillon Schneider du Creusot. Paris,* 1878, photograph, 1878, Paris, Léon et Lévy, © Léon et Lévy/Roger-Viollet
273 (t) Unknown, *1889 World Fair in Paris. Palace of gas industry,* photograph, 1889, Paris, Neurdein © Neurdein/Roger-Viollet
273 (b) Lenègre (publisher), *Exposition universelle de 1889,* 1889, map, 35 × 45 cm, Bibliothèque nationale de France, Public Domain
276–7 Jules Vacherot, *Parcs et jardins, album d'études,* 1925, Bibliothèque nationale de France, Public Domain
278–9, 284, 285 (t), 286–8 Christian Vogt, 2018, © Christian Vogt
290 Jouvet et Cie, *Carte géologique de la région française,* 1882, Atlas Map, 48 × 40 cm, Rumsey Collection, David Rumsey Map Collection, Public Domain
291 Institut Géographique National, *Carte géologique détaillée de la France: Paris,* 1966, cartographic survey, Institut Géographique National © IGN
292 (l) Hermann Julius Meyer, *Steinkohlenformation III,* 1908, from *Meyers grosses Konversations-Lexikon, ein Nachschlagewerk des allgemeinen Wissens,* Public Domain
292 ® *Carte montrant l'étendue de la zone qui a été recouverte par la mer depuis le début de la période éocène, illustration vintage gravé. Terre avant que l'homme–1886,* © Patrick Guenette / © 10/14/2019 123RF Limited 2005–2019
293 L. de Bernard, *Corps organisés fossiles de la Craie,* 1835, Bibliothèque nationale de France, Public Domain
294 Phillipe Buache, *Carte minéralogique où l'on voit la nature et la situation des terrains qui traversent la France et l'Angleterre / Dressée sur les observations et pour un mémoire de Mr Guettard,* 1746, atlas map, 31.5 × 27.5 cm, Bibliothèque nationale de France, Public Domain
295 Octave Keller, *Plan d'ensemble des carrières souterraines de Paris et du département de la Seine / dressé sous la direction de Mr. Octave Keller–dressé et dessiné par Mr. E. Vallet,* 1889, cartographic survey, 118 × 115 cm, Bibliothèque nationale de France, Public Domain
296 M. A. Leroux, *Hotel du petit journal,* facade, 1869
297 Georges Cuvier and Alexandre Brongniart, *Coupe théorique de divers Terrains, Roches et Minéraux qui entrent dans la composition du Sol du Bassin de Paris–Par MM. Cuvier et Alexandre Brongniart,* 1832, engraving, 32.5 × 27.5 cm, Bibliothèque nationale de France, Bibliothèque nationale de France, Public Domain
298 (l) Source unknown
198 (r) Charles Marville, *Buttes-Chaumont,* 1865, photograph, 24.7 × 37.9 cm, Bibliothèque historique de la Ville de Paris, Ville de Paris / BHVP / Roger-Viollet
299 Charles Marville, *Vue du parc des Buttes Chaumont d'après un dessin (prise de la rue de Crimée),* circa 1877, photograph, 23 × 37.5 cm, The History Collection / Alamy Banque d'Images
300 Source: *Carrières de France, Roche et minéraux industriels, Exploitations actives,* 2015 / BRGM / Société de l'indusrie Minérale / Republique française, Ministère de l'Écologie, du Développement durable et de l'Énergie
302, 305–9, 311 (b), 312 Francois David, © Vogt Landschaftsarchitekten AG
313 Patrick Syme, *Werner's Nomenclature of Colours: Adapted to Zoology, Botany, Chemistry, Minerology, Anatomy and the Arts,* 1814, (Washington: Smithsonian Books, 2018), plate "Whites" (no pagination) © Trustees of The Natural History Museum, London
314 © Michal Czerwonka, Courtesy of SCI-Arc
318 (tl) *Model showing proposed improvement,* © Herald-Examiner Collection/Los Angeles Public Library
318 (b) *A not-so-dry los Angeles River,* © Security Pacific Bank Collection / Los Angeles Public Library
319 (b) *Aerial view of water carrying aqueduct in outer Los Angeles, California,* © Shutterstock Photo
320 (b) *Signal Hill Oil Field,* © Spencer/ Herald Examiner Collection/ Los Angeles Public Library
321 (tl) *Hollywood car-chase scene,* © Los Angeles Times
321 (b) *Los Angeles aerial view,* Hayk Shalunts © Shutterstock Photo
322 (tl, b), 323 (b) © Joshua White, Courtesy of SCI-Arc
323 (tl) © Michal Czerwonka, Courtesy of SCI-Arc
336 Charles Marville, *Album du Bois de Boulogne,* 1858–1860, Bibliothèque nationale de France, département Fonds du service reproduction, RESERVE FOL-VE-1369, Public Domain
337 (t) Barthélemy d'Eyck, *Les Très Riches Heures du duc de Berry–Décembre,* ca. 1440, Tempera on Vellum, 13.6 × 22.5 cm, Musée Condé, Chantilly, Public Domain, photographer: R.M.N. / R.-G. Ojéda
337 (b) *Plan du Général du Chateau et Jardins de Vincennes,* 1739, Public Domain
338 Jean-Baptiste Camille Corot, *Rocks in the Forest of Fontainebleau,* ca. 1860–65, oil on canvas, 46 × 59 cm, National Gallery of Art, Washington D.C., Public Domain
339 Adolphe Alphand texts author, drawing by E. Hochereau, *Les promenades de Paris,* 1867–1873, Bibliothèque nationale de France, département Philosophie, histoire, sciences de l'homme, GR FOL-Z LE SENNE-68 (2 Planches), Public Domain
340 Charles Marville, *Album du Bois de Boulogne,* 1858–1860, Bibliothèque nationale de France, département Fonds du service reproduction, RESERVE FOL-VE-1369, Public Domain
341 (t) Agence Rol, *Bois de Vincennes, environs du stade,* 1923, 13 × 18 cm, Bibliothèque nationale de France, département Estampes et photographie, EI-13 (982), Public Domain
341 (b) Agence Rol, *Grévistes des transports publics parisiens au lac Daumesnil (Bois de Vincennes),* 1919, photography, 13 × 18 cm, Bibliothèque nationale de France, département Estampes et photographie, EI-13 (647), Public Domain

342 John G. Mark, *Bird's eye view Coney Island,* 1906, 26 × 46 cm, Geography and Map Division, Library of Congress, Washington D.C., Public Domain
343 Acte là ! / Fabrice Mathé / Olivier Rat, *Bois de Boulogne,* 2014, Paris, Mairie de Paris
344–5 *Plan of Paris with both Bois de Boulogne and Bois de Vincennes,* Bibliothèque de l'École des mines de Paris – MINES ParisTech, © Licence Ouverte Etalab
349 (tl) Académie Royale des Sciences, *Carte de Cassini (extrait),* 1750, Cartographic survey, n/a, Institute Géographique National © IGN
349 (tr) France. Service historique de l'armée de terre, *Carte de L'Etat major (extrait),* 1850, Cartographic survey, n/a, Institute Géographique National © IGN
349 Institute Géographique National, Carte IGN 1950 (bl), 2015 (br), Cartographic survey, n/a, Institute Géographique National © IGN
353–8, 361 (t), 363 Francois David, © Vogt Landschaftsarchitekten AG
364 *Buchenwald der Versuchsfläche bei Schluttenbach,* photo: Volker Griener/SMNK
366 Source: Poschlod, 2015 and Bundesamt für Naturschutz, 2001
367 Source: *Ökogramm nach Ellenberg*
368 Otto Wilhelm Thomé, *Flora von Deutschland, Österreich und der Schweiz,* 1885, Gera-Untermhaus, www.BioLib.de
369 Hans Carl von Carlowitz, *Sylvicultura Oeconomica,* 1713, Leipzig, Public Domain
370 Henri de Saint Michel, *München und Umgebung, Pfaffenhofen und Umgebung,* 1768, © Bayerische Vermessungsverwaltung
375 visuals unlimited, *the so-called "Drunken Forest of Black Spruce" in Fairbanks, Alaska, USA, where trees are collapsing into the ground due to the permafrost melting. September 2004,* © visuals unlimited / naturepl.com
376 (tl) © Isabelle Laurion
376 (tr) Laure Cailloce, *Buttes de pergélisol, ou palses, dans la région de Kuujjuarapik, au Nunavik,* 2014, 30.89 × 23.16 cm, © Laure Cailloce/ Takuvik/CNRS Photothèque
376 (ml) Bernhard Edmaier, *Ein Pingo nahe Tuktoyaktuk, Kanada,* © Bernhard Edmaier
376 (mr) Bernhard Edmaier, *Lena Delta,* © Bernhard Edmaier
376 (b) Source: *Vertikale Gliederung der breitengradabhängigen Permafrostzonierung,* from M. Ulrich
377 (t) Source: *Stadien der Thermokarstentwicklung,* from M. Ulrich
378 (t) *Moscow Suburbs 1818,* 1823, Public Domain
378 (b) Miguel.v, CC BY-SA 3.0 (b1), Mikksaaretalu, CC BY-SA 3.0 ee (b2), Alexey Sergeev (b3), Botaurus/Wikipedia (b4), PtG, CC BY-SA 3.0 (b5), Nicholas A. Tonelli, CC BY 2.0 (b6), Wikimedia Commons
380 Isaac Leviathan, Birch Grove, 1889, oil painting, Public Domain
382 (t) *Physiogeographical map,* Soviet Union, 1976, © GIN RAS laboratory of neotectonics and recent geodynamics, 2015–2018
382 (b) *Vegetation map of the Moscow Region from the Atlas of the Moscow Region,* published by the Main Directorate of Geodesy and Cartography under the Council of Ministers of the USSR, 1976, now the Federal Service for State Registration, Cadastre and Cartography
383 (t) Genplan Institute of Moscow, Original Natural Complexes of Moscow, © Genplan Institute of Moscow
384 National Atlas of Russia, *Resurs.F2 spacecraft, MK 4 camera. Scale about 1: 110,000,* satellite image, © Federal Agency for Geodesy and Cartography
385 (tl) Konstantin Yuon, *Picking Apples,* 1928, oil on canvas, 94 × 120 cm, © 2019, ProLitteris, Zürich
385 (tr) Unknown, *The Flowering of Cherry, All-Union Agricultural Exhibition,* 1939, © the funds of SPIB of Russia / State Public Historical Library 1863 – 2018
385 (bl) Video still from *How we live!* Production of the Central Documentary Film Studio Moscow, 1958, provided by www.net-film.ru/
385 (br) Eugenia Korobkova, *Citizens set off to storm the metropolitan gardens,* 2017, newspaper Komsomolskaya Pravda, © Evgenia Korobkov
386 (b) Ivan Ivanovich Shishkin, *At the edge of an oak forest,* 1882, oil painting, Public Domain
391 (t), 394 © Herzog & de Meuron
392 (1) *Pinus sylvestris,* Scots Pine, 2019, digital photograph, © Den Berk Boomkwekerijen
392 (2) Dominicus Johannes Bergsma, *Larix decidua* / European larch, © Dominicus Johannes Bergsma / Creative Commons Attribution-Share Alike 4.0 International
392 (3) *Quercus Rubra, Red oak,* © NetPS Plant Finder Tool #145462
392 (4) *Larix sibrica, Siberian Larch,* © NetPS Plant Finder Tool #J229-01
392 (5) *Tilia Cordata, Small leaved lime,* © NetPS Plant Finder Tool #42630
392 (6) *Populus tremula, Quaking Aspen,* © NetPS Plant Finder Tool #29929
392 (7) Willow, *Betula pendula, Silver Birch,* © Willow; under GNU Free Documentation License
392 (8) H. Zell, *Populus alba, Silver Poplar,* © H. Zell; Creative Commons Attribution-Share Alike 3.0 Unported
392 (9) Luana Teutzi, *Pyrus sp, Pear,* 2013, digital photograph, © iStock photo ID 181376734
392 (10) *Sorbus aucuparia, Rowan or Mountain ash,* © NetPS Plant Finder Tool #123979
392 (11) Michel Buchner, *Syringa vulgaris, Common Lilac,* photo courtesy NetPS Plant Finder Tool
392 (12) Blickwinkel, *Rosa canina*, *Dog rose,* stock photo, Alamy Stock Photo, Image ID: EBNRBP
392 (13) *Sambucus nigra, Elderberry,* © NetPS Plant Finder Tool #232790
392 (14) Chris Ireland-Jones, *Maianthemum bifolium, May Lily,* © Avon Bulbs
392 (15) Peganum *Campanula Latifolia Alba,* Bellflower, Public Domain; Creative Commons Attribution-Share Alike 2.0 Generic
392 (16) *Crataegus monogyna, Hawthorn,* © NetPS Plant Finder Tool #132604
392 (17) *Prunus padus, Bird Cherry,* © NetPS Plant Finder Tool #92480
392 (18) H. Zell, *Viburnum opulus, Guelder rose,* © H. Zell, CC BY-SA 3.0
392 (19) Max Licher, *Achillea millefolium, Yallow,* © Max Licher, CC BY-SA
392 (20) Graham Calow, *Galium verum, Ladies Bedstraw,* © www.naturespot.org.uk
392 (21) *Malus pumila, Apple tree,* Public Domain
392 (22) Luana Teutzi, *Pyrus sp, Pear tree,* 2013, digital photograph, © iStock photo ID 181376734
392 (23) *Prunus tomentosa, Cherry tree,* © NetPS Plant Finder Tool #251927
392 (24) *Prunus domestica var. Kolonovidnaja, Plum tree,* © Newblooms.com
396, 402 James Parsons, *The Acorn-Hog Economy of the Oak Woodlands of Southwestern Spain,* 1962, *Geographical Review,* vol. 52, no. 2
397 © Mauritius Images
398 Rui Boaventura, MEGAGEO, 2015
399 *Georg Leisner at the Anta da Cunha Baixa,* The Leisner Archive, photo: Vera Leisner
400 Photographer unknown, Instagram: sao_lourenco_do_barrocal
401 Hermann Adolph Köhler, 1897, Franz Eugen Köhler, Public Domain
403 Johann Christian Daniel Schreber, from *Die Säugthiere in Abbildungen nach der Natur, mit Beschreibungen,* 1739–1810, Public Domain
404 Source: EUFORGEN 2009
405–6 © APCOR
408–9 CBL T 413, folios 22v–23r, © The Trustees of the Chester Beatty Library, Dublin
410 A. Rouargu, *Constantinople,* 1855, Public Domain
411 (t) Stanislaw Chlebowski, *Turkish Women by the Fountain at the Sweet Waters of Asia,* 1873
411 (bl) © Google Earth

411 (br) Naci Yüngül, *The Distribution Network Plan and Fountains on the Old City,* ISKI
412 Prof. Dr. Kâzim çeçen, *Sinan's Water Supply System in Istanbul,* 1996, Istanbul, ISKI
414 (t) *Konstantinopel um 1850,* ca. 1850, Public Domain
414 (b) Source unknown
418 (b) Alberto Pasini, *Market Day in Constantinople,* 1877, oil on canvas, Public Domain
419 (b) William True, *An Illustration from The Innocents Abroad, Mark Twain,* 1869, Public Domain
421 (t) Giovanni Paolo Pannini, *Belisarius at the Gate of Constantinople,* 133 × 110 cm, Photo Courtesy of The Matthiesen Gallery, London
422 (m) Source unknown
422 (br) Moonik, *Door of the Imperial Council (Dîvân-ı Hümâyûn) in the Topkapı Palace in Istanbul,* 2012 © Moonik
424 (bl) *Aynalikavak Garden (Tersane Garden),* 1453, Gaznevi Album, Istanbul University Library T. 5461, 25b
424 (bm) Ivan Aivazovsky, *View of Constantinople by evening light,* 1846, oil on canvas, 120 × 189 cm, The Cottage palace museum, Peterhof, Public Domain
424 (br) Abdülcelil Çelebi Levnî and Seyyid Vehbi, *Garden scene of Sultan Ahmed III,* 1732, illumination on paper, Surname-i Vehbi
425 (bl) Ali. Amir Beg Shirwani, *Presentations of gifts to Sultan Süleyman the Magnificent,* 1558, Süleymanname, folio 412a, Public Domain
425 (bm) *Oud, çeng, and def in the palace garden,* early 16th century, from I. Ahmed's collection, Public Domain
425 (br) *Topkapı Sarayı in the time of Selim I,* 1584, depiction from the Hünername, Public Domain
428 (b) Vuillaume, *Le beau plan,* 1873, Antwerp, FelixArchief, Public Domain
429 (b) Aerial CGI of Droogdokken Park, © Van Belle & Medina Architects bvba / Vogt Landscape Ltd
430 *Cut and fill sections,* Droogdokken Park, © Van Belle & Medina Architects bvba
431 *Cut and fill plan,* Droogdokken Park, © Van Belle & Medina Architects bvba
434 Carte des Sols de la Belgique -Associations de sols Pedologie, prepared by R. Marechal & R. Tavernier 1970, drawn and printed by the Institut Cartographique Militaire Belge, 1971. Downloaded from the European Soil Data Centre, https://esdac.jrc.ec.europa.eu/content/carte-des-sols-de-la-belgique-associations-de-sols-pedologie, European Commission Joint Research Centre. Copyright by R. Marechal & R. Tavernier and the Institut Cartographique Militaire Belge 1970–1971
449 Lukas Ryffel, Cover, ETH Zürich, 2019
450 Heinrich C. Berann, *The Alps : Europe's top attraction all year round,* 1966–67, 42 × 80 cm, editor: Joint Publicity Commission of the Alpine Countries; painting by H.C. Berann, Innsbruck: Wagner'sche Univ.-Buchdruckerei Buchroithner & Co., Zentralbibliothek Zürich, Kartensammlung, Atelier Berann, Lans /Tirol, www.berann.com
452 (t) Source unknown
425 (b) *Pianta di Milano,* Istituto geografico militare, Firenze, Aprile 1937–XV
453 (t) Maurizio Pellegrini, *Ground Water in Alluvial Deposits Po and Veneto Plain,* from *the Atlante tematico d'Italia: Acque sotterranee,* by Roberto Melis and Servizio Cartografico (Mailand), (Milano: Touring Club Italiano, 1989–1992) , © Touring Club Italiano
453 (b) Lucio Gambi, *Drainage,* from *the Atlante tematico d'Italia: Bonifiche,* by Roberto Melis and Servizio Cartografico (Mailand), (Milano: Touring Club Italiano, 1989–1992), © Touring Club Italiano
454 (t) Source unknown
454 (m) *Veduta aerea del Parco Nord,* 1990, © Francesco Borella – Archivio Parco Nord Milano – Sesto San Goivanni
454 (b) Christian Hartmann, *Espenhain in der Po-Ebene,* 2012
456 Robert Smithson, Poster, *Movie Treatment for Spiral Jetty, Great Salt Lake, Utah,* 1970, offset lithograph on tan paper, 96.5 × 55.5 cm, Zurich, bpk / Cooper-Hewitt Smithsonian Design Museum / Art Resource, NY / Matt Flynn, © Holt/Smithson Foundation / 2019, ProLitteris,
457 (t) Leonardo da Vinci, *Atlantic Codex (Codex Atlanticus) f. 199 verso,* ca. 1507–1510, © Biblioteca Ambrosiana
457 (b) Giovanni Battista Clarici, *Carta dei dintorni di Milano,* 1580, © Comune di Milano – Raccolta delle Stampe "Achille Bertarelli"
458 (t) *Cursus Padi per Longobardiam a fonte usque ad ostia,* printed in the eighteenth century, property of Antonio Calvenzani
458 (b) Giovanni Brenna, *Pianta di Milano,* 1860, © Courtesy of the Harvard Map Collection, elaborated by Giorgio Stagni–www.stagniweb.it
459 (t) *Ponte del Naviglio, Bernate Ticino,* © Museo Storico Civico di Cuggiono
459 (m) *La conca di via Conca del Naviglio (Viarenna) fotografata alla fine del XIX secolo,* © Civico archivio fotografico Milano
459 (b) *Milano, la tranvia a vapore per Pavia, lungo la via Ascanio Sforza,* 1944, © Civico archivio fotografico Milano
460–1 © Image courtesy of OMA + Laboratorio Permanente
462 Pierre Jean François Turpin, *Darstellung der Urpflanze,* 1837, woodcut, Public Domain, in Anita Albus, *Die Kunst der Künste. Erinnerungen an die Malerei* (Frankfurt am Main: Eichborn Verlag, 1997), 374
463 Arnold Heim, *Bienenzucht, Eureka Canyon, Ventura County,* 1914, Glasdiapositiv, 8.5 × 10 cm, ETH-Bibliothek Zürich, Bildarchiv, Dia_023a-004, Public Domain CC BY-SA 4.0
464 Exhibition view of *Honigpumpe am Arbeitsplatz* by Joseph Beuys. documenta 6 (1977), © documenta archiv / Photo: Dieter Schwerdtle / © 2019, ProLitteris, Zurich
465 Source: *Bienenzeitung* 49. Jahrgang, August 1994, Mitteilungen des Deutschen Imkerbundes
466 *L'encyclopédie ou dictionnaire raisonné des sciences, des arts et des métiers sous la direction de Diderot et d'Alembert, tome 1,* 1762, photo © Ministère de la Culture – Médiathèque du Patrimoine, Dist. RMN-Grand Palais / image RMN-GP
467 Isaac Levitan, Пасека, ca. 1885, oil on canvas, 20.5 × 31 cm, Omsk Regional Museum of Fine Arts (Vrubel Museum), Omsk, Russia
469 © Carim Nahaboo
470 Source: V. Frisch, *Gelöste und ungelöste Rätsel der Bienensprache,* 1948
471 USDA Economic Research, *Pollinator Movements in the United States,* 2014, © ERS
473 Sebastian Wasek, *Via Giulia, Rome,* 2017, © age Fotostock
474 (b) Source: © 2019 GoogleEarth
476 (t) Berthold Werner, *Rom, Campo Santo Teutonico,* 2007, © Berthold Werner
480–1 Source: © 2019 GoogleEarth
482 *Jardin à quatre canaux entouré d'un mur, Hal-name,* le Livre de l'Exstase exécuté pour le prince Salim Mushkin-qalam, enlumineur, XVIIe siècle BnF, Manuscrits orientaux, Smith Lesouef oriental 198, fol. 2, © Bibliothèque nationale de France
483 (m) *Delkeskamp-Plan von 1864,* © Instituts für Stadtgeschichte Frankfurt am Main
483 (b) Howard, Ebenezer, *To-morrow: A Peaceful Path to Real Reform* (London: Swan Sonnenschein & Co., Ltd., 1898), Public Domain
484 Source unknown
485 (t, m) Wright, Frank Lloyd, *Broadacre City,* City Model, 1934/35 © 2019, ProLitteris, Zürich
485 (b) Christoph Bellin, *Schrebergärten, Kleingärten zwischen den Gleisen an der Haltestelle Westhafen der Berliner S-Bahn,* © christoph-bellin.de
486 (t) Donald Loggins, *Liz Christy Garden Community Garden,* 1973, © Donald Loggins
486 (b) Paul Debois, *Food from the Sky project,* © GAP Photos/ Paul Debois
488 Joel Sternfeld, *Highline New York,* © Joel Sternfeld
489 Unknown Artist, *Leicester Square,* London, circa 1910, © Depositphotos.com/ DarioStudios

490 A. Bodmer, *Nutzungszonenplan der Stadt Winterthur "Bodmerplan,"* 1926, in *Zeitschrift Wohnen*, vol. 6, no. 5, (1931), E-Periodica
492 Frank Mayer, *Winterthur - Töss - Eichliacker, Band I Grundlagen,* 1997, Winterthur, ZHAW Winterthur / Grundlagen aus Stadtarchiv Winterthur / Oederlin Daniel and Brossard Gilbert. *Architekturführer Winterthur Bd. 1. Ein Führer zur Baukunst in Winterthur von 1830 bis 1930,* (Zürich: vdf Hochschulverlag an der ETH Zürich, 1997)
493 (t) Mittelholzer, Walter, LBS_MH01-005836, ETH-Bibliothek Zürich, Bildarchiv/Stiftung Luftbild Schweiz
493 (b) Stadtgrenze: © Stadt Winterthur / Grundlagenkarte: Landeskarte 1:25'000 PK25: © Bundesamt für Landestopografie / Wald: © GIS Kanton Zürich / Park-Layer: © OpenStreetMap-Mitwirkende / Gartenstadt-Layer: Netzwerk Stadt und Landschaft NSL, Verbinden - Chancen nutzen, Schlussbericht Winterthur 2050 Studienprojekt 1, 2018, ETH Zürich
494 (t) Bridler und Völki Architekten, "Lageplan und Profile Wettbewerb Bebauung Vogelsangareal," 1911, E-Periodica, in *Schweizerische Bauzeitung,* vol. 57/58, no. 22 (1911)
494 (b) © *Das Werk* 1928, Band 15; E-Periodica
496 (t) Source: Stadtplan Winterthur
498 Unknown, *Flugplatz Dübendorf,* ca. 1938, photograph: gelatine silver print, detail, 10.5 × 14.5 cm, ETH-Bibliothek Zürich, Bildarchiv, Ans_05035-546, Public Domain
501 (t) Source: © 2019 GoogleEarth
501 (b) Flughafen Dübendorf, 1929, © BSF Swissphoto
505 (mr) Dufourkarte 1845-1865 / 1939 (swisstopo)
505 (br) Dübendorf Sonnenberg, Photo Schait, Dübendorf
506 Kolorierung des Dias durch Margrit Wehrli-Frey, *Avenue of plane trees in Nîmes,* 1937, Fotografie: glass-plate positive, hand colored, 8.5 × 10 cm, ETH-Bibliothek Zürich, Bildarchiv, CC BY-SA 4.0, photo: Leo Wehrli
507 *Palace of Chantilly with the gardens of André Le Nôtre,* 17th century, Public Domain
508 (t) *Regulierungs- und Erweiterungsplan der Stadt Rom,* 1882, watercolor, 120 × 160 cm, Rom, su concessione della Sovrintendenza - Archivio Capitolino
508 (b) *Contour Canal,* Studio Yan, Toulouse, in: L. T. C. Rolt, *From Sea to Sea: The Canal du Midi* (Allen Lane, A Division of Penguin Books Ltd, 1973)
509 (tl) Martabl/Blogger.com, 2013
509 (tr) *Allee in Meudon bei Paris,* ottefoto / photocase.de
509 (bl) Sven Högger, ETH Zürich, 2019
509 (br) Duke Farms Foundation, *Sycamore and London Plane Tree Allee,* 2014
511 (t) *Les Ponts Jumeaux,* Toulouse, Studio Yan, Toulouse, in: L. T. C. Rolt, *From Sea to Sea: The Canal du Midi* (Allen Lane, A Division of Penguin Books Ltd, 1973)
511 (b) Hans Leu, Lindenhof, 1504, Baugeschichtliches Archiv Stadt Zürich, Creative commons BY SA 4.0
512 (l) H. J. Redouté, *Platanus occidentalis L.,* Public Domain
512 (r) Frédéric Boissonas, *Vallée de Tempé,* 1910, Getty Museum, Public Domain
514 Lukas Ryffel, Case Studio, ETH Zürich, 2019
516-24, 530 (b), 531 (b), 532-3, 540, 541 (b), 542-3, 545 (b), 546 (b), 547 (b) © Giuseppe Micciché
526 (t) *Luftaufnahme Zürich HB und Limmat,* © Luftbilderschweiz.ch
526 (b) Johann Caspar Rahn, *Promenade im Platzspitz um 1815,* 1815, oil on canvas, Zürich, Baugeschichtliches Archiv Zürich
528 Bundesamt für Landestopografie swisstopo, *Geotechnische Karte der Schweiz 1:200'000,* 1967, reproduced by permission of swisstopo (JA100120)
529 (tl) *Sihlhochwasser am Platzspitz,* 1910, Baugeschichtliches Archiv der Stadt Zürich
529 (b) Kantonspolizei Zürich, 2005, Baudirektion des Kantons Zürich
534-5 Johannes Müller, *Müllerplan,* 1793, Stadtarchiv Zürich, Stadt Zürich, Open-Data
536 ETH-Bibliothek Zürich, Bildarchiv / Photographer: Comet Photo AG (Zürich) / Com_FC24-8009-0199 / CC BY-SA 4.0
538 Source: www.geo.admin.ch, © CNES, Spot Image, swisstopo, NPOC
544 Pieter Bruegel the Elder, *Children's Games,* Wikimedia Commons
547 (tl) © Veronica Paz & Jordi Simon, Ostia Antica, 2014
548 Archivesnormandie 1939-1945, *Bocage country at Cotentin Peninsula, Northern France,* Public Domain
549 Privatbesitz Röhricht, from Katrin Lesser, *UNESCO-Welterbe Hufeisensiedlung. Untersuchung der denkmalgeschützten Freiflächen und Konzeption für den zukünftigen Umgang,* Gutachten, Band I+II im Rahmen des Programmes Nationale Welterbestätten i.A. des BBSR, Berlin 2009/10
550 © National Trust Images/Derek Croucher
551 (t) Parker and Unwin, Broadway, Letchworth, 1905
551 (b) *Housing around Walden Place, Welwyn Garden City,* 1935, © Historic England
552 Erwin Barth, *Volkspark Rehberge, Berlin-Wedding, Grundriss Gesamtanlage,* 1927, watercolor ink painted on cardboard via blueprint, Architekturmuseum der Technischen Universität Berlin, Public Domain
553 (t) *Checking the angle of the clipped yew hedge, Great Dixter, East Sussex,* © Historic England Archive
553 (b) Photo: Caroll Hill
554 Ignatz Albrecht, *Abbildungen aller medizinisch-ökonomisch-technologischen Gewächse mit der Beschreibung ihres Gebrauches und Nutzens,* Wien, 1800, Public Domain
556 Source: EUFORGEN
557 Carl Augustus Lebschée, *Lithografie der Tanzlinde Peesten,* 1850, Public Domain
573, 576 (b), 577 (b), 578-9, 583, 587 © Florian Holzherr
581, 585 (t, bl) © Harms Metallguss
582 Source: © 2019 GoogleEarth
584 (t), 586 © Maren Brakebusch
585 (br) © Gerd Hartmann Maschinen- und Metallbau GmbH
588-9 *Plan von Treptow,* 1895, © Landesarchiv Berlin
590 *Große Liegewiese im Treptower Park nach der Gewerbeausstellung, um 1900,* © Museen Treptow-Köpenick
592 (t) *Luftbild des Hamburger Stadtparks, um 1928,* Heino Grunert, «Hamburger Reformgärten - Volksparkbewegung und Gartenkunstreform im beginnenden 20. Jahrhundert», in Claudia Horbas, Gisela Jaacks, Carsten Prange et al. (eds.), *Gartenlust und Blumenliebe. Hamburgs Gartenkultur vom Barock bis ins 20. Jahrhundert* (Ostfildern-Ruit: Hatje Cantz, 2006), 239, © Staatsarchiv Hamburg
592 (b) © hamburger-fotoarchiv.de
593 (t, m) Sven Högger, ETH Zürich, 2019
593 (b) Leberecht Migge, *Hamburg Fuhlsbüttel,* Public Domain
594 (t) © CNES, Spot Image, swisstopo, NPOC
594 (b) John Gwynn, *A Plan of Hyde-Park with the City and Liberties of Westminster & Showing the Several Improvements Propos'd,* 1766, Etching, Yale Center for British Art, © Paul Mellon Collection
595 (b) Sotheby's Institute of Art
597 Fritz Schumacher, *Freiflächensystem,* 1920-1923, Kölner Grün Stiftung: Erkundungsphase, in *Grüngürtel Impuls Köln* (Köln: Greven Verlag, 2013), 25, © Kölner Grün Stiftung
598 Friedrich Rothpletz, *Josefswiese,* 1915-1922, © Baugeschichtliches Archiv der Stadt Zürich (BAZ)
600 © HafenCity Hamburg GmbH / Franziska Husung
602 (tl) *Hamburger Stadt- und Vorortsbahnen,* 1912, Archiv der Hamburger Hochbahn AG
604, 605 (t), 608 (tl, b), 610 (b) © Giuseppe Micciché
604 (b), 606 (br), 608 (tl), 611 (b) © HafenCity Hamburg GmbH / Franziska Husung
611 (tl) G. F. Morrell, Public Domain
653 © Anne Gabriel-Jürgens

Interventions

I © Dafi Kühne

II (1) Julian Charrière, *The Blue Fossil Entropic Stories II,* 2013 (copyright the artist; © 2019, ProLitteris, Zurich) Courtesy DITTRICH&SCHLECHTRIEM, Berlin, Germany.
(2) Julian Charrière, *The Blue Fossil Entropic Stories I,* 2013 (copyright the artist; © 2019, ProLitteris, Zurich) Courtesy DITTRICH&SCHLECHTRIEM, Berlin, Germany.
(3) Julian Charrière, *The Blue Fossil Entropic Stories III,* 2013 (copyright the artist; © 2019, ProLitteris, Zurich) Courtesy DITTRICH&SCHLECHTRIEM, Berlin, Germany.

III © Christian Vogt

IV Olafur Eliasson, *The morning small cloud series,* 2006 (all the single images)
Olafur Eliasson, *The morning small cloud series,* 2006, photo: Fabian Birgfeld / PhotoTECTONICS (the composition of images)

V © Roni Horn, *Still Water (The River Thames, for Example), 1999,* 15 framed photographs and text printed on uncoated paper, 30½ × 41⅕ inches each (77.5 × 105.4 cm), Courtesy the artist and Hauser & Wirth

VI (1) © Andreas Greiner
(2–3) Katarina Schildgen and Paul Gasser, Agentur des Exponenten, GASAG Kunstpreis 2016, Andreas Greiner, © 2019, ProLitteris, Zürich
(4) © Andreas Greiner, photo by Theo Bitzer, 2016
(5–6) © Andreas Greiner, Installation View at Berlinische Galerie, photo by Theo Bitzer, 2016

VII (1–2) Andreas Greiner and Julian Charrière, *Dominions,* 2011, Detail, installation View, Dominions, Program e.V., Berlin, Germany, 2013 (copyright the artists; © 2019, ProLitteris, Zurich) Courtesy the artists
(3–7) Andreas Greiner and Julian Charrière, *Dominions,* 2011
(8–10) Andreas Greiner and Julian Charrière, *Dominions,* 2011–Detail, installation View, Dominions, Program e.V., Berlin, Germany, 2013 (copyright the artists; © 2019, ProLitteris, Zurich) Courtesy the artists

VIII (1) Julian Charrière, *Tropisme,* 2015, installation view, DITTRICH&SCHLECHTRIEM, Berlin, Germany (copyright the artist; © 2019, ProLitteris, Zurich). Photo by Jens Ziehe. Courtesy DITTRICH&SCHLECHTRIEM, Berlin, Germany.
(2) Julian Charrière, *Tropisme,* 2015, installation View, *For They That Sow the Wind,* Parasol Unit, London, United Kingdom, 2016 (copyright the artist; © 2019, ProLitteris, Zurich). Photo by Jack Hems. Courtesy Parasol unit foundation for contemporary art, London, United Kingdom.
(3) Julian Charrière, *Tropisme,* 2014, installation view, Polygon, Bugada & Cargnel, Paris, France, 2015 (copyright the artist; © 2019, ProLitteris, Zurich). Photo by Martin Argyroglo. Courtesy Bugada & Cargnel, Paris, France.
(4–5) Julian Charrière, *Tropisme,* photogravure, 2015 (copyright the artist; © 2019, ProLitteris, Zurich) Courtesy the artist
(6) Julian Charrière, *Tropisme,* 2014, installation view, Polygon, Bugada & Cargnel, Paris, France, 2015 (copyright the artist; © 2019, ProLitteris, Zurich). Photo by Martin Argyroglo. Courtesy Bugada & Cargnel, Paris, France.

IX © Christian Vogt

X (1–2) Julian Charrière, *We Are All Astronauts,* 2013, installation view, *For They That Sow the Wind,* Parasol Unit London, London, United Kingdom, 2016 (copyright the artist, © 2019, ProLitteris, Zurich). Photo by Jack Hems, Courtesy Parasol unit foundation for contemporary art, London, United Kingdom.
(3–4) Julian Charrière, *We Are All Astronauts,* 2013, installation view, *We Are All Astronauts,* Centre culturel suisse, Paris, France, 2014 (copyright the artist; © 2019, ProLitteris, Zurich). Photo by Martin Argyroglo. Courtesy Collection Musée cantonal des Beaux-Arts, Lausanne, Switzerland.
(5–6) Julian Charrière, *We Are All Astronauts,* 2013, installation view, *We Are All Astronauts,* Centre culturel suisse, Paris, France, 2014 (copyright the artist; © 2019, ProLitteris, Zurich). Photo by Martin Argyroglo. Courtesy Collection Musée cantonal des Beaux-Arts, Lausanne, Switzerland.

XI Scanning electron microscope capture, Andreas Greiner and Martina Heider (Bayerisches Polymerinstitut at Universität Bayreuth), 2016

XII (1–2) Julian Charrière and Julius von Bismarck, *Some Pigeons Are More Equal Than Others,* 2012, In Action Venice (copyright the artists; © 2019, ProLitteris, Zurich) Courtesy alexander levy, Berlin, Germany; DITTRICH & SCHLECHTRIEM, Berlin, Germany.
(3–4) Julian Charrière and Julius von Bismarck, *Some Pigeons Are More Equal Than Others,* 2012 (copyright the artists; © 2019, ProLitteris, Zurich). Courtesy the artists
(5) Julian Charrière and Julius von Bismarck, *Some Pigeons Are More Equal Than Others,* 2012, In Action Venice (copyright the artists; © 2019, ProLitteris, Zurich). Courtesy alexander levy, Berlin, Germany; DITTRICH & SCHLECHTRIEM, Berlin, Germany.
(6) Julian Charrière and Julius von Bismarck, *Some Pigeons Are More Equal Than Others,* 2012 (copyright the artists; © 2019, ProLitteris, Zurich). Courtesy the artists

XIII (1) Marguerite Humeau, *Vronski and Deborah (Lovers), Two elephants engineered to romantically fall in love with each other,* exhibition view, Palais de Tokyo, Paris. Polystyrene, white paint, acrylic parts, latex, silicone, nylon, 3 glass hormones containers, testosterone, oestrogen, adrenaline, dopamine, oxytocin, vasopressin, water pumps, water, powder-coated metal stand, sound, 188.7 × 200.7 × 301.9 cm (including stand), 2016, Credit: Spassky Fischer, Courtesy the artist, Clearing: New York/ Brussels
(2) Marguerite Humeau, *Echo, A matriarch engineered to die* (detail). Polystyrene, white paint, acrylic parts, latex, silicone, nylon, glass artificial heart, water pumps, water, potassium chloride, powder-coated metal stand, sound, 120.2 × 449.6 × 136.1 cm (including stand) + Glass-Heart 30 × 60 × 30 cm, 2016, Credit: Spassky Fischer, Courtesy the artist, Clearing: New York/Brussels
(3) Marguerite Humeau, *Félicie, A female engineered to be self-destructive–it gets drunk with ethanol that comes from a masala fruit,* exhibition view, Palais de Tokyo, Paris. Polystyrene, white paint, acrylic parts, latex, silicone, glass artificial masala fruit, ethanol, water pumps, water, nylon, powder-coated metal stand, sound, 82.3 × 332.1 × 209.5 cm (including stand), 2016, Credit: Spassky Fischer, Courtesy the artist, Clearing: New York/Brussels
(4) Marguerite Humeau, Echo, *A matriarch engineered to die,* exhibition view, Palais de Tokyo, Paris. Polystyrene, white paint, acrylic parts, latex, silicone, nylon, glass artificial heart, water pumps, water, potassium chloride, powder-coated metal stand, sound, 120.2 × 449.6 × 136.1 cm (including stand) + GlassHeart 30 × 60 × 30 cm, 2016, Credit: Spassky Fischer, Courtesy the artist, Clearing: New York/Brussels
(5) Marguerite Humeau, *Emmett, A male in artificial oestrus showing highly visible signs of aggressively,* exhibition view, Palais de Tokyo, Paris. Polystyrene, white paint, acrylic parts, latex, silicone, glass container, artificial black must, water pumps, water, nylon, powder-coated metal stand, sound, 162.3 × 391.2 × 300 cm (including stand), 2016, Credit: Spassky Fischer, Courtesy the artist, Clearing: New York/Brussels

Quotes

289 Claude Lévi-Strauss, *The Savage Mind* (Chicago: University of Chicago Press, 1966), 17. Translated from the French by George Weidenfield and Nicholson Ltd.
395 Elias Canetti, *Crowds and Power* (New York: The Viking Press, 1962), 84. Translated from the German by Carol Stewart
599 Anthony Vidler, Michel Foucault and Pamela Johnston. "Heterotopias." *AA Files,* no. 69 (2014), 18–22.

Index